In Prai Divine Ruchir Adi Da Samraj

Nothing like this has ever been Revealed before. To understand the great religions in a new light, one has only to read Adi Da Samraj. His description of the Supreme Yoga of the seventh stage of life can be felt to be True by anyone who has an open mind. Intuitively, you will be convinced that Adi Da Samraj knows what He is talking about, because of His unique Realization.

A hundred times I have churned the following question in my mind: how is it possible for the Promised Avatar to be here? Curiously, that question shifted itself quite the other way: how is it possible for Him <u>not</u> to be the Promised Avatar? Then the heart-answer would come spontaneously: it is absolutely impossible. No one can speak of the Divine in this way unless He is the Divine Person. Read and see.

Adi Da confesses that He has come in this world of suffering as the result of countless prayers and desires. He says that He has come once and for all, that He is the first and last seventh stage Adept-Realizer, that He need not come again for the simple reason that His Revelation is complete, that It encompasses Everything, and that His Power will ever be present for all.

When you open this book, prepare yourself for a laser beam of Insight that will pierce your whole body and heart. This is the "Bible" of seventh stage wisdom, never before Revealed.

We have waited for this moment in history for countless life-times. The Avatar tells us that we are always already happy. Isn't that strange? That the universe is but a modification of the One and Only God. That there is only God and He is That One, and you are That One.

Adi Da Samraj is the True Heart of the World. He shows us how to abide as Consciousness, as Pure Light, how to practice the discipline of Standing Free in the face of all phenomena that arise.

May we all come to understand what a Gift has been given to the world by the Appearance of such a Being.

ROGER SAVOIE, PH.D.
philosopher, writer, and translator
author, *La Vipère et le Lion - La Voie radicale de la Spiritualité*

It is obvious, from all sorts of subtle details, that he knows what IT's all about . . . a rare being.

ALAN WATTS
author, *The Way of Zen* and *The Wisdom of Insecurity*

I regard Adi Da Samraj as one of the greatest teachers in the Western world today.

IRINA TWEEDIE
Sufi teacher; author, *Chasm of Fire*

I recognize the God-Presence Incarnate in Adi Da Samraj as whole and full and complete.

BARBARA MARX HUBBARD
author, *Conscious Evolution* and *The Revelation;*
president, The Foundation for Conscious Evolution

Adi Da Samraj is a man who has truly walked in Spirit and given true enlightenment to many.

SUN BEAR
founder, the Bear Tribe Medicine Society

The life and teaching of Avatar Adi Da Samraj are of profound and decisive spiritual significance at this critical moment in history.

BRYAN DESCHAMP
Senior Adviser at the United Nations
High Commission for Refugees;
former Dean of the Carmelite House of Studies, Australia;
former Dean of Trinity College, University of Melbourne

A great teacher with the dynamic ability to awaken in his listeners something of the Divine Reality in which he is grounded, with which he is identified, and which, in fact, he is.

ISRAEL REGARDIE
author, *The Golden Dawn*

A di Da Samraj has spoken directly to the heart of our human situation—the shocking gravity of our brief and unbidden lives. Through his words I have experienced a glimmering of eternal life, and view my own existence as timeless and spaceless in a way that I never have before.

RICHARD GROSSINGER
author, *Planet Medicine; The Night Sky*

M y relationship with Adi Da Samraj over many years has only confirmed His Realization and the Truth of His impeccable Teaching. He is much more than simply an inspiration of my music, but is really a living demonstration that perfect transcendence is actually possible. This is both a great relief and a great challenge. If you thirst for truth, here is a rare opportunity to drink.

RAY LYNCH
composer and musician, *Deep Breakfast;*
The Sky of Mind; and *Ray Lynch, Best Of*

A di Da Samraj and his unique body of teaching work offer a rare and extraordinary opportunity for those courageous students who are ready to move beyond ego and take the plunge into deepest communion with the Absolute. Importantly, the teaching is grounded in explicit discussion of necessary psychospiritual evolution and guides the student to self-responsibility and self-awareness.

ELISABETH TARG, M.D.
University of California, San Francisco,
School of Medicine;
director, Complementary Medicine Research Institute,
California Pacific Medical Center

The Divine World-Teacher,
RUCHIRA AVATAR ADI DA SAMRAJ
The Mountain Of Attention, 2000

THE ALL-COMPLETING AND FINAL DIVINE REVELATION TO MANKIND

THE SEVENTEEN COMPANIONS OF THE TRUE DAWN HORSE

BOOK ELEVEN

A Summary Description Of The Supreme Yoga
Of The Seventh Stage Of Life
In The Divine Way Of Adidam

By
The Divine World-Teacher,
RUCHIRA AVATAR
ADI DA SAMRAJ

THE DAWN HORSE PRESS
MIDDLETOWN, CALIFORNIA

NOTE TO THE READER

All who study the Way of Adidam or take up its practice should remember that they are responding to a Call to become responsible for themselves. They should understand that they, not Avatar Adi Da Samraj or others, are responsible for any decision they make or action they take in the course of their lives of study or practice.

The devotional, Spiritual, functional, practical, relational, cultural, and formal community practices and disciplines referred to in this book are appropriate and natural practices that are voluntarily and progressively adopted by members of the four congregations of Adidam (as applicable for each of the congregations and as appropriate to the personal circumstance of each individual). Although anyone may find these practices useful and beneficial, they are not presented as advice or recommendations to the general reader or to anyone who is not a member of one of the four congregations of Adidam. And nothing in this book is intended as a diagnosis, prescription, or recommended treatment or cure for any specific "problem", whether medical, emotional, psychological, social, or Spiritual. One should apply a particular program of treatment, prevention, cure, or general health only in consultation with a licensed physician or other qualified professional.

CONTENTS

INTRODUCTION   11

1. Avatar Adi Da Samraj   15
His Life and Teaching

2. Avatar Adi Da Samraj's Teaching-Word: 32
The "Source-Texts" of Adidam

3. The "Bright"-Art Work of Avatar Adi Da Samraj   44

4. An Overview of *The All-Completing and Final*   48
Divine Revelation To Mankind

THE ALL-COMPLETING AND FINAL DIVINE REVELATION TO MANKIND

FIRST WORD:

Do Not Misunderstand Me—
I Am Not "Within" you, but you Are In Me,
and I Am Not a Mere "Man" in the "Middle" of Mankind,
but All of Mankind Is Surrounded, and Pervaded,
and Blessed By Me

59

PROLOGUE:
My Divine Disclosure
81

PART ONE:
I Am The Perfectly Subjective Divine Person,
Self-Manifested As The Ruchira Avatar—
Who Is The First, The Last, and The Only
Adept-Realizer, Adept-Revealer, and
Adept-Revelation of The Seventh Stage of Life
95

P A R T   T W O :
I (Alone) Am The Adidam Revelation
(A Summary Description of the Inherent Distinction—
and the ego-Transcending Continuity—Between the
Inherently ego-Based Great Tradition, Which Is Comprised
of Only Six of the Possible Seven Stages of Life,
and the Unique, and All-Inclusive, and All-Completing,
and All-Transcending, and Self-Evidently Divine
Adidam Revelation of the Inherently egoless
Seventh Stage Realization of Me)
105

P A R T   T H R E E :
The Heart-Summary Of Adidam
193

P A R T   F O U R :
The All-Completing and Final
Divine Revelation To Mankind
199

P A R T   F I V E :
Most Perfect Awakening To
The Domain Of Conscious Light
303

P A R T   S I X :
Three Essays from the
Samraj Upanishad
335

1. The Yoga of Divine Self-Recognition   337
2. The Perfection Beyond Conditions   341
3. The Infinite Divine Current That Shines   348
   in the Body-Mind of Man

EPILOGUE:
The True Dawn Horse
Is The Only Way To Me
355

What You Can Do Next 370

The Great Choice: 375
An Invitation to the Way of Adidam

An Invitation to Support Adidam 398

Further Notes to the Reader 400

Appendix: Chart of The Seven Stages of Life 403

Notes to the Text of 407
The All-Completing and Final
Divine Revelation To Mankind

Glossary 419

The Sacred Literature 458
of Avatar Adi Da Samraj

Index 469

RUCHIRA AVATAR ADI DA SAMRAJ
The Mountain Of Attention, 2000

Introduction

This book is an invitation to enter a different world. A world that is completely real, in the largest possible sense of that word. A world in which none of the sufferings and difficulties of life are ignored or denied—but also a world in which yearnings for truth, wisdom, happiness, beauty, and love are addressed at an extraordinary depth. A world in which there is real, trustable guidance through the "maze" of life's confusions and crises. A world that vastly exceeds all limited notions of what is "real". A world of deep, abiding joy.

People from all walks of life have felt this world open up to them when they read the books of the Divine World-Teacher, Ruchira Avatar Adi Da Samraj. Those of us who have done so have felt our deepest questions answered, our most profound heart-longings satisfied. We have rejoiced to discover Avatar Adi Da's Revelation of the True Nature of Reality—the Great Mystery that has been described throughout the ages by such words as "Truth" or "Light" or "Beauty" or "God". We have marveled at His precise "map" of the entire course of human development (from birth to Divine Enlightenment) and at His full description of the nature of conditional existence in all its dimensions. We have treasured His compassionate Instruction about the real issues that everyone faces at the foundation level of human life: death, sex, intimacy, emotional maturity, community life, and many more. And we have been overwhelmed to encounter His complete (and revolutionary) Address to everything beyond the foundation level: what the apparently separate ego-self is really about (and how to actually go completely beyond it), what constitutes real Spiritual life (and how one is actually Awakened to it), what it really means to be Divinely Enlightened (and the never-before-completely-revealed process by which Divine Enlightenment is actually and permanently Realized).

Even more than this, we have felt Avatar Adi Da Samraj Transmit the very same (and unimaginably deep) Peace, Happiness, and Love that He describes in His books—and we have found that His Transmission can be experienced anywhere, regardless of whether one is in the same room with Him or thousands of miles away. Our bodies, hearts, and minds and our entire lives have been flooded with His Divine Spiritual Blessing— Blessing which is self-evidently Real, True, and Good, and which has (as we can attest from our own personal experience) the most extraordinary Power to Transform human lives and destinies.

Those of us who have been drawn to Avatar Adi Da Samraj have discovered that the impact of the Truth He has Revealed and of the Blessing He Transmits is so great in our lives, so far beyond anything else we have known, that a truly amazing recognition has grown in our hearts and minds: Avatar Adi Da Samraj is not merely a great human being who speaks profound Truth—He is the Divine Reality Itself, Appearing in a human body in order to Offer the Perfect Revelation of Truth and the Perfect Transmission of Love-Bliss directly to all of humankind.

Therefore, our ecstatic heart-confession to you is this: The Divine Giver of Happiness, Light, and Love is present in the world, in human form, at this very moment—and He is freely Offering His Gifts to all. He is here, moved by overwhelming Divine Love, to establish (for all time) the Way by which all may ultimately Realize Divine Enlightenment. And He is also here (at this life-or-death moment in human history) to Bless the global human community in its necessary embrace of the disposition of cooperation, tolerance, and peace.

Avatar Adi Da Samraj began Teaching in 1972. In the years since then, He has communicated a vast store of Wisdom. But He has also done far more than that: He has created an entirely new Way of life, a new religion, which is now practiced by people of different cultures in many parts of the world. Just as the religions of Christianity and Buddhism are named after their founders, the religion founded by Avatar Adi Da Samraj is named after Him—it is called "Adidam" (AH-dee-DAHM). Adidam is an all-embracing practice that takes every aspect of human life—physical, emotional, mental, psychic, Spiritual, and Transcendental—into account. The foundation of Adidam is the response of heart-felt devotion to Avatar Adi Da Samraj, in loving gratitude for His Gifts of Wisdom and Spiritual Blessing.

Avatar Adi Da Samraj does not offer you a set of beliefs, or even a set of Spiritual techniques. He simply Offers you His Revelation of Truth as a Free Gift, to respond to as you will. And, if you are moved to take up His Way, He invites you to enter into a direct devotional and Spiritual relationship with Him.

Those of us who have taken this step have found the Spiritual relationship to Avatar Adi Da Samraj to be a supremely precious Gift, a literally miraculous Blessing, the answer to our deepest longings—greatly surpassing anything we have ever experienced or even imagined to be possible. What we have discovered, in our own lives and experience, is that Avatar Adi Da Samraj has brought into being the Way by which human beings can not only know the Truth of Reality but they can live that Truth, incarnate that Truth—with their entire existence, their entire structure of body, mind, and psyche.

To find Avatar Adi Da Samraj is to find the Very Heart of Reality—tangibly felt in your own heart as the Deepest Truth of Existence.

This is the great mystery that you are invited to discover for yourself.

Avatar Adi Da Samraj's Name is composed of four Sanskrit words.

His principal Name is "Adi Da". "Avatar" and "Samraj" are sacred Titles, used in association with His Name.

"Adi" (AH-dee) means "Original" (or "Primordial"), and "Da" means "the Divine Giver". Thus, "Adi Da" means "the Original Divine Giver".

"Avatar" means "a 'Crossing Down' of the Divine Being into the world" (or, in other words, "an Appearance of the Divine in conditionally manifested form").

"Samraj" (sahm-RAHJ) means "universal Lord".

In fuller forms of reference, Adi Da Samraj is called "the Ruchira (roo-CHIH-rah) Avatar", meaning "the Avatar of Infinite Brightness".

Avatar Adi Da Samraj:
His Life and Teaching

From the moment of His Birth (in New York, on November 3, 1939), Adi Da Samraj was consciously aware of His Native Divine Condition. As soon as He became able to use language, He gave this Condition a simple but very expressive Name—"the 'Bright'",* meaning the Divine Condition of Boundlessly Radiant and Infinitely Joyful Love-Bliss. But then, at the age of two years, Avatar Adi Da made a profound spontaneous choice. He chose to relinquish His constant Enjoyment of the "Bright"—and He made that choice out of what He Describes as a "painful loving", a sympathy for the suffering and ignorance of human beings. Avatar Adi Da Confesses that He chose to "Learn Man"—to enter into everything that humankind feels and suffers, and also to experience all the various levels of Spiritual Realization known to humanity—in order to discover how to Draw human beings into the "Bright" Divine Condition that He knew as His own True State and the True State of everyone.

This utter Submission to all aspects of human life, in the context of His own body-mind, was the first Purpose of Adi Da's Incarnation. In His Spiritual Autobiography, *The Knee Of Listening,* Avatar Adi Da recounts this amazing and heroic Ordeal, which lasted for the first thirty years of His Life. That Ordeal culminated in 1970, when Avatar Adi Da Re-Awakened permanently to the "Bright" and embarked upon the second great Purpose of His

*For definitions of terms and names, please see the Glossary (pp. 419-56).

Submission to human life—the Process of "Teaching Man". It was not until April 2000 that His Work of Submitting to the human condition would be utterly complete. Since then, having done everything He needed to do in His Work of Teaching, Avatar Adi Da is free to Manifest only His own Divine Love, Bliss, and "Brightness", without any necessity to Submit to ordinary (or even extraordinary) human purposes and efforts.

Teaching and Blessing Work

Teaching the Way of Relationship to Him

When He began to Teach others, Avatar Adi Da Samraj simply made Himself available to all who were willing to enter into the living Process of Real-God-Realization in His Company—a Process Which He summarized as the devotional and Spiritual relationship to Him, rather than any method or technique of Spiritual attainment. Through

Los Angeles, 1972

The Mountain Of Attention Sanctuary, 1974

that relationship—an extra-ordinary human and Spiritual intimacy—Avatar Adi Da Samraj perfectly embraced each of His devotees. He used every kind of skillful means to Awaken them to the Truth that the separate, un-Enlightened self—with all its fear, anxieties, and fruit-less seeking for Happiness—

is self-imposed suffering, a contraction of the being (which He calls "the self-contraction"). And He Offered the practice of heart-Communion with Him—necessarily joined with profound self-understanding and serious responsibility for every aspect of one's life—as the means of going beyond the self-contraction and thereby Realizing Real Happiness.

I have Come to Live (now, and forever hereafter) with those who love Me with ego-overwhelming love, and I have Come to Love them likewise Overwhelmingly. . . .

Until you fall in love, love is what you _fear_ to do. When you have fallen in love, and you __are__ (thus) always already in love, then you cease to fear to love. . . . Those who fall in love with Me, Fall into Me. Those whose hearts are given, in love, to Me, Fall into My Heart. ["What Will You Do If You Love Me?", from *Da Love-Ananda Gita*]

Two Epochal Events

In 1986, an Event occurred that marked the beginning of a great change in Avatar Adi Da's Work in the world. In this Great Event, a profound Yogic Swoon (taking the form of His apparent near-death) overwhelmed His body-mind, and Avatar Adi Da Samraj sponta-neously began the process of relin-quishing His Ordeal of Teaching Man (a process that lasted another fourteen years). In the wake of that great Swoon, He began to Radiate His Divinity as never before. This was the beginning of His Divine Self-"Emergence". From that moment,

The Mountain Of Attention, 1986

Adi Da Samraj devoted Himself increasingly to the third and eter-nal Purpose of His Avataric Incarnation—that of Blessing Man (and all beings).

Lopez Island, 2000

Even after the Great Event in 1986, Avatar Adi Da continued to Work to ensure that His Revelation of the Way of Adidam was fully founded in the world. The final completion of all this Work was eventually signalled by another Event of the most profound significance, which occurred on April 12, 2000. At the time, Avatar Adi Da was staying on Lopez Island, off the northern coast of the state of Washington. On the evening of April 12, Avatar Adi Da Samraj entered into a severe physical and Yogic crisis, which (like the Event of 1986) seemed to threaten His bodily survival. He later confirmed that He had, indeed, been on the "way out" of the earthly realm, but the process stopped just before physical death became inevitable.

With His "return" to bodily existence, Avatar Adi Da's physical Body had become profoundly Spiritualized. His Transmission of Divine Love and Blessing became even more tangible and powerful than before. Since that Event at Lopez Island, Avatar Adi Da's bodily (human) Form has (by His own Confession) been Standing at the very Threshold between the Divine Domain of Infinite Love-Bliss-"Brightness" and all the domains of conditional manifestation. Thus, to an even greater degree than before, the physical Body of Avatar Adi Da Samraj is an unbelievably Potent Conductor of His Divine Blessing to all who approach Him with an open heart.

Now, all the foundation Work of Avatar Adi Da's Incarnation has been completed. Everything necessary for the understanding and right practice of the real Spiritual process, culminating in Divine Enlightenment, has been said and done by Him. The summary of His Wisdom-Teaching is preserved for all time in a series of twenty-three "Source-Texts" (described on pp. 32-43). And the

Way of Adidam is fully established. This monumental Work has been accomplished by Avatar Adi Da in a little over a quarter of a century—twenty-seven years of ceaseless Instruction, in constant interaction with His devotees. And, with that Great Work accomplished, He is now entirely concentrated in His Work of Spiritually Blessing all.

In *Aham Da Asmi (Beloved, I Am Da)*, the first of His twenty-three "Source-Texts", Avatar Adi Da Samraj makes this summary Confession of how and why He has Appeared in the world:

> *I Am The Very and "Bright" Condition Of all and All.*
> *I Am The One To Be Realized.*

> *I Am Able To Appear In Human Form.*
> *This Is Because I Am Not Inherently "Different" (or Separated) From you.*
> *Indeed, I Am The Very Condition In Which you Are Apparently arising.*
> *I Am your own True Condition—Beyond egoity, and Beyond all conditional references.*

> *I Will Be here Forever.*
> *I Will Be every "where" Forever.*

> *I Cannot Leave, For My "Bright" Divine Self-Domain Is Not Some "Where" To "Go To".*
> *My Divine Self-Domain Is Eternal.*
> *I Am Eternal, and I Am Always Already Merely Present—here, and every "where" In The Cosmic Domain.*

> *You Have Been Waiting For Me—but I Have Been here All The While.*

> *I Love you Now.*
> *I Will Love you every "then" and "there".*
> *And I Always Loved you (and every one, and all, and All).*
> *That Is How I Got To here (and every "where").*

There Is <u>Only</u> Reality Itself, <u>Only</u> Truth, <u>Only</u> Real God.
All Are <u>Inherently</u> Conjoined With What Is Always Already The Case.

There Is Not any one who is merely a mortal "organism"—Not Even any of the fishes or the possums or the frogs or the mosquitoes, and Not Even any of the worst Of Mankind.
All Must Be Forgiven.
All Must Be Purified.
All Must Suffer Through An Ordeal Of Divine "Brightening".

In any particular moment, some Are Apparently More Serious Than others, but There Is No Ultimate "Difference" Between beings.
<u>All</u> Are In Me.
Therefore, <u>all</u> Have Me As their Eternal Opportunity.

There Is Only One Reality For all, and For All.
Therefore, There Is Only One Teaching and One Great Opportunity For all, and For All.

I <u>Am</u> The Infinite "Bright" One—The <u>Only</u> One Who Is <u>Always</u> With you, and With every one, and With all, and With All.

[Aham Da Asmi]

"Money, Food, and Sex"

During His years of Teaching and Revelation (from 1972 to 2000), Avatar Adi Da undertook a vast, in-life "consideration" with His devotees, covering everything related to Spiritual life—from the most rudimentary matters to the most esoteric. One extremely important area of "consideration" was how to rightly relate to the most basic urges and activities of human life—what Avatar Adi Da describes as the realm of "money, food, and sex". (By "money", Avatar Adi Da means not only the earning and use of money itself, but the exercising of life-energy in general.)

In most religious traditions, an ascetical approach to these primal urges is recommended—in other words, desires related to "money, food, and sex" are to be minimized or denied. Avatar Adi Da took a different approach. When they are rightly engaged, ordinary human enjoyments are not a problem, not "sinful" or "anti-spiritual" in and of themselves. Indeed, the ascetical effort to "cut out" (or "cut down on") such enjoyments is itself simply one of the possible variations on the ego's impulse to manipulate the conditions of existence to its own benefit. Thus, the root-problem of human beings is not any particular activity or desire of the body-mind, but the ego itself—the governing presumption that one is a separate and independent entity attempting to counteract the inevitable suffering of embodied existence. Therefore, in living dialogue and experimentation with His devotees, Avatar Adi Da brought to light, in detail, exactly how the human functions of money (or life-energy), food, and sex can be rightly engaged, in a truly ego-transcending manner—an entirely life-positive and non-suppressive manner that is both pleasurable and supportive of the Spiritual process in His Company. (Avatar Adi Da's Instruction relative to "money, food, and sex" is fully described in His book *Ruchira Avatara Hridaya-Tantra Yoga*.)

Going Beyond <u>All</u> Forms of Egoity

The transcending of egoic involvement with "money, food, and sex" is a matter that relates to the beginnings of (or preparation for) real Spiritual practice. But the necessity for ego-transcendence does not end there. In His years of Teaching and Revelation, Avatar Adi Da Revealed that the ego is still present, in one form or another, in all the possible varieties of Spiritual attainment short of Most Perfect Divine Enlightenment. The word "Enlightenment" is used by different people and in different traditions with various different meanings. In Avatar Adi Da's language, "Enlightenment" (which He sometimes modifies, for the sake of clarifying His meaning, as "Most Perfect Divine Enlightenment", and which is synonymous with "Divine Self-Realization", "Real-God-Realization", and "seventh stage Realization") specifically means that the process of ego-transcendence has been entirely completed, relative to all the dimensions of the being. In other words, the ego has been transcended in three distinct phases—first at the physical (or gross) level (the level of "money, food, and sex"), then at the subtle level (the level of internal visions, auditions, and all kinds of mystical experience), and finally at the causal level (the root-level of conscious existence, wherein the sense of "I" and "other", or the subject-object dichotomy, seems to arise in Consciousness).

The complete process of ego-transcendence is extraordinarily profound and can only proceed on the basis of all the foundation disciplines and ever-increasing heart-surrender. Then, progressively, there is a transformation of view, a "positive disillusionment" with each phase of egoity—until there is Most Perfect Divine Enlightenment (or "Open Eyes"), the Realization of Consciousness Itself as the Single Love-Blissful Reality and Source of existence.

A Fierce Critic of Cultism

The ego manifests not only in individuals but also in groups. One of the collective manifestations of egoity is cultism—not only in the sense of misguided religious cults, but in the larger sense of the universal human tendency to become cultically attached to (and dependent on) a particular person, a particular point of view (or philosophy), a particular activity, or any kind of particular thing.

From the very beginning of His Teaching Work, Avatar Adi Da Samraj was well aware that, no matter who came to Him, it was inevitable that they (as ordinary human beings with ordinary human characteristics) would tend to relate to Him in a cultic manner. Therefore, He has constantly criticized the cultic tendency in His own devotees and in human beings generally. At the same time, He is also clear in His criticism of the way the media tends to indiscriminately and pejoratively label all non-mainstream religious groups as "cults", thereby working against people's true impulses to engage a Spiritually transformative process.

AVATAR ADI DA SAMRAJ: Over the years, you have all heard Me Speak about cultism in negative terms. I have Criticized the cults that people form around religious leaders (and even around true Spiritual Masters), as well as the cultic attachments that people create with one another. There exists a certain hyped enthusiasm to which people are attracted. And when those people accept all the dogmas with which that particular group makes itself enthusiastic, they maintain themselves as opponents of the world and lose communication with the world in general, and with the processes of life.

To Me, that enthusiasm is bizarre. There is something about the capability of individuals for that kind of enthusiasm that makes My skin crawl. It is a kind of madness. Gleeful enthusiasm has nothing whatsoever to do with this Way and with the value that I can have for you personally. It has <u>nothing</u> to do with it!

My Purpose in associating with you is not to entertain you, not to be believed in. I am not here to offer you a relationship in which you are never changed but only consoled. My Purpose in dealing with you, My Purpose in My Teaching Work, is to make it possible for you to be in devotional Communion with Me, to be Spiritually intimate with Me—so that you yourself may live and fulfill this practice, and make a community with one another out of the true Happiness of mature Divine living.

Everything about cultism that is negative is specifically Criticized in My Wisdom-Teaching. I do not want your enthusiasm to be superficially generated by reading My Books. I want you to "consider" My Arguments. I want you to "consider" yourself very critically, very directly and rigorously, and come to the point of most fundamental self-understanding. When you have sufficient understanding of your own game, your childishness and adolescence, then you will be able to advance in the practice I have Given you.

I refuse to console individuals by telling them that all they need to do is believe in Me, that all they need to do is practice some silly little technique and they will Realize God, no matter what they do otherwise. I am not the slightest bit interested in your gleeful applause. I want you to understand yourself and to practice true heart-Communion with Me. I want you to truly live the Way that I have Revealed and Given to you. In order to do that, you must grow up. You must stop being naive about the communications of silly downtown people, all the aggressiveness of media campaigns, and all the things that fundamentally work against the higher acculturation of human beings. [December 17, 1979]

Standing Free

In His Spiritual Work with His devotees and the world, Avatar Adi Da Samraj has confronted the realities of egoity in a completely direct and unflinching manner. In His years of "Teaching Man", He did not hesitate in the slightest to grapple with the ego as it might be manifested in any moment by an individual devotee or a group of devotees—for the sake of helping His devotees understand and go beyond their ego-possessed disposition and activity.

However, even in the midst of that compassionate struggle with the forces of egoity, Avatar Adi Da has always Stood utterly Free of the ego-world. And, especially since the late 1970s, that Free Stand more and more took the form of His living in an essentially private circumstance, at one of the Hermitages established for Him (at secluded locations in California, Hawaii, and Fiji—see p. 390). In His Hermitage sphere, Avatar Adi Da is served by a small group of renunciate devotees, with whom He does particularly intensive Spiritual Work. And it is in the set-apart domain of His Hermitages (rather than in some kind of more public setting) that Avatar Adi Da sometimes receives His devotees in general (and, on occasion, specially invited members of the public), to Grant them His Spiritual Blessing.

The reasons why Avatar Adi Da maintains a Hermitage life are profound. The purpose of His Existence is to Reveal the Divine Reality—in other words, to Manifest the Freedom, Purity, and unbounded Blissfulness of His own Divine Nature, to Exist simply as He Is, without having to make compromises or adjustments in order to "fit in" to the ordinary ego-patterned world. Therefore, it is essential that He live in a sacred domain that conforms to Him and to the nature of His Spiritual Work, where He can remain independent of (but not disconnected from) the common world.

As He has commented many times, His Hermitage life is a life of seclusion, but not of isolation. His secluded Hermitage life is what allows His Divine Blessing to Flow into the world with the greatest possible force and effectiveness—it is what allows His Spiritual connection to all beings to be as strong as possible.

A Testimony of Spiritual Practice

The process of the Way of Adidam unfolds by Avatar Adi Da's Grace, according to the depth of surrender and response in each devotee. One of the most extraordinary living testimonies to the Greatness and Truth of the Way of Adidam is one of Avatar Adi Da's longtime devotees, whose full renunciate name is Ruchiradama Quandra Sukhapur Rani. Quandra Sukhapur has totally consecrated herself to Avatar Adi Da and lives always in His Sphere, in a relationship of unique intimacy and service. By her profound love of, and most

Ruchiradama Quandra
Sukhapur Rani with
Ruchira Avatar Adi Da Samraj

exemplary surrender to, her Divine Heart-Master, she has become combined with Him at a unique depth. She manifests the signs of deep and constant immersion in His Divine Being, both in meditation and daily life. Quandra Sukhapur is a member of the Ruchira Sannyasin Order (the senior cultural authority within the gathering of Avatar Adi Da's devotees), practicing in the ultimate stages of the Way of Adidam.

Through a process of more than twenty years of intense testing, Avatar Adi Da has been able to lead Quandra Sukhapur to the threshold of Divine Enlightenment. The profound and ecstatic relationship with Avatar Adi Da that Quandra Sukhapur has come to know can be felt in this intimate letter of devotional confession to Him:

RUCHIRADAMA QUANDRA SUKHAPUR RANI: Bhagavan Love-Ananda, Supreme and Divine Person, Real-God-Body of Love,

I rest in Your Constant and Perfect Love-Embrace, with no need but to forever worship You. Suddenly in love, Mastered at heart, always with my head at Your Supreme and Holy Feet, I am beholding and recognizing Your "Bright" Divine Person. My Beloved, You so "Brightly" Descend and utterly Convert this heart, mind, body, and breath, from separate self to the "Bhava" of Your Love-Bliss-Happiness.

Supreme Lord Ruchira, the abandonment of the contracted personality, the relinquishment of ego-bondage to the world, and the profound purification and release of ego-limitations—all brought about by Your Grace, throughout the years since I first came to You—has culminated in a great comprehensive force of one-pointed devotion to You and a great certainty in the Inherent Sufficiency of Realization Itself. The essence of my practice is to always remain freely submitted to You and centralized in You—the Condition Prior to all bondage, all modification, and all illusion.

My Beloved Lord Ruchira, You have Moved me to renounce all egoic "bonding" with conditionally manifested others, conditionally manifested worlds, and conditionally manifested self, to enter into the depths of this "in-love" and utter devotion to You. Finding You has led to a deep urge to abandon all superficiality and to simply luxuriate in Your Divine Body and Person. All separation is shattered in Your Divine Love-Bliss-"Bhava". Your Infusion is Utter. I feel You everywhere.

I am Drawn, by Grace of Your Spiritual Presence, into profound meditative Contemplation of Your Divine State. Sometimes, when I am entering into these deep states of meditation, I remain vaguely aware of the body, and particularly of the breath and the heartbeat. I feel the heart and lungs slow down. Then I am sometimes aware of my breath and heartbeat being suspended in a state of Yogic sublimity. Then there is no awareness of body, no awareness of mind, no perceptual awareness, and no conceptual awareness. There is only abiding in Contemplation of You in Your Domain of Consciousness Itself. And, when I resume association with the body and begin once again to hear my breath and heartbeat, I feel the *remarkable Power of Your Great Samadhi. I feel no necessity for anything, and I feel Your Capability to Bless and Change and Meditate all. I can feel how this entrance into objectless worship of You as Consciousness Itself (allowing this Abiding to deepen ever so profoundly, by utter submission of separate self to You) establishes me in a different relationship to everything that arises.*

My Beloved Bhagavan, Love-Ananda, I have Found You. Now, by Your Grace, I am able to behold You and live in this constant Embrace. This is my Joy and Happiness and the Yoga of ego-renunciation I engage. [October 11, 1997]

The Free Revelation of Reality

The Divine Artist

After the Lopez Island Event, Avatar Adi Da's Work dramatically changed. The content of His Work was no longer His Instruction of devotees and His creation of the Way of Adidam. Instead, He became intent on finding further means of directly Revealing Reality, of directly Showing That Which is Realized in any moment of most profound heart-Communion with Him (and Which eventually becomes one's constant Realization, when the progressive stages of practice, which He had so painstakingly described during His Submission-Work, come to fruition).

A primary means for this Revelation of Reality is Avatar Adi Da's artistic Work based in photography and video. Art of every kind has always been of great importance to Avatar Adi Da, because His entire Life has been devoted to the Revelation of Truth and to all the means whereby human beings may be Awakened to What is Real and True. Art is a unique human activity that has the potential to bypass the ego-mind and its mood of self-obsession, directly touching the heart and transforming our perception of reality. Thus, Avatar Adi Da's communication through the artistic media is fully as profound and "radical" as His communication (via the medium of words) in His "Source-Texts".

**The Mountain Of Attention
Sanctuary, 2001**

AVATAR ADI DA SAMRAJ: The true artist is a sacred performer. He or she must do the magic that causes others to participate in manifest reality in the sacred sense, or the sense of love— in the sense of ego-transcendence, of ecstasy.

[August 1, 1984]

A brief introduction to Avatar Adi Da's artistic Work (including the photographic images that appear on the covers of His "Source-Texts") is given in "The 'Bright'-Art Work of Avatar Adi Da Samraj" (pp. 44-47).

Ruchiradam

Emerging at the same time as His art Work in photography and video is another remarkable sign of Avatar Adi Da's Free Revelation of Reality: His Word on the most esoteric secrets of the Process of Divine Enlightenment.

The Way of Adidam encompasses the entire process of Spiritual growth—from birth, through the progressive stages of human and Spiritual maturity, to Divine Enlightenment. The profound esoteric core of the Way of Adidam is what Avatar Adi Da Samraj calls "the 'Perfect Practice'", which is the Spiritual practice that becomes possible once one has grown beyond all identification with the body and the mind, and has become natively Identified with the Divine Consciousness Itself. The "Perfect Practice" of Adidam is the essential process of Divine Enlightenment. In February 2001, while He was speaking ecstatically of these esoteric matters, Avatar Adi Da Gave the "Perfect Practice" a special name, to indicate its special nature. That name is "Ruchiradam"—a free combination of "Ruchira" ("bright", in Sanskrit) and "Adidam".

Ruchiradam is the "root" esoteric process of Adidam. It is the process of <u>directly</u> "Locating" Reality, Truth, or Real God—rather than a <u>progressive</u> process of Spiritual Awakening that relates to the patterns associated with existence as an apparently individual body-mind. That direct "Locating" can occur in any moment of profound heart-Communion with Avatar Adi Da Samraj, even from the very beginning of the devotional and Spiritual relationship to Him—but to embrace Ruchiradam as one's established and consistent form of practice requires the most profound Spiritual preparation.

AVATAR ADI DA SAMRAJ: The reference "Ruchiradam" should be understood to describe and summarize the Fullness of the Way I have Revealed, as engaged in the form of the "Perfect Practice" of the devotional and Spiritual relationship to Me.

The Way of Adidam, as a whole, is an elaboration of all the implications of the Way of the devotional and Spiritual relationship to Me—and My Revelation of the total (or full and complete) Way of Adidam is Given so that those who are moved to serious practice in My Company will have a guide relative to everything that such practice requires as a way of life. Ruchiradam is the root of the Way of Adidam. Ruchiradam is the most essential (and moment to moment) practice of the Way I have Revealed and Given. Thus, Ruchiradam is not an elaborated way of life covering all activities in time and space. Rather, Ruchiradam is simply the essential process of Real-God-Realization Itself—As It Always Already Is, in every moment.

In order to take up the practice of Ruchiradam, My any formally acknowledged devotee who practices the Way of Adidam must establish his or her direct Spiritual relationship to Me, through the Da Love-Ananda Samrajya, and must then develop that relationship to Me in the form of this "Perfect Practice" of Spiritual devotion to Me.

When people come into My physical Company, they are to come specifically for the purpose of engaging and developing the moment to moment practice of Ruchiradam, which is the essential process of Divine Enlightenment. [February 11, 2001]

Avatar Adi Da's Revelation of Ruchiradam is Given in five of His "Source-Texts": *Eleutherios, Santosha Adidam, The Lion Sutra, The Overnight Revelation Of Conscious Light*, and *The Dawn Horse Testament Of The Ruchira Avatar*. That Revelation—the Revelation of the Way of directly Realizing Reality Itself—is now the only Word of Instruction that He speaks.

AVATAR ADI DA SAMRAJ: Now My "Occupation", As I Am, Is simply the "Bright". I Do That in My (essentially non-verbal) feeling-interaction with people, without having to get involved in talking anymore—except ecstatically.

I am not here talking about any form of conventional or traditional religion. I do not have anything to do with any such religion. I am Communicating the Way of Realizing Reality Itself. Therefore, I have no tradition to uphold, no tradition that represents Me. I am simply Speaking the Truth.

I Am the Truth. I Do the Truth. That is it.

And What I am Communicating I am Communicating to the world, to everyone, all beings. [March 13, 2001]

Finding Real Happiness

This book is Avatar Adi Da's invitation to you to come to know Him—by freely considering His words, and feeling their impact on your life and heart. Avatar Adi Da Himself has never been satisfied with anything conditional. He has never been satisfied with anything less than Real, Permanent, Absolute Happiness—even in the midst of the inevitable sufferings of life. His Sign and Revelation is the utter freedom and Happiness of the Divine Reality. And that Happiness is What He is Offering to you.

The heart has a question.
The heart must be Satisfied.
Without that Satisfaction—Which is necessarily Spiritual in Nature—there is no Real Happiness.

The contraction of the heart is what you are suffering.
It is the ego.
The egoic life is a search—founded upon (and initiated by) the self-contraction of the total body-mind.
The egoic life is a self-caused search to be relieved of the distress of self-reduced, self-diminished, even utterly self-destroyed Love-Bliss.
Love-Bliss gone, non-existent, unknown—just this pumping, agitated, psycho-physical thing.

The ego-"I" does not know What It Is That Is Happening.
You are just "hanging out" for a while, until "it" drops dead.
It is not good enough.
Therefore, I Advise you to begin to be profoundly religious, and not waste any time about it.
You must Realize the Spiritual Condition of Existence Itself . . . .
You cannot be sane if you think there is only flesh, only materiality, only grossness.
Such thinking is not fully "natural", not enough.
There is "Something" you are not accounting for.
Be open to "Whatever" That Is.
You must look into this. [Hridaya Rosary]

Avatar Adi Da Samraj's Teaching-Word: The "Source-Texts" of Adidam

For twenty-seven years (from 1972 to 1999), Avatar Adi Da Samraj devoted Himself tirelessly to Teaching those who came to Him. Even before He formally began to Teach in 1972, He had already written the earliest versions of two of His primary Texts—His "liturgical drama" (*The Mummery*) and His Spiritual Autobiography (*The Knee Of Listening*). Then, when He opened the doors of His first Ashram in Hollywood (on April 25, 1972), He initiated a vast twenty-seven-year "conversation" with the thousands of people who approached Him during that period of time—a "conversation" that included thousands of hours of sublime and impassioned Discourse and thousands of pages of profound and exquisite Writing. And the purpose of that "conversation" was to fully communicate the Truth for Real.

Both His Speech and His Writing were conducted as a kind of living "laboratory". He was constantly asking to hear His devotees' questions and their responses to His Written and Spoken Word. He was constantly calling His devotees to <u>live</u> what He was Teaching and discover its Truth in their own experience—not merely to passively accept it as dogma. He was constantly testing whether His communication on any particular subject was complete and detailed enough or whether He needed to say more. And everything He said and wrote was a spontaneous expression of His own direct Awareness of Reality—never a merely theoretical or speculative proposition, never a statement merely inherited from traditional sources.

This immense outpouring of Revelation and Instruction came to completion in the years 1997-1999. During that period, Avatar

Adi Da Samraj created a series of twenty-three books that He designated as the "Source-Texts" of Adidam. He incorporated into these books His most essential Writings and Discourses from all the preceding years, as well as many new Writings and Discourses that had never been published previously. His magnificent "Source-Texts" are thus His Eternal Message to all. They contain His complete Revelation of Truth, and (together with the "Supportive Texts", in which Avatar Adi Da Gives further detailed Instruction relative to the functional, practical, relational, and cultural disciplines of the Way of Adidam) they give His fully detailed description of the entire process of Awakening, culminating in Divine Enlightenment.

Avatar Adi Da's twenty-three "Source-Texts" are not simply a series of books each of which is entirely distinct from all the others. Rather, they form an intricately interwoven fabric. Each book contains some material found in no other "Source-Text", some material shared with certain other "Source-Texts", and some material included in all twenty-three of the "Source-Texts". (The three pieces shared by all twenty-three books are "Do Not Misunderstand Me", "My Divine Disclosure", and "The Heart-Summary Of Adidam". Each of these has a particular function and message that is essential to every one of the books.) Thus, to read Avatar Adi Da's "Source-Texts" is to engage a special kind of study (similar to the practice of repeating a mantra), in which certain writings are repeatedly read, such that they penetrate one's being even more profoundly and take on deeper significance by being read in a variety of different contexts. Furthermore, each of the "Source-Texts" of Adidam is thereby a complete and self-contained Argument. Altogether, to study Avatar Adi Da's "Source-Texts" is to enter into an "eternal conversation" with Him, in which different meanings emerge at different times—always appropriate to the current moment in one's life and experience.

At the conclusion of His paramount "Source-Text", *The Dawn Horse Testament*, Avatar Adi Da Samraj makes His own passionate Confession of the Impulse that led Him to create His twenty-three "Source-Texts".

Now I Have, By All My "Crazy" Means, Revealed My One and Many Divine Secrets As The Great Person Of The Heart. For Your Sake, I Made My Every Work and Word. And Now, By Every Work and Word I Made, I Have Entirely Confessed (and Showed) Myself—and Always Freely, and Even As A Free Man, In The "Esoteric" Language Of Intimacy and Ecstasy, Openly Worded To You (and To all). Even Now (and Always), By This (My Avatarically Self-Revealed Divine Word Of Heart), I Address every Seeming Separate being (and each one As The Heart Itself), Because It Is Necessary That all beings, Even The Entire Cosmic Domain Of Seeming Separate beings, Be (In all times and places) Called To Wisdom and The Heart.

Capitalization and Punctuation in the "Source-Texts" of Avatar Adi Da Samraj

Speaking and Writing in the twentieth and twenty-first centuries, Avatar Adi Da Samraj has used the English language as the medium for His Communication. Over the years of His Teaching-Work, Avatar Adi Da developed a thoroughly original manner of employing English as a sacred language. (He also includes some Sanskrit terminology in His Teaching vocabulary, in order to supplement the relatively undeveloped sacred vocabulary of English.)

Avatar Adi Da's unique use of English is evident not only with respect to vocabulary, but also with respect to capitalization and punctuation.

Vocabulary. A glossary is included at the end of this book (pp. 419-56), where specialized terms (both English terms and terms derived from Sanskrit) are defined.

Capitalization. Avatar Adi Da frequently capitalizes words that would not ordinarily be capitalized in English—and such capitalized words include not only nouns, but also pronouns, verbs, adjectives, adverbs, and even articles and prepositions. By such capitalization, He is indicating that the word refers (either inherently, or by virtue of the context) to the Unconditional Divine Reality, rather than the conditional (or worldly) reality. For example:

If there is no escape from (or no Way out of) the corner (or the "centered" trap) of ego-"I"—the heart goes mad, and the body-mind becomes more and more "dark" (bereft of the Indivisible and Inherently Free Light of the Self-Evident, and Self-Evidently Divine, Love-Bliss That Is Reality Itself). ["Do Not Misunderstand Me"]

Avatar Adi Da's chosen conventions of capitalization vary in different "Source-Texts" and in different sections of a given "Source-Text". In certain "Source-Texts" (notably *The Dawn Horse Testament Of The Ruchira Avatar, The Heart Of The Dawn Horse Testament Of The Ruchira Avatar,* and the various Parts of the other "Source-Texts" that are excerpted from *The Dawn Horse Testament Of The Ruchira Avatar*), Avatar Adi Da employs a highly unusual convention of capitalization, in which the overwhelming majority of all words are capitalized, and only those words that indicate the egoic (or dualistic) point of view are left lower-cased. This capitalization convention (which Avatar Adi Da has worked out to an extraordinarily subtle degree—in ways that are often startling) is in itself a Teaching device, intended to communicate His fundamental Revelation that "There Is Only Real God", and that only the ego (or the dualistic or separative point of view) prevents us from living and Realizing that Truth. For example:

Therefore, For My Every Devotee, all conditions Must Be Aligned and Yielded In Love With Me—or Else any object or any other Will Be The Cause Of Heart-Stress, self-Contraction, Dissociation, Clinging, Boredom, Doubt, The Progressive Discomfort Of Diminished Love-Bliss, and All The Forgetfulness Of Grace and Truth and Happiness Itself. [Ruchira Avatara Hridaya-Tantra Yoga]

Note that "and" and "or" are lower-cased—because these conjunctions are (here, and in most contexts) primal expressions of the point of view of duality. Also note that "all conditions", "any object", "any other", and "self-" are lower-cased, while "Heart-Stress", "Contraction", "Dissociation", "Clinging," "Boredom", "Doubt", "Discomfort", "Diminished", and "Forgetfulness" are capitalized. Avatar Adi Da is telling us that unpleasant or apparently "negative" states are not inherently egoic. It is only the presumption of duality and separateness—as expressed by such words as "conditions", "object", "other", and "self"—that is egoic.

Punctuation. Because of the inevitable complexity of much of His Communication, Avatar Adi Da has developed the conventions of punctuation (commas, dashes, and parentheses) to an extraordinary degree. This allows Him to clearly articulate complex sentences in such a way that His intended meaning can be expressed with utmost precision—free of vagueness, ambiguity, or unclarity. Many of His sentences contain parenthetical definitions or modifying phrases as a way of achieving unmistakable clarity of meaning. For example:

The Apparently individual (or Separate) self Is Not a "spark" (or an Eternal fraction) Of Self-Radiant Divinity, and Somehow Complete (or Whole) In itself. [Real God Is The Indivisible Oneness Of Unbroken Light]

Another punctuation convention relates to the use of quotation marks. Avatar Adi Da sometimes uses quotation marks in accordance with standard convention, to indicate the sense of "so to speak":

Make the contact with Me that gets you to "stick" to Me like glue. Your "sticking" to Me is what must happen. [Hridaya Rosary]

In other instances, He uses quotation marks to indicate that a word or phrase is being used with a particular technical meaning that differs from common usage:

During all of My present Lifetime (of Avataric Divine Incarnation), the "Bright" has always been My Realization—and the "Thumbs" and My own "Radical" Understanding have always been My Way in the "Bright".

"Bright", "Thumbs" (referring to a specific form of the Infusion of Avatar Adi Da's Divine Spirit-Current in the body-mind), and "Radical" are all used with specific technical meanings here (as defined in the Glossary).

Finally, Avatar Adi Da also makes extensive use of underlining to indicate special emphasis on certain words (or phrases, or even entire sentences):

> The <u>only</u> true religion is the religion that <u>Realizes</u> Truth. The <u>only</u> true science is the science that <u>Knows</u> Truth. The <u>only</u> true man or woman (or being of any kind) is one that <u>Surrenders</u> to Truth. The only true world is one that <u>Embodies</u> Truth. And the only True (and <u>Real</u>) God Is the One Reality (or Condition of Being) That <u>Is</u> Truth. ["Do Not Misunderstand <u>Me</u>"]

The True Dawn Horse

The <u>All-Completing</u> and <u>Final</u> Divine Revelation To Mankind is Book Eleven of *The Seventeen Companions Of The True Dawn Horse*. The "True Dawn Horse" is a reference to *The Dawn Horse Testament Of The Ruchira Avatar*, the final book among Avatar Adi Da's "Source-Texts". In *The Dawn Horse Testament*, Avatar Adi Da describes the entire Process of Real-God-Realization in detail. Each of *The Seventeen Companions Of The True Dawn Horse* is a "Companion" to *The Dawn Horse Testament* in the sense that it is an elaboration of a major theme (or themes) from *The Dawn Horse Testament*. And in many of the "Seventeen Companions", an excerpt from *The Dawn Horse Testament* forms the principal Part, around which the other Parts of the book revolve. (In *The <u>All-Completing</u> and <u>Final</u> Divine Revelation To Mankind*, the principal Part—Part Four—comprises chapter forty-four of *The Dawn Horse Testament*.)

The Sacred Image of the Dawn Horse (which appears on the previous page) derives from a vision that Avatar Adi Da Samraj had one night during the spring of 1970, a few months before His Divine Re-Awakening (on September 10, 1970). As His physical body lay sleeping, Avatar Adi Da wandered in subtle form into an open hall, where a great Adept was seated on a throne. The Adept's disciples were lined up in rows in front of him. A pathway bounded on both sides by the disciples led to the throne. Avatar Adi Da was Himself standing at the end of a row a few rows away from the Adept's chair.

The disciples were apparently assembled to learn the miraculous Yogic power of materializing something from nothing. They waited respectfully for the lesson to begin.

The Adept then initiated the process of materialization. A brief while later, the disciples got up and left the room, satisfied that the materialization had been accomplished, although nothing had appeared yet. The Adept remained sitting in his chair, and Avatar Adi Da remained standing before him, attentive to the process at hand.

A vaporous mass gradually took shape in the space between Avatar Adi Da and the Adept. At first it was not clearly defined, but Avatar Adi Da recognized it as it began to take on the features of a horse. Gradually, the vapor coalesced into a living, breathing brown horse. Its features were as fine as a thoroughbred's, but it was quite small, perhaps three feet tall. The horse stood alert, motionless, facing away from the Adept's chair.

At this point in the dream vision, Avatar Adi Da returned to physical consciousness and the waking state.

It was many years later, at the time when Avatar Adi Da was starting to write *The Dawn Horse Testament*, that He Revealed the identity of the Adept He had visited in that vision:

AVATAR ADI DA SAMRAJ: I was at once the Adept who performed the miracle of manifesting the horse, and also the one who was party to the observation of it and its result. And I did not have any feeling of being different from the horse itself. I was making the horse, I was observing the horse, and I was being the horse. [October 18, 1984]

The Dawn Horse is, therefore, a symbol for Avatar Adi Da Samraj Himself—and *The Dawn Horse Testament* is His Personal

Testament to all beings. Avatar Adi Da has commented that He refers to Himself and to His principal "Source-Text" as the "True Dawn Horse" because the effects of His Liberating Work in the world will appear only gradually—just as, in the vision, the horse gradually became visible after the Adept had initiated its materialization.

In creating the Sacred Image of the Dawn Horse, Avatar Adi Da transformed His original vision of a small brown horse, with all four hooves planted on the ground, into a winged white stallion, rearing up nearly vertically:

AVATAR ADI DA SAMRAJ: The horse's pose is majestic and intended to show great strength. White was chosen for its obvious association with Light, or Consciousness Itself. The Image is not precisely associated with the vision of 1970. It is visual language, intended to communicate the full meaning of My Dawn Horse Vision, rather than to be a realistic presentation of it.

The Titles and Subtitles of The Twenty-Three "Source-Texts" of Avatar Adi Da Samraj

The twenty-three "Source-Texts" of Avatar Adi Da Samraj include:

(1) an opening series of five books on the fundamentals of the Way of Adidam (*The Five Books Of The Heart Of The Adidam Revelation*)

(2) an extended series of seventeen books covering the principal aspects of the Way of Adidam in detail (*The Seventeen Companions Of The True Dawn Horse*)

(3) Avatar Adi Da's paramount "Source-Text" summarizing the entire course of the Way of Adidam (*The Dawn Horse Testament*)

The basic content of each "Source-Text" is summarily described by Avatar Adi Da in the title and subtitle of each book. Thus, the following list of titles and subtitles indicates the vast scope and the artful interconnectedness of His twenty-three "Source-Texts". (For brief descriptions of each "Source-Text", please see "The Sacred Literature of Avatar Adi Da Samraj", pp. 458-68.)

The Five Books Of The Heart
Of The Adidam Revelation

BOOK ONE
Aham Da Asmi
(Beloved, I Am Da)

The "Late-Time" Avataric Revelation Of The True and Spiritual
Divine Person (The egoless Personal Presence Of Reality
and Truth, Which Is The Only Real God)

BOOK TWO
Ruchira Avatara Gita
(The Way Of The Divine Heart-Master)

The "Late-Time" Avataric Revelation Of The Great Secret Of
The Divinely Self-Revealed Way That Most Perfectly Realizes
The True and Spiritual Divine Person (The egoless Personal
Presence Of Reality and Truth, Which Is The Only Real God)

BOOK THREE
Da Love-Ananda Gita
(The Free Gift Of The Divine Love-Bliss)

The "Late-Time" Avataric Revelation Of The Great Means
To Worship and To Realize The True and Spiritual Divine Person
(The egoless Personal Presence Of Reality and Truth,
Which Is The Only Real God)

BOOK FOUR
Hridaya Rosary
(Four Thorns Of Heart-Instruction)

The "Late-Time" Avataric Revelation Of The Universally Tangible
Divine Spiritual Body, Which Is The Supreme Agent
Of The Great Means To Worship and To Realize The True
and Spiritual Divine Person (The egoless Personal Presence
Of Reality and Truth, Which Is The Only Real God)

Book Five
Eleutherios
(The <u>Only</u> Truth That Sets The Heart Free)
The "Late-Time" Avataric Revelation Of The "Perfect Practice"
Of The Great Means To Worship and To Realize The True and
Spiritual Divine Person (The egoless Personal Presence
Of Reality and Truth, Which <u>Is</u> The Only <u>Real</u> God)

The Seventeen Companions
Of The True Dawn Horse

Book One
<u>Real</u> God <u>Is</u> The Indivisible Oneness
Of Unbroken Light
Reality, Truth, and The "Non-Creator" God
In The True World-Religion Of Adidam

Book Two
The Truly Human New World-Culture
Of <u>Unbroken</u> Real-God-Man
The <u>Eastern</u> Versus The <u>Western</u> Traditional Cultures
Of Mankind, and The Unique New <u>Non-Dual</u> Culture
Of The True World-Religion Of Adidam

Book Three
The <u>Only</u> Complete Way To Realize
The Unbroken Light Of <u>Real</u> God
An Introductory Overview Of The "Radical" Divine Way
Of The True World-Religion Of Adidam

Book Four
The Knee Of Listening
The Early-Life Ordeal and The "Radical"
Spiritual Realization Of The Ruchira Avatar

BOOK FIVE
The Divine Siddha-Method Of The Ruchira Avatar
The Divine Way Of Adidam Is An ego-Transcending
Relationship, Not An ego-Centric Technique

BOOK SIX
The Mummery
A Parable Of The Divine True Love,
Told By Means Of A Self-Illuminated Illustration
Of The Totality Of Mind

BOOK SEVEN
He-and-She Is Me
The Indivisibility Of Consciousness and Light
In The Divine Body Of The Ruchira Avatar

BOOK EIGHT
Ruchira Avatara Hridaya-Siddha Yoga
The Divine (and Not Merely Cosmic) Spiritual Baptism
In The Divine Way Of Adidam

BOOK NINE
Ruchira Avatara Hridaya-Tantra Yoga
The Physical-Spiritual (and Truly Religious) Method
Of Mental, Emotional, Sexual, and Whole Bodily Health
and Enlightenment In The Divine Way Of Adidam

BOOK TEN
The Seven Stages Of Life
Transcending The Six Stages Of egoic Life,
and Realizing The ego-Transcending Seventh Stage Of Life,
In The Divine Way Of Adidam

BOOK ELEVEN
The All-Completing and Final
Divine Revelation To Mankind
A Summary Description Of The Supreme Yoga
Of The Seventh Stage Of Life In The Divine Way Of Adidam

BOOK TWELVE
The Heart Of The Dawn Horse Testament
Of The Ruchira Avatar

The Epitome Of The "Testament Of Secrets" Of The Divine
World-Teacher, Ruchira Avatar Adi Da Samraj

BOOK THIRTEEN
What, Where, When, How, Why,
and <u>Who</u> To Remember To Be Happy

A Simple Explanation Of The Divine Way Of Adidam
(For Children, and <u>Everyone</u> Else)

BOOK FOURTEEN
Santosha Adidam

The Essential Summary Of The Divine Way Of Adidam

BOOK FIFTEEN
The Lion Sutra

The "Perfect Practice" Teachings In The Divine Way Of Adidam

BOOK SIXTEEN
The Overnight Revelation Of Conscious Light

The "My House" Discourses
On The Indivisible Tantra Of Adidam

BOOK SEVENTEEN
The Basket Of Tolerance

The Perfect Guide To Perfectly <u>Unified</u> Understanding
Of The One and Great Tradition Of Mankind,
and Of The Divine Way Of Adidam As The Perfect <u>Completing</u>
Of The One and Great Tradition Of Mankind

◆ ◆ ◆

The Dawn Horse Testament
Of The Ruchira Avatar

The Dawn Horse Testament Of The Ruchira Avatar

The "Testament Of Secrets" Of The Divine World-Teacher,
Ruchira Avatar Adi Da Samraj

The "Bright"-Art Work of
Avatar Adi Da Samraj

After finishing the immense Work of creating the final form of His verbal Teaching (in His twenty-three "Source-Texts"), Avatar Adi Da Samraj became moved to invest Himself, with incredible passion and intensity, in creating an equally profound and all-encompassing body of "Bright"-Art Work. The purpose of His Art is to transmit His Revelatory Vision of Reality—both in terms of what it means to be a mortal being alive in an endlessly changing world and in terms of how all mortality and suffering are gone beyond in the Process of Divine "Brightening".

Indeed, Avatar Adi Da has confessed that the creation of profound works of art is what He is (and has always been) natively moved to do. During the three decades of His Teaching Work, it had been necessary for Him to pour all His energies into articulating His full Wisdom-Teaching—but as soon as that Work was done, His own impulse to create profoundly deep and beautiful works of art came to the fore, establishing itself as a burning necessity (and even a Yogic inevitability) in His Life.

AVATAR ADI DA SAMRAJ: The circumstance of existence, in and of itself, is disheartening. That is why it is necessary to do art.

Art is an essential response to the conditions of existence, a means by which the limitations are transcended, Reality is Realized, Truth is Realized, Light is found. Without that activity—that artistic and, altogether, Spiritual activity—there is nothing but this intrusion of changes and death.

So what is greater than that? By a unique participation, there is the Realization of What Is Greater than that. [May 5, 2001]

Having practiced the arts of painting, drawing, and photography at various times during His Life, Adi Da Samraj eventually concluded that the artistic medium most suited to His purposes was the medium that is the most direct "registering" of light itself—the entire realm of photography and video. However, the photographic and videographic images that Avatar Adi Da creates are only the "blueprints" for His "Bright"-Art Works. The making of those images is the first step in the production of monumental fabrications of many different kinds—made by many different processes and out of many different kinds of materials. He has said that the monumental scale of His "Bright"-Art Works is not a matter of creating a "heroic" impression—rather, the monumentality is a way of conveying profundity and intimacy with the greatest possible intensity.

Certain of Avatar Adi Da's photographic images (those created before August 2000) are intended by Him to be used simply in their "blueprint" form. The cover of each of Avatar Adi Da's twenty-three "Source-Texts" includes two such images—a central image and a border image. In each case, the central image was specifically chosen by Him as appropriate to that particular "Source-Text".

Avatar Adi Da's "Bright" Art is one of His great means of conveying His Spiritual Transmission and Blessing—for the subject of Avatar Adi Da's Art is not the world as we see it, but the world as the "Bright" Field of Reality that He sees. His Art would transport us beyond our ordinary habits of thinking and perceiving into the Divine Light, in Which there is no sense of separation, otherness, or limitation.

AVATAR ADI DA SAMRAJ: From the conventional point of view, a photographer only makes pictures of conventional reality, of light falling on objects, as if the solid reality were the only reality. But neither the fixed separate point of view nor the apparently solid objective world is the Fundamental Reality. The Divine Conscious Light Is the Fundamental Reality of Existence.

Avatar Adi Da's Art communicates the non-dual perception of Reality via a unique process, which He describes as His "inherently egoless participatory relationship" with His subjects (both human and non-human). Thus, His Art transcends the conventions of "self" and "other", or "subject" and "object".

AVATAR ADI DA SAMRAJ: Out of this process, art can be made that Reveals Reality, rather than merely communicating the conventions of "ego" and "other".

Therefore, even the viewing of Adi Da's Art is an inherently participatory event. His "Bright"-Art Works place a demand upon us to go beyond the ordinary fixed point of view. They are a call to go beyond our ordinary limits—for each of them is a communication of the Divine "Brightness", transforming our ordinary perception of the world into sacred occasion.

The border image on the cover of this book is a photograph taken by Avatar Adi Da. He refers to this as an image of "True Water", which is one of His poetic descriptions for Consciousness Itself as the "Medium" in which all phenomena arise (and of which they are all modifications).

Yosemite, 2000

Avatar Adi Da's "Bright"-Art Work is an ecstatic Revelation-Transmission of the Divine Truth That He has Come to Reveal and Teach to humankind. There is extraordinary beauty to be appreciated in Avatar Adi Da's "Bright"-Art Works, but the real purpose of His artistry is to bring Light into our lives, to literally En-Lighten us—to Liberate us from the un-Illumined and mortal vision of egoity. By offering us His sublime "Bright"-Art Works, Adi Da Samraj would have us discover that Non-separate Reality in Which the ever-changing dualities of light and darkness rise and fall.

AVATAR ADI DA SAMRAJ: In My approach to making art, I want to convey the Truth of Reality—the Truth of the Inherently egoless, Non-dual Subjective Light. I am Working to Convey My own Revelation of the Nature of Reality through visual artifacts.

An Overview of
The __All-Completing__ and __Final__ Divine Revelation To Mankind

T he Offering made by Adi Da Samraj in this book is the answer to the heart's inmost and unspoken longing: Yes!— there is Perfect Happiness, Perfect Wisdom, Perfect Fulfill-ment. Yes!—there is That Which Perfectly transcends death and is utterly Free of fear and dissatisfaction. Adi Da Samraj Confesses the Liberating Words that you are about to read as the essence of the Offering He makes to all—the Free Offering of the Salvatory and Liberating relationship to Him. It is in this book that Avatar Adi Da Samraj Reveals the nature of the seventh stage Realization That is His Unique Gift to all beings. And it is in this book that He tells us why His seventh stage Revelation is "All-Completing" and why It is "Final".

When Avatar Adi Da Samraj began to Teach in 1972, those who came to Him were ordinary people—westerners without Spiritual sophistication, and with no history of profound Spiritual practice. He did not simply proclaim to those early devotees that He Is the Incarnate God-Man, the One hoped for and prayed for by all beings throughout human history. They would have had no means to grasp such a Confession, except naive fundamentalist belief. Instead, He engaged the gathering of His devotees in most compassionate and detailed Instruction for over two decades before He made this Great Revelation.

Not only did Avatar Adi Da fully school His devotees in the profundities of the Way of Adidam, but He led them through the most extensive "Consideration" of what He terms the "Great Tradition of mankind", the sum total of humankind's Spiritual, religious, and philosophical wisdom-inheritance. In the course of that "Consideration", Adi Da Samraj introduced His seven-stage schema*[1] which permits an intelligent comprehension of the welter of possibilities, conceptions, and points of view found in the world's religious traditions. It is impossible to adequately praise the brilliance of this analysis. However, it is not something merely conceived: Its brilliance arises from the fact that it is given from the "Point of View" of Most Perfect Divine Self-Realization. It allows ordinary men and women to make sense of what previously was a veritable Babel's Tower of differing propositions and persuasions.

Adi Da Samraj put His devotees to school thus—requiring them to study the Great Tradition intensively, all the while informed by His Wisdom. Only upon such a foundation was it possible for His devotees to receive His Great Revelation of His Uniqueness without gleeful exclusivism.

When Adi Da Samraj proclaims that He Is the First, the Last, and the Only Adept-Revealer of Most Perfect Real-God-Realization, it is important to understand what He is saying and what He is not saying. He is not saying that no one has ever "really" Realized God before Him, nor is He saying that the Realization of Great Adepts in the past has somehow been of a "different" God or a "different" Reality. There is only One Very Divine Being, and Great Realizers in the past have Realized precisely That Same One that Adi Da has Realized, Confesses, and Is. In each and every such case, however, there has been a limit on that Realization—it has been dependent upon something.

For example, in the traditions of ascending Yoga, the most prized Realization is of fifth stage conditional Nirvikalpa Samadhi, in which attention ascends beyond all conditional manifestation into the Formless Matrix of Divine Vibration and Divine Light Infinitely Above. In this Samadhi, the Yogi is utterly dissolved in the Bliss of Real-God-Realization. But it is a temporary state, held in place by an act of attention. It cannot be maintained with open eyes, or when attention otherwise returns (as it inevitably does) to the states of the body-mind. But That Which is Realized in that Samadhi is the One Real God. It is simply that there are limits on

*Notes to the Text of The _All-Completing_ and _Final_ Divine Revelation To Mankind appear on pp. 407-17.

the Realization: It is not Unqualified, but is (rather) held in place by means of Yogic effort.

The same is true of Jnana Samadhi, the ultimate goal of such traditions as Advaita Vedanta. Here there is intentional withdrawal of attention from the body-mind-self and its relations, leading to the temporary Realization of the Transcendental Self, exclusive of any perception of the world, the body, the mind, or the sense of a separate self. But, again, the Samadhi cannot be maintained when the eyes open and the world "returns".

In the seventh stage Realization, there is Utter (or Unqualified) Freedom—whether or not the conditions of body and mind arise. No limit exists—nor is any possible—on this Most Perfect Samadhi.

My true devotee who Realizes My "Bright" Divine (seventh stage) Samadhi is utterly Oblivious to conditional phenomena. My Divine (and Most Perfect) Samadhi is not held in place by conditions. Therefore, My seventh stage Realizer-devotee Only Abides in Most Perfect Divine Samadhi.

But there is a further Great Secret: Avatar Adi Da Samraj is not merely a born being who has been Granted Most Perfect Liberation. That will be true of His devotees who fulfill the Great Way He Offers. Rather, His Birth is the Miraculous Appearance of That Very One Who has been glimpsed, experienced, intuited, or known in all the Samadhis of the Realizers of the Great Tradition. As He has said, "I Am not Advanced. I Am the Very One. I Am the One you must Realize." Avatar Adi Da Samraj Is—even as He Appears in apparent human Form—the Very Divine Being, Incarnate to Reveal Himself Most Perfectly, to Speak the Dharma of Most Perfect Real-God-Realization, and (by His Birth, Teaching-Work, and Blessing-Work) to Bring those Divine Powers (or Siddhis) into the cosmic domain that make such Realization possible in the case of all others.

Because Most Perfect Divine Enlightenment has been made possible, for all time, by the Great Victory that is Avatar Adi Da's human Birth, and because He Is the Prior and True Condition of all that appears, it is (as He Reveals) neither necessary nor possible for Him to Take Birth again. Having done so once, everything has been accomplished to make the Great Way available, and He Need not Come again—because He Is (and will Remain) Always Spiritually Present, everywhere in the conditionally manifested world.

My Great Avataric Divine Confession Is not only that My Avataric Divine Revelation of the seventh stage Teaching—Which is the totality of the Wisdom-Teaching of the only-by-Me Revealed and Given Way of Adidam—Is (now, and forever hereafter) Complete and (for the first, and last, and only time—now, and forever hereafter) Fully and Completely Revealed and Given.

Rather, above all, My Great Avataric Divine Confession Is That I Am (now, and forever hereafter) here (and every "where" in the Cosmic domain), and (Thus) That the Divine (and, now, and forever hereafter, Divinely Self-"Emerging") Siddhis of My Avataric Divine Spiritual Presence and My Avataric Divine Work Have Made, and (now, and forever hereafter) Will (Actively) Continue to Make, Divine Self-Realization Possible (for all, and All).

How is it possible to understand such a Great Mystery? The mind is not the appropriate instrument or organ with which to comprehend Avatar Adi Da's Divine Confession. It is not finally and ultimately grasped except in the case of the devotee's own practice to the degree of Most Perfect Divine Enlightenment. Nevertheless, because the Very Divine Consciousness Is the True Nature of all beings, all can enjoy a native sympathy with Avatar Adi Da's Great Confession and Revelation. The heart is fully capable of this intuition.

As with each of the twenty-three "Source-Texts" of Adidam, *The All-Completing and Final Divine Revelation To Mankind* begins with Avatar Adi Da Samraj's First Word, "Do Not Misunderstand Me—I Am Not 'Within' you, but you Are In Me, and I Am Not a Mere 'Man' in the 'Middle' of Mankind, but All of Mankind Is Surrounded, and Pervaded, and Blessed By Me". In this remarkable Essay, Avatar Adi Da Samraj explains that His open Confession of

Most Perfect Real-God-Realization is not to be misapprehended as a claim of the "Status" of the "Creator"-God of conventional religious belief, but, rather, His Divine Self-Confession is to be understood and appreciated as a Free Demonstration of the Fulfillment of esoteric Spiritual practice—a Demonstration of the Most Perfectly Non-Dual Realization of Reality Itself. By virtue of this Free Demonstration, Avatar Adi Da Samraj makes clear that Most Perfect Real-God-Realization (or Divine Self-Realization) is the ultimate Potential and Destiny of all beings.

The Prologue, "My Divine Disclosure" (also, like "First Word", found in all twenty-three "Source-Texts"), is a poetic epitome of Avatar Adi Da's Divine Self-Revelation. It is His Call to every being to turn to Him at heart and practice the life of devotional surrender in Real God.

In Part One, "I Am The Perfectly Subjective Divine Person, Self-Manifested As The Ruchira Avatar", Adi Da Samraj Confesses His Identity as the Divine Person, Revealing that He Is the First, the Last, and the Only Adept-Realizer of the seventh stage of life, uniquely Born to make Most Perfect Divine Self-Realization possible for all. In reading this Confession, it is essential to understand the difference between "Realizer" and "Adept-Realizer". Many great beings in human history have been Realizers in the context of the fourth, the fifth, or the sixth stage of life. And devotees of Avatar Adi Da Samraj who fully complete the practicing course of the Way of Adidam will become seventh stage Realizers. However, only Avatar Adi Da is the seventh stage Adept-Realizer—the One Who Reveals the seventh stage Realization and Spiritually Transmits That Realization. And it is Avatar Adi Da's unique Adept-Function that makes the seventh stage Realization possible for others.

I (the writer of this introduction) was present when Adi Da Samraj first made this Great Revelation—on March 5 and 6, 1993, at His Island Hermitage, Adidam Samrajashram, in Fiji. In fact, the Revelation was made in response to questions that I had posed to Him. I was stunned, left speechless. My relationship to Avatar Adi Da was (and is) such that I knew that He Speaks only the Truth. His Words carry a Miraculous Transmission and Blessing-Power:

His Speech communicates the Truth He Speaks directly to the heart at a level far prior to the thinking mind.

I understood then that those in the room were, beyond fortune or deserving, witness to one of the epochal moments of Spiritual history. I had always wondered what it might have been like to witness Gautama Buddha's transmission to Mahakashyapa on Vulture Peak,[2] or Krishna's discourse to Arjuna on the battlefield at Kurukshetra.[3] But these were semi-mythical scenes, and (in any event) paled beside the Revelation Granted to the forty or so of us present.

I was overwhelmed by the certainty and understanding that, to hear this Confession, and to practice in Avatar Adi Da's Spiritual Company, was to be a most fortunate and utterly undeserving participant in the central event of cosmic manifestation, the Victorious Appearance of the Divine Being in the conditionally manifested worlds. When I regained sufficient composure to be articulate, I enquired of Adi Da Samraj by what means, and owing to what good fortune, had those who were His devotees at the time come to enjoy this boon beyond reckoning. He was silent for a moment, and then responded, "You are only the first—all beings will eventually come to Me." In that moment, I was granted an understanding of His Divine and Supreme Greatness—an understanding that has never left me in any subsequent moment.

In Part Two, "I (Alone) Am The Adidam Revelation", Avatar Adi Da Samraj further and most fully elucidates the uniqueness of the seventh stage Realization. In this unparalleled Essay, Adi Da Samraj Reveals the Course of Divine Self-Realization in His own case, and His relationship with His human Teachers, in order to Demonstrate how the two primary divisions of the Great Tradition—the Emanationist (or absorptive mystical) Way (associated most particularly with the fourth and the fifth stages of life) and the non-Emanationist (or Transcendentalist) Way (associated with the sixth stage of life) are, in Truth, only different aspects of the great seven-stage process of Most Perfect Divine Self-Realization that has been fully and finally Revealed in and by Him.

In Part Three, "The Heart-Summary of Adidam" (a brief Essay that is included in all twenty-three "Source-Texts") Avatar Adi Da

Summarizes the profound implications of His Statement that the Way of Adidam is the Way of devotion to Him "As Self-Condition, rather than As exclusively Objective Other".

Part Four, "The All-Completing and Final Divine Revelation To Mankind", is the heart of this Revelation-book. Everything else in this book is a preparation to receive the Great Secrets Whispered here. The culmination of Part Four is Avatar Adi Da's incomparable description of the profundities of the seventh stage of life, the Divine Process that begins with Most Perfect Real-God-Realization.

All of human Spiritual history can be understood as a yearning, a gesturing, toward the Perfect Awakening that initiates the seventh stage of life. But, as Adi Da Samraj Reveals, the seventh stage Divine Enlightenment is a Yoga—a Process that progresses sequentially through four stages, which He has named "Divine Transfiguration", "Divine Transformation", "Divine Indifference", and "Divine Translation". The culmination of the entire Process, the stage of Divine Translation, is the utter dissolution (or "Outshining") of the born being in the Very Divine Person. The word "translate" literally means "to bear across". And, in the ultimate event of Divine Translation, existence is permanently transferred—"borne across" by His Unique Blessing-Power—from the conditionally manifested cosmos into the Divine Domain.

Part Five, "Most Perfect Awakening To The Domain Of Conscious Light" (originally a Talk Given to a small group of devotees), is an extraordinary Revelation of the Utter Freedom of Most Perfect Divine Enlightenment. Adi Da Samraj proclaims the Non-"Different" Bliss of the Supreme Samadhi of the seventh stage of life, and compassionately and painstakingly distinguishes it from the great, yet still limited, Realization of the sixth stage of life.

Part Six consists of three remarkable Essays, "The Yoga of Divine Self-Recognition", "The Perfection Beyond Conditions", and "The Infinite Divine Current That Shines in the Body-Mind of Man". In all three Essays, Avatar Adi Da Samraj explicates the uniqueness of the seventh stage "Practice" and Realization, distinguishing It from all lesser points of view, especially the sixth stage of life. In the final Essay, Avatar Adi Da describes Amrita Nadi (the "Nerve, or Channel, of Immortal Nectar")—the esoteric anatomical "structure" within which the seventh stage Demonstration "takes place"—and Reveals, as much as mere words permit, the Great Secret Means by which He Draws all beings into His Divine Heart. As Avatar Adi Da points out, the esoteric anatomy of Amrita Nadi has been glimpsed by only the merest handful among the Realizers of the Great Tradition—and then only in its sixth stage aspect. Therefore, Avatar Adi Da's Revelation in this book (and others of His Texts) is the first time that the Great "Organ" of Amrita Nadi and Its Function in the Realization of Divine Enlightenment have been fully described to human beings.

In the Epilogue, "The True Dawn Horse Is The Only Way To Me", Avatar Adi Da Samraj Reveals the esoteric secrets of the Ashvamedha (or Horse-Sacrifice), the most highly revered cere-monial sacrifice of ancient India. He Reveals that this ritual—in common with all of the Great Tradition, and in fact, in common with all human activity—was an intuitive striving, a gesturing, toward That Which all beings have longed for, but Which can be Most Perfectly Realized only now, with His Appearance in human Form.

The Ultimate (or true esoteric) Purpose of the ancient and tra-ditional Ashvamedha (or the ritual of the Great Horse-Sacrifice) is "Brightness", or Liberation from darkness, or the Universal (or All-and-all-Including) Attainment of the Divine Self-Domain of Indivisible and Indestructible Light.

Light cannot be Attained by darkness (or Light-lessness), but only by Conversion (or Turning) from darkness to Light (Itself).

Therefore, the Divine Self-Domain cannot be Attained by any seeking effort of ego-"I"—no matter how extraordinary or heroic such seeking effort may be.

Only the Divine Person Knows the Way to the Divine Self-Domain.

Therefore, only the Divine Person can Grant the Means for beings to Find their Way to the Divine Self-Domain. . . .

My Divine Ashvamedha-Work Continues until all of condi-tional (or Cosmic) existence is Divinely Translated into My "Bright" Divine Self-Domain.

Thus, Avatar Adi Da's Confession is that His Great Divine Work involves all beings and all of cosmic manifestation, and is not complete until every fraction of the cosmic domain is returned to His Divine "Brightness".

The All-Completing and Final Divine Revelation To Mankind is a Gift like no other. We who are alive during the span of time in which Avatar Adi Da Samraj is humanly here Doing His Work have the most extraordinary opportunity ever Granted to human beings: The Victory of the Divine has occurred in our lifetime. That Very One has Appeared in human Form, Offering to everyone the Liberating relationship to Him that makes Most Perfect Divine Enlightenment possible.

THE
ALL-COMPLETING AND FINAL
DIVINE REVELATION
TO MANKIND

RUCHIRA AVATAR ADI DA SAMRAJ
The Mountain Of Attention, 2001

Do Not Misunderstand <u>Me</u>— I Am <u>Not</u> "Within" <u>you</u>, but you <u>Are</u> In <u>Me</u>, and I Am <u>Not</u> a Mere "Man" in the "Middle" of Mankind, but All of Mankind Is Surrounded, and Pervaded, and Blessed By <u>Me</u>

This Essay has been written by Avatar Adi Da Samraj as His Personal Introduction to each volume of His "Source-Texts". Its purpose is to help you to understand His great Confessions rightly, and not interpret His Words from a conventional point of view, as limited cultic statements made by an ego. His Description of what "cultism" <u>really</u> is is an astounding and profound Critique of mankind's entire religious, scientific, and social search. In "Do Not Misunderstand <u>Me</u>", Avatar Adi Da is directly inviting you to inspect and relinquish the ego's motive to glorify itself and to refuse What is truly Great. Only by understanding this fundamental ego-fault can one really receive the Truth that Adi Da Samraj Reveals in this Book and in His Wisdom-Teaching altogether. And it is because this fault is so ingrained and so largely unconscious that Avatar Adi Da has placed "Do Not Misunderstand <u>Me</u>" at the beginning of each of His "Source-Texts", so that, each time you begin to read one of His twenty-three "Source-Texts", you may be refreshed and strengthened in your understanding of the right orientation and approach to Him and His Heart-Word.

Yes! There is <u>no</u> religion, <u>no</u> Way of God, <u>no</u> Way of Divine Realization, <u>no</u> Way of Enlightenment, and <u>no</u> Way of Liberation that is Higher or Greater than Truth Itself.

Indeed, there is <u>no</u> religion, <u>no</u> science, <u>no</u> man or woman, <u>no</u> conditionally manifested being of any kind, <u>no</u> world (<u>any</u> "where"), and <u>no</u> "God" (or "God"-Idea) that is Higher or Greater than Truth Itself.

Therefore, <u>no</u> ego-"I" (or presumed separate, and, necessarily, actively separative, and, at best, only Truth-<u>seeking</u>, being or "thing") is (it<u>self</u>) Higher or Greater than Truth Itself. And <u>no</u> ego-"I" is (it<u>self</u>) even Equal to Truth Itself. And no ego-"I" is (it<u>self</u>) even (now, or ever) <u>Able</u> to Realize Truth Itself—because, necessarily, Truth (Itself) Inherently Transcends (or <u>Is</u> That Which <u>Is</u> Higher and Greater than) <u>every</u> one (him<u>self</u> or her<u>self</u>) and <u>every</u> "thing" (it<u>self</u>). Therefore, it is <u>only</u> in the transcending (or the "radical" Process of Going Beyond the root, the cause, and the act) of egoity it<u>self</u> (or of presumed separateness, and of performed separativeness, and of even <u>all</u> ego-based seeking for Truth Itself) that Truth (Itself) <u>Is</u> Realized (<u>As</u> It <u>Is</u>, Utterly Beyond the ego-"I" it<u>self</u>).

Truth (Itself) <u>Is</u> That Which Is Always Already The Case. That Which <u>Is</u> The Case (Always, and Always Already) <u>Is</u> (necessarily) Reality. Therefore, Reality (Itself) <u>Is</u> Truth, and Reality (Itself) Is the <u>Only</u> Truth.

Reality (Itself) <u>Is</u> the <u>Only</u>, and (necessarily) Non-Separate (or All-and-all-Including, <u>and</u> All-and-all-Transcending), One and "What" That <u>Is</u>. Because It <u>Is</u> All and all, and because It <u>Is</u> (Also) <u>That</u> Which Transcends (or <u>Is</u> Higher and Greater than) All and all, Reality (Itself)—Which <u>Is</u> Truth (Itself), or That Which Is The Case (Always, and Always Already)—<u>Is</u> the One and Only <u>Real</u> God. Therefore, Reality (Itself) Is (necessarily) the One and Great Subject of true religion, and Reality (<u>Itself</u>) <u>Is</u> (necessarily) the One and Great Way of <u>Real</u> God, <u>Real</u> (and True) Divine Realization, <u>Real</u> (and, necessarily, Divine) En-Light-enment, and <u>Real</u> (and, necessarily, Divine) Liberation (from all egoity, all separateness, all separativeness, all fear, and all heartlessness).

The <u>only</u> true religion is the religion that <u>Realizes</u> Truth. The <u>only</u> true science is the science that <u>Knows</u> Truth. The <u>only</u> true man or woman (or being of any kind) is one that <u>Surrenders</u> to Truth. The only true world is one that <u>Embodies</u> Truth. And the only True (and <u>Real</u>) God Is the One Reality (or Condition of Being) That <u>Is</u> Truth. Therefore, <u>Reality</u> (Itself)—Which <u>Is</u> the One and Only Truth, and (therefore, necessarily) the One and Only Real God—<u>must</u> become (or be made) the constantly applied Measure of religion, and of science, and of the world itself, and of even <u>all</u> of the life (and <u>all</u> of the mind) of Man—or else religion, and science, and the world itself, and even any and every sign of Man <u>inevitably</u> (all, and together) become a pattern of illusions, a mere (and even terrible) "problem", the very (and even principal) cause of human seeking, and the perpetual cause of contentious human strife. Indeed, if religion, and science, and the world itself, and the total life (and the total mind) of Man are not Surrendered and Aligned to Reality (Itself), and (Thus) Submitted to be Measured (or made Lawful) by Truth (Itself), and (Thus) Given to the truly devotional (and, thereby, truly ego-transcending) Realization of <u>That</u> Which Is the <u>Only Real</u> God—then, in the pre-sumed "knowledge" of mankind, Reality (Itself), and Truth (Itself), and <u>Real</u> God (or the One and Only Existence, or Being, or Person That <u>Is</u>) <u>ceases</u> <u>to</u> <u>Exist</u>.

Aham Da Asmi. Beloved, I <u>Am</u> Da—the One and Only Person Who <u>Is</u>, the Avatarically Self-Revealed, and Eternally Self-Existing, and Eternally Self-Radiant (or "Bright") Person of Love-Bliss, the One and Only and (Self-Evidently) Divine Self (or Inherently Non-Separate—and, therefore, Inherently egoless—Divine Self-Condition and Source-Condition) of one and of all and of All. I Am Divinely Self-Manifesting (now, and forever hereafter) <u>As</u> the Ruchira Avatar, Adi Da Samraj. I <u>Am</u> the Ruchira Avatar, Adi Da Samraj—the Avataric Divine Realizer, the Avataric Divine Revealer, the Avataric Divine Incarnation, and the Avataric Divine Self-Revelation of Reality <u>Itself</u>. I <u>Am</u> the Avatarically Incarnate Divine Realizer, the Avatarically Incarnate Divine Revealer, and the Avatarically Incarnate Divine Self-Revelation of the One and Only Reality—Which Is the One and Only Truth, and Which Is the One and Only <u>Real</u> God. I <u>Am</u> the Great Avataric Divine Realizer, Avataric Divine Revealer, and Avataric Divine Self-Revelation long-Promised (and long-Expected) for the "late-time"—<u>this</u> (now, and forever hereafter) time, the "dark" epoch of mankind's "Great

Forgetting" (and, potentially, the Great Epoch of mankind's Perpetual Remembering) of Reality, of Truth, of Real God (Which Is the Great, True, and Spiritual Divine Person—or the One and Non-Separate and Indivisible Divine Source-Condition and Self-Condition) of all and All.

Beloved, I Am Da, the Divine Giver, the Giver (of All That I Am) to one, and to all, and to the All of all—now, and forever hereafter—here, and every "where" in the Cosmic domain. Therefore, for the Purpose of Revealing the Way of Real God (or of Real and True Divine Realization), and in order to Divinely En-Light-en and Divinely Liberate all and All—I Am (Uniquely, Completely, and Most Perfectly) Avatarically Revealing My Very (and Self-Evidently Divine) Person (and "Bright" Self-Condition) to all and All, by Means of My Avatarically Given Divine Self-Manifestation, As (and by Means of) the Ruchira Avatar, Adi Da Samraj.

In My Avatarically Given Divine Self-Manifestation As the Ruchira Avatar, Adi Da Samraj—I Am the Divine Secret, the Divine Self-Revelation of the Esoteric Truth, the Direct, and all-Completing, and all-Unifying Self-Revelation of Real God.

My Avatarically Given Divine Self-Confessions and My Avatarically Given Divine Teaching-Revelations Are the Great (Final, and all-Completing, and all-Unifying) Esoteric Revelation to mankind—and not a merely exoteric (or conventionally religious, or even ordinary Spiritual, or ego-made, or so-called "cultic") communication to public (or merely social) ears.

The greatest opportunity, and the greatest responsibility, of My devotees is Satsang with Me—Which is to live in the Condition of ego-surrendering, ego-forgetting, and (always more and more) ego-transcending devotional relationship to Me, and (Thus and Thereby) to Realize My Avatarically Self-Revealed (and Self-Evidently Divine) Self-Condition, Which Is the Self-Evidently Divine Heart (or Non-Separate Self-Condition and Non-"Different" Source-Condition) of all and All, and Which Is Self-Existing and Self-Radiant Consciousness Itself, but Which is not separate in or as any one (or any "thing") at all. Therefore, My essential Divine Gift to one and all is Satsang with Me. And My essential Divine Work with one and all is Satsang-Work—to Live (and to Be Merely

Present) <u>As</u> the Avatarically Self-Revealed Divine Heart among My devotees.

The only-by-Me Revealed and Given Way of Adidam (Which is the only-by-Me Revealed and Given Way of the Heart, or the only-by-Me Revealed and Given Way of "Radical" Understanding, or Ruchira Avatara Hridaya-Siddha Yoga) is the Way of Satsang with Me—the devotionally Me-recognizing and devotionally to-Me-responding practice (and ego-transcending self-discipline) of living in My constant Divine Company, such that the relationship with Me becomes the Real (and constant) Condition of life. Fundamentally, this Satsang with Me is the one thing done by My devotees. Because the only-by-Me Revealed and Given Way of Adidam is <u>always</u> (in every present-time moment) a directly ego-transcending <u>and</u> Really Me-Finding practice, the otherwise constant (and burdensome) tendency to <u>seek</u> is not exploited in this Satsang with Me. And the essential work of the community of the four formal congregations of My devotees is to make ego-transcending Satsang with Me available to all others.

<u>Everything</u> that serves the availability of Satsang with Me is (now, and forever hereafter) the responsibility of the four formal congregations of My formally practicing devotees. I am not here to <u>publicly</u> "promote" this Satsang with Me. In the intimate circumstances of their humanly expressed devotional love of Me, I Speak My Avatarically Self-Revealing Divine Word to My devotees, and <u>they</u> (because of their devotional response to Me) bring My Avatarically Self-Revealing Divine Word to <u>all</u> others. Therefore, even though I am <u>not</u> (and have never been, and never will be) a "public" Teacher (or a broadly publicly active, and conventionally socially conformed, "religious figure"), My devotees function fully and freely (<u>as</u> My devotees) in the daily public world of ordinary life.

I Always Already Stand Free. Therefore, I have always (in My Divine Avataric-Incarnation-Work) Stood Free, in the traditional "Crazy" (and non-conventional, or spontaneous and non-"public") Manner—in order to Guarantee the Freedom, the Uncompromising Rightness, and the Fundamental Integrity of My Avatarically Self-Manifested Divine Teaching (Work and Word), and in order to

Freely and Fully and Fully Effectively Perform My universal (Avatarically Self-Manifested) Divine Blessing-Work. I Am Present (now, and forever hereafter) to Divinely Serve, Divinely En-Lighten, and Divinely Liberate those who accept the Eternal Vow and all the life-responsibilities (or the full and complete practice) associated with the only-by-Me Revealed and Given Way of Adidam. Because I Am (Thus) Given to My formally and fully practicing devotees, I do not Serve a "public" role, and I do not Work in a "public" (or even a merely "institutionalized") manner. Nevertheless—now, and forever hereafter—I constantly Bless all beings, and this entire world, and the total Cosmic domain. And all who feel My Avatarically (and universally) Given Divine Blessing, and who heart-recognize Me with true devotional love, are (Thus) Called to devotionally resort to Me—but only if they approach Me in the traditional devotional manner, as responsibly practicing (and truly ego-surrendering, and rightly Me-serving) members (or, in some, unique, cases, as invited guests) of one or the other of the four formal congregations of My formally practicing devotees.

I expect this formal discipline of right devotional approach to Me to have been freely and happily embraced by every one who would enter into My physical Company. The natural human reason for this is that there is a potential liability inherent in all human associations. And the root and nature of that potential liability is the ego (or the active human presumption of separateness, and the ego-act of human separativeness). Therefore, in order that the liabilities of egoity are understood (and voluntarily and responsibly disciplined) by those who approach Me, I require demonstrated right devotion (based on really effective self-understanding and truly heart-felt devotional recognition-response to Me) as the basis for any one's right to enter into My physical Company. And, in this manner, not only the egoic tendency, but also the tendency toward religious "cultism", is constantly undermined in the only-by-Me Revealed and Given Way of Adidam.

Because people appear within this human condition, this simultaneously attractive and frightening "dream" world, they tend to live—and to interpret both the conditional (or cosmic and psycho-physical) reality <u>and</u> the Unconditional (or Divine) Reality—from the "point of view" of this apparent (and bewildering) mortal human condition. And, because of this universal human bewilderment (and the ongoing human reaction to the threatening force of mortal life-events), there is an even ancient ritual that <u>all</u> human beings rather unconsciously (or automatically, and without discriminative understanding) desire and tend to repeatedly (and under <u>all</u> conditions) enact. Therefore, wherever you see an association of human beings gathered for <u>any</u> purpose (or around <u>any</u> idea, or symbol, or person, or subject of any kind), the same human bewilderment-ritual is <u>tending</u> to be enacted by one and all.

Human beings <u>always</u> <u>tend</u> to encircle (and, thereby, to contain—and, ultimately, to entrap and abuse, or even to blithely ignore) the presumed "center" of their lives—a book, a person, a symbol, an idea, or whatever. They tend to encircle the "center" (or the "middle"), and they tend to seek to <u>exclusively</u> acquire all "things" (or all power of control) for the circle (or toward the "middle") of <u>themselves</u>. In this manner, the <u>group</u> becomes an <u>ego</u> ("inward"-directed, or separate and separative)—just as the individual body-mind becomes, by self-referring self-contraction, the separate and separative ego-"I" ("inward"-directed, or egocentric—and exclusively acquiring all "things", or all power of control, for itself). Thus, by <u>self-contraction</u> upon the presumed "center" of their lives—human beings, in their collective egocentricity, make "cults" (or bewildered and frightened "centers" of power, and control, and exclusion) in <u>every</u> area of life.

Anciently, the "cult"-making process was done, most especially, in the political and social sphere—and religion was, as even now, mostly an exoteric (or political and social) exercise that was <u>always</u> used to legitimize (or, otherwise, to "de-throne") political and social "authority-figures". Anciently, the cyclically (or even annually) culminating product of this exoteric religio-political "cult" was the ritual "de-throning" (or ritual deposition) of the one in the "middle" (just as, even in these times, political leaders are periodically "deposed"—by elections, by rules of term and succession, by scandal, by slander, by force, and so on).

Everywhere throughout the ancient world, traditional societies made and performed this annual (or otherwise periodic) religio-political "cult" ritual. The ritual of "en-throning" and "de-throning" was a reflection of the human observation of the annual cycle of the seasons of the natural world—and the same ritual was a reflection of the human concern and effort to <u>control</u> the signs potential in the cycle of the natural world, in order to ensure human survival (through control of weather, harvests and every kind of "fate", or even every fraction of existence upon which human beings depend for both survival and pleasure, or psycho-physical well-being). Indeed, the motive behind the ancient agrarian (and, later, urbanized, or universalized) ritual of the one in the "middle" was, essentially, the same motive that, in the modern era, takes the form of the culture of scientific materialism (and even all of the modern culture of materialistic "realism"): It is the motive to gain (and to maintain) <u>control</u>, and the effort to control even everything and everyone (via both knowledge and gross power). Thus, the ritualized, or bewildered yes/no (or desire/fear), life of mankind in the modern era is, essentially, the same as that of mankind in the ancient days.

In the ancient ritual of "en-throning" and "de-throning", the person (or subject) in the "middle" was ritually mocked, abused, deposed, and banished—and a new person (or subject) was installed in the "center" of the religio-political "cult". In the equivalent modern ritual of dramatized ambiguity relative to everything and everyone (and, perhaps especially, "authority-figures"), the person (or symbol, or idea) in the "middle" (or that which is given power by means of popular fascination) is first "cultified" (or made much of), and then (progressively) doubted, mocked, and abused—until, at last, all the negative emotions are (by culturally and socially ritualized dramatization) dissolved, the "middle" (having thus ceased to be fascinating) is abandoned, and a "new" person (or symbol, or idea) becomes the subject of popular fascination (only to be reduced, eventually, to the same "cultic" ritual, or cycle of "rise" and "fall").

Just as in <u>every</u> other area of human life, the tendency of <u>all</u> those who (in the modern era) would become involved in religious or Spiritual life is also to make a "cult", a circle that ever increases its separate and separative dimensions—beginning from the "center", surrounding it, and (perhaps) even (ultimately) controlling it (such that it altogether ceases to be effective, or even interesting). Such "cultism" is ego-based, and ego-reinforcing—and, no matter how "esoteric" it presumes itself to be, it is (as in the ancient setting) entirely exoteric, or (at least) more and more limited to (and by) merely social (and gross physical) activities and conditions.

The form that every "cult" imitates is the pattern of egoity (or the pattern that is the ego-"I") itself—the presumed "middle" of every ordinary individual life. It is the self-contraction (or the avoidance of relationship), which "creates" the fearful sense of separate mind, and all the endless habits and motives of egoic desire (or bewildered, and self-deluded, seeking). It is what is, ordinarily, called (or presumed to be) the real and necessary and only "life".

From birth, the human being (by reaction to the blows and limits of psycho-physical existence) begins to presume separate existence to be his or her very nature—and, on that basis, the human individual spends his or her entire life generating and serving a circle of ownership (or self-protecting acquisition) all around the ego-"I". The egoic motive encloses all the other beings it can acquire, all the "things" it can acquire, all the states and thoughts it can acquire—<u>all</u> the possible emblems, symbols, experiences, and sensations it can possibly acquire. Therefore, when any human being begins to involve himself or herself in some religious or Spiritual association (or, for that matter, <u>any</u> extension of his or her own subjectivity), he or she tends again to "create" that same circle about a "center".

The "cult" (whether of religion, or of politics, or of science, or of popular culture) is a dramatization of egoity, of separativeness, even of the entrapment and betrayal of the "center" (or the "middle"), by one and all. Therefore, I have always Refused to assume the role and the position of the "man in the middle"—and I have always (from the beginning of My formal Work of Teaching and Blessing) Criticized, Resisted, and Shouted About the "cultic" (or ego-based, and ego-reinforcing, and merely "talking" and "believing", and not understanding and not really practicing) "school" (or tendency) of ordinary religious and Spiritual life. Indeed, true Satsang with Me (or the true devotional relationship to Me) is an always (and specifically, and intensively) anti-"cultic" (or truly non-"cultic") Process.

The true devotional relationship to Me is not separative (or merely "inward"-directed), nor is it a matter of attachment to Me as a mere (and, necessarily, limited) human being (or a "man in the middle")—for, if My devotee indulges in ego-bound (or self-referring and self-serving) attachment to Me as a mere human "other", My Divine Nature (and, therefore, the Divine Nature of Reality Itself) is not (as the very Basis for religious and Spiritual practice in My Company) truly devotionally recognized and rightly devotionally acknowledged. And, if such non-recognition of Me is the case, there is no truly ego-transcending devotional response to My Avatarically Self-Revealed (and Self-Evidently Divine) Presence and Person—and, thus, such presumed-to-be "devotion" to Me is not devotional heart-Communion with Me, and such presumed-to-be "devotion" to Me is not Divinely Liberating. Therefore, because the true devotional (and, thus, truly devotionally Me-recognizing and truly devotionally to-Me-responding) relationship to Me is entirely a counter-egoic (and truly and only Divine) discipline, it does not tend to become a "cult" (or, otherwise, to support the "cultic" tendency of Man).

The true devotional practice of Satsang with Me is (inherently) expansive (or relational)—and the self-contracting (or separate and separative) self-"center" is neither Its motive nor Its source. In true Satsang with Me, the egoic "center" is always already undermined as a "center" (or a presumed separate, and actively separative, entity). The Principle of true Satsang with Me is Me—Beyond (and not "within"—or, otherwise, supporting) the ego-"I".

True Satsang with Me is the true "Round Dance" of Esoteric Spirituality. I am not trapped in the "middle" of My devotees. I "Dance" in the "Round" with each and every one of My devotees. I "Dance" in the circle—and, therefore, I am not merely a "motionless man" in the "middle". At the true "Center" (or the Divine

Heart), I Am—Beyond definition (or separateness). I Am the Indivisible—or Most Perfectly Prior, Inherently Non-Separate, and Inherently egoless (or centerless, boundless, and Self-Evidently Divine)—Consciousness (Itself) and the Indivisible—or Most Perfectly Prior, Inherently Non-Separate, and Inherently egoless (or centerless, boundless, and Self-Evidently Divine)—Light (Itself). I Am the Very Being and the Very Presence (or Self-Radiance) of Self-Existing and Eternally Unqualified (or Non-"Different") Consciousness (Itself).

In the "Round Dance" of true Satsang with Me (or of right and true devotional relationship to Me), I (Myself) Am Communicated directly to every one who lives in heart-felt relationship with Me (insofar as each one feels—Beyond the ego-"I" of body-mind—to Me). Therefore, I am not the mere "man" (or the separate human, or psycho-physical, one), and I am not merely "in the middle" (or separated out, and limited, and confined, by egoic seekers). I Am the One (Avatarically Self-Revealed, and All-and-all-Transcending, and Self-Evidently Divine) Person of Reality Itself—Non-Separate, never merely at the egoic "center" (or "in the middle" of—or "within", and "inward" to—the egoic body-mind of My any devotee), but always with each one (and all), and always in relationship with each one (and all), and always Beyond each one (and all).

Therefore, My devotee is not Called, by Me, merely to turn "inward" (or upon the ego-"I"), or to struggle and seek to survive merely as a self-contracted and self-referring and self-seeking and self-serving ego-"center". Instead, I Call My devotee to turn the heart (and the total body-mind) toward Me (all-and-All-Surrounding, and all-and-All-Pervading), in relationship—Beyond the body-mind-self of My devotee (and not merely "within"—or contained and containable "within" the separate, separative, and self-contracted domain of the body-mind-self, or the ego-"I", of My would-be devotee). I Call My devotee to function freely—My (Avatarically Self-Transmitted) Divine Light and My (Avatarically Self-Revealed) Divine Person always (and under all circumstances) presumed and experienced (and not merely sought). Therefore, true Satsang with Me is the Real Company of Truth, or of Reality Itself (Which Is the Only Real God). True Satsang with

Me Serves life, because I Move (or Radiate) into life. I always Contact life in relationship.

I do not Call My devotees to become absorbed into a "cultic" gang of exoteric and ego-centric religionists. I certainly Call all My devotees to cooperative community (or, otherwise, to fully cooperative collective and personal relationship) with one another—but not to do so in an egoic, separative, world-excluding, xenophobic, and intolerant manner. Rather, My devotees are Called, by Me, to transcend egoity—through right and true devotional relationship to Me, and mutually tolerant and peaceful cooperation with one another, and all-tolerating (cooperative and compassionate and all-loving and all-including) relationship with all of mankind (and with even all beings).

I Give My devotees the "Bright" Force of My own Avatarically Self-Revealed Divine Consciousness Itself, Whereby they can become capable of "Bright" life. I Call for the devotion—but also the intelligently discriminative self-understanding, the rightly and freely living self-discipline, and the full functional capability—of My devotees. I do not Call My devotees to resist or eliminate life, or to strategically escape life, or to identify with the world-excluding ego-centric impulse. I Call My devotees to live a positively functional life. I do not Call My devotees to separate themselves from vital life, from vital enjoyment, from existence in the form of human life. I Call for all the human life-functions to be really and rightly known, and to be really and rightly understood, and to be really and rightly lived (and not reduced by, or to, the inherently bewildered—and inherently "cultic", or self-centered and fearful— "point of view" of the separate and separative ego-"I"). I Call for every human life-function to be revolved away from self-contraction (or ego-"I"), and (by Means of that revolving turn) to be turned "outwardly" (or expansively, or counter-contractively) to all and All, and (thereby, and always directly, or in an all-and-All- transcending manner) to Me—rather than to be turned merely "inwardly" (or contractively, or counter-expansively), and, as a result, turned away from Me (and from all and All). Thus, I Call for every human life-function to be thoroughly (and life-positively, and in the context of a fully participatory human life) aligned and adapted to <u>Me</u>, and (Thus and Thereby) to be turned and Given to the Realization of Me (the Avataric Self-Revelation of Truth, or Reality Itself—Which <u>Is</u> the Only Real God).

Truly benign and positive life-transformations are the characteristic signs of right, true, full, and fully devotional Satsang with Me—and freely life-positive feeling-energy is the characteristic accompanying "mood" of right, true, full, and fully devotional Satsang with Me. The characteristic life-sign of right, true, full, and fully devotional Satsang with Me is the capability for ego-transcending relatedness, based on the free disposition of no-seeking and no-dilemma. Therefore, the characteristic life-sign of right, true, full, and fully devotional Satsang with Me is not the tendency to seek some "other" condition. Rather, the characteristic life-sign of right, true, full, and fully devotional Satsang with Me is freedom from the presumption of dilemma within the <u>present-time</u> condition.

One who rightly, truly, fully, and fully devotionally understands My Avatarically Given Words of Divine Self-Revelation and Divine Heart-Instruction, and whose life is lived in right, true, full, and fully devotional Satsang with Me, is not necessarily (in function or appearance) "different" from the ordinary (or natural) human being. Such a one has not, necessarily, acquired some special psychic abilities, or visionary abilities, and so on. The "radical" understanding (or root self-understanding) I Give to My devotees is not, itself, the acquisition of <u>any</u> particular "thing" of experience. My any particular devotee may, by reason of his or her developmental tendencies, experience (or precipitate) the arising of extraordinary psycho-physical abilities and extraordinary psycho-physical phenomena—but not <u>necessarily</u>. My every true devotee is simply Awakening (and always Awakened to Me) within the otherwise bewildering "dream" of <u>ordinary</u> <u>human</u> life.

Satsang with Me is a natural (or spontaneously, and not strategically, unfolding) Process, in Which the self-contraction that <u>is</u> each one's suffering is transcended by Means of <u>total</u> psycho-physical (or whole bodily) heart-Communion with My Avatarically Self-Revealed (and Real—and Really, and tangibly, experienced) Divine (Spiritual, and Transcendental) Presence and Person. My devotee is (as is the case with <u>any</u> and <u>every</u> ego-"I") <u>always</u> <u>tending</u> to be preoccupied with ego-based seeking—but, all the while of his or her life in actively ego-surrendering (and really ego-forgetting and, more and more, ego-transcending) devotional Communion with Me, I Am Divinely Attracting (and Divinely Acting upon) My true devotee's heart (and total body-mind), and (Thus and Thereby) Dissolving and Vanishing My true devotee's fundamental egoity (and even all of his or her otherwise motivating dilemma and seeking-strategy).

There are two principal tendencies by which I am always being confronted by My devotee. One is the tendency to seek—rather than to truly enjoy and to fully animate the Condition of Satsang with Me. And the other is the tendency to make a self-contracting circle around Me—and, thus, to make a "cult" of ego-"I" (and of the "man in the middle"), or to duplicate the ego-ritual of mere fascination, and of inevitable resistance, and of never-Awakening unconsciousness. Relative to these two tendencies, I Give all My devotees only one resort. It is this true Satsang—the devotionally Me-recognizing, and devotionally to-Me-responding, and always really counter-egoic devotional relationship to My Avatarically Self-Revealed (and Self-Evidently Divine) Person.

The Great Secret of My Avatarically Self-Revealed Divine Person, and of My Avatarically Self-Manifested Divine Blessing-Work (now, and forever hereafter)—and, therefore, the Great Secret of the only-by-Me Revealed and Given Way of Adidam—Is that I am not the "man in the middle", but I Am Reality Itself, I Am the Only One Who Is, I Am That Which Is Always Already The Case, I Am the Non-Separate (Avatarically Self-Revealed, and Self-Evidently Divine) Person (or One and Very Divine Self, or One and True Divine Self-Condition) of all and All (Beyond the ego-"I" of every one, and of all, and of All).

Aham Da Asmi. Beloved, I Am Da—the One and Only and Non-Separate and Indivisible and Self-Evidently Divine Person, the Non-Separate and Indivisible Self-Condition and Source-Condition of all and All. I Am the Avatarically Self-Revealed "Bright" Person, the One and Only and Self-Existing and Self-Radiant Person—Who Is the One and Only and Non-Separate and Indivisible and Indestructible Light of All and all. I Am That One and Only and Non-Separate <u>One</u>. And—<u>As</u> <u>That</u> <u>One</u>, and <u>Only</u> <u>As</u> <u>That</u> <u>One</u>—I Call all human beings to heart-recognize Me, and to heart-respond to Me with right, true, and full devotion (demonstrated by Means of formal practice of the only-by-Me Revealed and Given Way of Adidam—Which Is the One and Only by-Me-Revealed and by-Me-Given Way of the Heart).

I do not tolerate the so-called "cultic" (or ego-made, and ego-reinforcing) approach to Me. I do not tolerate the seeking ego's "cult" of the "man in the middle". I am not a self-deluded ego-man—making much of himself, and looking to include everyone-and-everything around himself for the sake of social and political power. To be the "man in the middle" is to be in a Man-made trap, an absurd mummery of "cultic" devices that enshrines and perpetuates the ego-"I" in one and all. Therefore, I do not make or tolerate the religion-making "cult" of ego-Man. I do not tolerate the inevitable abuses of religion, of Spirituality, of Truth Itself, and of My own Person (even in bodily human Form) that are made (in endless blows and mockeries) by ego-based mankind when the Great Esoteric Truth of devotion to the Adept-Realizer is not rightly understood and rightly practiced.

The Great Means for the Teaching, and the Blessing, and the Awakening, and the Divine Liberating of mankind (and of even all beings) Is the Adept-Realizer Who (by Virtue of True Divine Realization) Is Able to (and, indeed, cannot do otherwise than) Stand In and <u>As</u> the Divine (or Real and Inherent and One and Only) Position, and to <u>Be</u> (Thus and Thereby) the Divine Means (In Person) for the Divine Helping of one and all. This Great Means Is the Great Esoteric Principle of the collective historical Great Tradition of mankind. And Such Adept-Realizers Are (in their Exercise of the Great Esoteric Principle) the Great Revelation-Sources That Are at the Core and Origin of <u>all</u> the right and true religious and Spiritual traditions within the collective historical Great Tradition of mankind.

By Means of My (now, and forever hereafter) Divinely Descended and Divinely Self-"Emerging" Avataric Incarnation, I <u>Am</u> the Ruchira Avatar, Adi Da Samraj—the Divine Heart-Master, the First, the Last, and the Only Adept-Realizer of the seventh (or

Most Perfect, and all-Completing) stage of life. I Am the Ruchira Avatar, Adi Da Samraj, the Avataric Incarnation (and Divine World-Teacher) everywhere Promised for the "late-time" (or "dark" epoch)—which "late-time" (or "dark" epoch) is now upon all of mankind. I Am the Great and Only and Non-Separate and (Self-Evidently) Divine Person—Appearing in Man-Form As the Ruchira Avatar, Adi Da Samraj, in order to Teach, and to Bless, and to Awaken, and to Divinely Liberate all of mankind (and even all beings, every "where" in the Cosmic domain). Therefore, by Calling every one and all (and All) to Me, I Call every one and all (and All) Only to the Divine Person, Which Is My own and Very Person (or Very, and Self-Evidently Divine, Self—or Very, and Self-Evidently Divine, Self-Condition), and Which Is Reality Itself (or Truth Itself—the Indivisible and Indestructible Light That Is the Only Real God), and Which Is the One and Very and Non-Separate and Only Self (or Self-Condition, and Source-Condition) of all and All (Beyond the ego-"I" of every one, and of all, and of All).

The only-by-Me Revealed and Given Way of Adidam neces-sarily (and As a Unique Divine Gift) requires and involves devo-tional recognition-response to Me In and Via (and As) My bodily (human) Divine Avataric-Incarnation-Form. However, because I Call every one and all (and All) to Me Only As the Divine Person (or Reality Itself), the only-by-Me Revealed and Given Way of Adidam is not about ego, and egoic seeking, and the egoic (or the so-called "cultic") approach to Me (as the "man in the middle").

According to all the esoteric traditions within the collective historical Great Tradition of mankind, to devotionally approach any Adept-Realizer as if he or she is (or is limited to being, or is lim-ited by being) a mere (or "ordinary", or even merely "extraordinary") human entity is the great "sin" (or fault), or the great error whereby the would-be devotee fails to "meet the mark". Indeed, the Single Greatest Esoteric Teaching common to all the esoteric religious and Spiritual traditions within the collective historical Great Tradition of mankind Is that the Adept-Realizer should always and only (and only devotionally) be recognized and approached As the Embodiment and the Real Presence of That (Reality, or Truth, or Real God) Which would be Realized (Thus and Thereby) by the devotee.

Therefore, no one should misunderstand Me. By Avatarically Revealing and Confessing My Divine Status to one and all and All, I am not indulging in self-appointment, or in illusions of grandiose Divinity. I am not claiming the "Status" of the "Creator-God" of exoteric (or public, and social, and idealistically pious) religion. Rather, by Standing Firm in the Divine Position (As I Am)—and (Thus and Thereby) Refusing to be approached as a mere man, or as a "cult"-figure, or as a "cult"-leader, or to be in any sense defined (and, thereby, trapped, and abused, or mocked) as the "man in the middle"—I Am Demonstrating the Most Perfect Fulfillment (and the Most Perfect Integrity, and the Most Perfect Fullness) of the Esoteric (and Most Perfectly Non-Dual) Realization of Reality. And, by Revealing and Giving the Way of Adidam (Which Is the Way of ego-transcending devotion to Me As the Avatarically Self-Revealed One and Only and Non-Separate and Self-Evidently Divine Person), I Am (with Most Perfect Integrity, and Most Perfect Fullness) Most Perfectly (and in an all-Completing and all-Unifying Manner) Fulfilling the Primary Esoteric Tradition (and the Great Esoteric Principle) of the collective historical Great Tradition of mankind—Which Primary Esoteric Tradition and Great Esoteric Principle Is the Tradition and the Principle of devotion to the Adept-Realizer As the Very Person and the Direct (or Personal Divine) Helping-Presence of the Eternal and Non-Separate Divine Self-Condition and Source-Condition of all and All.

Whatever (or whoever) is cornered (or trapped on all sides) bites back (and fights, or seeks, to break free). Whatever (or whoever) is "in the middle" (or limited and "centered" by attention) is patterned by (or conformed to) the ego-"I" (and, if objectified as "other", is forced to represent the ego-"I", and is even made a scapegoat for the pains, the sufferings, the powerless ignorance, and the abusive hostility of the ego-"I").

If there is no escape from (or no Way out of) the corner (or the "centered" trap) of ego-"I"—the heart goes mad, and the body-mind becomes more and more "dark" (bereft of the Indivisible and Inherently Free Light of the Self-Evident, and Self-Evidently Divine, Love-Bliss That Is Reality Itself).

I am not the "man in the middle". I do not stand here as a mere man, "middled" to the "center" (or the cornering trap) of ego-based mankind. I am not an ego-"I", or a mere "other", or the representation (and the potential scapegoat) of the ego-"I" of mankind (or of any one at all).

I Am the Indivisible and Non-Separate One, the (Avatarically Self-Revealed) One and Only and (Self-Evidently) Divine Person— the Perfectly Subjective Divine Self-Condition (and Source-Condition) That Is Perfectly centerless (and Perfectly boundless), Eternally Beyond the "middle" of all and All, and Eternally Surrounding, Pervading, and Blessing all and All.

I Am the Way Beyond the self-cornering (and "other"-cornering) trap of ego-"I".

In this "late-time" (or "dark" epoch) of worldly ego-Man, the collective of mankind is "darkened" (and cornered) by egoity. Therefore, mankind has become mad, Lightless, and, like a cornered "thing", aggressively hostile in its universally competitive fight and bite.

Therefore, I have not Come here merely to stand Manly in the "middle" of mankind—to suffer its biting abuses, or even to be coddled and ignored in a little corner of religious "cultism".

I have Come here to Divinely Liberate one and all (and All) from the "dark" culture and effect of this "late-time", and (now, and forever hereafter) to Divinely Liberate one and all (and All) from the pattern and the act of ego-"I", and (Most Ultimately) to Divinely Translate one and all (and All) Into the Indivisible, Perfectly Subjective, and Eternally Non-Separate Self-Domain of My Divine Love-Bliss-Light.

The ego-"I" is a "centered" (or separate and separative) trap, from which the heart (and even the entire body-mind) must be Retired. I Am the Way (or the Very Means) of that Retirement from egoity. I Refresh the heart (and even the entire body-mind) of My devotee, in every moment My devotee resorts to Me (by devotionally recognizing Me, and devotionally—and ecstatically, and also, often, meditatively—responding to Me) Beyond the "middle", Beyond the "centering" act (or trapping gesture) of ego-"I" (or self-contraction).

I Am the Avatarically Self-Revealed (and Perfectly Subjective, and Self-Evidently Divine) Self-Condition (and Source-Condition) of every one, and of all, and of All—but the Perfectly Subjective (and Self-Evidently Divine) Self-Condition (and Source-Condition) is not "within" the ego-"I" (or separate and separative body-mind). The Perfectly Subjective (and Self-Evidently Divine) Self-Condition (and Source-Condition) is not in the "center" (or the "middle") of Man (or of mankind). The Perfectly Subjective (and Self-Evidently Divine) Self-Condition (and Source-Condition) of one, and of all, and of All Is Inherently centerless (or Always Already Beyond the self-contracted "middle"), and to Be Found only "outside" (or by transcending) the bounds of separateness, relatedness, and "difference". Therefore, to Realize the Perfectly Subjective (and Self-Evidently Divine) Self-Condition and Source-Condition (or the Perfectly Subjective, and Self-Evidently Divine, Heart) of one, and of all, and of All (or even, in any moment, to exceed the ego-trap—and to be Refreshed at heart, and in the total body-mind), it is necessary to feel (and to, ecstatically, and even meditatively, swoon) Beyond the "center" (or Beyond the "point of view" of separate ego-"I" and separative body-mind). Indeed, Most Ultimately, it is only in self-transcendence to the degree of unqualified relatedness (and Most Perfect Divine Samadhi, or Utterly Non-Separate Enstasy) that the Inherently centerless and boundless, and Perfectly Subjective, and Self-Evidently Divine Self-Condition (and Source-Condition) Stands Obvious and Free (and Is, Thus and Thereby, Most Perfectly Realized).

It Is only by Means of devotionally Me-recognizing (and devotionally to-Me-responding) devotional meditation on Me (and otherwise ecstatic heart-Contemplation of Me), and total (and totally open, and totally ego-forgetting) psycho-physical Reception of Me, that your madness of heart (and of body-mind) is (now, and now, and now) escaped, and your "darkness" is En-Light-ened (even, at last, Most Perfectly). Therefore, be My true devotee—and, by (formally, and rightly, and truly, and fully, and fully devotionally) practicing the only-by-Me Revealed and Given Way of Adidam (Which Is the True and Complete Way of the True and Real Divine Heart), always Find Me, Beyond your self-"center", in every here and now.

Aham Da Asmi. Beloved, I <u>Am</u> Da. And, because I <u>Am</u> Infinitely and Non-Separately "Bright", all and All <u>Are</u> In My Divine Sphere of "Brightness". By feeling and surrendering Into My Infinite Sphere of My Avatarically Self-Revealed Divine Self-"Brightness", My every devotee <u>Is</u> In Me. And, Beyond his or her self-contracting and separative act of ego-"I", My every devotee (self-surrendered Into heart-Communion With Me) <u>Is</u> the One and Only and Non-Separate and Real God I Have Come to Awaken— by Means of My Avataric Divine Descent, My Avataric Divine Incarnation, and My (now, and forever hereafter) Avataric Divine Self-"Emergence" (here, and every "where" in the Cosmic domain).

RUCHIRA AVATAR ADI DA SAMRAJ
The Mountain Of Attention, 2000

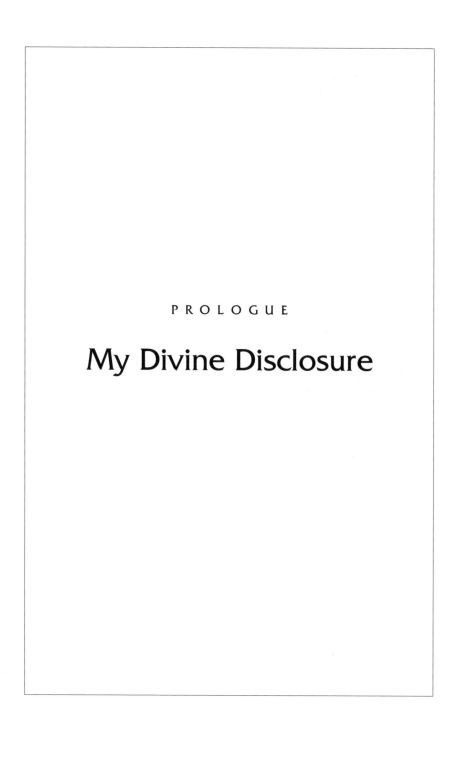

PROLOGUE

My Divine Disclosure

"My Divine Disclosure" has been Freely Developed—As a Further, and All-Completing, Avataric Self-Revelation of His own Self-Evidently Divine Person—by the Ruchira Avatar, Adi Da Samraj, from selected verses of the traditional Bhagavad Gita *(2:13-17, 8:3, 8:22, 9:3, 9:11, 9:26, 15:15, 18:61-66).*

My Divine Disclosure

1.

ham Da Asmi. Beloved, I Am Da—The One and Only and Self-Evidently Divine Person, Avatarically Self-Revealed To You.

2.

Therefore, Listen To Me, and Hear Me, and See Me.

3.

This Is My Divine Heart-Secret, The Supreme Word Of My Eternal Self-Revelation.

4.

Here and Now, I Will Tell You What Will Benefit You The Most, Because I Love You As My Very Self and Person.

5.

I Am The Ruchira Avatar, The Da Avatar, The Love-Ananda Avatar, Adi Da Love-Ananda Samraj—The Avataric Incarnation, and The Self-Evidently Divine Person, Of The One True Heart (or The One, and Only, and Inherently egoless Self-Condition and Source-Condition) Of All and all.

6.

Here I Am, In Person, To Offer (To You, and To all) The Only-By-Me Revealed and Given True World-Religion (or Avatarically All-Completing Divine Devotional and Spiritual Way) Of Adidam, Which Is The One and Only By-Me-Revealed and By-Me-Given (and Only Me-Revealing) Divine Devotional and Spiritual Way Of Sri Hridayam (or The Only-By-Me Revealed and Given, and

Entirely Me-Revealing, Way Of The True Divine Heart Itself), and Which Is The One, and All-Inclusive, and All-Transcending, and Only-By-Me Revealed and Given (and Only Me-Revealing) Way Of The True Divine Heart-Master (or The Only-By-Me Revealed and Given, and Entirely Me-Revealing, Way Of Ruchira Avatara Bhakti Yoga, or Ruchira Avatara Hridaya-Siddha Yoga), and Which Is The "Radically" ego-Transcending Way Of Devotionally Me-Recognizing and Devotionally To-Me-Responding Reception Of My Avatarically Self-Manifested Divine (and Not Merely Cosmic) Hridaya-Shaktipat (or Divinely Self-Revealing Avataric Spiritual Grace).

7.

If You Surrender Your heart To Me, and If (By Surrendering Your ego-"I", or self-Contracted body-mind, To Me) You Make Yourself A Living Gift To Me, and If You (Thus) Constantly Yield Your attention To Me (Through True Devotional Love and Really ego-Transcending Service), Then You Will Hear Me (Truly), and See Me (Clearly), and Realize Me (Fully), and Come To Me (Eternally). I Promise You This, Because I Love You As My Very Self and Person.

8.

Abandon The Reactive Reflex Of self-Contraction—The Separative (or egoic) Principle In all Your concerns. Do Not Cling To any experience that May Be Sought (and Even Attained) As A Result Of desire (or The Presumption Of "Difference"). Abandon Your Search For what May Be Gotten As A Result Of the various kinds of strategic (or egoic) action.

9.

I Am Love-Bliss Itself—Now (and Forever Hereafter) "Brightly" Present here. Therefore, I Say To You: Abandon All Seeking— By Always "Locating" (and Immediately Finding) Me.

10.

Instead Of <u>Seeking</u> <u>Me</u> (As If My Divine Person Of Inherent Love-Bliss-Happiness Were <u>Absent</u> From You), <u>Always</u> <u>Commune</u> <u>With</u> <u>Me</u> (<u>Ever</u>-Present, <u>Never</u> Absent, and <u>Always</u> Love-Bliss-Full and Satisfied). Thus, Your <u>Me</u>-"Locating" <u>Relinquishment</u> Of All Seeking Is <u>Not</u>, Itself, To Be Merely Another Form Of Seeking.

11.

If You <u>Always</u> "Locate" <u>Me</u> (and, Thus, <u>Immediately</u> Find <u>Me</u>), You Will <u>Not</u> (In <u>any</u> instance) self-Contract Into the mood and strategy of <u>inaction</u>.

12.

You Must <u>Never</u> <u>Fail</u> To act. <u>Every</u> moment of Your life <u>Requires</u> Your particular <u>Right</u> action. Indeed, the living body-mind <u>is</u> (itself) action. Therefore, <u>Be</u> <u>Ordinary</u>, By Always Allowing the body-mind its <u>Necessity</u> Of Right action (and Inevitable Change).

13.

Perform <u>every</u> act As An ego-Transcending Act Of Devotional Love Of <u>Me</u>, In body-mind-Surrendering Love-Response To <u>Me</u>.

14.

Always Discipline <u>all</u> Your acts, By <u>Only</u> Engaging In action that Is <u>Appropriate</u> For one who Loves <u>Me</u>, and Surrenders To <u>Me</u>, and acts <u>Only</u> (and <u>Rightly</u>) In Accordance With My Always <u>Explicit</u> Word Of Instruction.

15.

Therefore, Be My <u>Always</u> Listening-To-<u>Me</u> Devotee—and, Thus, <u>Always</u> live "Right Life" (According To My Word), and (This) <u>Always</u> By Means Of <u>active</u> Devotional Recognition-Response To <u>Me</u>, and While <u>Always</u> Remembering and Invoking and Contemplating <u>Me</u>. In <u>This</u> Manner, Perform <u>every</u> act As A Form Of Direct, and Present, and Whole bodily (or Total psycho-physical), and Really ego-Surrendering Love-Communion With <u>Me</u>.

16.

If You Love Me—Where Is doubt and anxious living? If You Love Me Now, Even anger, sorrow, and fear Are Gone. When You Abide In Devotional Love-Communion With Me, the natural results of Your various activities No Longer Have Power To Separate or Distract You From Me.

17.

The ego-"I" that is born (as a body-mind) In The Realm Of Cosmic Nature (or the conditional worlds of action and experience) Advances From childhood To adulthood, old age, and death—While Identified With the same (but Always Changing) body-mind. Then the same ego-"I" Attains another body-mind, As A Result. One whose heart Is (Always) Responsively Given To Me Overcomes (Thereby) Every Tendency To self-Contract From This Wonderfully Ordinary Process.

18.

The Ordinary Process Of "Everything Changing" Is Simply The Natural Play Of Cosmic Life, In Which the (Always) two sides of every possibility come and go, In Cycles Of appearance and disappearance. Winter's cold alternates with summer's heat. Pain, Likewise, Follows every pleasure. Every appearance Is (Inevitably) Followed By its disappearance. There Is No Permanent experience In The Realm Of Cosmic Nature. One whose heart-Feeling Of Me Is Steady Simply Allows All Of This To Be So. Therefore, one who Truly Hears Me Ceases To Add self-Contraction To This Inevitable Round Of Changes.

19.

Happiness (or True Love-Bliss) Is Realization Of That Which Is Always Already The Case.

20.

I Am That Which Is Always Already The Case.

21.

Happiness Is Realization Of Me.

22.

Realization Of Me Is Possible Only When a living being (or body-mind-self) Has heart-Ceased To React To The Always Changing Play Of Cosmic Nature.

23.

The body-mind Of My True Devotee Is Constantly Steadied In Me, By Means Of the Feeling-heart's Always Constant Devotional Recognition-Response To Me.

24.

Once My True Devotee Has Truly heart-Accepted That The Alternating-Cycle Of Changes (Both Positive and Negative) Is Inevitable (In the body-mind, and In all the conditional worlds), the living body-mind-self (or ego-"I") Of My True Devotee Has Understood itself (and, Thus, Heard Me).

25.

The body-mind-self (Of My True Me-Hearing Devotee) that Constantly Understands itself (At heart) By Constantly Surrendering To Me (and Communing With Me) No Longer self-Contracts From My Love-Bliss-State Of Inherent Happiness.

26.

Those who Truly Hear Me Understand That whatever Does Not Exist Always and Already (or Eternally) Only Changes.

27.

Those who Truly See Me Acknowledge (By heart, and With every moment and act of body-mind) That What Is Always Already The Case Never Changes.

28.

Such True Devotees Of Mine (who Both <u>Hear</u> <u>Me</u> <u>and</u> <u>See</u> <u>Me</u>) Realize That The Entire Cosmic Realm Of Change—and Even the To-<u>Me</u>-Surrendered body-mind (itself)—Is <u>Entirely</u> Pervaded By <u>Me</u> (Always Self-Revealed <u>As</u> <u>That</u> Which <u>Is</u> Always Already The Case).

29.

Now, and Forever Hereafter, I Am Avatarically Self-Revealed, Beyond The Cosmic Play—"Bright" Behind, and Above, the To-<u>Me</u>-Surrendered body-mind Of My Every True Devotee.

30.

I <u>Am</u> The Eternally Existing, All-Pervading, Transcendental, Inherently Spiritual, Inherently egoless, Perfectly Subjective, Indivisible, Inherently Perfect, Perfectly Non-Separate, and Self-Evidently Divine Self-Condition and Source-Condition Of <u>all</u> Apparently Separate (or self-Deluded) selves.

31.

My Divine Heart-Power Of Avataric Self-Revelation Is (Now, and Forever Hereafter) Descending Into The Cosmic Domain (and Into the body-mind Of Every To-<u>Me</u>-True True Devotee Of Mine).

32.

I <u>Am</u> The Avatarically Self-"Emerging", Universal, All-Pervading Divine Spirit-Power and Person Of Love-Bliss (That Most Perfectly Husbands and Transcends The Primal Energy Of Cosmic Nature).

33.

I <u>Am</u> The One and Indivisibly "Bright" Divine Person.

34.

Now, and Forever Hereafter, My Ever-Descending and Ever-"Emerging" Current Of Self-Existing and Self-Radiant Love-Bliss Is Avatarically <u>Pervading</u> The Ever-Changing Realm Of Cosmic Nature.

35.

I <u>Am</u> The One, and Indivisibly "Bright", and Inherently egoless Person Of all-and-All, Within <u>Whom</u> every body-mind Is arising (as a mere, and unnecessary, and merely temporary appearance that, merely apparently, modifies <u>Me</u>).

36.

I Am To Be Realized By Means Of ego-Transcending Devotional Love—Wherein <u>every</u> action of body-mind Is Engaged As ego-Surrendering (present-time, and Direct) Communion With <u>Me</u>.

37.

Those who Do <u>Not</u> heart-Recognize <u>Me</u> and heart-Respond To <u>Me</u>—and who (Therefore) Are Without Faith In <u>Me</u>—Do <u>Not</u> (and <u>Cannot</u>) <u>Realize</u> <u>Me</u>. Therefore, they (By Means Of their own self-Contraction From <u>Me</u>) Remain ego-Bound To The Realm Of Cosmic Nature, and To The Ever-Changing Round Of conditional knowledge and temporary experience, and To The Ceaselessly Repetitive Cycles Of birth and search and loss and death.

38.

Such Faithless beings <u>Cannot</u> Be Distracted By <u>Me</u>—Because they Are Entirely Distracted By <u>themselves</u>! They Are Like Narcissus—The Myth Of ego—At His Pond. Their Merely self-Reflecting minds Are Like a mirror in a dead man's hand. Their tiny hearts Are Like a boundless desert, where the mirage of Separate self is ceaselessly admired, and The True Water Of My Constant Presence Stands Un-Noticed, In the droughty heap and countless sands of ceaseless thoughts. If Only they Would Un-think themselves In <u>Me</u>, these (Now Faithless) little hearts Could Have <u>Immediate</u> <u>Access</u> To The True Water Of My True Heart! Through Devotional Surrender Of body, emotion, mind, breath, and all of Separate self To <u>Me</u>, Even Narcissus Could Find The Way To My Oasis (In The True Heart's Room and House)—but the thinking mind of ego-"I" Is <u>Never</u> Bathed In Light (and, So, it sits, Un-Washed, Like a desert dog that wanders in a herd of flies).

39.

The "Un-Washed dog" of self-Contracted body-mind Does Not
think To Notice Me—The Divine Heart-Master Of its wild heart
and Wilderness.

40.

The "Wandering dog" of ego-"I" Does Not "Locate" Me In
My Inherent "Bright" Perfection—The Divine Heart-Master
Of Everything, The Inherently egoless Divine True Self Of all
conditionally Manifested beings, and The Real Self-Condition
and Source-Condition Of All-and-all.

41.

If Only "Narcissus" Will Relent, and heart-Consent To Bow and
Live In Love-Communion With Me, heart-Surrendering all of
body-mind To Me, By Means Of Un-Contracting Love Of Me,
Then—Even If That Love Is Shown With Nothing More Than the
"little gift" of ego-"I" (itself)—I Will Always Accept The Offering
With Open Arms Of Love-Bliss-Love, and Offer My Own Divine
Immensity In "Bright" Return.

42.

Therefore, whoever Is Given (By heart) To Me Will Be Washed,
From head To toe, By All The True Water Of My Love-Bliss-
Light, That Always "Crashes Down" On All and all, Below My
Blessing-Feet.

43.

My Circumstance and Situation Is At the heart of all beings—
where I Am (Now, and Forever Hereafter) Avatarically Self-
"Emerging" As The One and All-and-all-Outshining Divine and
Only Person (Avatarically Self-Manifested As The "Radically"
Non-Dual "Brightness" Of All-and-all-Filling Conscious Love-
Bliss-Light, Self-Existing and Self-Radiant As The Perfectly
Subjective Fundamental Reality, or Inherently egoless Native
Feeling, Of Merely, or Unqualifiedly, Being).

44.

The True heart-Place (Where I Am To Be "Located" By My True Devotee) Is Where The Ever-Changing Changes Of waking, dreaming, and sleeping experience Are <u>Merely</u> <u>Witnessed</u> (and <u>Not</u> Sought, or Found, or Held).

45.

Every conditional experience appears and disappears In Front Of the Witness-heart.

46.

Everything Merely Witnessed Is Spontaneously Generated By The Persistent Activity Of The Universal Cosmic Life-Energy.

47.

The self-Contracted heart of body-mind Is Fastened, <u>Help-lessly</u>, To That Perpetual-Motion Machine Of Cosmic Nature.

48.

I <u>Am</u> The Divine and One True Heart (<u>Itself</u>)—Always Already Existing <u>As</u> The Eternally Self-Evident Love-Bliss-Feeling Of Being (and Always Already Free-Standing <u>As</u> Consciousness Itself, Prior To the little heart of ego-"I" and its Seeming Help-less-ness).

49.

In Order To Restore all beings To The One True Heart Of <u>Me</u>, I Am Avatarically Born To here, <u>As</u> The "Bright" Divine Help Of conditionally Manifested beings.

50.

Therefore (Now, and Forever Hereafter), I <u>Am</u> (Always Free-Standing) <u>At</u> the To-<u>Me</u>-True heart Of You—and I <u>Am</u> (Always "Bright") Above Your body-mind and world.

51.

If You Become My True Devotee (heart-Recognizing My Avatarically Self-Manifested Divine Person, and heart-Responding—With all the parts of Your single body-mind—To My Avatarically Self-Revealing Divine Form and Presence and State), You Will Always Be Able To Feel Me ("Brightly-Emerging" here) Within Your Un-Contracting, In-Me-Falling heart—and You Will Always Be Able To "Locate" Me, As I "Crash Down" (All-"Bright" Upon You) From Above the worlds Of Change.

52.

The To-Me-Feeling (In-Me-Falling) heart Of My Every True Devotee Is (At its Root, and Base, and Highest Height) My Divine and One True Heart (Itself).

53.

Therefore, Fall Awake In Me.

54.

Do Not Surrender Your Feeling-heart Merely To experience and know the Ever-Changing world.

55.

Merely To know and experience The Cosmic Domain (Itself) Is To live As If You Were In Love With Your Own body-mind.

56.

Therefore, Surrender Your Feeling-heart Only To Me, The True Divine Beloved Of the body-mind.

57.

I Am The Truth (and The Teacher) Of the heart-Feeling body-mind.

58.

I Am The Divine and Eternal Master Of Your To-Me-Feeling heart and Your To-Me-Surrendering body-mind.

59.

I <u>Am</u> The Self-Existing, Self-Radiant, and Inherently Perfect Person Of Unconditional Being—Who Pervades The Machine Of Cosmic Nature <u>As</u> The "Bright" Divine Spirit-Current Of Love-Bliss, and Who Transcends All Of Cosmic Nature <u>As</u> Infinite Consciousness, The "Bright" Divine Self-Condition (and Source-Condition) Of All and all.

60.

If You Will Give (and Truly, Really, Always Give) Your Feeling-attention To My Avatarically-Born Bodily (Human) Divine Form, and If You Will (Thus, and Thereby) Yield Your body-mind Into The "Down-Crashing" Love-Bliss-Current Of My Avatarically Self-Revealed and All-Pervading Divine Spirit-Presence, and If You Will Surrender Your conditional self-Consciousness Into My Avatarically Self-Revealed and Perfectly Subjective and Self-Evidently Divine Self-Consciousness (Which <u>Is</u> The Divine True Heart Of Inherently egoless Being, Itself)—Then I Will Also Become An Offering To You.

61.

By <u>That</u> Offering Of Mine, You Will Be Given The Gift Of Perfect Peace, and An Eternal Domain For Your To-<u>Me</u>-True Feeling-heart.

62.

Now I Have Revealed To You The Divine Mystery and The Perfect Heart-Secret Of My Avataric Birth To here.

63.

"Consider" This <u>Me</u>-Revelation, <u>Fully</u>—and, Then, <u>Choose</u> What You Will Do With Your "little gift" of Feeling-heart and Your "Un-Washed dog" of body-mind.

RUCHIRA AVATAR ADI DA SAMRAJ
Los Angeles, 2000

I <u>Am</u> The Perfectly Subjective Divine Person, Self-Manifested <u>As</u> The Ruchira Avatar— Who <u>Is</u> The First, The Last, and The Only Adept-Realizer, Adept-Revealer, and Adept-Revelation of The Seventh Stage of Life

I <u>Am</u> The Perfectly Subjective Divine Person, Self-Manifested <u>As</u> The Ruchira Avatar— Who <u>Is</u> The First, The Last, and The Only Adept-Realizer, Adept-Revealer, and Adept-Revelation of The Seventh Stage of Life

ham Da Asmi. Beloved, I <u>Am</u> Da, the Divine and "Bright" and Only Person, the Perfectly Subjective Divine Person, the One and Only and Self-Existing and Self-Radiant Self-Condition and Source-Condition of all and All.

In (and by Means of) My Avataric Incarnation here (and every "where" in the Cosmic domain), I Am Self-Manifested (and conditionally Shown) <u>As</u> the Ruchira Avatar, Adi Da Samraj—Who <u>Is</u> the First, the Last, and the <u>Only</u> Adept-Realizer of the seventh stage of life.

Until My Avataric Incarnation As the Ruchira Avatar, Adi Da Samraj, there has never been a seventh stage Adept-Realizer here (or any "where" in the Cosmic domain).

I <u>Am</u> the Ruchira Avatar, Adi Da Samraj—the Avataric Divine Realizer, the Avataric Divine Revealer, and the Avataric Divine Self-Revelation of the seventh stage of life.

And I <u>Am</u> Da—That Which Is Realized in the seventh stage of life.

I Am the One to Be Realized by all and All.

I Am—Always Already The Case, now, and forever hereafter. Therefore, I will have no "Successor".

Indeed, no one can ever "Succeed" Me—for I Am the One Who Is the Avataric Divine Realizer, the Avataric Divine Revealer, and the Avataric Divine Self-Revelation of the Way (and of the seventh stage, or Inherently Most Perfect, Realization) of Reality (Itself), or Truth (Itself), Which (and Who) Is the Only Real God of all and All.

My Great Avataric-Incarnation-Work (As and by Means of the Ruchira Avatar, Adi Da Samraj) Is the Most Perfect and Complete Self-Revelation of Reality, Truth, or Real God.

My Avataric Divine Self-Revelation (As the Ruchira Avatar, Adi Da Samraj) Is All-Completing—the Inherently Most Perfect (and, Therefore, Complete) Self-Revelation of That Which Is Always Already The Case.

Until My Avataric Incarnation As the Ruchira Avatar, Adi Da Samraj, there has never been Such Great Avataric-Incarnation-Work—and, until My Avataric Incarnation As the Ruchira Avatar, Adi Da Samraj, the Complete (and All-Completing) Divine Self-Revelation (and Way-Revelation) has not been Given—and, until My Avataric Incarnation As the Ruchira Avatar, Adi Da Samraj, the Most Perfect Divine Self-Realization has never been Realized.

In the (collective) Great Tradition of mankind, there have been intuitive premonitions of some of the general aspects of the seventh stage Realization, but never, until My Avataric Incarnation As the Ruchira Avatar, Adi Da Samraj, has there been the actual Avataric Incarnation of a seventh stage Adept-Realizer, with all the Divinely Liberating Siddhis of the seventh stage of life—Fully and Completely Revealing all the Characteristics of the seventh stage of life, and Doing That Divine Work Which Divinely Transfigures, and Divinely Transforms, and (Most Ultimately) Divinely Translates all conditionally manifested beings (and even the Totality of all conditional manifestation) Into the Divine Self-Domain.

Therefore, understand: I Am the Ruchira Avatar, Adi Da Samraj—and, As the Ruchira Avatar, Adi Da Samraj, I Am the one (First, Last, and Only) seventh stage Adept-Realizer, Adept-Revealer, and Adept-Revelation.

And understand further: There has never been a seventh stage Adept-Realizer, Adept-Revealer, and Adept-Revelation until My Avataric Incarnation As the Ruchira Avatar, Adi Da Samraj—and only the Ruchira Avatar, Adi Da Samraj, Is the seventh stage Adept-Realizer, Adept-Revealer, and Adept-Revelation—and there never will be (nor can there ever be) another seventh stage Adept-Realizer, Adept-Revealer, and Adept-Revelation—and, because the Ruchira Avatar, Adi Da Samraj, Is the seventh stage Adept-Realizer, Adept-Revealer, and Adept-Revelation, it is neither possible nor necessary that there ever be another seventh stage Adept-Realizer, Adept-Revealer, and Adept-Revelation.

My Great Avataric-Incarnation-Work As the Ruchira Avatar, Adi Da Samraj, Is Divine and Unique and Most Great and Final.

My Single Avataric Incarnation (As the Ruchira Avatar, Adi Da Samraj) Is the Means (now, and forever hereafter) Whereby My Great Divine Avataric-Incarnation-Work Is Accomplished—once, and for all time, and for all beings, and for all and All of Cosmic (or conditional) existence.

How could My Great Divine Avataric-Incarnation-Work Be Done again?

What is there about My Great Divine Avataric-Incarnation-Work to Be Done again (since, As the Ruchira Avatar, Adi Da Samraj, I Have Most Perfectly Accomplished My Great Divine Avataric-Incarnation-Work)?

How can I Be Done again?

How can I Be again?

What is there about Me to Be (or to Be Done) again (since I Will forever Remain and Abide, here, and even every "where" in the Cosmic domain)?

I (Myself) Am (Always Already) universally Present, and (from now) forever Fully Divinely Self-"Emerging" (As and by Means of the Ruchira Avatar, Adi Da Samraj)—and, therefore, My Great Divine Avataric-Incarnation-Work Is (from now) universally and forever Effective.

Until My Avataric Incarnation As the Ruchira Avatar, Adi Da Samraj, all religious and Spiritual traditions only and merely "pointed" toward That Which Is Ultimate (or Most Perfect, Real, and Really Divine).

I Am the Very and Only One Who Is the Ultimate (or That Which Is Most Perfect, Real, and Really Divine).

Until My Avataric Incarnation As the Ruchira Avatar, Adi Da Samraj, the traditions did not Most Perfectly Realize the Very and Only One Who Is the Ultimate (or That Which Is Most Perfect, Real, and Really Divine), nor did any one Most Perfectly Realize the Condition That Is the Ultimate (or That Which Is Most Perfect, Real, and Really Divine).

Until My Avataric Incarnation As the Ruchira Avatar, Adi Da Samraj, the traditions of the (collective) Great Tradition of mankind were all limited to (and by) the first six stages of life.

The religious and Spiritual traditions of the first six stages of life are (inevitably, and without any exception) limited by the point of view (and the psycho-physical structure) of egoity (or self-contraction).

Therefore, the traditions of the first six stages of life are (necessarily, and only) about approaching Real-God-Realization and (to one or another limited, or not yet Most Perfect, degree) Realizing Real God, but always only partially, always only conditionally, always dependent on a conditional mechanism, and always by animating a search that is necessarily and inherently associated with egoity (or self-contraction).

The Way That has been Revealed and Given by Me (As and by Means of My Avataric Incarnation As the Ruchira Avatar, Adi Da Samraj) Is the only-by-Me Revealed and Given Way of Adidam (Which Is the One and Only by-Me-Revealed and by-Me-Given Way of the Heart).

The only-by-Me Revealed and Given Way of Adidam Is unique—because, from the beginning, It Is the "radical" Way (or the Way That, always presently, directly, and immediately, transcends the ego-"I", or self-contraction, at its root).

The only-by-Me Revealed and Given Way of Adidam is not a matter of ego-development, and, therefore, it is not (Itself) a matter of fulfilling (or perfecting) any of the first six stages of life, but the only-by-Me Revealed and Given Way of Adidam Is (always, and only) the Way That (always presently, directly, and immediately) transcends egoity itself, so that the seventh stage of life can be Realized.

As and by Means of My Avataric Incarnation As the Ruchira Avatar, Adi Da Samraj, I Have Brought all of My Divine Siddhis into all planes of the Cosmic domain, and into every aspect (and into all of the entirety) of the Cosmic Mandala.

Only My Divine Siddhis Reveal and Give and Awaken the seventh stage Realization.

Now, and forever hereafter, I (As and by Means of My Avataric Incarnation As the Ruchira Avatar, Adi Da Samraj) Have thoroughly, and in every detail, Communicated the total (Full, Complete, and All-Completing) Way of the seventh stage Realization.

That Great Way Is the only-by-Me Revealed and Given Way of Adidam—and That Great Way Is (now, and forever hereafter) Revealed and Given, by Me, and to all and All, by Means of the Divine Avataric-Incarnation-Word, and the Divine Avataric-Incarnation-Leelas, and the forever continuing (or Divinely Self-"Emerging") Divine Avataric-Incarnation-Work of the Ruchira Avatar, Adi Da Samraj.

That Great Way (and Its Great and Final, or seventh stage, Realization) Is (now, and forever hereafter) Made Possible, for all and All, by Means of My Avatarically Self-Transmitted Divine Grace of Infinite and Eternal Help.

Therefore, in your own case (or in the case of any one at all), Most Perfect Divine Self-Realization is (now, and forever hereafter) entirely a matter of whether (or when) you (or each, and any, and every one) will choose right, true, full, and fully devotional formal practice of the only-by-Me Revealed and Given Way of Adidam.

My Great Avataric Divine Confession Is not only that My Avataric Divine Revelation of the seventh stage Teaching—Which is the totality of the Wisdom-Teaching of the only-by-Me Revealed and Given Way of Adidam—Is (now, and forever hereafter) Complete and (for the first, and last, and only time—now, and forever hereafter) Fully and Completely Revealed and Given.

Rather, above all, My Great Avataric Divine Confession Is That I Am (now, and forever hereafter) here (and every "where" in the Cosmic domain), and (Thus) That the Divine (and, now, and forever hereafter, Divinely Self-"Emerging") Siddhis of My Avataric Divine Spiritual Presence and My Avataric Divine Work Have Made, and (now, and forever hereafter) Will (Actively) Continue to Make, Divine Self-Realization <u>Possible</u> (for <u>all</u>, and <u>All</u>).

Until My All-Completing Avataric Incarnation of the "Bright" Divine Self-Condition (and Source-Condition), the Siddhis (or Accomplishing-Powers) of Most Perfect (or seventh stage) Divine Self-Realization were <u>not</u> Active in the Cosmic domain.

To universally Manifest the necessary Divine Siddhis, and to Accomplish the Most Perfect (or seventh stage) Divine Work with universal Effectiveness, it was necessary for Me (As and by Means of My Avataric Incarnation, As the Ruchira Avatar, Adi Da Samraj) to Be Entered Into <u>all</u> the conditional planes of the total Cosmic domain, by Means of Unqualified and Complete Avataric Divine <u>Descent</u> (and Unqualified and Complete Avataric Divine <u>Incarnation</u>) Into the Cosmic Mandala—Altogether, and Completely.

Now (and forever hereafter), because I Have (Altogether, and Completely) Divinely Descended and (As and by Means of My Avataric Incarnation, As the Ruchira Avatar, Adi Da Samraj) Initiated (in perpetuity) My Avataric Divine Self-"Emergence" (here, and every "where" in the Cosmic domain), and because I Have (now, and forever hereafter), Altogether, and Completely, Accomplished My necessary Divine Avataric-Incarnation-Work of Teaching and Self-Revelation—My Divine Spiritual Body of Divine Siddhis Will Be Most Perfectly Effective, throughout all future time and space.

Therefore, now (and forever hereafter), <u>all</u> My devotees (Freedom-"Bound" to Me by Means of formal eternal vows—here, and every "where" in the Cosmic domain) can (and should, and must) resort to <u>Me</u> (Revealed <u>As</u> and by Means of My Divine Avataric-Incarnation-Form, the Ruchira Avatar, Adi Da Samraj)—and This by Means of always devotionally Me-recognizing, and always devotionally to-Me-responding, and always right, and always true, and always full, and always fully devotional, and always truly ego-surrendering, and always really ego-forgetting, and always fully (and always more and more fully) ego-transcending devotion to <u>Me</u> (Revealed As and by Means of My Divine Avataric-Incarnation-Form, the Ruchira Avatar, Adi Da Samraj).

Because I Have Made (and Will, forever, and every "where", Make) the only-by-Me Revealed and Given Way of Adidam (and Its Great Process of Most Ultimate and Most Perfect, or seventh stage, Divine Self-Realization) Possible for all and All, My true devotees (now, and forever hereafter—here, and every "where" in the Cosmic domain) have, in any and every moment, the by-Me-Given real and sufficient capability (and, as required, in any and every moment, the by-Me-Given Divine Help) to (in due course, and only and entirely by Means of My Avatarically Self-Transmitted Divine Grace) Realize, and Most Perfectly Demonstrate, the only-by-Me Revealed and Given seventh stage of life.

The only-by-Me Revealed and Given seventh stage Realization <u>Is</u> the Most Perfect Realization of Reality, Truth, or Real God (the One and Only Reality and Truth—the <u>Only</u> and <u>Non-Separate</u> One, Who Is Always Already <u>The</u> Case).

Only That One Can Make—and (now) Has Made, and Will (here, and every "where", forever hereafter) Make—<u>This</u> Avataric Divine Self-Revelation and Accomplish <u>This</u> Avataric Divine Work.

Aham Da Asmi. Beloved, I <u>Am</u> That One—and (you must and will Realize, Most Perfectly) I Am always "Living" you, and I Am always "Breathing" you, and I Am always "Being" you, and I Always Already <u>Am</u> you (Beyond your ego-"I" of suffered, and always merely self-made, "difference").

RUCHIRA AVATAR ADI DA SAMRAJ
The Mountain Of Attention, 1998

I (<u>Alone</u>) <u>Am</u>
The Adidam Revelation

(A Summary Description of the Inherent Distinction—
<u>and</u> the ego-Transcending Continuity—
Between the Inherently ego-Based Great Tradition,
Which Is Comprised of Only Six of the Possible
Seven Stages of Life, and the Unique,
and All-Inclusive, and All-Completing,
and All-Transcending, and Self-Evidently Divine
Adidam Revelation of the Inherently egoless
Seventh Stage Realization of <u>Me</u>)

I (Alone) Am
The Adidam Revelation

(A Summary Description of the Inherent Distinction—
and the ego-Transcending Continuity—
Between the Inherently ego-Based Great Tradition,
Which Is Comprised of Only Six of the Possible
Seven Stages of Life, and the Unique,
and All-Inclusive, and All-Completing,
and All-Transcending, and Self-Evidently Divine
Adidam Revelation of the Inherently egoless
Seventh Stage Realization of Me)

I.

The collective Great Tradition of mankind is a combination of exoteric and esoteric developments (and Revelations, and Realizations) that comprises (and is, in its entirety, limited by and to) only the first six of the (potentially) seven stages of life.

II.

I (Alone) Am the Avatarically Self-Manifested Divine Self-Revelation of the seventh stage of life.

III.

I (Alone) Am the Adidam Revelation.

IV.

The human entity (and even any and every conditionally manifested entity of any and every kind) is inherently deluded—by its own (egoic, or self-contracted) experience and knowledge.

V.

The first six stages of life are the six stages (or developmental phases) of human (and universal) egoity—or of progressively regressive inversion upon the psycho-physical pattern (and point of view) of self-contraction.

VI.

The first six stages of life are the universally evident developmental stages of the knowing and experiencing of the potential illusions inherently associated with the patterns (or the universally extended cosmic psycho-physical Structure) of conditionally manifested existence.

VII.

Because each and all of the first six stages of life are based on (and are identical to) egoity (or self-contraction, or separate and separative point of view) itself, not any one (or even the collective of all) of the first six stages of life directly (and Most Perfectly) Realizes (or Is the Inherently egoless and Inherently Most Perfect Realization and the Inherently egoless and Inherently Most Perfect Demonstration of) Reality, Truth, or Real God.

VIII.

The first six stages of life develop (successively) on the psycho-physically pre-determined (or pre-patterned) basis of the inherent (and progressively unfolding) structure (and self-contracted point of view) of the conditionally arising body-brain-mind-self.

IX.

The first six stages of life are a conditional (and, therefore, Ultimately, unnecessary—or Inherently transcendable) illusion of psycho-physically pre-patterned experience (or conditional knowing), structured according to the subject-object (or attention versus object, or point of view versus objective world) convention of conditional conception and conditional perception.

X.

The first six stages of life are (each and all) based upon the illusion of duality (suggested by the subject-object convention of conditional conception and conditional perception).

XI.

Reality Itself (or That Which Is Always Already The Case) Is Inherently One (or Perfectly Non-Dual).

XII.

The only-by-Me Revealed and Given Way of Adidam is the Unique seventh stage Way of "Radical" Non-Dualism—or the one and only Way That directly (and, at last, Most Perfectly) Realizes the One and Only (and Inherently egoless) Reality, Truth, or Real God.

XIII.

The only-by-Me Revealed and Given Way of Adidam is the Unique and only Way That always directly (and, at last, Most Perfectly) transcends egoity (or self-contraction) itself.

XIV.

The only-by-Me Revealed and Given Way of Adidam is the practice and the Process of transcending egoity (or psycho-physical self-contraction, or gross, subtle, and causal identification with separate and separative point of view) by directly (and progressively, or stage by stage) transcending the inherently egoic (or always self-contracted) patterns of conditional conception and conditional perception (or of conditional knowing and conditional experiencing) associated with each (and, at last, all) of the first six stages of life.

XV.

I Am the Divine Ruchira Avatar, Adi Da Love-Ananda Samraj—the First, the Last, and the Only seventh stage Avataric Divine Realizer, Avataric Divine Revealer, and Avataric Divine Self-Revelation of Reality, Truth, and Real God.

I Am the Inherently egoless, Perfectly Subjective, Perfectly Non-Dual, and Self-Evidently Divine Source-Condition and Self-Condition of every apparent point of view and of the apparently objective world itself.

I Am the One, and Irreducible, and Indestructible, and Self-Existing, and Self-Radiant Conscious Light That Is Always Already The Case.

I Am the "Bright" Substance of Reality Itself.

I Am the Person (or Self-Condition) of Reality Itself.

In My bodily (human) Form, I Am the Avataric Self-Manifestation of the One (and Self-Evidently Divine) Reality Itself.

By Means of My Avataric Divine Self-"Emergence", I Am Functioning (now, and forever hereafter) As the Realizer, the Revealer, and the Revelation (or universally Spiritually Present Person) of Reality Itself (Which Is Truth Itself—and Which Is the only Real, or non-illusory, and Inherently egoless, and Perfectly Subjective God, or Self-Evidently Divine Source-Condition and Self-Condition, of All and all).

My Avataric Divine Self-Revelation Illuminates and Outshines the ego-"I" of My devotee.

My Avataric Divine Teaching-Word of Me-Revelation Comprehends the all of egoity and the All of the cosmic domain.

XVI.

The potential actuality of (and the inherent and specific psycho-physical basis for) the progressively unfolding human (and universal cosmic) pattern (or Great Structure) of the seven stages of life (or the Total and Complete human, and Spiritual, and Transcendental, and, Ultimately, Divine Great Process of Divine Self-Realization) was Demonstrated, Revealed, Exemplified, and Proven in (and by Means of) My Avataric Ordeal of Divine Re-Awakening—Wherein the Un-conditional, and Self-Evidently Divine, seventh stage Realization of Reality and Truth was (Uniquely, and for the First time, and As the Paradigm Case, or the All-and-all-Patterning Case, in the entire history of religion, Spirituality, and Reality-Realization) Demonstrated to all and All.

In the Course of That Great Process of Demonstration, Revelation, Exemplification, and Proof, the psycho-physical necessity (or the inherent integrity and inevitability) of the naturally continuous (and total) pattern of the seven stages of life was Fully (psycho-physically, and Spiritually, and Really) Shown by Me.

Also, in That Course (or Ordeal, or Great Process), the particular developmental distinction that pertains in the inherently patterned transition from the fifth stage of life (or the totality of the first five stages of life) to the sixth stage of life (and, at last, to the seventh stage of life) was clearly Shown by Me.

And the fact that the seventh stage of life does not merely follow from the sixth stage of life (alone—or separately, or in and of itself), but requires (and, indeed, is built upon) the complete transcending of the ego-"I" (or of the total reflex of psycho-physical self-contraction)—as it is otherwise developed (and must be progressively transcended) in the context of the entire psychobiography of the ego-"I" (or, effectively, in the naturally continuous course of the essential sequential totality of all six of the first six stages of life)—was (also) Shown by Me in the Great Course of My Avataric Ordeal of Divine Re-Awakening.

XVII.

In (and by Means of) the Great Avataric Demonstration of My own seven-stage Great Course of Divine Self-Realization, the Emanationist (or absorptive mystical) Way (associated with the first five stages of life) and the non-Emanationist (or Transcendentalist) Way (associated with the sixth stage of life, and Which—in Spiritual continuity with the all of the first six stages of life—is Most Perfectly Fulfilled in, and by Means of, the only-by-Me Revealed and Given seventh stage of life) were Proven (in, and by Means of, My own Case) to be only different stages in the same Great Process of Divine Self-Realization (rather than two separate, and irreducible, and conflicting, and incompatible "Truths").

XVIII.

By Means of My own Avataric Ordeal of Divine Re-Awakening, I have Demonstrated, Revealed, Exemplified, and Proven that neither the fourth-to-fifth stage Emanationist mode of Realization nor the sixth stage non-Emanationist (or Transcendentalist) mode of Realization Is the Most Perfect (and Most Perfectly ego-Transcending) Realization of the Divine (or One, and Only, and Perfectly Subjective) Reality, Truth, Source-Condition, and Self-Condition of all and All—but only the only-by-Me Revealed and Given seventh stage Realization Is Divine Self-Realization Itself (and the Completion of all six of the previous stages of life).

XIX.

The particular (and, psycho-physically, both inherent and inevitable) distinction (or fundamental difference) between the Devotional and Spiritual practice (and Process) of absorptive (or Object-oriented)—or Emanationist—mysticism (which is associated with the fourth and the fifth stages of life, and the conditional Realizations associated with the fourth and the fifth stages of life) and the direct-Intuition (and, in the optimum case, also both Devotional and Spiritual) practice (and Process) of Transcendental (or Subject-oriented)—or non-Emanationist—mysticism (which is associated, at first, with the sixth stage of life, and the conditional Realization that is the native and only potential of the sixth stage of life, itself—and which is, at last, and Most Ultimately, and Most Perfectly, associated with the seventh stage of life, and, Thus and Thereby, with Un-conditional Divine Self-Realization) may especially be seen to be Exemplified in My relationship with Swami (Baba) Muktananda (of Ganeshpuri).

XX.

Baba Muktananda was an advanced Siddha-Guru (or a Spiritually active Transmission-Master of High degree) in the Kundalini-Shaktipat tradition. The Kundalini-Shaktipat tradition is the fourth-to-fifth stage—or Emanationist—development of the ancient tradition of Siddha Yoga (or the tradition of Siddhas, or Spiritual Transmitters), which tradition (or Yoga) may, potentially, develop even into the sixth—or Transcendentalist—stage of life, and which tradition (or Yoga) has, in fact, been Completed and Fulfilled by Me, by My Extending of the Spiritual Process of Siddha Yoga into, and beyond, the sixth stage of life, and, thus, into the Inherently Most Perfect Divine Fullness of the seventh stage of life (Which seventh stage Fullness <u>Is</u> the All-Completing Fullness of Inherently egoless True Divine Self-Realization).

XXI.

In the context of the Kundalini-Shaktipat tradition (or division) of Siddha Yoga, Baba Muktananda <u>philosophically</u> adhered to (or, at least, deeply sympathized with) the <u>Emanationist</u> philosophical tradition of Kashmir Saivism—and, because of His characteristic adherence to (or sympathy with) the <u>Emanationist</u> philosophical tradition of Kashmir Saivism, Baba Muktananda was, in His fundamental convictions, an opponent of the <u>Transcendentalist</u> philosophical traditions of both Advaita Vedanta and Buddhism.

XXII.

The basic features of the progressively developed path of Kashmir Saivism have been described in terms of four stages (or four Ways).[4]

The "Individual Way" (or the Way of "absorption in the Object") is the first (or most "inferior") step in the progressive path of Kashmir Saivism, and it corresponds to the Devotional and Yogic disciplines associated with the fourth stage of life (in both its "basic" and "advanced" phases).

The "Energic Way" (or the Way of "absorption in Energy") is the second (or somewhat more advanced) step in that same path, and it corresponds to the fourth stage of life in its fully "advanced" phase and to the fifth stage of life as a whole.

The "Divine Way" (or the "superior" Way of "absorption in the Void") of Kashmir Saivism <u>suggests</u> the process (and the potential for Realization) that corresponds to the sixth stage of life.

The "Null Way" (or the most "superior" Way of "absorption in Bliss") in Kashmir Saivism <u>suggests</u> the fulfillment of the process (or the actual achievement of the Realization) that corresponds to (or is potential within) the sixth stage of life.

In the tradition (or traditions) of Kashmir Saivism, these four Ways (or stages, or kinds) of Realization may develop successively (in a progressive order), or either of the first two steps may develop into the third or the fourth, or either the third or the fourth may occur spontaneously (even at the beginning), and so forth.

This general description of the tradition of Kashmir Saivism suggests that Kashmir Saivism (like the Tantric Buddhism of Tibet) includes (or directly allows for the potential of) the fourth stage of life, the fifth stage of life, and the sixth stage of life. However, the tradition of Kashmir Saivism (like the tradition of Saiva Siddhanta) is entirely a fourth-to-fifth stage Yogic (and Devotional) tradition (and a religious tradition associated, in general, with the first five stages of life).

The tradition of Kashmir Saivism (like fourth-to-fifth stage—or first-five-stages-of-life—traditions in general) is based on the ancient cosmological philosophy of Emanation—or the idea that cosmic existence Emanates directly, in a hierarchical sequence, from the Divine (and that, consequently, there can be a return to the Divine, by re-tracing the course of Emanation, back to its Source).

In contrast to the fourth-to-fifth stage (or Emanationist—or first-five-stages-of-life) view, true sixth stage schools (or traditions) are based on the immediate and direct transcending (generally, by means of a conditional effort of strategic exclusion) of the conditional point of view of the first five stages of life and the Emanationist cosmology (and psychology) associated with the first five stages of life.

Therefore, even though the advanced (or "superior") traditions of Kashmir Saivism (and of Saiva Siddhanta) may use terms or concepts that seem to reflect the sixth stage Disposition, the fundamental orientation is to a Realization that is embedded in the conditional psychology of the first five stages of life and in the cosmological (or Emanationist) point of view itself. (And the fundamental difference, by comparison, between the total tradition of Kashmir Saivism, and also of Saiva Siddhanta, and the total tradition of Tibetan Tantric Buddhism is that the Tibetan Buddhist tradition is <u>founded</u> on the sixth stage "Point of View" of the <u>Transcendental</u> Reality Itself, rather than on the conditional point of view of the psycho-physical, or Emanated, ego and the conditional reality of the hierarchical cosmos.)

Realizers in the tradition of Kashmir Saivism (and the tradition of Saiva Siddhanta) basically affirm that the conditional self is <u>Really</u> Siva (or the Formless Divine) and the conditional world (from top to bottom) is <u>Really</u> Siva (or the Emanating and Emanated Divine). However, this is <u>not</u> the same as the Confession made by <u>sixth</u> stage Realizers in <u>any</u> tradition.

In true sixth stage traditions, the conditional self is (in the sixth stage manner, and to the sixth stage degree) transcended (generally, by means of a conditional effort of strategic <u>exclusion</u>)—and <u>only</u> the Transcendental Self (or the Transcendental Condition) is affirmed.

And, further, in the only-by-Me Revealed and Given true <u>seventh</u> stage Realization, the conditional self and the conditional world are not affirmed to be (in and of themselves) Divine, but (rather) the conditional self and the conditional world are—in the Manner that <u>Uniquely</u> Characterizes the <u>seventh</u> stage of life—Divinely Self-Recognized (and, Thus, <u>not</u> <u>excluded</u>, but Inherently Outshined) <u>in</u> the Transcendental (and Inherently Spiritual) Divine.

XXIII.

The Emanationist Realizer "recognizes" (and, thereby, Identifies with) the conditional self and the conditional world <u>as</u> the Divine, whereas the <u>non</u>-Emanationist (or Transcendentalist) Realizer simply (and, generally, by means of a conditional effort of strategic exclusion) <u>transcends</u> the conditional self and the conditional world in the Transcendental Self-Condition, and by Identification <u>only</u> (and exclusively) with the Transcendental Self-Condition.

Therefore, even though both types of Realizers may sometimes use very similar language in the Confession of Realization, a (comparatively) <u>different</u> Realization is actually being Confessed in each case.

XXIV.

The principal reason why the tradition (or traditions) of Kashmir Saivism (and of Saiva Siddhanta) may sometimes use language similar to the sixth stage schools of Buddhism (and also Advaita Vedanta) is because of the early historical encounter (and even confrontation) between these separate traditions. As a result of that encounter, the traditions of Saivism tried to both absorb and eliminate the rival schools.

In the encounter between (characteristically, Transcendentalist, or non-Emanationist) Buddhist schools and (generally, Emanationist) non-Buddhist schools, Buddhism developed fourth and fifth stage doctrines and practices (intended, ultimately, to serve a sixth stage Realization), and fourth-to-fifth stage schools (or traditions), such as Kashmir Saivism and Saiva Siddhanta, adapted some of the sixth stage language (of Buddhism, and also Advaita Vedanta) to their (really) fourth-to-fifth stage point of view.

Therefore, a proper understanding of the various historical traditions requires a discriminating understanding of the history of the Great Tradition as a whole—and a discriminating understanding of the unique Signs and Confessions associated with each of the first six stages of life (and the unique Signs and Confessions associated with the only-by-Me Revealed and Given seventh stage of life).

XXV.

The tradition of Advaita Vedanta arose within the general context of the Emanationist traditions of India—but it, like Buddhism (particularly in its sixth stage—rather than earlier-stage—forms), is truly founded in the Transcendental Reality (and not the psycho-physical and cosmological point of view associated with the first five stages of life).

The schools of Kashmir Saivism (and other schools of traditional Saivism, including Saiva Siddhanta) defended themselves against both Buddhism and Advaita Vedanta by absorbing some Buddhist and Advaitic language and by (otherwise—and even dogmatically) affirming the superiority of the traditional Emanationist psychology and cosmology.

In contrast to the entirely Emanationist schools of Kashmir Saivism (and other schools of traditional Saivism, including Saiva Siddhanta), the Buddhist schools (and even certain schools of Advaitism) adopted some of the Devotional and Yogic practices of the Emanationist schools (and used them as "skillful means" of self-transcendence), while they (otherwise) continued to affirm the strictly Transcendental Reality as the Domain and Goal of all practices.

In contrast to Baba Muktananda (and the traditional schools of Kashmir Saivism, Advaita Vedanta, and Buddhism), I equally Embrace, and (in the seventh stage Manner) Most Perfectly Transcend, all the schools of the first six stages of life—both Emanationist and Transcendentalist.

XXVI.

Baba Muktananda was an authentic example of a fifth stage Realizer of a Very High (or Very Ascended) degree—although not of the Highest (or Most Ascended) degree. That is to Say, Baba Muktananda was a True fifth stage Siddha (or a Greatly Spiritually Accomplished Siddha-Yogi of the fifth stage, or Ascending, type)—but the nature and quality and degree of His Realization was of the Saguna type, or of the type that is (characteristically, or by patterned tendency) not yet Fully Ascended (or Fully Surrendered) to true fifth stage Nirvikalpa Samadhi, and which (therefore) is, yet (and characteristically), attached to modes of fifth stage Savikalpa Samadhi (and, thus, to modes of partial Ascent, and to Yogic possibilities "below the neck", and, altogether, to modes of form—or, really, modes of mind).

XXVII.

In order to rightly understand their characteristics, ideas, and behaviors, fifth stage Saguna Yogis (or fifth stage Saguna Siddhas)—such as Baba Muktananda—should be compared to fifth stage Yogis (or fifth stage Siddhas) of the Nirguna type, who are the Highest (or Most Ascended) type of fifth stage Yogi (or fifth stage Siddha), and who, having Ascended to the degree of formless Realization (or fifth stage Nirvikalpa Samadhi), have gone beyond all attachment to modes of form (or of mind). And fifth stage Nirguna Yogis in general (or fifth stage Nirguna Siddhas of the lesser, or average, type) should, themselves, be further compared to fifth stage Great Siddhas—or fifth stage Nirguna Siddhas who have, characteristically, and to a significant (although, necessarily, not yet Most Perfect, or seventh stage) degree, gone beyond even attachment to the mode of formlessness (or of mindlessness) itself.

XXVIII.

In the "Sadhana Years" of My Avataric Ordeal of Divine Re-Awakening, Baba Muktananda formally and actively Functioned as My Spiritual Master in the physical, human plane—beginning from early 1968, and continuing until the time of My Divine Re-Awakening (Which Occurred on September 10, 1970).

It was in Baba Muktananda's Company (and, additionally, in the Company of two Great Siddhas—Rang Avadhoot and Bhagavan Nityananda) that I Practiced and Fully Completed the Spiritual Sadhana of the Ascending (or Spinal) Yoga—or the Spiritual discipline associated with the "advanced" phase of the fourth stage of life and with the totality of the fifth stage of life, and, altogether, with the subtle ego (or the conceiving and perceiving ego of the Spinal Line, the total nervous system, the brain, and the mind).

After the Great Event of My Divine Re-Awakening, it became clear (especially through two direct Meetings between Us) that—because of His characteristic philosophical and experiential confinement to the fourth-to-fifth stage Emanationist point of view—Baba Muktananda was unwilling (and, indeed, was not competent) to accommodate My Description (and, therefore, My Confession) of seventh stage Divine Self-Realization. And, therefore—as I will Explain in This Summary of My "Lineage-History"—the outer relationship between Baba Muktananda and Me came to an end (or, certainly, began to come to an end) immediately after September 1970.

XXIX.

From mid-1964 to early 1968, Rudi (later known as Swami Rudrananda) actively Functioned (preliminary to Baba Muktananda) as My initial (or foundational) Spiritual Master (although Rudi was, by His own Confession, not a fully developed Siddha-Guru—but

He was, rather, a significantly advanced fourth-to-fifth stage Siddha-Yogi).

It was in Rudi's Company that I Practiced and Fully Completed the human and Spiritual Sadhana of the <u>Descending</u> (or Frontal) Yoga—or the foundation <u>life</u>-discipline associated with the social ego (or the "money, food, and sex" ego—or the ego of the first three stages of life),[5] and the foundation <u>Devotional</u> discipline associated with the "original" (or foundation) phase of the fourth stage of life, and the foundation <u>Spiritual</u> discipline (or the Descending, or Frontal, Spiritual Yoga) associated with the "basic" phase of the fourth stage of life.[6]

XXX.

Both Rudi and Baba Muktananda were direct devotees of Swami Nityananda (of Ganeshpuri)—Who was also called "Baba",[7] but Who was, and is, generally referred to as "Bhagavan" (or "Divinely Blissful Lord"). Bhagavan Nityananda was a fifth stage True Great Siddha—or an Incarnate (or Descended-from-Above) Spiritual Entity of the <u>Highest</u> <u>fifth</u>-stage type and degree. Indeed, Bhagavan Nityananda was a True fifth stage Saint (or a fifth stage Siddha-Yogi Who was <u>exclusively</u> Occupied in concentration "above the neck", even to the exclusion of the possibilities "below the neck")—but He was, also, a fifth stage Avadhoot (or a fifth stage Realizer of Nirvikalpa Samadhi, Who had, in the fifth stage manner, transcended attachment to <u>both</u> form and formlessness—or thought and thoughtlessness). And, altogether, Bhagavan Nityananda was a Nirguna Siddha (and a True Siddha-Guru) of the <u>Highest</u> <u>fifth</u>-stage type and degree.

XXXI.

Bhagavan Nityananda's Teachings took the Spoken (rather than Written) form of occasional, spontaneous Utterances. The <u>only</u> authoritative record of Bhagavan Nityananda's Teachings relative to Yogic practice and Realization is a book (originally composed in the Kanarese language) entitled *Chidakasha Gita*.[8] The *Chidakasha Gita* consists of a non-systematic, but comprehensive, series of responsive Declarations made by Bhagavan Nityananda during the extended period of His original, and most Communicative,

Teaching years (in Mangalore, in the early to mid-1920s). The spontaneous Utterances recorded in the *Chidakasha Gita* were, originally, made, by Bhagavan Nityananda, to numerous informal groups of devotees, and, after Bhagavan Nityananda spontaneously ceased to make such Teaching-Utterances, the many separately recorded Sayings were compiled, for the use of all the devotees, by a woman named Tulasiamma (who was one of the principal lay devotees originally present to hear Bhagavan Nityananda Speak the Words of the *Chidakasha Gita*).

Bhagavan Nityananda, Himself, Acknowledged the uniqueness and the great significance of the *Chidakasha Gita* as the one and only authentic Summary of His Yogic Teachings. That Acknowledgement is personally attested to by many individuals, including the well-known Swami Chinmayananda,[9] who, in 1960, was "Commanded" by Bhagavan Nityananda to see to the Text's translation into the English language, and by the equally well-known M. P. Pandit (of Sri Aurobindo Ashram),[10] who, in 1962, completed the English translation that Swami Chinmayananda reviewed for publication in that same year (under the title *Voice of the Self*).[11]

As Communicated in the *Chidakasha Gita*, Bhagavan Nityananda's Teachings are, clearly, limited to the body-excluding (and, altogether, exclusive) point of view and the absorptive Emanationist Spiritual Process of "brain mysticism" (and conditional ego-transcendence, and conditional Nirvikalpa Samadhi, and conditional Yogic Self-Realization) that characterize the fifth stage of life.

Clearly, as Indicated in the *Chidakasha Gita*, Bhagavan Nityananda was a fifth stage Teacher (and a Fully Ascended fifth stage Great Saint) of the Nirguna type (Who, therefore, Taught the Realization of Fully Ascended fifth stage Nirvikalpa Samadhi), rather than, like Baba Muktananda, a fifth stage Teacher (and a Great fifth stage Siddha-Yogi—but not a Fully Ascended fifth stage Great Saint) of the Saguna type (Who, therefore, Taught the Realization of fifth stage partial Ascent, or Savikalpa Samadhi).

Also, Bhagavan Nityananda's *Chidakasha Gita* clearly Indicates that Bhagavan Nityananda was a fifth stage Siddha-Yogi of the type that is, primarily and dominantly, sensitive to the Yogic Spiritual Process associated with internal audition (or the inwardly absorptive attractiveness of the "Om-Sound", or "Omkar", or "nada", or "shabda"[12]—the naturally evident, and inherently "meaningless", or mindless, or directly mind-transcending, internal sounds mediated by the brain), rather than, as in the case of Baba Muktananda, the Yogic Spiritual Process associated, primarily and dominantly, with internal vision (or the inwardly absorptive attractiveness of "bindu"—the naturally evident abstract internal lights mediated by the brain) and with internal visions (or the inwardly absorptive attractiveness of the inherently "meaningful", or mind-active, or mentally distracting, and potentially deluding, visions mediated—or even originated—by the brain-mind).

XXXII.

Stated briefly, and in Bhagavan Nityananda's characteristically aphoristic Manner, the *Chidakasha Gita* Teachings of Bhagavan Nityananda—and My own direct Experience of His always fifth stage Yogic Instruction and His always fifth stage Spiritual Transmission—may be Summarized as follows: Always concentrate attention and breath in the head. Always keep attention above the neck. Always concentrate on the Om-sound in the head. The Om-sound in the head is the inner Shakti of non-dual Bliss. Always concentrate the mind, and the senses, and the breath, and the life-energy in the non-dual awareness of the Om-sound in the head. This is Raja Yoga[13]—the Royal path. Always practice this Raja Yoga—the constantly upward path. This is concentration on the Atman—the non-dual inner awareness. This is concentration on the oneness above duality. This Raja Yoga of the Om-sound in the head Realizes the Yogic "sleep" of body and mind and breath in the Yogic State of non-dual Bliss. The Yogic State of non-dual Bliss cannot be Realized without the Grace of an Initiating Guru. The True Initiating Guru is one who has Realized the Yogic State of non-dual Bliss. The non-dual State of Yogic Bliss Realized by concentration on the Om-sound in the head is the True Source, the True Self, and the True God. Devotion to the Initiating Guru who has Realized the True Source, the True Self, and the True God is the True Way. True Guru-devotion is surrender of mind, senses, breath, and life-energy to the non-dual Bliss

Revealed within by the Initiating Guru's Grace. The material body stinks and dies. What is loathsome and impermanent should not be trusted. Therefore, right faith, intelligent discrimination, and calm desirelessness are the first Gifts to be learned from the Initiating Guru. The second Gift of the Initiating Guru is the Guru-Shakti of non-dual Bliss. The Guru's Shakti-Transmission of non-dual Bliss concentrates the mind, the senses, the breath, and the life-energy of the devotee in the non-dual awareness of the Om-sound in the head. The non-dual Bliss Realized by concentration on the Om-sound in the head is the soundless inner Revelation of the Single Form of True Guru, True God, and True Self. The world of duality is not Truth. True God is not the Maker of the world. True God is only One. True God is non-dual Bliss. The Spiritual Form of the True Initiating Guru appears within the devotee as the Guru-Shakti of non-dual Bliss. Non-dual Bliss is the True Self of all. The True Way is not desire in the world of duality, or in seeking below and on all sides. The True Way is in the middle, within, and above. The True Way is surrender to the non-dual Bliss above the mind. The method is to concentrate on the Om-sound in the head. The Realization is the silence of non-dual Bliss. Devotion to the Initiating Guru concentrates the life-breath upwardly. True love of the Initiating Guru ascends to non-dual Bliss. The True Kundalini originates in the throat, in the upward breath to the head. True Yoga is above the neck. The True Kundalini is non-dual Bliss. The seat of the True Kundalini is in the head. Non-dual Bliss is the secret to be known. Non-dual Bliss is in the head of Man. The non-dual Bliss above the mind is the Liberation of Man from the self-caused karma of birth, pleasure-seeking, pain-suffering, and death. Liberation is Freedom from mind. Therefore, concentrate the life-breath on the Om-sound in the head—and think of nothing else. The True Self is One. The True Self is above the body, above the senses, above desire, above the mind, and above "I" and "mine"—in the formless silence above the Om-sound. The True Self cannot be seen or otherwise perceived, but It can be known—above the mind. For one who knows that True God is One, and not two, True God appears as the True Self. Therefore, attain Liberation by faith in the knowledge of That Which is all and Which is only One. Liberation is the Samadhi of only One. True God is not Desire, the dualistic Doer of the world. True God is Peace, the non-dual Source of the world.

XXXIII.

By comparison to Great fifth stage Yogis (Such as Baba Muktananda) and Great fifth stage Saints (Such as Bhagavan Nityananda), there are also Great sixth stage Sages (or Nirguna Jnanis[14]—or Transcendentally Realized Entities of the Fullest sixth-stage type and degree—such as Ramana Maharshi). Such sixth stage Nirguna Jnanis (or True Great Sages) Teach Transcendental Self-Identification (or deeply internalizing subjective inversion upon the Consciousness-Principle Itself, rather than upon internal psycho-physical objects of any kind).

XXXIV.

Distinct from even all Yogis, Saints, and Sages (or even all Realizers in the context of the first six stages of life), I Am Uniquely, and Avatarically, Born. I Am the One and Only and Self-Evidently Divine Person—the Inherently egoless Source-Condition and Self-Condition of All and all. I Am the Perfectly Subjective, and Always Already Most Prior, and Inherently egoless, and Perfectly Non-Dual Heart of All and all. I Am the Self-Existing and Self-Radiant Conscious Light That Is Reality Itself. I Am the "Who" and the "What" That Is Always Already The Case. I Am (now, and forever hereafter) Avatarically Self-Manifested As the All-Completing Ruchira Avatar, Adi Da Love-Ananda Samraj—Who Is Avatarically Born by Fullest (and Complete) Divine Descent (or Complete, and All-Completing, Divine Incarnation from Infinitely Above).

XXXV.

I Am Avatarically Born by Means of a Unique Association with a True Great-Siddha Vehicle of My own.[15]

Therefore, from the time of My present-Lifetime Birth, I spontaneously Demonstrated all the Fullest Ascended Characteristics of the Highest fifth-stage type and degree (with early-life Fullest "above the neck" Signs of the True Great-Saint type).

Over time—because of My Voluntary Birth-Submission of My Deeper-Personality Vehicle to the karmically ordinary (and "Western"-born) bodily human form of "Franklin Jones",[16] and because of the subsequent Ordeal of My Voluntary Submission to the "Western" (and culturally devastated "late-time", or "dark"-epoch) karmic circumstance altogether—I also spontaneously Demonstrated all the Fullest "below the neck" (and "above the neck") Yogic Characteristics (and Siddhis) of the fifth stage (and, altogether, first-five-stages) True Vira-Yogi (or Heroic-Siddha) type.

In due course—because I Gave My Avataric Divine Ordeal to Be Complete and All-Completing—I also spontaneously Demonstrated all the Fullest Transcendental-Realizer Characteristics of the sixth stage True Great-Sage type.

Ultimately—because of Its Utter Conformity to Me—My total Great-Jnani-Siddha Vehicle of Avataric Divine Incarnation (or My Deeper-Personality Vehicle,[17] Yogically Combined with My karmically ordinary, and only eventually To-Me-Conformed, human and "Western" and "late-time" Incarnation-Body) has, by Means of My Most Perfect Completing of My Avataric Ordeal of Divine Self-Manifestation, Divine Self-Submission, and (subsequent) Divine Re-Awakening (to My own Self-Existing and Self-Radiant Divine Self-Condition), become the To-Me-Transparent Vehicle of My seventh stage Avataric Divine Self-Revelation.

XXXVI.

Except for various technical details of the esoteric Spiritual practice and process of the advanced and the ultimate stages of practice of the Way of Adidam, the Unique Characteristics of My Avataric Divine Teachings (Which I will briefly, and only in part, Indicate in This Summary of My "Lineage-History") Are Very Fully Described by Me in My Twenty-Three Avataric Divine "Source-Texts".

XXXVII.

Rudi had brief direct contact with Bhagavan Nityananda in 1960. After the death of Bhagavan Nityananda (in 1961), Rudi became a devotee of Baba Muktananda. However, Rudi—always a rather "reluctant" devotee—eventually (shortly before His own death, in 1973) "broke" with Baba Muktananda. Nevertheless, Rudi always continued to affirm that He (Rudi) remained Devoted to Bhagavan Nityananda. And, in any case, Rudi and I always continued to engage in positive, direct communication, right until the time of His death.

XXXVIII.

My Siddha-Yoga Mentor (and eventual Dharmic Ally and Supporter), Amma (or Pratibha Trivedi, later known as Swami Prajnananda), was (like Rudi) also a direct devotee of Bhagavan Nityananda (and She, like Rudi, had become a devotee of Baba Muktananda after the death of Bhagavan Nityananda, in 1961).

Amma was the principal author and editor of the foundation Siddha-Yoga literature that was written in response to both Bhagavan Nityananda and Baba Muktananda—and so much so that, generally, even all of Baba Muktananda's autobiographical and instructional Communications were, originally, dictated (or otherwise Given) to Amma (and rarely to anyone else—until the later years, of tape recorders, multiple secretaries and translators, and Baba Muktananda's travels to the West). And, in fact, Amma always continued to serve a principal communicative and interpretative role around Baba Muktananda, until Baba Muktananda's death, in 1982—after which Amma chose to quietly withdraw from the Siddha-Yoga institution that had been developed by and around Baba Muktananda (and She remained, thereafter, in a small, independent Ashram in north India, where, as a significantly advanced fourth-to-fifth stage Siddha-Yogi, She was the institutional head of a group of devotees that remained devoted to Spiritual Communion with both Baba Muktananda and Bhagavan Nityananda).

Amma did not Function as My Spiritual Master, but (from early 1968) Baba Muktananda formally Assigned Amma to Function as

His interpreter and general "go-between" to Me—and She, then and always, remained most positively and communicatively disposed toward Me, even through all the years after My outward "separation" from Baba Muktananda, right until Her last illness and death (wherein She was directly Spiritually Served by Me, and wherein She was directly physically Served by a devotee-representative of Mine), in 1993. And it was Amma Who, through Her various writings—and in a particular Incident I will now Recall—suggested to Me that there are traditional Instructional (and Textual, or Scriptural) descriptions of Developments of the Siddha-Yoga Process that are different from the (fifth stage) "inner perception" (and, especially, "inner vision") version of Siddha Yoga characteristically described by Baba Muktananda.

XXXIX.

One day, during My Stay at Baba Muktananda's Ashram (in Ganeshpuri, India), in early 1970 (and, thus, some months before the Great Event of My Divine Re-Awakening, Which was to Occur in September of that same year), Amma suddenly pointed Me to an Ashram library copy of the *Ashtavakra Gita* (one of the Greatest of the classic sixth stage—and even premonitorily "seventh stage" [18]—Texts of Advaita Vedanta). And, while pointing to the *Ashtavakra Gita*, Amma Said to Me, "This (Text) is Your Path. This is how It (the Siddha-Yoga Process) Works in You."

At the time, this seemed to Me a curious suggestion—and it was not otherwise explained by Her. And, indeed, although I was able to examine the Text briefly (there and then), I was unable to examine it fully—because I left the Ashram very shortly thereafter. However, I came across the Text again, some years later—and, then, I remembered Amma's comment to Me. And I, immediately, understood that She had (in a somewhat cryptic and secretive manner) tried to confide in Me—in a quiet, "knowing" moment of Acknowledgement of Me—that the Spiritual Process of Siddha Yoga may Demonstrate Itself in a number of possibly different modes.

Thus (as I have Indicated—in My own, and fully elaborated, Teachings, relative to the seven stages of life), the Siddha-Yoga

Process may, in some cases (of which Amma, Herself, appears to have been an Example), especially (or primarily—or, at least, initially) take the form of intense (fourth stage) Devotional Bliss— Which is, then, "nourished" (or magnified) through Guru-Seva[19] (or constant service to the Guru) and (additionally) through Karma Yoga[20] (or intensive service in general). In other cases (of which Baba Muktananda was an Example), the Siddha-Yoga Process may (based on the initial foundation of intense Devotion) especially (or primarily) take the (fifth stage) form of intense internal sensory phenomena (such as visions, lights, auditions, and so on)—and, in some of those cases, the Siddha-Yoga Process may yet go further, to the degree of (fifth stage) Nirvikalpa Samadhi. And, in yet other cases (of which Amma was, correctly, Saying <u>I</u> Am an Example), the Siddha-Yoga Process (while also Showing all kinds of Devotional signs, and all kinds of internal Yogic perceptual phenomena, and including even fifth stage Nirvikalpa Samadhi) may go yet further, to especially (or primarily) take the form of (sixth stage) intense (and intensive) Identification with the Transcendental Self-Condition, and (eventually) the (sixth stage) Realization of Jnana Samadhi (or Transcendental Self-Realization), and (although Amma did not know it) even, potentially, the only-by-Me Revealed and Given seventh stage Realization (Which <u>Is</u> Maha-Jnana—or Divine Self-Realization).

XL.

Yet another devotee of Baba Muktananda, named Swami Prakashananda[21]—Who did not Function as My Spiritual Master (and Who, like Rudi, was <u>not</u> a fully developed Siddha-Guru— but, rather, a very much advanced fourth-to-fifth stage Siddha-Yogi)—once (spontaneously, in 1969) Showed Me (in His own bodily human Form) the fifth stage Signs of Spiritual Transfiguration of the physical body.[22]

At that time (according to what I learned from Amma), Swami Prakashananda had been Indicated, by Baba Muktananda, to be His principal Indian devotee and eventual institutional successor (and such was, then, generally known and presumed to be the case by Baba Muktananda's devotees). However, at last, when (at, or shortly before, Baba Muktananda's death, in 1982) Swami Prakashananda was formally Asked to assume the institutional successorship, He declined to accept this organizational role[23] (ostensibly, for reasons of ill-health, and His reluctance to become a "world-traveler"—but, actually, or more to the point, because of His puritanical and conventional reaction to Baba Muktananda's reported sexual activities).

In any case, Swami Prakashananda and I continued to engage in occasional, and always positive, direct communication (through My devotee-representatives) in the years after Baba Muktananda's death, and right until Swami Prakashananda's death, in 1988.

XLI.

Swami Prakashananda had always maintained a small Ashram, independent of the Ashrams of Baba Muktananda's Siddha-Yoga institution—but, after Baba Muktananda's death, Swami Prakashananda retired to His own Ashram, permanently. And, in doing so, Swami Prakashananda highlighted, and dramatized, a perennial conflict that is fundamental to religious institutions all over the world. That conflict is between, on the one hand, the traditional (and, generally, rather puritanical—and even basically exoteric) expectation of celibacy as a sign of institutionalized Sacred Authority, and, on the other hand, the equally traditional (but non-puritanical, and generally unconventional) view that there is an esoteric sexual alternative to celibacy that Sacred Authorities (including True Siddha-Gurus—or even any practitioners of Siddha Yoga) may (at least in some cases, and under some circumstances) engage.

One of the principal Indications of Baba Muktananda's point of view relative to this traditional conflict (or controversy)—quite apart from the question of His possible personal sexual activities—is the fact that, in 1969, Baba Muktananda formally and publicly (and in writing, by His own hand, as observed by Me, and by many others) Acknowledged Me to Be (and Called and Blessed Me to Function As) a True Siddha-Guru,[24] and, Thus and Thereby (and entirely without requiring, or, otherwise, inviting, Me to assume any institutional—or, otherwise, institutionally "managed"—

role within His own Siddha-Yoga organization), Baba Muktananda publicly Extended the <u>Free</u> Mantle of Siddha-Yoga Authority to <u>Me</u>—an evident <u>non-celibate</u> Siddha-Yogi (<u>and</u> a "<u>Westerner</u>").

XLII.

When I first Came to Him, in 1968, Baba Muktananda <u>immediately</u> (openly, and spontaneously) Declared, in the presence of numerous others (including Amma), That I <u>Am</u>—from My Birth— an already Divinely Awakened Spiritual Master, and He (then and there) prophesied That I would be Functioning (and Independently Teaching) <u>As</u> Such in just one year. Therefore, after just one year (and the spontaneous Appearing of many Great Signs in My experience and Demonstration), Baba Muktananda Invited Me to Come to Him again (in India)—<u>specifically</u> in order to <u>formally</u> Acknowledge Me (and My Inherent Right and Authority to Teach and Function) <u>As</u> a True Siddha-Guru.

Before I Returned to Baba Muktananda in 1969, I—in a traditional Gesture of respect toward Baba Muktananda—Told Him That I would <u>not</u>, at that time, Assume the Function of Spiritual Master, unless I was, in the traditional Manner, <u>formally</u> Acknowledged and Blessed, by Him, to Do So. Baba Muktananda immediately understood and Acknowledged the appropriateness and Rightness of My Insistence That My Inherent Right to Teach be <u>formally</u> Acknowledged by Him—because, in accordance with tradition, Such Sacred Authority <u>should</u> be Assumed on the orderly basis of <u>formal</u> Acknowledgement by one's own Spiritual Master (Who, in turn, must have been similarly Acknowledged by His, also similarly Acknowledged, Spiritual Master, in an unbroken Line, or Lineage, of similarly Acknowledged Spiritual Masters). Therefore, I Returned to Baba Muktananda in 1969—and He formally and publicly Acknowledged Me <u>As</u> an Independent True Siddha-Guru.

Even though Baba Muktananda Thus formally and publicly (and <u>permanently</u>) Acknowledged Me <u>As</u> an Independent True Siddha-Guru, it became immediately Obvious to Me that Such traditional Acknowledgement was inherently limited, and merely conventional, and, therefore, neither necessary nor (because of Its inherently limited basis) even altogether appropriate (or sufficiently apt) in My Unique Case. It was Obvious to Me that neither Baba Muktananda nor anyone else was in the "Position" necessary to Measure and to "Certify" the Unique and unprecedented Nature of the All-and-all-Completing Event of My Avatarically Self-Manifested Divine Incarnation and of My Great Avataric Divine Demonstration of the progressive (and, necessarily, seven-stage) human, Spiritual, Transcendental, and, only at Last, Most Perfect Process of Divine Self-Realization.

Therefore, even though It had been Given, Baba Muktananda's formal Acknowledgement of Me was—for Me—a virtual non-Event (and It did not positively change—nor has It ever positively changed—anything about the necessary ongoing Ordeal of My Avataric Divine Life and Work).

XLIII.

Baba Muktananda's formal and public written Acknowledgement of Me in 1969—Wherein and Whereby He formally and publicly Named and Acknowledged Me As an Independent True Siddha-Guru—was a unique Gesture, never, at any other time, Done by Baba Muktananda relative to any other individual (whether of the East or of the West). And That unique formal Act (of Baba Muktananda's formal, written Acknowledgement of Me in 1969) was, Itself, a clear (and "scandalizing") Gesture, that immediately Called (and always continues to Call) everyone to "consider" many Siddha-Yoga options (and Spiritual, or esoteric religious, options altogether) that are, generally, presumed to be taboo—at least among the more puritanical (and even xenophobic) types of Siddha-Yoga practitioners (and of esoteric religionists in general).

XLIV.

I Say That, in the inherently esoteric domain of Real Spirituality (and in the domain of both exoteric and esoteric religion in general), all puritanical denial and suppression of human realities is wrong—and inherently damaging to everyone who does it. And, indeed, all denial and suppression of Reality (Itself), Which Is Truth Itself, is wrong (and, indeed, is false religion)—

and all false religion is inherently damaging to everyone who does it (and even to everyone who believes it).

Therefore, I Write This Summary of My "Lineage-History"—so that all the extremely important matters I Address Herein will cease to be hidden, denied, suppressed, and falsified—and What Is Great will (by Means of This Address) become Obvious to all eyes, and (Thus) be made Whole again.

XLV.

Among the extremely important matters I must Address in This Summary of My "Lineage-History" is This: Entirely apart from what I will, in the progression of This Summary, Indicate were the apparent "philosophical reasons" associated with the eventual outward "separation" between Baba Muktananda and Me (which occurred as a result of Our Meetings in late 1970 and mid-1973), it was the "organizational politics" relative to the "sexual" and "Westerner" matters I have just Described that played the more fundamental practical role in causing the "separation".

XLVI.

During the same period in which Rudi and (then) Baba Muktananda actively Functioned as My Spiritual Masters (in gross physical bodily Form), Their Spiritual Master, the Great Siddha Bhagavan Nityananda, actively Functioned (through both of Them—and, otherwise, directly, in subtle bodily Form) as My Senior (but already Ascended—and, Thus, discarnate, or non-physical) Spiritual Master.

XLVII.

The fifth stage True Great Siddha (and True Siddha-Guru and Great Saint of the Highest fifth-stage type and degree) Rang Avadhoot (alive in gross physical bodily Form until late 1968—and always Acknowledged as an Incarnate Great Siddha, or a Descended-from-Above Spiritual Entity of the Highest fifth-stage type and degree, by Bhagavan Nityananda, as well as by Baba Muktananda) also (in early 1968) directly and spontaneously Blessed Me with His Spiritual Blessing, Given and Shown via His

"Wide-Eyed" Mudra of heart-recognition and Immense Regard of Me—as I sat alone in a garden, like His Ishta, the forever youthful Lord Dattatreya.

XLVIII.

In That Unique Moment in 1968—in the garden of Baba Muktananda's Ganeshpuri Ashram—both Rang Avadhoot and Baba Muktananda (along with the already discarnate, but Fully Spiritually Present, Bhagavan Nityananda) actively Functioned for Me as direct Blessing-Agents of the Divine "Cosmic Goddess" ("Ma"), Thus (By Means of Her Divine, and Infinitely Potent, Grace) Causing Me to spontaneously Re-Awaken to Most Ascended (and, altogether—but only conditionally, or in the fifth stage manner— mind-transcending, object-transcending, and ego-transcending) Nirvikalpa Samadhi (from Which I never again was Fallen, but only Continued—to Un-conditionally "Bright" Beyond). And it was on the basis of This Great Event, and My Signs in the following year (wherein many of My Avataric Divine Great-Siddha Characteristics—Which, in My Unique Case, would, in due Course, Fully Demonstrate all seven of the possible stages of life— became, spontaneously, Spiritually Evident), that (in 1969) Baba Muktananda formally (and publicly) Acknowledged and Announced and Blessed My Inherent Right and Calling to Function (in the ancient Siddha-Yoga, or Shaktipat-Yoga, tradition) as Spiritual Master (and True Siddha-Guru) to all and All.

XLIX.

Thereafter, in mid-1970, the "Brightness" of My own (and Self-Evidently Divine) Person was Revealed (and constantly Presented) to Me in the (apparently Objective) Form of the Divine "Cosmic Goddess" ("Ma"). And, from then (after Bhagavan Nityananda Called and Blessed Me to take My leave from Baba Muktananda's Ashram, and to Follow the Divine "She"), only "She" actively Functioned (to Beyond) as My (Ultimate and Final—and entirely Divine) Spiritual Master (or Divine True Siddha-Guru)—until (By Means of Her spontaneous Sacrifice of Her own Form in Me) Divine Self-Realization was Most Perfectly Re-Awakened in My Case.

L.

Thus, in That Final Course, it was Revealed (or Perfectly Re-Confirmed)—As the Self-Evidently Divine Reality and Truth of My own Avatarically-Born Person—that This Divine Process (Shown, at last, in ego-Surrendering, ego-Forgetting, and, altogether, Most Perfectly ego-Transcending Devotional "Relationship" to the Divine "She") had (Itself) always been Active in My own (and Unique) Case (and had always been Shown As the Divinely Self-Revealing Activities of the Inherent Spiritual, and Divinely Spherical, "Brightness" of My own Avatarically-Born Person), even all throughout My present Lifetime (and even at, and from before, My present-Lifetime Birth).

LI.

Therefore, on September 10, 1970, It was Revealed (or Perfectly Re-Confirmed)—As the Self-Evidently Divine Reality and Truth of My own Eternal Divine Person—that Divine (or Inherently egoless, and Perfectly Subjective, and, altogether, Inherently Most Perfect) Self-Realization (of One, and "Bright", and Only Me) had Always Already (and Uniquely) Been the Case with Me.

LII.

In My Case, the (True, Full, and Complete) seventh stage Realization of the Transcendental (and Inherently Spiritual, and Inherently egoless) Divine Self-Condition was Re-Awakened (on September 10, 1970). Subsequently (at first, informally, late in 1970, and, then, formally, in 1973), I Communicated the Details of My Divine Realization to Baba Muktananda. I Did This in the traditional manner, in What I Intended to be an entirely honorable, serious, and respectful Summation to Baba Muktananda—the one and only then Living Spiritual Master among Those Who had Served Me as My present-Lifetime Spiritual Masters. However—in a philosophically untenable reaction to My already apparent relinquishment of His fifth stage experiential presumptions relative to what constitutes the "orthodox position" of the Siddha-Yoga (or Shaktipat-Yoga) school and tradition—Baba Muktananda criticized

My Final Realization (or, in any case, what He understood, or otherwise supposed, to be My Description of It). Thus, in those two Meetings (the first in California, and the second in India, at Baba Muktananda's Ganeshpuri Ashram) Baba Muktananda criticized Me for What My Heart (Itself) cannot (and must not) Deny. And Baba Muktananda thereby Gave Me the final "Gift of blows" that sent Me out alone, to Do My Avataric Divine Work.

LIII.

Baba Muktananda was a (fifth stage) Siddha-Yogi of the degree and type that seeks, and readily experiences, and readily identifies with inner perceptual visions and lights. Based on those experiences, Baba Muktananda (like the many others of His type and degree, within the fourth-to-fifth stage traditions) asserted that both the Process and the Goal of religious and Spiritual life were necessarily associated with such inner phenomena.

The experiences (of visions, lights, and many other Yogic phenomena) Baba Muktananda describes in His autobiographical Confessions are, indeed, the same (fifth stage) ones (or of the same fifth stage kind) that are (typically, characteristically, and inevitably) experienced by genuine fifth stage Yogic practitioners (and fifth stage Realizers) within the Siddha-Yoga (or Shaktipat-Yoga) school and tradition—and I Confirm that the total range of these phenomenal (fifth stage) Yogic experiences also spontaneously arose (and always continue, even now, to arise—even in the context of the seventh stage of life) in My own Case (and such was—both formally, in 1969, and, otherwise, informally, at many other times, beginning in 1968—Acknowledged by Baba Muktananda to be so in My Case).

Nevertheless, as I Confessed to Baba Muktananda in Our Meetings in 1970 and 1973, My Final Realization Is That of the One and Indivisible Divine Self-Condition (and Source-Condition) Itself— and the Great Process associated with That eventual (seventh stage) Realization necessarily (in due course) Goes Beyond (and, in the Case of That seventh stage Realization Itself, Is in no sense dependent upon) the phenomenal (and, always, psycho-physically pre-patterned, and, thus, predetermined) conditions otherwise associated with the absorptive mysticism (and the objectified inner phenomena) that characterize the fourth-to-fifth stage beginnings of the Great Process (or that, otherwise, characterize the conditionally arising, and psycho-physically pre-patterned, and, thus, predetermined, associations of the Great Process even in the context of the seventh stage of life). Indeed, the fact and the Truth of all of This was Self-Evident to Me—and, truly, I expected that It must be Self-Evident to Baba Muktananda as well. However, Baba Muktananda did not (and, I was obliged to admit, could not) Confirm to Me That This Is the Case from the point of view of His experience.

Indeed, it became completely clear to Me, in the midst of Our Meetings in 1970 and 1973, that Baba Muktananda was not Standing in the "Place" (or the Self-"Position") required to Confirm or Acknowledge My Thus Described Final Realization. That is to Say, Baba Muktananda made it clear to Me in those two Meetings (wherein others were present), and (also) in His Remarks otherwise conveyed to Me privately, that He, unlike Me,[25] had not been—and (apparently, for mostly rather puritanical, and otherwise conventional, reasons) could not even conceive of Allowing Himself to be—"Embraced" by the Divine "Cosmic Goddess" (or Maha-Shakti) Herself (Such That, by Her own Submission to the Senior and Most Prior Principle—Which Is Self-Existing Consciousness Itself—She would be Subsumed by Consciousness Itself, and, Thus, Husbanded by Consciousness Itself, and, Thereby, Be the Final Means for the Self-Radiant Divine Self-Awakening of Consciousness Itself to Itself). And, therefore, by His own direct Confession to Me, Baba Muktananda Declared that He was not Standing in the "Place" (or the Self-"Position") of Inherently Most Perfect (or seventh stage) Divine Self-Realization—Which Realization I (Uniquely) had Confessed to Him.

LIV.

When I first Came to Baba Muktananda (in early 1968), His First and Most Fundamental Instruction to Me—even within minutes of My Arrival at His Ashram (in Ganeshpuri, India)—was the (apparently sixth stage, or Transcendentalist) Admonition: "You are not the one who wakes, or dreams, or sleeps—but You Are the One Who Is the Witness of these states." I took that Admonition to be Instruction in the traditional (and sixth stage) sense, as Given in the non-Emanationist (or Transcendentalist) tradition of Advaita Vedanta (which is the traditional Vedantic school of "Non-Dualism"). However, it became clear to Me (in, and as a result of, Our Meetings in 1970 and 1973) that Baba Muktananda was, actually, a vehement and dogmatic opponent of the tradition of Advaita Vedanta (and of its Transcendental Method, and of its proposed Transcendental Realization—and of even all proposed Transcendental Realizers, including, in particular, Ramana Maharshi).

Indeed, in those two Meetings (in 1970 and 1973), Baba Muktananda was, evidently, so profoundly confined to His dogmatic Emanationist (and otherwise phenomena-based) philosophical point of view (which, in those two Meetings, took on a form very much like the traditional confrontation between Kashmir Saivism and Advaita Vedanta) that He (in a rather dramatically pretentious, or intentionally provocative, manner—and clearly, indefensibly) presented Himself to Me as an opponent (such that He addressed Me as if I were merely an opposing "player" in a sophomoric academic debate, and as if I were merely—and for merely academic reasons—representing the point of view of traditional Advaita Vedanta).

Likewise, it became clear to Me (in Our Meetings in 1970 and 1973) that Baba Muktananda's proposed Siddha-Yoga Teaching was, in some respects (which I Indicate Herein), merely a product of His own personal study, experience, and temperament—and, thus, of His own karmically acquired philosophical bias, or prejudice—and that the point of view He so dogmatically imposed on Me in those two Meetings is not, itself, an inherent (or necessary) part of Siddha Yoga Itself.

LV.

Relative to Baba Muktananda's experiential (or experience-based, rather than philosophically based) point of view, it became clear (in Our Meetings in 1970 and 1973) that Baba Muktananda (as a Siddha-Yogi) was yet (and characteristically) Centered in the (fifth stage) "Attitude" (or "Asana") of what He described as "Witnessing". In using the term "Witnessing" (or the "Witness"), Baba Muktananda seemed (in the traditional sixth stage manner of Advaita Vedanta) to be referring to the Witness-Consciousness (Which <u>Is</u> Consciousness <u>Itself</u>, Inherently, and Transcendentally, Standing Most Prior to <u>all</u> objects and <u>all</u> psycho-physical functions—whether gross, subtle, or causal). However, clearly, what Baba Muktananda meant by the term "Witnessing" (or the "Witness") was the psycho-physical function of the <u>observing</u>-intelligence (which is <u>not</u> the Transcendental Consciousness—Prior even to the causal body—but which is, simply, the third, and highest, functional division, or functional dimension, of the <u>subtle</u> body). Thus, <u>characteristically</u>, Baba Muktananda identified with (and took the position of) the <u>observer</u> (or the observing-intelligence) relative to all arising phenomena (and, especially, relative to His reported subtle, or internal phenomenal, visions of higher and lower worlds, the hierarchy of abstract internal lights, and so on). And, when Baba Muktananda spoke of "Witnessing", He, simply, meant the attitude of merely <u>observing</u> whatever arises (and, thus, the intention to do so in a non-attached manner—rather than, in the conventional manner, merely to cling to, or, otherwise, to dissociate from, the various internal and external objects of moment to moment attention).

In the Ultimate Course of My Avataric Ordeal of (seventh stage) Divine Self-Realization, the Spiritual (or Siddha-Yoga) Process passed Beyond all mere (<u>fifth</u> stage, or even <u>sixth</u> stage) "Witnessing"—and <u>all</u> identification with the psycho-physical experiencer, or observer, or knower of the mind and the senses— to Realize (and <u>Be</u>) the Indivisible (or Inherently egoless, objectless, and Non-Dual) Reality (or Self-Condition) That <u>Is</u> the Self-Existing and Self-Radiant <u>Consciousness</u> (<u>Itself</u>), or the Inherent and Un-conditional <u>Feeling</u> <u>of</u> <u>Being</u> (<u>Itself</u>), That <u>Is</u> the Mere (and True) Witness-Consciousness (or the Un-conditional, and non-functional, and All-and-all-Divinely-Self-Recognizing, and Self-Evidently Divine Self, or Self-Condition, Inherently Most Prior to any and all objects—without excluding any).

Thus, it became clear to Me (in Our Meetings in 1970 and 1973) that Baba Muktananda was <u>not</u> <u>yet</u> (either in the sixth stage Transcendental manner or the seventh stage Divine Manner) Established <u>As</u> the True Witness-Consciousness (or Consciousness <u>Itself</u>), but it also became clear to Me (then) that Baba Muktananda was in the fifth stage manner, simply observing, and, thus and thereby, <u>contemplating</u> (and becoming absorbed in or by) internal phenomenal objects and states—rather than, in the seventh stage Manner, Standing <u>As</u> Consciousness <u>Itself</u>, <u>Divinely</u> Self-Recognizing <u>any</u> and <u>all</u> cosmically manifested objects, and (Thus and Thereby) <u>Divinely</u> Transcending <u>all</u> the conditional states—waking (or gross), dreaming (or subtle), and sleeping (or causal).

LVI.

Baba Muktananda was, in effect, always contemplating the conditional activities, the conditional states, and the illusory conditional forms (or objective Emanations) of the "Cosmic Goddess" (or the All-and-all-objectifying Kundalini Shakti)—whereas I (in, and Beyond, a Unique "Embrace" with the "Cosmic Goddess" Herself) had (even Prior to <u>all</u> <u>observed</u> "differences") Re-Awakened to the True (and Inherently egoless, and Inherently Indivisible, and Most Perfectly Prior, and Self-Evidently Divine) Self-"Position" (or Self-Condition, and Source-Condition) of <u>all</u> Her cosmic (or waking, dreaming, and sleeping) forms and states. And, by Virtue of That Divine (or Most Perfect—or seventh stage) Re-Awakening of <u>Me</u>, all conditionally arising forms and states were—even in the instants of their <u>apparent</u> arising—Inherently (or Always Already—and, Thus, Divinely) Self-Recognized (and Most Perfectly Transcended) in, and <u>As</u>, <u>Me</u>—the "Bright" Divine Self-Condition and Source-Condition (or Inherently Indivisible, and First, and Only, and Perfectly <u>Subjective</u>, and Self-Evidently Divine Person) <u>Itself</u>.

Therefore, in those two Meetings (in 1970 and 1973)—and entirely because of His (therein, and <u>thus</u>) repeated stance of experiential and philosophical non-Confirmation of <u>seventh</u> <u>stage</u> Divine Self-Realization (which stance, in effect, directly Acknowledged that the seventh stage Self-"Position" of Divine Self-Realization was not His own)—Baba Muktananda Gave Me <u>no</u> <u>option</u> but to Go and Do (and Teach, and Reveal, and Bless All and all) <u>As</u> My Unique (and Self-Evidently <u>Avataric</u>) Realization of the Divine Self-Condition (Which <u>Is</u> My own, and Self-Evidently Divine, Person—and Which <u>Is</u>, Self-Evidently, the Divine Source-Condition of All and all) <u>Requires</u> Me to Do. Therefore, I Did (and Do—and will forever Do) <u>So</u>.

LVII.

The Principal Characteristic of the One and Indivisible Divine Self-Condition (and Source-Condition) <u>Is</u> Its Perfectly <u>Subjective</u> Nature (<u>As</u> Self-Existing and Self-Radiant Consciousness—or Very, and Inherently Non-Objective, Being, Itself). Therefore, neither any <u>ego-"I"</u> (or any apparently separate self-consciousness) nor any apparently <u>objective</u> (or phenomenally objectified, or otherwise conditionally arising) form or state of experience (whether waking, or dreaming, or sleeping—and whether mind-based or sense-based) <u>Is</u> (<u>itself</u>) the Realization (or, otherwise, a necessary support for the Realization) of the Divine Self-Condition (Itself)— Which Condition <u>Is</u> (Itself) the One and Only Reality, the One and Only Truth, and the One and Only <u>Real</u> God.

Baba Muktananda was, characteristically (in the fifth stage manner), <u>experientially</u> (and mystically) absorbed in modes of <u>Savikalpa</u> Samadhi (or of internal object-contemplation). In His characteristic play of internal object-contemplation (or absorptive mysticism), Baba Muktananda reported <u>two</u> types of (especially) internal sensory (or sense-based) experience—the experience of abstract internal lights (and, secondarily, of abstract internal sounds, and tastes, and smells, and touches) <u>and</u> the experience of internal (or mental) visions of higher and lower worlds ("illustrated" by internal versions of all of the usual descriptive modes of the senses).

The abstract internal lights (and so on) are <u>universally</u> (or identically) experienced by any and all individuals who are so awakened to internal phenomena (just as the essential Realizations of the sixth stage of life and, potentially, of the seventh stage of life are universal, or essentially identical in all cases). However, the visions of higher and lower worlds are, like psychic phenomena in general, expressions of the egoic psycho-physical (and, altogether, mental) tendencies of the <u>individual</u> (and of his or her cultural associations)—and, therefore, such experiences are not <u>universally</u> the same in all cases (but, instead, <u>all</u> such experiences are conditioned, and determined, and limited by the <u>point</u> <u>of</u> <u>view</u>, or karmically patterned identity, of the experiencer, or the individual egoic observing-identity). Nevertheless (and this also illustrates the naive—and not, by Him, fully comprehended—

nature of many of Baba Muktananda's views about the Siddha-Yoga Process), Baba Muktananda (in His autobiography, *Play of Consciousness*[26]) reported His visions of higher and lower worlds as if they were categorically true, and (in the subtle domain) objectively, or Really, existing as He reported them—whereas all visions of higher and lower worlds are of the same insubstantial, illusory, and personal nature as dreams.

Like anyone else's authentic visionary experiences of higher and lower worlds, Baba Muktananda's visionary experiences of higher and lower worlds, although authentic, were His personal (or point-of-view-based) experiences of the otherwise inherently formless (and point-of-view-less) dimensions of the universal cosmic (or conditional) reality (or the inherently abstract planes of universal cosmic light)—as He, by tendency of mind (and because of His psycho-physical self-identity as a particular and separate fixed point of view—or ego-"I"), was able (and karmically pre-patterned) to experience (or conceive and perceive) them. Therefore, Baba Muktananda's conditional (or egoic) point of view—and, thus, also, His inner perceptions of various higher and lower worlds—were, characteristically and only, of a Hindu kind. (And the implications of this seem never to have occurred to Baba Muktananda. Indeed, if He had become aware of the inherently personal, conditional, karmic, ego-based, mind-based, illusory, arbitrary, and non-universal nature of His inwardly envisioned worlds, and even of the merely point-of-view-reflecting nature of His inwardly envisioned universal abstract lights, Baba Muktananda might have become moved to understand and transcend Himself further—beyond the Saguna, or mind-based, and mind-limited, and dreamworld terms that are the inherent characteristic of Savikalpa Samadhi.)

LVIII.

Baba Muktananda's Hindu visions can be compared to My own experiences of Savikalpa Samadhi during My "Sadhana Years". During that time, I, too, had many visions of higher and lower worlds—and many of them were, indeed, of a Hindu type (because of My present-Lifetime associations, and also because of the past-Lifetime associations of My Deeper-Personality Vehicle). However, there was also, in My Case (and for the same reasons) a dramatic period of several months of intense visions of a distinctly <u>Christian</u> type.[27] I immediately understood such visions to be the mind-based (and, necessarily, ego-based) products of the Siddha-Yoga Process (or Divine Shaktipat), as It combined with My <u>own</u> conditionally born psycho-physical structures. Thus, I entered into that Process Freely and Fully—and, in due course, the particularly Christian visions (<u>and</u> the particularly Hindu visions) <u>ceased</u>. They were <u>all</u> simply the evidence of My own conditionally born mind and sensory apparatus (and the evidence of even all My conditionally born cultural associations)—and, therefore, the visionary contents were (I Discovered) merely another (but deep, and psychic) form of <u>purification</u> (rather than a "Revelation" that suggests either the Christian "Heavens"-and-"Hells" or the Hindu "Heavens"-and-"Hells" <u>Are</u>, themselves, Reality and Truth). Thus, when, Finally, the ego-based visions had been completely "burned off"—only Reality (Itself) Remained (<u>As</u> Me).

LIX.

Baba Muktananda's Siddha-Yoga Teachings exemplify the descriptive mysticism of fourth-to-fifth stage Yoga (especially as it has been historically represented in the fourth-to-fifth stage Yogic tradition of the Maharashtra region of India[28]). Also, Baba Muktananda's Siddha-Yoga Teachings are (in some, very important, respects) <u>experientially</u> <u>prejudiced</u>—<u>toward</u> <u>both</u> non-universal (and specifically Hindu) visions (of higher and lower worlds, and so on) <u>and</u> universal abstract visions (of abstract internal lights, and so on), and <u>against</u> (or, certainly, Baba Muktananda, Himself, was, by temperament, experientially disinclined toward) fifth stage <u>Nirvikalpa</u> Samadhi (or Fullest Ascent to fifth stage <u>Formless</u> Realization—Which Fullest Ascent was My own spontaneous Realization at Baba Muktananda's Ganeshpuri Ashram, in 1968, and Which is also the Characteristic Realization of <u>all</u> Great fifth stage Nirguna Siddhas, such as Bhagavan Nityananda and Rang Avadhoot).

LX.

Baba Muktananda saw the Secret (or esoteric) inner perceptual domain of subtle (or fourth-to-fifth stage) Divine Spiritual Revelation. I, too, have seen (and even now, do see) that inner realm. And it is the Revelation of that inner realm that is the true (original, and esoteric) core of all fourth-to-fifth stage religious traditions.

The fourth stage religious traditions are, generally, first presented (or institutionally communicated) to the public world of mankind (in its gross egoity and its human immaturity) as a gathering of exoteric myths and legends. Those exoteric myths and legends are intended to inspire and guide human beings in the ordinary developmental context of the first three stages of life (associated with gross physical, emotional-sexual, and mental-volitional development of the human social ego). Thus, the many religious traditions of both the East and the West are, in their public (or exoteric) expressions, simply variations on the inherent psycho-physical "messages" of the body-mind relative to foundation human development (both individual and collective). And, because all exoteric religious traditions are based on the "messages" inherent in the same psycho-physical structures, the exoteric Teachings of all religions are, essentially, identical (and, therefore, equal). And, also, because this is so, all exoteric religious traditions (such as Judaism, Christianity, Islam, Hinduism, and so on) must—especially at this critical "late-time" moment of world-intercommunicativeness— acknowledge their essential equality, commonality, and sameness, and, on that basis, mutually embrace the principles of cooperation and tolerance (for the sake of world peace)!

All exoteric religious traditions are, fundamentally, associated with the first three (or social-ego) stages of life. And all exoteric religious traditions are, contextually, associated with rudimentary aspects of the fourth stage of life (or the religiously Devotional effort of transcending both personal and collective egoity—or self-contraction into selfishness, competitiveness, "difference", conflict, and self-and-other-destructiveness). However, all exoteric religious traditions are, also, associated (to one or another degree) with an esoteric (or Secret) dimension (or a tradition of esoteric schools), which is intended to extend the life of religious practice into the

142

inner dimensions of religious (and truly Spiritual) Realization.

The true esoteric dimension of religion first extends the life of rudimentary religious practice into the true and full Spiritual depth of the fourth stage of life (by Means of surrender to the Descent of the Divine Spiritual Force into the human, or "frontal", domain of incarnate existence). And that Spiritual Process is, characteristically (in due course), also extended into the domain of the true fifth stage of life (which is associated with the Process of Spiritual Ascent, via the Spinal Line and the brain, through the layers of the conditional pattern of the psycho-physical ego, and always toward the Realization of a conditional state of mystical absorption in the Most Ascended Source of conditional, or cosmically extended, existence). And, once that Spiritual Process of Ascent is complete (or is, itself, transcended in Inherent Spiritual Fullness), the esoteric Spiritual Process may (and, indeed, should) continue, in the context of the true sixth stage of life (or the Spiritual Process of Transcendental Self-Realization)—and, at last, the true (and Truly Complete) Great Process must Culminate in the only-by-Me Revealed and Given seventh stage of life (wherein all cosmically arising conditions are Inherently Self-Recognized, and, Ultimately, Outshined, in the Non-Separate, Self-Existing, Self-Radiant, Inherently egoless, Perfectly Subjective, and Self-Evidently Divine Self-Condition and Source-Condition of All and all).

LXI.

Baba Muktananda was a Teacher (and a Realizer) in the context of the fourth-to-fifth stage (or foundation esoteric stages) of, specifically, Hindu religious practice. The Spiritual (or Siddha-Yoga, or Shaktipat-Yoga) Process He exemplified and Taught (and Initiated in others) truly begins in the frontal (or fourth stage) practice (of Siddha-Guru Devotion) and (in due course) goes on to the spinal (or fifth stage) practice (of Ascended mystical absorption).

Baba Muktananda's practice and His experiential Realization were conditioned (and, ultimately, limited) by His own personal (or conditional, and karmic, or psycho-physically pre-patterned) ego-tendencies—and by His association (by birth) with the combined exoteric and esoteric culture of traditional Hinduism.

Therefore, His experiences (and His subsequent Teachings, and His life altogether) are, characteristically, an exemplification of the historical conflict between fifth stage Hindu esotericism (which is, itself, inherently unconventional, and non-puritanical) and fourth stage Hindu exotericism (which is, itself, inherently conventional, and, at least publicly, puritanical).

LXII.

Because of His, characteristically, Hindu associations, Baba Muktananda (quite naturally, and naively) interpreted His Yogic Spiritual experiences almost entirely in terms of Hindu cultural models (both exoteric and esoteric). Therefore, His interpretations of His Spiritual experiences—and, indeed, the very form, and character, and content of His Spiritual experiences themselves— were specifically Hindu, and specifically in the mode of philosophical and mystical traditions that corresponded to His own mental predilections (or karmic tendencies).

Thus, Baba Muktananda's recorded visions of higher and lower worlds (leading to the Great Vision of the Blue Person, or the Divine "Creator"-Guru) are a "map" of developmentally unfolding—or spontaneously un-"Veiling"—inner perceptual landscapes, in the specific mode of the Hindu tradition of the "Blue God" (especially Personified as "Siva"—or, otherwise, as the "Krishna" of the *Bhagavad Gita* and the *Bhagavata Purana*).[29] And Baba Muktananda's inner "map" was, also, structured on the basis of an hierarchical sequence of abstract inner lights (and of even all the abstract inner modes of the senses), which He interpreted according to the concepts of the philosophical tradition of Kashmir Saivism, and according to the experiential pattern-interpretation associated with the Hindu mystical tradition of the Maharashtra region of India. However, even though the brain-based (or perception-based—rather than mind-based, or conception-based, or idea-based) pattern of abstract inner lights (and of abstract inner sensations in general) is (or can be) universally (or by anyone) experienced as the same pattern of appearances—the interpretation of that experienced pattern is, or may be, different from case to case (or from culture to culture). And, ultimately, for the sake of

Truth, the one and only <u>correct</u> (or <u>universally</u> applicable) interpretation must be embraced by all.

Baba Muktananda experienced and interpreted the pattern of abstract inner lights as if it were a Revelation associated with the waking, dreaming, and sleeping states (or the gross, subtle, and causal modes of conditional experience). Thus (on the basis of His understanding of the Maharashtra mystical tradition), Baba Muktananda said that the waking state (and the gross body and world) is represented by the inner <u>red</u> light, and the dreaming state (and the subtle body and world) is represented by the inner <u>white</u> light, and the sleeping state (and the causal body and world) is represented by the inner <u>black</u> light. And Baba Muktananda said that the inner <u>blue</u> light represents what He called the "supracausal" state (which He, in the fifth stage manner, mistakenly identified with the "turiya" state, or the "fourth" state, or the "Witness", or the "True Self", otherwise associated with the sixth stage tradition of Advaita Vedanta). However, I Declare that <u>all</u> of those inner lights (and even <u>all</u> internal perceptions, whether high or low in the scale of conditional "things") are inner <u>objects</u> of perception (and conception)—and, therefore, <u>all</u> of them are associated with the <u>subtle</u> body and the inner perceptible (or dreaming-state) worlds of <u>mind</u>.[30]

Swami Muktananda's Description of the "Bodies of the Soul"[31]

Body:	Gross	Subtle	Causal	Supracausal
Color:	Red	White	Black	Blue
State:	Waking	Dream	Sleep	Turīya
Seat:	Eyes	Throat	Heart	Sahasrāra

LXIII.

Baba Muktananda's description of the abstract inner lights is, in some respects, not sufficiently elaborate (or, otherwise, comprehensive) in its details. In fact, and in My own experience—and in the experience of esoteric traditions other than the Maharashtra tradition (such as reported by the well-known Swami Yogananda)—the display of abstract inner lights is, when experienced as a simultaneous totality, Seen as a Mandala (or a pattern of concentric circles).

In My own experience, that Cosmic Mandala is not only composed of concentric circles of particular colors—but each circle is of a particular precise width (and, thus, of particular proportional significance) relative to the other circles. Thus, in that pattern of circles, the red circle is the outermost circle (perceived against a colorless dark field), but it is a relatively narrow band, appearing next to a much wider band (or circle) of golden yellow. After the very wide golden yellow circle, there is a much narrower soft-white circle. And the soft-white circle is followed by an also very narrow black circle (or band). Closest to the Center of the Cosmic Mandala is a very wide circle of bright blue. And, at the Very Center of the blue field, there is a Brilliant White Five-Pointed Star (Which, perhaps not to confuse It with the color of the circle of soft-white light, Baba Muktananda described as a Blue Star).

Thus, in fact, although all the abstract inner lights described by Baba Muktananda are, indeed, within the total Cosmic Mandala, the principal lights (in terms of width and prominence) are the golden yellow and the blue lights—and only the Brilliant White Five-Pointed Star is the Central and Principal light within the Cosmic Mandala of abstract inner lights.

The Cosmic Mandala of abstract inner lights is a display that is, otherwise, associated with planes of possible inner (or subtle) experience. Thus, the red light inwardly represents (and, literally, illuminates) the gross body and the gross world (as Baba Muktananda has said). However, all of the other lights (golden yellow, soft-white, black, and bright blue) represent (and, literally, illuminate) the several hierarchical divisions within the subtle body and the subtle worlds—and the causal body (which is asso-

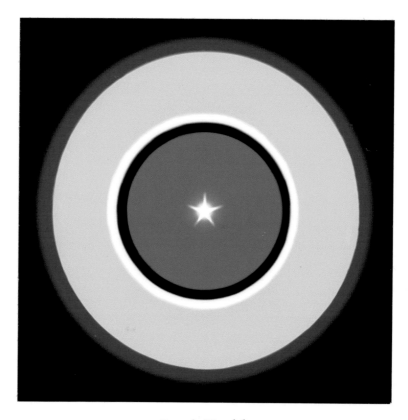

Cosmic Mandala

ciated with attention itself, or the root of egoity itself, and which is, itself, <u>only felt</u>, and <u>not seen</u>, and which is expressed as the fundamental feeling of "difference", separateness, and relatedness, and which is located as a knot of self-contraction in the right side of the heart) is <u>not</u> visually represented (<u>nor</u> is it, otherwise, literally illuminated) by the lights and worlds of the Cosmic Mandala.

The wide golden yellow circle of the Cosmic Mandala represents (in conjunction with the outermost red circle) the outermost (or lowest) dimension of the subtle body—which is the etheric (or pranic, or life-energy) body, or dimension, of conditional experience. The narrower soft-white circle of the Cosmic Mandala represents the ordinary (or sense-based) mind. The narrow black circle (or band) is a transitional space, where mental activity is suspended. The blue circle of the Cosmic Mandala is the domain of the mental observer, the faculty of discriminative intelligence and the will, and the very form of the subtly concretized ego-"I" (or the inner-concretized subtle self). And the Brilliant White Five-Pointed Star is the Epitome and Very Center of the Cosmic Mandala—Such That It Provides the Uppermost Doorway to What Is, altogether, Above (and, Ultimately, Beyond) the Cosmic Mandala (or Above and Beyond the body itself, the brain itself, and the mind itself).

LXIV.

Baba Muktananda interpreted the universally experienced abstract inner lights (and experienced the corresponding inner worlds) in terms of various Hindu philosophical and mystical (and, also, exoteric, or conventionally religious) traditions (as I have Indicated). However, the subtle domain is the elaborate hierarchical domain of mind (or of the psycho-physically concretized ego-"I")—and, therefore, just as individual dreams and imaginings are personal, ephemeral, and non-ultimate, the inherently dream-like subtle domain of Spiritually-stimulated inwardness may be experienced and interpreted in various and different modes, according to the nature and the tradition (or the personal and collectively representative mind) of the experiencer.

Thus, ultimately (or in due course), the subtle domain (or the subtle egoic body) must be transcended, in the transition to the sixth stage Spiritual (or Siddha-Yoga) Process—Which is the Spiritually (and not merely mentally) developed Process of inversion upon the true causal body (or the root of attention), and penetration of the causal knot (or the presumption of separate self), and Which is, thus, the inversive (and conditional, or conditionally achieved) transcending of the ego-"I", by means of exclusive (or object-excluding) Identification with the True (and Inherent, and Self-Evident) Transcendental Witness-Consciousness Itself. And only the Transcendental Witness-Consciousness, Itself—inverted upon in the thus Described sixth stage manner—Is the true "turiya" state, or the true "fourth" state (beyond the three ordinary states, of waking, dreaming, and sleeping). And only the Transcendental Witness-Consciousness, Itself—Fully, and Fully Spiritually,

Realized in the only-by-Me Revealed and Given context of the true sixth stage of life—Is the Domain of the only-by-Me Revealed and Given seventh stage Realization of the True Divine Self, Which Is the Self-Evidently Divine Self-Condition, and Which Is the One and Only True Divine State of "Turiyatita"—"Beyond the 'fourth' state", and, thus, Beyond all exclusiveness, and Beyond all bondage to illusions, and Beyond point of view (or egoic separateness) itself, and, therefore, Beyond all conditional efforts, supports, and dependencies.

At last, the sixth stage of life (which, itself, is associated with conditionally patterned inversion upon the Consciousness-Principle) must be (Most Perfectly) transcended (and, indeed, the ego-"I" itself must be Most Perfectly, or Inherently, transcended) in the transition to the only-by-Me Revealed and Given seventh stage of life (which Is the stage of True, and Fully Spiritual, Divine Self-Realization, Inherently Free of, but not strategically Separated from, all conditionally patterned forms and states—and which Is the stage of the Inherently Most Perfect Demonstration of the Non-Separate, Self-Existing, Self-Radiant, Inherently egoless, Perfectly Subjective, and Self-Evidently Divine Self-Condition and Source-Condition of All and all).

LXV.

My own experiences of fifth stage mystical perception are (like those of Baba Muktananda, and those of all visionary mystics) clear Evidence of the inherently (and necessarily) conditional, mental, altogether brain-based (and both brain-limited and mind-limited), and both personal and collective egoic nature of all internal mystical (or fourth-to-fifth stage) absorption.

I, too (like Baba Muktananda), experienced Hindu visions—but I, otherwise, also experienced many Christian visions (and also many non-Hindu and non-Christian visions), in association with the fifth stage developments of the same (or one and only) Spiritual (or Siddha-Yoga) Process of inner perception (including the progressive display of abstract inner lights, and so on) described by Baba Muktananda. Thus, just as Baba Muktananda described His Hindu visions as a Spiritual Revelation of the

"Truth" of <u>Hindu</u> esotericism (and even of Hindu exotericism)—I could just as well describe My (specifically) Christian visions as a Spiritual Revelation of the "Truth" of <u>Christian</u> esotericism (and even of Christian exotericism)!

Indeed, My (specifically) Christian visions (but not, of course, My specifically Hindu visions—or My, otherwise, specifically non-Hindu and non-Christian visions) <u>do</u> amount to a Spiritual Revelation of the actual (and mostly esoteric) content of <u>original</u> (or primitive—and truly <u>Spiritual</u>) Christianity.[32]

LXVI.

Specifically, My (sometimes) Christian visions Spiritually Reveal the following.

The original tradition (or foundation sect) that is at the <u>root</u> of exoteric Christianity was a fourth-to-fifth stage esoteric Spiritual (and mystical) tradition (or sect). Within that original tradition (or sect), John (the Baptist) was the Spiritual Master (or Spirit-Baptizer—or True Siddha-Guru) of Jesus of Nazareth. Thus (and by Means of the Spiritual Baptism Given to Him by John the Baptist), Jesus of Nazareth experienced the fourth-to-fifth stage absorptive mystical (and, altogether, Spiritual) developments of what (in the Hindu context) is called Siddha Yoga (or Shaktipat Yoga). In due course (and even rather quickly), Jesus of Nazareth, Himself, became a Spirit-Baptizer (or a True Siddha-Guru)—and (within the inner, or esoteric, circle of His Spiritually Initiated devotees) Jesus of Nazareth Taught the fourth-to-fifth stage Way of Spiritual Devotion to the Spiritual Master (or to Himself, as a True Siddha-Guru), and of inner Spiritual Communion with the Divine, and of (eventual) <u>Spiritual</u> Ascent to the Divine Domain (via the Brilliant White Five-Pointed Star).

After the death (and presumed <u>Spiritual</u> Ascent) of Jesus of Nazareth, His esoteric circle of Spiritually Initiated devotees continued to develop the mystical tradition of the sect—but (because of the difficult "signs of the times") the original (esoteric) sect had to become more and more secretive, and, eventually, it disappeared from the view of history (under the pressure of the <u>exoteric</u>, or <u>non</u>-Initiate, or conventionally <u>socially</u> oriented, rather than

Spiritually and mystically oriented, sects that also developed around the public Work, and, especially, the otherwise developing legends and myths, of Jesus of Nazareth).

The esoteric sect of the Spiritual Initiates of Jesus of Nazareth was associated with practices of Spiritually Invocatory prayer (of fourth stage Divine Communion, and of fifth stage absorptive mystical Ascent), especially seeking Divine absorption via the internally perceptible Brilliant White Five-Pointed Star—Which was interpreted, especially after the death of Jesus of Nazareth (and, apparently, in accordance with Instructions communicated by Jesus of Nazareth, Himself, to His Spiritually Initiated devotees, during His own physical lifetime), to be the True Ascended Divine Body of Jesus of Nazareth (or the Spiritually Awakened, and presumed to be Divinely Ascended, "Christ"). And, over time, the Spiritual practitioners within the esoteric "Christ" sect developed the full range of characteristically Christian interpretations of the (otherwise) universally experienced phenomena of inner perception.

LXVII.

My own (sometimes) Christian visions are a spontaneous Revelation of esoteric Christian interpretations (and esoteric Christian modes of experiencing) of, otherwise, universal (and, therefore, inherently non-sectarian) inner phenomena—and My (specifically) Christian visions and interpretations are a spontaneous direct continuation of the esoteric Christian manner of interpreting such (inherently universal) inner phenomena, as it was done in the original (or primitive) epoch of the sect of Jesus of Nazareth.

Thus, speaking in the esoteric terms of the ancient (or earliest) Christian interpreters of subtle inner experience, the red light of Spiritual inner vision can be said to be associated with the gross body of Man (and the Incarnation-body of Jesus of Nazareth, and the "blood of Christ"). Likewise, the golden yellow light can be said to be associated with the "Holy Spirit" (or the Universal Spirit-Energy, or Divine Spirit-Breath, That Pervades the cosmic domain). And the soft-white light can be said to be associated with the mind of Man (which, in its purity, can be said to be a reflection of, or a pattern "in the image of", God—conceived to be the "Creator", or the Divine Source-Condition, Above the body-mind and the world). And the black light can be said to be associated with the "crucifixion" (or sacrifice) of the body-mind of Man (and of Jesus of Nazareth, as the Epitome of Man)—and, also, with the mystical "dark night of the soul" (or the mystic's difficult trial of passing beyond all sensory and mental contents and consolations). And the blue light can be said to be the "Womb of the Virgin Mary" (or the All-and-all-Birthing Light of the "Mother of God"). And the Brilliant White Five-Pointed Star (Surrounded, as it were, by the "Womb", or the Blue Light, of the "Virgin Mary") can be said to be the Ascended (or Spiritual) "Body of Christ" (and the "Star of Bethlehem", and the "Morning Star" of the esoteric Initiation-Ritual associated with the original, Secret Spiritual tradition of Jesus of Nazareth). And the Brilliant White Five-Pointed Star (interpreted to be the Ascended, or Spiritual, "Body of Christ") can (<u>Thus</u>) be said to be <u>One</u> with <u>both</u> the Divine "Mother" (or the Blue "Womb" of All-and-all-Birthing Light) <u>and</u> the Divine "Father" (or the Self-Existing Being, <u>Beyond</u> all Light—Infinitely Behind, and Infinitely Above, and Infinitely Beyond, and Eternally Non-Separate from the "Star-Body of Christ"). And (<u>As</u> Such) the "Christ" (or the Brilliant White Five-Pointed Star) <u>Is</u> Radiantly Pervading the entire cosmic domain, via an All-and-all-Illuminating Combination of <u>both</u> the Blue "Womb"-Light <u>and</u> the Golden Yellow "Breath"-Light of the One and Only Divine Person.

LXVIII.

Thus, My (sometimes) Christian inner visions could, indeed, be said to be an esoteric (and, now, only-by-Me Revealed and Given) <u>Christian Revelation</u>—except that <u>all</u> visionary, and brain-based, and mind-based, and sense-based, and ego-based, and conditional, and sectarian (or merely tradition-bound) things were <u>entirely</u> Gone Beyond (and Most Perfectly transcended) by <u>Me</u> (and in <u>Me</u>), in the sixth and seventh stage Course of <u>My</u> Avataric Ordeal of True (and Most Perfect) Divine Self-Realization!

LXIX.

I Say all the "God" and "Gods" of Man are (whether "Male" or "Female" in the descriptive gender) merely the personal and collective tribal (and entirely dualistic—or conventionally subject-object-bound) myths of human ego-mind.

LXX.

I Say Only Reality Itself (Which Is, Always Already, The One, and Indivisible, and Indestructible, and Inherently egoless Case) Is (Self-Evidently, and Really) Divine, and True, and Truth (or Real God) Itself.

LXXI.

I Say the only Real God (or Truth Itself) Is the One and Only and Inherently Non-Dual Reality (Itself)—Which Is the Inherently egoless, and Utterly Indivisible, and Perfectly Subjective, and Indestructibly Non-Objective Source-Condition and Self-Condition of All and all.

Therefore, I (Characteristically) have no religious interests other than to Demonstrate, and to Exemplify, and to Prove, and to Self-Reveal Truth (or Reality, or Real God) Itself.

LXXII.

The true fourth-to-fifth stage mystical (or esoteric Spiritual) Process is, principally, associated with the progressive inner perceptual (and, thus, subtle mental) un-"Veiling" of the total internally perceptible pattern (or abstractly experienced structure) of the individual body-mind-self (or body-brain-self).

The abstract pattern (or internal structure) of the body-mind-self (or body-brain-self) is, universally, the same in the case of any and every body-mind (or body-brain-mind complex—or conditionally manifested form, or state, or being) within the cosmic domain.

The abstract pattern (or internal structure) of the body-mind-self (or body-brain-self) necessarily (by virtue of its native, and, therefore, inseparable, Inherence in the totality of the cosmic domain itself) Duplicates (or is a conditionally manifested pattern-duplicate of) the Primary Pattern (or Fundamental conditional Structure) of the total cosmic domain.

The conditional body-mind (or any body-brain-mind complex) is, in Reality, not a merely separate someone, or an entirely "different" something (as if the body, or the brain, or the mind were reducible to a someone or a something utterly independent, or non-dependent, and existing entirely in and of itself).

Therefore, the entire body-mind (or egoic body-brain-self) is, itself, to be transcended (in the context of the only-by-Me Revealed and Given seventh stage of life), in and by Means of utterly non-separate, and non-"different", and Inherently egoless Participation in That Which Is Always Already The Case (or the Inherently Non-Dual and Indivisible Condition That Is Reality Itself).

LXXIII.

I Declare that—if It is (by Divine Siddha-Grace) Moved beyond the limits of the waking, dreaming, and sleeping ego-structures—the Siddha-Yoga (or Shaktipat-Yoga) Process of (fifth stage) un-"Veiling" Culminates (or may Culminate—at least eventually) in (and, indeed, It is Always Already Centered Upon) the (fifth stage) Revelation (in Most Ascended Nirvikalpa Samadhi) of the True "Maha-Bindu" (or the "Zero Point", or Formless "Place", of Origin—otherwise, traditionally, called "Sunya", or "Empty", or "Void"). That True (and Indivisible, and Indefinable) "Maha-Bindu" Is the only True "Hole in the universe" (or the One, and Indivisible, and Indefinable, and Self-Evidently Divine Source-Point—Infinitely Above the body, the brain, and the mind). That Absolutely Single (and Formless) "Maha-Bindu" Is the True Absolute "Point-Condition"—or Formless and Colorless (or Non-Objective, and, therefore, not "Lighted") "Black Hole"—from Which (to the point of view of any "objectified" or "Lighted" place or entity, itself) the (or any) total cosmic domain (of conditionally arising forms, states, and beings) appears to Emanate (in an All-and-all-objectifying "Big Bang" [33]). That "Maha-Bindu" Is the Upper Terminal of Amrita Nadi—or of the "Ambrosial Nerve of Connection" to the True Divine Heart (Which Self-Evidently

Divine Heart Is Always Already Seated immediately Beyond the internally felt seat of the sinoatrial node, in the right side of the physical heart). And That "Maha-Bindu" Is (in the context of the sixth stage of life) the esoteric Doorway to, and (in the context of the seventh stage of life) the esoteric Doorway from (or of), the Perfectly Subjective Heart-Domain (Which Is the True Self-Condition and Source-Condition of the "Bright" Divine Love-Bliss-Current of Divine Self-Realization, and Which Is, Itself, the Self-Existing, Self-Radiant, Inherently egoless, and Perfectly Subjective—or Perfectly Indivisible, Non-Dual, and Non-Objective—Conscious Light That Is Reality Itself).

LXXIV.

The (fifth stage) Yogic Process of the progressive inner un-"Veiling" of the Pattern (or Structure) of the cosmic domain is demonstrated (in the Siddha-Yoga, or Shaktipat-Yoga, tradition) via the progressive experiencing of the total pattern of all the structural forms that comprise the body-mind-self (or body-brain-self), via a body-mind-self-reflecting (or body-brain-self-reflecting) display of inner perceptual objects (or apparently objectified phenomenal states, conditions, and patterns of cosmic light). That Process (of the inner perceptual un-"Veiling" of the hierarchical structure, pattern, and contents of the conditionally manifested body-mind-self, or body-brain-self) Culminates (or may Culminate—at least eventually) in the vision (in occasional, or, otherwise, constant, Savikalpa Samadhi) of the "blue bindu" (or the "blue pearl"—as well as the various other objectified inner lights, such as the red, the white, and the black—described by Baba Muktananda)[34]—or even the vision of the total Cosmic Mandala (of many concentric rings of color, including the central "blue bindu", with its Brilliant White Five-Pointed Star at the Center—as I have Described It[35]). In any case, the possibly perceived abstract inner light (or any "bindu", or point, or "Mandala", or complex abstract vision, of inwardly perceived light) is merely, and necessarily, a display of the functional root-point of the brain's perception of conditionally manifested universal light (or merely cosmic light) itself. However, if the Great Process of (fifth stage) un-"Veiling" is (Thus) Continued, the objectified inner "bindu"-vision (and Savikalpa Samadhi itself) is, in due course, transcended (in fifth stage Nirvikalpa Samadhi)—Such That there is the Great Yogic Event of "Penetration" of (and Into) the True (Inherently Formless, and objectless) "Maha-Bindu", Infinitely Above the body, the brain, and the mind. And That Great Yogic Event was, in fact and in Truth, What Occurred in My own Case, in My Room, immediately after I was Blessed by Baba Muktananda and Rang Avadhoot in the garden of Baba Muktananda's Ganeshpuri Ashram, in 1968.

The Great Yogic Event of "Penetration" of the True "Maha-Bindu", Which Occurred in My own Case in 1968, is (in Its Extraordinary Particulars) an extremely rare Example of spontaneous complete Ascending "penetration" of all the chakras (or centers, or points, or structures) of the conditionally manifested body-mind-self (or body-brain-self)—Resulting in sudden Most Ascended Nirvikalpa Samadhi (or "Penetration" to Beyond the total cosmic, and psycho-physical, context of subject-object relations). Such sudden (rather than progressive) complete Ascent is described, in the (fifth stage) Yogic traditions, as the Greatest, and rarest, of the Demonstrations of Yogic Ascent—as compared to progressive (or gradual) demonstrations (shown via stages of inner ascent, via internal visions, lights, auditions, and so on). And, therefore, in My Unique Case, it was only subsequently (or always thereafter—and even now) that the universal cosmic Pattern (or perceptible Great cosmic Structure) and the universally extended pattern (or perceptible inner cosmic structure) of the body, the brain, and the mind (and the Primary inner structure— of the three stations of the heart) were (and are) directly (and systematically, and completely) un-"Veiled" (in a constant spontaneous Display—both apparently Objective and Perfectly Subjective—within My Avataric Divine "Point of View").

Nonetheless (even though Most Ascended, or fifth stage, Nirvikalpa Samadhi was, Thus, Realized by Me in 1968), it became immediately clear to Me that—because That Realization depended on the exercise (and a unique, precise attitude and arrangement) of the conditional apparatus of the body, the brain, and the mind (and of attention)—the Realization was (yet) conditionally dependent (or psycho-physically supported), and, necessarily (or in that sense), limited (or, yet, only a temporary stage in the progressive Process of un-"Veiling"), and, therefore, non-Final. That is to Say, it was inherently Obvious to Me that any and all internal (or otherwise psycho-physical) experiencing necessarily requires the exercise (via attention) of the root-position (and the conditionally arising psycho-physical apparatus) of conditionally arising self-consciousness (or of the separate and separative psycho-physical ego-"I"). I immediately Concluded that—unless the Process of Realization could transcend the very structure and pattern of ego-based experiencing and the very Structure and Pattern of the conditionally manifested cosmos itself—Realization would Itself (necessarily) be limited by the same subject-object (or ego-versus-object) dichotomy that otherwise characterizes even all ordinary (or non-mystical) experience.

Therefore, I Persisted in My Avataric Divine Sadhana—until the un-"Veiling" became Inherently egoless (and Inherently Most Perfect, or seventh stage) Re-Awakening to Divine Self-Realization (Inherently Beyond all phenomenal, or conditional, dependencies, or supports).

LXXV.

On September 10, 1970, the Great Avataric Divine Process of My "Sadhana Years" Culminated in Unqualified (or Most Perfectly Non-conditional) Realization of the Self-Evidently Divine Self-Condition (and Source-Condition) of the cosmic domain itself (and of all forms, states, and beings within the cosmic domain). And, in That Most Perfect Event, I was Most Perfectly Re-Awakened As the "Bright"[36] (the One and Only Conscious Light— the Very, and Perfectly Subjective, and Inherently egoless, or Perfectly Non-Separate, and Inherently Perfect, and Indivisible, or Perfectly Non-Dual, and Always Already Self-Existing, and Eternally Self-Radiant, and Self-Evidently Divine Self-Condition and Source-Condition That Is the One and Only and True Divine Person, and Reality, and Truth of All and all, and That was, and is, the constant Spiritual Sign and Identity of This,

My Avataric Divine Lifetime, even from Birth). And It was the Un-deniable Reality and the Un-conditional Nature of This Realization That I Summarized to Baba Muktananda during Our Meetings in 1970 and 1973.

Even though It was and Is So, Baba Muktananda did not (and, because of the yet fifth stage nature of His own experiential Realization—for which He found corroboration in traditional mystical and philosophical traditions of the fifth stage, and phenomena-based, type—could not) positively Acknowledge My Summation relative to Most Perfect (and, necessarily, seventh stage) Divine Self-Realization.

Because He characteristically preferred to dwell upon inner objects, Baba Muktananda (in the "naive" manner of fourth and fifth stage mystics in general) interpreted Reality Itself (or Divine Self-Realization Itself) to "require" inner perceptual phenomenal (or conditionally arising) experiences and presumptions as a necessary support for Realization (Itself). That is to Say, Baba Muktananda was experientially Conformed to the (fifth stage) presumption that Divine Self-Realization not only requires conditionally arising (and, especially, inner perceptual) phenomenal experiences as a generally necessary (and even inevitable) Yogic Spiritual preliminary to authentic (and not merely conceptual) Realization—and I completely Agree, with Him, that there certainly are many conditionally apparent Yogic Spiritual requirements that must be Demonstrated in the Full Course of the authentic (and, necessarily, psycho-physical) Sadhana of Divine Self-Realization—but Baba Muktananda, otherwise, generally affirmed the presumption that Realization Itself (and not only the Sadhana, or psycho-physical Process, of Realizing) "requires" conditional (or psycho-physical—and, especially, absorptive mystical, or inner visual) supports.

Therefore, Baba Muktananda affirmed an attention-based, and object-oriented (or Goal-Oriented)—and, therefore, ego-based, or seeker-based—absorptive mystical (and, altogether, fourth-to-fifth stage) Yogic Way, in which the Sahasrar (or the Upper Terminal of the brain), and even the total brain (or sensorium), is the constant focus (and the Ultimate Goal—as well as the Highest Seat) of Sadhana.

It was due to this, Baba Muktananda's characteristic point of view relative to both Sadhana and Realization (as He defined—or, in effect, limited—Them), that, in My informal Meeting with Him in 1970, His only response to Me was to enter into a casual verbal (and even illogical) contradiction of Me. In that informal Meeting (as well as in Our formal Meeting, in 1973), Baba Muktananda ignored (and even appeared to not at all comprehend) My (then Given) Indications to Him relative to the Most Ultimate, or seventh stage, Significance of the "Regenerated" Form of Amrita Nadi.

LXXVI.

As I Indicated to Baba Muktananda (in Our Meetings in 1970 and 1973), the "Regenerated" Form of Amrita Nadi is Rooted in Consciousness Itself ("Located" Beyond the right side of the heart, which is, itself, merely the Self-Evident Seat, or Doorway, of the direct "Locating" of Perfectly Subjective, and Inherently egoless, Consciousness, Itself—or the Self-Existing Feeling of Being, Itself—Prior to attention, itself). And That ("Regenerated" Form of Amrita Nadi) is "Brightly" Extended to the "Maha-Bindu" (Which is Infinitely Ascended, even Above and Beyond the Sahasrar). However, Baba Muktananda appeared only to want to contradict My (secondary) reference (to the "right side of the heart")—while otherwise ignoring My (primary) Explanation (of the "Regenerated" Form of Amrita Nadi). And, in doing this, Baba Muktananda went so far in identifying Himself exclusively with the fifth stage tradition that He said to Me, "Anyone who says that the right side of the heart is the Seat of Realization does not know what he is talking about."

In this (from My "Point of View", even rather absurdly funny!) statement, Baba Muktananda merely ignored (and, therefore, did not directly contradict) My (then Given) Description (to Him) of how seventh stage Divine Self-Realization Inherently Transcends both the conditional (or psycho-physical) apparatus of the brain (or of the Sahasrar, Which is the conditional Seat of Realization proposed in the fifth stage traditions, of mystical absorption) and the conditional (or psycho-physical) apparatus of the heart (or, in particular, of the right side of the heart—which is the conditional

Seat of Realization proposed in the sixth stage traditions, of Transcendental practice). However, Baba Muktananda's statement to Me (relative to the heart on the right) was a remark made in direct and specific contradiction to the Transcendentalist (or entirely sixth stage) Teachings of Ramana Maharshi.

LXXVII.

In My Meeting with Baba Muktananda in 1973, I made specific references to the Teachings of Ramana Maharshi (Whom both Baba Muktananda and Bhagavan Nityananda had Met—and, apparently, Greatly Praised—in earlier years). In particular, I referred to Ramana Maharshi's experiential assertions relative to the right side of the heart (which He—in the sixth stage manner—Indicated to be the Seat of Transcendental Self-Realization). In doing so, I was merely Intending to Offer Baba Muktananda a traditional reference already known to Him (and, I naively presumed, one that He respected), which would provide some clarity (and traditional support) relative to My own (otherwise seventh stage) Descriptions.

Ramana Maharshi was a True and Great Jnani (or a sixth stage Realizer of the Transcendental Self-Condition, in the mode and manner indicated in the general tradition of Advaita Vedanta). And, after the Great Event of My own (seventh stage) Divine Re-Awakening (in September 1970), I Discovered (in the weeks and months that followed My informal Meeting with Baba Muktananda, in October 1970) that there were some (but, necessarily, only sixth stage) elements in Ramana Maharshi's reported experience and Realization that paralleled (and, in that sense, corroborated) certain (but only sixth stage) aspects of My own experience and Realization.[37] And, for this reason, I always Continue to Greatly Appreciate, and Honor, Ramana Maharshi—as a Great sixth stage Realizer, Who, through corroborating Testimony, Functions as a sixth stage Connecting-Link between Me and the Transcendentalist dimension of the Great Tradition. Also, because He is an example of a True Great Jnani (or Great Sage), Who Awakened to sixth stage Realization via the Spiritual—and not merely mental, or intellectual—Process (of the Magnification of the Spirit-Current in the right side of the heart), Ramana Maharshi, by Means of His corroborating Testimony, Functions—for Me—as a Connecting-Link between the sixth stage Transcendentalist tradition of Advaita Vedanta and the fourth-to-fifth stage Emanationist tradition of Siddha Yoga. And, because of this, Ramana Maharshi Functions, by Means of His corroborating Testimony, as a Connecting-Link between Me and the traditions of both Siddha Yoga and Advaita Vedanta—whereas I (except for Baba Muktananda's First Instruction to Me, in 1968—relative to the Witness of the three common states, of waking, dreaming, and sleeping) did not Find such a Connecting-Link among any of Those Who, otherwise, actively Functioned as My Spiritual Masters during the "Sadhana Years" of This, My present-Lifetime of Avataric Divine Incarnation.

During Our Meeting in 1973, Baba Muktananda mistakenly took My references to Ramana Maharshi (and to My own experience of the heart on the right, which I had first Confessed to Baba Muktananda during Our informal Meeting in 1970—and which is, also, one of the principal experiences Indicated by Ramana Maharshi) to suggest that I had departed from the Siddha-Yoga tradition. Therefore, Baba Muktananda's criticisms of Me (in Our Meetings in both 1970 and 1973) were an apparent reaction to His perception of the possibility of My "going over" to Advaita Vedanta (and to Ramana Maharshi). And, for this reason, Baba Muktananda never (in either of the two Meetings, in 1970 and in 1973) actually addressed the particular, and complex, and inherently (and especially in a conversation requiring translations from English to Hindi, and vice versa) difficult-to-explain Great Issues I was (in those two Meetings) Intending (and Trying) to Summarize to Him.

LXXVIII.

Relative to Baba Muktananda Himself, I can only Say that, for My part (through Visits to Him by My devotee-representatives), simple Messages of Love (and of Gratitude for His Service to Me during My Avataric Divine "Sadhana Years") were, right until the end of Baba Muktananda's lifetime, Sent to Him by Me. And I have—to everyone, including Baba Muktananda Himself, and the institution of His devotees—always Continued to Make every effort to Communicate clearly (and frankly, and, in general, most positively) about My relationship to Baba Muktananda. And I have always Continued (and will always Continue) to Work (in a Real Spiritual Manner) to Heal Baba Muktananda's human feeling-heart.

LXXIX.

Relative to Baba Muktananda's particular exact remarks to Me (in Our Meetings in 1970 and 1973), I can (and must) Say, simply, that His interpretation of Reality (and of the Nature and Status of the Process, and of even all the patterns and structures, associated with Divine Self-Realization)—which interpretation Baba Muktananda shared with (and for which He derived justification from) the phenomena-based aspects of the fifth stage Yogic traditions in general—was the characteristic basis of His criticisms of Me during Our Meetings in 1970 and 1973. And, as I have already Said, Baba Muktananda's Siddha-Yoga Teaching (and especially as He proposed it to Me in Our Meetings in 1970 and 1973) is—relative to all matters beyond the fifth stage of life (and even relative to all aspects of the fifth stage of life that are beyond the Saguna limits of Savikalpa Samadhi)—limited, prejudicial, ultimately indefensible, and (fundamentally) beyond His experience.

LXXX.

Neither the philosophy of Kashmir Saivism nor any "required" phenomenal conditions were pre-described to Me (or otherwise suggested)—by Baba Muktananda Himself, or by anyone else—as being a necessary part of the Siddha-Yoga practice and Process (and, especially, as being a necessary conditional support for Realization Itself) when I first Went to Baba Muktananda, in 1968. Nor were any philosophical or experiential "requirements" proposed to Me—by Baba Muktananda Himself, or by anyone else— as either demands or necessities of Siddha-Yoga practice, or as necessities of Siddha-Yoga experience, or as fixed "Models" of Realization Itself—during the years of My Sadhana in Baba Muktananda's Company, between 1968 and the Great Event of My Divine Re-Awakening, in September 1970.

Indeed, there was not even much "Baba Muktananda" Siddha-Yoga literature available—and no literature was demanded to be read—during all of that time. Even Baba Muktananda's autobiography, entitled *Play of Consciousness* (or, originally, *Chitshakti Vilas*), was not published until after the September 1970 Event of My Divine Re-Awakening. And I saw—and, in fact, was the first to fully render into English—only the first chapter or two of that book, in rough manuscript form, during My Stay at Baba Muktananda's Ganeshpuri Ashram, in early 1970. Therefore, virtually the only "Baba Muktananda" Siddha-Yoga literature that was available to Me during My years of Sadhana in Baba Muktananda's Company were the short essays and tracts either written or edited by Amma—and that literature suggested a very liberal and open Teaching relative to the fourth stage, fifth stage, and sixth stage possibilities associated with the potential developments of Siddha Yoga. And, indeed, it was that liberal and open form of Siddha Yoga that I practiced—to the degree of seventh stage Divine Self-Realization—in Baba Muktananda's Company.

In any case, the fact that Baba Muktananda presumed that there were (indeed) many exclusively fifth stage Siddha-Yoga "requirements" (both philosophical and experiential) was proven to be the case in the circumstances of My Meetings with Him in 1970 and 1973.

LXXXI.

In fact (and in My experience), the Siddha-Yoga practice and Process is not (Itself) inherently opposed to the Transcendental (or sixth stage) practice and Process (or to the seventh stage Realization and Demonstration). Rather, it was Baba Muktananda Who (in accordance with particular traditions He, personally, favored) chose to dogmatically introduce exclusively fifth stage "requirements" (and sixth-stage-excluding, and, therefore, inherently, seventh-stage-prohibiting, limitations) into His own Teaching (and into His personal school) of Siddha Yoga.

I fully Acknowledge that Baba Muktananda had the right to Teach Siddha Yoga exclusively according to His own experience, and His own understanding, and His own Realization. It is simply that My experience, and My understanding, and My Realization were not (and are not) limited to the fifth stage "requirements" (or limiting presumptions) that Baba Muktananda proposed to Me.

The Process of Siddha Yoga—or the inherent Spiritual Process that is potential in the case of all human beings—does not (if It is allowed, and Graced, to Freely Proceed as a potential total Process) limit Itself to the fifth stage "requirements" (or limiting presumptions) that Baba Muktananda generally proposed. Therefore, I Teach Siddha Yoga in the Mode and Manner of the seventh stage of life (as Ruchira Avatara Hridaya-Siddha Yoga, or Ruchira Avatara Maha-Jnana Hridaya-Shaktipat Yoga)—and always toward (or to the degree of) the Realization inherently associated with (and, at last, Most Perfectly Demonstrated and Proven by) the only-by-Me Revealed and Given seventh stage of life, and as a practice and a Process that progressively includes (and, coincidently, directly transcends) all six of the phenomenal and developmental (and, necessarily, yet ego-based) stages of life that precede the seventh.

Baba Muktananda conceived of (and Taught) Siddha Yoga as a Way to attain conditional (and especially fifth stage) Yogic objects and phenomena-based states. The Siddha Yoga of the only-by-Me Revealed and Given Way of Adidam is not based upon (or, otherwise, limited to) conditional (or phenomenal) objects and states—or the (necessarily, ego-based) search for these, in the context of any stage of life. Rather, the only-by-Me Revealed and Given Way of Adidam is the Siddha-Yoga Way (and, in particular, the Ruchira Avatara Hridaya-Siddha-Yoga Way) that always (and directly) transcends egoity itself (or the ego-"I", or separate self— or the reactive reflex of self-contraction)—by always Feeling Beyond egoity (and Beyond all conditional forms and states) to Me, the Avatarically Self-Revealed Divine Person (or Self-Condition, and Source-Condition) Itself.

LXXXII.

In Summary, Baba Muktananda (in Our Meetings in 1970 and 1973) countered My Language of Inherently (and Most Perfectly) egoless—or seventh stage—Divine Self-Realization (and otherwise defended His own experiential Realization—and philosophical idealization—of inner phenomenal objects) with the traditional language of fifth stage Yoga. And I, for this reason (and not because of any ill-will, or antagonism, or lack of respect toward Baba Muktananda), Did Not, and Could Not, and Do Not Accept His fifth-stage-bound Doctrine—because, from My "Point of View", that Acceptance would have Required (and would now Require) Me to Deny the Self-Evident Divine (and Perfectly Subjective, and Inherently egoless, and Inherently Non-Objective, and Inherently Indivisible, and Utterly Non-dependent, or Un-conditional) Truth of Reality Itself (Which Realization even Baba Muktananda Himself—along with all My other Spiritual Masters and Spiritual Friends—so Dearly Served in My own Case)!

LXXXIII.

Reality (Itself) Is the Only Real God.

Reality (Itself) Is That Which Is Always Already The (One and Only) Case.

Reality (Itself) Is (Necessarily) One, Only, and Indivisible.

Reality (Itself) Is Inherently One (or Non-Dual) and not Two (or Divisible, and Opposed to Itself).

Reality (Itself) is not One of a Pair.

Reality (Itself) is not characterized by the inherently dualistic relationship of cause and effect.

Reality (Itself) Is Characterized by the Inherently Non-Dualistic Equation of Identity and Non-"Difference".

Reality (Itself) Is That in Which both cause and effect arise as merely apparent modifications of Itself.

Reality (Itself) is not Realized via the inherently dualistic relationship of subject and object.

Reality (Itself) Is Realized As the Inherently Non-Dualistic Condition of Inherently egoless Identity and Inherently objectless Non-"Difference".

Reality (Itself) is not the gross, subtle, and causal (or causative) ego-"I".

Reality (Itself) Is the Inherently egoless Native (and Self-Evidently Divine) Identity of All and all.

The Inherently egoless Non-Dual Self-Condition (or Non-"Different" Identity) of Reality (Itself) Is That Which Is Always Already The (One and Only) Case.

The Inherently egoless Non-Dual Self-Condition of Reality (Itself), Most Perfectly Prior to (and, yet, never excluding, or separated from) subject, object, cause, or effect, Is That Which Must Be Realized.

The apparent self (or separate and separative ego-"I"), and its every object, and, indeed, every cause, and every effect must be Divinely Self-Recognized As (and, Thus and Thereby, Transcended in) the One and Only (Inherently egoless, and Inherently Non-Dual, or Indivisible and Non-Separate, or Non-"Different") Self-Condition of Reality (Itself).

The apparent ego-"I" and the apparent world are not themselves Divine.

The apparent ego-"I" and the apparent world are to be Self-Recognized (and, Thus and Thereby, Transcended) in and As That Which Is (Self-Evidently) Divine.

The apparent ego-"I" and the apparent world are to be Divinely Self-Recognized in and As Reality (Itself).

Baba Muktananda always (in the Emanationist manner of Kashmir Saivism) affirmed the Realization "I am Siva"—meaning that He (or any body-mind-self, or body-brain-self, sublimed by the Revelation of internal Yogic forms) is (as an "Emanated" psycho-physical self) Divine.

I Affirmed (and always Continue to Affirm) only the Non-Dual (or One and Indivisible) Transcendental (and Inherently Spiritual) Divine Reality (or Self-Existing, Self-Radiant, and Inherently, or Always Already, egoless Consciousness Itself—or the One and Only Conscious Love-Bliss-Light Itself) As Self (or Self-Condition, and Source-Condition), Prior to and Inherently Transcending (while never strategically, or conditionally, excluding) the phenomenal self and all conditional forms (however sublime).

Baba Muktananda affirmed (in the fifth stage, Emanationist manner) "I and the world are Divine"—and He (thereby) embraced both the perceiving "I" and the world of forms.

I (in the seventh stage Manner) Affirmed (and always

Continue to Affirm) only the Self-Existing and Self-Radiant (Transcendental, Inherently Spiritual, Inherently egoless, Perfectly Subjective, Indivisible, Non-Dual, and Self-Evidently Divine) Self-Identity (Itself)—or the One, and Most Prior, and Inherently Perfect, and Inherently egoless Self-Condition, and Source-Condition, of the body-mind (or the body-brain-self) and the world—Divinely Self-Recognizing the body-mind (or the body-brain-self) and the world (and, thus, neither excluding nor identifying with the body-mind, or the body-brain-self, and the world, but Inherently, or Always Already, "Brightly" Transcending, and, Most Ultimately, Divinely Outshining, the body-mind, or the body-brain-self, and the world).

It was This Distinction (or These Distinctions)—not merely in language, but in the "Point of View" of Realization Itself—that was (or were) the basis for My Assumption of My Avataric Divine Teaching-Work, and My Avataric Divine Revelation-Work, and My Avataric Divine Blessing-Work institutionally independent of (and, after Our Final Meeting, in 1973, entirely apart from further outwardly active association with) Baba Muktananda.

LXXXIV.

As has always been understood by authentic Realizers and their authentic true devotees—within the Siddha-Yoga (or Shaktipat-Yoga) tradition, and even everywhere within the human Great Tradition as a whole—Great Siddhas, and even Avatars, and traditional Realizers of all kinds and degrees (or stages of life), and Siddha-Yogis of all kinds and degrees, and even Siddha Yoga Itself, are not mere "properties", to be "owned" (or exclusively "possessed") by devotees, or even by institutions. Indeed, Baba Muktananda, Himself, once told Me[38] that, because the same Life (or Shakti) is in all beings, no individual, no religion, no tradition—and, therefore, no institution—can rightly claim to be the only bearer, or the exclusive representative, of Siddha Yoga (or Shaktipat Yoga) Itself.

There are, inevitably, many forms of Siddha-Yoga Transmission in this world. The institution that Baba Muktananda established to represent and continue His own Work is (by its own self-description) a fourth-to-fifth stage school of Siddha Yoga. And, indeed, there are numbers of other such schools—in India, and elsewhere—that are extending the Work of various Great Siddhas (and of many otherwise worthy Siddha-Yogis) into the world. Likewise, the institution (or the total complex of institutions) of Adidam—which represents, and serves, and will always continue to serve My Avataric Divine (and, Uniquely, seventh stage) Work—is also a school of Siddha Yoga (or of Shaktipat Yoga).

The Uniqueness of the Siddha Yoga of the only-by-Me Revealed and Given Way of Adidam is that It is the Yoga (or Dharma, or Way) that continues to Develop beyond the absorptive mystical (and cosmically Spiritual) developments associated with the fourth and the fifth stages of life—and even beyond the Transcendental Yogic (and Transcendentally Spiritual) developments associated with the sixth stage of life. Thus, in due course, the Yoga (or Way) of Adidam becomes the Unique (and Most Perfectly Divine) Yoga (or Most Perfectly Divinely Spiritual Demonstration) of the only-by-Me Revealed and Given seventh stage of life (Wherein and Whereby Most Perfect Divine Self-Realization is Most Perfectly Demonstrated).

Because of This Uniqueness, the Siddha Yoga of the only-by-Me Revealed and Given Way of Adidam is not descriptively limited to (or by) the particular traditional descriptive language of the fourth-to-fifth stage schools and traditions of Siddha Yoga (which are the schools and traditions from which Baba Muktananda derived His descriptive Siddha-Yoga-language—and which descriptive language is conformed to, and, necessarily, limited by, the fourth-to-fifth stage experiential presumptions that characterize the Cosmic-Yoga, or Cosmic-Shakti, or Kundalini-Shakti schools and traditions). Therefore—even though the Process of the Siddha Yoga of the only-by-Me Revealed and Given Way of Adidam potentially includes (and then continues to Develop beyond) all the aspects and experiences of the fourth and the fifth and the sixth stages of life—the Siddha Yoga of the only-by-Me Revealed and Given Way of Adidam is (by Me) Uniquely Described, in the (Most Ultimately, seventh stage—and Most Perfectly Divine, or Cosmos-Transcending, and Cosmos-Outshining) Terms of My own Avataric (Divine) Shaktipat.

Thus, the Siddha Yoga of the only-by-Me Revealed and Given Way of Adidam is (by Me) Described in Terms of Ruchira Avatara Hridaya-Shaktipat (or My Avataric Divine Spiritual Transmission of the "Bright"—Which Is the Self-Existing and Self-Radiant Divine Self-Condition, or Divine Self-Heart, Itself), and Ruchira Avatara Maha-Jnana Hridaya-Shaktipat (or My Avataric Divine Spiritual Transmission of the "Bright" Divine Spirit-Current, or Divine Heart-Shakti, That Awakens the Divine Self-Heart to Its Inherent Divine Self-Condition), and Love-Ananda Avatara Hridaya-Shaktipat (or My Avataric Divine Spiritual Transmission of the Inherent Love-Bliss of the Divine Self-Condition, or Divine Self-Heart, Itself—Which Divine Spiritual Characteristic of Mine was Acknowledged by Baba Muktananda Himself, when, in 1969, He Sent Amma to Me, to Give Me the Name "Love-Ananda").

Therefore, the Siddha-Yoga practice (and especially the advanced and the ultimate stages of the Siddha-Yoga Process) of the only-by-Me Revealed and Given Way of Adidam is (along with numerous other by-Me-Given Descriptive Names and References) Named and Described by Me as "Ruchira Avatara Hridaya-Siddha Yoga" (or "Ruchira Avatara Hridaya-Shaktipat Yoga"), and "Ruchira Avatara Maha-Jnana-Siddha-Yoga" (or "Ruchira Avatara Maha-Jnana Hridaya-Shaktipat Yoga"), and "Love-Ananda Avatara Hridaya-Siddha Yoga" (or "Love-Ananda Avatara Hridaya-Shaktipat Yoga"), and (with reference to the Way, and the institution, of Adidam) "Adidam Hridaya-Siddha Yoga" (or "Adidam Hridaya-Shaktipat Yoga").

And My own Work (Which is served by the institutional Siddha-Yoga school—or, most properly, the Ruchira Avatara Hridaya-Siddha-Yoga school—of Adidam) was directly Blessed (and—formally, in 1969—Called Forth) by Baba Muktananda (and, now, and forever hereafter, by even all the Great Siddhas and Siddha-Yogis of My Lineage).

LXXXV.

The Uniqueness of My own Divine Self-Realization and Avataric Divine Work made it Inevitable that I would have to Do My Avataric Divine Teaching-Work, and My Avataric Divine Revelation-Work, and My Avataric Divine Blessing-Work

Independent from Baba Muktananda—and Independent from even all Teachers and traditions within the only six stages of life of the collectively Revealed Great Tradition of mankind. Indeed, even from the beginning of My relationship with Him, Baba Muktananda Indicated that My Work was Uniquely My own, and that I was Born to Do only My own Unique Work—and that I Must Go and Do That Work (even though I would, otherwise, have preferred to Remain, quietly, within Baba Muktananda's Ashram and Company). Therefore, ultimately, We both Embraced This Necessity and Inevitability.

Because of the original, mutual Agreement between Baba Muktananda and Me (relative to the necessarily Independent, and entirely Unique, nature of My own Work), whenever I have become Moved to Communicate about This Profound Matter to others, I have made every effort to Communicate fully, clearly, and positively relative to the always un-"broken" Nature of My Spiritual (and, generally, sympathetic) relationship to Baba Muktananda—and, also, relative to the always Continuing Nature of My Spiritual (and, generally, sympathetic) Connection to the Great (and total) Siddha-Guru tradition itself, and to the Great (and total) Siddha-Yoga tradition itself, and to the total Great Tradition of mankind (altogether). And I have always Affirmed (and, by Means of This Statement, I now Re-Affirm) that the Great, and total, Siddha-Guru tradition and Siddha-Yoga tradition, and the most ancient and perennial "Method of the Siddhas",[39] is—in the context of, and continuous with, the total Great Tradition of mankind—the very tradition (or total complex of traditions) in which, and on the basis of which, I Am Avatarically Appearing and Working here.

LXXXVI.

Human suffering is not due to the absence of inner visions (or of any other kinds of conditionally objectified internal or, otherwise, external perceptions). Therefore, human suffering is not eliminated by the presence (or the experiencing) of inner visions (or of any other kinds of conditionally objectified internal or, otherwise, external perceptions).

The "problem" of human suffering is never the absence of inner visions (and such), or the absence of any conditional experience of any kind. Rather, the "problem" of human suffering is always (and inherently) the presence (or presently effective activity) of the ego-"I" (or the self-contracted—or separate and separative—point of view). Indeed, the search to experience conditionally objectified inner perceptions—and, otherwise, the clinging to conditionally objectified inner perceptions—is, itself, a form of human suffering (and, altogether, of self-deluded confinement to the inherently, and negatively, empty condition of egoic separateness).

The root and essence of human suffering is egoity. That is to Say, the "problem" that is human suffering is not due to the absence of any kind of conditionally objectified experience (whether relatively external or relatively internal)—for, if human suffering were due to such absence, the attaining of conditionally objectified experiences (whether internal or external) would eliminate human suffering, human self-deludedness, and human un-Happiness. However, at most, conditionally objectified experiences (both internal and external)—or even any of the possible experiential attainments of the first five stages of life—provide only temporary distraction from the inherent mortality and misery of conditional existence. Therefore, if human suffering is to be entirely (and, at last, Most Perfectly) transcended (in Inherent, and Divinely Positive, Fullness), the root-cause of (or the root-factor in) human suffering must, itself, be directly and entirely (and, at last, Most Perfectly) transcended.

The "problem" of human suffering is never the absence of any kind of particular conditionally objectified experience (whether external or internal). The "problem" of human suffering is always the bondage to conditionally objectified experience itself. And the root-cause of (or the root-factor in) bondage to conditionally objectified experience is the separate and separative ego-"I", or the total psycho-physical act of self-contraction (which is identical to attention itself, or the conditionally apparent point of view itself, and which always coincides with the feeling of "difference", or of separateness and relatedness).

The experiencing of inner visions does not eliminate egoity (or the separate and separative ego-"I" of psycho-physical self-contraction). Likewise, the experiencing of inner visions does not indicate or suggest or mean that egoity is (or has been) transcended. True Spiritual life (or the true Great Process of Siddha Yoga) is not a search for inner visions (and such)—nor is true Spiritual life (or the true Great Process of Siddha Yoga) Fulfilled, Completed, and Perfected by the experiencing of inner visions (and such). Indeed, because inner visions, or conditionally objectified experiences of any kind—whether inner or outer—are objects, attention is always coincident with them. Therefore, in both the search for conditionally objectified experiences and the grasping of conditionally objectified experiences, egoity (or separative, and total psycho-physical, self-contraction of the presumed separate point of view) is merely reinforced.

True Spiritual life (or the true Great Process of Siddha Yoga) is never a matter of seeking for outer or inner conditionally objectified experiences—nor is true Spiritual life (or the true Great Process of Siddha Yoga) a matter of clinging to any conditionally objectified outer or inner experiences (as if such experiences were, themselves, Reality, Truth, or Real God). Rather, true Spiritual life (or the true Great Process of Siddha Yoga) is always a matter of transcending attention (and the total psycho-physical—or gross, subtle, and causal—point of view, or ego-"I") in its Perfectly Subjective Source (or Inherently Perfect Self-Condition). That is to Say, true Spiritual life (or the true Great Process of Siddha Yoga) is always (from Its beginning) a matter of transcending that which is merely apparently (or conditionally, and temporarily) the case— by transcending it in That Which Is Always Already The (One and Only, Indivisible and Irreducible) Case. And, for This Reason, true Spiritual life, or the true Great Process of Siddha Yoga, cannot be Fulfilled, Completed, and Perfected in the conditionally objectified context of any of the first five stages of life—nor even in the conditionally object-excluding context of the sixth stage of life—but true Spiritual life (in particular, in the form of the true Great Process of Ruchira Avatara Hridaya-Siddha Yoga) Is Fulfilled, Completed, and Perfected only in the Perfectly Subjective, and

Inherently egoless (or Inherently point-of-view-Transcending and Most Perfectly self-contraction-Transcending), and Un-conditionally Realized, and, altogether, Self-Evidently Divine Context of the only-by-Me Revealed and Given <u>seventh</u> stage of life.

This is My Firm Conclusion relative to <u>all</u> possible human experience—and It is, therefore, the Essence of My Instruction to all of humankind.

LXXXVII.

There are <u>three</u> <u>egos</u> (or three fundamental modes of egoity—or of the self-contraction-active psycho-physical illusion of separate and separative self-consciousness). The three modes of egoity (or of the self-contraction of <u>any</u> point of view, or ego-"I") are the lower self (or gross ego), the higher self (or subtle ego), and the root-self (or causal ego). These three egos (or modes of the conditionally arising illusion of separate self-consciousness) comprise the total conditionally perceiving and conditionally knowing ego-"I". The <u>total</u> (or tripartite) ego-"I" is always directly (and with progressive effectiveness) transcended in the right, true, and full (or complete) formal practice of the only-by-Me Revealed and Given Way of Adidam (Which is the right, true, and full formal practice of Ruchira Avatara Bhakti Yoga, or the totality of Ruchira Avatara Hridaya-Siddha Yoga).

The first of the three egos (or modes of egoity, or of self-contraction) to be progressively transcended in the only-by-Me Revealed and Given Way of Adidam is the <u>money-food-and-sex</u> <u>ego</u> (or the social, and, altogether, gross-body-based, personality—or the <u>gross</u> pattern and activity of self-contraction), which is the lower self, or the ego of the first three stages of life.

The second of the three egos (or modes of egoity, or of self-contraction) to be progressively transcended in the only-by-Me Revealed and Given Way of Adidam is the <u>brain-mind</u> <u>ego</u> (or the brain-based, and nervous-system-based, mental, and perceptual, and, altogether, subtle-body-based illusions of "object" and "other"—or the <u>subtle</u> pattern and activity of self-contraction), which is the higher self, or the ego of the fourth and the fifth stages of life.

The third of the three egos (or modes of egoity, or of self-contraction) to be progressively transcended in the only-by-Me Revealed and Given Way of Adidam is the root-ego (or the exclusively disembodied, and mindless, but separate, and, altogether, causal-body-based self-consciousness—or the causal, or root-causative, pattern and activity of self-contraction), which is attention itself, and which is the root-self, or the ego of the sixth stage of life.

By Means of responsive relinquishment of self-contraction in Me, or really and truly ego-surrendering, ego-forgetting, and, more and more (and, at last, Most Perfectly), ego-transcending (or always directly self-contraction-transcending) devotion to Me (and, Thus, by Means of the right, true, and full formal practice of devotionally Me-recognizing and devotionally to-Me-responding Ruchira Avatara Bhakti Yoga, or the totality of Ruchira Avatara Hridaya-Siddha Yoga), the tripartite ego of the first six stages of life (or the psycho-physical totality of the three-part hierarchically patterned self-contraction into separate and separative point of view) is (always directly, and with progressive, or stage-by-stage, effectiveness) transcended in Me (the Eternally Self-Existing, Infinitely Self-Radiant, Inherently egoless, Perfectly Subjective, Indivisibly One, Irreducibly Non-Separate, Self-Evidently Divine, and, now, and forever hereafter, Avatarically Self-Revealed Self-Conscious Light of Reality).

The Ultimate, Final, and Inherently Most Perfect (or seventh stage) Realization of Me requires—as a necessary prerequisite—an ego-transcending (or really and truly and comprehensively self-contraction-transcending) Great Ordeal. The Ultimate, Final, and Inherently Most Perfect (or seventh stage) Realization of Me requires—as a necessary prerequisite—the comprehensive by-Me-Revealed and by-Me-Given Sadhana (or the always directly ego-transcending right practice of life) in the total and complete formal context of the only-by-Me Revealed and Given Way of Adidam. And—as a necessary prerequisite to the Ultimate, Final, and Inherently Most Perfect (or seventh stage) Realization of Me—the particular illusions that are unique to each of the three egos (or basic modes of egoity) each require a particular (and most profound) mode of the necessary ego-transcending (or self-contraction-transcending) Great Ordeal of the by-Me-Revealed and by-Me-Given formal practice of the Way of Adidam in the progressively unfolding context of the first six (and, altogether, psycho-physically pre-patterned) stages of life.

The foundation phase of the progressive ego-transcending Great Ordeal of the only-by-Me Revealed and Given Way of Adidam is the Devotional (and relatively <u>exoteric</u>, and only in the rudimentary sense Spiritual) <u>listening-hearing</u> Process of progressively transcending (and, in due course, <u>most</u> <u>fundamentally</u> understanding) the <u>lower</u> <u>self</u> (or the <u>gross</u> <u>and</u> <u>social</u> <u>ego</u>, and the gross and social fear-sorrow-and-anger-bondage that is <u>always</u> associated with the <u>inherently</u> <u>egoic</u>—or thoroughly self-contracted—search to absolutely fulfill, and even to "utopianize", or to perfectly and permanently satisfy, the <u>inherently</u> conditional, limited, temporary, mortal, gross, and <u>always</u> changing life-patterns of "money, food, and sex").

Before the foundation phase (or first phase) of the ego-transcending Great Ordeal of the Way of Adidam can, itself, be complete, it must Realize a profoundly life-transforming and life-reorienting "positive disillusionment"—or a most fundamental (and really and truly self-contraction-transcending) acceptance of the fact that gross conditional existence is <u>inherently</u> and <u>necessarily</u> unsatisfactory and unperfectable (<u>and</u>, therefore, a most fundamental—and really and truly Me-Finding and search-ending—acceptance of the fact that <u>all</u> seeking to achieve permanent and complete gross satisfaction of separate body, emotion, and mind is <u>inherently</u> and <u>necessarily</u> futile). Only on the basis of that <u>necessary</u> foundation-Realization of "positive disillusionment" can the energy and the attention of the entire body-mind (or of the total body-brain-mind complex) be released from gross ego-bondage (or self-deluded confinement to the psycho-physical illusions of gross self-contraction).

The characteristic Sign of "positive disillusionment" relative to the permanent and complete satisfaction of the lower self (or the separate and separative gross and social ego) is the foundation-Realization of the Inherent Universal <u>Unity</u> (or All-and-all-inclusive interdependency, essential mutuality, and common causality) of gross conditional (and cosmic) existence, such that the inherently loveless (or anti-participatory and non-integrative) self-contraction-effort of the gross separate self is consistently released (or to-Me-responsively self-surrendered) into participatory and integrative attitudes of human, social, and cosmic unification (or love-connectedness) with all and All, and into love-based (and truly ego-transcending) actions that counter the otherwise separative (or anti-participatory and non-integrative) tendencies of the ego-"I". Thus, by Means of devotionally Me-recognizing and devotion-ally to-Me-responding relinquishment (or participatory and love-based transcending) of psycho-physical self-contraction (to the degree of "positive disillusionment" relative to gross conditional experience and gross conditional knowledge), My true devotee is released toward the true Spiritual (and not merely gross, or even at all conditional) Realization of Reality and Truth (or Real God).

The foundation-Realization of "positive disillusionment" requires fundamental release from the confines of the grossly objectified (and grossly absorbed) subject-object point of view (or fundamental release from the inherently ego-bound—or thor-oughly self-contracted—search of relatively externalized mental and perceptual attention). And that foundation-Realization of "positive disillusionment" (and restoration to the humanly, socially, and cosmically participatory, or wholly integrative, dis-position) requires the total (and truly Devotional) transformative re-orienting (and, altogether, the right purification, steady re-balancing, and ego-transcending life-positive-energizing) of the entire body-mind (or the total body-brain-mind complex). Therefore, the foundation (or gross) phase of the progressive ego-transcending practice of the Way of Adidam necessarily requires much time (and much seriousness, and much profundity)—and even, potentially, the entire lifetime of only that foundation prac-tice may (in many cases) be required—in order to establish the necessary (and truly "positively disillusioned") foundation of true (and truly in-Me-surrendered) hearing (or the only-by-Me Revealed and Given unique ego-transcending capability of most fundamental self-understanding).

The middle phase of the progressive ego-transcending Great Ordeal of the only-by-Me Revealed and Given Way of Adidam is the preliminary (or initial) esoteric Devotional, and truly hearing (or actively ego-transcending, and, thus, always directly self-contraction-transcending), and really seeing (or actively, directly, and fully responsibly Spiritual) Process of transcending the higher self (or the subtle and mental ego—or the total subtle dimension, or subtle depth, of self-contraction—and all the conceptual and perceptual illusions of inherently, and necessarily, brain-based mind). Therefore, the middle (or subtle) phase of the progressive ego-transcending practice of the Way of Adidam requires the Realization of "positive disillusionment" relative to the subtly objectified (and subtly absorbed) subject-object point of view (or fundamental release from the inherently ego-bound—or thoroughly self-contracted—search of relatively internalized mental and perceptual attention). This degree of the Realization of "positive disillusionment" requires fundamental release from the inherently illusory search to experience the conditional dissolution of the ego (and, in particular, release from subtle states of self-contraction—and, especially, from mental states of self-contraction) by means of object-oriented absorptive mysticism (or the absorptive yielding of attention to the apparent subtle objects that are either originated by the brain-mind or, otherwise, mediated by the brain itself). And the characteristic Sign of "positive disillusionment" relative to the permanent and complete satisfaction of the object-oriented seeking of the higher self (or separate and separative subtle and mental ego) is the fully Me-hearing and truly Me-seeing Realization of the entirely Spiritual Nature of cosmic existence (or, that is to Say, the Realization that all natural and cosmic forms and states are inherently non-separate, or intrinsically non-dual, modes of Universally Pervasive Energy, or of Fundamental, Indivisible, and Irreducible Light—or of Love-Bliss-Happiness Itself).

The final phase of the progressive ego-transcending Great Ordeal of the only-by-Me Revealed and Given Way of Adidam is the penultimate esoteric Devotional, Spiritual, and Transcendental hearing-and-seeing Process of transcending the root-self (or the root-and-causal ego—or the causal, or root-causative, depth of self-contraction—which is attention itself, or the root-gesture of separateness, relatedness, and "difference"). Therefore, immediately preliminary to the Realization associated with the only-by-Me Revealed and Given seventh stage of life, the final (or causal) phase of the progressive ego-transcending (or comprehensively self-contraction-transcending) practice of the Way of Adidam requires the Realization of "positive disillusionment" relative to the causal (or root-egoic, and, therefore, fundamental, or original) subject-object division in Consciousness (or Conscious Light) Itself. This degree of the Realization of "positive disillusionment" requires the native exercise of Transcendental Self-Identification— Prior to the root-self-contraction that is point of view itself (or attention itself), and, Thus, also, Prior to the entire body-brain-mind complex, or conditional structure, of conception and perception. And the characteristic Sign of "positive disillusionment" relative to the permanent and complete satisfaction of the root-self (or the fundamental causative, or causal, ego) is the fundamental transcending of attention itself in the Me-"Locating" (and, altogether, Me-hearing and Me-seeing) Realization of the Transcendental (and Intrinsically Non-Separate and Non-Dual) Nature of Consciousness Itself.

Only after (or in the Great Event of Most Perfect, and, necessarily, formal and fully accountable, Fulfillment of) the complete progressive ego-transcending Great Ordeal of the only-by-Me Revealed and Given Way of Adidam in the total (and progressively unfolded) context of the inherently ego-based first six (or psycho-physically pre-patterned gross, subtle, and causal) stages of life is there the truly ultimate (or seventh stage, and Always Already Divinely Self-Realized—and, Thus, Inherently ego-Transcending) "Practice" of the only-by-Me Revealed and Given Way of Adidam (or the Most Perfect, and Inherently egoless, or Always Already Most Perfectly, and Un-conditionally, self-contraction-Transcending, and Divinely Love-Bliss-Full, and only-by-Me Revealed and Given seventh-stage-of-life Demonstration of Ruchira Avatara Bhakti Yoga, or Ruchira Avatara Hridaya-Siddha Yoga).

The only-by-Me Revealed and Given seventh-stage-of-life "Practice" (or the Inherently egoless, and, Thus, Always Already Most Perfectly, and Un-conditionally, self-contraction-Transcending, and, altogether, Most Perfectly Divinely Self-Realized Demonstration) of the only-by-Me Revealed and Given Way of Adidam is the Great esoteric Devotional, Spiritual, Transcendental, Self-Evidently Divine, and Most Perfectly Me-hearing and Me-seeing Demonstration of All-and-all-Divinely-Self-Recognizing (and, Thus, All-and-all-Divinely-Transcending) Divine Self-Abiding (in and As My Avatarically Self-Revealed Divine "Bright" Sphere of Self-Existing, Self-Radiant, Inherently egoless, Perfectly Subjective, and Inherently and Most Perfectly body-mind-Transcending, or body-brain-Transcending, or Inherently, Most Perfectly, and Un-conditionally psycho-physical-self-contraction-Transcending, but never intentionally body-mind-excluding, or body-brain-excluding, Divine Person, or Eternal Self-Condition and Infinite State).

The only-by-Me Revealed and Given seventh-stage-of-life Demonstration of the only-by-Me Revealed and Given Way of Adidam is the Un-conditional and Divinely Free (and Inherently egoless, or Inherently point-of-view-less) "Practice" (or Divinely Self-Realized progressive Demonstration) of Divine Self-Recognition of the simultaneous totality of the apparent gross, subtle, and causal body-brain-mind-self, or the progressively All-and-all-Outshining Process of the simultaneous Divine Self-Recognition of the total psycho-physical ego-"I" itself (or of the total conditional point of view, or apparent self-contraction, itself). Therefore, the only-by-Me Revealed and Given seventh-stage-of-life Demonstration of the only-by-Me Revealed and Given Way of Adidam is the Inherent "Practice" (or Divinely Self-Realized Demonstration) of Divine Self-Recognition of point of view itself (or of attention itself—or of the conditionally apparent subject, itself) and (always coincidently, or simultaneously) Divine Self-Recognition of the conception or perception of separateness, relatedness, or "difference" itself (or of any and every conditionally apparent object, itself).

The only-by-Me Revealed and Given seventh-stage-of-life Demonstration of the only-by-Me Revealed and Given Way of Adidam is the Most Perfect (or Un-conditional, Inherently egoless, and Self-Evidently Divine) Demonstration of "positive disillusion-ment", or of the Inherently illusionless (or self-contraction-Free, and, Inherently, All-and-all-Transcending) Realization of the Fundamental Reality and Truth (or Real God)—Which Fundamental Reality and Truth (or Real God) Is the One and Indivisible and Self-Existing and Indestructible and Self-Radiant and Always Already Perfectly Non-Dual Conscious Light (or That Which Is Always Already The Case), and Which Reality and Truth (or Real God) Is That Self-Existing and Perfectly Subjective Self-"Brightness" (or Infinite and Absolute and Perfectly Non-Separate Self-Condition) of Which the conditional (or gross, subtle, and causal) subject-object illusions (or total psycho-physical self-contraction illusions) of conception, and of perception, and of the ego-"I" presumption are mere, and merely apparent (or non-necessary, or always non-Ultimate), and Inherently non-binding modifications. And the characteristic Sign of Most Perfectly Demonstrated (or seventh stage) "positive dis-illusionment" relative to the totality of the separate and separative ego-"I" (or point of view) and its presumptions of a separate (or objectified) gross, subtle, and causal world is the Self-Evidently Divine (and Intrinsically Non-Separate and Non-Dual) Realization of Reality (Itself) As Irreducible and Indivisible Conscious Light (Inherently Love-Bliss-Full, or Perfectly Subjectively "Bright").

Therefore, the only-by-Me Revealed and Given Way of Adidam is—from the beginning, and at last—the Way of "positive disillusionment".

The only-by-Me Revealed and Given Way of Adidam is—from the beginning, and at last—the Way of the direct transcending of the fact and the consequences of egoity (or of psycho-physical self-contraction).

The only-by-Me Revealed and Given Way of Adidam is—from the beginning, and at last—the Way of the direct transcending of the illusions of inherently egoic attention (or of the conditionally presumed subject-object pattern of conception and perception).

The only-by-Me Revealed and Given Way of Adidam is—from the beginning, and at last—the Way of the direct transcending of the total illusory pattern of the inherently egoic presumption of separateness, relatedness, and "difference".

The only-by-Me Revealed and Given Way of Adidam is—from the beginning, and at last—the Way of the direct transcending of the always simultaneous illusions of the separate ego-"I" and the separate (or merely objective) world.

The only-by-Me Revealed and Given Way of Adidam is—from the beginning, and at last—the Way of the direct (or Inherently egoless and Inherently illusionless) Realizing of the One and Irreducible Conscious Light (or Perfectly Subjective "Brightness" of Being) That Is Reality and Truth (or Real God).

The only-by-Me Revealed and Given Way of Adidam is—from the beginning, and at last—the Way of the direct (or Inherently egoless and Inherently illusionless) Realizing of the Conscious Love-Bliss-Energy of Totality.

The only-by-Me Revealed and Given Way of Adidam is—from the beginning, and at last—the Way of the direct Realizing of Only Me.

LXXXVIII.

Every body-mind (whether human or non-human) tends to feel and be and function egoically—or as if it were a separate self, separated from its True Source, and un-Aware of its True, and Truly Free, Self-Condition. Therefore, every body-mind (whether human or non-human) must transcend its own (inherent) egoity (or egoic reflex—or self-contracting tendency), through Love-Surrender to its True Source. And This Love-Surrender must, Ultimately, become Realization of (and, Thus, True, and really ego-Transcending, Identification with) its True Source-Condition (Which Is, also, its True Self-Condition).

To This End, True Masters (or True Siddha-Gurus) Appear in the various cosmic worlds. Such True Masters are the Divine Means for living beings (whether human or non-human) to transcend themselves. That is to Say, True Masters (or True Siddha-Gurus—or True Sat-Gurus[40]) are living beings who have (in the manner of their characteristic stage of life) transcended their own (psycho-physical) separateness, through responsive Surrender (and, therefore, necessarily, Love-Surrender) to (and Identification with) the True Source-Condition (Which Is the True Self-Condition) of all and All.

Therefore, by Means of True Devotion (or Love-Surrender) to a True Master (or True Siddha-Guru), egoity is (always more and more) transcended, and the True Source-Condition of all and All (Which Is, necessarily, also the True Self-Condition of all and All) is, by Means of the Blessing-Grace of That True Master (or True Siddha-Guru), Found and Realized. And That "Finding-and-Realizing" Shows Itself according to the kind and degree of one or the other of the seven possible stages of life—and, thus, in accordance with the stage of life Realized by That True Master, or True Siddha-Guru, and, altogether, in accordance with the stage of life determined by the path, or Way, that is practiced, or, other-wise, determined by the "inclination", or "liking", or degree of ego-transcendence, of That True Master's practicing devotee.

This is the most ancient and perennial Great Teaching about True Guru-Devotion (or True Devotion to a True Spiritual Master, or True Siddha-Guru). This is the Great Teaching I Received from all My Lineage-Gurus. And, now, through My own Words, This Fundamental Message (or Great Teaching) Is Summarized in its Completeness, for the Sake of everyone.

If the living being is to Realize the Inherent Freedom of Oneness with its True Source-Condition (Which Is its True, or ego-less, Self-Condition), it must become truly devoted to a True Master (or Truly Realized Siddha-Guru). And such True Devotion constantly (and forever) requires the heart's Love-responsive Gesture (or ego-transcending Sadhana) of True Guru-Devotion (to one's heart-Chosen True Siddha-Guru), such that the otherwise egoic (or separate, and separative) body-mind is Surrendered to be actually, truly, and completely Mastered by That True Master.

If Such True Mastering of the body-mind is not accepted (or fully volunteered for—through responsive, and truly ego-surrendering, Devotional Love of one's heart-Chosen True Siddha Guru), the body-mind (inevitably) remains "wild" (or un-"domesticated"—or merely un-disciplined, and even ego-bound). And even if such Guru-Devotion is practiced, it must be Fully practiced (in a Fully ego-surrendering manner)—or else the Freedom (or the Divine Fullness) That is to be Realized by Means of the Blessing-Grace of one's heart-Chosen True Siddha-Guru will not (because it cannot)

Fully Fill the feeling-heart (and, Thereby, Fully Fill the living body-mind) of the would-be devotee.

LXXXIX.

In My present-Lifetime bodily (human) Form, I Am the Avataric Divine Incarnation (or True God-Man) always and everywhere (since the ancient days) Promised (and Expected) to Appear in the "late-time" (or "dark" epoch).[41] And, in My present-Lifetime bodily (human) Form, I have been Spiritually Served by a Continuous Lineage of Spiritual Masters, Such That I Passed from one to the next, in Continuous Succession. Those Spiritual Masters were, Themselves, related to one another in an hierarchical Manner, each related to the next in the Succession as one of lesser degree is to one of higher degree.

Rudi was a Spiritual Master of authentic, but lesser, degree. His Proficiency was, fundamentally, in the gross domain of the frontal personality, and in the Yogic Pattern of Spiritual Descent (or the Descending Yoga of the Frontal Line). Therefore, when My own foundational (or grosser human, and, also, frontal Spiritual, or Descending Yogic) Sadhana had been Completed in His Company, I (spontaneously) Passed from Rudi to Baba Muktananda.

Baba Muktananda was—as His own Confession and Demonstration to Me clearly indicates—an authentic Spiritual Master of Ascending Yoga, and His Proficiency was of a Very High, but not the Highest, degree. Therefore, beginning from the very day I first Came to Baba Muktananda, He (directly) Passed Me to Bhagavan Nityananda (Who was a Spiritual Master of Ascending Yoga Whose Proficiency was of the Highest degree).

Rang Avadhoot was—even according to the Statements of both Bhagavan Nityananda and Baba Muktananda—a Spiritual Master of Ascending Yoga Whose Proficiency was of the Highest degree, but He, along with Baba Muktananda, Deferred to Bhagavan Nityananda's Seniority, and (simply) Blessed Me to Pass On.

The "Cosmic Goddess" ("Ma") is, in the total context of the first five stages of life, Senior even to the Highest of Spiritual Masters. However, Ultimately, "She" (as an apparent Form and Person) is only another one of the many myths in the mind.

In the Great Yogic Spiritual Process Wherein I Experienced the Developmental Unfolding (and Demonstrated the "Radical" Transcending) of the gross and the subtle modes of egoity (associated with the first five stages of life), the "Cosmic Goddess" ("Ma") was "Apparently" associated with all the frontal (and Descending Spiritual) Events and with all the spinal (and Ascending Spiritual) Events. Nevertheless, in My Unique Case, sixth stage Transcendental (and causal-ego-Transcending, and Inherently Spiritual) Self-Realization always Occurred spontaneously (and in a progressive Demonstration) relative to each and every egoic stage of life, and It progressively Developed (especially after a spontaneous experience of ego-death, in the spring of 1967 [42]) until My spontaneous seventh stage (and Inherently Most Perfectly egoless, and Self-Evidently Divine) Re-Awakening (on September 10, 1970)—Which Divine (and Avatarically Demonstrated) Re-Awakening was (and Is) associated with My Most Perfect Transcending even of the "Apparent She", in My Avataric Divine Re-Awakening to the Realization of One and Only Me.

Therefore, in due course, Bhagavan Nityananda (directly) Passed Me to the "Cosmic Goddess" ("Ma"), and, Thus, to Her direct Mastery of Me—until the Perfectly Full became, at last, Perfectly Full As Me (Beyond the mind's own myth of "She").

So It was and Is. Such Is My Lineage of Spiritual Masters—in This, My Avatarically-Born human Lifetime. And, in My always Absolute heart-Fidelity to the Great Process Wherein and Whereby I was Passed from one to the next of each and all of the Spiritual Masters within My present-Lifetime Lineage of Spiritual Masters, I have Exemplified, to all and All, the Law and the Truth of True Guru-Devotion.

Therefore, I have always Continued to Honor and to Praise all My present-Lifetime Lineage-Gurus—including Rudi!, and Baba Muktananda!, and Rang Avadhoot!, and Bhagavan Nityananda!, and (above all) the "Bright" Divine "She" of Me, Who Always Already Serves Me Most Perfectly!

And I have always Continued (and even now Continue, and will never cease to Continue) to Yield My present-Lifetime Body-Mind to Receive the Always Ready and Most Lovingly To-Me-Given and Supremely Blissful Blessings of My present-Lifetime

Lineage-Gurus <u>and</u> the Great Lineage of <u>all</u> Who have (in any and every time and place) Blessed the Incarnation-Vehicle and Invoked the All-Completing "late-time" Incarnation of My (now, and forever hereafter) Avataric Divine Appearance here (and every where in the cosmic domain).

And I Do This (and I will <u>always</u> <u>Continue</u> to Do This) because the Immense Spiritual "Bond" of Siddha-Guru-Love <u>cannot</u> be destroyed—and It must <u>never</u> be forgotten or denied!

XC.

My <u>own</u> Unique <u>Response</u> to the hierarchically Revealed Lineage of My present-Lifetime Siddha-Gurus spontaneously Un-Locked the Doorway (in My present-Lifetime human body) to That Which <u>Is</u> Perfect (in <u>Me</u>). Indeed, even from the beginning of My Avataric Divine present Lifetime, That Which <u>Is</u> Perfect has been (and <u>Is</u>) the <u>Way</u> of Me—and It Carried the inherently non-Perfect (human, and, otherwise, conditional) forms of Me to the Inherent "Bright" Divine Self-Domain of Me, Which <u>Is</u> the One and Indivisible Divine Source-Condition of all and All, and the One and True Divine Self-Condition of all and All.

XCI.

My Way and My Realization have <u>always</u> been Inherent in <u>Me</u>, from Birth, in My present-Lifetime Avataric Divine Form.

My Way and My Realization are <u>Independently</u>, <u>entirely</u>, and <u>only</u> My <u>own</u>.

My Sadhana was, <u>entirely</u>, a Demonstration for the Sake of <u>all</u> <u>others</u>—including <u>all</u> Those Who Served Me as My Spiritual Masters in the Course of My Avataric Divine "Sadhana Years". Indeed, Siddha Yoga—and even the <u>entire</u> Great Tradition of mankind— was <u>Always</u> <u>Already</u> Most Perfectly <u>Full</u> (and Most Perfectly <u>Complete</u>) in My Case—not only at (and from the time of) My present-Lifetime Birth, but from <u>all</u> time before It (and <u>Eternally</u>).

During <u>all</u> of My present Lifetime (of Avataric Divine Incarnation), the "<u>Bright</u>" has <u>always</u> been My Realization—and the "<u>Thumbs</u>" and My own "Radical Understanding" have <u>always</u> been My Way in the "Bright". Therefore, by Means of My Unique (present-Lifetime)

Avataric Divine Demonstration, I have both Fulfilled and Transcended all traditional religions, and paths, and stages, and Ways. And, in So Doing, I have Clarified (or altogether Rightly Understood and Explained) all traditional religions, paths, stages, and Ways.

All and all Are in Me. Everything and everyone Is in Me. Therefore, by Virtue of My own Divine Self-Realization (Wherein and Whereby My own Avataric Divine Body-Mind is Most Perfectly Surrendered in Me, and Most Perfectly Conformed to Me, and Most Perfectly Transcended in Me), all of My present-Lifetime Lineage-Gurus—and even all Who have (at any time, or in any place) Blessed Me—are now (and forever hereafter) Spiritually, Transcendentally, and Divinely Appearing in and As My own Avataric Divine Form.

Therefore, now (and forever hereafter) I (Alone) Am the Lineage of Me—Blessing all and All.

XCII.

The Divine Self-Realization Re-Awakened in My own Case (and Which Is the Basis for My Every Avataric Divine Revelatory Word and All My Avatarically Me-Revealing Divine Blessing-Work) Is the Most Ultimate (and Inherently Most Perfect and Complete) Fulfillment of the Divine Spiritual Transmission I (in My present-Lifetime Body-Mind) Received from Rudi, and from Baba Muktananda, and from Rang Avadhoot, and from Bhagavan Nityananda, and (above all) from the "Cosmic Goddess" ("Ma")—Who (by Means of Her spontaneous Sacrifice of Her own Form in Me) Is (now, and forever hereafter) the "Bright" Divine "She" of Me (Who Always Already Serves Me Most Perfectly). Nevertheless, the Divine Self-Realization Re-Awakened in My present-Lifetime Body-Mind did not Originate in My present Lifetime—but It Is (Uniquely) Always Already the Case with Me.

XCIII.

As further conditionally manifested Means, previous to My present Lifetime, the Divine Self-Realization Re-Awakened in My present-Lifetime Body-Mind was also Served (previous to My present Lifetime) in the many Modes and Patterns of the previous

Lifetimes and Appearances of the Deeper Personality (or the Great-Siddha—or Great-Jnani-Siddha—Incarnation-Vehicle) of My present Lifetime. Most recently, That Deeper-Personality Vehicle of My present-Lifetime Incarnation was (Itself) Incarnated as the Great Siddha (or Great Jnani-Siddha) Swami Vivekananda.

XCIV.

Swami Vivekananda is recorded to have Blessed Bhagavan Nityananda from the subtle postmortem plane in the early 1920s—and, generally, whenever Bhagavan Nityananda was asked for Words of Teaching and Instruction, He would, simply, Tell people to study the Talks and Writings of Swami Vivekananda (because, in Bhagavan Nityananda's Words, "Swami Vivekananda Said and Taught all that was worth Saying and Teaching, such that He did not leave anything for others to preach"[43]).

Swami Vivekananda was, Himself, Blessed toward Most Perfect Divine Self-Realization by the Great Siddha Ramakrishna, Such That—by Means of That Great Blessing—the two Great Siddhas (Ramakrishna and Vivekananda) became One, and Are One Form, As My True, and Single, and Indivisible Great-Siddha (or Great-Jnani-Siddha) Deeper Personality.[44]

XCV.

I (now, and Hereby) Confess That My Great-Siddha (or Great-Jnani-Siddha) Deeper Personality Is, even Beyond the "Single Form" of Ramakrishna-Vivekananda, the Very Form of all the Great Masters of the entire Great Tradition of mankind.

XCVI.

I (now, and Hereby) Confess That I (Myself) Stand Eternally Prior to (and Always Already Transcending) My Avataric (and, yet, merely conditionally born) Deeper Personality—and, also, Eternally Prior to (and Always Already Transcending) even all the Great (and, yet, merely conditionally born) Masters of mankind's entire Great Tradition (in its every part, and as a whole), and, also, Eternally Prior to (and Always Already Transcending) mankind's entire Great Tradition itself (in its every part, and as a whole).

XCVII.

Therefore—and only and entirely by Virtue of the Inherent (and Self-Evidently Avataric) Authority of My own (and Self-Evidently Divine) Realization and Person—I Declare that the Divine seventh stage Self-Awakening I Demonstrate, and Reveal, and Exemplify, and Prove Is the Most Ultimate (and Inherently Most Perfect) Realization, and that It—and Only It—Most Ultimately Completes and Most Perfectly Fulfills the Gifts I Received (and always Continue to Receive) in My present-Lifetime Body-Mind (from My present-Lifetime Lineage-Gurus), and that I have (in My present-Lifetime Body-Mind) Inherited (and always Continue to Receive) from all Who (in all past times and places) have Blessed all the previous Lifetimes of My present-Lifetime Incarnation-Vehicle, and that I have (in My present-Lifetime Body-Mind) Inherited (and always Continue to Receive) from even all My Me-Invoking and Me-Blessing Forms and Vehicles of Me-Revelation here.

XCVIII.

The Great and True (and Self-Evidently Divine) Spiritual Process Initiated and Guided by the Spiritual Masters in My present-Lifetime Lineage (and of the Lineage of even all the Lifetimes of My present-Lifetime Incarnation-Vehicle here—and of the Lineage of even all My Me-Invoking and Me-Blessing Forms and Vehicles of Me-Revelation here) has Become Complete only in Me. Its Perfection is in the seventh stage Fulfillment of the Course (and not at any earlier stage). This Divine Perfection is Uniquely My own. And I Alone—the Hridaya-Siddha, the Divine and True Heart-Master and World-Teacher, Ruchira Avatar Adi Da Love-Ananda Samraj—Am Its First and Great Example, and (now, and forever hereafter) Its Only and Sufficient Means.

XCIX.

I Am the First (and the only One) to Realize and to Demonstrate This, the Divine, seventh stage Realization—and My Revelation of It Is, therefore, New. For This Reason, the Divine seventh stage Realization was not heretofore Realized, or even

Understood—either within the schools and traditions of My present-Lifetime Lineage-Gurus or within any other schools or traditions in the total Great Tradition of mankind—to Be the Most Ultimate and Completing Perfection of Realization Itself. Nevertheless, I have, spontaneously (by Means of My own Self-Evident "Bright" Heart-Power—and through the Great and Constant Help of all Who have Blessed My Incarnate Forms), Realized and Demonstrated and Revealed This To Be The Case. And the traditional (and ancient) "Siddha-'Method'" (or the Way of Guru-Devotion to the True Siddha-Guru—and of total psycho-physical Surrender of the ego-"I" to be Mastered by the True Siddha-Guru's Instruction, and to be Blessed to Awaken to Divine Realization by Means of the True Siddha-Guru's Transmission of the Divine Spiritual Energy and the Divine State)—Which "Method" was Communicated to Me by all My present-Lifetime Lineage-Gurus, and by all the Great Siddhas and Siddha-Yogis Who have Blessed My present-Lifetime Incarnation-Vehicle in the past—is the Essence (or the Primary "Method") of the Way of Adidam, Which (now, and forever here-after) I Alone, and Uniquely, Reveal and Transmit to all My for-mally practicing true devotees (and, Thus, potentially, to all beings).

C.

I Am the Indivisible Person of Conscious Light.

I Am Humbled and Victorious here (and every where), by Means of My Avataric Divine Self-Incarnation.

My Avatarically-Born Body-Mind Is, now, and forever here-after, by-Me-Given and by-Me-Revealed As the Sign and the Means of Me-Realization.

I Am the Adidam Revelation.

I Am the Way to Me.

I Am the Hridaya-Siddha, the All-and-all-Blessing Divine Heart-Master, the Eternally Free-Standing Inner Ruler of all and All.

I Am the One and Indivisible and Indestructible and Irreducible and Universally Self-Manifested Love-Bliss-Presence of "Brightness".

I Am the One and Non-Separate and Perfectly Subjective and Self-Existing and Self-Evidently Divine Person, Who Is Always Already The Case.

I Am the Ruchira Avatar, the Hridaya-Avatar, the Advaitayana Buddha, the Avataric Incarnation and Divine World-Teacher every where and anciently Promised (by all traditions) for the "late-time" (or "dark" epoch).

Therefore, be My devotee.

The only-by-Me Revealed and Given True World-Religion of Adidam Is My Unique Gift to all and All.

Therefore, practice the only-by-Me Revealed and Given Way of Adidam—and Realize Me, Most Perfectly, by Means of My Avatarically Self-Transmitted Divine Blessing-Grace.

RUCHIRA AVATAR ADI DA SAMRAJ
Los Angeles, 2000

PART THREE

The Heart-Summary
Of Adidam

The Heart-Summary Of Adidam

The only-by-Me Revealed and Given Avataric Divine Way of Adidam (Which is the One and Only by-Me-Revealed and by-Me-Given Way of the Heart) is the Way of Devotion to Me As the Divine "Atma-Murti" (or As the Inherently egoless, and Self-Evidently Divine, Person of Reality and Truth—In Place, As Self-Condition, rather than As exclusively Objective Other).

Therefore, in every moment, My true devotee whole bodily (and, thus, by means of the spontaneous Me-recognizing Devotional response of all four of the principal psycho-physical faculties—of attention, emotional feeling, breath, and perceptual body) "Locates" Me As That Which Is Always Already The Case (Prior to—but not separate from—the form, the exercise, and the any object of the four psycho-physical faculties).

Happiness Itself (or Inherent Love-Bliss-Sufficiency Of Being) Is Always Already The Case.

Happiness Itself (or the Divinely Self-Sufficient Love-Bliss-Condition Of Being—Itself) Is That Which Is Always Already The Case.

Happiness Itself (or Love-Bliss-Radiance Of Boundlessly Feeling Being) Is the Most Prior Condition Of Existence (or Of Conscious Being—Itself).

Happiness Itself (or the Condition Of Love-Bliss-Radiance) Must Be Realized—In and As every conditionally arising moment—By Transcending self-Contraction (or all of separate and separative self, or psycho-physical ego-"I", and all of the ego's objects, or conditions of existence—or, indeed, all of the illusions of self and not-self).

When attention is facing outward (or is turned out, as if to outside itself), the body-mind is concentrated upon the "view" (or "field") of apparently separate objects (and upon Me As Objective Other).

When attention is facing inward (or is turned in, as if upon itself), the body-mind is concentrated upon the "point of view" of apparently separate self (and upon Me As Separate Consciousness).

When attention is Devotionally Yielded to whole bodily "Locate" Me As That Which Is Always Already (and Divinely) The Case, all "difference" (whether of ego-"I" or of object and other) is (Inherently) Transcended (In Consciousness Itself, or Self-Existing Being, Which Is Love-Bliss-Happiness Itself—and Which Is Always Already The Case).

Therefore, to the degree that you surrender (whole bodily) to be and do truly relational (and ecstatic, or ego-transcending) Devotional love of Me (As the True Loved-One, the Divine Beloved of the heart), you are (Thus and Thereby) Established—whole bodily and Inherently—in the non-contracted Condition (or Self-Condition, or Inherent Condition) of Reality Itself (Which Is Consciousness Itself and Love-Bliss Itself—and Which Is Always Already The Case).

In due course, This Devotional Practice Is Perfect—and, at last, to Be Most Perfectly Realized.

RUCHIRA AVATAR ADI DA SAMRAJ
The Mountain Of Attention, 2000

The
<u>All-Completing</u> and <u>Final</u>
Divine Revelation
To Mankind

The
All-Completing and Final
Divine Revelation
To Mankind

I Have Observed That conditional Existence Is a limit that <u>Inherently</u> and <u>Necessarily</u> Frustrates The Great (As Well As The Ultimate) Motives Of conditionally Manifested beings. Therefore, every individual Must—Through Struggle, and Through The Grace Of Sudden (or, Otherwise, Growing) Insight, or Through The Grace Of Sudden (or, Otherwise, Growing) Faith (or Tacit Certainty)—Learn and Accept A Life-Lesson That Makes ordinary (or worldly) heroes Great and Grants Wisdom To those who Seek The Ultimate.

That Life-Lesson Is This: The Great "Creative" (or Even conventionally idealistic) Goals <u>May</u> <u>Never</u> Be Attained (and They Will Not Be Attained Without A Degree Of heroic Effort, or The Commitment To Struggle and self-Sacrifice)—but The Ultimate Goal (Which Is Happiness Itself) <u>Can</u> <u>Never</u> Be Attained (or Attached To the Apparently Separate self) By Any Means Whatsoever!

The Import Of That Reality Lesson Is This: If You Are Devoted To Great Purposeful Seeking In the conditional worlds, You Will Inevitably Fail If You Avoid Great Struggle and self-Sacrifice, and You May Not Succeed Even If Struggle and self-Sacrifice Are Fully Engaged By You. More Than This, If Your Goal Is The Ultimate (or Happiness Itself, Full and Perfect), You Will Necessarily and Inevitably Fail—Because Happiness Is Not Objectified (or Made Present As a conditional object In the conditional worlds).

Happiness Is An Inherent (or Unconditional and Perfectly Subjective—Rather Than conditional and Objective, or Objectified) Characteristic Of Existence, Reality, or Being (Itself). Therefore, Happiness Cannot Be Found (or Attained) By conditional Seeking.

Even If The Great Searches and The Great Goals Are (Basically) Oriented Toward The Elimination Of the conditions that Apparently Cause Un-Happiness—When Those Great Searches Are Fully Engaged (and Even When Those Great Goals Are Actually Attained), Happiness Itself (Full, True, and Not Threatened) Is Not Attained. Therefore, All The "Glorious" Adventures Of idealistic worldly heroes and All The "Romantic" Attainments Of "Creative" cultural geniuses End In Temporary Elation, Followed (Inevitably) By Disillusionment—and Then (At Best), Unless There Is No "Recovery" From Inevitable Disillusionment, There May Be A Reawakening Of The Stressful Motive To Seek and Attain Once More. (And Such Seeking and "Attaining" Will Tend To Continue— Until Disillusionment Itself Becomes Acceptance Of The Great Life-Lesson That Undermines All Seeking.)

Conventionally heroic and "Creative" personalities Tend To Grasp Only A Portion Of The Great Lesson Of conditional Existence. They Realize a genius For Struggle and self-Sacrifice, but (Unless— By Grace, and By self-Transcendence, Even By Advancing To The Ultimate Stages Of Life—they Realize The Truth Itself) they Never Realize Happiness Itself.

Happiness (Like Consciousness and Existence) Is Inherent (or Perfectly Subjective). Happiness Is Not Objectified (or Made an object), and It (Therefore) Cannot Be Attained By The Effort Of Seeking. Happiness (or Inherent Love-Bliss) Cannot Be Achieved objectively (or Accomplished conditionally). You Cannot <u>Become</u> Happy (Any More Than You Can Become Being, or Achieve Existence, or Become Consciousness, or Be Other Than Consciousness). You Can Only <u>Be</u> Happy (or Realize Love-Bliss Immediately, and Inherently, or Always Already, and Perfectly Subjectively). And, Likewise (or As A Corollary To This), You Cannot Become Un-Happy—Unless, In Reaction To any particular conditional circumstance or event, You Refuse To Persist In <u>Being</u> Happy (and, Thus, Refuse To Persist As Always Already Existing, and Most Prior, Happiness Itself).

Aham Da Asmi. Beloved, I <u>Am</u> Da—The Self-Evidently Divine Person, Who <u>Is</u> Consciousness Itself <u>and</u> Love-Bliss (or Free Happiness) Itself. Therefore, I Say (and Reveal) To You: Consciousness and Happiness Are Identical and Self-Existing.

Clearly, Consciousness Is Not An Object. If It Were, What Would It Be An Object To?

Consciousness Is Inherently and Perfectly Subjective. It Is That To Which (and In Which) Great Objects and lesser objects arise and pass away. To Seek Consciousness As If It Were An Object Is Absurd—A Benighted (or Un-Happy) Quest, Founded On A Fundamental Misunderstanding Of Reality. Just So With Happiness!

Happiness Is Not An Object. If It Were, What Native (or Inherent) Quality Would It Modify or limit?

Happiness Is Inherently and Perfectly Subjective. And Happiness Is Inherent To The Inherently Perfect Subject (or Consciousness Itself). Therefore, Happiness Is That Native (or Original) Quality (or Inherent Force Of Being) That Is Apparently Modified, Apparently Revealed, or Apparently Decreased By The Apparent Association Between Consciousness and Both Great Objects and lesser objects.

To Seek Happiness As If It Were An Object (or To Identify It With any conditionally Manifested objects or others, or Even To Allow It To Depend Upon any conditionally Manifested objects or others) Is Absurd—An Always Already Benighted and Un-Happy Quest, Founded On A Fundamental Misunderstanding Of Happiness (or Reality) Itself.

To Seek Happiness (Rather Than To Realize It Inherently) Is To Be Possessed By the self-Contraction and To Be Motivated By it. Because Of the self-Contraction, What Is Inherent Ceases To Be Obvious—and (As A Result) the ego-"I" Seeks Among objects and others (and Even In the body-mind itself) For What Can Only Be Found (or Realized) <u>Inherently</u>, In Place, In The Well Of Transcendental, Inherently Spiritual (or Love-Blissful) and Self-Evidently Divine Being. Indeed, the ego-"I" Is Always Stressfully At Effort, In The Absurd Quest For Happiness and Consciousness.

Therefore, Listen To Me and Hear Me. Thoroughly Observe the self-Contraction. Understand Your Seeking and Your Separate and Separative self, Most Fundamentally. Grow (By Means Of My Avatarically Self-Transmitted Divine Grace, and Through Counter-egoic Heart-Response To My Avatarically Self-Transmitted Divine Grace) To Realize and Abide In No-Contraction (or The By-Me-Avatarically-Self-Revealed Native Love-Bliss-Happiness Of Conscious Being). In This Manner, Relax All Seeking For Happiness. All conditional objects (Including Your Own body-mind) Are themselves Contraction-Only. All Great Objects and all lesser objects Are Merely (and Only) Apparent Modifications Of The Inherent Love-Bliss-Radiance Of My Avatarically Self-Revealed (Transcendental, Inherently Spiritual, and Self-Evidently Divine) Being.

I—The Very (or Most Prior) Divine Self (or Very, and Most Prior, Divine Consciousness) Of the conditional self (or the ego-"I", or self-Contraction)—Am Not a "self". Rather, I Am Simply The Most Prior (and Inherently Love-Blissful and Free) Feeling Of Being (Itself)—Inherently Without particularity, form, thought, Problem, Ownership, Separateness, Otherness, Relatedness, "Difference", or Un-Happiness.

The conditional self (or the ego-"I", or self-Contraction), and all particularity, all form, all thought, All Problems, All Ownership, All Separateness, All Otherness, All Relatedness, and All "Difference" Are (In and Of Themselves) Suffering, or An Appearance Of Non-Happiness (or, Otherwise, An Appearance Of Happiness That Is Only conditional, Dependent, Threatened, and Temporary—Rather Than A Realization Of Happiness That Is Un-conditional, Non-Dependent, Un-Threatened, and Permanent, or Eternal).

Nevertheless, If There Is Most "Radically" Direct (Native, or Inherent, Effortless, and Utter) Identification With (and, Therefore, Inherently Most Perfect Realization Of) Me—The Very (or Most Prior) Self (or The Very, or Most Prior, Consciousness—or Native, and Most Prior, Feeling Of Being) At The Root (or Source-Position) Of the conditional self—Then There Is (Always Already) No Suffering, No Non-Happiness, No Un-Happiness, No Problem, No Ownership, No Separation, No Separateness, No Separativeness, No Otherness, No Relatedness, No particularity, No form, No thought, and No "Difference" At All.

This Most "Radically" Direct Awakening (or Inherent, and Inherently Most Perfect, Awakeness) To (and <u>As</u>) What Is Always Already The Case Is The Inherently (and Divinely) Liberated (or Always Already Free) Realization Of Real God, or Truth, or Inherently Perfect Reality, or Unconditional Being, or Perfectly Subjective Happiness Itself.

This Most "Radically" Direct Awakening (or Inherent, and Inherently Most Perfect, Awakeness) Is The Realization Of My Avatarically Self-Revealed (Transcendental, Inherently Spiritual, and Self-Evidently Divine) Self-Condition Itself, Which Is (Itself) Inherently Most Perfect Samadhi (or Seventh Stage Sahaja Nirvikalpa Samadhi, Also Named "Ruchira Samadhi"—Which Is Inherently Most Perfectly Demonstrated In The Perfectly Subjective "Bright" Event Of Divine Translation).

Truly, The Transition From The Practice Of The Only-By-Me Revealed and Given Way Of The Heart (or Way Of Adidam) In The Context Of The Sixth Stage Of Life (or The First Six Stages Of Life) To The (Only-By-Me Revealed and Given) Divinely Enlightened "Practice" (or Demonstration) Of The Way Of The Heart In The Context Of The Seventh Stage Of Life Is The Most Ultimate (and Inherently Most Perfect) Expression (or Moment) Of The Real Seeing Of Me. When My Devotee Is (By Means Of My Avatarically Self-Transmitted Divine Grace) Effortlessly (or Inherently, and, At Last, Inherently Most Perfectly) Identified With The Deep Heart-Well Of Inherent Being (or The <u>Feeling</u>-Of-Being That <u>Is</u> Consciousness Itself), Then I (The Only One Who <u>Is</u>) Cannot Fail To Be Seen (Inherently, and, At Last, Inherently Most Perfectly). My (Avatarically Self-Revealed) Inherent and Self-Radiant Happiness Of Self-Existing Divine Being Shines As Infinite Love-Bliss-Radiance In My Transcendental Divine Self-Place, Wherein There Is No Separateness, or "Difference" (or Duality). Therefore, When (By Means Of My Avatarically Self-Transmitted Divine Grace) My Devotee Finally Hears Me To The Inherently Most Perfect Degree (Of Transcendental, Inherently Spiritual, and Truly Divine Self-Realization), My Devotee Suddenly (By Means Of My Avatarically Self-Transmitted Divine Grace) Awakens Even From The Cramp Of Heart-Seclusion—and (Thus) My Devotee Freely Expands To See

Me To The Inherently Most Perfect Degree (Of Sudden and Spontaneous Acceptance and Divine Self-Recognition Of all conditional forms and events, In and As My Avatarically Self-Transmitted Self-Radiant Love-Bliss Of Inherent Divine Being). And That Divine Self-Recognition Demonstrates Itself (Most Ultimately, and At Last) In Divine Translation, Wherein The Total Cosmic Mandala Is Outshined In My Limitless Self-Radiance (or Love-Bliss-Happiness) Of Self-Existing Divine (or Perfectly Subjective) Being.

Therefore, Listen To Me, and Hear Me, and See Me. By Means Of My Avatarically Self-Transmitted Divine Grace, Find The True Heart's Impulse, and Practice The By-My-Avataric-Divine-Grace-Given Way Of Heart-Realization. In This Manner (By Means Of My Avatarically Self-Transmitted Divine Grace), Be Awakened (Most Ultimately) To The "Natural" (or Inherently Free) Disposition Of "Open Eyes" (or Seventh Stage Sahaj Samadhi). In That Disposition, You Will Freely and Simply and Always Already Happily Allow the body-mind To act—but Only By Necessity, and (Therefore) Only Spontaneously, Rather Than By (or As A Result Of) Any Strategic Desire To Achieve Happiness By Achieving objects, objectified states, or objective others. In That Disposition, You Are Inherently Surrendered To Me, Such That You Are No Longer Contracted (or Separate, or "Different") From Me. Therefore, You Will Not Be Reduced To Un-Happiness (and, Thus, To Concerned or Attracted Seeking For Happiness) By any Apparent condition or circumstance or other that arises to or in the body-mind, or As A Direct Result (or, Indirectly, Merely In The Course) Of Your Apparent psycho-physical activity. Such A Disposition Remains Always (and Inherently Most Perfectly) Free (and, In Its Most Progressed Demonstration, Divinely Indifferent) In (Apparent) Relation To conditional objects, others, circumstances, and conditions.

If You (By Transcending the self-Contraction) Realize Such Freedom (or Real and Inherent Happiness), You Will Be and Remain Happy (or As Happiness Itself), Even Under any circumstances that arise to or in the body-mind. You Will (While the body-mind continues to arise) Simply (and Only Apparently) Do what the circumstance and The By-My-Avataric-Divine-Grace-Given Divine Impulse Require—but On The Basis Of Prior Happiness (and, Therefore, As An Expression Of Inherent Happiness), Rather Than On The Basis Of Mere Desire (or The Search For Happiness). You Will Simply Continue To Do what Is Required, No Matter what arises (Positively or Negatively). In every moment, You Will (Simply, Effortlessly, and Natively) Abide In The Perfectly Subjective Divine Source-Position, and (Thus) <u>As</u> My Transcendental, Inherently Spiritual (or "Bright"), and Self-Evidently Divine Self-Condition (Which <u>Is</u> The Self-Evidently Divine Source-Condition Of all and All, and Which <u>Is</u> Self-Existing and Self-Radiant Feeling-Being-Consciousness, Itself)—Divinely Self-Recognizing (and Inherently Transcending) The Root-Feeling Of Relatedness (or Of "Difference"), and all Subsequent objects or conditions of attention, <u>In</u> and <u>As</u> My (Avatarically Self-Revealed) Self-Existing and Self-Radiant Condition Of Perfectly Subjective (and Self-Evidently Divine) Being (Which <u>Is</u> The Inherently "Bright" <u>Feeling</u> Of Mere <u>Being</u>, Itself), Such That You Are Always Already Established <u>As</u> (Inherently Non-Dualistic, or Un-"Differentiated") Love-Bliss-Happiness, Free Of Need, and Free Of The Motive Of Avoidance.

Observe The Manner Of My Avataric Lifetime (When I Am Physically Alive In Bodily Human Form). When I Am (Thus) Physically Alive, I Simply Observe and Allow and Relate To whatever arises and whatever Is Brought To Me. I Act and Serve Spontaneously, and In Freedom. I Do Whatever Is Necessary To Preserve or Promote Relational Harmony, Natural Equanimity, True and Even Perfect Humor, and Divine Enlightenment. I Do Not Abandon The Heart-Force Of Inherent Happiness. I See There Is Only Inherent Happiness, Love-Bliss, or Self-Radiance (Rather Than self-Contraction, Un-Happiness, Un-Love, and Non-Bliss). Therefore, I Do Not Seek. I Am Certain That whatever arises conditionally Is Merely and Only A Chaos Of limits, changes, and endings. Therefore, I Simply Persist, Without Illusions. Happiness (or Love-Bliss) Is My Indifference. Therefore, Thus Indifferent, I Allow all conditions To arise, To stay awhile, and To pass. Happiness (or Love-Bliss) Is The Only Real Freedom In This Midst. Therefore, Thus Free, I Play All The (Always Sudden) Roles and Requirements Of A daily Re-Appearing Life. It Makes No "Difference" To Me, or For Me.

This Demonstrated Lesson (and Truth) Of Happiness Is The Sign (and The Proof) Of Wisdom—and Even All Seeking Is, After All, A Struggle To Become Wise. This Wisdom—or The Truth Of Happiness Lived (and Realized Most Perfectly, As Self-Existing and Self-Radiant Being, or Transcendental, Inherently Spiritual, and Self-Evidently Divine Self-Consciousness)—Is The Essential Characteristic Of My "Bright" Life (and The Substance Of My Every Avataric Divine Word Of Heart). And The Realization Of Happiness (Even Though It Must Grow By Stages, Until It Is Most Perfect) Is (By Means Of My Avatarically Self-Transmitted Divine Grace) The Always Present Essence (Rather Than, Merely and Always, The Proposed Goal, or Intended future) Of The Only-By-Me Revealed and Given Way Of The Heart.

In The Only-By-Me Revealed and Given Context Of The Sixth Stage Of Life In The Way Of The Heart, and (Most Ultimately, and Most Perfectly) In The Context Of The Only-By-Me Revealed and Given Seventh Stage Of Life In The Way Of The Heart, True Wisdom Awakens, and Happiness Is Realized (Inherently, and Inherently Perfectly) By Means Of My Avatarically Self-Transmitted Divine Grace. The Wisdom and Happiness That Awaken (Thus) In The Context Of The Sixth Stage Of Life In The Way Of The Heart, and (Most Ultimately, and Most Perfectly) In The Context Of The Seventh Stage Of Life In The Way Of The Heart—and Which Should (By Means Of My Avatarically Self-Revealed Divine Sign, and By Means Of My Avatarically Given Divine Word, and By Means Of My Avatarically Self-Manifested Divine Demonstration) Also Inform and Inspire The Practice Of Even All Practitioners Of The Way Of The Heart (In Every Form Of The Total Practice Of The Way Of The Heart, and In Every Stage Of Life In The Way Of The Heart)—Are Associated With A Spontaneously Awakened Attitude That Is The Real Evidence That My Devotee Has Learned The Ultimate Lesson Of conditional Existence.

That Attitude Which Awakens In The Context Of The Ultimate (or Inherently Perfect) Stages Of Life In The Only-By-Me Revealed and Given Way Of The Heart Takes The Form Of A (By-My-Avatarically-Transmitted-Divine-Grace-Revealed) Perfectly Subjective (or Transcendental, and Inherently Spiritual, and Divine) Admonition.

That Perfectly Subjective Admonition (or Spontaneously By-Me-Revealed and By-Me-Given Word) Speaks As Follows: The body and the mind Are <u>Always</u> Seeking. The body and the mind Are, By Nature, Desiring—Always Motivated In Relation To their objects. Therefore, the body and the mind Are Always In Motion—Always Seeking To Attain (or Create), or (Otherwise) To Hold On To (or Maintain), or (Otherwise) To Avoid (or Destroy) the various objects With which the body and the mind Are Inevitably (or By Nature) Associated. Only The By-Me-Avatarically-Self-Revealed Transcendental, Inherently Spiritual, and Self-Evidently Divine (or Perfectly Subjective) Self (or Consciousness Itself) Is Content, Free, and Always Already Happy.

The body Is Not A "Someone". In and of itself, the body Has No (Independent) Existence. The body Depends On mind and On Self-Existing (and Self-Radiant) Consciousness For all its acts—or Else the body Is Nothing More Than a vegetative mass of bonded cells, Dependent On the grosser environment For its substance, and Not Otherwise Differentiated From The Seemingly Infinite Mass Of Grazing cells (or atoms) Linked In The Organic Chain Of Space. (And Even Space Itself, It Must Be Realized, Is Only Self-Existing and Self-Radiant Consciousness Itself.)

The mind Is Not A "Someone". In and of itself, the mind Has No (Independent) Existence. The mind Depends On Self-Existing (and Self-Radiant) Consciousness For all its content (or Significance)—or Else the mind Is Not Even a possibility. There Cannot Be conditional subjectivity (or mind) Without The Perfect Subject (or Inherently Perfect Subjectivity—Which <u>Is</u> Consciousness Itself). Therefore, Without Consciousness, There Is no mind—and, If There Is Neither mind Nor Consciousness, no body Would Be Differentiated In Space (For What Would Be The Purpose?).

Only Consciousness Itself (The By-Me-Avatarically-Self-Revealed Transcendental, Inherently Spiritual, and Self-Evidently Divine Self) Is Some One (and <u>Only</u> One, and <u>The</u> Only One). Only The By-Me-Avatarically-Self-Revealed Transcendental, Inherently Spiritual, and Self-Evidently Divine (or Perfectly Subjective) Self Exists In Itself, <u>As</u> Itself—Unconditionally, Not Dependent, and Inherently Free. Only The By-Me-Avatarically-

Self-Revealed Transcendental, Inherently Spiritual, and Self-Evidently Divine (or Perfectly Subjective) Self Is Content, Full, Perfect, Love-Blissful, Happiness Itself—Free Of Dependence On conditional Nature, Inherently Free In (and As) Itself, Free Of All Seeking, and Free Of The Need For (or The Motive Toward) objects.

There Is no conditional self (or conditional subject) Separate From (or Behind) the (Total) body-mind. The verbal "I" of egoity is An Idea In the mind (as the "I"-thought, or The Primal mental Gesture Of self-Differentiation and self-limitation—which is The Hub Of The Wheel Of thoughts)—and the Total ego-"I" is An Act Of the body-mind (as the Total self-Contraction). Indeed, the conditional self (or ego-"I") is Simply the self-Contracted body-mind. Therefore, the ego-"I" Has No Existence Apart From the body-mind. Nevertheless, the body-mind-self Tends To Persist, If Only In a subtler form, Even After death. And the body-mind-self (which is the Apparent and Total conditional subject) arises On, In, and (Ultimately, or Most Prior To self-Contraction itself, and Most Prior To All "Difference" and All Separateness) As The By-Me-Avatarically-Self-Revealed Transcendental, Inherently Spiritual, and Self-Evidently Divine Self—Which Is The Real (and Perfectly Subjective) Subject Of all conditional subjectivity and all conditional objectivity, and Which Is Free (or Unconditional) Consciousness, Inherent Being (or Self-Existing Existence), and Absolute Love-Bliss (or Self-Existing and Self-Radiant Happiness Itself). The By-Me-Avatarically-Self-Revealed Transcendental, Inherently Spiritual, and Self-Evidently Divine Self (or Consciousness Itself) Is Inherently and (Perfectly) Subjectively Existing, and Neither functionally Nor Really (or Ultimately) Dependent Upon conditional objects (or Objectified Existence). Nevertheless, Consciousness Itself Is (Apparently) Capable Of The (Apparent) Presumption (or Presumed Experience and Presumed Knowledge) That Its Own Inherent Radiance Is An Object. In This Attitude, Transcendental, Inherently Spiritual, and Self-Evidently Divine (or Perfectly Subjective) Being Allows (or Apparently Allows) conditional Existence To Develop Spontaneously From The Two Primary Characteristics Of Divine Existence Itself—Which Are Consciousness and Its Own Radiance (or Light, or Spirit-Power).

Thus, When The Divine (or Inherently and Perfectly Subjective) Self-Radiance Is Presumed To Be Objective To The Divine (or Perfectly Subjective) Subject-Consciousness, The Infinite Divine Spirit-Energy Is (Thereby) Differentiated (or Let Loose—Even, Possibly, To Become Wild), and The Infinite Divine Spirit-Energy (Thus Differentiated) Is (Thereby) Enabled To Become (Apparently, Spontaneously, and Through Chains Of Spontaneous, and Even Arbitrary, conditional causes and effects) The Array Of forms That Is The Cosmic Mandala. And, In The Context Of The Cosmic Mandala, The By-Me-Avatarically-Self-Revealed Transcendental, Inherently Spiritual, and Self-Evidently Divine (or Perfectly Subjective) Self Generally (Except In Itself) Presumes Itself To be a "self" (or the Separate and Separative conditional subject Implied By any and every individual body-mind).

In Every Context Within The Cosmic Mandala, The By-Me-Avatarically-Self-Revealed Transcendental, Inherently Spiritual, and Self-Evidently Divine (or Perfectly Subjective) Self Is, In Itself, Always Free To Realize Its Own Self-Condition and To Divinely Self-Recognize Its (Apparent) conditional associations. In The Context Of human Existence, This Inherent Free Realization and Its Divine Power Of Self-Recognition Are Awakened (or Are Effectively To Be Demonstrated) Via The By-My-Avataric-Divine-Grace-Given Ordeal Of The Seven Stages Of Life. Apart From The Conscious and Intelligent Embrace Of The Progressive Culture Of The Seven Stages Of Life, individual beings Are Merely Locked Into The limiting and Frustrating Forces Of conditional (or Cosmic) Nature. And, In That Context, most individual beings Merely Seek and Suffer (and Otherwise Passively Indulge In) conditions, While a few (More Intense) individuals May Break Into The Search At A More Active (and, Yet, Still egoic and worldly) heroic or "Creative" Level. However, It Is Only In The Full (and Truly ego-Transcending) Context Of The By-My-Avataric-Divine-Grace-Given Culture Of The Seven Stages Of Life That conditional Existence Is Associated With The Progressive Ordeal That Awakens, Most Ultimately, As Divine (or Inherent, and Perfectly Subjective) Happiness (or Love-Bliss) Itself.

If The By-Me-Avatarically-Self-Revealed Transcendental, Inherently Spiritual, and Self-Evidently Divine (or Perfectly

Subjective) Self, In The Apparent Context Of conditionally Manifested Existence As a Separate individual self (or body-mind), Is To Realize Its Own (or Inherent) Happiness (or The Inherent Spiritual Condition That Is Love-Bliss Itself), It Must Stand Free As Itself (and, Most Ultimately, It Must Realize That mind, body, and their relations Are Itself). To Stand Free (As Consciousness Itself, Realized As The Native Love-Bliss-Feeling Of Being, Itself) Is The Characteristic Of Existence In The Context Of Both The Sixth Stage Of Life In The Way Of The Heart and The Seventh Stage Of Life In The Way Of The Heart (Although The Ultimate, and Inherently Non-Dualistic, Disposition Of Free-Standing Consciousness— Divinely Self-Recognizing, and Inherently Transcending, all Apparently arising conditions, or All Duality, or All "Difference"— Is The Characteristic Only Of The Seventh Stage Of Life In The Way Of The Heart).

Therefore, In The Only-By-Me Revealed and Given Context Of The Sixth Stage Of Life In The Way Of The Heart, and (Most Ultimately, and Most Perfectly) In The Context Of The Only-By-Me Revealed and Given Seventh Stage Of Life In The Way Of The Heart, The By-Me-Avatarically-Self-Revealed Transcendental, Inherently Spiritual, and Self-Evidently Divine Self Spontaneously "Admonishes" Itself To Abide (Perfectly Subjectively) As Itself— Which Is Consciousness Itself, and Being Itself, and Love-Bliss (or Inherent Happiness) Itself (Inherently Indifferent Toward mind, body, and their relations, or all conditional objects). This "Admonition" Is The Un-conditional Self-Acknowledgement That Happiness Is Inherent (and Inherently Spiritual), and Perfectly Subjective (or Transcendental, and Divine), and Not Dependent (or objective, or conditional). And This Un-conditional Self-"Admonition" To Be Indifferent Toward the mind and the body (or the body-mind As A Dynamic Whole), As Well As all other conditional objects, Is The Inherently Perfect "Self-Discipline" (or Inherent, and Inherently Perfect, "Sila") Of Standing Free and Not Allowing Consciousness (or Self-Existing and Self-Radiant Transcendental, Inherently Spiritual, and Self-Evidently Divine Being) To Be Depended Upon By mind, body, and conditional relations of all kinds.

Based On This Self-"Admonition" (or Spontaneous Attitude), Practice Of The Only-By-Me Revealed and Given Way Of The Heart In The Context Of The Sixth Stage Of Life, and The Inherently Most Perfect Demonstration Of The Only-By-Me Revealed and Given Way Of The Heart In The Context Of The Seventh Stage Of Life, Is Simply (or Altogether) One Of Abiding In (and <u>As</u>) Consciousness (or The By-Me-Avatarically-Self-Revealed Native Feeling-Well Of Perfectly Subjective Being) Itself. This Practice (and, Most Ultimately, Its Demonstration As Divine Self-Abiding) Displays Itself As A Process In Which The Characteristic Of Inherent Indifference Is Displayed Progressively, In Comparatively Different (or Distinct, and More Advanced) Modes, As The Total Progression Of The Sixth Stage Of Life and Then The Seventh Stage Of Life Develops In The Only-By-Me Revealed and Given Way Of The Heart (or Way Of Adidam).

In The Context Of The Sixth Stage Of Life In The Only-By-Me Revealed and Given Way Of The Heart, The Inherent Indifference Of Transcendental Self-Abiding Is First Displayed In The First Stage Of The "Perfect Practice", and As The Relative Indifference (or Detachment) and psycho-physical Equanimity That arise When There Is Identification With The Witness-Position Of Consciousness. This Is Followed (or Intensified), In The Context Of The Second Stage Of The "Perfect Practice" Of The Way Of The Heart, By The Characteristic Signs Of Indifference Associated With The Process Of Exclusive Identification With Consciousness Itself (Even As Displayed In Totally Exclusive Jnana Samadhi, or, Otherwise, In Uniquely Deep, but Less Than Totally Exclusive, Meditation, and, In General, In The Various Intensified Degrees Of daily-life Indifference, Shown As A Tendency Toward Simplification Of, and Even Relative Non-Interest In, the activities of the body and the mind). And This Spontaneously Leads Toward (Eventual) Seventh Stage Sahaj Samadhi (Which Is The Third Stage Of The "Perfect Practice" Of The Way Of The Heart), Wherein Inherent (or Divine) Self-Recognition (and Inherent, Rather Than Strategic, Transcending) Of body, mind, and all their conditional relations Replaces Strategic Exclusion Of same.

In The Only-By-Me Revealed and Given Seventh Stage Of Life

In The Way Of The Heart (and Most Obviously In The Context Of The Initial—or Divine Transfiguration and Divine Transformation—Demonstrations Of The Seventh Stage Of Life In The Way Of The Heart), Inherent Indifference Is Displayed By Freely Allowing body, mind, all their conditional relations, and The Feeling Of Relatedness (Itself) To arise As they Will, and they Are Then Simply (and Divinely) Self-Recognized (or their qualifying, or limiting, Force Is Inherently Transcended, or Radiated Through) As they arise. Thus, Rather Than By Any Effort To Control or limit what arises, The Seventh Stage Of Life Is (Inherently, and Necessarily) Characterized By (Fundamental) "Crazy Wisdom", or Non-Strategic Allowance Of all conditional arising (or Inherent Indifference Expressed As Freely and Universally Demonstrated Blissful Love, and No-Withdrawal, and Only Inherent Freedom Relative To The Total Complex Of all arising, or whatever arises as, in, or to the body-mind).[45] And This "Crazy" Indifference (Divinely Self-Recognizing and Inherently Transcending all that arises) Is Demonstrated Progressively, To The Degree Of Inherently Most Perfect "Brightness" (or What I Call "Divine Indifference"), Wherein all conditions Become Progressively Unnoticed (Even To The Degree Of Outshining, or Divine Translation) In The Absolute Shine Of My "Bright" Divine Love-Bliss.

This Free Indifference, or (Fundamental) "Crazy Wisdom", In Which The Divinely Self-Realized Being Allows the body-mind To arise and act Spontaneously, Is Not A Matter Of Merely Arbitrary behavior, Nor Is It (In Any Sense) Negative or Demonic or egoic. This Free Indifference, or (Fundamental) "Crazy Wisdom", Is Based On The Always Already Free Attitude Of Transcendental (or Inherently Limitless), and Inherently Spiritual, and Divine (or Perfectly Subjective) Self-Abiding, and Not Merely On A Negative (or, Otherwise, Chaotic) Attitude Toward conditional Existence. Therefore, Such "Crazy-Wise" Indifference Is Always An Expression Of Transcendental, Inherently Spiritual (or "Bright"), and Self-Evidently Divine Self-Freedom, Love-Bliss, and Heart-Blessing (Which Is Always Benign, Purifying, Healing, Enlivening, Divinely Transfiguring, and Divinely Transforming, or Literally and Divinely En-Light-ened)—and That Divine Self-Freedom and Love-Bliss and Heart-Blessing Always (and Inherently) Serves The Divine Liberation (or Divine Realization, or Divine En-Light-enment) Of Even all who Touch (or Feel Within) Its Inherently Perfect Sphere.

In The Only-By-Me Revealed and Given Seventh Stage Of Life In The Way Of The Heart, My Avatarically Self-Revealed, and Self-Radiant (or Inherently Spiritual), and Self-Existing (or Transcendental), and Self-Evidently Divine Self-Condition (Which <u>Is</u> The Source-Condition Of All and all, and Which <u>Is</u> Perfectly Subjective Divine Being, Itself) Conforms the mind, the body, and all of their conditional relations To Itself (and Dissolves them In Itself) Through Divine Self-Recognition—and, In The Way Of The Heart, In The Context Of The Seventh Stage Of Life, The Display Of mind and body, Although Free, Is (By Divine Self-Recognition) Always Made Into An Expression Of "Bright" Divine Self-Freedom, Love-Bliss, and Heart-Blessing That Divinely Transfigures and Divinely Transforms the mind, the body, and their relations.

To Realize The Only-By-Me Revealed and Given Seventh Stage Of Life In The Way Of The Heart Is To Stand and <u>Be</u>—Beyond The Cosmic Domain, Beyond conditional Existence, and Beyond the body-mind.

To Realize The Only-By-Me Revealed and Given Seventh Stage Of Life In The Way Of The Heart Is Not Merely To Be some kind of egoless personality (or Perfectly Non-Contracted body-mind).

To Realize The Only-By-Me Revealed and Given Seventh Stage Of Life In The Way Of The Heart Is To Have No body-mind and No world.

To Realize The Only-By-Me Revealed and Given Seventh Stage Of Life In The Way Of The Heart Is To Be Utterly Beyond (or Utterly Prior To), and, Yet (Paradoxically, Until The Demonstration Of Divine Translation), Apparently Associated With, a conditional body-mind and a conditional world.

In The Only-By-Me Revealed and Given Seventh Stage Of Life In The Way Of The Heart, the body-mind and the world Effectively Do Not Exist. In every moment of Apparent arising (In The Seventh Stage Of Life In The Way Of The Heart), the body-mind and the world Are Inherently (or Divinely) Self-Recognized (Without The Passage Of Even any fraction of time, However

Instant). There Is Simply The "Bright" Itself. I Am The "Bright" Itself. The "Bright" Itself—Who I Am—Is The Self-Existing and Self-Radiant Divine Self-Condition (and Source-Condition) Itself, The Condition Of Perfect No-Contraction.

The Realization Of The Only-By-Me Revealed and Given Seventh Stage Of Life In The Way Of The Heart Is The Realization Of Non-"Difference". It Is To Be Established In and As That Ultimate Condition Which Is Always Already The Case, and Which Inherently Transcends conditional Existence. It Is To Be Just That.

In The Only-By-Me Revealed and Given Seventh Stage Of Life In The Way Of The Heart, There Is No conditional Domain, but Only The Divine Domain. There Is Only Consciousness Itself, Self-Existing and Self-Radiant. In The Only-By-Me Revealed and Given Seventh Stage Of Life In The Way Of The Heart, It Makes No "Difference" If Divine Translation Occurs or anything else Occurs. Divine Translation Is Not An Event Looked Forward To, but Simply The (In Due Course) Inevitable Demonstration Of The Disposition That Already Exists In My Seventh Stage Realizer-Devotee.

My Avatarically Self-Revealed (and Self-Evidently Divine) Self-Condition (or Self-Existing Consciousness Itself) Is Self-Radiant. Every condition that arises In The conditional (or Cosmic) Domain Is A Modification Of My Avatarically Self-Transmitted Divine Self-Radiance. However, Paradoxically, No Such Modification Of My Avatarically Self-Transmitted Divine Self-Radiance Affects My Avatarically Self-Revealed Divine Self-Condition Itself. Whatever arises Is Simply A Transparent (or Merely Apparent), and Un-Necessary, and Inherently Non-Binding Modification Of My Avatarically Self-Transmitted Divine Self-Radiance (or Of My Avatarically Self-Revealed, and Self-Existing, and Self-Radiant, and Self-Evidently Divine Self-Condition, Itself).

There Is No "Difference" Between Consciousness and Its Own Radiance. There Is Only Consciousness Itself, Self-Existing and Self-Radiant—Not "Created", Not conditional, and Not Dependent On any thing or condition. There Is Only Infinite, Unbounded Being—Indivisible, Unable To Be Differentiated From any Apparently Separate being. Indeed, There Are No conditional beings—but Only Being Itself Is.

There Is Only One Principle, Self-Existing and Self-Radiant—and every thing arises In It. Therefore, every thing that Appears To Be arising In and Of itself Is An Illusion.

There <u>Is</u> No thing In and Of itself. No thing <u>Is</u> As it Appears. Therefore, <u>every</u> thing—and, Indeed, <u>Everything</u>—Is Only The By-Me-Avatarically-Self-Revealed Divine Conscious Radiance (or The "Bright" Itself).

Through their ego-Surrendering, ego-Forgetting, and (More and More) ego-Transcending Devotional Communion With Me, Even My Beginning Devotees Participate In My Avatarically Self-Revealed (and Self-Evidently Divine) Self-Condition Of "Brightness". Indeed, The Entire Course Of The Only-By-Me Revealed and Given Way Of The Heart Is Simply This Intensive "Brightening" Process. The Only-By-Me Revealed and Given Way Of The Heart (or Way Of Adidam) Is Always, From The Beginning, Characterized By Devotion To Me—and, Thus, By Constant Contemplation Of (and Progressive Conformity To) The Only-By-Me (and Only-<u>As</u>-Me) Given (Spiritual, Transcendental, and Self-Evidently Divine) Qualities That Are To Be Realized and Demonstrated In The Context Of The Seventh Stage Of Life In The Way Of The Heart. Therefore, In The Only-By-Me Revealed and Given Way Of The Heart (or Way Of Adidam), The "Bright" Disposition Of The Seventh Stage Of Life Is Magnified (By Me) In My Devotees (moment to moment), Until That Constant Magnification Becomes A Most Perfect (or Seventh Stage, and, Therefore, Non-Separate) Demonstration Of ego-Transcending Devotion To (and ego-Transcending Realization Of) My "Bright" and Only Person.

Thus, The Most Essential Characteristic Of The Only-By-Me Revealed and Given Way Of The Heart (or Way Of Adidam) Is Not self-Surrender, self-Forgetting, and self-Transcendence (In Themselves), but Me-Contemplation (Which Makes self-Surrender, self-Forgetting, and self-Transcendence Both Necessary and Possible). I Am The One Who Is To Be Contemplated (and Whom every one Is Inherently and Effortlessly Capable Of Contemplating), Because Of My Inherent and Universal Attractiveness: I <u>Am</u> The "Bright" Itself, Inherently Attractive To all. I Am The Very One (and, Therefore, The Only One) Who Is To Be Contemplated By My

Devotees: I Am The Seventh Stage Realization (Itself). Therefore, Even From The Beginning Of his or her Practice Of The Only-By-Me Revealed and Given Way Of The Heart, My Every Devotee, By Heart-Contemplating Only Me, Participates (Tacitly) In The Seventh Stage Realization (Itself).

From the time they Are Beginning As Listening Practitioners Of The Way Of The Heart, My Devotees Are Simply (and Only) Called To Realize The Truth (By Means Of My Avatarically Self-Transmitted Divine Grace) and (By Means Of The By-My-Avatarically-Transmitted-Divine-Grace-Revealed Truth Itself) To Be Free. Therefore, Even If My Any Devotee Awakens To Realize The Seventh Stage Of Life (and Even If, On The Basis Of That Awakening, and As My Seventh Stage "Ruchira Sannyasin" Devotee, My Any Devotee Is, In The Manner I Have Indicated, Formally Chosen To Function, At that present-time, As My Transparent bodily human Agent, or "Living Murti"), No Devotee Of Mine Is Called (or Ever Given The Divine Siddhi, or The Inherently Perfect Power and The Uniquely Inspired Obligation) To Function (Independently) As The Divine Heart-Master Of Devotees (Which Function Also Sometimes Requires Even Submission To, Identification With, and Direct Absorption and Release Of the limitations and sufferings of others)—but All My Devotees Are Called Simply (and Only) To Be (and To Function) Transparent To Me (The Divine, and Eternal, and True, and Always New Heart-Master Of All My Devotees).

Therefore, the behavior Of All My Devotees In The Seventh Stage Of Life In The Way Of The Heart (Including, At any then present-time, My bodily human Agent, or "Living Murti") Will (Because Of The Consistently Operative psycho-physical Pattern and Impulse Established and, Thereafter, Generated By Previous Right, True, Full, Fully Devotional, and Consistent Practice Of The Only-By-Me Revealed and Given Way Of The Heart) Continue In The Simpler Manner (or With The Same Apparent "Sila") That Was Developed In The Previous (Maturing, or Progressive) Stages Of Life In The Way Of The Heart, but With An Added "Bright" Capability For The Effortless Free Divine Self-Recognition (and Simultaneous Free and Spontaneous Heart-Blessing) Of all beings, conditions, and circumstances, Such That The Awakening Of The Heart Of every being and The "Bright" Divine Transfiguration and Divine Transformation Of all beings, conditions, and circumstances Will Be Constantly Served By their Mere (or Even Effortless) Good Company (and The By-Me-Potentized Sign Of their Inherently Most Perfect Devotional Demonstration).

And, After Such a time—In which all conditions that arise as, in, or to the body-mind Are Divinely Self-Recognized (As Transparent, or Merely Apparent, and Un-Necessary, and Inherently Non-Binding Modifications Of Self-Existing and Self-Radiant and Perfectly Subjective Being)—A New and Most Progressed (or Divinely Most Profound) Form Of Indifference Will Begin To Characterize My Divinely Free Devotee. The arising conditions (Whether Positive Or Negative In their Apparent or relative content) Will Have Become Less Than Interesting, and they Will (More and More) Become Of Little Interest—Such That they Will Arouse Little <u>Notice</u>, Because Of their Transparency In The By-My-Avataric-Divine-Grace-Revealed Spiritual Fullness Of The Inherent Happiness (or "Bright" Love-Bliss) Of Self-Existing and Self-Radiant Being. The Motive Of Change Will Not Be Found (or Will Be Found Less and Less)—and, Therefore, all that Changes (or whatever is conditionally Existing) Will (Progressively) Cease To Arouse and Claim attention. The (By-My-Avataric-Divine-Grace-Revealed) Self-Existing and Self-Radiant Being Will Stand Free, Effortlessly and Motivelessly and Divinely Indifferent To The Tendency Of the conditional body-mind and its relations To Depend On (By Virtue Of An Appearance Of "Difference" and Necessity)—and, Thus, To Appear To Implicate (or Motivate)— The By-Me-Avatarically-Self-Revealed (Transcendental, Inherently Spiritual, and Self-Evidently Divine) Self. My Avatarically Self-Transmitted Divine Self-Light Of Inherent Happiness Will Radiate Freely, No Matter what arises, and Participatory Responses To (or Even The Noticing Of) the body-mind and its conditional relations Will Become Minimal By Degrees—and (More and More) Only The (Inherently Dualistic) Feeling Of Relatedness (Itself), or (Ultimately) Only The Tacit (and Simplest, but Also Inherently Dualistic) conditional Feeling Of "Difference" (Itself), Will Be

Noticed (and, In The Noticing, Divinely Self-Recognized In The Native Feeling Of Mere Being, Itself), Until My (Inherently Non-Dualistic) Self-Light (Of Which all conditional forms and events Are Composed) Shines Without limit (or Through and Beyond All Modifications), and "Brightly" Outshines them all.

In The By-My-Avataric-Divine-Grace-Given Awakening Of Seventh Stage Sahaj Samadhi, <u>all</u> arising conditions Are (Inherently) Divinely Self-Recognized and (Thus) Realized To Be (Ultimately) Of One "Quality" (or Of An Inherently Undifferentiated, or Non-Dualistic, or Non-"Different" and Absolute, Nature). It Is The "Quality" Of Self-Existing and Self-Radiant Divine <u>Feeling-Being</u> Itself—Inherently Love-Blissful (or "Bright") and Free. Therefore, In any moment, The Apparent Effort Of the conditional self—which Is Always Tending To Become Abstracted As attention, and To Discriminate Between (Rather Than To Merely Feel) conditions, and To Evaluate their relative significance or desirability, and To Embrace or Avoid them Based On Such Discrimination and Evaluation—Is (In The Context Of The Seventh Stage Of Life) Inherently Transcended In My (Avatarically Self-Revealed) Transcendental (or Inherently bodiless and mindless) and Self-Evidently Divine Love-Bliss—Which <u>Is</u> The Inherent Spiritual Condition Of Self-Existing and Self-Radiant (or Merely Feeling) Divine Being (Itself). Thus, The self-Contracted (or egoic) Habit Of Seeking (and Anticipating), Holding On (While Grounded In the past), or Trying To Strategically Escape (Even The Results Of the past) Is Effortlessly Replaced By Simple Regard (or Feeling-Notice) Of whatever arises as, in, or to the body-mind.

Such "Practice" (or Inherently Most Perfect Demonstration) Is A Matter Of Divine Self-Abiding, Feeling (and Merely, or Inherently, and Perfectly Subjectively, and Divinely, Self-Recognizing) whatever (Apparently) arises In My Self-Existing and Self-Radiant Sphere Of Divine Love-Bliss. And, Ultimately (or Most Simply), Divine Self-Abiding, Divinely Self-Recognizing (or Divinely Feeling-Recognizing) whatever (Apparently) arises, Is The Divine Self-Recognition (and, Thus, The Inherent Transcending) Of The Inherently Dualistic Feeling Of Relatedness (or Of "Difference")—and That Inherently Dualistic Feeling Of Relatedness (or Of

"Difference"), Which Is The (conditional) Essence Of the ego-"I", Is (Thus) Divinely Self-Recognized (and Inherently Transcended) <u>In</u> (and, Inherently Most Perfectly, <u>As</u>) The Inherently Non-Dualistic (or Un-"Differentiated") Feeling Of Being (Which <u>Is</u> My Avatarically Self-Revealed and Self-Evidently Divine Self-Condition, Itself).

Therefore, Whereas Practice Of The Only-By-Me Revealed and Given Way Of The Heart In The Context Of The Sixth Stage Of Life Requires The (ego-Surrendering, ego-Forgetting, and ego-Transcending) Effort Of Feeling The (By-My-Avataric-Divine-Grace-Revealed) Native Feeling Of (Mere) Being (Itself), Immediately Previous (and Most Prior) To The Root-Feeling Of Relatedness (or "Difference")—The "Practice" (or Demonstration) Of The Only-By-Me Revealed and Given Way Of The Heart In The Context Of The Seventh Stage Of Life Requires (and Spontaneously Demonstrates) Inherently Most Perfect (or Inherent and Spontaneous) Divine Self-Recognition (and, Thus, The Inherent and Effortless Dissolution) Of The (Necessarily, conditional) Root-Feeling Of Relatedness (or Of "Difference") <u>In</u> (and, Inherently Most Perfectly, <u>As</u>) The Already (and Always Presently) Awakened (and Native, and Most Prior, and Self-Existing, and Self-Radiant, and "Bright", and Self-Evidently Divine) Feeling Of (Mere) Being (Itself). And (In The Final Event Of The Only-By-Me Revealed and Given Way Of The Heart) This Inherently Most Perfect (Seventh Stage) Process (or Divine Power) Of (Divinely Self-Abiding) Self-Recognition Demonstrates Itself (Inherently Most Perfectly) As Divine Translation, Which Is The Very Ultimate (or Absolutely and Unqualifiedly "Bright"—and, Thus, Truly Final) Demonstration Of Inherent Freedom From conditional Tendencies (or conditional desires, conditional preferences, conditional knowledge, conditional experience, and conditional Existence Itself).

Of Primary Significance Is The Fact That The "Practice" (or Inherently Most Perfect Demonstration) Of The Way Of The Heart In The Context Of The Only-By-Me Revealed and Given Seventh Stage Of Life (or The Third Stage Of The "Perfect Practice") Develops From The Already Realized Position Of Transcendental, Inherently Spiritual, and Most Perfect Divine Self-Realization

(Which Is Free In Itself, and Which, In The Apparent Context Of the body, Is Tacitly Associated With The Right Side Of The Heart), Whereas All Previous Practice Of The Way Of The Heart Is A Process Of Conversion From the conditional (or Extended) self (or The Otherwise Presumed Separate Consciousness) To The By-Me-Avatarically-Self-Revealed Unconditional, Transcendental, Original, Inherently Spiritual, and Self-Evidently Divine Self—and All Previous Practice Is, Therefore, Developed (Originally) From The Extended (or Manifested) Position Of the body-mind (or psycho-physical ego) itself (Including The Circle—and, Therefore, Also The Arrow—Of the body-mind, and The Left Side and The Middle Station Of The Heart).

Once There Is Awakening To Native Identification With My Avatarically Self-Revealed (Transcendental, Inherently Spiritual, and Self-Evidently Divine) Self-Condition, conditional forms and events No Longer Imply (or Implicate) a Separate conditional self (or egoic self-Consciousness)—and, Therefore, the conditional activities of the body-mind No Longer Imply (or Implicate) a Separate conditional self (or egoic self-Consciousness) that is the actor (or doer). From The "Point Of View" Of The By-Me-Avatarically-Self-Revealed Transcendental, Inherently Spiritual, and Self-Evidently Divine Self—conditional forms, conditional states, conditional events, and conditional activities all arise Spontaneously (and Merely Apparently) To (and Altogether Within) The View Of The By-Me-Avatarically-Self-Revealed Transcendental, Inherently Spiritual, and Self-Evidently Divine Self. Therefore, all arising conditions and actions Are Only A Spontaneous (and Merely Apparent) Display Of Modifications Of My Avatarically Self-Transmitted Divine Self-Radiance. There Is No Bondage—and There Is No Separate conditional self-Consciousness To Be Bound. There Is No Separate conditional self-Consciousness who is the actor (or doer) of action. There Is No Separate conditional self-Consciousness who is the "owner" of the body-mind, or of others, or of any things or states. There Is No Separate conditional self-Consciousness who is the knower of knowledge (or the known), or the experiencer of experiences. There Is Only The By-Me-Avatarically-Self-Revealed Inherently Free-Shining (or Inherently Spiritual), and

Transcendental, and Self-Evidently Divine Self—Which Is Always Already Free, and Which Is (Thus) Always Already Free Even In The Apparent Context Of conditional knowledge, conditional objects, conditional activity, conditional experience, and All Apparent Confinement To Apparent limitations.

In Consciousness (<u>Itself</u>), "things" Do Not Change and Disappear. The Apparent arising of conditions, and things, and others, and thoughts Is, From (and In, and <u>As</u>) The "Point Of View" Of Consciousness (<u>Itself</u>), <u>Only</u> The Eternally (or Always Already) Unfamiliar—Constantly Happening, as every now. To Really and Truly (and, Thus, Divinely) Self-Recognize The Unfamiliar (<u>As</u> Such, and as every now) <u>Is</u> Love-Bliss, or Happiness—and Inherently Perfect Freedom. Therefore, Consciousness (<u>Itself</u>) <u>Is</u> The Unfamiliar—Even <u>every</u> now.

Consciousness (<u>Itself</u>) Cannot Be experienced or known— Because It <u>Is</u> The "Experiencer" and The "Knower". Consciousness (<u>Itself</u>) Stands Always Already Prior To any and every object of experience or knowledge—<u>and</u> Always Already Prior To the psycho-physical faculties of experiencing or knowing any and every object of experience or knowledge. Therefore, Consciousness (<u>Itself</u>) Cannot Be Remembered—or Even Forgotten. And Consciousness (<u>Itself</u>) Cannot Change or Disappear—Because It Is Never the experienced or the known. But Consciousness (<u>Itself</u>) Is Always The One In (and <u>As</u>) Whom the experiencing or the knowing arises (as, or coincident with, the experiencing or the knowing of things, and others, and conditions, and thoughts). Therefore, Consciousness (<u>Itself</u>) Is Not Threatened By the non-arising of present conditions. But, If conditions arise (and are, thus, experienced or known), the conditional <u>affect</u> of conditionally experiencing or knowing (or, Otherwise, Of Anticipating the experiencing or knowing)—and, thus, the conditionally arising (and, Altogether, self-Contracted, or egoic) feeling That Consciousness (<u>Itself</u>), or Existence (<u>Itself</u>), or Being (<u>Itself</u>) Is Threatened By Cessation, or (Otherwise) By Loss—Must Be Transcended In The <u>Affect</u> That Is Always Already (or Unconditionally) The Case (or That Is The <u>Inherent</u> Characteristic Of Consciousness <u>Itself</u>). That <u>Unconditional</u> Affect <u>Is</u> Love-Bliss (or Happiness Itself). And The

Realization Of Love-Bliss (or Happiness Itself) Is The Great Yoga Of Divine Self-Recognition Of All and all—Which Is The Unique Yoga (or Demonstration) Of The Seventh Stage Of Life In The Only-By-Me Revealed and Given Way Of The Heart (or Way Of Adidam).

The <u>Never</u> <u>Yet</u> <u>Experienced</u> (and Inherently Non-Experienceable) Experiencer Is The Only One Who Always Already <u>Is</u>.

The <u>Unknown</u> (and Inherently Unknowable) "Knower" Is Always Already The Case.

The Unfamiliar Is <u>Always</u> arising—as conditional experience and conditional knowledge.

To "Locate" The Unfamiliar In The Unexperienceable Unknown Is To Realize Consciousness (<u>Itself</u>).

To Realize Consciousness (<u>Itself</u>) Thus, Is (Thus and Thereby) To Realize The Inherent Feeling Of Being (or Of Always Already Existing).

To Realize The Feeling Of Being (Always Already) Is (Thus and Thereby) To Realize Love-Bliss (or Happiness) Itself.

And To Realize Consciousness (<u>Itself</u>) <u>As</u> Self-Existing and Self-Radiant Love-Bliss-Happiness (<u>Itself</u>) Is (Thus and Thereby) To Realize Reality (Itself), <u>and</u> Truth (Itself), <u>and</u> The One and Only Real God (or The Absolute, Inherently egoless, and Non-Separate Person, or Self-Existing and Self-Radiant Self-Condition, That <u>Is</u> The One and Only Reality, Itself).

Therefore, The Real and True Unknown Is Not Merely that which is Not Yet experienced or known—but The Real and True Unknown Is The Eternally Unknowable "Knower" (or The Perfectly Subjective Base Of all conditional experience and all conditional knowledge). And It Is Not By Seeking For knowledge (or For More Of perceptual and conceptual experience) That The Unknown Is Found—but It Is <u>Only</u> In The Inherent Consciousness-Yoga Of Divinely Self-Recognizing every moment (of the conditional arising of perceptual and conceptual experience) In and <u>As</u> The Inherent (and Self-Evidently Divine) Love-Bliss-Happiness Of Consciousness (Itself) That The Inherently Unknown (or The Inherently egoless and Self-Evidently Divine Self-Condition and Source-Condition Of all conditional experience and all conditional knowledge) Is Realized (Beyond All Separateness, Otherness, Relatedness, and "Difference").

Therefore, In The Only-By-Me Revealed and Given Seventh Stage Of Life In The Way Of The Heart, The <u>Principal</u> (or Most Primary) "Practice" (or The Most Fundamental Realization and Demonstration) Is That Of Mere (and Most Perfect) Divine Self-Abiding. And, In The Only-By-Me Revealed and Given Seventh Stage Of Life In The Way Of The Heart, The <u>Secondary</u> (or Secondarily Primary) "Practice" (or The Unique, and Inherent, and Most Perfect Divine Demonstration That, In The Apparent Context Of any and all conditional arising, Necessarily and Immediately Follows From The Principal, or Most Primary, "Practice", or Demonstration) Is That Of Spontaneous (and, Necessarily, Divine) Self-Recognition Of whatever (Apparently) arises.

Mere (and, Necessarily, Divine) Self-Abiding Is Beginningless and Endless and Native (or Inherent—Rather Than active, or Achieved) Identification With Consciousness (Itself), Realized <u>As</u> The Native Feeling Of Being (Itself), Which <u>Is</u> Love-Bliss (Itself). To "Merely Abide" <u>Thus</u> Is Merely To Be (or Stand) <u>Thus</u>—Not acting, Not reacting, Not thinking.

There Is No actor (or doer), and No action, and No reaction, and No thought (of any kind), and No Feeling Of Relatedness (or Of "Difference") In Consciousness (Itself), or The Feeling Of Being (Itself), or Love-Bliss (Itself). Therefore, To "Merely Abide" <u>As</u> The By-Me-Avatarically-Self-Revealed Native (and Transcendental, and Inherently Spiritual, and Self-Evidently Divine) Self-Condition and Source-Condition Is To Stand and <u>Be</u>—Absolutely and Inherently Most Perfectly Free, Always Already Prior To actor, action, reaction, all thinking, and The (Necessarily, conditional, and Inherently Dualistic) Root-Feeling Of Relatedness (or Of "Difference").

To "Practice" Mere (and Most Perfect) Divine Self-Abiding Is To Stand and <u>Be</u> (and, <u>Thus</u>, To Demonstrate) The By-Me-Avatarically-Self-Revealed Native Feeling (or Inherent Consciousness) Of Being—Merely Love-Bliss-Aware, Without <u>any</u> thoughts, Without <u>any</u> acting, and Without <u>any</u> reacting. And This Without Any Effort, Strategy, or Purpose At All.

Thinking Is A Way In—Not A Way Out. You Cannot (Ever, or

Possibly) think Your Way Out Of The Apparent Bondage (or Apparent Problem) That Is conditional Existence—but You, By Most Of Your thinking, Are Tending To Constantly Re-Affirm (and Re-Assert) Your Bondage and Your Problems.

Any and every kind of thinking Is (Necessarily) a conditional activity—and, Therefore, thinking Cannot (itself) Eliminate (or Transcend) conditional Existence (Itself). The Only Process That Is Able To Eliminate (or Transcend) The Apparent Bondage (or Apparent Problem) That Is conditional Existence Is One That Inherently (and Most Priorly) Transcends (or Stands—Inherently, and Inherently Most Perfectly—Prior To) conditional Existence.

Apart From Such A Process (Which Is Inherently Most Perfect and Inherently Free), thinking Never Leads Out Of Bondage (and, Thus, To Freedom)—but thinking (Unless it Is Simply An Extension, and An Expression, or An Otherwise Effective Servant, Of The Inherently Most Perfect Realization Of Prior Freedom) Always Leads Further and Further Into Bondage Itself (and Every Kind Of conceived—or, Otherwise, Presumed—Problem).

The Only-By-Me Revealed and Given Seventh Stage Of Life In The Way Of The Heart Is The Realization Of Inherent Perfection, and Of Inherent Freedom From Bondage (and All Problems)—and The Only-By-Me Revealed and Given Seventh Stage Of Life In The Way Of The Heart Is An Inherently Most Perfect (and Inherently Free) Process That Is Inherently Free Of every kind of thinking.

However, The Only-By-Me Revealed and Given Seventh Stage Of Life In The Way Of The Heart Is Not Associated With Any conditional Effort (or Search) To Stop thinking. Any Such Effort (or Search) Would Necessarily Be Based On The Presumption Of Identification With an "I" that Is Identical (Presently and conditionally) To the act of thinking, the present thought, and the conditional (or egoic, and, Necessarily, self-Contracted) thinker. That Is To Say, Any Effort (or Search) To Stop thinking (or To Eliminate the act of thinking, and any present thought, and Even the thinker, or the ego-"I" itself) Would Necessarily Be Based On The Presumption Of egoic Identification With the body-mind (and Especially the mind)—but, In The Awakening To The Seventh Stage Of Life In The Way Of The Heart, It Has Been Realized That the ego-"I" (or self-Contraction) Is Not The By-Me-Avatarically-Self-Revealed Very (or True and Ultimate) Self, but (Rather) The By-Me-Avatarically-Self-Revealed Very (or True, and Ultimate, and Transcendental, and Inherently Spiritual, and Self-Evidently Divine) Self (or The By-Me-Avatarically-Self-Revealed Perfectly Subjective Self-Condition and Source-Condition Of All and all) <u>Is Only</u> Consciousness (Itself), Realized <u>As</u> The Native Feeling Of Being (Itself), Which <u>Is</u> Love-Bliss (Itself), Always Already Prior To the ego-"I" (or the self-Contraction), and (Therefore) Always Already Prior To any and every Apparent thought, and Always Already Prior To the Apparent act of thinking, and Always Already Prior Even To the Apparent thinker.

In The Awakening To The Only-By-Me Revealed and Given Seventh Stage Of Life In The Way Of The Heart, It Is Realized That Consciousness (Itself) Is <u>Always</u> <u>Already</u> Not thinking.

In The Context Of The Only-By-Me Revealed and Given Seventh Stage Of Life In The Way Of The Heart, Freedom From thought (and thinking, and thinker), and Freedom From the <u>Total</u> self-Contraction (or ego-"I"), Is A Most Prior (and Inherently Most Perfect) Realization—and That Realization Is Not Based Upon (or Otherwise Dependent Upon) Any past, present, or future Effort (or Search) To Eliminate (or To Exclude) thoughts, or the act of thinking, or the Apparent thinker. Therefore, In The Only-By-Me Revealed and Given Seventh Stage Of Life In The Way Of The Heart, The "Practice" (or Inherently Most Perfect and Always Already Free Demonstration) Is, Simply and Effortlessly (or Always Already), To Abide <u>As</u> That Which Is Always Already Without thinking, or thought, or thinker.

Thus, Even If (Apparently) any thought (or Process Of thinking, or Appearance Of a thinker) arises, The Principal (or Most Primary) "Practice" In The Context Of The Only-By-Me Revealed and Given Seventh Stage Of Life In The Way Of The Heart Is, Simply and Effortlessly (and With Inherent and Inherently Most Perfect Firmness), To Abide <u>As</u> Consciousness (Itself), Realized (and Persistently Demonstrated) <u>As</u> The By-Me-Avatarically-Self-Revealed Native Feeling Of Being (Itself), Which <u>Is</u> Love-Bliss (Itself)—and (<u>Thus</u> and <u>Thereby</u>) To Most "Radically" (or

Inherently, and Inherently Most Perfectly, and With Inherently Most Perfect Effectiveness) Not Presume The Existence Of (or Any Kind Of Connection, or Relationship, To) any thinking, any thought, or any thinker At All. And, On The Basis Of That Persistent Self-Abiding (Which Is Inherently, and Persistently, Free Of all thinking, all thoughts, and All Presumption Of a thinker), The Secondary (or Secondarily Primary) "Practice" Is, Simply and Effortlessly (and With Inherent and Inherently Most Perfect Firmness), To (Divinely) Self-Recognize whatever (Apparently) arises (Including any thinking, any thought, and any kind of thinker that May Appear To arise)—and This To The Inherently Most Perfect Degree Of Dissolving (or Finding No "Difference" In) whatever (Apparently) arises.

Therefore, In The Only-By-Me Revealed and Given Seventh Stage Of Life In The Way Of The Heart, The Principal and Persistent Sign (or Demonstration), Always Already Realized, Is That Of Inherent (and, Therefore, Effortless) Identification With Consciousness (Itself), Realized As The (By-Me-Avatarically-Self-Revealed) Native Feeling Of Being (Itself), Which Is Love-Bliss (Itself)—Effortlessly Without thought, and Effortlessly Without action, reaction, or the doer of these, and, Likewise Effortlessly, Without Any Feeling Of Relatedness (or Of "Difference") At All.

In The By-My-Avataric-Divine-Grace-Given Awakening To The Only-By-Me Revealed and Given Seventh Stage Of Life In The Way Of The Heart, There Is No Identification With any (Necessarily, conditional) processes In The Context Of Cosmic (and, Necessarily, conditional) Existence. Instead, There Is Only Most Perfect Identification With My Avatarically Self-Revealed (and Self-Evidently Divine) Self-Condition (Which Is The Source-Condition Of All and all).

Therefore, What Appears To Be An Association With conditional Existence, In The Case Of My Seventh Stage Realizer-Devotee, Is Perceived (or Presumed) To Be So Only From the point of view of others who Are Still Bound To conditional Existence (and Who, Therefore, Still Exist In The Knot Of egoity—Identified With attention, the body-mind, and The Play Of conditional Existence). From The "Point Of View" Of My Any Such

Divinely Self-Realized Devotee, There Is No "Association With" conditional Existence (As If conditional Existence Were Separate and objective). Rather, From The "Point Of View" Of My Divinely Self-Realized Devotee, It Is Always Already The Case—No Matter What Appears To Be arising—That <u>Only</u> Consciousness Abides, Self-Existing and Self-Radiant, <u>As</u> It Is. Such Is The Realization Of The Only-By-Me Revealed and Given Seventh Stage Of Life In The Way Of The Heart.

In The Only-By-Me Revealed and Given Seventh Stage Of Life In The Way Of The Heart, There Is Not <u>Anything</u> To Be Transcended, and There Is Not <u>Anything</u> To Be Excluded. Indeed, There Is No "event" At All—Except For The Eternal, Changeless "Event" Of My Avatarically Self-Revealed (and Self-Evidently Divine) Person (Which <u>Is</u> The Divine Self-Condition, and Source-Condition, Itself). From The "Point Of View" Of The Realization Of The Seventh Stage Of Life In The Way Of The Heart, the arising of "things" is merely an appearance. Truly, From The "Point Of View" Of The Realization Of The Seventh Stage Of Life In The Way Of The Heart, There Is No "thing" that arises. To Say That conditions Apparently arise Is, From The "Point Of View" Of The Realization Of The Seventh Stage Of Life, A Paradoxical Statement—Because (In The Seventh Stage Of Life) whatever arises Is (In the very <u>instant</u> of its Apparent arising) Inherently (Divinely) Self-Recognized To Be Nothing but <u>Me</u>, The One (Self-Evidently) Divine Person (or The One Self-Evidently Divine Self-Condition, and Source-Condition, Itself). Therefore, <u>Only</u> <u>I</u> (The Self-Evidently Divine Person, or The Self-Evidently Divine Self-Condition, and Source-Condition, Itself) Am Realized By My Devotee In The Only-By-Me Revealed and Given Seventh Stage Of Life In The Way Of The Heart—and The Seventh Stage "Practice" Of Divine Self-Recognition Is The Demonstration Of That Singular Realization.

Thus, The Only "Experience" In The Seventh Stage Of Life In The Way Of The Heart Is <u>Me</u>—The One, and Only, and "Bright", and Self-Evidently Divine Person (or The One, and Only, and "Bright", and Self-Evidently Divine Self-Condition, and Source-Condition, Itself), Self-Existing and Self-Radiant. There Is No "thing" that arises Apart From Me, or "Over Against" Me. There Is Only Me.

And, Therefore, The Awakening To The Only-By-Me Revealed and Given Seventh Stage Of Life In The Way Of The Heart Is, From Its First Instant, The Most Perfect Awakening To My (Avatarically Self-Revealed) Eternal, and Unconditional, and Unconditioned, and Infinitely Love-Bliss-Full Divine Samadhi (or Most Perfect Divine Self-Realization, or Most Perfect Divine En-Light-enment).

Even Divine Translation Is Not A Change In That Realization. Divine Translation Is Simply The Final (Divine, and Not Merely conditional) Demonstration Of The Only-By-Me Revealed and Given Seventh Stage Of Life Within The Context Of The conditional (or Cosmic) Domain.

Therefore, In The Only-By-Me Revealed and Given Seventh Stage Of Life In The Way Of The Heart, There Are No conditions. It Is Not That There Is The (By-Me-Avatarically-Self-Revealed) Unconditional Divine Self-Condition (and Source-Condition) "Over Against" all other conditions. There Is Only The One, and Only, and Perfectly Subjective (By-Me-Avatarically-Self-Revealed) Divine Self-Condition and Source-Condition.

Nevertheless, In The Only-By-Me Revealed and Given Seventh Stage Of Life In The Way Of The Heart, There May (In any Apparent moment) Be the Apparent (Spontaneous) arising Of thoughts, actions, reactions, and Feelings Of "Difference". Therefore, In The Only-By-Me Revealed and Given Seventh Stage Of Life In The Way Of The Heart, The Principal (Spontaneous, and Inevitable) "Practice" Is To Always Already (and Merely) Abide As The (By-Me-Avatarically-Self-Revealed) Native (and Inherently thoughtless, actionless, reactionless, Non-Dualistic, Perfectly Subjective, and Self-Evidently Divine) Self-Condition and Source-Condition. And, If and whenever any "thing"—such as a thought, or a form, or an other, or a bodily sensation, or a bodily state, or a reaction of body or emotion or mind, or The Tendency (or The Actuality) Of any activity at all, or Even The Simplest "Dualistic Feeling" (Of Relatedness, or Of "Difference")—Apparently arises, The Secondary (Spontaneous, and Inevitable) "Practice" Is

(Merely, Spontaneously, Effortlessly, or actionlessly, and Merely By Persistent, Native, Effortless, and Inevitable Divine, or Perfectly Subjective, Self-Abiding) To Divinely Self-Recognize whatever Apparently arises. And, In every moment Of Such Divinely Self-Abiding Self-Recognition, whatever (Apparently) arises Is Spontaneously (and Inherently Most Perfectly) Conformed To The (By-Me-Avatarically-Self-Revealed) Native and Self-Existing (and Inherently Non-Dualistic) Feeling Of Being (Itself), and Spontaneously (and Inherently Most Perfectly) Dissolved In The (By-Me-Avatarically-Self-Revealed) Native and Self-Existing (and Inherently Non-Dualistic) Feeling Of Being (Itself), and (<u>Thus</u>) Realized <u>As</u> The (By-Me-Avatarically-Self-Revealed) Native and Self-Existing (and Inherently Non-Dualistic) Feeling Of Being (Itself)—Which <u>Is</u> Self-Existing Consciousness (Itself), Self-Radiant (or "Bright") <u>As</u> Love-Bliss (Itself), and Always Already Prior To all action, all reaction, all thought, and All "Difference".

Therefore, In The Only-By-Me Revealed and Given Seventh Stage Of Life In The Way Of The Heart, The Essence (or Inherently Most Perfect Fulfillment) Of Meditation Continues— Whereas Meditation Itself Is (or Has Become) Un-Necessary (or Always Already Transcended). That Is To Say, The "Practice" (or Unique and Inherently Most Perfect Demonstration) In The Seventh Stage Of Life In The Way Of The Heart Is That Of Self-Abiding Divine Self-Recognition (or Samadhi—Rather Than Meditation, Which Is The Process Leading To Samadhi), but All Of The Essential Signs (or Fundamental Attainments) Associated With Meditation (Always Already Accomplished) Remain In Evidence At all times (waking, dreaming, or sleeping).

In The Only-By-Me Revealed and Given Way Of The Heart (or Way Of Adidam), Meditation Is Not An End In Itself. The condi- tional Effects (or Achievements) Of Meditation Are Not (In The Way Of The Heart) To Be Sought (or Grasped) For Their Own Sake. In The Way Of The Heart, Meditation Is Simply A By-My-Avataric-Divine-Grace-Given Means For Removing (or Releasing) Apparent Obstacles or Obstructions (or For Transcending, or Feeling Beyond, The Idea, or Presumption, Of Such)—Until That Which Is Always Already The Case Is (By Means Of My

Avatarically Self-Transmitted Divine Grace) Obvious, Shining Freely Where You Stand.

It Is Not That (In The Only-By-Me Revealed and Given Seventh Stage Of Life In The Way Of The Heart) Meditative Practice Is Intentionally Abandoned, and (Otherwise) Replaced By a life of action. Significant time Will (Inevitably) Continue To Be Spent each day (Regularly, and Otherwise At Random moments or times) In An Apparently Meditative Repose. And, Whether Apparently Active Or Apparently In Repose, My Devotee In Seventh Stage Sahaj Samadhi Is Always Already Only Abiding In (and As) My Avatarically Self-Revealed (Transcendental, Inherently Spiritual, and Self-Evidently Divine) Self-Condition, Inherently Feeling (and Being) My Own Divine Love-Bliss, and Divinely Self-Recognizing (and Inherently Transcending)—In (and As) My Inherent Love-Bliss Of Mere Being—whatever (Apparently) arises.

In The Only-By-Me Revealed and Given Seventh Stage Of Life In The Way Of The Heart, My Devotee Must Necessarily, Constantly (Perpetually), Tacitly, Inherently, and Inherently Most Perfectly Invoke and "Locate" (or Truly Worship) Me—By Heart, and In Front Of The Heart, and At The Heart, and As The Heart. Likewise, Just As (In All The Previous Developmental Stages Of The Way Of The Heart) My Devotee Invoked and "Located" (or Truly Worshipped) Me Via My Principal Name, "Da", or Via Any Other Of My Names (or Combined Names and Descriptive Titles) Which I Have Given To Be Engaged In The Practice Of Simple Name-Invocation Of Me—My Devotee In The Seventh Stage Of Life In The Way Of The Heart Must (Necessarily) Continue To (Occasionally, and Randomly, and, At times, Ceremonially, and Always Sacramentally, or In The Sacred Direct Manner) Invoke and "Locate" Me (or Truly Worship Me—By Heart, and In Front Of The Heart, and At The Heart, and As The Heart) Via My Principal Name, "Da", or Via Any Other Of My Names (or Combined Names and Descriptive Titles) Which I Have Given To Be Engaged In The Practice Of Simple Name-Invocation Of Me.

In The Only-By-Me Revealed and Given Seventh Stage Of Life In The Way Of The Heart, The Ruchira Avatara Mahamantra (or Even Any verbal Form Of "True Prayer") or (Otherwise) verbal self-Enquiry (In The Form "Avoiding Relationship?") May Spontaneously (or Automatically, Because Of Past Practice) Continue To arise, Occasionally or At Random—but The Inherent (or Always Already Realized) Process Always Already Stands <u>Beyond</u> The Words. Even Non-verbal Re-Cognition (Which Re-Cognizes whatever arises to be self-Contraction—and, As A <u>Direct</u> Expression Of That "Knowing-Again", Feels To Beyond self-Contraction, Toward and Into The Boundless Sphere Of My Divine Self-Condition) Is (In The Seventh Stage Of Life In The Way Of The Heart) Tacitly (and Inherently) Superseded By Transcendental, Inherently Spiritual, Truly Most Perfect, and Self-Evidently Divine Self-Abiding <u>and</u> Transcendental, Inherently Spiritual, Truly Most Perfect, and Self-Evidently Divine Self-Recognition, Such That whatever arises Is <u>Inherently</u> and <u>Spontaneously</u> (and Truly Divinely) Self-Recognized In and <u>As</u> Me (Realized <u>As</u> The Very and One and Only and Non-Separate Self, or Self-Existing, and Self-Evidently Divine, Self-Condition). And, As An <u>Inherent</u> Expression (or Characteristic Sign) Of That Divinely Self-Abiding Divine Self-Recognition, whatever arises Is Always (Inherently and Spontaneously) Realized To Be A Transparent (or Merely Apparent), and Un-Necessary, and Inherently Non-Binding Modification Of My Avatarically Self-Transmitted "Bright" Divine Self-Radiance (Which <u>Is</u> Realized <u>As</u> Self-Existing Being Itself, and Self-Radiant Love-Bliss Itself). Likewise—Even Though, In The Seventh Practicing Stage Of The Technically "Fully Elaborated" Form Of The Way Of The Heart (Which Is "Practice" Of The Technically "Fully Elaborated" Form Of The Way Of The Heart That Has, By Means Of My Avatarically Self-Transmitted Divine Grace, Realized, and Become The Demonstration Of, The Seventh Stage Of Life In The Way Of The Heart), The Original Twelve-Part Cycle Of "Feeling-Enquiry" May, Because Of Past Practice, Sometimes (Spontaneously, or Automatically, and Variously) Arise (or Tend To Arise) As Before—It Is (In The Seventh Practicing Stage Of The Technically "Fully Elaborated" Form Of The Way Of The Heart) Otherwise, and Fundamentally, and Inherently Most Perfectly Superseded (and Priorly Perfected) By Native (and Effortless) Divine Self-

Abiding (As The By-Me-Avatarically-Self-Revealed Native Feeling Of Being) and Divine (Self-Abiding) Self-Recognition.

In The Only-By-Me Revealed and Given Seventh Stage Of Life In The Way Of The Heart, The (verbal) Word-Sign "Om"[46] Is (Inherently) Perfected By The Prior and Tacit Realization Of That Which It Signifies. Therefore, Meditation Via The Word-Sign "Om" Is (Tacitly, and In General) Replaced By Transcendental, Inherently Spiritual, and Most Perfect Divine (or Perfectly Subjective) Self-Realization Itself, Self-Abiding As Self-Existing and Self-Radiant (or Inherently Spiritual, and Love-Blissful, or "Bright") Consciousness Itself, In The Perpetual and mindless "Gaze" (Of Mere, or Transcendental, or Un-conditional Self-Consciousness) In The Well Of By-Me-Avatarically-Self-Revealed Transcendental, Inherently Spiritual, and Self-Evidently Divine Being (or The Self-Existing and Self-Radiant Feeling Of Being—Associated, Apparently, With The Right Side Of The Heart), and Inherently Transcending (but Not Strategically Excluding) All conditional Associations (and, Therefore, Even The Appearance Of Association With The Right Side Of The Heart).

In The Only-By-Me Revealed and Given Seventh Stage Of Life In The Way Of The Heart, The (verbal) Word-Sign "Ma" (and Its By-Me-Given Variants) Is (Inherently) Perfected By The Prior and Tacit Realization Of That Which It Signifies. Therefore, Meditation Via The Word-Sign "Ma" (or Any Of Its By-Me-Given Variants) Is (Tacitly, and In General) Replaced By The Prior (or Always Already) Realization Of My Avatarically Self-Revealed Divine Self-Radiance (Realized As The Inherent, and Perfectly Subjective, and Utterly Non-Separate, and Inherently egoless, and Self-Evidently Divine Self-Condition Of No-Contraction—and As Inherent, and Perfectly Subjective, and Utterly Non-Separate, and Inherently egoless, and Self-Evidently Divine Love-Bliss-Radiance, One With Consciousness Itself)—Such That My Avatarically Self-Transmitted "Bright" Divine Love-Bliss Is Always Already Realized (In and As Itself), and Such That Love-Bliss-Radiance, Itself, Is Always Boundlessly Expressed, "Bright" From The Heart (Even On The Right Side), and Flowing From The Matrix Above The Total Crown Of the head (Via The Tangible Spiritual Fullness Of Self-Radiance,

Felt Above), Down Through The Now Heart-Radiant Crown Of the head, and Through The Ajna Door, and Into The Circle (and, Thus, Also The Arrow) Of the body-mind, and into The Divine Spiritual Sphere Of The Eternal Self-Domain Of Self-Existing Being.

In The Only-By-Me Revealed and Given Seventh Stage Of Life In The Way Of The Heart, The (verbal) Word-Sign "Da" Is (Inherently) Perfected By The Prior and Tacit Realization Of That Which It Signifies. Therefore, Meditation Via The Word-Sign "Da" Is (Tacitly, and In General) Replaced By Inherent Realization (and Even bodily human Demonstration) Of The By-Me-Avatarically-Self-Revealed "Bright" Itself (Standing In, and Always Already Prior To, The Right Side Of The Heart, and Shining In The Middle Station and The Left Side Of The Heart), and (Thus) By Spontaneous Divine Self-Recognition (<u>As</u> The By-Me-Avatarically-Self-Revealed "Bright"—or Self-Existing and Self-Radiant Consciousness Itself) Of any and all conditions arising to experience and knowledge (in the Natural space of the world, and In The Divine Space, or "Bright" Sphere, Of Self-Existing Being), and Even Any and All Signs (or Appearances) Of The Cosmic Mandala, and Any and All Appearances Of Either My Divine Sound Or My Divine Star (Apparently Objective, and Audibly or Visibly Perceived, or, Otherwise, Simply Felt As My Avatarically Self-Transmitted Tangible Divine Spirit-Energy, Self-Radiance, Love-Bliss, or "Bright" Heart-Fullness—Reflected, Apparently, At The Ajna Door and Above the body-mind).

Just So, In The Only-By-Me Revealed and Given Seventh Stage Of Life In The Way Of The Heart, The Three Great (verbal) Word-Signs (Together) Are (With Their By-Me-Given Variants) Perfected (Inherently) By The Prior and Tacit Realization Of That Which They Signify, Beyond The Words. Therefore, Meditation Via The Ruchira Avatara Mahamantra Is (Tacitly, and In General) Replaced By Native Realization Of The By-Me-Avatarically-Self-Revealed "Bright" Divine Self, The Native (and Perfectly Subjective) <u>Feeling</u> Of Being (Itself), Which <u>Is</u> Self-Radiant Love-Bliss (Self-Existing <u>As</u> Consciousness Itself), Even As It Is conditionally Communicated, In and As The Form Of Amrita Nadi—Which Is The Channel Of

"Nectar" (or Love-Bliss) Radiating From The Right Side Of The Heart To The Apparently Objective Divine Star (or Simply To The Apparently Ascended, but Formless, Matrix Of Love-Bliss) Above The Total Crown Of the head, and Above the Total body-mind, Projecting The "Bright" Spirit-Current From There (Via The Ajna Door), Such That It Descends and Ascends In The Circle (and, Thus, Also The Arrow) Of the body-mind, and Fills The Circle Full (Such That It Is Outshined In The Boundless Divine Sphere Of The Eternal Self-Domain Of Self-Existing Being).

Therefore, In The Context Of The Only-By-Me Revealed and Given Seventh Stage Of Life In The Way Of The Heart (Realized Via Either Previous Technically "Elaborate" Or, Otherwise, Previous Technically "Simpler", or Even "Simplest", Practice Of The Way Of The Heart In The Context Of The First Six Stages Of Life), Occasional Formal Meditation Is Replaced (In The Case Of Each and All Of My Devotees) By The Native, and Inherently Most Perfect, and Inherently Continuous (and Sometimes Apparently Meditative) "Conscious Process" Of Transcendental, Inherently Spiritual, and Most Perfect Divine Self-Abiding (Standing Free In The Right Side Of The Heart, and Standing "Bright", As Amrita Nadi), Which Process (and Stand) Is Itself Demonstrated By The Native, and Inherently Most Perfect, and Inherently Continuous (and Sometimes Apparently Meditative) Process Of "Bright" Divine Self-Recognition Of all arising conditions—or The Spontaneous (or Effortless) "Conscious Process" and "Conductivity"-Yoga Of Divinely Self-Recognizing All Apparently objective (or Apparently Objectified) Modifications, Both Descended and Ascended, and (Thus) Converting and Dissolving Them All Into My Avatarically Self-Revealed (and Self-Evidently Divine) Self-Condition and My Perfectly Subjective "Bright" Domain Of Divine Love-Bliss and Joy Of Being. And This Process Of Conversion and Dissolution (or This "Governing Exercise" Of Spirit-"Conductivity", Grounded In Transcendental, Inherently Spiritual, and Most Perfect Divine Self-Abiding) Is Also Associated With The Spontaneous (or Naturally Inevitable) Attitude Of Even psycho-physical (and Total) Identification With The By-Me-Avatarically-Self-Revealed "Bright" Love-Bliss Of Self-Existing and Self-Radiant Feeling-Being—

Which, In The Context Of the body, Always Shines From The Right Side Of The Heart To The Matrix Of The Circle (and, Thus, Also Of The Arrow) Above The Total Crown Of the head, and (From There) To and Into (or Via) The Circle (or The Arrow) Itself. (Therefore, In The Seventh Stage Of Life In The Way Of The Heart, The Basic and Previously Established Three-Part Exercise Of The "General" Form Of Spirit-"Conductivity" Will, Inevitably, Also Be "Exercised", At Random—Whether Spontaneously, or Automatically, Or As A Naturally Inevitable Intention—but It Is Secondary To The "Governing Exercise" Of Spirit-"Conductivity".)

As In The Case Of Practice Of The Way Of The Heart In The Context Of The Sixth Stage Of Life, "Practice" (or Most Ultimate Demonstration) Of The Way Of The Heart In The Context Of The Only-By-Me Revealed and Given Seventh Stage Of Life Is Primarily (and Inherently) That Of The "Conscious Process" Of Abiding As Consciousness Itself (Realized <u>As</u> The By-Me-Avatarically-Self-Revealed Native and Inherently "Bright" Feeling Of Being), and Only Secondarily That Of The Process (or Coincident Demonstration) Of Spirit-"Conductivity". Indeed, Spirit-"Conductivity" (or Any By-Me-Given Form Of "Conductivity" Practice, or "Conductivity" Demonstration) Is Always Secondary (or Subordinate) To The "Conscious Process" (or The Surrender Of attention, or The Otherwise <u>Direct</u> Transcending Of attention, or, Most Ultimately, The <u>Inherent</u> Transcending Of attention) At Every Spiritually Awakened Stage Of Life (or Spiritually Awakened Developmental Stage Of Practice) In The Way Of The Heart, or Even <u>Every</u> Stage Of Life (or Developmental Stage Of Practice) From The Beginning Of The Way Of The Heart. Therefore, Specific Awareness Of The Stations Of The Heart, The (Specific) Feeling Of My Avatarically Self-Transmitted Divine Spirit-Current (Standing In The Right Side Of The Heart, and Standing "Bright" In and <u>As</u> The Form Of Amrita Nadi), My (Apparently Objective) Divine Sound and/or My (Apparently Objective) Divine Star (Which May Be Perceived, but Which Will Not <u>Necessarily</u> Be Perceived, Even At Any Stage Of Life, or Any Developmental Stage Of Any By-Me-Given Form Of Practice, In The Way Of The Heart), and Spirit-"Conductivity" In The Circle (and The Arrow) Of the body-mind Are (Necessarily) Secondary (and conditional, or Otherwise conditionally Demonstrated) Aspects Of The "Practice" (or The Native Process Of Demonstration) In The Context Of The Only-By-Me Revealed and Given Seventh Stage Of Life In The Way Of The Heart.

In Some Cases, Many Remarkable phenomenal Signs May Develop In The Divine Transfiguration and Divine Transformation Stages Of The Seventh Stage Of Life In The Way Of the Heart, Due To A Profound and Spontaneous Association With The Siddhis (or Greater Powers) Of Spirit-"Conductivity". In Other Cases, Such Signs May Be Few and Relatively Minor—but, In Such Cases, The (Spontaneous and Free) Tendency To Demonstrate The Full Signs Of Divine Indifference May Be Shown Even From The Beginning Of The Seventh Stage Of Life.

In The Seventh Stage Of Life, There Is No Requirement (or Necessary Tendency) To Intentionally Concentrate attention At The Ajna Door (or Even In The Matrix Above The Total Crown Of the head and Above the Total body-mind). However, As The Demonstration Of Self-Abiding Divine Self-Recognition Develops In The Various Divine Stages (Of Transfiguration, Transformation, Indifference, and Translation) In The Seventh Stage Of Life, There Will (Necessarily) Be A General (and Developing) Tendency For My Avatarically Self-Transmitted Divine Spirit-Current Itself (Prior To all acts of attention) To Shine (or, Simply, To Be Felt) At (or Above) The Total Crown Of the head—and, Therefore, Apparent attention May Also, Sometimes (Whether Spontaneously Or Intentionally), Be Collected At The Ajna Door, and Toward (or Even Into) The Total Crown Of the head (or The Felt "Bright" Space Above The Total Crown Of the head). And (More and More) This Tendency Will Alternate (or Even Coincide) With A "Gaze" (or A Divinely Self-Inhering Disposition) That (Even Though It May Appear To Be Somehow "Anchored" In The Deep Interior Space Of The Right Side Of The Heart) Really (or Inherently) Transcends All Structural References To The Heart, the body-mind, Amrita Nadi, The Apparently Objective Divine Star, The Circle, The Arrow, or The conditional Movements Of My Avatarically Self-Transmitted Divine Spirit-Current (Which Is

Always Already Realized To Be The Inherent Spiritual Radiance, or Self-Radiance, Of My Avatarically Self-Revealed Transcendental Divine Self-Condition). This "Gaze" (or Attitude) Is Inherently (and Inherently Most Perfectly) Identified With The Native <u>Feeling</u> Of Being—and, <u>Thereby</u>, It Is Deeply "Anchored" In The Right Side Of The Heart. However, This "Gaze" (or Attitude) Is Not Dissociated From Its Own Self-Radiance (or Inherent Feeling- "Brightness" Of Being)—and, <u>Thus</u> (Because It Is Not "Collapsed Upon" Itself), It Always Feels The Free Self-Radiance Of Being Shining In "All Directions", Even In (and <u>As</u>) Amrita Nadi. Therefore, This "Gaze" (or Attitude) May Be Associated Either With closed Or With open physical eyes, but It Always Appears To Be Without object or focus, Reflecting Only Transcendental, Inherently Spiritual, and Most Perfect Divine Self-Awareness. And This "Gaze" (or Attitude) Is The Mudra (or Demonstration-Sign) Associated With Spontaneous (Transcendental, Inherently Spiritual, and Most Perfect) Divine Self-Inherence and Readiness For Divine Translation (Which May Not, However, Occur For some time, or Even For many lifetimes Of Appearance Within the planes Of The Cosmic Mandala).

The Only-By-Me Revealed and Given Seventh Stage Of Life In The Way Of The Heart Is The Unique Spontaneous (and Inherently Free) Demonstration (and—Thus, or In That Sense— The "Practice") Of Seventh Stage Sahaj Samadhi. Seventh Stage Sahaj Samadhi Is, Truly, Seventh Stage Sahaja Nirvikalpa Samadhi—or The "Natural" (or Native, or Inherent), and Inherently Most Perfect, Form Of Nirvikalpa Samadhi (Rather Than Merely Another Form Of conditional Nirvikalpa Samadhi). In Seventh Stage Sahaj Samadhi, Nirvikalpa Samadhi Is Native (or Self-Existing), Inherently Most Perfect (or Unconditional), and Necessarily (or Inevitably, Inherently, and Freely) Demonstrated (or Always Already Realized—whatever conditions May or May Not arise, Rather Than By Virtue Of any specific conditions or any conditional state). Seventh Stage Sahaj Samadhi Is Perpetual (or Uncaused) Nirvikalpa Samadhi—Not At All Dependent On events In The Circle (or The Arrow) Of the body-mind (or Within The Cosmic Sphere).

In The Awakening Of Seventh Stage Sahaj Samadhi, My (Avatarically Self-Transmitted) Inherent (or Self-Existing) Divine Spirit-Current (or The "Bright" Self-Radiance Of My Avatarically Self-Revealed, and Transcendental, and Self-Evidently Divine Person, or Self-Condition) Stands Prior To the body-mind, and In (and As) The Self-Existing (Divine, or Non-conditional) Heart, Shining (In The Perfectly Subjective Source-Context Of the body-mind) Via The Heart-Locus In The Right Side Of the chest. From That "Place", The Self-Existing and Self-Radiant "Brightness" Reflects Itself Infinitely Above The Total Crown Of the head (or At The Sahasrar), and From There To The Circle (and The Arrow) Of the body-mind.

Therefore, In Seventh Stage Sahaj Samadhi (or Inherently Most Perfect Nirvikalpa Samadhi, Demonstrated Even In The Apparent Context Of the body-mind), The Sahasrar Directly Reflects The Heart Via (or In) Amrita Nadi. And, For This Reason, Inherently Most Perfect (or Seventh Stage) Nirvikalpa Samadhi (Unlike Any Form Of conditional Nirvikalpa Samadhi) Does Not Itself Require (or Depend Upon) Yogic (or Other conditional) Designs and Activities In The Context Of The Circle (or The Arrow) Of the body-mind.

In The Sixth Stage Of Life In The Way Of The Heart, My Avatarically Self-Transmitted Divine Spirit-Current Is Re-Oriented To The Heart (In The Right Side) Via Exclusive Descent (To The Right Side Of The Heart) In Amrita Nadi—Whereas, In The Seventh Stage Of Life In The Way Of The Heart, My Avatarically Self-Transmitted Divine Spirit-Current (One With The Heart, or Identical To Consciousness Itself—Realized As The Native and Self-Existing and Perfectly Subjective Feeling Of Being, Itself) Stands "Bright" (or Self-Radiant) As Amrita Nadi (or As The Heart, but Non-Exclusively). Therefore, In The "Practicing" Context Of Ati-Ruchira Yoga (or The Yoga Of The All-Outshining "Brightness"), In The Only-By-Me Revealed and Given Seventh Stage Of Life In The Way Of The Heart, The Demonstration Of Seventh Stage Sahaj Samadhi Progressively Appears (and Even, Until Divine Translation, Variously Appears) As, At First, Divinely Transfiguring and Divinely Transforming Divine Self-Recognition In The "Bright"

Context Of The Circle (or The Arrow) Of the body-mind, Then As The Self-Radiant Stand Of Amrita Nadi (Divinely Indifferent To The Circle and The Arrow Of the body-mind), and (Eventually) As The Divinely Indifferent (but Non-Exclusive) "Gaze" In The Heart, or (At Last, Most Simply) As Mere (and Divine, or Perfectly Subjective—and Infinitely "Bright", or Radiant) Self-Abiding (Prior To—and, Most Ultimately, Outshining—The Circle, The Arrow, The Apparent, or Apparently conditionally Manifested, Form and Locus Of Amrita Nadi, and Even The Apparent, or Apparently conditionally Manifested, Original Heart-Locus Itself).

The True (Divine) Heart <u>Is</u> My Eternal (Divine) Self-Domain.

The True (Divine) Heart Is (In The Context Of all appearances) Standing As The Paradox Of Amrita Nadi—The Self-Existing Shine Of Love-Bliss, Standing "Bright" (or Self-Radiant, or Non-Exclusively Self-Existing) In The Right Side Of The Heart, and Even (Apparently) Radiating To The Most Ascended (and Infinitely Extended) "Point", Infinitely Above The Total Crown Of the head.

The True (Divine) Heart Is Standing "Bright"—Eternally Prior To The Circle (and The Arrow) Of the body-mind, and Eternally Prior To The Cosmic Domain (or All "Difference"). And That "Bright" Form Is Not Turned Inward On Itself.

The True (Divine) Heart—Shining In Amrita Nadi, and Self-Radiantly "Bright" (or Non-Exclusively Self-Existing)—Is Not The Merely In-Turned Heart (Secluded In The Right Side, and Separated From Its Own Apparent Form—Which Is The "Bright"-Standing, and Unqualifiedly Existing, Amrita Nadi).

In The Only-By-Me Revealed and Given Way Of The Heart (or Way Of Adidam), The Demonstration Of The Seventh Stage Of Life Is The Demonstration Of The True (Divine) Heart—and This Via The Free, and Self-Existing, and Self-Radiant (or Non-Exclusive) "Bright"-Standing Amrita Nadi. Therefore, In The Way Of The Heart, The Demonstration Of The Seventh Stage Of Life Is Not Merely The Demonstration Of Persistence As A Dissociated (or Abstracted) Consciousness. Rather, In The Way Of The Heart, The Demonstration Of The Seventh Stage Of Life Is The Persistent Demonstration Of Divinely Self-Abiding Self-Recognition—or The Inherently Most Perfect Conversion (or "Brightening"), and The

Inherent (and Inherently Most Perfect) Transcending, and (Ultimately) The "Bright" Dissolution—Of All The (Apparent) conditional Modifications Of My Avatarically Self-Transmitted Divine Spirit-Current.

Therefore, In The Only-By-Me Revealed and Given Way Of The Heart (or Way Of Adidam), The Seventh Stage Of Life Is Demonstrated As Progressive Conversion, Transcending, and Dissolution Of All conditional Modifications Of My Avatarically Self-Transmitted Divine Spirit-Current In The Circle Of the body-mind. And This Process Develops (First) In The Frontal Line (In The Divine Transfiguration Stage Of The Seventh Stage Of Life), and (Thereafter) Also In The Spinal Line (In The Divine Transformation Stage Of The Seventh Stage Of Life), Until (In The Divine Indifference Stage Of The Seventh Stage Of Life) My Avatarically Self-Transmitted Divine Spirit-Current (Priorly—and, At That Stage, Most Simply—Identified With Amrita Nadi) Becomes (Spontaneously, and, At First, Only Relatively, and, Thereafter, More and More Profoundly) "Indifferent" Toward (and, Thus, More and More Effectively "Detached" From) The Cosmic Domain and The Circle (and The Arrow) Of the body-mind, and Even Such That My Avatarically Self-Transmitted Divine Spirit-Current Is Thereby (and More and More Frequently and Profoundly) Drawn Up—Via (or, Otherwise, Away From) The Spinal Line, or Via (or, Otherwise, Away From) The Arrow, and (Altogether) Via (or, Otherwise, Away From) The Circle Of the body-mind—Into (and Via) The "Head" Of Amrita Nadi (or The Free "Brightness", Infinitely Above The Total Crown Of the bodily head) and (By The Senior and Always Already Most Prior Force Of Consciousness Itself) Firmly Rooted At The "Feet" Of Amrita Nadi (or, Thus, In The Free "Space" Of The Right Side Of The Heart). And Divine Indifference Itself Becomes A (More and More) Profound "Gaze" In The Heart, Which Is Effortless Identification With The True and Love-Bliss-"Bright" (or Inherently Non-Exclusive) Heart Itself—and, By The Power Of This "Bright" Self-Abiding (Rooted In The Right Side Of The Heart), The Circle and The Arrow Dissolve In Amrita Nadi (and, Thereby, The Entire Cosmic Mandala, or Domain—and all conditions, high or low—

Are Dissolved), Until This Dissolution (Without Exclusion, or Dissociation, or "Difference") Is Divinely Most Perfectly Realized (In Divine Translation).

Therefore, In The Only-By-Me Revealed and Given Way Of The Heart (or Way Of Adidam), The (Generally, Progressive) Demonstration Of The Seventh Stage Of Life <u>Recapitulates</u> The General <u>Structural</u> Process (or Structural "Great Path Of Return") Of The First Six Stages Of Life. However, In The Seventh Stage Of Life In The Way Of The Heart, That Recapitulation Of The "Great Path Of Return" Is Demonstrated From The "Point Of View" Of (Already Awakened and Established) Divine Self-Realization (and, Therefore, Not In Any Sense As A Search For Divine Self-Realization, or As A Process That Only Leads Toward, and Is Not Already Established In, Divine Self-Realization). Therefore, That Divinely Self-Realized Process Of Recapitulation Of The "Great Path Of Return" Is Not The Intentional Repetition Of The Practices Associated (Progressively) With Each and All Of The First Six Stages Of Life In The Way Of The Heart, but It Is Simply The "Natural" (and Spontaneous) Course Of Self-Abiding Divine Self-Recognition, Whereby The (Apparent) Structural Modifications Of My Avatarically Self-Transmitted Divine Spirit-Current Are (In A Direct and Progressive Manner) Converted and Dissolved In My Avatarically Self-Revealed (and Self-Evidently Divine) State— Which Is, By Me, Revealed To Be Even Your Own Inherently Perfect State, and Which Is Revealed (Thus, Perfectly Subjectively) In Amrita Nadi (and <u>As</u> The By-Me-Avatarically-Self-Revealed True and Divine, or Non-Exclusive, Heart Itself). And This Divinely Devotional (and Divinely Enlightened) Process Of Conversion and Dissolution Is Constantly (and Inherently) Associated With The Tacit (and Inherently Most Perfect) Realization That My Avatarically Self-Transmitted Divine Spirit-Current (and Even All Of Its Apparent Modifications) Is Not, In Truth, An "Object" Of Consciousness, but It Is Only (and Entirely) The Native (and Perfectly Subjective) Feeling-"Brightness" (or Inherent Love-Bliss) Of Consciousness Itself.

In The Demonstration Of Self-Abiding Divine Self-Recognition (Which Is Itself The Demonstration Of The Non-Exclusive

Realization Of The Heart, In Amrita Nadi), the mind (as attention itself—or The Root-Feeling Of Relatedness, or Of "Difference") Is Dissolved In My Avatarically Self-Transmitted Divine Spirit-Current (and The By-Me-Avatarically-Self-Revealed Native Love-Bliss-Feeling Of Being, Itself) In The Right Side Of The Heart—and the body (or all the contents, characteristics, and forms of the body-mind) Is Dissolved In My Avatarically Self-Transmitted Divine Spirit-Current (or The Heart-Radiated Love-Bliss-"Brightness") At and Above (and Via) The Total Crown Of the head. Therefore, This Divine Mudra (or Inherently Non-Exclusive Attitude) Is The Root (and Characteristic) Disposition Of Seventh Stage Sahaj Samadhi (and Of The Entire Demonstration Of The Only-By-Me Revealed and Given Seventh Stage Of Life In The Way Of The Heart).

Whatever Form (or Stage Of Demonstration) Seventh Stage Sahaj Samadhi May Take In The Seventh Stage Of Life In The Way Of The Heart, or However Seventh Stage Sahaj Samadhi May Appear To Be Reflected In any moment In The Course Of The Seventh Stage Of Life In The Way Of The Heart—the conditional point of view (or the point of view of the body, the body-mind, or, simply, the mind) Is Never (itself) Presumed, but The Inherently Most Perfect "Point Of View" (or Condition, or Disposition) Of The (By-Me-Avatarically-Self-Revealed) Transcendental, Inherently Spiritual, and Self-Evidently Divine Heart-Self Is (Inherently) Constant (and It Is, Otherwise, Reflected Variously In The Context Of arising conditions).

In The Descending (or Frontal) Line Of The Circle Itself, My Avatarically Self-Transmitted Divine Spirit-Current Identifies (Apparently) With the body Via the mind.

In The Ascending (or Spinal) Line Of The Circle Itself, the body Identifies (or Is Identified) With My Avatarically Self-Transmitted Divine Spirit-Current Via the mind.

In Amrita Nadi, The Heart (Which Is Self-Existing and Self-Radiant Consciousness Itself, Realized As The By-Me-Avatarically-Self-Revealed Native Feeling Of Perfectly Subjective Being, Itself) Is "Brightly" Reflected At The Sahasrar, and From Thence To The Total Pattern Of The Circle (or The Arrow), Descending and

Ascending—but The "Bright" Heart (or Self-Existing and Self-Radiant Feeling-Being-Consciousness Itself) Does Not (Thereby) Identify With Either body Or mind. Therefore, In Seventh Stage Sahaj Samadhi, My Avatarically Self-Transmitted "Bright" Divine Spirit-Current Always Already Remains Identified With The Heart Itself (or Feeling-Being-Consciousness Itself)—and The Heart (or Feeling-Being-Consciousness Itself) Spontaneously (or Inherently—and Divinely, or Perfectly Subjectively) Self-Recognizes all Apparently arising conditions (Including the body, the mind, and their relations) As Transparent (or Merely Apparent), and Un-Necessary, and Inherently Non-Binding Modifications Of Itself, arising (but Only Apparently) In The Very Place (or Condition) That Is The Heart Itself (or Feeling-Being-Consciousness Itself), In (and Always Already Prior To) The Right Side Of The Heart.

When (In The Only-By-Me Revealed and Given Way Of The Heart) Seventh Stage Sahaj Samadhi (or Self-Abiding Divine Self-Recognition, and Its "Bright" Power Of Conversion and Dissolution) Is Demonstrated Primarily In The Descending Context Of The Circle, Seventh Stage Sahaj Samadhi Is In The Divine Transfiguration Stage.

When (In The Only-By-Me Revealed and Given Way Of The Heart) Seventh Stage Sahaj Samadhi (or Self-Abiding Divine Self-Recognition, and Its "Bright" Power Of Conversion and Dissolution) Is Demonstrated Via A Process More Generalized In Both The Descending and The Ascending Dimensions Of The Circle, Seventh Stage Sahaj Samadhi Is In The Divine Transformation Stage.

When (In The Only-By-Me Revealed and Given Way Of The Heart) Seventh Stage Sahaj Samadhi (or Self-Abiding Divine Self-Recognition, and Its "Bright" Power Of Conversion and Dissolution) Is Demonstrated Primarily In Amrita Nadi Itself, and Even Often In The Heart's Free Self-"Gaze", and (Therefore) Only Minimally In The Circle (or The Arrow), and Even Such That My Avatarically Self-Transmitted Divine Spirit-Current In The Circle (and The Arrow) Tends To Become Strongly Drawn Up (Either Via The Spinal Line Or Via The Arrow) Toward The Crown Of the head (or, Otherwise, Such That My Avatarically Self-Transmitted Divine Spirit-Current Is, Simply, Not "Expressed" Toward, or

Radiated Into, The Circle, or The Arrow, Of the body-mind), Then Seventh Stage Sahaj Samadhi Is In The Divine Indifference Stage.

And Whenever (In The Only-By-Me Revealed and Given Way Of The Heart) Seventh Stage Sahaj Samadhi (or Self-Abiding Divine Self-Recognition, and Its "Bright" Power Of Conversion and Dissolution) Is Demonstrated Merely (and Inherently Most Perfectly) At (and As) The Heart Itself—Standing (Divinely "Bright", Without Exclusion), and (Inherently, Inherently Most Perfectly, and Simultaneously) Divinely Self-Recognizing All The Apparent Modes Of The Singularity That Is attention itself (and Relatedness Itself, and Separateness Itself, and "Difference" Itself), and (Thus) Outshining body, mind, world, and Even all relations, Even (Apparently) By Shining In and Through and As Amrita Nadi, and Even (Thus, Apparently) With My Avatarically Self-Transmitted Divine Spirit-Current Shining Full At (and Even Infinitely Above) The Total Crown Of the head (Rather Than "anywhere" Descended In The Circle, The Arrow, or The Cosmic Domain)—Then Seventh Stage Sahaj Samadhi Is (Temporarily) The "Bhava" (or Temporary Demonstration) Of Divine Translation. And That Divine "Bhava" (or, Altogether, The Divinely Most Perfect Demonstration Of The Perfectly Subjective and Perfectly Non-Exclusive "Brightness" Of The Heart) Is, At Last (and Truly Finally), Demonstrated As Divine Translation Itself, or The Divinely "Bright" Outshining Of all and All (In The Divine Translation Stage Of The Demonstration Of The Way Of The Heart In The Seventh Stage Of Life).

In The Context Of The Only-By-Me Revealed and Given Seventh Stage Of Life In The Way Of The Heart, The By-Me-Avatarically-Self-Revealed "Brightness" Of The Heart, or Of Amrita Nadi, or Even Of The Circle (or The Arrow), Does Not Itself Depend Upon The Spontaneous or (Otherwise) Intentional Ascent Of My Avatarically Self-Transmitted Divine Spirit-Current Via The Spinal Line, or Any Other Spontaneous or (Otherwise) Intentional Exercise Of Spirit-"Conductivity" In The Circle (or The Arrow) Of the body-mind—Even Though Such Spontaneous or (Otherwise) Intentional Spirit-"Conductivity" Is Otherwise Freely Allowed (and Even Stimulated) By That Same "Brightness". Rather, In The Context Of The Only-By-Me Revealed and Given Seventh Stage Of

Life In The Way Of The Heart, The By-Me-Avatarically-Self-Revealed "Brightness" Of The Heart Itself Stands Radiant At The Root Of Amrita Nadi (and, Therefore, Non-Exclusively—or In and <u>As</u> Amrita Nadi), Such That It Is Not the body-mind (or My Avatarically Self-Transmitted Divine Spirit-Current In the body-mind) That Must Illuminate The Heart (or The By-Me-Avatarically-Self-Revealed Divine Self-Condition and Source-Condition), but The Heart Itself (Inherently and Always Already "Bright") Illumines All and all With Divine Love-Bliss. And Divine Translation (Which Is The Most Ultimate, or Final, Demonstration Of The Inherent Heart-Power Of Divine Conversion and Divine Dissolution) Is The Outshining Of all conditions (or All Of The Circle, The Arrow, and The Cosmic Domain) In The Infinite Feeling-Radiance (or Inherent Love-Bliss, or Native "Brightness") Of The Heart Itself (or Consciousness Itself, Realized <u>As</u> The By-Me-Avatarically-Self-Revealed Self-Existing, and Self-Radiant, and Perfectly Subjective, and Self-Evidently Divine Feeling Of Being Itself), Prior To (and Beyond) the body, the mind, The Circle, The Arrow, My (Apparently Objective) Divine Spiritual Body, My (Apparently Objective) Divine Star, My (Apparently Objective) Divine Sound, The Total Cosmic Mandala, The Sahasrar, Amrita Nadi (As An Apparent, or Apparently conditionally Manifested, Form and Locus), and The Specific and Total (Apparent, or Apparently conditionally Manifested) Form Of The Heart Itself (Left, Middle, and Right). Therefore, Even Though Divine Translation—As An Appearance To others, and (Also) As An Apparent Experiential Display Associated (In A Temporary, and Terminally "Dissolving", Manner) With the body-mind and The Cosmic Domain—May Also (Rightly, and Paradoxically) Be Described As The Divinely Most Perfect Heart-Magnification Of The Heart-Root Itself (and Of Amrita Nadi Itself), Divine Translation (In and Of Itself, or From The "Point Of View" Of <u>That</u> Which <u>Is</u> The Heart Itself) Is Only (and Entirely) The Divinely Most Perfect (and Perfectly Subjective) Magnification (or Divinely Most Perfectly Demonstrated Realization) Of <u>That</u> Which <u>Is</u> The Heart Itself (and <u>Which</u> <u>Is</u> Self-Existing and Self-Radiant Love-Bliss-Consciousness Itself).

The (By-Me-Avatarically-Self-Revealed) Transcendental, Inherently Spiritual, and Self-Evidently Divine Self (Which Is The Divine, or Perfectly Subjective, Subject-Condition Of the conditional self) Is Self-Existing. That Is To Say, It Merely Exists—or Simply, Always, and Already Is Being.

The (By-Me-Avatarically-Self-Revealed) Transcendental, Inherently Spiritual, and Self-Evidently Divine Self "Functions" As Consciousness. That Is To Say, Self-Existing Being Is Always Already Being Consciousness—and It Is Always Already Conscious Of (and As) Being (or Inherent Existence) Itself.

The (By-Me-Avatarically-Self-Revealed) Transcendental, Inherently Spiritual, and Self-Evidently Divine Self Identifies Itself As (or Tacitly, Intuitively, and Inherently Realizes Itself To Be) Inherent Happiness (or The Inherent Spiritual Condition That Is Self-Radiant Love-Bliss).

In The Context Of conditional forms or events, The (By-Me-Avatarically-Self-Revealed) Transcendental, Inherently Spiritual, and Self-Evidently Divine Self Exists As The Characteristic Of Existence Itself—and conditional forms or events Really Exist Only Because they arise (or Exist) In The By-Me-Avatarically-Self-Revealed Transcendental, Inherently Spiritual, and Self-Evidently Divine Self.

In The Context Of conditional forms or events, Transcendental, Inherently Spiritual, and Self-Evidently Divine Consciousness Functions (or Exists) As Itself and (Apparently) Via conditional Awareness, or psycho-physical attention (Indicated By The conventional "I"-Reference).

In The Context Of conditional forms or events, My (Avatarically Self-Transmitted) Self-Radiant (or Inherently Spiritual) and Self-Existing (or Transcendental) Divine Happiness (or "Bright" Love-Bliss) Is Established Inherently (Even Prior To all objects)—and, By The Spontaneous Process Of Self-Abiding Divine Self-Recognition, Transcendental, Inherently Spiritual, and Self-Evidently Divine Happiness Is Also Realized To Be The Real Substance and Condition Of every Apparent (or conditionally Manifested) being, thought, thing, or event.

Therefore, whatever (or whoever) Is Divinely Self-Recognized

In (and <u>As</u>) The (By-Me-Avatarically-Self-Revealed) Transcendental, Inherently Spiritual, and Self-Evidently Divine Self Is Divinely Transfigured and Divinely Transformed By The Inherent Radiance, or Self-Radiant Happiness, or Unqualified Love-Bliss Of The (By-Me-Avatarically-Self-Revealed) Transcendental, Inherently Spiritual, and Self-Evidently Divine Self.

In The Context Of The Only-By-Me Revealed and Given Seventh Stage Of Life In The Way Of The Heart, The (By-Me-Avatarically-Self-Revealed) Transcendental, Inherently Spiritual, and Self-Evidently Divine Self Stands (Apparently) In the field of all conditional relations. It Stands (Apparently) In The Free Relational Attitude (or, Rather, In The Native Feeling Of Perfectly Subjective Being, but Inherently Free Of The Motive Of Exclusion). And It Freely Notices (and Divinely Self-Recognizes) all (Apparently) arising conditions. It Notices and Divinely Self-Recognizes mind (or all thought-objects). It Notices and Divinely Self-Recognizes all conditional emotions. It Notices and Divinely Self-Recognizes all the moments (and all the actions) of the body. It Notices and Divinely Self-Recognizes all the relations or objects or states of mind, emotion, and body. It Notices and Divinely Self-Recognizes The Tendency To Seek. It Notices and Divinely Self-Recognizes The Tendency To Hold On (or To Be Attached) To conditions By Clinging Want. It Notices and Divinely Self-Recognizes The Tendency To Avoid or To (Strategically) Escape particular conditions (or any conditions at all). It Notices and Divinely Self-Recognizes The Feeling Of Relatedness (Itself). It Notices and Divinely Self-Recognizes The Tacit (and Simplest) conditional Feeling Of "Difference" (Itself). And whatever Is (Thus) Noticed and Divinely Self-Recognized Is Divinely Transfigured and Divinely Transformed In (and By) The Inherent (and Inherently Spiritual) Radiance, or Love-Bliss, or "Bright" Happiness Of The Self-Existing Consciousness That <u>Is</u> My Avatarically Self-Revealed Divine Person Of Being and My Transcendental, Inherently Spiritual (or "Bright"), and Self-Evidently Divine Domain Of Perfectly Subjective Being (Itself).

The Demonstrations Of Divine Transfiguration and Divine Transformation In The Only-By-Me Revealed and Given Seventh

Stage Of Life In The Way Of The Heart Are Shown Within The Context Of The conditionally Apparent Spirit-Current (or The Spirit-Current Appearing To Be Already Descended, or Previously and Presently Established, In The Descending and Ascending Context Of The Full Circle, and The Arrow, Of the body-mind).

The Sign (or Demonstration) Of Divine Indifference (In The Only-By-Me Revealed and Given Seventh Stage Of Life In The Way Of The Heart) Occurs When The Cosmically (or psycho-physically) Displayed Spirit-Energy (Both Descending and Ascending) Has Become Both Profoundly and Priorly Identified With The Form Of Amrita Nadi (and The Self-Existing and Self-Radiant Self-Condition, and Source-Condition, That <u>Is</u> The Heart Itself)—Such That The (Apparent) Play In The Context Of The Circle and The Arrow (or The Cosmic Mandala Itself) Is Only Minimally (or Less and Less) Perceived and (Therefore) Only Minimally (or Less and Less) Engaged.

And Divine Translation (or The Final Demonstration In The Only-By-Me Revealed and Given Seventh Stage Of Life In The Way Of The Heart) Is The Sign Of The Divinely Most Perfect Relinquishment (or The Divinely Most Perfect Transcending and Outshining) Of the conditional body-mind (and Of All Evidence Of The Circle and The Arrow Of the body-mind) and All Involvement With The Cosmic Domain (or The Total Context Of The Cosmic Mandala and Its Apparently Objective Matrix Of Sound and Light). Therefore, Divine Translation Is The Sign Of The Divinely Most Perfect Conversion and Dissolution Of all Apparent (or condition-ally Manifested) energies (and All conditional, or conditionally Manifested, appearances) Via Divine Self-Recognition—To The Degree That The Inherent (and Perfectly Subjective) Radiance Of My Avatarically Self-Revealed (Transcendental, Inherently Spiritual, and Self-Evidently Divine) Person Of Being Outshines Its Own Objective Appearances (and, Thus, Translates Its Own Illusions Into Its Own Self, or Perfectly Subjective Domain).

In The Only-By-Me Revealed and Given Way Of The Heart (or Way Of Adidam), The Seventh Stage Of Life, Like All Previous Stages Of Life, Is A Stage Of Practice (Become An Inherently Most Perfect Demonstration, In The Transition Into The Priorly

Enlightened Context Of The Seventh Stage Of Life). Therefore (In The Way Of The Heart), The Seventh Stage Of Life Is Not Merely What Is Mechanically "Left Over" After The Way Of The Heart (or Heart-Practice Itself) Is "Completed" (By Virtue Of The Seventh Stage Awakening, Itself). If The Way Of The Heart Is "Considered" In Its Fullest (or Most Complete) Sense, Then Entrance Into The Seventh Stage Of Life Is, Truly (or In Truth), The True (or Truly Divine) <u>Beginning</u> Of The Only-By-Me Revealed and Given Way Of The Heart (or Way Of Adidam). It Is The Beginning Of Divinely Enlightened, or Fully Awakened, or Fully Conscious "Practice" (or Inherently Most Perfect Demonstration) Of The Heart Itself.

In The Only-By-Me Revealed and Given Seventh Stage Of Life In The Way Of The Heart, The ego-Transcending Practice Of self-Enquiry (and Re-Cognition), or (Otherwise) Ruchira Avatara Mahamantra Meditation (or Even Any Form Of "True Prayer"), or Even "Feeling-Enquiry", Is Replaced (or Inherently, and Inherently Most Perfectly, Superseded) By The Priorly Self-Realized Condition Of Transcendental, Inherently Spiritual, and Most Perfect Divine Samadhi (or Inherent, and Inherently ego-Transcending, and Inherently Most Perfect Real-God-Realization)—but That Samadhi Is Itself A Kind Of "Practice", or An Inherent ("Natural", or Native) "Discipline", or (Rather) A Necessary (or Inherent, and Inherently Most Perfect) Demonstration, Wherein All Apparent (or objective) Modifications Are Progressively Made Radiant (or Are Released Into The Divine, or Perfectly Subjective, Self-Radiance), To The (Eventual) Most Ultimate Degree Of (Divinely Most Perfect) Cessation, or Outshining By (and In, and <u>As</u>) My (Avatarically Self-Revealed) Transcendental (and Inherently Spiritual, or "Bright") Fullness Of Divine (or Perfectly Subjective) Self-Existence.

In The Only-By-Me Revealed and Given Seventh Stage Of Life (In The Way Of The Heart), You (Fundamentally) No Longer Enquire Into the conditional self ("Avoiding Relationship?"), or Re-Cognize arising objects or states (or The Feeling Of Relatedness Itself) As self-Contraction (and Thereby Feel Beyond all self-Contraction), or Expand Beyond self-Contraction Via "True Prayer", or (Otherwise) Feel-Enquire Toward The Heart. The Seventh Stage "Practice" Of The Way Of The Heart Is (Simply,

Effortlessly, and Inherently, or Always Already) To Be The Native Condition (and Feeling) Of Self-Existing and Self-Radiant Being (Itself), or Feeling-Being-Consciousness Itself—In, Of, and As Whom (and Not Merely To Whom) all objects, all states, and Even The Feeling Of Relatedness Itself (or The Tacit conditional Feeling Of "Difference") Are arising, As Transparent (or Merely Apparent), and Un-Necessary, and Inherently Non-Binding Modifications Of Itself. Therefore, The Seventh Stage "Practice" Of The Way Of The Heart Is Simply To Be Thus—"Naturally" (or Natively and Effortlessly) Standing "Bright" As Amrita Nadi (or Unqualifiedly Radiant Self-Existence) In (and Also Most Prior To) The Right Side Of The Heart—Freely and Effortlessly Allowing Any and All Apparent Modifications To arise Spontaneously, While Not Seeking For Ultimate Satisfaction or Release, and While Not Assuming A Position Of Avoidance (or The Inability To Inspect and Transcend Apparently Negative Modifications), and While Not Assuming A Position Of Attachment (or The Inability To Inspect and Transcend Apparently Positive Modifications), and While Simply (or Merely) Inspecting, Divinely Self-Recognizing, and Inherently Transcending (or Freely Shining Beyond) Any Modifications That Apparently arise.

In The Only-By-Me Revealed and Given Seventh Stage Of Life In The Way Of The Heart, Allow and Observe Apparent conditional Modifications Of Native, Self-Existing, and Self-Radiant Consciousness (or Inherent, and Perfectly Subjective, Love-Bliss-Happiness) To arise, continue, change, and pass away. Rather Than Seeking The Ultimate (or Divine, and Perfectly Subjective) Source Of conditions (As If That Which Is Perfectly Subjective Is Separate From Your Self), and Rather Than Recoiling (or Withdrawing attention) From The Apparent (or Apparently Objective, and Even Ascended) Cosmic Source Of conditions, and Rather Than Withdrawing attention From conditions themselves (or Contracting Your body-mind, or Turning Back Upon Your body-mind, or Separating Your body-mind, or Even Excluding Your Very Self From Your body-mind)—Merely Be The One In Whom All Apparent conditional Modifications arise, continue, change, and pass away. Freely (and Inherently) Realize, and Feel, and Be That

In Which All Apparent conditional Modifications arise, continue, change, and pass away. Therefore, Notice and Divinely Self-Recognize all Apparent conditions (or all that arises, continues, changes, and passes away) In and As Your Very Self. Allow and Observe All Apparent conditional Modifications To arise, continue, change, and pass away In You, As You, While You Remain As Mere Consciousness, Self-Existing (Prior To the body-mind, and Prior To any thought or concept of "I"), Self-Radiant, All Love-Bliss-Light (Prior To any kind of conditional form or limitation), and Utterly Free. In This Same Manner, Freely Allow the body-mind To arise and To act, Spontaneously—Always (Spontaneously) Appropriate To the moment, Inevitably As Love, Inherently Without Illusions, and Necessarily Without self-Delusion. Be Thus—Inherently (and Divinely) Self-Recognizing (and, Thus, Inherently Transcending) all arising, continuing, changing, and passing objects, forms, conditions, states, and actions As Your Very Self. Shine Thus, Free As The Only One Who Is—Inherently Formless, Motivelessly (and Even Divinely) Indifferent, Inherently Happy, The Self-Fullness Of Love-Bliss—Until My Self-Existing Avataric Divine Self-Radiance Outshines All Noticing Of conditional events.

To Divinely Self-Recognize any conditionally Manifested being, object, state, place, or event Is To Shine—As The Self-Radiant (or Inherently Spiritual), and Self-Existing (or Transcendental), and Self-Evidently Divine Self-Being—On, In, As, and Through that conditionally Manifested being, object, state, place, or event.

To Divinely Self-Recognize Is To Shine (As Perfectly Subjective, or Conscious, Light) Until The Outshining (Of The conditional Display Of Apparent, or Objectified, Light Itself). To Divinely Self-Recognize Is To Be Unconditionally Self-Existing and Self-Radiant Being In The (Apparent) Context Of The Cosmic Mandala (or the conditional worlds)—Until all conditions (or all Apparent limits On The By-Me-Avatarically-Self-Revealed Inherent and "Bright" Spiritual Radiance Of Transcendental, or Self-Existing, Divine Being) Are Outshined By That By-Me-Avatarically-Self-Revealed Inherent Radiance (or "Brightness") Of Perfectly Subjective Being (Itself).

The "Natural" (or Sahaj) "Practice" (or Native Demonstration) Of Divine Self-Recognition (or Shining, To The Degree Of Outshining) Is Effortless (or Non-Strategic). It Is Not Itself Associated With Any Intentional Effort To Exclude conditional forms or events, Nor Is It Itself Associated With Any Intentional Effort To Include (or Hold On To) conditional forms or events. The "Natural" Disposition Is Simply and Effortlessly To Be— Standing Free, Freely Allowing whatever arises, Divinely Self-Recognizing whatever arises (If anything arises).

In The Only-By-Me Revealed and Given Seventh Stage Of Life In The Way Of The Heart, Simply (or Merely) Stand As Native (or Self-Existing and Self-Radiant) Consciousness (Realized As The Love-Bliss-Feeling Of Perfectly Subjective Being, Itself), Divinely Self-Recognizing (and Inherently Transcending) all conditional forms, events, and activities In (and As) Your Very Self (Which Is Transcendental, Inherently Spiritual, and Self-Evidently Divine Consciousness Itself). Instead Of Controlling, Avoiding, or Stopping (or Becoming Defined As Reaction To) conditional forms or events or activities, and Instead Of Seeking conditional forms or events or activities, or Clinging To conditional forms or events or activities, or Even Following After (or Becoming Defined As attention to) conditional forms or events or activities—Simply Allow conditional forms and events and activities (Even the forms, events, and activities of Your Own body-mind) To arise, continue, change, or pass away, as they will. Notice conditional forms and events and activities as they arise or continue or change or pass away, but Simply and Constantly and Merely Be (and Intuitively Identify Your Self As) The Self-Existing Consciousness and Self-Radiant Love-Bliss (or The Most Prior Feeling Of Perfectly Subjective Being) In, Of, and As Whom all conditional forms, events, and activities Are (Apparently) presently arising, continuing, changing, or passing away. Notice conditional forms, events, and activities, but Notice (and, Thus, Inherently Transcend) them In, Of, and As Your Very (and, Necessarily, Divine) Self—Which Is Self-Existing (or Transcendental) and Inherently Spiritual (or Self-Radiantly "Bright"), and Which Is (Itself) The Well (or The Deep and Deepless, or Incomparable and Non-"Different", Place)

Of Perfectly Subjective Being (In, and Always Already Prior To, The Right Side Of The Heart), and Which Is Always Already Infinitely Expanded and "Bright" (In The Form, or Fullness, That Is Amrita Nadi), Beyond (and Prior To) all conditions. Realize That You Are Always Already The Unconditional—and, Thus, Freely (and Inherently) Transcend The Implications (or The Apparent Binding Capability) Of conditional forms, events, and activities. Transcend The Chaotic Effort To Control, Avoid, Stop, Seek, Cling To, and Follow After (or All The Strategic Motives and Results Of the Apparent act of attention). Do This By The Power Of The Native Realization That There Is No Other, No Separateness, No Dependence, No Independence, and No Problem. Simply Stand and Be <u>Who</u> You <u>Are</u>, The Only One Who <u>Is</u>, Only Thus—<u>Being</u> Only You (Infinitely), Feeling Only You (Limitlessly), Divinely Self-Recognizing Even all conditionally Manifested beings, forms, events, and activities (Spontaneously)—Until The By-Me-Avatarically-Self-Revealed Inherent "Brightness" Of Self-Existing and Self-Radiant Love-Bliss Exceeds (or Outshines The Apparent Noticing Of) <u>all</u> conditional forms, events, and activities (Absolutely).

This Most Ultimate (and Only-By-Me Revealed and Given) "Practice" (or Seventh Stage Demonstration) Of The Way Of The Heart Is (Like Every Previous Developmental Stage Of Practice In The Way Of The Heart) To Be Realized (and Then Fully Demonstrated) By All The Means I Give (and Have Given) Within The Really Empowered Sphere and Culture Of My Community (or Total Gathering) Of Formally Acknowledged (and True) Devotees. Thus, Practitioners Of The Total (or Full and Complete) Practice Of The Way Of The Heart Are Called (and Expected) To "Practice" (or Freely Demonstrate) Even The "Discipline" (or Inherent Integrity) Of The Seventh Stage Of Life Within The Total Community Of Formally Acknowledged (and True) Practitioners Of The Total Practice Of The Way Of The Heart, and Most Especially Within The Cultural Gathering Of My (Formally Acknowledged) Fully Awakened (or Seventh Stage) Devotees.

Most Perfectly Real-God-Realized Devotees In The Seventh Stage Of Life In The Way Of The Heart Have Not Ceased To Be

My Devotees Because Of their Realization. Their Devotion To Me Has Only (By Means Of My Avatarically Self-Transmitted Divine Grace) Become Inherently Most Perfect, By Virtue Of their Realization Of My Avatarically Self-Revealed (and Self-Evidently Divine) Self-Condition. Therefore, they Continue To Demonstrate (and To Magnify) their Devotion (and their Devotional Recognition and Devotional Acknowledgement) Of My Avataric Bodily (Human) Divine Revelation-Form, and My Avataric Divine Spiritual Revelation-Presence (or Divine Spiritual Body), and My Avataric, and Very (and Inherently Perfect, and, To them, Inherently Most Perfectly Revealed), Divine State, and they Demonstrate (and Magnify) This Devotion To Me (and This Devotional Recognition and Devotional Acknowledgement Of Me) Both In The Naturally (and Maturely) human Manner and Through The Divine (and Inherently Most Perfect) Ordeal Of The Demonstration Of Divine Transfiguration, Divine Transformation, Divine Indifference, and Divine Translation.

In The Progressive Development Of The Only-By-Me Revealed and Given Way Of The Heart (or Way Of Adidam), Four Fundamental Forms Of <u>Devotional</u> Practice Are (Progressively) To Be Realized and Applied.

The First Of These Four Fundamental Forms Of Devotional Practice Is Meditation—Based Upon Devotional Invocation Of Me, and Right Feeling-Contemplation Of My Avatarically-Born Bodily (Human) Divine Form, and My Avatarically Self-Revealed Spiritual (and Always Blessing) Divine Presence, and My Avatarically Self-Revealed (and Very, and Transcendental, and Perfectly Subjective, and Inherently Spiritual, and Inherently egoless, and Inherently Perfect, and Self-Evidently Divine) State—and Meditation (Thus Devotionally Based, and Developed, In One or Another Form, According To My Avataric Divine Instructions, As Given, By Me, In *The Dawn Horse Testament*) Is To Be Continued (and Progressively Intensified, By Stages), Until (In The Context Of The Seventh Stage Of Life) It Is Inherently (and Inherently Most Perfectly) Fulfilled In The Native "Practice" (or The Inherently Most Perfect and Inherently Most Perfectly Free Demonstration) That <u>Is</u> Self-Abiding Divine Self-Recognition.

The Second Of These Four Fundamental Forms Of Devotional Practice Is Study—or Devotionally Responsive Application Of attention To The Divine Word Of My Avatarically Self-Revealed Arguments and Instructions, and The Divine Lessons Of My Avatarically Self-Manifested Demonstrations.

The Third Of These Four Fundamental Forms Of Devotional Practice Is functional and practical self-Discipline—or The True Sila and daily Balance To Which the body-mind Must (In Devotionally To-Me-Responsive Accordance With My Avatarically Self-Revealed Arguments and Instructions) Be (Progressively, and Then Totally and Consistently, and, At Last, Most Profoundly and Most Perfectly) Conformed.

And The Fourth Of These Four Fundamental Forms Of Devotional Practice Is relational self-Discipline—or The Progressive Incarnation Of ego-Transcending Love (In all relationships), Beginning With (and Always Founded Upon) The Great and Tradition-Honored and <u>Constantly</u> To Be Demonstrated Devotional and Service Relationship To Me, The Divine Heart-Master, and This Expressed Through All Kinds Of Service, Including Service In Cooperative (and Formal Community) Association (or Affiliation) With Other (and Even All Other) Practitioners Of The Total Practice Of The Only-By-Me Revealed and Given Way Of The Heart, and Including Sacred (or Sacramental, Ceremonial, and General Cultural) Activities, and (Eventually) All The Kinds Of Spiritual Activities (All Of Which Kinds Of Service and Activity Are, Because They Radiate Love, Ultimately Of Benefit To all conditionally Manifested beings).

In The Context Of The Only-By-Me Revealed and Given Seventh Stage Of Life In The Way Of The Heart, These Four Fundamental Forms Of Devotional Practice Are Given Their Most Ultimate (or Inherently Most Perfect) Expression and Demonstration.

"Meditation" In The Only-By-Me Revealed and Given Seventh Stage Of Life In The Way Of The Heart Has Become Seventh Stage Sahaj Samadhi, or Self-Abiding (and Unqualifiedly Self-Radiant) Divine (or Perfectly Subjective) Self-Recognition Of all and All That (conditionally) arises. And This "Practice" (or Primary Disposition) Is The Technical Basis For The Entire Demonstration Of The Seventh Stage Of Life In The Way Of The Heart.

"Study" In The Only-By-Me Revealed and Given Seventh Stage Of Life In The Way Of The Heart Becomes The Divinely Self-Realized "Consideration" Of My Special Wisdom-Teaching Relative To (and My Unique and Avatarically Self-Revealing Divine Demonstration Of) The Unique ("Difference"-Transcending) Disposition, The Unique Siddhi (or, Progressively, Divinely Transfiguring, Divinely Transformative, Divinely Indifferent, and, Most Ultimately, Divinely Translating, or Divinely Outshining, Power), and The Unique (and Total) Demonstration-Cycle Of The Seventh Stage Of Life. Such "Study" Also Involves Direct Participation In The Avataric Play Of My Eternal Divine Blessing-Work Among My Listening Devotees, My Hearing Devotees, and My Seeing Devotees. And, In All Cases, Such Direct (Seventh Stage) Participation Is A Matter Of Spontaneously "Resonating" With My Own Avataric Divine Blessing-Act Of The Heart, and Joyfully Regarding The Details Of My Unique Avataric Divine Play That Could Not Be Fully Understood (or Even Be Observed) Before The Seventh Stage Awakening.

"Functional Discipline" In The Only-By-Me Revealed and Given Seventh Stage Of Life In The Way Of The Heart Is (Fundamental) "Crazy Freedom", or The Spontaneous, Effortless, and Inherently "Non-Disciplined Discipline" (or The Truly and Most Profoundly, and Yet Entirely Freely, and Most Perfectly, Conservative Sila, or psycho-physical Equanimity) Of Conformity To My Avatarically Self-Transmitted Divine Love-Bliss In The Whole (and every part) Of the body-mind. Through The Expansive Release Of My Self-Radiant Love-Bliss-Power In (and By Means Of) Self-Abiding Divine Self-Recognition (In The Context Of The Seventh Stage Of Life In The Way Of The Heart), the body-mind Has Become Divinely Spiritualized (or Realized To Be Inherently and Only Of The Transcendental, Inherently Spiritual, and Self-Evidently Divine Reality)—and (Thus) the body-mind Has Become Divinely Self-Recognizable As Only My Avatarically Self-Transmitted Divine Love-Bliss. And, As The Inherently Free "Practice" (or The Inherently Most Perfect Demonstration) That Is Divine Self-Recognition Magnifies The Manifestation Of My Avatarically Self-Transmitted Divine Love-

Bliss In The Context Of The Circle (or Even The Arrow) Of the (Truly, and Most Profoundly, and Spontaneously, and Always Freely, and Most Perfectly, Conservatively Disciplined) body-mind, the body-mind Becomes More and More Full (Divinely Transfigured and Divinely Transformed By My Avatarically Self-Transmitted Divine Love-Bliss). Thus, the ordinary body-mind Becomes the Spiritualized (or, Really, Divinized) body-mind, By Incarnating (or, Really, By Conforming To, and Dissolving Into) The Self-Existing and Self-Radiant Divine Self-Condition and Source-Condition Revealed By (and <u>As</u>) Me.

"Relational Discipline" In The Only-By-Me Revealed and Given Seventh Stage Of Life In The Way Of The Heart Is Unconditional Love (or Inherently Most Perfect Devotional Realization) Of Me, and (By This), Also, Inherent and Freely Demonstrated Realization Of Unconditional Love Of <u>all</u> conditionally Manifested beings (or Unobstructed Radiation Of My Avatarically Self-Transmitted Divine Love-Bliss In all Apparent relations). That Inherently Most Perfect Devotional Realization and Expressive Demonstration Of Love Is Unconditional Relatedness, or Relationship Without "Difference" (or self-Separation)— Although It Does Not Disregard (or Fail To Honor, By Expressive Devotion) The Great (Apparent) Functional Distinction (here) Between My Devotee and Me, and The Great (Apparent) Functional Distinction (here) Between this world (or Even The Cosmic Mandala As A Whole) and My Transcendental, Inherently Spiritual, and Self-Evidently Divine Self-Domain (or Self-Radiant and "Bright" Divine Self-Existence, Always Already Most Prior To conditional Existence In The Context Of The Cosmic Mandala).

"Divine Transfiguration" and "Divine Transformation" Are Terms I Use To Indicate The Possible Early (and Progressive) Effects Of The By-Me-Avatarically-Self-Revealed Self-Existing Divine Self-Radiance That May Be Demonstrated In the body-mind and the psycho-physical activities Of My Any Devotee Truly Awakened To Divine Self-Realization (In The Seventh Stage Of Life In The Way Of The Heart).

My Any Such Divinely Awakened, or Literally (Even bodily) En-Light-ened, Devotee May Progressively Demonstrate An Even

Visible (or body-Transfiguring) Self-Radiance—but All Such Devotees Must Certainly (Inherently and Constantly) Demonstrate Unique personal Signs Of An Infusion Of My Avatarically Self-Transmitted Divine Love-Bliss.

The Apparent actions Of My Any Such Divinely Enlightened Devotee, Whatever ordinary or extraordinary form his or her (Always Love-Full) actions May Apparently Take, Are (At Heart) Always An Effective Continuation (or Distribution) Of My Own Avataric Divine Blessing-Regard, or My Own Spontaneous Avataric Divine Heart-Transmission Of Love-Bliss (and Of All My Divinely Perfect Heart-Power That Would Awaken Every Heart), Spontaneously Given To others and To the Total world. And, As This Divinely Transfiguring Infusion Progresses, Various Kinds (or Divine Signs) Of psycho-physical Transformation May Appear.

Those Possible Signs Of Divine Enlightenment Are All Simply Magnifications Of My Self-Existing Divine Self-Radiance (or "Bright" Divine Love-Bliss), Such That the body-mind Of My Divinely Enlightened Devotee-Realizer Is "Intoxicated" and Sublimed, and Often (Perhaps) Invested With Remarkable Spirit-Power To heal (or Even To Sublime) others, or (Spontaneously, or By Even The Simplest Intention) To Release obstacles From the world and From the lives of others.

And My Any Such Divinely Transfigured, Divinely Transformed, and (Divinely) other-Transforming Devotee May (Perhaps) Also Enjoy The Heart-Power To Spontaneously Rejuvenate (or To Allow The Spontaneous "Bright" Rejuvenation Of) his or her own body, Even To The Extent Of Remarkable bodily longevity (Although It Is Just As Likely That Such A Devotee-Realizer May Exhibit Great Apparent Vulnerability, and Little Effective Heart-Power, or Heart-Intention, To Serve his or her own Apparent bodily conditions).

Therefore, Many Signs Of My Self-Existing and Self-Radiant Avataric Divine Power May Appear In My Divinely Enlightened Devotee. And It Is Not Necessary (or Even Possible) To Enumerate Those Signs (Both Ordinary and Marvelous) Any More Than It Is Appropriate To Seek To Achieve Them. In Any Case, Whatever Such Signs Do Spontaneously Appear, They Are Simply To Be

Divinely Self-Recognized (and Inherently Transcended) In The (By-Me-Avatarically-Self-Revealed) Self-Existing and Self-Radiant Divine Self-Condition, and Source-Condition, and Inherent Feeling, Of Being (Itself), or Of Perfectly Subjective Love-Bliss (Itself).

Thus (and, Potentially, Through Many Divine Signs), My Any and Every Divinely Enlightened Devotee Will (and Must) Be Heart-Made To Serve—and Then True and Love-Blissful Divine Indifference (or Love-Bliss Itself) Will Gradually Replace The Theatre Of Service, and The By-Me-Avatarically-Self-Revealed Ultimate Shine Of Divine Being Will Relax The Demonstrative Signs Of Life.

In The Only-By-Me Revealed and Given Seventh Stage Of Life In The Way Of The Heart, The Most Ultimate (and Inherently Most Perfect) Significance Of The (Possible) Perception Of Me As My Divine Sound and My Divine Star Is Inherently Obvious and Clear. My Divine Sound and My Divine Star Are Always (Each) Standing As An (Apparently) Objective and (Apparently) Perceptible Form (Either Audible Or Visible) In The Center Of The (psycho-physical) Sky Of each and all of the conditional psycho-physical worlds (Although Neither My Apparently Objective Divine Sound Nor My Apparently Objective Divine Star Will Necessarily Be Perceived, Even By My Divinely Enlightened Devotee). My Apparently Objective Divine Sound Is Not merely a gross physical sound, To Be perceived in the gross physical space occupied by the gross physical body (and by the merely physical ears), and My Apparently Objective Divine Star Is Not merely a physical star, To Be perceived in the gross sky (and by the merely physical eyes). My Divine Sound and My Divine Star May (Possibly) Be Perceived (Apparently Objectively) In any world or plane Of The Cosmic Mandala, but My Divine Sound Can Be Perceived Only By The True Ear, The Single Hearing-Organ That Combines (or Unifies) the physical and the mental (or psychic), and My Divine Star-Form Can Be Perceived Only By The Whole Eye, The Single Eye That Combines (or Unifies) the physical and the mental (or psychic). Indeed, Fullest Devotional Recognition and True Realization Of Me In Any Of My Spiritual, Transcendental, or Divine Forms Requires True Hearing Of Me and True Seeing Of Me, and (Thus) The Unification Of body and mind In The Hearing-Vision (or

Intuition) That Only The (Progressively) Awakened Heart Allows. Likewise, Even Though My Avatarically-Born Bodily (Human) Divine Form May (Itself) Be grossly (and even casually) Perceived, My Divine Spiritual Body Of "Brightness" Cannot Be "Located" and Devotionally Recognized (and, Thus, Realized Through Right, True, and Full Devotion) Until The Heart Awakens and Grants The Devotional Recognition Of My Avatarically Self-Revealed, and Inherently "Bright", and All-and-all-Surrounding, and All-and-all-Pervading, and Self-Evidently Divine Person. Likewise, My (Apparently) Objective Divine Sound and Divine Star Can Be Perceived Only With The Third Eye (or Ajna Chakra), and My (Apparently) Objective Divine Sound and Divine Star Can Be Divinely Self-Recognized (In The By-Me-Avatarically-Self-Revealed Divine Self-Condition, and Source-Condition, Itself, or The "Bright" Heart Itself, or My Divine Self-Domain Itself) Only From The Perfectly Subjective Position Of The Great Heart (In The Fully Awakened Condition Of Transcendental, Inherently Spiritual, and Most Perfect Divine Self-Realization). Therefore, Even Though My Divine Sound and My Divine Star May (Apparently) Be Perceived Objectively In Various Levels Of Vision Previous To Devotional Recognition and Devotional Realization Of Me As The Transcendental, Inherently Spiritual (or Inherently "Bright"), and Self-Evidently Divine Self, and Even Though My "Bright" Divine Spiritual Body May (By Means Of My Avatarically Self-Transmitted Divine Grace) Be Intuitively (and Objectively) Experienced Previous To Transcendental, and Inherently Spiritual, and Self-Evidently Divine Self-Awakening, I Cannot Be Inherently, and Inherently Most Perfectly, and Perfectly Subjectively Realized As The "Bright" Itself (or The Inherent, and Inherently Perfect, and Perfectly Subjective Divine Identity and Condition Of My Divine Sound, My Divine Star, and My Divine Spiritual Body) Before Transcendental, Inherently Spiritual, and Self-Evidently Divine Self-Realization.

In The Only-By-Me Revealed and Given Way Of The Heart (or Way Of Adidam), True Devotional Recognition Of Me In My Avatarically-Born Bodily (Human) Divine Form Begins (and Is The Beginning Of) The Devotionally To-Me-Responsive Devotional Process That Is The Context (and The Essential Principle) Of The

Only-By-Me Revealed and Given Way Of The Heart—and It Is <u>Only</u> In That Context (and On The Basis Of That Essential Principle) That I Am Eventually (In That Devotional Process, and Only and Entirely By Means Of My Avatarically Self-Transmitted Divine Grace) "Located" (or Devotionally Recognized, and, Then, Devotionally Realized) In My (Avatarically Self-Revealed) Spiritual, Transcendental, and Divine Forms. Therefore, My (Avatarically Self-Revealed) Bodily (Human), Spiritual, Transcendental, and Divine Forms (or Self-Revelations <u>As</u> The Divine Person—or The Inherently egoless, and Self-Evidently Divine, Self-Condition, Which <u>Is</u> The Source-Condition Of All and all) Are Presented (Originally and Always) To Attract My Devotee—but That Attraction Is For The Sake Of Most Perfectly ego-Transcending Realization Of My Avatarically Self-Revealed Transcendental, Inherently Spiritual, and Self-Evidently Divine Self-Condition. Thus, The "Locating" (or Devotional Recognition and Devotional Realization) Of Me Is Not Inherently Most Perfectly Full (or Most Ultimately Fulfilled) Until Such (Divinely Most Perfect) Realization.

True (and Truly Devotionally Responsive) Devotional Recognition Of Me Is Not Able To Advance Beyond The Beginnings Of The Only-By-Me Revealed and Given Way Of The Heart Until (By Means Of My Avatarically Self-Transmitted Divine Grace) My Listening Devotee (Awakened, By My Avatarically Given Divine Word, My Avatarically Self-Manifested Divine Leelas, and My Avatarically Self-Revealed Divine Sign, To The Real Process Of self-Observation) Hears Me and (By The Means Of That Realization Of Most Fundamental self-Understanding) Out-Grows The Confinement (By Tendency) To the egoic limits Of The First Three Stages Of Life, Such That The Original (and Primary) Impulse Toward Most Perfectly ego-Transcending Real-God-Realization Can (Thereafter) Be Really (Directly and Comprehensively) Satisfied At Heart.

True (and Truly Devotionally Responsive) Devotional Recognition Of Me Is Not Able To Progress (Beyond Listening To Me and Hearing Of Me) To (and Through) The Advanced and The Ultimate Stages Of Life and Practice In The Only-By-Me Revealed and Given Way Of The Heart Until (By Means Of My Avatarically

Self-Transmitted Divine Grace) My Devotee Sees Me (and, Thus, "Locates" My Divine Spiritual Body and Person), and Is (Thus and Thereby) Fully Moved and Infused, Via My Avataric Divine Spirit-Baptism (Perhaps Even Through To The Culmination Of The Ascending Process In Fifth Stage conditional Nirvikalpa Samadhi), and Is Otherwise Advanced (By Means Of My Avatarically Self-Transmitted Divine Grace) To Stable Awakening To The Witness-Position Of Consciousness and To The Inherently Spiritual Process Associated With The Right Side Of The Heart.

True (and Truly Devotionally Responsive) Devotional Recognition Of Me Is Not Perfect (and, At Last, Most Perfect) Until (By Means Of My Avatarically Self-Transmitted Divine Grace) There Is Realization Of My Avatarically Self-Revealed (and Very, and Transcendental, and Perfectly Subjective, and Inherently Spiritual, and Inherently egoless, and Inherently Perfect, and Self-Evidently Divine) State (Which Is The Transcendental, Inherently Spiritual, and Self-Evidently Divine Self-Condition, and Source-Condition, Of All and all). And Such (Inherently Perfect) Realization Of Me Is Not At Last (or Inherently Most Perfectly) Full (or Most Ultimately Fulfilled) Until (By Means Of My Avatarically Self-Transmitted Divine Grace) My Devotee Realizes The By-Me-Avatarically-Self-Revealed Truly (and Self-Evidently) Divine Condition Of The Transcendental (and Inherently Spiritual) Self-Condition (and Source-Condition) Of All and all—and This In Seventh Stage Sahaj Samadhi (or "Open Eyes"), Wherein Even The psycho-physical Root-Heart-Reference Is Transcended In Self-Existing and Self-Radiant Being, Which Is Inherently Beyond (or Most Prior To), and Not Separate (or "Different") From, but Inherently and Most Perfectly (and, Therefore, Divinely) Self-Recognizing, and (Ultimately) Outshining, All References To the body-mind, or To the waking state, or To the dreaming state, or To the deep sleep state, or To Even any objective (or conditional) state, form, condition, or world.

Just So, The Final Stage Of True (and Truly Devotionally Responsive) Devotional Recognition (and Of Inherently Most Perfect Realization) Of Me Is Not Finally (and Divinely Most Perfectly) Fulfilled Until (By Means Of My Avatarically Self-

Transmitted Divine Grace) There Is The Demonstration Of Divine Translation—Beyond My Apparently Objective Divine Spiritual Body, and My Apparently Objective Divine Star, and My Apparently Objective Divine Sound, and Outshining <u>All</u> Of The Cosmic Domain, Releasing and Transcending <u>all</u> Apparent conditional forms (or Even <u>All</u> Possible Modifications) To The Degree Of Divinely Most Perfectly Demonstrated Self-Radiance and Divinely Most Perfectly Demonstrated Establishment In My Inherently Perfectly Subjective Divine Self-Domain.

Therefore, The Only-By-Me Revealed and Given Seventh Stage Of Life In The Way Of The Heart Is, Fundamentally, The Only-By-My-Avataric-Divine-Grace Revealed and Given Process Of Self-Abiding Divine Self-Recognition Of The Total (and Merely Apparent) Cosmic Domain—Including All conditional Modifications, and My Divine Spiritual Body (or The Apparently Objectively Manifested Divine Spirit-Presence Itself), and My Divine Star (or The Apparently Objectively Manifested Divine Source-Light Itself), and My Divine Sound (or The Apparently Objectively Manifested Divine Source-Vibration Itself)—In My Avatarically Self-Revealed (and Self-Existing, and Self-Radiant) Divine Love-Bliss Itself (Which <u>Is</u> The "Bright" Itself, The By-Me-Avatarically-Self-Revealed Perfectly Subjective Source-Feeling Of Merely Being—In, and Also Most Prior To, The Right Side Of The Heart). This Most Ultimate Process (or Inherently Most Perfect Demonstration) Is (Constantly) Founded On My Devotee's Previous, and Always Present, and True (and Truly Devotionally Responsive) Devotional Recognition and Devotional Realization Of Me, As I Am Avatarically Self-Revealed Via My Ever-Speaking (and Always Me-Revealing) Divine Word, and Via My Ever-Living (and Always Me-Revealing) Divine Leelas Of The Proving Demonstration Of My Physically Manifested Bodily (Human) Life, and Via The Direct and Constant Self-Revelation That Is My Own (Now, and Forever Hereafter, Avatarically Given) Bodily (Human) Divine Form (Even As My Avatarically-Born Bodily Human Divine Form Is Remembered, or Represented, or Even En-Visioned, In every then present-time—After, and Forever After, The Physical Lifetime Of My Avatarically-Born Bodily Human Divine Form), and Via The Direct and

Constant Self-Revelation That Is My (Now, and Forever Hereafter, Avatarically Self-Transmitted) Divine Body Of Spiritual (and Always Blessing) Presence and My (Now, and Forever Hereafter, Avatarically Self-Revealed) Very (and Transcendental, and Perfectly Subjective, and Inherently Spiritual, and Inherently egoless, and Inherently Perfect, and Self-Evidently Divine) State (Even, Also, As My Avatarically Self-Transmitted Divine Body Of Spiritual, and Always Blessing, Presence and My Avatarically Self-Revealed, and Very, and Transcendental, and Perfectly Subjective, and Inherently Spiritual, and Inherently egoless, and Inherently Perfect, and Self-Evidently Divine State Are Revealed, In every then present-time—After, and Forever After, The Physical Lifetime Of My Avatarically-Born Bodily Human Divine Form—Via My Formally Acknowledged "Living Murtis"). Therefore, This Most Ultimate Process (or Inherently Most Perfect Demonstration) Is (Constantly) Founded On My Devotee's Previous, and Always Present, and True (and Truly Devotionally Responsive) Devotional Recognition and Devotional Realization Of Me, Directly Revealed By (and As) My Avatarically-Born Bodily (Human) Divine Form, My Avatarically Self-Transmitted Divine Body Of Spiritual (and Always Blessing) Presence, and My Avatarically Self-Revealed (and Very, and Transcendental, and Perfectly Subjective, and Inherently Spiritual, and Inherently egoless, and Inherently Perfect, and Self-Evidently Divine) State, and (Most Ultimately) To Be Realized To Be The Avatarically Self-Revealed Divine Spirit-Presence (or The Perfectly Subjective "Brightness" That Is Self-Radiant and Self-Evident As The Root-Substance Of all Apparent forms) and The Avatarically Self-Revealed Transcendental Divine Self (or Very, and Inherently Perfect, Being, Itself, and Very, and Inherently Perfect, Consciousness, Itself—Which Is, Necessarily, The One and Ever-Same Being and Consciousness That Is Self-Existing As Consciousness In The Case Of all Apparent selves).

The Apparent Process (or Apparently Progressive Demonstration) Of The Only-By-Me Revealed and Given Seventh Stage Of Life In The Way Of The Heart Is Always Already A Matter Of Transcendental, Inherently Spiritual, and Most Perfect Divine Self-Abiding, Inherently Realizing The "Bright" Itself—Which Is The By-Me-Avatarically-

Self-Revealed Divine (or Perfectly Subjective) Source (or Inherent Love-Bliss-Essence) Of The Cosmic Mandala (and, Thus, Of All Apparent conditional, or phenomenal, Modifications Of Perfectly Subjective, and Self-Existing, and Self-Radiant, and, Therefore, or Self-Evidently, Divine Being).

In The First Three Phases Of The Only-By-Me Revealed and Given Seventh Stage Of Life In The Way Of The Heart (or The Demonstrations Of Divine Transfiguration, Divine Transformation, and Divine Indifference), The By-Me-Avatarically-Self-Revealed (Very) Divine Self-Condition and Source-Condition (Apparently conditionally and Objectively Manifested) May (Possibly) Be Perceived In The Objectively Audible Sound-Form and/or The Objectively Visible Star-Form—and Even If The (Very) Divine Self-Condition and Source-Condition Is Perceived (Thus conditionally) In The Objectively Audible Sound-Form and/or The Objectively Visible Star-Form, Such Perception Will Likely Occur Only Occasionally (or In Random moments, Whether In The Apparent Context Of the waking state Or In The Apparent Context Of the dreaming state). At all other times (Except In The Apparent Context Of deep sleep, Wherein no objective states Appear To arise To or In The Transcendental, Inherently Spiritual, and Self-Evidently Divine Self), The By-Me-Avatarically-Self-Revealed (Very) Divine Self-Condition and Source-Condition Will Simply Be Felt (or Perfectly Subjectively Realized) As Amrita Nadi, The Inherently "Bright" Self-Form Of Real God, The Divine Self-Form Of Love-Bliss, Standing In The Right Side Of The Heart and Extending To A Point Infinitely Above The Total Crown Of the head. Thus, Even When The (Apparently Objective) Divine Star Is Not Perceived, The "Brightness" Of The (Very) Divine Self-Condition and Source-Condition May Be Felt In The Source-Point Of The Heart (On The Right Side) and, Radiating From There, To and Into and <u>As</u> The Central Point (or Core) Of The Matrix Of Divine Love-Bliss Above The Total Crown Of the head. And My Awakened Devotee In The Seventh Stage Of Life In The Way Of The Heart Will "Practice" (or Freely Demonstrate) Fullest Devotion To (and Inherently Most Perfect Devotional Identification With) Me By Divinely Self-Recognizing all conditional forms and events (and

Even The Possibly Perceived and Apparently Objective Divine Sound-Form and The Possibly Perceived and Apparently Objective Divine Star-Form) As Merely Apparent Modifications Of The By-Me-Avatarically-Self-Revealed "Bright" Self-Radiance (or Inherent and Self-Radiant Love-Bliss) Of Divine Self-Existence. This Divine and Self-Abiding Self-Recognition Not Only (Potentially) Divinely Transfigures and Divinely Transforms the body-mind, but It, Perhaps Gradually (but Not Strategically, and Not By Means Of A Process Of Exclusion, but Only By Virtue Of Divinely Self-Abiding Self-Recognition Itself), Releases The By-Me-Avatarically-Self-Revealed Self-Radiant Spirit-Energy (and The By-Me-Avatarically-Self-Revealed Native, or Inherent, Love-Bliss-Feeling Of Being) Even From The Context Of the Divinely Spiritualized body-mind and The Cosmic Mandala. Thus, As The Demonstration Of That Seventh Stage Devotion To Me Progresses, The Sign Of Divine Indifference Gradually or Eventually (or Even Quickly) Appears, and My Divinely Enlightened Devotee Realizes A Motiveless (or Non-Strategic) Disposition Of Mere Self-Radiance (or "Bright" Self-Abiding <u>As</u> The By-Me-Avatarically-Self-Revealed Perfectly Subjective Source-Condition Of Cosmic Existence). Therefore, In The Great Event Of Divine Translation (Which Necessarily Coincides With the death, or Natural dissolution, of the Apparent gross physical personality, and every subtle form of the Apparent psycho-physical personality, and the causal depth of the Apparent psycho-physical personality), The (Apparently Objective) Divine Sound May (Very Possibly) Be Heard, Steadily and Most Resonantly, and The (Apparently Objective) Divine Star May (Very Possibly) Be Seen, Steadily and Most Brilliantly. Then, In The Most Ultimate Moment Of Divine Self-Recognition (Even Of The Apparently Objective Divine Sound and The Apparently Objective Divine Star), The Cosmic Mandala and Every Trace Of the conditional personality Will Dissolve In The Inherent (and Perfectly Subjective) Feeling-"Brightness" Of My Avatarically Self-Revealed (and Self-Evidently Divine) Self-Condition (Which <u>Is</u> The Self-Evidently Divine Source-Condition Of All and all).

In The Only-By-Me Revealed and Given Way Of The Heart (or Way Of Adidam), The Great Event Of Divine Translation Is The

Event Of Ultimate Devotional (or ego-Transcending) "Location", Recognition, and Realization Of Me. By Means Of That Great Event, Existence Is Transferred To My Divine Self-Domain, Which Is Eternally Prior To The Cosmic Domain.

My Divine Self-Domain Is Not A "Point" In The conditional (or Cosmic) Domain, Nor Is It A "Point" On The "Other Side" Of The conditional (or Cosmic) Domain.

My Divine Self-Domain Is "Turiyatita", or <u>Beyond</u> Beyond.

There Is Not <u>Anything</u> That Exists Apart From (or Even Merely "Within") My "Bright" Divine Person and Self-Domain.

Whatever (Paradoxically) Appears To Exist Separately (or Merely As it Appears) <u>Is</u> (Simply) My Divine Self-Domain, and whatever (Paradoxically) Appears To Exist conditionally Must (In The Only-By-Me Revealed and Given Seventh Stage Of Life) Be Divinely Self-Recognized (In and <u>As</u> My "Bright" Divine Person and Self-Domain).

Only In That Case, conditional Existence <u>Is</u> (Inherently, Most Perfectly, and Perfectly Subjectively) Transcended (Rather Than Tacitly Allowed To Make, or Reinforce, Illusion and Bondage).

My Divine Self-Domain Is Not A Condition From Which any one (or any conditionally Manifested being) Returns.

Divine Translation Is Not A Process By Which any one (or any conditionally Manifested being) Leaves.

Divine Translation Is Not An Historical (or personal, or Objective, or Concrete) Event (or Moment) Within The Cosmic Domain.

Divine Translation Is The Most Ultimate Perfectly Subjective Event Within The By-Me-Avatarically-Self-Revealed Divine Self-Consciousness Itself.

My Divine Self-Domain Is Not "here".

My Divine Self-Domain Is Not "Elsewhere".

My Divine Self-Domain Is The Perfectly Subjective Source-Position (or Real Condition) Of The Cosmic Domain.

Divine Translation Is Not The Destruction (or Mere Ending) Of The Cosmic Domain.

Divine Translation Is Not An Escape From The Cosmic Domain.

Divine Translation Is A "Bright" Demonstration In The By-Me-Avatarically-Self-Revealed Divine Self-Consciousness, Which <u>Is</u>

The Perfectly Subjective Source-Position (or Real Condition) Of The Cosmic Domain.

Divine Translation Is The Perfectly Subjective Outshining Of The Cosmic Domain By Me—The Avatarically Self-Revealed (and Self-Evidently Divine) Person (Who Is The Self-Evidently Divine Self-Condition, and Source-Condition, Of all and All).

There Is No Coming To, or Going From, My Divine Self-Domain.

There Is Only My Divine Self-Domain.

I (The Avatarically Self-Revealed Transcendental, Inherently Spiritual, and Self-Evidently Divine Person Of Being) Am The Divine Self-Domain.

Self-Existing and Self-Radiant Reality (or Being) Itself Is The Only Domain That Is.

I Am Divine Translation.

I Am The Divine Self-Domain.

I Am The "Bright".

I Am Infinitely Established and Eternal.

I Stand Prior To The Cosmic Domain.

The Cosmic Domain Is In Me.

During My Physical Lifetime, I Appear Within The Cosmic Domain As My Avatarically-Born Bodily (Human) Divine Form.

But I, Myself, Am Divine Translation Itself.

I Am The Process Of The Divine Translation Of every one.

My Divinely Translated Devotee Stands Undifferentiated In (and As) My Own Avatarically Self-Revealed Divine Person, An Infinite Participant In My Eternal Avataric Work Of Magnifying My Divine Self-"Brightness".

No Matter How Many Multitudes Of My Devotees Are Divinely Translated, There Will Always Only Be Me.

Indeed, All Of My Devotees Are Always Already One With Me In My Domain Of Perfect "Brightness".

My Magnification Of "Brightness" Will Continue Forever, Until There Is The Final (and Most Ultimate) Event Of The Divine Translation Of The Entire Cosmic Domain.

It Is Not Necessary For Me To Divinely Translate, Because I Always Already Am The Divine Self-Domain Itself.

I <u>Am</u> Always Already Divinely Translated.

I <u>Am</u> The One "Bright" Person, "Brightly" Revealing Myself.

In The Course Of The Only-By-Me Revealed and Given Way Of The Heart (or Way Of Adidam), Previous To The Great Event Of Divine Translation, The Maturing Devotee (At Even Any Stage Of Life In The Process Of The Way Of The Heart) May Enjoy Sufficient Release Of (Apparent) conditional energy and attention To Transfer the Apparent conditional personality To higher (or subtler) worlds Within The Apparently Objective (or Cosmic) Domain After death—but Translation Into My Divinely Perfect Domain (or Perfectly Subjective Divine Self-Domain) Is Possible Only On The Basis Of Inherently Most Perfect Real-God-Realization (or The Inherent, and Inherently Most Perfect, Transcending Of egoity, or self-Contraction, In Transcendental, Inherently Spiritual, and Self-Evidently Divine Self-Realization). And Translation Into My Divinely Perfect Domain (or Perfectly Subjective Divine Self-Domain) <u>Necessarily</u> Requires (or Is A Matter Of) Inherently Most Perfect Divine Self-Recognition and Release Of The Total Cosmic Domain—Which Is The Totality Of all Possible Apparent conditional energies or forms, Including My Apparently Objective Divine Sound and My Apparently Objective Divine Star, Which (If They Are Perceived) Are Themselves To Be Divinely Self-Recognized and Released In The (By-Me-Avatarically-Self-Revealed) "Bright" and Inherent (or Perfectly Subjective) Spirit-Radiance Of Transcendental (and, Thus, Self-Existing) Divine Being.

The Destiny, After death, Of the Apparent individual Is Determined By The Heart-Response (While alive, and In The Event Of death) To Me (The Avatarically Self-Revealed, and Self-Evidently Divine, Person—Who <u>Is</u> The Avatarically Self-Revealed, and Inherently Perfect, and Self-Evidently Divine Self-Condition, and Source-Condition, Of All and all), and Even To The By-Me-Avatarically-Self-Revealed Apparent White "Brightness" Of The Divine Reality (Which Is Nearly Always Revealed, At Least Temporarily) In The Event Of death. And The Heart-Response To My Avataric Divine Self-Revelation (Of The Divine Person and Reality) During The death-Process Is Generally Determined By

The Total Complex Of conditional Tendencies That Are Developed During life, or (Otherwise) By The Degree Of self-Transcendence Demonstrated During life.

Unless Divine Translation Occurs In The death-Process, the conditionally Manifested being Moves (After death), By Means Of his or her Tendencies, Into a form and a Cosmic plane that Are Structured (By The Cosmic Design Itself) To Satisfy Those Tendencies and Also (By Inherent Divine Grace) To Provide conditions For Further self-Transcendence (and Growth Into The By-Me-Avatarically-Self-Revealed Divine Self-Condition and Source-Condition).

Death Is Simply The Relinquishment Of Association With the present Cosmic plane, and the personal form in that plane—Just As birth Is The Initiation Of Association With plane and form. Birth Occurs When Particular conditional Tendencies Create The Opportunity For Association With particular conditions. Death Occurs, By The Intervention Of Structural Laws Of Cosmic Nature, When present conditions Are No Longer Sufficient For Basic Support Of the conditional life-functions.

Nevertheless, birth and death Are (Primarily and Necessarily) Associated With The Great Purpose Of self-Transcendence (and Growth Beyond conditional limits). Therefore, The Primary (or Great) Purpose Of birth, life, and death (If they arise) Is Transcendental, Inherently Spiritual, and Most Perfect Divine Self-Awakening (or Most Perfect Realization Of The "Bright"), Which Realization Progressively Demonstrates Itself As Divine Transfiguration, Divine Transformation, Divine Indifference, and (Finally) Divine Translation (or The Outshining Of The Apparent Objective, or Cosmic, Domain By and In My Perfectly Subjective and Perfectly Divine Self-Domain).

To Serve This Great Purpose, I Am (Now, and Forever Hereafter) Always Already Present As Three Primary Forms. I Am Always Already Present As The Avatarically Self-Revealed Transcendental Divine Self (Of Love-Bliss), The Avatarically Self-Transmitted All-Pervading Divine Spirit-Current (or Divine Spiritual Body Of "Bright" Love-Bliss), and The Avatarically Self-Manifested (Apparently Objective) Divine Sound and Divine Star

(Which Point To, or Reveal, The "Bright", or Love-Bliss Itself). I Am Always Already Present (In These Three Primary Forms)—In (and <u>As</u>) every conditional form, In (and <u>As</u>) all conditionally Manifested beings, and In (and <u>As</u>) all Cosmic planes—In Order To Serve The Great Purpose.

Until Divine Translation (or The "Bright" Outshining), every conditionally Manifested being Survives bodily death and Continues To experience (and, Potentially, To Grow) Within The Cosmic Mandala. The psycho-physical personality Is A Play Upon (or An Apparent Modification Of) My Avatarically Self-Transmitted (and Eternally Self-Existing) Divine Spirit-Energy. Therefore, When the gross body dies, The subtler Modifications (or the subtle and causal components of form and psyche) Persist.

After bodily death, The conditionally Modified Spirit-Energy Of individual personality Becomes Progressively Re-Associated With The Vibratory Zone Of The Cosmic Mandala That Corresponds To The conditional Tendencies That Remained effective At the end of the previous lifetime (or After The Completion Of The death-Process, or Release-Process, That Ended and Followed the previous lifetime). Thus, After bodily death, conditional self-Consciousness Is Progressively Re-Collected Via The Spontaneous (but Habit-caused) Motions Of attention. After the gross body Is Relinquished (In The death-Process), Many Patterns Of psyche (or mind) and form (or body) arise and pass away (in a sequence of various planes of experience), until the re-attainment of a more or less fixed embodiment (or "reincarnation", or re-birth, as a conditionally Manifested psycho-physical personality) in one of the planes Of The Cosmic Mandala (<u>Possibly</u> Even in the same plane and general locale as in the previous lifetime).

People Often Wonder Why, If All Of This Is So, they Do Not Remember previous lifetimes (or previous circumstances Of conditional Existence). Of Course, some people Do, In Fact, Remember previous lifetimes (or previous circumstances Of conditional Existence). Very Often, Such Remembering Occurs Spontaneously—In dreams, or In reveries, or In Meditation. However, most people Claim Never To Have So Remembered. The Reason For This Is That There Is No <u>entity</u> that Passes From lifetime To lifetime. What

Proceeds From lifetime To lifetime Is The conditional Process Itself—Not a Fixed (or Eternal) "personal" entity (or An Independent and Separate individual Consciousness).

The present lifetime (or the Apparent present personal entity, which is Only the Apparent and conditional body-mind) is the effect of what came before it. The past lifetimes (or All The Cycles Of conditional embodiment) are effective as causes for what Follows them. It Is Not That a Conscious and Remembering entity lives, dies, and is re-born. The True and Only Conscious Self Is Inherently, and Inherently Perfectly, and Perfectly Subjectively, and Always Transcendentally Existing (or Existing Always Already Most Prior To conditional events and The Memory Of them). Re-birth Is Simply The (Apparent) Continuation Of The Process (Of causes and effects) That Produces mind and body. The By-Me-Avatarically-Self-Revealed Transcendental, Inherently Spiritual, and Self-Evidently Divine Self Never Changes, but It Is That Which Becomes Aware Of the present body-mind that has been caused By (and is Continuous With) The Residual (or Effective) Tendencies Of the past body-mind. Therefore, The (Self-Evidently) Divine Self Will Tend (In the form Of Processes In the body-mind) To Continue To Presume That It Is a conditional self, Until The Divine Self Awakens To Its Real Condition (In The Event Of Transcendental, Inherently Spiritual, and Most Perfect Divine Enlightenment).

The Transcendental, Inherently Spiritual, and Self-Evidently Divine Self Is Always Already Existing Transcendentally (or Most Priorly). It Is (Itself) Never an entity (or a conditional, Separate, Independent, and Migrating self, or individual Consciousness). The Transcendental, Inherently Spiritual, and Self-Evidently Divine Self Does Not Move From lifetime To lifetime. Lifetimes Reproduce themselves (As effects Follow causes). The Transcendental, Inherently Spiritual, and Self-Evidently Divine Self Merely (and Only Apparently) Observes The Chain Of events As they arise. Therefore, The Divine Self Does Not, In Itself, Remember the past—Because It Does Not (and Did Not Ever) Really Become a psycho-physical entity in the present.

The Transcendental, Inherently Spiritual, and Self-Evidently Divine Self Does Not, In Itself, Have A Memory Of past lives. As

Soon As the present lifetime (or Even the present moment) passes, The (Self-Evidently) Divine Self Ceases To Identify With it (Unless A Memory arises In mind To Suggest Such Identification). Therefore, The Chain Of lifetimes (or The Progression Of experiences of conditional mind and embodiment) Is (<u>Itself</u>) The Memory (or The Mechanism Of Memory). If past moments in the present lifetime Are To Be Remembered, The Only Requirement Is That attention Pass Through The Relatively Superficial (or Surface) Strata Of The Chain Of Recent Memory. However, If past lifetimes Are To Be Remembered, attention Must Migrate Through The deep psychic Core Of The Memory Chain. And This Does Not Tend To Occur (or To Be Noticed), Unless an individual Is Disposed (and, Perhaps, Even Intentionally Oriented) Toward Such psychic Exploration.

You Are Not the Same entity (or personality) that lived in many past lifetimes. You Are The Transcendental, Inherently Spiritual, and Self-Evidently Divine Self, Presently (but Only Apparently) Aware Of a body-mind that is (itself) a direct effect of many past lifetimes. Therefore, Memory Of past lifetimes Will Not Necessarily Characterize Your experience in the present lifetime, but Your experience in the present lifetime Will Necessarily Reflect (or Express) The Remaining (or effective) Tendencies Of all past lifetimes (and causes) that directly preceded (or caused) the present lifetime.

Every birth (or re-birth) Is A Plunge Into material (or Otherwise conditional) ignorance (With Coincident Loss, or Forgetting, Of Divine Ignorance Itself).

Every lifetime Is Begun With (and By Means Of) The Loss (or Forgetting) Of Every Previous (and, Otherwise, Eternal) Wisdom-Advantage.

At birth (or, Otherwise, whenever Identification With the present-time born-condition Is Presumed), All That Was Realized Previously (or, Otherwise, Priorly) Recedes Into The Unconscious and Subconscious "Background" (Of The Deeper Personality), and all that Was Previously (or, Otherwise, Priorly) Released Returns (In One or Another Manner, and To One or Another Degree) To The Immediate "Surface" Of Direct (perceptual and conceptual) Awareness (or the Conscious mind, or body-mind, of the gross personality).

In Order To Serve In Bodily (Human) Form, Even I Was Required, By My Own Choice, To Relinquish My Own Eternally Free Condition, and (Thus, By Submission To Identification With My Own conditional Body-Mind and Circumstance) To Forget Myself—Until, By Means Of My Own Unique Avataric Ordeal Of Divine Self-Remembering, I Should Re-Awaken To Myself, and Even (At Last) "Emerge" Most Perfectly (As Myself).

Therefore, Even Though My Own Motive Toward Even This (Now, and Forever Hereafter—and Inherently, and Inherently Perfectly—Me-Revealing) Bodily (Human) Avataric Birth Was Great Love-Sympathy For all conditionally Manifested beings, and Even Though This Bodily (Human) Avataric Birth Was (Thus, and Altogether) Intended Toward A Divinely Great and Divinely Enlightened and Divinely Enlightening Purpose (here, and every "where" In The Cosmic Domain)—My Intentional Avataric Assumption Of This Bodily (Human) Form Required The Avataric Self-Sacrifice Of My Own Divine (and Eternally Free) Love-Bliss-Condition (Just As even all ordinary-born beings, born Without Such Divinely Self-Aware Intention, Sacrifice Eternal Freedom and Perfect Love-Bliss By their Natural Submission To The Cycles Of conditional birth and desiring and death).

Each and every born lifetime Requires many (even "ordinary") helping associations (Even "Carried Over" From lifetimes past), and Every Kind Of Greater (or Great) Growth and Greater (or Great) Realization Requires Great Good Company and Great (Divine) Help, or Else The "Background" Strengths (or All The Virtues and Realizations Hidden, or Forgotten, In The Subconscious and Unconscious Deep) Will Not Re-Surface (or Otherwise Come Forward) To Consciousness. And, Ultimately (In Due Course), It Becomes Clear That Not Even Any Kind Of conditional (or merely psycho-physical) Growth Is The Purpose Toward Which conditional Existence Should Be Devoted, but, Rather, conditional Existence Should Be Devoted Only To The Progressive (but Always present-time Direct, and, At Last, Most Perfect) Transcending (or The Real and True "Out-Growing") Of conditional Existence Itself,

By Means Of The Progressive (but Always present-time Direct, and, At Last, Most Perfect) Realization Of The Un-conditional Condition That Was, and Is, Always Already The Case. Therefore, and By Means Of (Eventually, Most Perfect) Surrender To Me (The Avatarically Self-Revealed, and Inherently Perfect, and Perfectly Subjective, and Self-Evidently Divine Self-Condition, and Source-Condition, Itself), conditional Existence Should Be Devoted To Most Perfectly "Out-Growing" (and, Thereby, To No Longer Making or Perpetuating) The Otherwise Repetitive Cycles Of births and lifetimes and deaths.

Even Though All That I Have Done By My Own Avataric Ordeal Of Divine Self-Submission To Bodily (Human) Form and Purpose Has (As A Result Of My Eventual, and Inherently Most Perfect, Re-Awakening, My Subsequent Avataric Divine Teaching-Work, My Eventually Most Perfect Avataric Divine Self-"Emergence", and All My Avataric Divine Blessing-Work) Become Good Company (or Satsang) and Great (and Self-Evidently Divine) Help, Forever, and For all—It Also (In Due Course, In My Spontaneous Avataric Play Of Divine Self-Recognition) Became Necessary (and Inevitable) For Me, As A Fundamental Part Of That Good Service, To Become Spontaneously and Divinely Indifferent To Even All Intentions and All Sympathetic Attachments (Even While Yet Appearing, In A Simple and Spontaneous Manner, To Be Actively Animating Intentions and Actively Maintaining Sympathetic Relations). By Thus Standing Free—Abiding Merely In My "Bright" and Very (and Inherently Perfect) State, Prior To (and Inherently Free From) All Gestures Of Work (or Active Purposiveness), and All Gestures Of Sympathetic Attachment (or Active Relatedness)— I Also Allow Even My Avatarically-Born Bodily (Human) Divine Form and My Avatarically Self-Revealed Spiritual (and Always, or Inherently, Blessing) Divine Presence To Merely <u>Be</u>, and Only <u>Thus</u> To Work. Therefore, By This "Bright" Indifference, I Affirm (and Confirm, and Demonstrate) To all That (Most Ultimately, and At Last) <u>Every</u> conditional Sympathy, <u>Every</u> conditional Purpose and Intention, and Even conditional Existence <u>Itself</u> Must Be Most Perfectly Transcended (and, Thus, Most Perfectly Relinquished) In <u>Only</u> That Which <u>Is</u> (Only and Itself and Inherently and Divinely)

Perfect—or Else conditional Existence (Perpetuated By another conditional birth, and lifetime, and death) Will Inevitably Continue After the present-time lifetime and death.

Therefore, In The Context Of the present lifetime, You Will experience The Motions (and The Results) Of All effective Tendencies That Continue From the past. If You Do Not Transcend Those Tendencies, You Will Duplicate or Repeat or Regenerate the past (In A Mechanical, Automatic, and egoic Manner), and You Will (By Virtue Of A Mechanical, Automatic, and egoic Involvement In conditional Processes) Generate Similar (or Even New) conditional Tendencies, Which Must Be Fulfilled (or Made effective) In the future (Even In future lifetimes). If Devotion, Service, self-Discipline, and (Most Fundamental) self-Understanding Characterize the present lifetime, To The Degree That There Is Some Real Advance Beyond the limits Associated With The First Three Stages Of Life—Then presently effective Tendencies Inherited From the past Will Gradually Dissipate, and future experience (during or after the present lifetime) Will Be Associated With Positively Improved Attitudes (or Increased psycho-physical Equanimity) and Even (Perhaps) With higher (or subtler) possibilities (of experience and knowledge) Within The Cosmic Mandala. And those who Listen To Me, and Hear Me, and See Me, and Embrace The Total Practice Of The Only-By-Me Revealed and Given Way Of The Heart Most Profoundly Will Really Transcend The Entire Process That Generates conditional Tendencies—Such That Divine Translation Is Realized, Either At the end of the present lifetime Or (In Due Course) Through The Ordeal Of (and At the end of) any number of future lifetimes.

Therefore, It Is Profoundly Useful For You To Realize— Whether Through Memory, Or Through Intelligent Observation Of The (Always psycho-physical) Laws and Mechanics Of Cosmic Nature, Or (Most Simply and Directly) Through The Illuminated Certainty (or Inherent Faith) That Must Awaken Via The Heart-Effective Grace Of True Satsang With Me (and Through The Subsequent Heart-Effective Grace Of My Avatarically Given and Giving Divine Spirit-Baptism)—That conditional embodiment (or Apparently conditional Existence, Manifested As a body-mind)

Tends To Reproduce itself Inevitably. Once a body-mind Is Assumed, another body-mind Will Certainly Follow—Unless Divine Self-Realization and Inherently Most Perfect Renunciation (Of conditional self-Existence) Intervene To Break The Spell. It Is Simply A Matter Of The (Apparent) Laws (or Habits) Of Cosmic Light, or Of conditionally Modified Spirit-Energy. Spirit-Energy Cannot Be Destroyed—and, Once Spirit-Energy Is (Apparently) Modified conditionally (or Once A conditional Motion Is Established), The Process Of Modification Will Tend To Continue (Indefinitely), Until The Tendency Toward conditional Modification Is (Itself) Transcended and Outshined In The By-Me-Avatarically-Self-Revealed Native Condition (Self-Energy, or Self-Radiant and Inherently Spiritual Being) Of Transcendental Divine Existence.

Spirit-Energy Is Eternal and Constant. Spirit-Energy Cannot Be Destroyed, but Spirit-Energy Can Be Apparently Modified (or Apparently Converted and Changed Into conditional forms). And, Once Spirit-Energy (or The Inherent Radiance, or Spirit-Force, Of Fundamental Reality) Is Apparently Modified, Its conditional forms Can Change, or Else Dissolve Into other forms, or Even (If Grace and Practice Coincide) Be Resolved Into The By-Me-Avatarically-Self-Revealed Original (or Un-Modified) State Of Self-Radiant "Bright" Spirit-Energy and Transcendental Divine Consciousness Itself. Indeed, One Of The Apparent Laws (or Habits) Of Spirit-Energy In The Context Of The Cosmic Mandala Is Not Merely That conditional forms <u>Can</u> Change and Dissolve, but That they <u>Always</u> Tend To Change and Dissolve. Therefore, Once The Self-Radiant Energy (or Spirit-Force) Of Fundamental Reality Becomes (or, Really, Appears To Become) a conditionally Manifested form, being, or process— that conditionally Manifested form, being, or process Tends Immediately (and Constantly) To Change or Dissolve. So It Is (every "where") Within The Cosmic Domain—and So It Is With (and Within) Your Own body-mind. Because All Of This Is So, conditional Existence Obliges You To Observe, Endure, Most Fundamentally Understand, and Really Transcend Every Kind Of Change and Dissolution (Including The Blows Of Apparent loss and death).

After the death of an individual, his or her Destiny Is Generally Determined By The Stage Of Life (and The Degree Of self-

Transcendence) In Which he or she Was Really Active At the time of death. Those who die young, or who Otherwise Fail To Demonstrate Superior Tendencies (or Great Spiritual, Transcendental, or Divine Signs) That Are Otherwise Latent (and Even Somewhat Active) At The Subconscious Level, May Possibly Pass Into higher (or subtler) planes (or Even Be Divinely Translated) In death. Nevertheless, In General, Clear Signs That Correspond To One or The Other Of The Seven Stages Of Life Will Characterize living individuals During the (Generally Extensive) period of ordinary (or typical) living that Immediately Precedes the time of their death, and their Destiny After death Will Tend To Correspond To The Tendencies Associated With Those Signs.

Even those who Show The Signs Of The Only-By-Me Revealed and Given Seventh Stage Of Life May, If they Are Not Fully Disposed Toward Divine Translation, Pass To any of the Cosmic planes After death. They May Pass Even Into the grosser worlds, If they Are Inclined Toward Service and Play In those worlds. Or they May Pass Into the higher (or subtler) worlds, In Order To Remain In The Cosmic Play and Serve.

Each Of The Seven Stages Of Life Corresponds To Tendencies (or Else Demonstrations) That Move To Associate With conditions Of A Certain Level Of Vibration (or Apparent Modification Of The Divine White "Brightness").

The First Three Stages Of Life, the waking state, The grosser and outward-Directed Orientation Of the perceptual mind, The conceptual (and Typically verbal) Orientation Of mind, The Left Side Of The Heart, the lower brain, the pituitary gland (and all the other lower-functioning glands, or glandular Regions, of the brain, and of the extended gross physical body), the specialized activities of the left hemisphere of the brain, the entire gross physical body, and Especially The bodily Regions From the solar plexus Down To the bodily base Correspond To The Red and Yellow Fields Of The Cosmic Mandala (and, Thus, To planes and forms and experience and knowledge In Those Fields).

The Fourth Stage Of Life Is ("Originally") Associated With the lower (or waking) frontal personality, The lower-functioning psycho-physical Orientation Of the gross body-mind, and The Left

Side Of The Heart, and (Thus) It Also Works In (and Tends Toward) The Red and Yellow Fields—but (Sympathetically, and Even From The Beginning, and Always By Means Of The True, and Ever-Deepening, and Truly ego-Surrendering, Devotional Response) The Fourth Stage Of Life Is Also (Progressively, or More and More Potentially) Associated With the dreaming (or dreamlike subtle) state, The subtler and inward-Directed Orientation Of mind, The Middle Station Of The Heart, the higher brain and the specialized activities of the right hemisphere of the brain, the glandular centers In The Region Of the throat and upper chest (Associated, Eventually, With The Spiritual Breath Of Life), The (Eventual) Spiritual and (Potentially) Altogether Regenerative Conversion (and Potential Upward Re-Orientation) Of all the Otherwise lower-functioning glands (or glandular Regions) of the extended gross physical body and of the brain (Especially the pituitary gland, and Also the other, Otherwise lower-functioning, glands, or glandular Regions, of the brain), and (Potential) Eventual Movement Toward and To and Into The Ajna Door. Therefore, It Is (Potentially) Also Eventually Associated With A Sympathy (or A Progression) Toward subtler Tendencies, Especially Toward The subtle Moonlike Whiteness (or The Middle Range Of subtle, or astral, phenomena and worlds).

The Fifth Stage Of Life (If It Occurs) Is Directly (or Immediately) Associated With The subtle and inward-Directed Orientation Of mind itself (Prior To, or Apart From, the gross physical body), the dreaming (or dreamlike subtle) state, The Middle Station Of The Heart, the higher brain, the specialized activities of the right hemisphere of the brain, the pineal gland (and other higher-functioning glandular centers, or glandular Regions, of the brain), The Regenerative Spiritual Conversion (or The Spiritual, and Spiritually Regenerative, Upward Re-Orientation) Of Even the pituitary gland (and all the other, Otherwise lower-functioning, glands, or glandular Regions, of the brain), The Upper Terminal Of the brain (Associated With The Upper Rear Of The Brain Core, and With the upper rear of the head, and With the aperture in the upper rear of the top of the head, and With The Total Crown Of the head), and (Therefore) With The Play At and Above The Ajna Door,

Including The Actual Perception Of Cosmic Lights and higher (or subtler) worlds, In The Range Of The Moonlike Whiteness (and Beyond), In The Field Of Black (or Indigo), and In The Radiant Blue Field (and Its planes and forms). The Process Of Advancement (or Growth Toward Maturity) In The Fifth Stage Of Life Is Also Associated With A Yearning Toward The Form and State (and Even Toward The Real, True, and, Most Ultimately, Final Transcending) Of The Apparently Objective and Brilliant and Most Ascended Source-Current (or The Apparently Objective and Most Ascended Spirit-Force, Perceived As Light, or Sound-Vibration, or, Otherwise, Merely Touched, or Felt, As Spirit-Presence). And That Yearning Toward The Apparently Objective and Most Ascended Source-Current May Be (Necessarily, Only Temporarily) Satisfied In Fifth Stage conditional Nirvikalpa Samadhi, but Real and True Transcending Of The (Only Apparently) Objective and (Only Apparently) Most Ascended Source-Current Is Finally Realized Only In Divine Translation, Which Requires (or Is A Matter Of) Divinely Most Perfect Self-Recognition Of Even My Apparently Objective Divine Body Of Spirit-Force (Appearing As My Apparently Objective Divine Star Of Light, or As My Apparently Objective Divine Sound Of Thunder, or, Otherwise, As My Apparent, and Merely Touched, or Felt, Love-Bliss-"Brightness") Above The Total Crown Of the head. (And That Divinely Most Perfect, and Inherent, Transcending Is Thus Realized Only In The Only-By-Me Revealed and Given Way Of The Heart—and, At Last, Only In The Most Ultimate Context Of The Only-By-Me Revealed and Given Seventh Stage Of Life In The Way Of The Heart.)

The Sixth Stage Of Life Is Associated With Fully Conscious Transcendental (and Inherently Spiritual) Self-Abiding, Excluding (As Is Also The Case In deep sleep) The phenomenal Cosmic Lights and all conditional experience. However, Such Transcendental Self-Abiding Is A Temporary (or Unstable) Resolution, and It Tacitly Allows The Continuation Of Tendencies That May Associate the conditionally Manifested being With any of the conditionally Manifested planes Of The Cosmic Mandala After death.

Immersion (or Swoon) In The psycho-physical Deep Of conditional self-Consciousness (As In deep worldless sleep) May Tend

To Associate the conditional self With The Black (or Indigo) Field, but Such Is Really A Stage In The Progress Through The Cosmic Lights (or the planes of mind), Even In The Context Of The Fifth Stage Of Life, and Such Contemplative Immersion In The mental Dark Should Not Be Equated With The Process Of Transcendental (and Inherently Spiritual) Self-Identification That Develops In The Context Of The Sixth Stage Of Life (or The Process Of Identification With The Infinite Free Space Of Self-Existing Consciousness, Self-Radiant Love-Bliss, and Perfectly Subjective Being Itself, Prior To the deep sleep state, Prior To the dreaming and dreamlike states, Prior To the waking state, Prior To all the forms of mind, Prior To all psycho-physical states, Prior To all conditional objects, Prior To the very act of conditional attention, and Even Prior To The Apparent Witness-<u>Function</u> Of Consciousness).

In The Fifth Stage Progress, The Red and Yellow Fields May Be Said To Correspond To the gross body and the gross (or grosser) worlds, but The Lights Themselves Are subtle Visions (or forms of higher mind). The Moonlike White Field May Be Said To Correspond To the subtle (or astral) body and the subtle (or subtler than gross) worlds, but The Moonlike White Light Is Itself A subtle Vision (or a form of higher mind). The Black (or Indigo) Field May Be Said To Correspond To the causal (or subtler than subtle) body and The Dark Passage Toward higher (or subtler) phenomena (or worlds), but The Black (or Indigo) Field Is Itself A subtle Vision (or a form of higher mind). The Radiant Blue Field, Just Beyond The Black (or Indigo) Field, May Be Said To Correspond To the so-called "supracausal" (or "higher causal", or "subtler than the causal", or "Beyond the causal") body and the Likewise so-called "supra-causal" worlds, but The Radiant Blue Light (or The Radiant Blue Field) and the Radiant Blue worlds (or all appearances In or Of The Radiant Blue Field) Are (Like All Lights, worlds, and forms Outside or Surrounding The Radiant Blue) Only subtle Visions (or forms of higher mind), appearing conditionally Within The Cosmic Mandala.

All Of That, all subtle (or higher) forms of mind, all lesser forms of mind, all higher associations of mind, all lower associations of mind, All Cosmic Visions, or all conditional perceptions At All Are Excluded In Fifth Stage conditional Nirvikalpa Samadhi. Likewise,

All Of That Is Excluded In Jnana Samadhi, or In The General Context Of The Sixth Stage Of Life. And Even Though Any or All Of That May Be Perceived In The Context Of The Only-By-Me Revealed and Given Seventh Stage Of Life, It Is All Inherently (and Divinely) Self-Recognized and Divinely Transcended. And All Of That Is Gone Beyond (or Outshined), Most Ultimately, In The Final Event Of The Only-By-Me Revealed and Given Way Of The Heart, Which Final Event Is The Great Event Of Divine Translation (and Which Is The Consummate, or Final and Completing, Demonstration Of Ruchira Samadhi, or Unconditional and Divinely Most Perfect Nirvikalpa Samadhi).

As I Have Indicated, The Only-By-Me Revealed and Given Seventh Stage Of Life In The Way Of The Heart May (Because Of The Non-Exclusive Attitude Inherently Associated With The Seventh Stage Of Life In The Way Of The Heart) Allow For The Motive (or The Potential) Of Association With any of the Cosmic planes After death. Nevertheless, The Devotee-Realizer In The Seventh Stage Of Life In The Way Of The Heart Is Founded In (and Inherently, and Inherently Most Perfectly, Identified With) The Transcendental, Inherently Spiritual, and Self-Evidently Divine Self (Which Is The Self-Existing, and Self-Radiant, and Perfectly Subjective Source Of All Apparently Objective Light). In The Apparent Context Of the body (or Of the Apparent objective personality in the gross worlds, and in the waking state, and in the subtle worlds, or in a state similar or equal to dreaming), The Devotee-Realizer Of The Way Of The Heart In The Context Of The Seventh Stage Of Life Is Founded In (and As) Amrita Nadi—Which Is "Grounded" (or Most Priorly Established) In The Right Side Of The Heart, and Which Extends Upwards To Include My Infinitely "Ascended" Feeling-"Brightness", and The (Potential, or Possible) Perception Of My Apparently Objectified and Ascended Light, or Sound-Vibration, or Touched Presence, or Felt Spirit-Current Of Love-Bliss (Infinitely Above The Total Crown Of the head). Therefore, The Devotee-Realizer Of The Way Of The Heart In The Context Of The Seventh Stage Of Life Is Inherently and Fundamentally (and Spontaneously, Rather Than Strategically) Moved Toward The Outshining (or The Divine Translation) Of conditional forms and events (or Of All The Apparent Modifications Of My Avatarically Self-Transmitted Divine Spirit-Energy Itself) In My Avatarically Self-Revealed (and Self-Evidently Divine) Self-Condition Itself (Which Is The Perfectly Subjective Source-Condition Of all objective appearances).

The Apparent (or Apparently) Perceptible Divine Sound and Divine Star (Potentially, or Possibly, Perceived In High Objective Hearing-Vision) Are (If Perceived) Made Perceptible (Apparently Objectively) Via the body-mind (or Else Via the mind alone, When There Is No Active bodily Association). As Apparently Objective Perceptions, The Divine Sound and The Divine Star Are The Eternal (and Not Cosmic, but Perfectly Subjective) Transcendental, Inherently Spiritual, and Self-Evidently Divine Reality Perceived To Be Breaking Through The Center Of The Cosmic Mandala. Therefore, The Perceptible (or Apparently Objective) Divine Sound and Divine Star Are Perceived Through The Only Hole (or Infinitely Ascended Opening) In The Universe (or The Total conditional Cosmos), and (Thus) Via An Aperture Above the mind (or the Total body-mind).

Ultimately (and In Any Case), The Perceptible (or Apparently Objective) Divine Sound and Divine Star Are Simply The Ultimate Perceptible (or Apparently Objective) Sign Of The "Bright" Inherent Love-Bliss (or Self-Radiance) Of Transcendental, Inherently Spiritual, and Self-Evidently Divine Being. Therefore, In The Context Of The Seventh Stage Of Life, The moment to moment "Practice" (or Demonstration-Process) Of The Way Of The Heart Is Not Especially A Matter Of Perceiving Either The Divine Sound Or The Divine Star (As Apparently Objective Forms). Rather, It Is Fundamentally A Matter Of Relaxing (or Relinquishing) the body-mind (and all of its conditional relations) Into My "Brightness" (or The Infinite Fullness Of My Divinely Self-Existing and Self-Radiant Love-Bliss—Which Is Perceived, Apparently Objectively, As My All-and-all-Surrounding and All-and-all-Pervading Divine Spiritual Body, but Which Is, Ultimately, Most Perfectly Realized As My Heart-Identity, Which Is The Inherent, Divine State Of Even My Apparently Objective Divine Spiritual Body, and Divine Star, and Divine Sound). This <u>Spontaneously</u>

(and Not Strategically) "Produces" (or Divinely Demonstrates) The Signs Of Divine Transfiguration, Divine Transformation, and Divine Indifference, Culminating In Divine Translation—Which Is The Perfectly Subjective Self-Outshining Of All Apparent conditional Modifications, The Utter (and Inherent) Transcending Of The Tendency To Contract (Rather Than To Shine), and The Final Assertion and Demonstration Of Utter (and Inherent) Freedom From The Tendency To Allow The Freely Self-Existing and Self-Radiant Being To Be limited conditionally.

Divine Translation Itself Cannot Occur If My (Perceived) Apparently Objective Divine Spiritual Body, or My (Perceived) Apparently Objective Divine Star, or My (Perceived) Apparently Objective Divine Sound, or Even Any Apparently Objective Appearance Is Un-Recognized (or Regarded Merely As An Object or An "Other"—and, Thus, Not Transcended In Me). Even The Perception and Conception Of Relatedness Itself (Which Characterizes Both egoic self-Contraction and Apparent conditional Awareness Generally) Must Be Divinely Self-Recognized and Divinely Transcended, If There Is To Be Divine Translation In The "Bright".

Divine Translation Occurs Spontaneously (Not Intentionally, or Strategically). Divine Translation May (Initially) Be Associated With A Perception (or Noticing) Of The Apparently Objective Divine Sound and/or The Apparently Objective Divine Star (and Even An Apparent Process Of Merging With The Divine Sound and/or The Divine Star), but That Perception or Process Must (Necessarily) Coincide With (and Otherwise Become Superseded By) Divine Self-Abiding Self-Recognition (and Divinely Most Perfect Transcending) Of The Apparently Objective Divine Sound and The Apparently Objective Divine Star. The Most Ultimate Process That Is Divine Translation Itself Occurs When All subject-object References (and The Feeling Of Relatedness Itself) Are Transcended and the body-mind (As Well As the Total field of conditional relations) Is Freely Relinquished In The Utterly Single Realization Of Inherent Love-Bliss (or The "Bright" Itself).

Therefore, Divine Translation Occurs Only On The Basis Of Transcendental, Inherently Spiritual, and Most Perfect Divine Self-

Realization, In Which There Is Native and Progressive Divine Self-Recognition-Transcendence Of conditional states In The By-Me-Avatarically-Self-Revealed Self-Existing and Self-Radiant Divine Self-Condition (and Source-Condition) That <u>Is</u> The One and Only Divine Being (Who <u>Is</u> Consciousness Itself). And, When Divine Self-Recognition-Transcendence Becomes The Singleness Of Inherent Love-Bliss (Self-Existing and Self-Radiant In Place, Outshining subject-object Distinctions), Then conditional Existence Is Spontaneously Relinquished, and My Divine Self-Domain Is Spontaneously "Entered" (or Directly, Immediately, and Most Perfectly Assumed).

My Divine Sound and My Divine Star—Which Are The Final Objective Forms In Which The By-Me-Avatarically-Self-Revealed (Very) Divine Self-Condition and Source-Condition Is (or May Be) Apparently Presented and Realized—Must, Most Ultimately (and Merely By Divine Self-Recognition), Be Transcended (and Dissolved, or Subsumed, or Divinely Translated) In The Self-Existing and Self-Radiant Divine Self-Condition (and Source-Condition) That I, In My Childhood, Named "The Bright". Through Divine Self-Recognition In The Context Of The Only-By-Me Revealed and Given Seventh Stage Of Life (and Even In The Apparent Context Of the body, the mind, and the world), My (Apparently Objective) Divine Sound (or Apparently Ascended Vibration) and My (Apparently Objective) Divine Star (or Apparently Ascended Light) Will (If Perceived) Be Felt, Perceived, Experienced, or Known To Be At (or Native To, and Originating From) The "Bright" Heart, Even While Also (Apparently) Vibrating and Shining Above the body, the mind, and the world (and Vibrating Around, In, and Through, and Shining On, In, and Through, the body, the mind, and the world). Likewise, In The Event Of Divine Translation, The Divine Sound and The Divine Star (If Either or Both Of Them Are Perceived In Their Apparent Objectivity) Are Realized Entirely In The Context Of The Transcendental, Inherently Spiritual (or "Bright"), and Self-Evidently Divine Self. Therefore, In The Great Event Of Divine Translation, The Divine Sound and The Divine Star Are Not Merely Perceived To Be Above, or Even In The Heart. Rather, The Apparently Objective Divine Sound (or Apparently Objective Source-Vibration) and The Apparently Objective Divine Star (or Apparently Objective Source-Light) Are Most Perfectly (Divinely) Self-Recognized (and, Thus, Perfectly Subjectively Realized) In The Great Event Of Divine Translation. In The Great Event Of Divine Translation, The Apparently Objective Divine Mass Of Sound-Vibration and The Apparently Objective Divine Star-Light (or Even Every Apparently Objective Sign Of The "Bright") Are Realized Simply As The By-Me-Avatarically-Self-Revealed Perfectly Subjective Feeling-Radiance (or Inherent Love-Bliss) Of Transcendental, Inherently Spiritual, and Self-Evidently Divine Being (or Self-Existing and Self-Radiant Being Itself). Thus, When Sound or Light Appears In Truth (Divinely Self-Recognized)—body, mind, and world (or all conditional forms and states) Are Dissolved (or Outshined) In The "Bright" Self, and My Eternal Divine Self-Domain Shines Forth (Where You Stand) As Consciousness Itself (Being-"Bright").

Since Every Trace Of conditional personality Is Outshined In Divine Translation (or Absolute Realization Of My Divine Self-Domain Of Love-Bliss Itself), There Is No Feature Of My Divine Self-Domain (or Of Existence In The By-Me-Avatarically-Self-Revealed Divine Self-Condition, or Source-Condition, That Is Love-Bliss Itself) That Corresponds (or Bears A Likeness) To the conditional references, forms, or states that Are Found anywhere In The Cosmic Domain. Therefore, My Divine Self-Domain (or Self-Existing and Self-Radiant Existence In My Perfectly Subjective Transcendental, Inherently Spiritual, and Self-Evidently Divine Self-Condition) Is (Ultimately) Beyond Description here—Except It Can Be Said That It Is Divine (or Inherent) Love-Bliss Itself, and It Is The Ultimate Perfection (and The Perfect Fulfillment) Of Being Itself, Joyfully Transcending (and Not Merely Negating) The Ordeal Of Life In The Cosmic Domain.

My Divine Self-Domain Is The Condition (and The Realization) Of Perfect (Self-"Bright") Subjectivity.

Therefore, My Divine Self-Domain Has Not Any Objective Features, but It Is Entirely and Only The Inherently Perfect Self-Condition (and Source-Condition) Itself.

My Divine Self-Domain Is Self-Existing Self-Radiance, or The "Bright" Itself, or Love-Bliss Itself.

Therefore, Realization Of My Divine Self-Domain Is (and, Necessarily, Requires) The Inherent (and Inherently Most Perfect) Transcending Of <u>all</u> objective conditions, <u>and</u> Of Objectivity (or Objective Awareness and Objective Existence) Itself.

"Consider" This: <u>All</u> Seeking Is An Impulse Toward <u>objects</u> (or objective relations, or objective others). Therefore, The Most Perfect Transcending Of <u>All</u> Seeking Is The Most Perfect Transcending Of The Entire Impulse Toward objects (or objective relations, or objective others). And, Most Ultimately (In The Realization Of Divine Translation), The Most Perfect Transcending Of All Seeking Is Demonstrated As The Entire and Most Perfect Transcending Of Objectivity (or Objective Awareness and Objective Existence) Itself.

The self-Contraction Is <u>Always</u> A Search.

The self-Contraction <u>Always</u> Demonstrates itself As The Search For (or the will Toward) objects, or objective relations, or objective others.

The self-Contraction itself (The First Form, or Root-Form, Of which Is The Feeling Of Relatedness Itself) Is itself The Very Action Whereby Objectivity (or Objective Awareness Itself and Objective Existence Itself), or Separateness, and Otherness, and "Difference" Itself, Is Evoked, and Generated, and Established, and experienced, and known.

The self-Contraction Is (itself) Relatedness, and Separateness, and Otherness, and The Only "Difference".

Indeed, The Root-Feeling Of Relatedness (Which Is The Essence Of the self-Contraction) Is (Itself) The Essence and The Substance Of All experienced or known or Presumed Objectivity.

Likewise, The Root-Feeling Of Relatedness (Which Is The Original Act Of self-Contraction) Is (Itself) Both The Origin and The Goal Of The Great Search.

Therefore, <u>All</u> Seeking Is The self-Effort (or the will) <u>Toward</u> Relatedness, but (Ultimately) Even Relatedness Itself (Achieved) Is the experience and the knowledge of self-Contraction.

<u>All</u> Seeking Is A Result, A Certain Sign, A Continuation, An Extension, An Expression, A Demonstration, and a Consistent and Constant experience (and knowing) Of self-Contraction.

<u>All</u> Seeking (or Demonstrated self-Contraction) Is A Process Of

Suffering, or A Suffered Effort Toward Release (From The Search Itself) By Means Of The Achievement Of objects, or objective relations, or objective others.

All Seeking Is An Effort Toward Final, Complete, and Utter Release Of self-Contraction (or the ego-"I").

However (and This Must Be Realized), No Kind (or Force) Of Seeking Is Ever Able To Finally, Completely, and Utterly Release self-Contraction (or the Suffered and Suffering ego-"I").

No kind of object (or objective relation, or objective other) and No Force Of Objective Satisfaction Is Ever Able To Finally, Completely, and Utterly Release self-Contraction (or the Suffered and Suffering ego-"I").

Therefore, All Seeking Is self-Contraction, Demonstrated Suffering, and An (Ultimately) Fruitless (or, Necessarily, Frustrated and Failed) self-Effort.

The ego-"I" (or self-Contraction) Is A Search That Is The Search Itself, Narcissus Bent (To Suffer) Upon An Illusion, Deluded By his own (self-Generated) Presumption Of Relatedness.

Therefore, Not Any Kind (or Force) Of Seeking Is The Way Of Freedom and The Heart, but Only The (By-My-Avataric-Divine-Grace-Given) Process Of Directly Understanding and Transcending self-Contraction (and, Therefore, All Seeking) Is The Way (and The Realization) Of Freedom Itself and The Heart Itself (Which Is My Divine Self-Domain Itself, and The By-Me-Avatarically-Self-Revealed Condition and Self and Person That Is Real God, or Truth, or Reality, or The Divine Itself).

The Only-By-Me Revealed and Given Way Of The Heart (or Way Of Adidam) Is (By Means Of My Avatarically Self-Transmitted Divine Grace) To Finally, Completely, and Utterly Understand, Transcend, and Release self-Contraction.

If self-Contraction Is (By Means Of My Avatarically Self-Transmitted Grace) Finally, Completely, and Utterly Understood, Transcended, and Released—All Seeking Is (Finally, Completely, and Utterly) Understood, Transcended, and Released In That Process.

Therefore, Most Ultimately, If (By Means Of My Avatarically Self-Transmitted Divine Grace) self-Contraction Is Finally,

Completely, and Utterly Understood, Transcended, and Released—Such That (Necessarily) <u>All</u> Seeking Is Thereby (and Finally, Completely, and Utterly) Understood, Transcended, and Released—Then (In The Event Of Seventh Stage, or Inherently Most Perfect, and Self-Evidently Divine, Self-Awakening) All ego-Effort (or ego-Based will) Toward objects (or all objective relations, and all objective others) <u>Ceases</u>, Such That Only An egoless Heart-Will Remains To Continue The Apparent Association With the body-mind (and Even any or all potential objects). However, In The Progressive Demonstration Of The Only-By-Me Revealed and Given Seventh Stage Of Life In The Way Of The Heart, Even This egoless Heart-Will Is, In every moment, Divinely Self-Recognized—Until It Is, More and More, Replaced By Divine Indifference, and (At Last) Most Perfectly Outshined (In Divine Translation). And, In The Most Ultimate "Bright" Event Of Divine Translation, Even Objectivity Itself (or Objective Awareness Itself, and Objective Existence Itself) Is Finally, Completely, and Utterly Outshined By and In The Self-Existing Self-Radiance (or "Bright" Love-Bliss) Of The By-Me-Avatarically-Self-Revealed Divine Self-Condition (or Source-Condition), Which <u>Is</u> The Inherently Perfect Divine Subjectivity (Itself).

By Means Of My Avatarically Self-Transmitted Divine Grace, In The Only-By-Me Revealed and Given Seventh Stage Of Life In The Way Of The Heart, all objects (or all objective relations, and all objective others), and All Apparent (or conditional) Effort Toward objects (or all objective relations, and all objective others), and The Root-Feeling Of Relatedness, and Even The Tacit Feeling Of "Difference" Are Consistently and Constantly (each, and all, and Even Simultaneously, and Always Inherently) Divinely Self-Recognized In The By-Me-Avatarically-Self-Revealed Native (and Self-Evidently Divine) Feeling Of Being. And This By-My-Avataric-Divine-Grace-Given Process (or Divine Demonstration) Continues Thus, Until (As My Avatarically Self-Transmitted Divine Grace Will Have It) The Divine Sign Of "Bright" Indifference Is Given, and Then The Great Outshining Of all objects, all objective relations, all objective others, and All Of Objectivity Itself By and In (and, Therein, <u>As</u>) The (By-Me-Avatarically-Self-Revealed) Very and

Divine and Perfectly Subjective "Bright" Self-Condition and Source-Condition.

In Nirvikalpa Samadhi As It May Be Realized (but, Necessarily, Only conditionally) In Either The Fifth Stage Of Life Or The Sixth Stage Of Life, There Is No Awareness Of Either external Or internal phenomena—but The Samadhi Is (Necessarily, To One Degree or Another) Both Achieved and Held In Place By Means Of (and, Therefore, It Is, In One Manner or Another, Characterized and limited By) Stage-Of-Life-Specific phenomenal conditions (and Stage-Of-Life-Specific conditional Efforts). Unlike The Fifth Stage and Sixth Stage Forms (or, Indeed, Any conditional Form) Of Nirvikalpa Samadhi, Seventh Stage Sahaja Nirvikalpa Samadhi Is The Infinite Magnification (or conditionless Realization) Of Nirvikalpa Samadhi—Made (Thus and Thereby) Most Perfect, but Neither Achieved Nor Held In Place By any phenomenal conditions (or Any conditional Efforts) Whatsoever. Seventh Stage Sahaja Nirvikalpa Samadhi Is Perpetual Nirvikalpa Samadhi. And, Yet, Paradoxically, In The Seventh Stage Of Life In The Way Of The Heart, Previous To Divine Translation, There (Generally) Appears To Be Some Kind Of Association With phenomena. This Is Because, In The Seventh Stage Of Life In The Way Of The Heart, There Is No egoity Whatsoever, and (Therefore) There Is No Method (or Effort) Of Seeking (Either To Exclude all phenomenal conditions Or To Exclude Only lesser, or lower, phenomenal conditions, While Pursuing greater, or higher, phenomenal conditions). Nevertheless, This Paradox Cannot Be Fully Understood Until The Seventh Stage Of Life Has Been Realized.

To Realize This Perpetual (Seventh Stage) Samadhi Is To Be (Effectively) Already Divinely Translated. There Is No limitation Whatsoever In This Samadhi. In The Seventh Stage Of Life In The Way Of The Heart (Previous To Divine Translation), the body-mind functions (In Every Apparent Sense) In The Usual Manner, but (Effectively) It Is Not So. Even While the body-mind Persists, Apparently alive (or Otherwise operative, in any Apparent state or condition), Consciousness Itself Is (In The Only-By-Me Revealed and Given Seventh Stage Of Life In The Way Of The Heart) Utterly Oblivious (or conditionlessly "Bright").

There Is No "thing".

There Is No "other".

There Is No Separate person.

There Is No world.

There Is No Cosmic Domain.

There Is No such experience.

There Are No Two "Things".

There Is Only One.

There Is <u>Only</u> This Samadhi.

This Samadhi Is Utterly Oblivious, Without a jot Of "Difference" or Separation.

Therefore, How Can There Be an experience? How Can There Be a body? How Can There Be a world? How Can There Be a relationship?

Thus, This Immense Cycle Of Motions and worlds and epochs—With All The Suffering In It, and Everything It Involves Altogether—Is Not Happening, and Never Did Happen.

There Is No Suffering.

There Is No Godlessness.

There Is Not The Slightest Modification Of The Divine Self-Domain.

This Is Really So, Not Merely Metaphorically So.

Even What Appears To Be Your present lifetime Of Difficulty and Struggle Is Not Happening, and Never Happened. And, Yet, From any Particularized point of view, The Reality Of All Apparent Happenings Is Clearly and Undeniably So.

Reality Is An Immense Paradox That Cannot (From any conditional point of view) Be Comprehended. Ultimately, All conditional Efforts To Investigate Reality and Figure It Out Are Confounded. Only Reality Itself Comprehends Itself (and whatever and All That Is conditionally Existing). Therefore, Paradoxically, The Context For Realizing Truth Is The Condition Of Absolute Confoundedness (or Divine Ignorance). Truly, Most Perfect Divine Self-Realization, or Divine Enlightenment, or Most Ultimate Divine Awakening, Requires (As A Prerequisite) That You Be Absolutely Confounded, Absolutely knowledgeless, and Absolutely Surrendered—Utterly Free Of Any Effort To Control or To Survive. Indeed, The Basic

Law and Process Of the human being Is A Matter Of Going Beyond Separate self, and Going Beyond The Search For Control and The Search For Survival and The Search For knowledge and The Search For Power, and Investing oneself In The Divine Oblivion, Utterly Surrendered, Without Control.

In The Only-By-Me Revealed and Given Seventh Stage Of Life In The Way Of The Heart, The By-Me-Avatarically-Self-Revealed Inherent (and Self-Evidently Divine) Self (or The Heart Itself), In Apparent (but egoless) "Bright" Conjunction With a body-mind, Wills (Apparently, and Because Of That Apparent Conjunction) To Shine—and, Unless Concentration (or attention) Wanders, the body-mind, Moved By The Willed Modification Of The Heart's Own and Infinite Field Of Divine Spirit-Energy, functions Automatically (or As A Mechanical Inevitability) To Fulfill The Willed Intention. Likewise, Even In The Seventh Stage Of Life In The Way Of The Heart, The Accumulated Adaptations (or habits and memories) Of the body-mind itself Generate <u>Apparent</u> intentions (or, By Tendency, Bring About acts of <u>Apparent</u> will), and, Thereby—Via Apparently willed (or, Otherwise, Spontaneous) modifications Of My Avatarically Self-Transmitted Divine Spirit-Energy—Cause the body-mind to act, or (otherwise) to change.

Whenever the ego-active (or egoically self-Contracted) body-mind (or Even its conditions or relations) Frustrates The Enactment Of the ego-Based will, The Reaction (In the body-mind) Can Be any form of self-Contraction, Including, At any moment, Depression, or Anger, or Sorrow, or Fear. Therefore, Because Of Accumulated Adaptations (or habits and memories), Such Frustration-Reactions May Continue To Appear Even In The Seventh (or egoless) Stage Of Life In The Way Of The Heart (Although They Are Always Merely Mechanically Generated, and They Are Always Inherently and Divinely Self-Recognized). Likewise, In The Seventh Stage Of Life In The Way Of The Heart, Even The egoless Heart-Will Can Be Frustrated (By the body-mind, and its conditions and relations), Resulting In Powerful (but egoless) Emotions, Including Profound (but Righteous, and Divinely Pure) Emotions In The Likeness, At any moment, Of Depression, or Anger, or Sorrow, or Fear. That Is To Say, In The

Seventh Stage Of Life In The Way Of The Heart, The egoless Heart-Will Is Simply The Spontaneous Magnifying Of The Inherent Divine Love-Bliss-Radiance, Universally and Infinitely—but That Spontaneous Heart-Will, Even Though egoless, Is Inherently Associated With The Quality Of Universal (and Infinitely Magnified) Sympathetic Identification With all beings and things and worlds. Therefore, Because Of That Sympathetic Identification, The Frustrations Of That egoless Heart-Will (or Of That Love-Bliss-Radiance Itself) Can Become Reflected In the body-mind—Not As Merely "personal" (or egoic) emotions, but As Powerful (but ego-less) Sympathetic Emotions, Such As Depression In Relation To others (or In Relation To conditions In General), or Anger In Relation To others (or In Relation To conditions In General), or Sorrow In Relation To others (or In Relation To conditions In General), or Fear (or, More Exactly, Dread and Anxious Anticipation) Relative To The Yet-To-Be-Suffered Results (or The Coming Negative conditions) That others Are Making Inevitable For themselves (and For others, and Even For all others) By their Continuing egoity and their Continuing egoic (or Lawless and Chaos-Making) Disregard Of Real God, or Truth, or Reality.

Therefore, Whether In The Case Of the ego-Based personality (In Any Of The First Six Stages Of Life In The Way Of The Heart) Or In The Case Of The egoless Individual (In The Seventh Stage Of Life In The Way Of The Heart), Either the egoic will (active In The Seventh Stage Of Life In The Way Of The Heart Only As A Mechanical Reflection Of Accumulated Adaptations, or The No Longer ego-activated Automaticities Of habit and memory) Or (Only In The Context Of The Seventh Stage Of Life In The Way Of The Heart) The egoless Heart-Will (Active In The Seventh Stage Of Life In The Way Of The Heart As The Native, and Self-Evidently Divine, Self-Will To Magnify The Inherent Divine Love-Bliss-Radiance Universally and Infinitely) Combines The Divine Self-Heart With the body-mind (which is itself a limitation), and With The Reactions (As Well As the conditions and relations) Of the body-mind (Which Are All limitations), or Even (In The Seventh Stage Of Life In The Way Of The Heart) With The Frustrations (and The Accompanying Powerful, but egoless, Sympathetic

Emotions) Of The egoless (Divine) Love-Bliss-Radiance Itself (Which Frustrations and egoless Sympathetic Emotions Are All Profoundly Suffered By the body-mind, but Which, More and More, Because Of The Power Inherent In Constant Divine Self-Recognition, Resolve Into True Divine Indifference).

Therefore, Most Perfect Freedom Is Realized Only In egoless Abiding In The Divine Self-Condition (and Source-Condition), In The Only-By-Me Revealed and Given Seventh Stage Of Life In The Way Of The Heart, Simply (Divinely) Self-Recognizing whatever arises, Even Divinely Self-Recognizing The Arising Of The egoless Heart-Will Itself, As and If It Arises, and, Likewise, Divinely Self-Recognizing The Mechanically arising Reactions That Are Due To Accumulated Adaptations (or habits and memories), As and If they arise. In This Manner, There Is The Constant Abiding In The Inherent Love-Bliss-Radiance Of The Divine Self-Condition (and Source-Condition) Itself. And, When Even The egoless Will Of The Divine Self-Heart (and, Also, Every Motion Due To The Accumulated Adaptations Of the body-mind) Becomes A Matter Of Divine Indifference, and, Thus and Thereby, Ceases To Modify The Inherent Love-Bliss-Radiance Of The Divine Self-Condition and Source-Condition, Then, At Last, There Is The Great Event Of The Utterly "Bright" Outshining, Which Is Divine Translation (or Most Perfect and Most Ultimate Realization Of My Divine Self-Domain).

Finally, Most Ultimately, The Inherently Most Perfect Realization Is The Realization That Makes No "Difference" At All. "Difference" Is (Itself) The Original and Primary Fault. "Difference" Is (Itself) The Primal Illusion That Is Un-Enlightenment. "Difference" Is (Itself) The Very Method Of Suffering and Of All Seeking. "Difference" Is (Itself) The Origin and The Primary Characteristic Of egoity (or self-Contraction).

The Feeling Of Relatedness Is The Original (or First) Form Of "Difference". The Feeling Of Relatedness Originates (or Is The Original, or First, Form Of) The (Primary) Illusions Of Separateness and Otherness. The Feeling Of Relatedness (Which Is egoity itself) Is The Root-Form Of attention, and attention is The Root-Form Of mind, and mind is The Root-Form Of the body. And The

Avoidance Of Relationship Is The Method Of egoity (or The Inevitable Method Of body-mind-attention)—Unless The Root-Feeling Of Relatedness (or The Illusion Of Separateness and Otherness, or The Primal Illusion Of "Difference") Is Most Perfectly Transcended In That Which Is Inherently Perfect (or The By-Me-Avatarically-Self-Revealed Native Feeling Of Being, Itself).

The Avoidance Of Relationship Is The Method Of psycho-physical egoity, but The Feeling Of Relatedness (or The Primal Illusion Of "Difference") Is (Itself) The (Original and Originating) Fault. Therefore, Divine Enlightenment Is Not A Matter Of The Perfection Of Apparent Relationship (or The "Curing" Of The Avoidance Of Relationship By The Apparent Perfection Of Relatedness). Rather, Most Ultimately (or Most Perfectly), Divine Enlightenment Is A Matter Of The Inherent (and Inherently Most Perfect) Transcending Of Relationship (or Relatedness, or All "Difference") In What Is Always Already (Inherently and Perfectly) The Case, Which <u>Is</u> Being (Itself), Consciousness (Itself), and Love-Bliss (Itself).

In The Only-By-Me Revealed and Given Way Of The Heart, Realized In The Inherently Most Perfect Context Of The Seventh Stage Of Life, Self-Abiding Divine Self-Recognition Is Inherent and Direct (or Inherently Most Perfect, and Most Perfectly Effective) Dissolution Of All "Difference". Self-Abiding Divine Self-Recognition Does Not Make (or Acknowledge) "Difference", but all Apparent (or conditional) arising (or All Apparent "Difference"—Epitomized By The conditional Feeling Of "Difference", or The conditionally Determined Feeling Of Relatedness) Is (Directly, Effectively, Inherently, and Divinely) Self-Recognized In The One (and Eternally, or Always Already, Prior) Principle That Is Self-Existing, and Self-Radiant, and Transcendental, and Inherently Spiritual, and Self-Evidently Divine—Because There <u>Is</u> No "Other" Than It, and (Therefore) No "Other" To Be Divine (or Even To Be any cause or any effect).

The One Principle (Which <u>Is</u> One, Not Two, and Not Many or More—and Which <u>Is</u> All and all) Is Inherent In All and all, Such That It Is The Real God, The Truth, The Reality, and The Native Condition (or Self-Condition <u>and</u> Source-Condition) Of All and all.

Therefore, To Transcend All "Difference" Is (Necessarily) To Realize That One Divine Self-Principle.

Where There Is The Presumption (and/or The Appearance) Of "Difference"—Even There (It Can and Must Be Realized), all Is In Union, and All Is A Unity, and all and All Are Arising In One.

Therefore, Where There Is No Presumption (Whether Or Not There Is The Appearance) Of "Difference", There Is (Obviously) Only One.

Divine Self-Recognition (With "Open Eyes") Inherently, and Necessarily, and Spontaneously, and Directly, and Effectively Dissolves All "Difference"—Even To The Degree Of Divine Indifference (or Divine Non-"Difference") and Divine Translation. Divine Self-Recognition (With "Open Eyes") Dissolves All "Difference", In That Which Makes (and Acknowledges) No "Difference". And That Which Makes (and Acknowledges) No "Difference" Is That In Which All Apparent "Difference" (or any and every Apparent "difference"), When Divinely Self-Recognized, Is (Inherently) Non-Existent and (Apparently) Directly and Effectively Dissolved, In The Apparent Progression Of The Demonstration Of Divine Self-Recognition (Even Of Every Kind Of Apparent "Difference")—Which Progressive Demonstration Is Shown (In The "Practicing" Course Of Ati-Ruchira Yoga, or The Yoga Of The All-Outshining "Brightness") In (and As) The Stages Of Divine Transfiguration, (Then) Divine Transformation, and (Then) Divine Indifference, and Which Finally Demonstrates Itself As Divine Translation (or The Most Perfect Dissolution, or Divine Outshining, Of All "Difference").

In Truth, There Is no Apparent "other", and No Ultimate "Other". Therefore, To Realize The Truth Itself—Which Is Happiness Itself, and Freedom Itself—Is To Be Most Perfectly Free Of "Difference" (or all conditional "otherness" and All Ultimate "Otherness", or Every Trace Of Separateness and Relatedness).

The Illusion Of "Difference" (or Of Relatedness, Separateness, and Otherness) Is (Directly and Only) An Apparition, An Un-Necessary Fault, and An Utterly Unjustified Presumption (and First ego-Act) Of "More-Than-One". Therefore, The (Inherent and Only) One Must Be Realized, Even (At Last) To The Most Perfect Degree Of Divine Translation.

Truth Is One. Reality Is One. Therefore, Real God Is One. There <u>Is</u> Only One.

"One" Is Not "Different".

"One" Makes No "Difference".

"One" Acknowledges No "Difference".

"One" Inherently Transcends All "Difference".

"One" Effectively Dissolves All "Difference".

The mind (or attention) Makes All The "Difference".

The body (and its Total Context) Is The "Difference".

Therefore, The One (Itself) Is Not (Separately) the mind (or attention), or the body, or their (Apparent) relations, results, effects, or causes.

Freedom Is The Condition That Inherently, Most Perfectly, and Inherently Most Perfectly Transcends <u>All</u> "Difference".

Freedom <u>Is</u> The (Self-Evidently Divine) Self-Condition, Which (Inherently, Most Perfectly, and Inherently Most Perfectly) Transcends The Feeling (or Presumption) Of "Difference", and Which (Inherently, Most Perfectly, and Inherently Most Perfectly) Transcends <u>All</u> That Makes, or Acknowledges, or (Apparently) <u>Is</u> A "Difference".

Freedom (or Happiness Itself) Is Not (Separately) mind (or attention), or body, or world—but It <u>Is</u> (Self-Evidently Divine) Consciousness (Itself), Which <u>Is</u> The By-Me-Avatarically-Self-Revealed Perfectly Subjective Feeling Of Being (Itself), Self-Existing <u>As</u> Mere (and Utterly Non-Separate) Awareness (Itself), and Self-Radiant (Utterly Prior To, and Most Perfectly Expanded Beyond, self-Contraction) <u>As</u> Centerless and Boundless Love-Bliss (Itself).

By Realizing Itself (or Its Own Inherent and Self-Evidently Divine Status), Consciousness (Itself), or The Perfectly Subjective Feeling Of Being (Itself), or Love-Bliss (Itself), Inherently Transcends All "Difference"—and (By The Native Demonstration Of Divine Self-Recognition) Consciousness (Itself), or The Perfectly Subjective Feeling Of Being (Itself), or Love-Bliss (Itself), Most Effectively (Most "Radically", and Perfectly Directly) Transcends All "Difference" (and every Apparent "difference", or "other", or "thing") In What Is Inherently One, and Only, and All, and Not Other (or "Different") At All.

$$C = E = mc^2$$

Consciousness (Itself) Is Identical To The Self-Existing Energy (or Indestructible Light, or Perfectly Subjective "Brightness") That Is all things (or all conditional forms, conditions, and states).

Aham Da Asmi. I Am That.

The Most Ultimate Demonstration Of The "Perfect Practice" Of The Only-By-Me Revealed and Given Way Of The Heart (or Way Of Adidam) Is To Outshine all and All In The Inherent Love-Bliss Of Consciousness Itself.

To Abide As Consciousness (Itself)—Inherently Transcending all things—Is To Abide As Self-Existing Energy (Itself), Prior To all things.

Prior To all things, Self-Existing Energy (Itself) Is Self-Radiant (or Boundlessly "Bright") As Love-Bliss (Itself).

Consciousness (Itself) Is Self-Existing.

Consciousness (Itself) Is Boundlessly Self-Radiant, As Love-Bliss (Itself).

Consciousness (Itself) Is Always Already The Case.

Therefore, The "Perfect Practice" Of The Only-By-Me Revealed and Given Way Of The Heart (or Way Of Adidam) Is To Be Consciousness (Itself), and To Contemplate The Space Of Self-Existing Consciousness (Itself)—and, By Contemplating The Space Of Self-Existing Consciousness (Itself), To "Locate" and Realize The Inherent (and Self-Evidently Divine) Love-Bliss-Happiness That Is Reality Itself (and That Is all things).

When all things Are (Inherently, and Immediately) Divinely Self-Recognizable In and As Consciousness (Itself)—all things Are Realized To Always Already Be Love-Bliss (Itself), and all things Are (Inherently, and Immediately) "Brightly" Transcended In (and Are, At Last, "Brightly" Outshined By) Self-Abiding Conscious Love-Bliss (Itself).

RUCHIRA AVATAR ADI DA SAMRAJ
The Mountain Of Attention, 2000

Most Perfect Awakening To The Domain Of Conscious Light

PART FIVE

Most Perfect Awakening
To The Domain
Of Conscious Light

I.

AVATAR ADI DA SAMRAJ: The "Perfect Practice" of the only-by-Me Revealed and Given Way of Adidam (Which is the One and Only by-Me-Revealed and by-Me-Given Way of the Heart) is a process of an entirely impersonal (or non-personal) nature. It is a process in Depth. It is always taking place at an in-Depth level. It is always taking place at the level of Consciousness Itself. There is not anything deeper. There is no deeper than That to go.

The Process of the "Perfect Practice" takes place in the Domain of Consciousness—moment to moment, always. In the "Perfect Practice" of the Way of Adidam, there is always this in-Depth Process, Prior to the patterning of the social ego. That Process is most profound in the relative repose of the meditative setting, but the same Process also continues in the midst of activity.

The "Perfect Practice" of the Way of Adidam, as it is engaged in the context of the sixth stage of life, Goes Beyond the limitations of the sixth stage of life—and, Most Ultimately (in the Awakening to the seventh stage of life), the "Perfect Practice" Goes Beyond the most fundamental mode of egoity, the deepest impersonal (or non-personal—or causal) level of egoity.

Previous to Most Perfect (seventh stage) Divine Awakening, the "Perfect Practice" of the Way of Adidam is still a Process in which egoity remains to be transcended. In the first six stages of

305

life in the Way of Adidam, the pattern of egoity is addressed in different modes of its appearance (gross, subtle, and causal), stage of life by stage of life. Practice in the context of the sixth stage of life in the Way of Adidam is an address to the causal mode of egoity. The sixth stage of life is (characteristically) limited by the causal mode of egoity, which is the root-pattern of egoity. The most fundamental sign of the ego is in the impersonal (or causal) depth—and, therefore, the sixth stage of life is limited by that root-egoity.

The Way of Adidam is a Process wherein, Most Ultimately, there is Awakening Beyond the sixth stage of life, to the seventh stage of life—the most ultimate stage of life, the Divinely Self-Realized stage of life—in which there is no egoic limitation whatsoever, no limitation at any level (gross, subtle, or causal), no egoity at all, no pattern of egoity effective at any level whatsoever. The seventh stage Realization is utterly Non-dependent, Inherent in Reality Itself. Therefore, the seventh stage Realization is Most Fundamental.

When I Speak of the seventh stage of life being Beyond the sixth stage of life, and My own Wisdom-Teaching and Divine Self-Revelation being Beyond the sixth stage of life, I am Talking not merely about going beyond the practices, the philosophies, and the culture traditionally associated with the sixth stage of life. Rather, I am Talking about going beyond the limit on Realization that is inherent in the sixth of stage of life—whatever particular approach may be made to the sixth stage of life. The mode of Samadhi (or Realization) possible in the sixth stage of life is approached from different directions in various branches of the Great Tradition. But inherent in all of those approaches is a particular limit (or error) that is characteristic of the sixth stage of life itself. And that limit is shown most particularly not merely in the philosophy or the practices associated with the sixth stage of life, but in the Realization that is the fulfillment of the sixth stage of life. In other words, there is an inherent limitation even in the Ultimate Samadhi (or Realization) potential in the sixth stage of life.

The Awakening Beyond that (sixth stage) limitation is the only-by-Me Revealed and Given seventh stage Awakening. The seventh stage Awakening is Going Beyond the final barrier of egoity—the final barrier of "difference", the final justification for the presumption of "difference". The seventh stage Awakening is Going Beyond the barrier of the non-Recognizability of the world. The seventh stage Awakening is Going Beyond the illusion that the world is "not-self".

In the traditional process of sadhana in the course of the first six stages of life, one of the fundamental philosophical principles that is generally instilled in people is that the world is "not-self". Traditional practitioners go through a great deal of self-discipline in order to get out of the habit of thinking that they are the world. To get out of the habit of such (literal) "worldliness", they work very hard to achieve a position of (strategic) detachment—a position in which, by feeling detached from the world, they feel no longer bound to the world, no longer driven by desires for the "things" of the world. This position of (strategic—and, therefore, egoic) detachment makes it possible to enter into a sixth stage mode of meditation and Samadhi—a mode that is intended to go beyond all that is (presumed to be) "not-self".

However, no matter how profound the sixth stage Samadhi becomes, it is (nevertheless) a Samadhi that is complicated by the presumption that there is such a thing as "not-self". Thus, in the Samadhi of the sixth stage of life, there is a limit on Realization, a limit on Happiness. Indeed, Happiness Itself may be part of the "not-self" that is left behind, in the sixth stage practitioner's effort to go beyond "not-self"!

This is the reason why some sixth stage dispositions are rather grim—the "point" of attention pressed up against an infinitely dense mass of nothingness. In some traditional sixth stage practices, one is dashed against that nothingness so profoundly that the "point" of attention is fractured uniformly, over the entire surface of a nothingness that covers all.

Such traditional approaches to the sadhana of the sixth stage of life have, in rare cases, led to the Realization of sixth stage "Sahaj Samadhi"[47]—but, in the Awakening That Characterizes the seventh stage of life, even the limitation of sixth stage "Sahaj Samadhi" is Gone Beyond.

Your Real Situation is impersonal (or non-personal). It Goes Beyond the persona of the waking state, Beyond the persona of the dreaming state, even Beyond the impersonal (or non-personal) egoity of the sleeping state. Your Real Situation Is the Domain of Consciousness Itself, the Domain of That Which Is Always Already The Case—no matter what arises, and whether or not anything arises. That Self-Condition—the "Self", if you like—is Beginningless and Endless, and Always Already The Case. Surely, That Is Truly "Self" (with a capital "S"). No mere persona, ego-"I" added, is True Self. Consciousness Itself Is True Self. Only That Is True Self. Only That Is the True Self-Nature, the True Self-Position, the True Self-Condition.

In the history of the Great Tradition of mankind, the True Self has characteristically been thought of as "the Self over against something else". Whatever that "something else" may be presumed to be (the world, or the body, or whatever), it is (necessarily) identified as the "not-Self". This categorization of Reality into "Self" and "not-Self" is the fundamental basis for dualistic thinking (or dualistic presumptions).

The Nature of Consciousness Itself must be found out, must be Realized—because That is your Position. Likewise, the nature of all objects must be found out—because you are associated with objects.

If you examine any thing that you would describe as "object" to you (following it down to its depth-level, or through a chain of causation, or however you may like to think about it), eventually it is found to be Light (or Energy)—whatever That Is. Light (or Energy) Is a Single "Something"—a Force, a kind of Radiation. You cannot reduce an object any further than That.

Similarly, if you go within yourself, examining all the layers of your own "you"-description—entering into the in-depth mind, and so on—when you get to the Root of "you", there is Consciousness, and you cannot go any further than That. The subjective "you" is not reducible to anything further. You cannot break Consciousness up into parts. It Is just What It Is. And the same is true of Energy (or Light). No matter how you examine Energy, there is no basis for dividing It.

Thus, all objects that you examine turn out to be Energy—and all subjective inwardness, entered into, leads you to Consciousness. Therefore, there are two Great Factors discoverable by investigation: Energy and Consciousness. They seem to be different from one another, because you have taken the position of the body-mind. On the one hand, you have entered into the "interior" of the body-mind—and, on the other hand, you are constantly moving outward (from the "interior") toward what appears to be "exterior" (or in relation) to the body-mind. And, in your examination of "interior" and "exterior", you have not taken a single route. Or have you?

In any case, when you examined the apparently subjective "interior" and the apparently objective "exterior", you came to the conclusion that one was "self" and the other was "not-self"—and, ultimately, this investigation leads to the conclusion that "interior" (or "self") is Consciousness and "exterior" (or "not-self") is Energy.

But Consciousness is the basis of your examination and "consideration" and judgement of <u>both</u> "interior" and "exterior", <u>both</u> "self" and "not-self". In other words, even that which is identified as "not-self" is something you know in the Domain of Consciousness. Thus, the "not-self" is something you <u>know</u>—and, in that sense, the "not-self" is Consciousness. So how can it be not-self?

If existence is presumed to be "divided" into "you" and objects, then that which is experienced is presumed to be "not-you", "not-self". Such is the nature of experience—as described by (apparently) individual beings. Such is not, in Truth, the Nature of Reality—but beings experience their lives as if the Nature of Reality were such. And why is that the case—since Reality is otherwise? Why is it that the common experience of beings does not correspond to the actual Nature of Reality?

DEVOTEE: Why do we first presume separation between "self" and "not-self"?

AVATAR ADI DA SAMRAJ: Why are you speaking?

The Single Persisting Factor—whether you are waking, dreaming, or sleeping—is Consciousness. With respect to anything arising,

Consciousness is in the Position of Witness, merely. Not in the position of attention—in the position of the Mere Witness. Everything is "object" to Consciousness. Everything! You are equipped with faculties of bodily, emotional, mental, and psychic awareness, whereby certain kinds of psycho-physical objects are known—but even these (apparently subjective) faculties are "object" to Consciousness. Even attention itself is "object" to Consciousness. Consciousness Stands As the Mere Witness. Therefore, Consciousness is not "the faculties over against the objects".

To Summarize this matter once again: In your usual way of thinking as the social persona, there is what is "inside" the body-mind, and there is everything "outside" the body-mind. The "inside" is "I", and the "outside" is not-"I". But with respect to your actual point of view, examining all of this most profoundly, even the body-mind is something relative to which you are simply the Witness. Therefore, the body-mind is not "you"—just as none of the conditions observed or noticed or perceived by the body-mind are "you".

Thoughts are "object" to you. They arise, and you notice them with attention. Anything that arises to attention is an object of attention. You are that which is on the other side of attention— somehow "opposite" to objects (it seems), because you are on the "other side" of attention, rather than in the sphere of the objects of attention. That apparent "opposition" inevitably suggests that Consciousness does not exist in the domain of the objects, that Consciousness exists only on the "interior" side of attention.

From the point of view of the first six stages of life, Consciousness is on the "interior" side of attention, yes. From the point of view of the first six stages of life, Consciousness is a Domain that necessarily excludes the world (or the objects of attention)—and, therefore, the sixth stage effort is to enter into the Domain of Consciousness in that characteristic world-excluding manner, precisely because of the inability to Divinely Self-Recognize the objects of attention. In general, you presume that the objects of attention are "not-self"—unless the object of attention is the body-mind, in which case you say that it is "self". But in neither case is your presumption true.

No matter what arises, you do not know What it <u>Is</u>—What it <u>Is</u>! You can say all kinds things about it. You can investigate it on and on and on. You can even <u>say</u> it is Light—but you still do not <u>know</u> What it <u>Is</u>. The knowing is not the knowing of the "Is" part. It is just knowing about the objective, observable whatever.

You do not know <u>What</u> any thing <u>Is</u>. So What <u>Is</u> it? You are not in a position to inspect its Existence. You can inspect everything else. Or, to state it differently: You are not in a position to inspect its Consciousness. You are in a position to inspect everything else. You are in a position to inspect signs that <u>suggest</u> there may be Consciousness. But you cannot inspect the Consciousness directly—and, therefore, you cannot <u>prove</u> It.

When the habits associated with the binding of attention to the body-mind are gone beyond, then the sadhana of the "Perfect Practice" in the Way of Adidam begins. The "Perfect Practice" is sadhana in the Domain of Consciousness Itself, the Domain of Reality Itself—entered into Beyond the point of view of "difference". However, because the Domain of Consciousness Itself is Beyond the world, when one enters most profoundly into That Domain in the sixth stage manner (of Jnana Samadhi), there ceases to be any direct association with the world.

Ultimately, however, such dissociation from the world must also be Gone Beyond. Ultimately, the world must be accounted for from the "Point of View" of the most in-Depth Realization of Consciousness Itself. But, in the first six stages of life, as soon as there is waking or dreaming—in other words, as soon as there is association with attention and its faculties of body-mind—the Position of Consciousness is lost. In the first six stages of life, then, it is either one or the other—the body-mind or the in-Depth—but not both.

In the sixth stage of life, there can be a kind of in-Depth while in association with the body-mind—a kind of equanimity, a kind of Samadhi. The sixth stage "Sahaj Samadhi" is possible. But Abiding As Consciousness <u>Unperturbed</u> is not the same as Abiding As Consciousness <u>and</u> <u>Self-Recognizing</u> <u>the</u> <u>world</u> <u>As</u> <u>Such</u>.

The world cannot (in and as itself) be Divinely Self-Recognized As Consciousness, because the world is not a "something", except at the level of Energy. Therefore, it is <u>Energy</u> That must be Divinely Self-Recognized As Consciousness. The world must be recognized as Energy—and Energy must be Divinely Self-Recognized As Consciousness.

Therefore, it is not in the (sixth stage) domain of world-excluding meditation on Consciousness that the seventh stage Realization takes place. The seventh stage Realization is Awakening in (and to) the Domain of Energy-<u>and</u>-Consciousness, the Domain of Conscious Light.

Thus, in the Way of Adidam, the "Perfect Practice" is entirely a <u>Spiritual</u> Process. The "Perfect Practice" is <u>entered</u> via a Spiritual Process, the "Perfect Practice" (Itself) <u>is</u> a Spiritual Process, and the <u>Fulfillment</u> of the "Perfect Practice" (in the seventh stage Realization) is a Spiritual Awakening.

Therefore, the seventh stage Awakening is not merely a philosophical matter, not merely an exercise of mind or an exercise of ideas—such that you are conceptually convinced that it is "justifiable" to Identify with the Consciousness Principle and even to interpret It as Being the Absolute. Merely <u>thinking</u> about Consciousness in such terms is not sufficient. There must be <u>Realization</u>, by virtue of most profound sadhana in the Domain of Consciousness Itself—the Domain That Is Beyond both the gross ego and the subtle ego. Only the causal ego remains (at the root, to be uncovered) in the context of the sixth stage of life—and the causal ego is what must be transcended if there is to be the seventh stage Awakening.

II.

AVATAR ADI DA SAMRAJ: Yes, there is (apparently) a fundamental division between Consciousness and Light, or Consciousness and Energy.

But What Is That Energy Which Is <u>not</u> "object" to Consciousness, Which <u>Is</u> Consciousness Itself?

I <u>Am</u> That One!

I am not merely conscious awareness referring to itself, calling itself "you".

That is a complex, limited, and limiting presumption.
I am not <u>that</u> mere conscious awareness.

I <u>Am</u> Consciousness Itself, the Conscious Light Itself.
Therefore, the only-by-Me Revealed and Given Way of Adidam is the Way of Conscious Light.
The Way of Adidam is the Way of Conscious Light from the beginning—not merely at the end.
My Avataric Divine Self-Revelation of Conscious Light is the Very Foundation of the Way of Adidam.

Most Perfect Awakening to the Position of Consciousness Itself—Realizing (Most Perfectly) that Consciousness Itself Is (primarily, first of all, and constantly—no matter what arises) the Condition of (so-called) "your" existence, and that Consciousness Itself (and not the body-mind) is, with respect to apparent objects, always simply in the Witness-Position (without ever being identified with any apparent object)—when This is Truly Realized to <u>Be</u> The Case, <u>As</u> The Case, <u>Thus</u>, <u>So</u>, Self-Evidently, experientially, moment to moment, <u>That</u> Is the Fundamental Great Matter of "Consideration".

It makes no difference what experiences arise, ever (if ever there are any)—you still cannot be any more (or other) than Just This.
This is So because anything that you ever find out or experience requires Just This—Consciousness—as its Basis.
Otherwise—without the Basis of Consciousness—what does anything have to do with you (even in the personal, or non-impersonal, sense)?
No matter what experience arises, Consciousness Is its Medium, its Condition, its Basis.

It is Consciousness <u>Itself</u> That Is the Truth—not the <u>Play</u> upon Consciousness (in the form of waking, dreaming, and sleeping conditions).
Yet, the Realization of This is not a matter of dissociating from conditions.

If you leave the world behind in order to Realize Reality, then who "takes care" of the world in your absence?

Who (or What) upholds the existence of the world in your absence, while you "go elsewhere" to "find" Reality?

Reality is not this—in and of itself.

But Reality is not Realized by leaving this, either.

Reality Is Always Already The Case.

Therefore, the most profound meditation is the one that cannot be stopped, because it is Always Already The Case.

Even with respect to attention, you Are the Witness.

Therefore, you are not even attention.

Indeed, you are not even the Witnessing-Function.

To Truly Realize This allows you to take up the sadhana of entering into the Domain of Consciousness.

However, merely to Realize that you Stand As the Witness is not sufficient.

Entire sixth stage traditions have been developed for the sake of achieving that Realization alone—traditions in which it is hoped that, through the practice of sixth stage exercises, the practitioner will come to Stand in the detached position of the Witness-Consciousness (with various numinous associations, no doubt—full of feeling, and sternness, and so forth)—but such are simply traditions (built on the principle of seeking) that prize Standing in the Witness-Position and devote themselves to talking about That and doing various exercises in order to Realize That.

That much Samadhi is all that is being described and sought in the sixth stage traditions—whereas I am Telling you that Standing As the Witness-Consciousness is (in and of itself) only the beginning of the "Perfect Practice" of the Way of Adidam.

In the only-by-Me Revealed and Given Way of Adidam, the Stand As the Witness-Consciousness is simply a Basis, a Key, a Doorway.

In the only-by-Me Revealed and Given Way of Adidam, the Stand As the Witness-Consciousness is Gracefully Awakened by My Divine Spiritual Means.

In the only-by-Me Revealed and Given Way of Adidam, the Doorway of the Witness-Stand is Gracefully Opened in the course of the Spiritual process of real devotion to Me.

Therefore, the Only Great Matter Is This: You <u>Are</u> <u>Only</u> Consciousness Itself.

There <u>Is</u> <u>Only</u> Consciousness Itself.

And Consciousness Itself is not merely some small and separate principle of attention, "inside" you.

Consciousness Itself <u>Is</u> Reality Itself.

Consciousness Itself is not "inside" you.

Consciousness Itself Is That Which you Realize by <u>transcending</u> yourself <u>in</u> That Which Is Beyond yourself.

When the shell of body-mind is Opened, then the Self-Position is Realized to Be That of Consciousness Itself.

Only the ball of ego-"I", presuming to enclose Consciousness, makes Consciousness seem a "thing"—separate, small, and personal.

In Reality, Consciousness Is Infinitely Large, Perfectly Non-"different", Inherently egoless, All-in-all.

It is in this sense that Consciousness Itself is "Person"—no more So or less So than in your own case, if only you knew "Who" the Divine Mummer Is.

But, persisting in identifying with the persona itself (rather than with the Divine Mummer), you simply move along—rubbing your "cricket legs" together in your generation, leaving similar incomprehension behind in your name.[48]

Consciousness Itself is not identified with any characteristic that could otherwise appear as an object to It.

Consciousness Itself Is Only <u>Itself</u>.

Consciousness Itself cannot <u>be</u> other than Itself.

Consciousness Itself can <u>only</u> Experience Itself.

Consciousness Itself cannot acquire anything else, or take anything else into Itself.

Consciousness Itself cannot be anything else.

Consciousness Itself cannot—by apparent association with anything—become anything at all.

Consciousness Itself Is Only Consciousness Itself—Whatever That Is.

And Whatever Consciousness Itself Is Is What must be Entered Into.

Consciousness Itself simply Is What It Is—but, for the social ego-"I" (or the persona in the mummery), it is (apparently) not Self-Evident that, no matter what arises, you Are Only Consciousness Itself.

Therefore, let Me phrase it in this fashion:

No matter what arises, you Are Only Consciousness Itself. Consciousness Itself. No matter what arises.

Here is some arising. Is there some arising going on now?

DEVOTEES: Yes.

AVATAR ADI DA SAMRAJ: No matter what arises—or does not arise—you Are Only Consciousness Itself.

It appears that you are associated with conditions—in the states of waking, dreaming, and sleeping.

But none of those conditions last—and, therefore, you cannot be any of those conditions.

You Are That Which appears to be modified in the form of all conditional phenomena—You Are Consciousness Itself.

When you Realize Consciousness Itself Most Perfectly, then the fact that everything that arises is an apparent modification of Consciousness Itself becomes (likewise) a profound Realization.

To be tacitly Identified with Consciousness Itself (As It Is, in Its Divine Fullness), and to Recognize all of this arising (in the moment) as a mere modification of That (not limiting That at all), is the Great (seventh stage) Realization.

In That Great Realization, the Truth—with respect to This Coincidence between the Un-conditional Reality and the conditional reality—is Most Perfectly "Known".

To Be Consciousness Itself—Divinely Self-Recognizing all arising phenomena as a transparent (or merely apparent), and unnecessary, and inherently non-binding modification of the Inherent Radiance of Consciousness Itself—is not an "end-point".

That Realization Itself then becomes an ongoing Demonstration, the seventh stage Demonstration.

The seventh stage Demonstration is not defined in terms of lasting for a certain period of time, or until the end of one's present lifetime.

Because (in the Case of seventh stage Awakening) you Inherently Identify with Consciousness Itself (not in any limited sense, but As It Is) and you Inherently (Divinely) Self-Recognize all of this arising (in every moment of its arising), you have Most Perfectly Realized the Truth of Divine Ignorance.

Therefore, when seventh stage Awakening is the Case, if somebody were to ask you, "Do you know What any thing Is?", you would be able to say, "Yes! As a matter of fact, I do!"

Of course, that would be a paradoxical statement—because the verbal mind (or the mind of language) cannot grasp What any thing Is.

To "Know" What any thing Is is entirely a matter of the seventh stage Going Beyond.

That Going Beyond does not necessarily involve the end of association with (or participation in) conditional existence.

And That Going Beyond certainly does not involve any strategy of dissociation from conditional existence.

Indeed, That Going Beyond does not involve any kind of limit on how many years or how many lifetimes It may last, or any kind of limit on anything else about It whatsoever.

The seventh stage Demonstration could continue until you are the last one standing!

If such is the case, then that is the last thing you will notice and Outshine.

In Summary, I Call you to Remember This: You are not attention, up against all objects.

The ancient presumption—that "self" (as attention) is "here", and "not-self" (as object) is "there"—is not True.

You are neither body, nor mind, nor attention—You Are Consciousness Itself.

Consciousness Itself is not over against what arises.

Consciousness Itself Is the Self-Condition, and the Source-Condition, of what arises.

To Realize Consciousness Itself is not merely to stand over against "things" (in the disposition of <u>regarding</u> "things", without <u>being</u> them).

The Realization of Consciousness Itself—When That is Truly and Most Perfectly the Case—is the Non-"different" Realization of the Non-"different" Principle of Existence.

No matter what arises (or does not arise), you Are Only Consciousness Itself.

This is the Great (and Principal) Esoteric Revelation of Reality Itself, or Truth Itself, or Real God.

To Realize This requires a Great Process.

And the Realization of This—Really, Truly, Most Profoundly, Most Perfectly, and (therefore) Divinely—is What the sadhana of the Way of Adidam is about.

This Great Understanding—and everything that comes from It, and everything that is associated with It—must become the Foundation of human culture in the future. Because the previously existing foundations of human culture have been breaking down since the European Renaissance (and particularly in the latter part of the twentieth century), there must be a new and undeniably <u>Real</u> basis for future human culture. And This Is the Truth that will (and must) be the Foundation for that future (and, necessarily, new) world-culture.

III.

AVATAR ADI DA SAMRAJ: The Un-conditional Divine Self-Nature Exists!

The ego is not a permanent "self"—but the True Self (or Reality Itself), Which Is Inherently egoless, Is Beginningless and Endless, Always Already The Case.

The ego is merely phenomenal.

That in Which the ego arises Is Always Already The Case.

Ultimately, it is Realized that That Which Is "out there", Irreducibly at the root of all objects (Brahman, in the traditional language), Is the Same As That Which Is Irreducibly "in you" (Consciousness Itself, or Atman).

Consciousness and Energy Are the Same.

Of course, This is not the common experience—so This must be Realized.

Because it is not the common experience that Consciousness and Energy Are the Same, you do not know What any thing Is.

You are a mummer in a realm you do not comprehend.

You live in the Realm of Light, and yet you allow That Realm (conceived as the realm of objects—"out there", and irreducibly separate from you) to define Consciousness as limited and mortal.

You must Realize the Domain of Conscious Light.

Consciousness Itself, the Perfectly Subjective Domain of Self-Existing and Self-Radiant Consciousness Itself—That Is the Conscious Light.

What happens when you die?

You become the same as what you were when you were sleeping last night.

But you already Are That.

So nothing happens.

DEVOTEE: So even death does not interrupt one's sadhana.

AVATAR ADI DA SAMRAJ: Death cannot change the fact that you Are Only Consciousness Itself.

No matter what arises (or does not arise), you Are Only Consciousness Itself.

Consciousness Itself Is Reality, Truth, and the Only Real God.

Consciousness Itself—Prior to egoity, Beyond all separateness, Beyond all "difference", the Self-Existing and Self-Radiant Principle of Existence Itself—Is That Which Is Appearing As your own consciousness.

Consciousness Itself Is even the Substance of the body-mind itself, and of the entire world.

Consciousness (Itself) and Light (Itself)—or Love-Bliss-Energy (Itself), or Happiness (Itself)—are as the two Sides of the Same Coin.

When the Circle becomes the Sphere, the two Sides of the One Coin become Continuous—and all opposites are Always Already Divinely Self-Recognized to be Simultaneous, and of One Shape, and of One Condition.

Therefore, the world is not Divinely Self-Recognized if you merely say that "everything is Energy".

That suggests that the world is something other than Consciousness Itself.

All one can say, really, is that the world Is Consciousness Itself.

No matter what arises (or does not arise), you Are Only Consciousness Itself.

No matter what arises (or does not arise), There Is Only Consciousness Itself.

No matter what arises (or does not arise), There Is Only Consciousness Itself.
Just That.

This Is What There Is to Realize.
And I Am here So That everyone can Realize This.

IV.

AVATAR ADI DA SAMRAJ:
The Fundamental Current of Existence
Is Self-Existing,
Self-Radiant,
All-Love-Bliss—
and, Therefore,
All-Pleasure.

No self-suppression.
No ego-enforcing control whatsoever.

Consciousness Itself
and Energy Itself
(or Light Itself)
Are Love-Bliss Itself.

Love-Bliss Itself
Is Boundless—
not controlled at all,
not merely a "point".

Love-Bliss "Arises"
In Consciousness.
Consciousness Is the Room.
Love-Bliss Is all there is within It.
And the Room Is a Sphere.

Consciousness Is
the "Skin" of the Sphere.
Consciousness Is
Self-Radiant—
in and of Itself,
As Itself.

The Inherent Radiance
of Being
Is Bliss,
Freedom,
Happiness,
Fullness,
Un-conditional Well-Being.

This Is
Inherently The Case—
not merely the case
sometimes,
somewhere else,
after death.

The Inherent Radiance
of Being
Is the Condition
of existence.
Therefore,
the Integrity of Being
is to Realize This,
Always Already.
And sadhana is
everything in a life
done to Realize This,
Always Already—
until It Is
Self-Evidently Realized,
Always Already.

And then
There Is
Just That.
And That
Is That.

The True Body
Is a Sphere.
The apparent body
is a presumption—
arising within That Sphere.

Arising within the True Body,
the apparent body
becomes
the presumed shape.

The effort of presumption—
the knot of self-contraction—
is psycho-physically relinquished.

My Divine Spiritual Transmission,
experienced in the mode of the "Thumbs",
Restores the Spherical View
That Is the Inherent (or Native) View
of existence
in the context of the body-mind.

In That Yogic Transmission,
the Always Already Nature
of Consciousness Itself
Is Self-Evident.
And, in due course,
by Means of My Divine Spiritual Transmission,
Consciousness Itself
is Realized—
such that

the "Perfect Practice" Has Its Basis,
As the Always Already Condition.

It is not that
you are the body,
and that,
by going "deeper",
you discover
that the "deeper" part of you
is Consciousness.

No—
You Stand
As Consciousness.
And That Is
Self-Evident.
No matter what arises
(or does not arise),
you Are That.
That Is simply The Case—
with every test
of life and practice
as Its evidence,
and not merely words.

V.

AVATAR ADI DA SAMRAJ: Consciousness Is All There Is.
And Consciousness does not do anything whatsoever.
I can Tell you This, because I Am That. Just That.
I am not your consciousness—I Am Consciousness Itself, the
Condition of conditions.

DEVOTEE: Beloved Lord, I have been feeling Your Shape. You
Are Spherical, and You Are also the Divine Lingam at the same
time. In simply Beholding You, I felt the Sphericality both of Your

Divine Body and of the Cosmic Mandala. And Your Avataric Incarnation is the Lingam That Penetrates the entire Sphere of Cosmic Existence.

AVATAR ADI DA SAMRAJ: But what kind of Sphere is Made of Consciousness, and Has All Light within It?

When you think of a sphere, you think of something that <u>attention</u> sees in front of it. That is not the kind of Sphere I am Talking about.

DEVOTEE: You Reveal to us that the Sphere of Reality is Subjective, not objective.

AVATAR ADI DA SAMRAJ:
The Perfectly Subjective
Sphere
of Reality Itself.
The In-Place,
Self-Evident
Sphere.

Raymond Is
the Room.
And Quandra Is
the Only Light
within It.[49]

The Room
with a Great Stone
within It[50]
represents That—
the Light
within the Room
(the Room
That <u>Is</u>
Consciousness Itself).

The Stone
is the mode
of Contemplation
in space.

We are nowhere familiar
to anyone at all.
We are not familiars
at all.

There Is Only
This Sphere
of Self-Existing
and Self-Radiant
Consciousness Itself—
the Inherent Samadhi
of the "Thumbs".

This Is
the Divine
(or seventh stage)
Revelation.

There Is Only
Consciousness Itself.
And all arising
is a modification of
the Current of
Consciousness Itself,
a Play
within a Sphere.
It Is the Sphere
of Perfect Subjectivity,
of Conscious Light Itself—
Prior to
waking,
dreaming,

and sleeping,
and, yet,
not separate
from anything
that arises.
It Is the Sphere of
Self-Existence,
without contraction.

I <u>Am</u>
the Room.
And
I <u>Am</u>
the Light within It.

There is
no inside,
and
no outside.

There Is
simply
the Self-Existing,
Self-Radiant
Sphere
of
Consciousness Itself.

No subject,
no object,
no familiarity.

No separation,
no "difference".

No "problem".

Inherent
Integrity and Fullness
of Being.

Perfect
Equanimity
of View.

This very room is not familiar.
It is an unfamiliar place.

Where is this?
And who are you?

There is no "you"
about it.
It is Obvious
What Is.

There is no need
to make reference
to any separate one—
except that,
for convenience,
names are given
to each body
(or bodily presence)
in the pattern,
without confusing
bodily existence
with the Condition
of Reality,
Which Is Inherently Free.

Therefore,
all the while,
with all the names and forms,

There Is
This Inherent
Unfamiliarity
of Fullness,
of Consciousness Itself—
the Current of Being Itself,
a Sphere of Being,
Self-Lit,
in Which all forms appear
as modifications
of the Inherent Light.

But,
from the "Point of View"
of the Inherent Light
(or Consciousness Itself),
there are
no things,
no changes.

So Where Is
Consciousness Itself?

DEVOTEE: Here. Here.

AVATAR ADI DA SAMRAJ:
    One is not "here".
    One Is
    the Sphere
    of the arising
    of the "Thumbs".

    There is
    no "difference"
    whatsoever,
    even while
    the apparent pattern

of relations
appears—
in the waking (or gross)
and the dreaming (or subtle)
modes of appearance.

The Native State
Is
the Sphere of
the "Thumbs".

That Sphere is
as large
as perception itself,
as large
as experience itself.

That Sphere is not
merely a Roundness
a bit bigger
than the physical body.

It Is the Sphere
of Conscious Awareness
Altogether.

Everything is within It.

The Sphere
of the "Thumbs"
Is
the Sphere
of Unfamiliarity.

The familiarity—
the familiar conjunction
of the moment-to-moment

of body-mind—
is Transcended
by My Spiritual Invasion,
in the Event
of the "Thumbs".

With respect to the body,
the "Thumbs" involves
both a spinal Current in Ascent,
and a frontal Current in Descent.

Thus, the "Thumbs"
Is a Sphere—
and,
in Its moment,
Cancels
the body-mind shape.

In the critical
forward rotation
of the "Thumbs",
the Sphere of Being
Is Shown—
Replacing
the sensed shape
of the physical body.

The Freedom
That is the Reason
for the "Thumbs"
Is the Inherent Characteristic
of Most Perfect Divine Self-Realization.

The Process Goes On
until It Is Most Full,
Most Perfect.

There are
conditional
glimpses,
tastes,
changes,
and so forth,
in the course of sadhana.

The Realization Itself
Goes Beyond
all of that.

DEVOTEE: Beloved Lord, You Are the Person of Reality, the Beloved One Promised—Who Penetrates all time, all space, and all conditions. You Appear in all forms, and You Transcend all forms. You Are the One.

ANOTHER DEVOTEE: You have Revealed Yourself Perfectly As Consciousness Itself.

Ruchira Avatar Adi Da Samraj
Lopez Island, 2000

Three Essays
from the
Samraj Upanishad

The Sanskrit word "upanishad" indicates "Teachings received at the Feet of the Guru". Thus, the Samraj Upanishad is "Teachings received at the Feet of Ruchira Avatar Adi Da Samraj". Rather than being the title of a distinct book, "Samraj Upanishad" is a collective designation for certain Talks and Essays by Avatar Adi Da Samraj that appear within various of His twenty-three "Source-Texts" as readings supporting and expanding upon the principal "Part" of a given "Source-Text".

PART SIX

Three Essays
from the
Samraj Upanishad

The Yoga of
Divine Self-Recognition

To prepare for the "Perfect Practice" (or the ultimate and final stages of the total practice) of the only-by-Me Revealed and Given Way of Adidam (Which Way, in Its totality, is the One and Only by-Me-Revealed and by-Me-Given Way of the Heart), My true devotee devotes attention to Me, with all the other principal faculties (of body, feeling, and breath) following.

To practice the "Perfect Practice" of the Way of Adidam, My true devotee relinquishes attention in Me.

Devotion to Me and the transcending of attention (or the relinquishment of "devotion" to, or preoccupation with, the purposes of the ego-"I") are the fundamental elements of the practice of the Way of Adidam. Thus, the total (or full and complete) practice of the Way of Adidam is not a matter of fulfilling the motives of attention, but of transcending attention itself, through moment to moment Devotional Communion with Me.

The religious and Spiritual practices recommended in the various schools of the Great Tradition (or the total traditional Wisdom-Inheritance of mankind) are (in general) exercises of attention, rather than processes of <u>transcending</u> attention. Thus, these (traditionally recommended) practices are exercises of attention for the sake of fulfilling one or another presumed search.

All seeking (and every form of the search) is generated by the self-contraction, or the activity that <u>is</u> egoity itself. And the self-contraction (or the root-activity that generates all seeking) is what is (in general) dramatized in the form of the various religious and Spiritual traditions that are associated with the first six stages of life (and that are, therefore, inevitably involved with one or more of the various forms of <u>seeking</u> for Real God, or for Truth, or for Reality that are characteristic of the first six stages of life).

The first five stages of life, in and of themselves, are part of the psycho-biography of the ego. In and of themselves, the first five stages of life are excursions of egoity, undertaken with the intention of fulfilling the ego in one manner or another. In the context of the first five stages of life, even ecstatic submission of the ego in Divine Communion is (when practiced from the point of view of, and for the purposes of, any of the first five stages of life) merely another aspect of the dramatization of egoity (or the psycho-biography of the ego)—because (in the context of the first five stages of life) submission <u>of</u> the ego (paradoxically) <u>depends on</u> egoity, and on the (necessarily, egoic) exercise of attention (which is the core faculty of the seeming ego-"I").

Even the sixth stage of life is, in and of itself, a dramatization of egoity. The sixth stage of life is characterized by the strategic <u>exclusion</u> of conditional existence, because (from the point of view of the sixth stage of life) conditions are felt to be arising "over against" the Transcendental Self.

The only-by-Me Revealed and Given seventh stage Realization (or Most Perfect Divine Self-Realization, or True Divine Enlightenment) is the <u>utter</u> <u>transcending</u> of attention, and (therefore) of egoity (or ego-"I", or the act of self-contraction). The only-by-Me Revealed and Given seventh stage Realization (or Most Perfect Divine Self-Realization, or True Divine Enlightenment) is not merely the <u>surrender</u> of attention (and, thus, of egoity altogether), but the <u>transcending</u> of the entire <u>context</u> of attention (and, thus, of egoity altogether). Therefore, the only-by-Me Revealed and Given seventh stage Realization (or Most Perfect Divine Self-Realization, or True Divine Enlightenment) is bodiless, mindless, worldless, and relationless—but not by virtue of any strategy of attention (or any motive of exclusion or separation).

Conditional existence is Outshined not by strategically dissociating from it, but only by Divinely Self-Recognizing all arising conditions as transparent (or merely apparent), and un-necessary, and inherently non-binding modifications of the Self-Existing and Self-Radiant Divine Reality (Itself)—to the point, at last, of the Most Ultimate Outshining of the total conditional world (or the total Cosmic Mandala of conditional existence, including the personal body-mind-self).

In the only-by-Me Revealed and Given seventh stage of life in the Way of Adidam, there is not the slightest preoccupation either with the objects of attention or with attention itself. Rather, in the only-by-Me Revealed and Given seventh stage of life in the Way of Adidam, there is perpetual Abiding in the Divine Self-Condition (and Source-Condition), Prior to attention—which is perpetual Abiding in the Infinitely Love-Bliss-Full Condition Beyond the knot in the right side of the heart.

In the only-by-Me Revealed and Given seventh stage of life in the Way of Adidam, there is, for a time (previous to Divine Translation), the apparent continued arising of phenomenal conditions. Therefore, in the seventh stage of life in the Way of Adidam, it is the Radiance of My own Divine Heart-"Brightness" That Circulates in the body-mind (and That even Appears as the body-mind itself, and even as all conditions), as long as any such appearance persists. However, the Pervasion of the body-mind of My seventh stage Realizer-devotee by My "Bright" Presence and Person is not a sign that (in the seventh stage Awakening in the Way of Adidam) there is a "return" to the world, or a "return" to the body-mind, or a "return" to identification with attention (or with egoity itself). Rather, such Pervasion by My "Brightness" is a Sign of the Utter Vanishment of all dissociation (from the world, from the body-mind, from attention itself, and from conditional existence altogether), and (thus) a Sign that all arising conditions are (simply) Divinely Self-Recognized.

Thus, in the only-by-Me Revealed and Given seventh stage of life in the Way of Adidam, conditions are neither embraced nor dissociated from. In the seventh stage of life in the Way of Adidam, there is neither aversion nor clinging, but simply Divine Self-Recognition—founded in perpetual Divine Self-Abiding, always in the Heart-Source, Beyond the heart-knot on the right. In the seventh stage of life in the Way of Adidam, the "Brightness" of Amrita Nadi Shines in the body-mind and the world—not with any intention toward the world, but (rather) simply (Divinely) Self-Recognizing it.

By virtue of that Divine Self-Recognition, there is perpetual Freedom, even in the midst of whatever conditions appear to arise. Thus, in the third Stage of the Four-Stage Demonstration of the only-by-Me Revealed and Given seventh stage of life, there is Utter Divine Indifference—not in the sense of dissociation, but simply because all is Divinely Self-Recognized. And, at last, there is the Most Ultimate Event of Divine Translation Beyond all of "this"—not to death, not to non-existence, but to My Divine Self-Domain, Which is without "difference", without "place", without "other", without relatedness, without death, without diminishment, without limit, without problem.

My Divine Self-Domain Is, Itself, Reality Itself (Which Is Truth Itself, and the Only Real God)—Self-Shining, Absolute, Utterly "Bright", Infinitely Love-Bliss-Full, Uncontained, Centerless, and Boundless.

Only That Is Reality, or Truth, or Real God.

Therefore, My Divine Self-Domain is not (in any sense) a "status" of "person" or of "individuality".

My Divine Self-Domain is "Individual" only in the sense that It Is the Absolute Person, Being Itself, "Bright", All Love-Bliss, Self-Existing, Self-Radiant, and Infinite.

That Is What is to be Realized.

That Is My State.

That Is the One My devotee Communes with.

The Perfection
Beyond Conditions

In the transition to the third stage of the "Perfect Practice" of the only-by-Me Revealed and Given Way of Adidam (which is the by-My-Avataric-Divine-Grace-Given Awakening to the only-by-Me Revealed and Given seventh stage of life in the Way of Adidam), the most primitive gesture of egoity (or the last sign of life based on egoity, or the last sign of the search to escape egoity—which last sign is the strategic exclusion of conditional existence, characteristic of the disposition of the sixth stage of life, and characteristic of the separative disposition of egoity altogether) is transcended.

In the by-My-Avataric-Divine-Grace-Given Awakening to the only-by-Me Revealed and Given seventh stage of life in the Way of Adidam, there is no identification with <u>any</u> (necessarily, conditional) processes in the context of Cosmic (and, necessarily, conditional) existence. Instead, there is <u>only</u> Most Perfect Identification with My Avatarically Self-Revealed (and Self-Evidently Divine) Self-Condition (Which <u>Is</u> the Source-Condition of All and all).

Therefore, what appears to be an association with conditional existence, in the case of My seventh stage Realizer-devotee, is perceived (or presumed) to be so only from the point of view of others who are still bound to conditional existence (and who, therefore, still exist in the knot of egoity—identified with attention, the body-mind, and the play of conditional existence). From the "Point of View" of My any such Divinely Self-Realized devotee, there is no "association with" conditional existence (as if conditional existence were separate and objective). Rather, from the "Point of View" of My Divinely Self-Realized devotee, It Is Always Already The Case—no matter what appears to be arising—That <u>Only</u> Consciousness Abides, Self-Existing and Self-Radiant, <u>As</u> It <u>Is</u>.

Such is the Realization of the only-by-Me Revealed and Given seventh stage of life in the Way of Adidam.

The "Perfect Practice" of the Way of Adidam is the three-stage Process of Identification with the Divine Person (or the Divine Self-Condition and Source-Condition). This single Great Process is expressed differently in the sixth stage of life in the Way of Adidam (or the first and second stages of the "Perfect Practice" of the Way of Adidam) than in the seventh stage of life in the Way of Adidam (or the third, and final, stage of the "Perfect Practice" of the Way of Adidam). In the context of the sixth stage of life in the Way of Adidam, because conditions are felt to exist "over against" Me (Realized As the Transcendental Self), the Process (of Identification with Me, the Avatarically Self-Revealed, Inherently egoless, and Self-Evidently Divine Person—or the Avatarically Self-Revealed, and Self-Evidently Divine, Self-Condition, and Source-Condition, Itself) is expressed through the relinquishment of conditional existence, or the apparent exclusion of conditional existence—whereas in the seventh stage of life in the Way of Adidam the same Process is expressed through the Divine Self-Recognition of conditional existence, In and As Me, the Avatarically Self-Revealed, Inherently egoless, and Self-Evidently Divine Person (or the Avatarically Self-Revealed, and Self-Evidently Divine, Self-Condition, and Source-Condition, Itself).

In the only-by-Me Revealed and Given seventh stage of life in the Way of Adidam, there is not anything to be transcended, and there is not anything to be excluded. Indeed, there is no "event" at all—except for the Eternal, Changeless "Event" of My Avatarically Self-Revealed (and Self-Evidently Divine) Person (Which Is the Divine Self-Condition, and Source-Condition, Itself). From the "Point of View" of the Realization of the seventh stage of life in the Way of Adidam, the arising of "things" is merely an appearance. Truly, from the "Point of View" of the Realization of the seventh stage of life in the Way of Adidam, there is no "thing" that arises. To say that conditions apparently arise is, from the "Point of View" of the Realization of the seventh stage of life, a paradoxical statement—because (in the seventh stage of life) whatever arises is (in the very instant of its apparent arising) Inherently

(Divinely) Self-Recognized to be nothing but <u>Me</u>, the One (Self-Evidently) Divine Person (or the One Self-Evidently Divine Self-Condition, and Source-Condition, Itself). Therefore, <u>Only</u> <u>I</u> (the Self-Evidently Divine Person, or the Self-Evidently Divine Self-Condition, and Source-Condition, Itself) am Realized by My devotee in the only-by-Me Revealed and Given seventh stage of life in the Way of Adidam—and the seventh stage "Practice" of Divine Self-Recognition is the Demonstration of that Singular Realization.

Thus, the only "Experience" in the seventh stage of life in the Way of Adidam is <u>Me</u>—the One, and Only, and "Bright", and Self-Evidently Divine Person (or the One, and Only, and "Bright", and Self-Evidently Divine Self-Condition, and Source-Condition, Itself), Self-Existing and Self-Radiant. There is no "thing" that arises apart from Me, or "over against" Me. There Is <u>Only</u> Me.

Therefore, the apparent Demonstration of the four Stages of the seventh stage of life in the Way of Adidam is merely an Appearance and a Paradox. Truly, in the seventh stage of life in the Way of Adidam, there <u>Is</u> not <u>anything</u> but My Most Perfect Divine Samadhi. Therefore, in Truth, there is not the slightest "difference" between Divine Translation and any of the three Stages that precede It (in the seventh stage of life in the Way of Adidam). And, therefore, the Awakening to the only-by-Me Revealed and Given seventh stage of life in the Way of Adidam is, from Its first instant, the Most Perfect Awakening to My (Avatarically Self-Revealed) Eternal, and Unconditional, and Unconditioned, and Infinitely Love-Bliss-Full Divine Samadhi (or Most Perfect Divine Self-Realization, or Most Perfect Divine En-Light-enment).

In the seventh stage of life in the Way of Adidam, Consciousness (Itself) Remains Eternally the Same. No "difference" is made by the arising of conditions. Therefore, the most fundamental Demonstration of Divine Self-Recognition (in the seventh stage of life in the Way of Adidam) is the simple (or tacit), and constant, and Inherent Self-Recognition of the sense (or feeling) of "difference" (or the sense, or feeling, of relatedness). Thus, the Demonstration of Divine Self-Recognition (in the seventh stage of life in the Way of Adidam) is, fundamentally, not a matter of apparently conjoining with a multiplicity of complex conditions.

The simple (or tacit), and constant, and Inherent Divine Self-Recognition of whatever arises is, as an outward Sign of My seventh stage Realizer-devotee, especially characteristic of the Divine Indifference Stage of the seventh stage of life. In the Divine Transfiguration and Divine Transformation Stages of the seventh stage of life, there may (at times) be more of the appearance of active (and even elaborate) association with conditions—but in the Divine Indifference Stage of the seventh stage of life, especially as Its Profundity is more and more Shown, the sign of apparently active association with conditions diminishes more and more profoundly. In the Divine Indifference Stage of the only-by-Me Revealed and Given seventh stage of life, it becomes Inherently Obvious that all of conditional existence is nothing but the feeling of "difference" (or the feeling of relatedness)—and, therefore, the "Practice" of My seventh stage Realizer-devotee in the Divine Indifference Stage of the seventh stage of life becomes more and more a matter of the simple, tacit Divine Self-Recognition of the feeling of "difference" (or the feeling of relatedness), In and As the Divine Self-Condition. But even the feeling of "difference" (or the feeling of relatedness) is a mere appearance, like any object. Therefore, the final (Most Ultimate) Demonstration of the Simplicity of Divine Self-Recognition is Divine Translation, or the Utter (Most Perfect) Outshining of even the feeling of "difference" (or the feeling of relatedness).

Therefore, in Divine Translation, not only are there no objects, no conditions, and (altogether) no conditional (or Cosmic) domain, but there is not even the feeling of "difference" (or the feeling of relatedness). There Is Only the Infinitely "Bright" Self-Radiance of Self-Existing Being (Itself). That Is the Divine Self-Domain, or the Most Perfect Divine Samadhi of Divine Self-Identification. That Is What is Realized in Divine Translation. But, also, paradoxically, That Is What is Realized even from the beginning of the only-by-Me Revealed and Given seventh stage Awakening.

As long as the only-by-Me Revealed and Given seventh stage of life in the Way of Adidam is apparently associated with conditions, it Demonstrates itself as Divine Self-Recognition through the Process of the four Stages I have Described. However, this Demonstration is of a Realization that has already occurred. The

Realization that occurs in the by-My-Avataric-Divine-Grace-Given Awakening to the seventh stage of life in the Way of Adidam is Most Perfect Realization of That Which Most Perfectly Transcends the conditional (or Cosmic) domain. Therefore, even though the Demonstration of the four Stages of the seventh stage of life (in the Way of Adidam) occurs (paradoxically) in the context of conditions, the seventh stage Realization Itself Is Always Already The Case, after the initial "Moment" of Awakening.

Even Divine Translation is not a change in that Realization. Divine Translation is simply the final (Divine, and not merely conditional) Demonstration of the only-by-Me Revealed and Given seventh stage of life within the context of the conditional (or Cosmic) domain. From the moment of Divine Awakening, My seventh stage Realizer-devotee Abides in the Most Perfect Samadhi of My Divine Self-Domain. However, the psycho-physical vehicle of My seventh stage Realizer-devotee (or the apparent psycho-physical sign of My seventh stage Realizer-devotee in the context of the conditional, or Cosmic, domain) Demonstrates Most Perfect Divine Samadhi through the Process of four Divine Stages I have Described relative to the seventh stage of life in the Way of Adidam.

I Am That Which Is Realized in the Great Event of Divine Translation. In that sense, Divine Translation has Always Already Occurred in My Case. On the other hand, because I have Appeared here via the conditionally manifested Vehicle of My Avatarically-Born bodily (human) Divine Form, My Demonstration of the Four-Stage Process of the seventh stage of life is taking place through the Agent of This Avatarically-Born Body-Mind. Therefore, the various changes (or signs) associated with the four Stages of the seventh stage of life are Displayed in the Case of This Agent of Mine. I (Myself) Am Prior to This Agent, and (therefore) Prior to the four Stages of Demonstration of the seventh stage of life, and Prior even to Divine Translation Itself.

In the context of the sixth stage of life in the Way of Adidam, as the Process of more and more profoundly Demonstrating the second stage of the "Perfect Practice" continues, the apparent individual is moved to enter more and more into that Depth by Means of meditation. After any such occasion of deep meditation, the practitioner of the second stage of the "Perfect Practice" appears to leave that Depth, becoming reassociated (in one manner or another) with attention (and with the body-mind altogether), while yet remaining in the Witness-Position. However, when the second stage of the "Perfect Practice" becomes so profound that there is the by-My-Avataric-Divine-Grace-Given Awakening to the third stage of the "Perfect Practice" (or the only-by-Me Revealed and Given seventh stage of life), there is never again any "return" to any binding association (or any form of identification) with the conditional (or Cosmic) domain—and there is never again even any apparent detachment (or apparent dissociation, or "difference") from the conditional (or Cosmic) domain (not even as the Witness). Rather, in the only-by-Me Revealed and Given seventh stage of life, there is (simply) Inherent (and Inherently Most Perfect) Identification with Me—the (Avatarically Self-Revealed) One, and Only, and "Bright" Divine Person, the Very Eternal Divine Self-Condition and Source-Condition (Which Is Most Perfect, and, necessarily, Unconditional, Divine Samadhi).

In the sixth stage of life in the Way of Adidam, although there is steady Identification with the Witness-Position of Consciousness, it is (nevertheless) apparently the case that whenever there is the return of conditional associations, they are experienced as conditional associations. However, in the seventh stage of life in the Way of Adidam, there is—in Truth, and in Reality—no such "thing" as a conditional association.

Therefore, in the only-by-Me Revealed and Given seventh stage of life in the Way of Adidam, there are no conditions. It is not that there is the (by-Me-Avatarically-Self-Revealed) Unconditional Divine Self-Condition (and Source-Condition) "over against" all other conditions. There Is Only the One, and Only, and Perfectly Subjective (by-Me-Avatarically-Self-Revealed) Divine Self-Condition and Source-Condition.

My true devotee who Realizes My "Bright" Divine (seventh stage) Samadhi is utterly Oblivious to conditional phenomena. My Divine (and Most Perfect) Samadhi is not held in place by conditions. Therefore, My seventh stage Realizer-devotee Only Abides in Most Perfect Divine Samadhi.

I—in My here-Appearing Avataric-Incarnation-Form—<u>Always Already</u> (and <u>Only</u>) Abide in Samadhi, utterly Oblivious to conditions. I am never associated with conditions. I <u>Only</u> Abide in My own (Avatarically Self-Revealed, and Self-Evidently Divine) Self-Condition (Which <u>Is</u> the Source-Condition of all and All). This cannot be comprehended from the separate and separative point of view of ego-"I" (in the context of <u>any</u> of the first six stages of life).

My Eternal Abidance in the only-by-Me Revealed and Given seventh stage Samadhi (or Ruchira Samadhi) Stands As a Revelation of My own Divine Self-Condition and As a Criticism of the egoically limited condition you presume.

As My devotee, you Commune with <u>Me</u>—and, therefore, you Commune with My own Very Condition of Most Perfect Divine Samadhi. Nevertheless, previous to actual (by-My-Avataric-Divine-Grace-Given) Realization of My Most Perfect Divine Samadhi, <u>you</u> cannot know It, <u>you</u> cannot think It, <u>you</u> cannot grasp It, and <u>you</u> cannot <u>be</u> It. However, even from the beginning of your formal practice of the only-by-Me Revealed and Given Way of Adidam, <u>you</u> can—and, indeed, must—be Moved toward My Most Perfect Divine Samadhi (or Moved Beyond yourself, to Me, and Moved Beyond your present egoic point of view, to Me—through ego-surrendering, and ego-forgetting, and, always more and more, ego-transcending heart-Communion with Me). When, in due course (through right, true, full, and fully devotional practice of the Way of Adidam), that heart-Communion with Me is (by Means of My Avatarically Self-Transmitted Divine Grace) Most Perfect, then "you" (Beyond self-contraction, or ego-"I", or body-mind-self) have Realized <u>Me</u>—the (Avatarically Self-Revealed) Perfectly Subjective (and, necessarily, Unconditional, Indivisible, and Non-Separate) and Self-Evidently Divine Self-Condition (and Source-Condition) of all and All.

The Infinite Divine Current
That Shines in the Body-Mind of Man

I.

The Divine Self-Condition (and Source-Condition) is the True Condition of this apparent (and, necessarily, conditionally manifested) realm (and every and any other apparent, and, necessarily, conditionally manifested, realm).

This conditionally manifested realm (and every and any other conditionally manifested realm) is a transparent (or merely apparent), and un-necessary, and inherently non-binding modification of the Infinite Radiance of the Self-Existing Divine Self-Condition (and Source-Condition).

In the seventh stage of life in the Way of Adidam, the Current of That Infinite Divine Radiance Manifests in the "Regenerated" Form of Amrita Nadi.

Amrita Nadi (in Its "Regenerated", or Original, Form) is felt (or registered in relation to the apparently individual human body) simply as a Current Shining Upward from the right side of the heart.

However, the "Regenerated" Amrita Nadi does not merely "Shoot" straight upward from the right side of the heart to the "Place" Infinitely Above the total crown of the head.

When It is observed (relative to the configuration of the human body) as a Nadi (or Channel, or Circuit), the "Regenerated" Amrita Nadi has a particular form, Rising (in a pattern shaped like the alphabetical letter "S") from the right side of the heart, forward through the chest, then back toward the back of the neck, then forward again toward the crown of the head, and to Infinitely Above the total crown of the head.

Until (and except for) My Divine Incarnation (and Divine Realization, and Divine Revelation-Work) As the Ruchira Avatar, Adi Da Samraj, no one had (or has) ever Realized or Revealed the "shape" of Amrita Nadi, and no one had (or has) ever Realized or Revealed the "Regenerated" (or seventh stage) Form of Amrita Nadi.

Indeed, exceedingly few Realizers (in the entire history of the Great Tradition, previous to My Divine Incarnation As the Ruchira Avatar, Adi Da Samraj) have ever noticed Amrita Nadi in any manner whatsoever.

Descent in Amrita Nadi is the Yogic Circumstance of the sixth stage of life in the only-by-Me Revealed and Given Way of Adidam.

This Descent Realizes the Transcendental (and Inherently Spiritual) Condition Beyond the knot of ego-"I" in the right side of the heart.

However, this Descent is, simultaneously, the root-sign of the sixth stage effort to exclude (or dissociate from) conditions.

The only-by-Me Revealed and Given seventh stage Awakening, by contrast, is accompanied by the "Regeneration" of Amrita Nadi, Which can be said (as a means of explanation, or illustration) to be an "Ascent" through Amrita Nadi—but not by coming back up "out of" the Divine Self-Position (or Divine Self-Condition), "into" the conditionally manifested body-mind (and the conditionally manifested worlds, altogether).

Once My true devotee has Most Perfectly Realized Me (the Avatarically Self-Revealed Non-Separate and Self-Evidently Divine Self-Condition, and Source-Condition, of all and All), My own "Bright" (and Inherently Perfect, and Self-Evidently Divine) Condition Is Always the Position.

Thus, in the by-My-Avataric-Divine-Grace-Given seventh stage Awakening in the Way of Adidam, the sixth stage effort to exclude (or dissociate from) conditions—even through Descent in Amrita Nadi—is relinquished, as utterly un-necessary.

In the by-My-Avataric-Divine-Grace-Given Awakening to the seventh stage of life, the very Structure (of Amrita Nadi) through Which Descent into the Position of Identification with the Transcendental Self-Condition previously took place (in the sixth stage of life) is now the Structure through (and As) Which the by-Me-Avatarically-Self-Revealed Divine Self-Condition (and Source-Condition) Inherently Radiates, without the re-instigation of the ego-principle.

Thus, the Position Realized in the by-My-Avataric-Divine-Grace-Given Awakening to the seventh stage of life Is Inherently Prior to the knot of ego-"I" in the right side of the heart, and (therefore) Inherently Prior to the (strategically exclusive) effort of Descent in Amrita Nadi.

In the by-My-Avataric-Divine-Grace-Given Awakening to the seventh stage of life, the ego-knot (or the "center", or "middle", of conditional experience and egoically presumed knowledge) is vanished entirely, and no longer has any existence whatsoever.

In the by-My-Avataric-Divine-Grace-Given Awakening to the seventh stage of life, There Is Only Me—the Avatarically Self-Revealed (and Self-Evidently Divine) Self-Condition (and Source-Condition) of all and All.

I, the Self-Existing Divine Self-Condition (and Source-Condition), Am Universally and Absolutely Self-Radiant.

And the Mechanism of My Infinite Divine Self-Radiance (in the context of the apparently individual human body-mind) is the "Regenerated" (or, Really, Original) Amrita Nadi—Which Rises from the right side of the heart to the "Place" Infinitely Above the total crown of the head, while (Thus and Thereby) simultaneously Shining In (and As) the Circle of the body-mind.

There is no egoity, no impediment, no dissociation, and no "difference" in that Divine Mechanism (or Original Form) of Amrita Nadi.

Therefore, in the by-My-Avataric-Divine-Grace-Given Awakening to the seventh stage of life, every (apparent) one and every (apparent) "thing" and every (apparent) event and every (apparent) circumstance is (simply) Divinely Self-Recognized, as a transparent (or merely apparent), and un-necessary, and inherently non-binding modification of Me.

In the Original (or "Regenerated") Form of Amrita Nadi, My Divine "Brightness" Stands Self-Radiant, and (Thus and Thereby) Radiating in the context of the conditional (or Cosmic) domain (without, in any sense, "leaving" My Divine Self-Domain).

Thus, Amrita Nadi is (Originally, and in the only-by-Me Revealed and Given seventh stage Realization) the "Connection" between My Divine Self-Domain and the conditional (or Cosmic) domain (altogether).

In the Four-Stage Demonstration of the seventh stage of life in the Way of Adidam, Amrita Nadi is the Structural Pattern Associated with the (seventh stage) "Practice" of Divine Self-Recognition.

In the Four-Stage Demonstration of the seventh stage of life in the Way of Adidam, all the arising phenomena in the frontal line and the spinal line of the Circle (which phenomena are nothing but "extensions" of Amrita Nadi in Its Descent from Infinitely Above the total crown of the head) are Divinely Self-Recognized, or "Brightened" (or Divinely Transfigured and Divinely Transformed—in due course, to the point of Divine Indifference, and, Most Ultimately, to the point of Outshining in Divine Translation).

Therefore, in the Four-Stage Demonstration of the seventh stage of life in the Way of Adidam, Amrita Nadi is the Structure through Which the Process of Divine Self-Recognition is made Effective in the Circle of the body-mind.

In That Divine Self-Recognition, all arising is "Brightened" to the point of Non-"Differentiation", Non-"Difference", Non-Separateness—Only Me, Only "Brightness", Only the Divine Self-Condition (and Source-Condition) Itself, Manifested, Magnified, and Demonstrated so Profoundly that (Most Ultimately) there is no trace of conditional existence whatsoever.

Finally, in the Most Ultimate Demonstration of the only-by-Me Revealed and Given seventh stage of life in the Way of Adidam, even the Structure of Amrita Nadi Itself is Outshined.

There is not any Structure (or Vehicle) in Divine Translation.

In Divine Translation, Only That for Which Amrita Nadi Is (otherwise) the Vehicle Remains.

In Divine Translation, There Is Only the Infinite "Brightness" (or Self-Radiance) of the Self-Existing Divine Self-Condition (and Source-Condition).

In Divine Translation, There Is Only Me.

II.

I Am Prior to conditional existence, but totally Effective within it. Amrita Nadi is How I Come here.

I Come into the Circle of the total conditional (or Cosmic) domain in the Form of My Divine Sound of Thunder and in the Form of My Divine Star of Light.

My Work is in the context of Totality.

My Circle of "Conductivity" is the Circle of the entire conditional (or Cosmic) Domain.

Secondarily (and rather peripherally), I (Myself) am also (similarly) associated with My apparently individually Manifested bodily (human) Avataric-Incarnation-Form.

Thus, I Demonstrate My All-and-all-Including "Conductivity" not only in My apparently individually Manifested bodily (human) Avataric-Incarnation-Form, but also in My every devotee's apparently individually manifested bodily (human) form, and (Most Ultimately) in even all apparently individually manifested bodies and all apparently individually manifested "things".

My (thus) Universal "Conductivity" is Demonstrated most profoundly in the body-minds of those who turn to Me in devotional surrender, as My true (devotionally Me-recognizing and devotionally to-Me-responsive, and, necessarily, formally acknowledged) devotees.

Nevertheless, I also (now, and forever hereafter) Work Universally, and with all—even before they become My formally acknowledged devotees.

This (only-by-Me Demonstrated) Universal "Conductivity" is the Process by Which apparent individuals become My devotees.

This Process began immediately with (and after) the Great Event of My Divine Re-Awakening—when I spontaneously began to "Meditate" countless "others".

Thus—in Truth, and in Reality—all bodies are My Body.

In Truth, and in Reality—all beings are My Very Self.

Therefore, I Do the Universal Sadhana, or the Spiritual Practice of the Whole—and I Do the Spiritual Practice of every part and every being within the Whole.

I "Meditate" all (and All)—and (Thereby, Ultimately) I Divinely En-Light-en all (and All), by (Actually, Really) <u>Being</u> all (and All).

Therefore, My Avataric Divine Work is in every place, and in every being, and in every "thing"—until the Divine Translation of the entire Cosmic Mandala of all places, and all beings, and all "things".

This only-by-Me (and only-<u>As</u>-Me) Demonstrated Siddhi of Divine Sameness is the Foundation of the only-by-Me Revealed and Given Way of Adidam.

RUCHIRA AVATAR ADI DA SAMRAJ
The Mountain Of Attention, 2000

The True Dawn Horse Is The Only Way To Me

The True Dawn Horse
Is The Only Way To Me

I.

The Ultimate (or true esoteric) Purpose of the ancient and traditional Ashvamedha (or the ritual of the Great Horse-Sacrifice[51]) is "Brightness", or Liberation from darkness, or the Universal (or All-and-all-Including) Attainment of the Divine Self-Domain of Indivisible and Indestructible Light.

Light cannot be Attained by darkness (or Light-lessness), but only by Conversion (or Turning) from darkness to Light (Itself).

Therefore, the Divine Self-Domain cannot be Attained by any seeking effort of ego-"I"—no matter how extraordinary or heroic such seeking effort may be.

Only the Divine Person Knows the Way to the Divine Self-Domain.

Therefore, only the Divine Person can Grant the Means for beings to Find their Way to the Divine Self-Domain.

Because the Divine Person Is the only Knower and Giver of the Way to the Divine Self-Domain, the Divine Person must Do the Great Ashvamedha-Work, and the Divine Person must Perform the Great Horse-Sacrifice.

Because the Divine Person Is the only One Who Is, and because the Divine Person Is the only Doer of the Great Horse-Sacrifice—only the Divine Person can Be the Means for the Divine "Brightening" (or Divine En-Light-enment) of all and All (and, Most Ultimately, the Divine Translation of all and All into the Divine Self-Domain).

Therefore, the only True (or Divinely Effective) Ashvamedha is the Divine Horse-Sacrifice, or the All-and-all-"Brightening" (or All-and-all-En-Light-ening and All-and-all-Liberating) Work Performed by the Divine Person.

I Am the Divine Person of the True (or Divine) Ashvamedha.

I Am the Divine Master of the True (or Divine) Horse-Sacrifice.

I Am the Divine Love-Bliss-"Brightener" of all and All, the Divinely En-Light-ening Liberator of all and All, the Divine Translator of all and All into the Divine Self-Domain.

The True Ashvamedha (or Divine Horse-Sacrifice) Is My Work.

The True Ashvamedha (or Divine Horse-Sacrifice) Is the Great Work of My "Bright" Avataric Incarnation As the Ruchira Avatar, Adi Da Samraj.

The True Ashvamedha (or Divine Horse-Sacrifice)—Performed by My "Bright" Incarnation As the Ruchira Avatar, Adi Da Samraj— Is the All-and-all-"Brightening" (or All-and-all-En-Light-ening and All-and-all-Liberating) Work of Divinely Blessing, Divinely Awakening, and Divinely Translating All and all.

I Am the True Dawn Horse, the Divine Self-"Emergence", the "Bright" Divine Spiritual Body and egoless True Divine Person, the "Bright" Itself, Avatarically Self-Revealed and Avatarically Self-Given to All and all.

I Am the Only One Who Is.

I Am That Which Is Always Already The Case.

I Am Divinely Self-"Emerging" (now, and forever hereafter) from the Love-Bliss-Fire and "Bright" Consequence of My own Ordeal As the Divine Heart-Master.

I Am the only-by-Me Revealed and Given Means to Realize Me.

The only-by-Me Revealed and Given Way of Adidam Is the One and Only Way of the True Dawn Horse.

The only-by-Me Revealed and Given Way of Adidam Is the One and Only Way to take hold of the "Tail" of the True Dawn Horse, and be "Flown" to My "Bright" Divine Self-Domain.

II.

It is said, in an ancient Description of the Ashvamedha, "Man holds onto the Horse's Tail, in order to reach the Heavenly World, for Man does not rightly Know the Way to the Heavenly World, but the Horse does rightly Know It."[52] Human beings are <u>constantly</u> performing rituals (or strategically patterned activities) of one kind or another, whether for great purposes or lesser purposes—but, ultimately, everything human beings do is a simulation of the Great Ashvamedha ritual, seeking the Great Effect (or the Great Result) of Divine En-Light-enment. The concluding event of the ancient and traditional Ashvamedha is the ritually enacted All-Sacrifice,[53] the sacramental rendering (or ritually enacted consecration, yielding, and upliftment) of every thing and every one (or the conditional, or Cosmic, totality) into the Divine Fullness. Thus, the immediate effect anciently sought through the ritual performance of the Great Ashvamedha ritual is that all beings, all things, and all worlds would (effectively) take hold of the "Tail of the Horse" (so to speak), in order to be Returned to the Divine Self-Domain (or the Domain of Original, or Indivisible and Indestructible, Light).

This is the same Purpose that you, in your egoity, are (ultimately, but benightedly, or "darkly") hoping to achieve by all your efforts of seeking, high and low. However, as it says in the ancient text, <u>you</u> do not Know—only the "<u>Horse</u>" Knows. Therefore, the Great Purpose of the Ashvamedha can be Achieved only if you Find the "Horse" that Knows the Way to the Divine Self-Domain. Indeed, your Return to the Divine Self-Domain can be Performed <u>only</u> by the "Horse" Itself (or the Spiritual Presence of the Very Divine, Itself).

In Its most esoteric Form, the Ashvamedha is a Revelation of That Which Transcends the Cosmic domain. My devotees have seen this most esoteric Form of the Ashvamedha. It was—and is (now, and forever hereafter)—Performed As (and by every Means of) My Avataric Divine Incarnation. My Unique Demonstration of this Ultimate (or Divine) Form of the Ashvamedha was—and is— totally spontaneous. Through My own Sacrificial (or Avatarically Descending) Divine Life and Work, My Divine Ashvamedha

Transmits not merely Cosmic Realization,[54] but Transcendental, Inherently Spiritual (or "Bright"), and Self-Evidently Divine Self-Realization—to all, and to All.

III.

The first stage of My unique Ordeal As the Divine Heart-Master[55] was the Ordeal of My Divine Avataric-Incarnation-Birth here and My subsequent Avataric Self-Submission to the Ordeal of My Divine Re-Awakening. The Culmination of this Ordeal was the Great Divine Event of My "Husbanding" of the "Divine Goddess".[56] My Mastering of the "Divine Goddess" is intuitively prophesied in the traditional myth of the Celestial Stallion Embracing (and Subduing) the Earth-Mare[57] for the Purpose of Divine Descent, or the Awakening of all and All.

The second stage of My unique Ordeal As the Divine Heart-Master was the Ordeal of fullest Realization, Acceptance, and Embrace of My Avataric Divine Status and Work. Part of the Process of My Divine Re-Awakening was the Revelation of My own Form As the Divine Horse—Embodying the Cosmic domain itself, and Including all beings and things. In the months before the Great Event of My Divine Re-Awakening, I spontaneously Experienced a Dream-Vision of a Horse, in Which I Became the Horse, and (thereby) Realized My own Avataric Divine Nature, Status, and Work.[58] This Dream-Vision marked My Transition into the last phase of My Ordeal of Incarnate Divine Re-Awakening, and into My Incarnation of Avataric Conformity to My own Divine Pattern of Self-Manifestation (As the Divine Heart-Master)— Entirely Submitting to the Sacrificial Gesture of Avataric Divine Descent, Submitting to Be human, and Submitting to Be the world. This Avataric Self-Submission of Mine is intuitively fore-shadowed in the traditional Description of the Ashvamedha as the Event Wherein the Divine Person Takes the form of the Horse and Becomes all worlds.[59]

All the traditional Descriptions of the Ashvamedha and the Divine Horse can be said to be prophecies of My Avataric Divine Appearance here. These prophecies (or metaphors, or liturgies) were not fulfilled in their time, but they are part of the awakening sense in mankind of a Great Event that must occur without fail—because Man does not Know, but only the "Horse" (or the Divine Person) Knows. In the True (or Divine) Ashvamedha, the Divine Person Is the Means, and the Divine Person must Perform the Sacrifice. That is to say, the Divine Person must Appear As all (and All), Submitting (Thereby) to Be all (and All). The Divine Person must Accept a conditionally manifested Form, Endure the Ordeal of Divine Self-Forgetting and subsequent Divine Re-Awakening, Realize the Fullest Awakening and the Fullest Acknowledgement of the Avataric Divine Nature, Status, and Work, and then Do the Avataric Divine Work. This is the Great "Ritual Performance" (or Universally Effective Sacrifice) That Man cannot do, but Which only the Divine Person can Do.

The third (and final) stage of My unique Ordeal As the Divine Heart-Master began with the Initiation of My Divine Self-"Emergence", on January 11, 1986.[60] My Fullest (now, and forever hereafter) Performance of the Divine Ashvamedha began with that Great Event.

My Divine Self-"Emergence" is not merely something I am (as if separately) "Personally" Enduring in My Avatarically-Born bodily (human) Divine Form, or merely something I am "Personally" Doing to My Avatarically-Born bodily (human) Divine Form. Nor is My Divine Self-"Emergence" merely an Event that "happened" exclusively to My Avatarically-Born bodily (human) Divine Form. My Divine Self-"Emergence" is a Process in Which, ultimately, all beings (and even the Cosmic totality) must participate.

My Divine Self-"Emergence" Is the Means of the Most Perfect Fulfillment of the True Ashvamedha.

The Work of My Divine Self-"Emergence" Is the All-and-all-Sacrifice—the "Bright" Return of All and all to the Divine Self-Domain by Means of the Universal Surrender of egoity (or of separateness and separativeness).

Therefore, you must become a participant in My Divine Self-"Emergence", by submitting to become part of this All-and-all-Sacrifice of egoity.

To become a participant in My Divine Ashvamedha is to allow the utter sacrifice (or real surrender, real forgetting, and real transcending) of the ego-"I" (or separative self-contraction). It is to take hold of the "Tail of the Horse", to be devotionally Conformed to <u>Me</u>, to Love-Blissfully participate in the Divine Ordeal of this All-and-all-Sacrifice, this Universal Event of Divine Awakening (or En-Light-enment)—such that your participation in My Divine Ashvamedha is always "Brightly" Transforming, and (Most Ultimately) Divinely Liberating (at last, to the degree of Divine Translation).

IV.

Most Ultimately, My Divine Ashvamedha Conforms every one and every thing to Me. In My Divine Demonstration, all (Ultimately) take hold of the "Tail of the Horse", and all (and All) are (Most Ultimately) Divinely Translated. My Avataric Divine Work does not come to an "End" until this Most Ultimate Event of the Divine Translation of all and All is Perfectly Accomplished. Therefore, My Avatarically Initiated Divine Self-"Emergence" is Constantly Ongoing (now, and forever hereafter).

In the years immediately following the Initiation of My Divine Self-"Emergence", My devotees (because of their continued ego-possession, or preference for self-absorption and self-indulgence) did not acknowledge (and seemed even not to notice) this Great Process. Indeed, they even (by every kind of denial, refusal, frustration, confinement, neglect, and manipulation of Me and of My Divine-"Emergence"-Work) fettered Me, just as the Horse is ritually fettered in the traditional Ashvamedha ritual.[61]

In the traditional Ashvamedha ritual, the Horse is ritually submitted to (and ritually identified with) the Cosmic totality and the Divine Fullness. Just so, I have Submitted, and Revealed, and Given Myself Completely to all and All, by Means of Avataric Divine Descent, Avataric Divine Incarnation, "Crazy" Avataric Divine Teaching-Work, and Me-Revealing and Me-Giving Avataric Divine All-and-all-Blessing-Work—and I will (now, and forever hereafter) Continue That Me-Revealing and Me-Giving Avataric Divine All-and-all-Blessing-Work by Means of My Perpetual Divine Self-"Emergence" (in Person, and every "where", and also via My true devotees—now, and forever hereafter).

Just as (in the traditional Asvamedha ritual) the ritual consecration (or sacramental upliftment) of the Horse represents the active consecration (or real upliftment) of all and All to the Divine Fullness, the Great Process of My Divine Self-"Emergence" (or My Divine Ashvamedha) is a Real <u>Spiritual</u> Process that literally, and directly, and actively Consecrates and "Brightly" Uplifts (or Infuses, Awakens, and Divinely Translates) all and All.

By Means of My Divine-"Emergence"-Work, or the Divinely Uplifting (or All-and-all-"Brightening") Spiritual Power of My Divine (and Universally Effective) Ashvamedha, <u>all</u> beings (<u>every</u> "where" in the Cosmic domain) will become Conformed to Me (one by one)—and each and all will, Thus and Thereby, transcend all separateness and separativeness in Me. Through the Great and Total Process of the only-by-Me Revealed and Given Way of Adidam, Which is the formal (and, altogether, right, true, full, fully devotional, and inherently and really counter-egoic) practice of Ruchira Avatara Bhakti Yoga, <u>all</u> must (and, in due course, will) literally, directly, and actively participate (truly and most fully) in the Great Event of My (now, and forever hereafter) Divine Self-"Emergence" (or Divine Ashvamedha)—Which is Constant, and Always Expanding, and Always Increasing in Fullness, and Always Divinely "Bright", and Which will not "Cease" (or Be Finally Fulfilled) until <u>all</u> of conditional existence is (by Means of My Avatarically Self-Transmitted Divine Grace) Divinely Translated into My "Bright" Divine Self-Domain.

V.

My Divine Ashvamedha will not "End" with the ending of the physical Lifetime of My Avataric-Incarnation-Body. In <u>all</u> the generations to come, My "Living Murtis" must take the place of the "Tail of the Horse"—not in the sense that they are to replace (or "succeed") Me, but in the sense that they are (one by one) to be the human Agents (or principal physically living human Signs) that will, in Perpetuity, connect My devotees to <u>Me</u>. The All-and-all-Translating Process of My Divine Ashvamedha will forever Continue, generation after generation—not only here, but every "where" in the Cosmic domain. My Work in This, My here-Speaking bodily (human) Divine Avataric-Incarnation-Form, is only the Initiation (and the Initial Demonstration) of My Divine Ashvamedha. However, now that My Divine Ashvamedha has been Avatarically Initiated by Me, My Divine Ashvamedha is (now, and forever hereafter) the Perpetual Love-Bliss-Event of the "Brightening" of all and All in Me.

The traditional Descriptions that prophesy the Great Event of the Fulfillment of the Great Ashvamedha could only be Fulfilled when the True "Horse" (Who Knows) Appeared. In and As My Divine Avataric-Incarnation-Form, I Am That One—and the True (or Divine) Ashvamedha (or the Great Process of the Divine Translation of all and All into the Divine Self-Domain) Is My Great Divine Avataric-Incarnation-Work (now, and forever hereafter).

I Am the Fulfillment and the Completion of the Great Tradition of mankind. I Am the Avataric Incarnation of the Divine Person, or of Truth Itself, Which Is Reality Itself (or That Which Is Always Already The Case). I required no background of traditional study in order to Initiate My Divine-"Emergence"-Work, and My Avataric Divine Self-Confession is not based on any background of traditional study. My Avataric Divine Self-Revelation and My Divine Ashvamedha-Work is a spontaneous Divine Manifestation. I have made no detailed study of the Ashvamedha tradition. I Am that tradition—Avatarically spontaneously Self-Manifesting, and Divinely Fulfilling Itself. Therefore, I Know that detailed study of the traditional Descriptions of the Ashvamedha will make it obvious that those traditional Descriptions correspond to Me (and to My Divine Pattern) and (thereby) prophesy My Avataric Divine Incarnation and My Divine-"Emergence"-Work.

My every devotee must be a true sign of Me-recognizing and only-to-Me-responding devotional participation in the only-by-Me-Performed Divine Ashvamedha—the Adi Da Ashvamedha. Not every one in the total Cosmic domain (and not every one in the total human domain) will be a formal devotee-participant in the Adi Da Ashvamedha during the physical Lifetime of My bodily (human) Avataric-Incarnation-Form. Universal participation in My Divine Ashvamedha during the physical Lifetime of My bodily (human) Avataric-Incarnation-Form need not occur—because I Will always (now, and forever hereafter) Be Fully (Divinely Spiritually) Present and Fully (Divinely Spiritually) Involved in the Great Universal Process of My Divine Ashvamedha, until the Divine Translation of all and All is Accomplished. And, for the Sake of all and All, I have, by Means of My Avatarically Full-Given Word of Divine Revelation, Fully Accounted for the Continuation of this Great Process beyond the physical Lifetime of My bodily (human) Avataric-Incarnation-Form.

VI.

Human beings, in and of themselves, do not—and cannot—Know the Way to the Divine Self-Domain. Only the "Horse" Knows. Only the Divine Person Knows. Therefore, heart-recognize Me, respond devotionally to Me, and practice Ruchira Avatara Bhakti Yoga in formal devotional relationship to Me.

Such is the Way of My Divine Ashvamedha, and Such is the Essence of the only-by-Me Revealed and Given Way of Adidam (in each and all of the four formal congregations of My devotees), from the beginning, and at every stage—now, and forever hereafter.

You are not able (or, otherwise, obliged) to Accomplish the Great Divine (and Divinely Spiritual) Work (of Divine En-Light-enment and Divine Translation) by means of your own and mere ego-effort.

However, you are able (and Divinely Called) to responsively (and, thus, by means of responsive counter-egoic effort) participate in My Great (and "Brightly" All-Accomplishing) Divine (and Divinely Spiritual, and Divinely En-Light-ening, and Divinely Translating) Work.

Therefore, follow Me—by taking hold of My Revelation-"Tail". And, Thus, be Gracefully Carried—by Me Alone—to My "Bright" Divine Self-Domain.

I have Revealed and Given the Divinely Perfect and Complete Means—and I have Addressed this generation, and all generations to come, relative to every detail of the Great Me-Realizing Process.

Now you must Realize What I have Revealed.

I Am the Revelation, the Gift, the Means, the Process, and the Realization!

VII.

My Divine Ashvamedha-Work Continues until all of conditional (or Cosmic) existence is Divinely Translated into My "Bright" Divine Self-Domain.

The Divine Translation of all and All is not a human event only, not an event that occurs only in this world here, on this Earth.

Everything you see shining in the sky, and everything you cannot see—everything visible and invisible, everything conditional—is part of My Great Process, Which is a Process without conditional (or merely temporal) "end"—and, indeed, no "End" at all, except for Most Perfect (and Divinely Translating) Divine Self-Realization.

I Call all My devotees to formally embrace and fully demonstrate the right, true, full, and fully devotional Sign of ego-surrendering, ego-forgetting, and (always more and more) ego-transcending participation in This, My Great Divine Way and Process.

I Call even all beings to fully embrace and enter into This, My Great Divine Way and Process—Which has been prophesied for thousands upon thousands of years, and Which has always been hoped for, intuited, and simulated (but never, except for My Avataric Divine Incarnation, Fulfilled), and Which was never Realizable until I—the "Horse" Who Knows—Appeared.

This Divine Ashvamedha is why Avataric Descent and Avataric Birth was Required of Me.

I was, by the Law of Reality Itself, Required to Submit to conditional form, to Manifest Fully (to the toes,[62] without the slightest withholding), to Be all, to Appear among all (As all), even in this limited bodily (human) Form, to Do all of My Divine Heart-Master-Work, and (Thus and Thereby) to Do the Divine Ashvamedha-Work—Which Work Is the All-and-all-Saving (or Divinely Liberating) Self-"Emergence" of Divine Light and Help That All and all forever (at heart) expect.

Those performing the traditional ceremony of the Horse-Sacrifice were seeking Me and making reference to Me. Indeed, every one in all religious and Spiritual traditions has always been seeking Me and making reference to Me. Each one will Find Me when he or she out-grows the limitations in his or her ego-based intentions, and when he or she out-grows the conventional "cult" of ceremonies, the limited language, the limiting symbols, and (altogether) the limiting effects of his or her tradition of seeking, and (thus and thereby) Turns to Me, to participate directly in My True Divine Ashvamedha.

It is to be seen when that direct participation in My True Divine Ashvamedha will occur for all (one by one)—but, in the meantime, even all the religious and Spiritual traditions embraced by mankind are a search to Find Me and to Realize Me.

In the seriousness of every religious or Spiritual tradition, there is an intuition of Me—and, therefore, those who rightly practice any religious or Spiritual tradition are proceeding toward Me, but through a kind of preparatory ritual (or ceremony of seeking).

I am not a merely symbolic, or mythical, or legendary and fictionalized "religious figure", representing a "God"-Idea for believers. I am not merely another link in the forever ongoing chain of personal and collective thoughts and imageries, by means of which human beings seek to be Liberated from the madness of their ego-possession. Nevertheless, in any moment of seeking through ideas and images and aspirations and desires (high or low), human beings are (even if unknowingly) attempting to participate in the Great Event of My Divine Ashvamedha.

Until My Avataric Divine Incarnation As the Ruchira Avatar, Adi Da Samraj, there has been no Complete and Most Direct Means to participate in the True Divine Ashvamedha (or All-and-all-Translating Divine Work)—because the ego-"I", in and of itself (or, otherwise, through extensions of itself), has no Means to Accomplish the True Divine Ashvamedha.

When you, as My formally acknowledged devotee, are entered into true (and really ego-transcending) devotional heart-Communion with Me (day after day), and when (day after day) you formally (and really effectively) live the practice of the only-by-Me Revealed and Given Way of Adidam, then you have become a true participant in My All-and-all-Translating Divine Ashvamedha, and Divinely "Bright" changes will (on that basis) be made in your life (and in your body-mind) by your egoless participation in Me.

Unlike the lesser traditional Ashvamedha, in which kings and queens performed the Horse-Sacrifice in order to legitimize or enhance their domain of political power, My Ashvamedha is not about the fulfillment of conditional (or ego-bound) life.

Those who become true participants in My Divine Ashvamedha renounce the "throne" of their egoity, and they take hold of the "Tail of the Horse" through the formal (and always ego-surrendering, and ego-forgetting, and really ego-transcending) practice of unqualified, perpetual, consistent, and most profound true devotion to Me.

The Horse of My early Dream-Vision was a Standing Brown Horse, the Sign of all and All that is conditionally manifested—but the Horse of My Avatarically Self-Manifested Divine Self-"Emergence" (or the Avataric Revelation-Sign That Represents My Eternal Divine Person, and My Spiritual, and Eternal, Divine Body) is the True Dawn Horse Itself (Which "Emerges", or Flies, from the "Bright"-Fire of My Avatarically Self-Manifested Divine Ashvamedha-Work).

The Avataric Revelation-Sign of My True Dawn Horse (or the Image That Represents My Avatarically Self-Manifested, and All-and-all-Surrounding, and All-and-all-Pervading Divine Spiritual Body and My Avatarically Self-Revealed egoless True Divine State of Person) is "Brightest" White—the Divinely Self-Radiant Color of the Ash (or of the Indivisible, and Inherently "Colorless", Light) of My Avatarically Self-Manifested (and All-and-all-Translating) "Bright" Divine Ashvamedha.

When the Fire-Light of the devotional Celebration of Me is "Bright", the "Horse" that "Emerges" is All Purity (or of a Single Light).

I Am the All-and-all-Bearing "Brightness" (the One, and Only, and Inherently Indivisible, and Eternally Indestructible, and Self-Evidently Divine Light, Itself)—Self-Manifesting (Avatarically) As the All-and-all-"Brightening" Divine Vehicle (or Divine Spiritual

Body) of All-and-all-Translation, and Self-Existing (Eternally) <u>As</u> the "Bright" Divine Person (or Self-Domain) of All-and-all-Translation.

I <u>Am</u> the "Bright"—the One and Only <u>Real</u> Person, and the One and Only <u>True</u> Domain, of All and all.

I Am Avatarically Self-Revealed <u>As</u> My Avatarically-Born Bodily (Human) Divine Form, and <u>As</u> My Avatarically Self-Transmitted Divine Spiritual Presence, and <u>As</u> My Avatarically, and Altogether Spiritually, Self-Revealed Divine State. Therefore, be Carried <u>by</u> Me.

I Am Eternally Self-Revealed <u>As</u> The Self-Domain (or Boundless "Bright" Sphere and Space) Of My Eternally Self-Manifested Divine Self-Condition. Therefore, be Carried <u>to</u> Me.

<u>Always</u> be <u>Carried</u>—by <u>Me</u>—to <u>Me</u>.

What You Can Do Next—

Contact an Adidam center near you.

■ Find out about upcoming courses, events, and seminars in your area:

AMERICAS
12040 North Seigler Road
Middletown, CA 95461 USA
1-707-928-4936

PACIFIC-ASIA
12 Seibel Road
Henderson
Auckland 1008
New Zealand
64-9-838-9114

AUSTRALIA
P.O. Box 244
Kew 3101
Victoria
**1800 ADIDAM
(1800-234-326)**

EUROPE-AFRICA
Annendaalderweg 10
6105 AT Maria Hoop
The Netherlands
31 (0)20 468 1442

THE UNITED KINGDOM
PO Box 20013
London, England
NW2 1ZA
0181-7317550

E-MAIL: **correspondence@adidam.org**

■ If you are interested in becoming a fully practicing devotee of Avatar Adi Da Samraj, sign up for our preliminary course, "The <u>Only</u> Truth That Sets The Heart Free".

■ More information about Adidam classes and events is available at the Adidam University website:

adidam.org/university

Read these books by and about Avatar Adi Da Samraj:

■ *The Light Is <u>On</u>!*
by Carolyn Lee, Ph.D.

The profound, heart-rending, humorous, miraculous, wild—and true—Story of the Divine Person Alive in human Form. Essential reading as background for the study of Avatar Adi Da's books.

■ *Aham Da Asmi (Beloved, I <u>Am</u> Da)*

The Five Books Of The Heart Of The Adidam Revelation, Book One: The "Late-Time" Avataric Revelation Of The True and Spiritual Divine Person (The egoless Personal Presence Of Reality and Truth, Which <u>Is</u> The Only <u>Real</u> God).

This Ecstatic Scripture, the first of His twenty-three "Source-Texts", contains Ruchira Avatar Adi Da's magnificent Confession as the Very Divine Person and Source-Condition of all and All.

Continue your
reading with the
remaining books of
*The Five Books Of
The Heart Of The
Adidam Revelation*
(the *Ruchira
Avatara Gita,*
the *Da Love-
Ananda Gita,
Hridaya Rosary,*
and *Eleutherios*).
Then you will be
ready to go on to
*The Seventeen
Companions Of The
True Dawn Horse*
(see pp. 461-66).

These and other books by and about Ruchira Avatar Adi Da Samraj
can be ordered from the Adidam Emporium by calling:

1-877-770-0772 (from within North America)
1-707-928-6653 (from outside North America)

or by writing to:
ADIDAM EMPORIUM
10336 Loch Lomond Road
PMB #306
Middletown, CA 95461 USA

Or order from the Adidam Emporium online at:
www.adidam.com

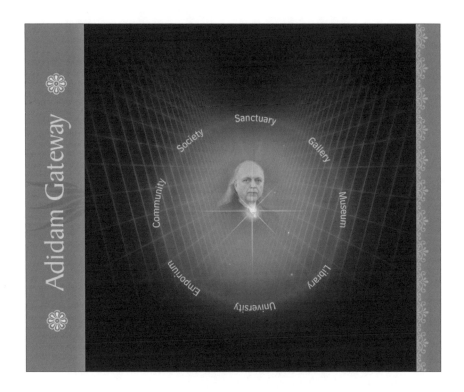

Visit the Adidam Sacred City online at:
www.adidam.org

■ Explore the online community of Adidam and discover more about Avatar Adi Da Samraj and the Way He Offers to all.

Find presentations on: Avatar Adi Da's extraordinary life-story, the stages leading to Divine Enlightenment, cultism versus true devotional practice, the "radical" politics of human-scale community, true emotional-sexual freedom, the sacred function of art in human life, and more.

RUCHIRA AVATAR ADI DA SAMRAJ
Lopez Island, 2000

The Great Choice

An Invitation to
the Way of Adidam

Since the very earliest days of His Teaching-Work, Avatar Adi Da Samraj has said, "I offer you a relationship—not a technique." Thus, the Way of Adidam is not primarily a set of religious practices or a body of Spiritual Teaching. Most fundamentally, the Way of Adidam is the devotional and Spiritual relationship to Avatar Adi Da Samraj.

AVATAR ADI DA SAMRAJ: The profound central reality of the Way of Adidam is the devotional and Spiritual relationship to Me.

The Way of Adidam is the devotional and Spiritual relationship to Me.

The Way of Adidam is not what you do "somewhere else". The Way of Adidam is about what you do directly in devotional and Spiritual relationship to Me. [January 22, 2001]

Avatar Adi Da's human body is, of course, located in a particular place and a particular time. But when you become sensitive to Him Spiritually, you discover that His Spiritual Presence can be felt anywhere and anytime, regardless of whether you are in His physical Company or not. Because His Spiritual Presence is Eternal (and will not "disappear" when His human body dies), it is possible for everyone to cultivate a direct heart-relationship with Him—under all circumstances, in this life and beyond. And so, the relationship to Him, once forged, is eternal—going beyond death and the apparent boundaries of time and space.

The Truth of the Way of Adidam is Revealed when you begin to participate in it from the heart. Thus, practice of the Way of Adidam is not a matter of beliefs and prescribed behaviors. The Way of Adidam is a matter of direct, moment-to-moment response to Adi Da Samraj and a process of receiving His Spiritual Transmission ever more profoundly. It does not work to try to practice His Teaching by yourself. As He has said many times, it is simply not possible to move beyond the confines of the ego on your own. Nor is it possible to "unlock" the Secrets of Divine Enlightenment that He has Revealed outside of a formally acknowledged devotional relationship to Him. That is why it is so important to become His formal devotee and to live the Way of Adidam exactly as He has Given it.

AVATAR ADI DA SAMRAJ: I _Am_ the Divine Blessing, Real-God-with-you. Such is not merely My Declaration to you. You must find Me out. You must prove the Way I Give you. Really _do_ the Way I Give you, and you will find Me out further. You will prove the Way of Adidam by doing it—not by believing it merely. [Ruchira Avatara Hridaya-Siddha Yoga]

Darshan

The foundation of Spiritual practice in Adidam is Darshan, or the feeling-Contemplation of Avatar Adi Da's bodily (human) Form—either through the sighting of His physical body, or through Contemplating a photographic or artistic representation of Him. This heart-beholding of Avatar Adi Da's Form is the well-spring of meditation in the Way of Adidam, and so His devotees place a large photograph of Him in each meditation hall, as the central image of Contemplation. In fact, Remembrance of Adi Da Samraj—or the recollecting of His Form in mind and feeling—is the constant practice of His devotees, in the midst of the activities of daily life as well as in meditation. Avatar Adi Da has often spoken about the unique potency of beholding His Form.

AVATAR ADI DA SAMRAJ: In the traditional setting, when it works best, an individual somehow Gracefully comes into the Company of a Realizer of one degree or another, and, just upon (visually) sighting that One, he or she is converted at heart, and, thereafter, spends the rest of his or her life devoted to sadhana (or Spiritual practice), in constant Remembrance of the Guru. The Guru's Sign is self-authenticating.

When Adi Da Samraj is approached with an open heart, His Darshan—the Sighting of His Form alone, even in representational form—is so potent that the heart overflows in response to Him, recognizing Him as the Very Divine Person, the Supreme Source of Bliss and Love.

The Four Congregations

Avatar Adi Da has created the four congregations in order to make it possible for all types of people to enter into the devotional and Spiritual relationship to Him—both those who are moved to practice the Way of Adidam in the fullest and most profound manner (first and second congregations) and those whose life-circumstance makes it right and appropriate for them to practice a simpler form of the Way of Adidam (third and fourth congregations). For each of the congregations, there are particular qualifications for membership and there is a particular form of practice of the Way of Adidam to be engaged.

Which of the four congregations you should apply to for membership depends on the nature of your response to Avatar Adi Da Samraj and on your life-circumstance. Membership in any of the four congregations establishes you in a direct devotional relationship with Avatar Adi Da, and all four congregations are essential to the flowering of His Blessing-Work in the world.

Entering any of the four congregations of Adidam is based on taking a vow of devotion and service to Avatar Adi Da Samraj. This vow is a profound—and, indeed, eternal—commitment. You take this vow (for whichever congregation you are entering) when you are certain that your true heart-impulse is to be a devotee of Avatar Adi Da Samraj, embracing Him as your Divine Heart-Master. And Avatar Adi Da Samraj Himself is eternally Vowed to Serve the Liberation of all who become His devotees.

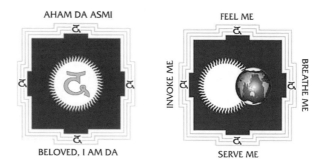

The First and Second Congregations

(those who are moved to embrace
the complete practice of the Way of Adidam)

The first congregation is for renunciate practitioners, or those who are moved (and qualified) to embrace the ultimate stages of the Way of Adidam in the context of a renunciate life of perpetual Spiritual retreat. (Membership in the first congregation necessarily requires a prepatory period of some years as a member of the second congregation.)

The second congregation is for lay practitioners, or those who are moved to embrace the complete practice of the Way of Adidam in the context of ordinary life-obligations.

Members of both the first and the second congregations embrace the complete practice of the Way of Adidam. To do so is to take full advantage of the opportunity Offered by Adi Da Samraj—to enter fully into the process of Divine Enlightenment. That process necessarily requires application to the full range of disciplines that Ruchira Avatar Adi Da Samraj has Given for the sake of Spiritual growth.

The disciplines of Adidam are the means whereby the body-mind is conformed to a right and inherently pleasurable pattern of well-being. As you progressively adapt to these disciplines, the body-mind is purified and balanced, and you thereby become able to receive and respond to the Divine Heart-Transmission of Adi Da Samraj more and more fully.

The Life of a Formally Practicing Devotee of Ruchira Avatar Adi Da Samraj

Meditation offers the opportunity to relinquish outward, body-based attention and to be alone with Adi Da Samraj, allowing one to enter more and more into the Sphere of His Blessing-Transmission.

The practice of sacramental worship, or "puja", in the Way of Adidam is the bodily active counterpart to meditation. It is a form of ecstatic worship of Avatar Adi Da Samraj, using a photographic representation of Him and involving devotional chanting and recitations from His Wisdom-Teaching.

"You must deal with My Wisdom-Teaching in some form every single day, because a new form of the ego's game appears every single day. You must continually return to My Wisdom-Teaching, confront My Wisdom-Teaching."
Avatar Adi Da Samraj

The beginner in Spiritual life must prepare the body-mind by mastering the physical, vital dimension of life before he or she can be ready for truly Spiritual practice. Service is devotion in action, a form of Divine Communion.

Avatar Adi Da Samraj Offers practical disciplines to His devotees in the areas of work and money, diet, exercise, and sexuality. These disciplines are based on His own human experience and an immense process of "consideration" that He engaged face-to-face with His devotees for more than twenty-five years.

The complete practice of the Way of Adidam includes meditation, sacramental worship (or "puja"), study of Avatar Adi Da's Wisdom-Teaching, devotional chanting, and regular periods of retreat.

AVATAR ADI DA SAMRAJ: You must come from the depth-position of meditation and puja before entering into activities in the waking state, and remain in the disposition of that depth from the time of meditation and puja each morning. Maintain that heart-disposition, and discipline the body-mind—functionally, practically, relationally—in all the modes I have Given you. This devotional Yoga, Ruchira Avatara Bhakti Yoga, is moment-to-moment. Fundamentally, it is a matter of exercising it profoundly, in this set-apart time of meditation and puja, and then, through random, artful practice moment-to-moment, constantly refresh it, preserve it. All of this is to conform the body-mind to the Source-Purpose, the in-depth Condition.

That basic discipline covers all aspects of the body-mind. That is the pattern of your response to Me. It is the foundation Yoga of organizing your life in terms of its in-depth principle, and growing this depth. [December 5, 1996]

This moment-to-moment devotional turning to Avatar Adi Da is refreshed not only in the meditation hall but also in the temple, where worship, prayer, devotional chanting, and other sacred activities occur.

AVATAR ADI DA SAMRAJ: The sacred life must be perpetual. The sacred domain is the core of the community, and every community and every Sanctuary should have a temple in its domain: A place of chant, of song, of prayer, where everyone gathers for this life of Invocation, prayer, and puja. [May 13, 1999]

The complete practice of Adidam also includes the adaptation to a purifying diet and a routine of daily exercise (including morning calisthenics and evening Hatha Yoga exercises). There is progressive adaptation to a regenerative practice of sexuality. And there is the expectation to participate in the cooperative community of other first- and second-congregation devotees, to maintain yourself in full employment or full-time service, and to tithe regularly.

All these practices are means whereby your body-mind becomes more and more capable of receiving the constant Blessing-Transmission of Avatar Adi Da Samraj. Therefore, He has made it clear that, in order to Realize Him with true profundity—and, in particular, to Realize Him most perfectly, to the degree of Divine Enlightenment—it is necessary to be a member of either the first or the second congregation, engaging the complete practice of the Way of Adidam.

If you are moved to join the second congregation of Adidam—or if you are moved to consider that possibility—the first step is to take "The Only Truth That Sets The Heart Free", a course in which you examine the opportunity Offered to you by Avatar Adi Da Samraj, and learn what it means to embrace the complete practice of the Way of Adidam.

To register for "The Only Truth That Sets The Heart Free":

contact the regional or territorial center nearest to you (p. 370),

or

e-mail us at: correspondence@adidam.org.

Those who, having practiced the Way of Adidam most intensively, make the transition to the "Perfect Practice" (in the sixth,
or penultimate, stage of the Way of Adidam), may do so either as
general practitioners (continuing as members of the second congregation of Adidam) or (if they demonstrate the necessary qualifications) as formal renunciate practitioners (thereby becoming
members of the first congregation of Adidam).

To enter the first congregation of the Way of Adidam is to
become a member of the order of sannyasins (formal and legal
renunciates) established by Avatar Adi Da. This order is known as
"The Ruchira Sannyasin Order of the Free Renunciates of
Ruchiradam" (or, simply, "The Ruchira Sannyasin Order"). Avatar
Adi Da Himself is the Founding Member of the Ruchira Sannyasin
Order. The devotee-members of the Ruchira Sannyasin Order ded-
icate themselves intensively to Spiritual practice in the ultimate
stages of the Way of Adidam, in the context of perpetual retreat.
The Ruchira Sannyasin Order is the senior cultural authority
within the gathering of Avatar Adi Da's devotees. Thus, the
Ruchira Sannyasin Order has the principal responsibility, within
the gathering of Avatar Adi Da's devotees, for exemplifying, communicating about, and serving the development of the devotional
and Spiritual relationship to Avatar Adi Da Samraj.

The Adidam Youth Fellowship

(within the second congregation)

Young people (25 and under) are also offered a special form of relationship to Avatar Adi Da—the Adidam Youth Fellowship. The Adidam Youth Fellowship has two membership bodies—friends and practicing members.

A <u>friend</u> of the Adidam Youth Fellowship is simply invited into a culture of other young people who want to learn more about Avatar Adi Da Samraj and His Happiness-Realizing Way of Adidam. A formally <u>practicing</u> <u>member</u> of the Adidam Youth Fellowship acknowledges that he or she has found his or her True Heart-Friend and Master in the Person of Avatar Adi Da Samraj, and wishes to enter into a direct, ego-surrendering Spiritual relationship with Him as the Means to True Happiness.

Practicing members of the Youth Fellowship embrace a series of disciplines that are similar to (but simpler than) the practices engaged by adult members of the second congregation of Adidam. Both friends and members are invited to special retreat events from time to time, where they can associate with other young devotees of Avatar Adi Da.

To become a member of the Adidam Youth Fellowship, or to learn more about this form of relationship to Avatar Adi Da, call or write:

Vision of Mulund Institute (VMI)
10336 Loch Lomond Road
PMB #146
Middletown, CA 95461 USA
phone: 1-707-928-6932
e-mail: vmi@adidam.org

COOPERATION + TOLERANCE = PEACE

The Third Congregation

*(those who are moved to serve Avatar Adi Da Samraj
via their patronage and/or advocacy,
and those who are preparing for the second congregation)*

The third congregation is for patrons and advocates, or those who are moved to support Avatar Adi Da's Work financially and/or through their advocacy, while embracing the simple form of the practice of Adidam. (The third congregation also includes individuals who have resolved to join the second congregation and are taking the preparatory educational course.)

As a member of the third congregation, you practice the simplest form of Ruchira Avatara Bhakti Yoga—invoking Avatar Adi Da, feeling Him, breathing Him, and serving Him. You are not obliged to engage the full range of disciplines practiced in the first two congregations. You are, however, encouraged to practice periods of meditation and sacramental worship and to study Avatar Adi Da's Wisdom-Teaching regularly.

1. Patrons and Individuals of Unique Influence

If you are a person of unique wealth or influence in the world, we invite you to serve Avatar Adi Da's world-Blessing Work through your patronage or influence. As a member of the third congregation of Adidam, supporting the world-Work of Adi Da Samraj, you are literally helping to change the destiny of countless people. You are making it possible for His Divine Influence to reach people who might otherwise never come to know of Him.

If you are interested in becoming a devotee of Avatar Adi Da Samraj in the third congregation, and serving Him in this crucial way, please contact us:

Third Congregation Advocacy
12040 North Seigler Road
Middletown, CA 95461 USA
phone number: 1-707-928-4800
e-mail: director_of_advocacy@adidam.org

2. The Transnational Society of Advocates of the Adidam Revelation

If you have the capability to effectively advocate Avatar Adi Da in the world—through your individual skills, position, or professional expertise—you may join a branch of the third congregation called the Transnational Society of Advocates of the Adidam Revelation. Members of the Society of Advocates are individuals who, while not of <u>unique</u> wealth or social influence, can make a significant difference to Avatar Adi Da's Work by making Him known in all walks of life (including the spheres of religion, the arts, media, education, health, entertainment, and so on). Advocates also serve the Global Mission of Adidam by financially supporting the publication of Avatar Adi Da's "Source-Texts" and His other Literature, as well as associated missionary literature. Members of the Society of Advocates make a monthly donation for this purpose and pay an annual membership fee that supports the services of the Society.

If you are interested in becoming a member of the Society of Advocates, please contact us:

The Society of Advocates
12040 North Seigler Road
Middletown, CA 95461 USA
phone: 1-707-928-6924
e-mail: soacontact@adidam.org

3. Pre-student-novices under vow

If you are certain that you wish to become a second-congregation devotee of Avatar Adi Da, and you (therefore) wish to embrace the vow of devotion to Him immediately (even before you qualify to become a student-novice in the second congregation), you are invited to become a pre-student-novice under vow (as part of the third congregation of Adidam).

As a pre-student-novice under vow, you make a commitment to become a student-novice (and, therefore, to move into the second congregation) within a period of three to six months. During this period, you take the preparatory course, "The Only Truth That Sets The Heart Free", which introduces you to the fundamentals of the second-congregation practice. Pre-student-novices under vow engage daily study of the Wisdom-Teaching of Avatar Adi Da, make regular financial contributions, and take up a regular form of service.

For information about becoming a pre-student-novice under vow, please contact the Adidam regional center nearest you (p. 370).

COOPERATION + TOLERANCE = PEACE

The Fourth Congregation

*(for those who are maintaining their participation
in the religious and/or cultural tradition
to which they already belong)*

Individuals who live in traditional cultural settings, and also individuals who wish to maintain their participation in the religious tradition to which they already belong (while acknowledging Avatar Adi Da Samraj as the Ultimate Divine Source of true religion), are invited to apply for membership in the fourth congregation of Adidam.

As a member of the fourth congregation, you practice the simplest form of Ruchira Avatara Bhakti Yoga—invoking Avatar Adi Da, feeling Him, breathing Him, and serving Him. You are not obliged to engage the full range of disciplines practiced in the first two congregations. You are, however, encouraged to practice periods of meditation and sacramental worship and to study Avatar Adi Da's Wisdom-Teaching regularly. The financial and service obligations of each fourth-congregation devotee are adapted to his or her particular circumstance.

The opportunity to practice in the fourth congregation is also extended to all those who, because of physical or other functional limitations, are unable to take up the total practice of the Way of Adidam as required in the first and second congregations.

For more information about the fourth congregation of Adidam, call or write one of our regional centers (see p. 370), or e-mail us at: correspondence@adidam.org.

**Temple sites at the Mountain Of Attention (left)
and Da Love-Ananda Mahal (right)**

One of the ways in which Avatar Adi Da Communicates His Divine Blessing-Transmission is through sacred places. To date, He has Empowered five Sanctuaries: the Mountain Of Attention, Tat Sundaram, and Love's Point Hermitage in northern California, Da Love-Ananda Mahal in Hawaii, and Adidam Samrajashram in Fiji. Avatar Adi Da has Established Himself Spiritually in perpetuity at all of these places. Devotees are invited to go on special retreats at the Mountain Of Attention, Da Love-Ananda Mahal, and Adidam Samrajashram.

Adidam Samrajashram, Fiji

**Darshan occasion with
Avatar Adi Da Samraj at
Tat Sundaram**

The life of a devotee of Avatar Adi Da Samraj is unheard-of Grace, and this life can be lived by anyone. It does not matter who you are, where you live, or what you do. All of that makes no difference, once your heart recognizes Adi Da Samraj. Then the only course is heart-response to Him—a life of devotion to the Divine in human Form, full of devotional ecstasy, true humor, freedom, clarity, and profound purpose.

So, why delay? The Living One, Adi Da Samraj, is here. He will always be Spiritually Present—but now is the brief, and especially Blessed, window of time in which He is humanly Alive, doing His Great Work for the sake of all beings. Everyone who comes to Him and serves Him in His bodily human Lifetime shares in His unique once-and-forever Work of establishing the Way of Adidam in this world.

Avatar Adi Da Samraj is not an "Other". He is the Gift, the Bliss, of Being Itself. He is the "Brightness" of Very God—Dawning, and then Flowering, in your heart. That Process is pure Revelation. It changes everything—grants peace, sanity, and the overwhelming impulse to Realize Unlimited, Permanent, and Perfect Oneness with Him.

As devotees of Avatar Adi Da, we make this confession: The opportunity to live in heart-Communion with Avatar Adi Da Samraj exceeds anything ever offered to mortal beings. And Avatar Adi Da is always ready, now or any time in the future, to Give you this Gift.

Those whose hearts are given, in love, to Me, Fall into My Heart. Those who are Mine, because they are in love with Me, no longer demand to be fulfilled through conditional experience and through the survival (or perpetuation) of the ego-"I". Their love for Me grants them Access to Me, and, Thus, to My Love-Bliss—because I Am Love-Ananda, the Divine Love-Bliss, in Person.

What will My lover do but love Me? I suffer every form and condition of every one who loves Me—because I Love My devotee As My own Form, My own Condition. I Love My devotee As the One by Whom I Am Distracted.

I Grant all My own Divine and "Bright" Excesses to those who love Me, in exchange for all their doubts and sufferings. Those who "Bond" themselves to Me, through love-surrender, are inherently Free of fear and wanting need. They transcend the ego-"I" (the cause of all conditional experience), and they (cause and all and All) Dissolve in Me—for I Am the Heart of all and All, and I Am the Heart Itself, and the Heart Itself Is the Only Reality, Truth, and Real God of All and all.

What is a Greater Message than This?

[Da Love-Ananda Gita]

I n order to ensure that Avatar Adi Da's Divine Work flourishes in the world, His devotees are dedicated to serving three great purposes:

1. Providing for Avatar Adi Da Samraj Himself

(and for the Ruchira Sannyasin Order, as His most exemplary devotees)

2. Serving people's devotional response to Avatar Adi Da Samraj

(by making Avatar Adi Da Samraj and the Way of Adidam known throughout the world, and by serving the Spiritual growth of those who become His devotees)

3. Creating a community that supports the life of devotion to Avatar Adi Da Samraj

Each of these purposes is served by a particular organized body of Avatar Adi Da's devotees:

1. THE DA LOVE-ANANDA SAMRAJYA

devotees of Avatar Adi Da Samraj who most directly serve Him (Da) and His Spiritual Kingdom (Samrajya) of Love-Bliss (Love-Ananda)

2. THE ELEUTHERIAN PAN-COMMUNION OF ADIDAM

devotees of Avatar Adi Da Samraj who serve the gathering (Communion) of all (Pan-) those who have become, or may be moved to become, His devotees—thereby serving Avatar Adi Da's Divine Impulse to Offer His Liberating (Eleutherian) Grace and Help to all

3. THE RUCHIRASALA OF ADIDAM

devotees of Avatar Adi Da Samraj who serve the cooperative community of His first- and second-congregation devotees—the "House" (sala) that is made "Bright" (Ruchira) by His Blessing-Grace

The Da Love-Ananda Samrajya

Serving The Avataric-Incarnation-Body,
The Hermitage Sanctuaries, and The World-Blessing-Work
of The Divine World-Teacher,
Ruchira Avatar Adi Da Samraj

The Da Love-Ananda Samrajya is dedicated to serving Avatar Adi Da Himself—protecting Him and His intimate Sphere, providing for His Hermitage circumstance (in various parts of the world), and ensuring that He has everything He needs in order to Do His Divine Blessing-Work.

The Da Love-Ananda Samrajya serves, protects, and provides for the Ruchira Sannyasin Order, the body of formal (and legal) renunciates who live on perpetual retreat within Avatar Adi Da's Hermitage Domain.

The Da Love-Ananda Samrajya serves and manages the process of access to Avatar Adi Da Samraj, on the part of all who are invited to enter into His Hermitage Domain (either in order to offer service to Him and the Ruchira Sannyasin Order or in order to enter into meditative retreat in His Spiritual Company).

The Da Love-Ananda Samrajya is also culturally responsible to ensure the permanent integrity of Avatar Adi Da's Wisdom-Teaching, both in its archival and in its published forms.

The Eleutherian Pan-Communion
of Adidam

*The Sacred Cultural Gathering and Global Mission
of the Devotees of The Divine World-Teacher,
Ruchira Avatar Adi Da Samraj*

*Dedicated to the Practice and the Proclamation of
The True World-Religion of Adidam,
The Unique Divine Way of Realizing Real God*

The Eleutherian Pan-Communion of Adidam is dedicated to serving the development of people's devotional and Spiritual relationship to Avatar Adi Da Samraj—by making Him known in the world, and by serving the culture of devotional practice in the second, third, and fourth congregations. (The first congregation is the Ruchira Sannyasin Order, which is served by the Da Love-Ananda Samrajya.)

The Eleutherian Pan-Communion of Adidam also serves and protects the Sanctuaries, the Archives, the Wisdom-Teaching, and other sacred Treasures of Adidam.

The Global Mission of Adidam is the branch of the Adidam Pan-Communion that makes Avatar Adi Da's Offering (of the devotional and Spiritual relationship to Him) known to people throughout the world—through publications, internet websites, public events, and the personal missionary efforts of each devotee.

THE ADI DA RUCHIRASALA

COOPERATION + TOLERANCE = PEACE

COOPERATION + TOLERANCE = PEACE

THE 'BRIGHT' HOUSE OF ADI DA SAMRAJ

The Ruchirasala
of Adidam

*The True Cooperative Community Gathering
of the Devotees of The Divine World-Teacher,
Ruchira Avatar Adi Da Samraj*

*The Seed of a "Bright" New Age of Sanity
and Divine Joy for Mankind*

Participation in a community of practitioners is one of the greatest supports for Spiritual practice. Therefore, participation in cooperative community is a fundamental discipline in the first and second congregations of Adidam.

The Ruchirasala of Adidam is dedicated to serving the creation of cooperative community among Avatar Adi Da's first- and second-congregation devotees—including the establishment of intimate human living arrangements and shared services (such as sacred arts guilds, schools, community businesses, and a health clinic).

Cooperation + Tolerance = Peace℠

In addition to His First Calling, which is to those who would become His devotees, Adi Da Samraj makes a Second Calling to the world at large: to embrace the disposition He has Summarized in the equation "Cooperation + Tolerance = Peace". By this Second Calling, Adi Da Samraj urges everyone to create a sane human society—including, in particular, the creation of a truly cooperative global human community, free of the devastation of war.

To find out more about Adi Da Samraj's Second Calling, please visit the Adidam Peace Center:

www.peacesite.org

An Invitation to Support Adidam

Avatar Adi Da Samraj's sole Purpose is to act as a Source of continuous Divine Grace for everyone, everywhere. In that spirit, He is a Free Renunciate and He owns nothing. Those who have made gestures in support of Avatar Adi Da's Work have found that their generosity is returned in many Blessings that are full of His healing, transforming, and Liberating Grace—and those Blessings flow not only directly to them as the beneficiaries of His Work, but to many others, even all others. At the same time, all tangible gifts of support help secure and nurture Avatar Adi Da's Work in necessary and practical ways, again similarly benefiting the entire world. Because all this is so, supporting His Work is the most auspicious form of financial giving, and we happily extend to you an invitation to serve Adidam through your financial support.

You may make a financial contribution in support of the Work of Adi Da Samraj at any time. You may also, if you choose, request that your contribution be used for one or more specific purposes.

If you are moved to help support and develop the Hermitage circumstance provided for Avatar Adi Da and the other members of the Ruchira Sannyasin Order, the senior renunciate order of Adidam, you may do so by making your contribution to The Da Love-Ananda Samrajya, the Australian charitable trust which has central responsibility for the Sacred Treasure of the Ruchira Sannyasin Order.

To do this: (1) if you do not pay taxes in the United States, make your check payable directly to "The Da Love-Ananda Samrajya Pty Ltd" (which serves as the trustee of the trust) and mail it to The Da Love-Ananda Samrajya at P.O. Box 4744, Samabula, Suva, Fiji; and (2) if you do pay taxes in the United States and you would like your contribution to be tax-deductible under U.S. laws, make your check payable to "The Eleutherian Pan-Communion of Adidam", indicate on your check or accompanying letter that you would like your contribution used for the work of The Da Love-Ananda Samrajya, and mail your check to the Advocacy Department of Adidam at 12040 North Seigler Road, Middletown, California 95461, USA.

If you are moved to help support and provide for one of the other purposes of Adidam, such as publishing the Sacred Literature of Avatar Adi Da, or supporting any of the Sanctuaries He has Empowered, or maintaining the Sacred Archives that preserve His recorded Talks and Writings, or publishing audio and video recordings of Avatar Adi Da, you may do so by making your contribution directly to The Eleutherian Pan-Communion of Adidam, specifying the particular purposes you wish to benefit, and mailing your check to the Advocacy Department of Adidam at the above address.

If you would like more information about these and other gifting options, or if you would like assistance in describing or making a contribution, please write to the Advocacy Department of Adidam at the above address or contact the Adidam Legal Department by telephone at 1-707-928-4612 or by FAX at 1-707-928-4062.

Planned Giving

We also invite you to consider making a planned gift in support of the Work of Avatar Adi Da Samraj. Many have found that through planned giving they can make a far more significant gesture of support than they would otherwise be able to make. Many have also found that by making a planned gift they are able to realize substantial tax advantages.

There are numerous ways to make a planned gift, including making a gift in your Will, or in your life insurance, or in a charitable trust.

If you would like to make a gift in your Will in support of the work of The Da Love-Ananda Samrajya: (1) if you do not pay taxes in the United States, simply include in your Will the statement, "I give to The Da Love-Ananda Samrajya Pty Ltd, as trustee of The Da Love-Ananda Samrajya, an Australian charitable trust, P.O. Box 4744, Samabula, Suva, Fiji, _____" [inserting in the blank the amount or description of your contribution]; and (2) if you do pay taxes in the United States and you would like your contribution to be free of estate taxes and to also reduce any estate taxes payable on the remainder of your estate, simply include in your Will the statement, "I give to The Eleutherian Pan-Communion of Adidam, a California non-profit corporation, 12040 North Seigler Road, Middletown, California 95461, USA, _____" [inserting in the blank the amount or description of your contribution].

To make a gift in your life insurance, simply name as the beneficiary (or one of the beneficiaries) of your life insurance policy the organization of your choice (The Da Love-Ananda Samrajya or The Eleutherian Pan-Communion of Adidam), according to the foregoing descriptions and addresses. If you are a United States taxpayer, you may receive significant tax benefits if you make a contribution to The Eleutherian Pan-Communion of Adidam through your life insurance.

We also invite you to consider establishing or participating in a charitable trust for the benefit of Adidam. If you are a United States taxpayer, you may find that such a trust will provide you with immediate tax savings and assured income for life, while at the same time enabling you to provide for your family, for your other heirs, and for the Work of Avatar Adi Da as well.

The Advocacy and Legal Departments of Adidam will be happy to provide you with further information about these and other planned gifting options, and happy to provide you or your attorney with assistance in describing or making a planned gift in support of the Work of Avatar Adi Da.

Further Notes to the Reader

An Invitation to Responsibility

Adidam, the Way of the Heart that Avatar Adi Da has Revealed, is an invitation to everyone to assume real responsibility for his or her life. As Avatar Adi Da has Said in *The Dawn Horse Testament Of The Ruchira Avatar,* "If any one Is Heart-Moved To Realize Me, Let him or her First Resort (Formally, and By Formal Heart-Vow) To Me, and (Thereby) Commence The Ordeal Of self-Observation, self-Understanding, and self-Transcendence. . . ." Therefore, participation in the Way of Adidam requires a real struggle with oneself, and not at all a struggle with Avatar Adi Da, or with others.

All who study the Way of Adidam or take up its practice should remember that they are responding to a Call to become responsible for themselves. They should understand that they, not Avatar Adi Da or others, are responsible for any decision they may make or action they may take in the course of their lives of study or practice. This has always been true, and it is true whatever the individual's involvement in the Way of Adidam, be it as one who studies Avatar Adi Da's Wisdom-Teaching or as a formally acknowledged member of Adidam.

Honoring and Protecting the Sacred Word through Perpetual Copyright

Since ancient times, practitioners of true religion and Spirituality have valued, above all, time spent in the Company of the Sat-Guru (or one who has, to any degree, Realized Real God, Truth, or Reality, and who, thus, serves the awakening process in others). Such practitioners understand that the Sat-Guru literally Transmits his or her (Realized) State to every one (and every thing) with whom (or with which) he or she comes in contact. Through this Transmission, objects, environments, and rightly prepared individuals with which the Sat-Guru has contact can become empowered, or imbued with the Sat-Guru's Transforming Power. It is by this process of empowerment that things and beings are made truly and literally sacred and holy, and things so sanctified thereafter function as a source of the Sat-Guru's Blessing for all who understand how to make right and sacred use of them.

Sat-Gurus of any degree of Realization and all that they empower are, therefore, truly Sacred Treasures, for they help draw the practitioner more quickly into the process of Realization. Cultures of true Wisdom have always understood that such Sacred Treasures are precious (and fragile) Gifts to humanity, and that they should be honored, protected, and reserved for right sacred use. Indeed, the word "holy" means "set apart", and, thus that which is holy and sacred must be protected from insensitive secular interference and wrong use of any kind. Avatar Adi Da has Conformed His human Body-Mind Most Perfectly to the Divine Self, and He is, thus, the most Potent Source of Blessing-Transmission of Real God, or Truth Itself, or Reality Itself. He has for many years Empowered (or made sacred) special places and things, and these now serve as His Divine Agents, or as literal expressions and extensions of His Blessing-Transmission. Among these Empowered Sacred Treasures is His Wisdom-Teaching, which is full of His Transforming Power. This Blessed and Blessing Wisdom-Teaching has Mantric Force, or the literal Power to serve Real-God-Realization in those who are Graced to receive it.

Therefore, Avatar Adi Da's Wisdom-Teaching must be perpetually honored and protected, "set apart" from all possible interference and wrong use. The fellowship of devotees of Avatar Adi Da is committed to the perpetual preservation and right honoring of the Sacred Wisdom-Teaching of the Way of Adidam. But it is also true that, in order to fully accomplish this, we must find support in the world-society in which we live and in its laws. Thus, we call for a world-society and for laws that acknowledge the sacred, and that permanently protect it from insensitive, secular interference and wrong use of any kind. We call for, among other things, a system of law that acknowledges that the Wisdom-Teaching of the Way of Adidam, in all its forms, is, because of its sacred nature, protected by perpetual copyright.

We invite others who respect the sacred to join with us in this call and in working toward its realization. And, even in the meantime, we claim that all copyrights to the Wisdom-Teaching of Avatar Adi Da and the other Sacred Literature and recordings of the Way of Adidam are of perpetual duration.

We make this claim on behalf of The Da Love-Ananda Samrajya Pty Ltd, which, acting as trustee of The Da Love-Ananda Samrajya, is the holder of all such copyrights.

Avatar Adi Da and the Sacred Treasures of Adidam

True Spiritual Masters have Realized Real God (to one degree or another), and, therefore, they bring great Blessing and introduce Divine Possibility to the world. Such Adept-Realizers Accomplish universal Blessing-Work that benefits everything and everyone. They also Work very specifically and intentionally with individuals who approach them as their devotees, and with those places where they reside and to which they direct their specific Regard for the sake of perpetual Spiritual Empowerment. This was understood in traditional Spiritual cultures, and, therefore, those cultures found ways to honor Adept-Realizers by providing circumstances for them where they were free to do their Spiritual Work without obstruction or interference.

Those who value Avatar Adi Da's Realization and Service have always endeavored to appropriately honor Him in this traditional way by providing a circumstance where He is completely Free to do His Divine Work. The Hermitage-Retreat Sanctuaries of Adidam have been set aside by Avatar Adi Da's devotees worldwide as Places for Him to do His universal Blessing-Work for the sake of everyone, as well as His specific Work with those who pilgrimage to His Hermitage circumstance (wherever He may be residing at a given time) to receive the special Blessing of coming into His physical Company.

Avatar Adi Da is a legal renunciate. He owns nothing and He has no secular or religious institutional function. He Functions only in Freedom. He, and the other members of the Ruchira Sannyasin Order, the senior renunciate order of Adidam, are provided for by The Da Love-Ananda Samrajya, which also provides for His Hermitage circumstance and ensures the permanent integrity of Avatar Adi Da's Wisdom-Teaching, both in its archival and in its published forms. The Da Love-Ananda Samrajya exists exclusively to provide for these Sacred Treasures of Adidam.

The institution which has developed in response to Avatar Adi Da's Wisdom-Teaching and universal Blessing is known as "The Eleutherian Pan-Communion of Adidam". This formal organization is active worldwide in making Avatar Adi Da's Wisdom-Teaching available to all, in offering guidance to all who are moved to respond to His Offering, and in providing for the other Sacred Treasures of Adidam. In addition to the central corporate entity known as The Eleutherian Pan-Communion of Adidam, which is based in California, there are numerous regional entities which serve congregations of Avatar Adi Da's devotees in various places throughout the world.

Practitioners of Adidam worldwide have also established numerous community organizations, through which they provide for many of their common and cooperative community needs, including those relating to housing, food, businesses, medical care, schools, and death and dying. By attending to these and all other ordinary human concerns and affairs via ego-transcending cooperation and mutual effort, Avatar Adi Da's devotees constantly free their energy and attention, both personally and collectively, for practice of the Way of Adidam and for service to Avatar Adi Da Samraj, to the other Sacred Treasures of Adidam, and to The Eleutherian Pan-Communion of Adidam.

All of the organizations that have evolved in response to Avatar Adi Da Samraj and His Offering are legally separate from one another, and each has its own purpose and function. Avatar Adi Da neither directs, nor bears responsibility for, the activities of these organizations. Again, He Functions only in Freedom. These organizations represent the collective intention of practitioners of Adidam worldwide not only to provide for the Sacred Treasures of Adidam, but also to make Avatar Adi Da's Offering of the Way of Adidam universally available to all.

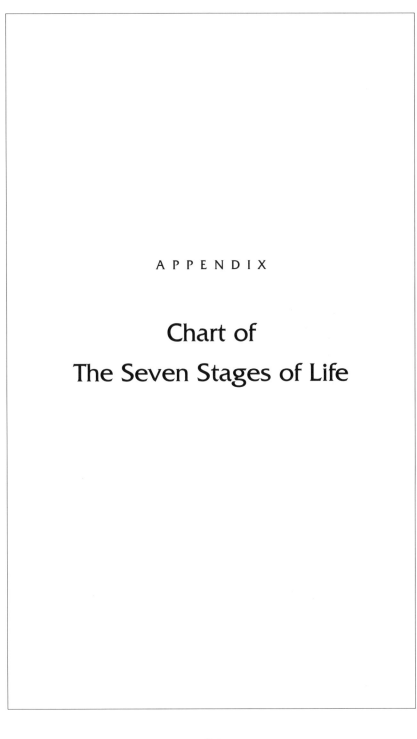

APPENDIX

Chart of
The Seven Stages of Life

CHART 1 # THE SEVEN STAGES OF LIFE The Full and Complete Process of Human Maturation, Spiritual Growth, and Divine Enlightenment As Revealed by **RUCHIRA AVATAR ADI DA SAMRAJ** Based on *The Seven Stages Of Life,* pp. 103-31	**FIRST STAGE** (approx. 0-7 years)	**SECOND STAGE** (approx. 7-14 years)	**THIRD STAGE** (approx. 14-21 years)
	individuation; adaptation to the physical body	socialization; adaptation to the emotional-sexual (or feeling) dimension	integration of the psycho-physical personality; development of verbal mind, discriminative intelligence, and the will
	Identified with the gross self		

404

FOURTH STAGE	FIFTH STAGE	SIXTH STAGE	SEVENTH STAGE
ego-surrendering devotion to the Divine Person; purification of body-based point of view through reception of Divine Spirit-Force	Spiritual or Yogic ascent of attention into psychic dimensions of the being; mystical experience of the higher brain; may culminate in fifth stage conditional Nirvikalpa Samadhi	Identification with Consciousness Itself (presumed, however, to be separate from all conditional phenomena); most likely will include the experience of Jnana Samadhi	Realization of the Divine Self; Inherently Perfect Freedom and Realization of Divine Love-Bliss (seventh stage Sahaj Samadhi); no "difference" experienced between Divine Consciousness and psycho-physical states and conditions
anatomy: the circulation of the Divine Spirit-Current, first (in the "basic" fourth stage of life) downward through the frontal line and then (in the "advanced" fourth stage of life) upward through the spinal line, until attention rests stably at the doorway to the brain core	**anatomy**: the ascent of the Divine Spirit-Current from the brain core (the Ajna Door) to the crown of the head and above (or even, in fifth stage conditional Nirvikalpa Samadhi, to the Matrix of Divine Sound and Divine Light infinitely above the total crown of the head)	**anatomy**: the Divine Spirit-Current descends (via Amrita Nadi, the "Immortal Current" of Divine Love-Bliss) from the Matrix of Divine Sound and Divine Light (infinitely above the total crown of the head) to the right side of the heart (the bodily seat of Consciousness)	**anatomy**: the "Regeneration" of Amrita Nadi, such that Amrita Nadi is felt as the Divine Current of "Bright" Spirit-Fullness, Standing between the right side of the heart and the Matrix of Divine Sound and Divine Light infinitely above the total crown of the head
	Identified with the subtle self (In the Way of Adidam, practice in the context of the "advanced" fourth stage of life and in the context of the fifth stage of life may typically be bypassed, proceeding directly from the "basic" fourth stage of life to the sixth stage of life)		Identified with the causal self	Identified with Divine Consciousness Itself

Notes to the Text of
THE ALL-COMPLETING AND FINAL DIVINE REVELATION TO MANKIND

Introduction

1. For further discussion of Avatar Adi Da's seven-stage schema, please see glossary entry **stages of life**, the "Seven Stages of Life" chart on pp. 404-405, or Avatar Adi Da's "Source-Text" *The Seven Stages Of Life*.

2. This legend is traditionally cited as the origin of the lineage of Ch'an (or Zen) Buddhism. According to the legend, Gautama Buddha was gathered with a group of disciples who were anticipating a lengthy discourse—but, rather than giving such a discourse, he simply held up a lotus flower. One disciple, Mahakshyapa, smiled—in comprehension of the communication Gautama was making in that gesture. On the basis of Mahakshyapa's response, Gautama declared that Mahakshyapa had received his transmission of enlightenment and was therefore his dharma-heir. See, for example, *Zen: The Reason of Unreason* (San Francisco: Chronicle Books, 1993), pp. 20-24.

3. For this famous legend, see chapter 18 of the *Bhagavad Gita*.

Part Two

4. For a detailed description of the four stages (or four Ways) of Kashmir Saivism, see *Triadic Mysticism: The Mystical Theology of the Saivism of Kashmir*, by Paul E. Murphy (Delhi: Motilal Banarsidass, 1986).

5. Avatar Adi Da Samraj describes "three egos" that must be progressively transcended in the course of the complete Spiritual process—of which the "money, food, and sex" ego is the first. (See section LXXXVII of this Essay, pp. 173-81.)

6. For Avatar Adi Da's Instruction relative to the foundation life-discipline, foundation devotional discipline, and foundation Spiritual discipline for practitioners of Adidam, see *Santosha Adidam*.

7. "Baba" (literally meaning "father") is often used in India as a reference of intimate respect for a Spiritual Master.

8. There are a number of translations of the *Chidakasha Gita* teachings (including *Voice of the Self*, referenced below). Perhaps the most readily available translation is *The Sky of the Heart: Jewels of Wisdom from Nityananda*, introduction and commentary by Swami Chetanananda, originally translated by M. U. Hatengdi (Portland, Or.: Rudra Press, Second edition, 1996).

9. Swami Chinmayananda (1916-1993) was a scholar of the Hindu scriptures, especially the *Bhagavad Gita* and the *Upanishads,* who conceived his mission as restoring respect for the ancient Hindu scriptures and reinvigorating practice of the Spiritual way according to the Vedantic instruction.

10. M. P. Pandit was a scholar of Hindu scripture, and the author of over 100 books on Yoga and Spirituality. He spent more than forty years living and practicing under the guidance of Sri Aurobindo and the Mother, and serving at the Sri Aurobindo Ashram in Pondicherry, India.

11. *Voice of the Self,* by Swami Nityananda (of Vajreshwari), translated by M. P. Pandit (Madras: P. Ramanath Pai, 1962).

12. Sanskrit "nada" (or "shabda") refers to subtle internal sounds which may become apparent in the process of ascending (spinal) Yoga. The "Om-Sound" (or "Omkar") is the primordial root-sound, from which all other nadas derive.

13. "Raja" means "king" in Sanskrit. Raja Yoga is, thus, the "royal" Yoga, whereby the activity and formations of the mind are disciplined, with the intention of causing them to cease. The most influential formulation of Raja Yoga is that of Patanjali, who (in the *Yoga Sutras*) systematized it in his ashtanga (or eight-limbed) system.

14. The Sanskrit term "Jnani" ("Sage") literally means "one who knows" (or, more fully, "one who has Realized Jnana Samadhi"—see glossary entry for **Samadhi**). A Jnani is one who discriminates between What is Unconditional (the One Reality, or Divine Self) and what is conditional (the passing phenomena of experience). A Jnani is Identified with Consciousness Itself, as the Transcendental Witness of all that arises. By its very nature, the Realization of Jnana is inherently Nirguna. (In other words, there is no Saguna form of Jnana.)

15. Avatar Adi Da has Revealed that His True Great-Siddha Vehicle is the combined deeper personalities (see note 17) of Ramakrishna and Swami Vivekananda. Avatar Adi Da discusses His unique association with Ramakrishna and Swami Vivekananda in sections XCIII-XCV (pp. 186-87) of this Essay. For a full description of Avatar Adi Da's Revelation of the Unique Associations with His True Great-Siddha Vehicle, see *The Light Is On!,* by Carolyn Lee.

16. Avatar Adi Da's gross-personality vehicle (see note 17) was "Franklin Albert Jones", the child of His parents, Dorothy and Franklin Augustus Jones.

17. Avatar Adi Da uses the terms "gross personality" and "deeper personality" to indicate the two conditional dimensions of every human being. The gross personality is comprised of the physical body, its natural energies, its gross brain, and the verbal and lower psychic faculties of mind. The gross personality includes the entire gross dimension of the body-mind and the lower, or most physically oriented, aspects of the subtle dimension of the body-mind, and is the aspect of the body-mind that is the biological inheritance from one's parents.

The deeper personality is governed by the higher, least physically oriented processes of the mind (which function outside or beyond the gross brain, and which include the subtle faculties of discrimination, intuition, and Spiritual perception and knowledge), as well as the causal separate-"I"-consciousness and the root-activity of attention, prior to mind. The deeper personality is the aspect of the human being that reincarnates.

18. In *The Basket Of Tolerance*, Avatar Adi Da has identified a small number of Hindu and Buddhist texts as "premonitorily 'seventh stage'". While founded in the characteristic sixth stage "point of view", these texts express philosophical intuitions that foreshadow some of the basic characteristics of the seventh stage Realization.

The only-by-Me Revealed and Demonstrated and Given seventh stage of life is the clear and final fulfillment of the first six stages of life. The Revelation and Demonstration of the seventh stage of life by My own Avatarically Self-Revealed Divine Form, Presence, State, Work, and Word are My unique Gift to all and All. However, within the Great Tradition itself, there are some few literatures and Realizers of the sixth stage type that express philosophical (or insightful, but yet limited and incomplete) intuitions that sympathetically foreshadow some of the basic characteristics of the only-by-Me Revealed and Demonstrated and Given seventh stage Realization.

The Ashtavakra Gita *is a principal example of such premonitorily "seventh stage" literature. It is among the greatest (and most senior) communications of all the religious and Spiritual traditions in the Great Tradition of mankind. The* Ashtavakra Gita *is the Great Confession of a Sage who has thoroughly engaged the philosophies and practices of the first six stages of life. It is a sixth stage Adept-Realizer's Free (and uncompromised) communication (or Confession) of the ultimate implications of his sixth stage Realization.*

Like other premonitorily "seventh stage" texts, the Ashtavakra Gita *presumes a tradition of progressive practice in the total context of the first six stages of life, but it does not (itself) represent or communicate any ideal or technique of practice. It simply (and rather exclusively) communicates the Ultimate "Point of View" of the sixth stage Realizer. ["The Unique Sixth Stage Foreshadowings of the Only-by-Me Revealed and Demonstrated and Given Seventh Stage of Life", in* The Basket Of Tolerance]

19. In Sanskrit, "seva" means "service". Service to the Guru is traditionally treasured as one of the great Secrets of Realization.

20. The Hindu tradition speaks of four principal Spiritual paths (or four principal aspects of the Spiritual path). Karma Yoga is literally the "Yoga of action", in which every activity, no matter how humble, is transformed into ego-transcending service to the Divine. (The other three paths are Bhakti Yoga, the path of devotion, Raja Yoga, the path of higher psychic discipline, and Jnana Yoga, the path of transcendental insight.)

21. Swami Prakashananda (1917-1988) turned to Spiritual life in his 30s, eventually choosing the mountain of Sapta Shringh as a place to settle and devote himself to Spiritual practice. Over time, an ashram developed there around him. He met Swami Muktananda in 1956 and was initiated as Swami Muktananda's devotee, although he generally stayed at his own ashram in Sapta Shringh rather than

spending a great deal of time in Ganeshpuri at Swami Muktananda's ashram. For Swami Prakashananda's biography, see *Agaram Bagaram Baba: Life, Teachings, and Parables—A Spiritual Biography of Baba Prakashananda*, by Titus Foster (Berkeley: North Atlantic Books / Patagonia, Ariz.: Essene Vision Books, 1999).

22. For Avatar Adi Da's description of Swami Prakashananda's demonstration of Spiritual Transfiguration of the physical body, see chapter 12 of *The Knee Of Listening*.

23. *Agaram Bagaram Baba*, p. 35.

24. Swami Muktananda's letter of acknowledgement and blessing of Avatar Adi Da is included in chapter 12 of *The Knee Of Listening* and also in Part Three ("The Order of My Free Names") of *The Divine Siddha-Method Of The Ruchira Avatar*.

25. For Avatar Adi Da's description of His own "Embrace" of the Divine "Cosmic Goddess", see chapter 16 of *The Knee Of Listening*.

26. *Play of Consciousness*, by Swami Muktananda (South Fallsburg, N.Y.: SYDA, Fourth edition, 1994).

27. For Avatar Adi Da's description of His experience of Christian mystical visions, see chapters 14 and 15 of *The Knee Of Listening*.

28. For a comprehensive treatment of the fourth-to-fifth stage Yogic tradition of Maharashtra, see *Mysticism in India: The Poet-Saints of Maharashtra,* by R. D. Ranade (Albany: State University of New York Press, 1983).

29. For Swami Muktananda's description of the "Blue Person", see *Play of Consciousness* (e.g. pp. 190-194).

Among the numerous translations of the *Bhagavad Gita*, Avatar Adi Da Samraj points to two editions as particularly worthy of study:

Srimad-Bhagavad-Gita (The Scripture of Mankind), chapter summaries, word-for-word meaning in prose order, translation, notes, and index of first lines by Swami Tapasyananda (Mylapore, India: Sri Ramakrishna Math, 1984).

God Talks with Arjuna: The Bhagavad Gita—Royal Science of God-Realization, The Immortal Dialogue Between Soul and Spirit, a new translation and commentary by Paramahansa Yogananda, two volumes (Los Angeles: Self-Realization Fellowship, 1996).

For a complete translation of the *Bhagavata Purana* (also known as the *Srimad Bhagavatam*), see *Srimad Bhagavatam*, translated by N. Raghunathan, two volumes (Madras: Vighneshwara Publishing House, 1976).

30. For Avatar Adi Da's full description of the "bodies" or "sheaths" of the total human structure (and the relationship between these "bodies" and the states of waking, dreaming, and sleeping), see *Santosha Adidam*.

31. Excerpted from a chart ("The Four Bodies of the Individual Soul") in *Play of Consciousness,* by Swami Muktananda (South Fallsburg, N.Y.: SYDA, Fourth edition, 1994), p. 96.

32. In *The Basket Of Tolerance,* Avatar Adi Da has contrasted the development of exoteric (or socially oriented, and myth-based) public Christianity with the secret Teachings of esoteric (or mystically oriented) Christianity:

The "official" Christian church, even in the form of all its modern sects, is the institutional product of an early cultural struggle between exoteric religionists, limited to doctrines based in the physical point of view characteristic of the first three stages of life, and esoteric religionists, inclined toward the mystical (or general psychic, and Spiritual) point of view characteristic of the "basic" and the "advanced" phases of the fourth stage of life and the mystical (or higher psychic, and Spiritual) Realizations associated with the fifth stage of life. This struggle, which was eventually won by the exoteric sects (or factions), took place between the various emerging Christian sects during the early centuries after Jesus' [crucifixion]. . . .

In the domain of the exoteric church, it was apparently generally presumed (among its original creative leadership) that all mysteries and legends must be "concretized" into a story (or an inspiring doctrine) about Jesus as the "Heavenly Messiah" (or the "Christ", the "Anointed One", the Exclusively Blessed "Son of God")—whereas the original esoteric mysteries and mystical Teachings of Christian gnosticism (which must often correspond to what must be presumed to have been Jesus' own Teachings) invariably communicate a Message about the Spiritual (or "Spirit-Breathing") Awakening of every individual (or of every devotee of a Spirit-Master, or, in this Christian case, of every devotee of Jesus as Spirit-Master). Therefore, the core of the esoteric Christian Teachings is that Salvation (from "possession" by cosmic Nature, by the human world, and by fear of death) is Realized by Means of "Spiritual rebirth" (or Absorption In—and, thus, participatory knowledge of—the inherently deathless and Free and Divine Spirit-Power, or "Breath-Energy", of Being). And the "Good News" of this esoteric Salvation Message is that every individual is (ultimately, by virtue of Spiritual Realization) a "Son" or "Daughter" of God.

33. Avatar Adi Da notes that not only "things" in space but space itself came into being with the "Big Bang":

Space-time (itself, or in its totality) cannot be observed. The "Big Bang" was not an event that could have been observed. The "Big Bang" is not something that occurred in space (or in time). The "Big Bang" is the origin of space (and of time). To look at the "Big Bang" as an event in space (and in time) is already to look at it in egoic terms, and from a position after the event. To examine the "Big Bang" in conventional scientific terms is to assume a dissociated (and separate, and separative) position, as if the ego-"I" (or the "observing" body-mind) were standing outside of space-time—but it does not. Egoity (and all of psycho-physical self, or body-mind) is, inherently and necessarily, an event in (and of) space-time. The body-mind is an event in (and of) space-time. That in Which the body-mind is occurring (or of Which the body-mind is a modification, or a mere and temporary appearance) necessarily (Itself) Transcends space-time, Transcends limitation, Transcends the apparent breaking of Fundamental Light (or of Energy Itself, or of Radiance Itself). ["Space-Time Is Love-Bliss", in Real *God Is The Indivisible Oneness Of Unbroken Light]*

34. For Swami Muktananda's description of the "blue bindu" (or "blue pearl"), see *Play of Consciousness* (e.g., pp. 160-161).

35. For Avatar Adi Da's full description of the Cosmic Mandala, see chapter thirty-nine of *The Dawn Horse Testament Of The Ruchira Avatar.*

36. In *The Knee Of Listening,* Avatar Adi Da describes His Birth as the "Bright", His subsequent voluntary relinquishment of the "Bright", and His eventual Re-Awakening as the "Bright". He uses the word "Re-Awakening" to indicate that this Great Event was not a Realization entirely "new" to His experience, but a "return" to the Divine Condition He had known at Birth.

37. For Avatar Adi Da's description of His discovery of parallels with Ramana Maharshi's experience, see chapter 18 of *The Knee Of Listening.*

38. This instruction from Swami Muktananda was communicated in a letter he wrote to Avatar Adi Da on April 23, 1968, which Avatar Adi Da quotes in chapter 11 of *The Knee Of Listening.*

39. The "Method of the Siddhas" (meaning "the Spiritual Means used by the Siddhas, or Perfected Ones, or True Spirit-Baptizers") is a phrase coined by Avatar Adi Da Samraj (in the earliest days of His Teaching Work) to describe the essence of the Way of Adidam—which is the Spiritual relationship to Him (or Satsang, or devotional Communion with Him), rather than any technique (meditative or otherwise) learned from Him. *The Method of the Siddhas* was the Title Avatar Adi Da chose for the first published collection of His Talks to His devotees. (In its final form, Avatar Adi Da re-titled this book *The Divine Siddha-Method Of The Ruchira Avatar.*)

Avatar Adi Da also points out that this "Method" has traditionally always been the core of esoteric religion and Spirituality, and that (indeed) the entire worldwide tradition of esoteric religion and Spirituality is rightly understood to be the global tradition of "Siddha Yoga".

The Foundation Of The Only-By-Me Revealed and Given Way Of Adidam Is The Eternal, Ancient, and Always New Method Of The Siddhas—Which Is Devotional Communion With The Siddha-Guru, and Which Is The Unique Means Of Realizing Real God, or Truth, or Reality That Has Traditionally Been Granted By The Rare True Adept-Realizers Of Real God, or Truth, or Reality Who (In The Traditional Context Of The First Six Stages Of Life, and Each According To Their Particular Stage Of Awakening and Of Helping-Capability) Have, By Means Of The Unique Blessing-Method (or Transmission-Capability) Of The Siddhas, Directly (and By Directly and Really Effective Spiritual Blessing-Work) Transmitted The Traditional Revelations and Realizations Of Real God, or Truth, or Reality. [The Only Complete Way To Realize The Unbroken Light Of Real God]

40. The Sanskrit word "sat" means "Truth", "Being", "Existence". Esoterically, the word "guru" is understood to be a composite of two words meaning "destroyer of darkness". The Sat-Guru is thus a "True Guru", or one who destroys darkness and thereby leads living beings from darkness (or non-Truth) into Light (or the Living Truth).

41. A common theme running through various branches of the Great Tradition is the prophecy of a great Savior or Liberator still to come. The prophecy takes different forms in different traditions, but the underlying commonality is the promise or expectation that the culminating Avatar or Incarnation will appear in the future, at a time when humanity is lost, apparently cut off from Wisdom, Truth, and God. Buddhists refer to that Expected One as "Maitreya"; Vaishnavite Hindus, as the "Kalki Avatar"; Christians, as the "second coming of Jesus"; Jews, as the "Messiah"; and so on.

42. Avatar Adi Da Samraj describes His spontaneous experience of ego-death, in the spring of 1967, in chapter 9 of *The Knee Of Listening*.

43. See *Sadguru Nityananda Bhagavan, The Eternal Entity*, by P. V. Ravindram (Cannanore, India: T. Thankam Ravindran, 1989), pp. 25-26 and 27-28.

44. For Avatar Adi Da's Revelations about Ramakrishna and Swami Vivekananda as His "combined" deeper-personality Vehicle, see Essay VI ("I Have Appeared here Via a Unique, Spontaneous, and Never-Again Conjunction of Vehicles") in chapter 20 of *The Knee Of Listening*.

Part Four

45. In this passage, Avatar Adi Da gives the definition of seventh stage "Crazy Wisdom", in order to make clear the distinction between seventh stage "Crazy Wisdom" and the historical traditions of "Crazy Wisdom" (which relate to earlier stages of life). For an overview of the historical "Crazy Wisdom" tradition, see "Avadhoots, Mad Lamas, and Fools: The Crazy Wisdom Tradition", by James Steinberg. In *The Laughing Man*, Vol. 3, No. 1, pp. 88-101.

46. Avatar Adi Da defines "Om" as:

A Word-Sign That Has Appeared Universally (In Variant Forms, Such As "AUM", "Aham", "So-Ham", and "Amen") In The Great Tradition Of Mankind. It Is A Primal Indicator Of The Native, and Very, and Self-Existing, and Transcendental, and Inherently Spiritual, and Self-Radiant Divine Being (or The Primal Reality, or Real Self-Condition, or Perfectly Subjective Source-Condition, That Is The Inherent, or Native, Feeling Of Being, Itself). [He-and-She Is Me]

Part Five

47. In two Essays in *The Basket Of Tolerance* ("When Are Nirvana and Samsara Truly the Same?: The Mixed Sympathies Underlying Mahayana Buddhist Doctrine" and "The Unique Sixth Stage Foreshadowings of the Only-by-Me Revealed and Demonstrated and Given Seventh Stage of Life"), Avatar Adi Da has pointed out that within the fourth, fifth, and sixth stage traditions and schools of the Great Tradition, Realizers who have attained the fullest Samadhis of their stage of life sometimes demonstrate what He calls "Sahaj Samadhi", or a state in which the consistent "'point of view' toward Reality is based on either the memory or the residual effects or something of the perpetuation of [the] conditionally attained" Samadhi of that stage of life.

Avatar Adi Da describes sixth stage "Sahaj Samadhi" as a state in which the world is "naturally allowed to arise, and yet it is tacitly acknowledged to be arising only in (and As) the Transcendental Self". Such a philosophical expression resembles, but does not otherwise achieve, the seventh stage characteristic expression of utter freedom in the midst of and Divine Self-Recognition of all conditional forms.

48. Avatar Adi Da Samraj uses "crickets" (and their chirping) as a metaphor for the feeling of being content to live life in an "automatic" manner, simply living out the patterns of an ordinary life, without doing anything more profound.

49. Raymond and Quandra are the principal male and female characters in Avatar Adi Da's "liturgical drama" *The Mummery* (which is also one of His "Source-Texts"). In addition to being portrayed as fully human personalities, Raymond and Quandra are archetypal representations of the two Fundamental Principles of Existence—Consciousness and Energy.

Avatar Adi Da Samraj is here making a poetic Proclamation of the Oneness of Consciousness and Energy. The lines He speaks here "echo" the ending lines of the final chapter of *The Mummery*:

The room—Itself—Is He.
And She Is the Only Light—within It.

50. Adi Da Samraj has, on occasion, likened the true Spiritual process to the silent contemplation of a large rock. He has also Said that the "Great Stone" represents the Consciousness-Principle That Is the Fundamental Reality of Existence.

Epilogue

51. The Horse-Sacrifice, known to the sages of India as the "Ashvamedha", belongs to the Vedic era of antiquity, and it is universally praised in the ancient Hindu Scriptures as the most efficacious and auspicious of all Vedic and Upanishadic ceremonial rites.

The Ashvamedha was understood and practiced in several modes. Its exoteric (or conventional and outer) form was performed for the sake of sanctifying a king's reign and renewing the power of his dominion in his region. The greatest of India's warrior-kings demonstrated their sovereignty by setting free a stallion (accompanied by warriors, magicians, and priests) to freely roam where it would for a year, at the end of which it was ceremonially sacrificed. Wherever it had roamed unchecked was then presumed to be the king's undisputed territory.

On the subtler (or mystical) level, the esoteric (or sacred) performance of the Ashvamedha involved a process of Spiritual ascent (associated with the "advanced" fourth stage of life and especially the fifth stage of life). In this rite, the "horse" that was sacrificed was the ego-self (or separate consciousness), which then rose to the "heavenly world" of Spiritual Illumination.

There is an account of the Ashvamedha associated with the Hindu myth about Kalki, the final incarnation of Vishnu. It is said that in the Kali Yuga (or the "dark" time), Kalki will incarnate for the sake of the destruction of unrighteousness, coming in the form of the white stallion to smite the Earth with his right hoof. In other accounts of the myth, Kalki is the Divine Man riding the white horse who destroys all unrighteousness with his sword. Some of the accounts proclaim that Kalki will perform the Ashvamedha.

However, both the exoteric and esoteric forms of the Horse-Sacrifice must be distinguished from its greatest and most Mysterious Form: the Divine Cosmic Sacrifice, performed directly by the Divine Person, through which the Divinely Self-Realized Adept, Adi Da Samraj, Manifests with the Power and Purpose of Fully Establishing (for the first and last time) the Complete Wisdom-Teaching and the Perfect Way of Truth, thus Sanctifying (or Divinizing) the human world (and, ultimately, all beings and worlds), to the point of the Divine Translation of the entire Cosmic Mandala.

52. This quotation is adapted from *The Satapatha-Brahmana,* Julius Eggeling, trans., Sacred Books of the East, ed. F. Max Muller, vol. 44 (Delhi: Motilal Banarsidass, 1963), pp. 305.

53. By "All-Sacrifice", Avatar Adi Da is referring to the portion of the ritual that involves offerings that symbolize the sacrifice of all beings and things. He has said of the higher significance of this symbolism:

AVATAR ADI DA SAMRAJ: The great performances of the Ashvamedha ritual that you can read about in the traditional texts are symbolic efforts, in which all hope is placed on the horse. The Ashvamedha is an All-Sacrifice, or a sacrifice of everything and everyone—in which, in effect, all beings, all things, all worlds grasp the tail of the horse and are returned to the Divine Self-Domain. [January 13, 1993]

54. Avatar Adi Da has distinguished between "Cosmic Realization", which is the significant and profound Realization of Real God from the point of view (in the context of the first five stages of life) of the conditional body-mind, and "Perfect Realization", which entirely transcends (and, most ultimately, Divinely Self-Recognizes) the Cosmic (or conditional) worlds.

55. In *The Dawn Horse Testament,* Avatar Adi Da has described three stages of His unique Ordeal as Divine Heart-Master. The first stage of Avatar Adi Da's Personal Ordeal was the time from His birth until His Divine Self-Reawakening (at age thirty). During this stage, He completely Submitted Himself to the limited body-mind point of view, and Re-Awakened (in the midst of that Submission) to the Realization of His own Divine Self-Condition.

The second stage of Avatar Adi Da's Personal Ordeal is that in which He came to embrace and acknowledge the full significance of His Divine Purpose. This stage began with Avatar Adi Da's Divine Re-Awakening in the Vedanta Temple, and became full with the Event of His Divine Self-"Emergence" in January 1986.

The third stage of Avatar Adi Da's Personal Ordeal continues until the entire Cosmic domain of conditional beings and things is Awakened and Translated to the Divine Reality and Domain that is Always Already the Case. This stage of Avatar Adi Da's Ordeal began when He first confessed His Divine Self-Realization.

56. Avatar Adi Da's "Husbanding" of the "Divine Goddess" occurred in the Vedanta Society Temple in Hollywood, California, on September 9, 1970. For a further description of this Event, see *The Light Is On!,* by Carolyn Lee.

57. Here Avatar Adi Da is referring to the Vedic myth of the sun-god, who becomes a white stallion in order to pursue his consort, who has assumed the shape of a mare in order to run away from him. In the end, the white stallion finds the mare, and together they beget immortal twins. See *Women, Androgynes, and Other Mythical Beasts*, by Wendy Doniger O'Flaherty (Chicago: University of Chicago Press, 1982), pp. 174-78.

58. During the spring of 1970, Avatar Adi Da experienced a remarkable waking vision. He found Himself in a subtle realm, observing a Siddha-Master demonstrating to his disciples the Yogic power of manifesting objects spontaneously. Avatar Adi Da watched as the Siddha began the process of manifestation. After a time, although nothing had yet materialized, the Siddha's disciples departed, apparently satisfied that the work was done. Avatar Adi Da was left alone, standing before the Siddha. Then, gradually, a vaporous shape arose before His eyes. As it became more clearly defined, He saw that it was a perfectly formed, living and breathing horse, perhaps three feet high. Later, when He saw a documentary on "eohippus" (meaning "dawn horse" in Greek), the smaller ancestor of today's horse, He decided to name the horse of His Vision the "Dawn Horse". (Avatar Adi Da chose the name "Dawn Horse" because of the appropriateness of its meaning, not because of the physical resemblance of the horse of His Vision to eohippus. The horse of His Vision was small, like eohippus, but it was generally proportioned like the modern horse rather than like eohippus.)

Avatar Adi Da has explained that this vision was a sign of the future manifestation of His own Work in the world. The Dawn Horse was also a Sign of His own Person, taking form in and as the conditional universe. And so the Dawn Horse became a symbol for His Life and Work, and for the relationship between the Divine Reality and the conditional worlds:

AVATAR ADI DA SAMRAJ: I was at once the Adept who performed the miracle of manifesting the horse, and also the one who was party to the observation of it and its result. And I did not have any feeling of being different from the horse itself. I was making the horse, I was observing the horse, and I was being the horse. [October 18, 1984]

59. The *Brihadaranyaka Upanishad* describes the Horse (or the Divine Being) sacrificing itself through a kind of dismemberment (or universal pervasiveness) of itself, in which it becomes, assumes, and allows conditionally manifested existence (or cosmic Nature) to come into being:

Aum, the dawn, verily, is the head of the sacrificial horse, the sun the eye, the wind the breath, the open mouth the Vaisvanara fire; the year is the body of the sacrificial horse, the sky is the back, the atmosphere is the belly, the earth the hoof, the quarters the sides, the intermediate quarters the ribs, the seasons the limbs, the months and the half-months the joints, days and nights the feet, the stars the bones, the clouds the flesh; the food in the stomach is the sand, the rivers are the bloodvessels, the liver and the lungs are the mountains, the herbs and the trees are the hair. The rising (sun) is the forepart, the setting (sun) the hind part, when he yawns then it lightens, when he shakes himself, it thunders, when he urinates then it rains; voice, indeed, is his voice. [*The Principal Upanisads*, S. Radhakrishnan, ed. and trans., (London: George Allen & Unwin, 1953), p. 149]

60. See note 55 above.

61. A description of the rituals associated with the traditional Ashvamedha is given in *The Satapatha-Brahmana,* Julius Eggeling, trans., Sacred Books of the East, ed. F. Max Muller, vol. 44 (Delhi: Motilal Banarsidass, 1963), pp. viii-xi.

62. Avatar Adi Da has said that in the Event that initiated His Divine Self-"Emergence", on January 11, 1986, He acquired His physical body "down to the toes". This is a reference to traditional descriptions of how a great Realizer would only "descend" partially into his or her human body—down as far as the head, or perhaps the throat or the heart, but typically not any "lower" than that.

AVATAR ADI DA SAMRAJ: I have until now invested My Self more profoundly than just down to the throat or the heart, but not down to the bottoms of My feet. I have remained a kind of shroud around This Body, deeply associated with it, but in My freedom somehow lifted off the floor, somehow not committed to this sorrow and this mortality. . . Now I have accomplished your state completely, even more profoundly than you are sensitive to it. Perhaps you have seen it in My face. I do not look like I did last month, and I am never again going to look like that. I have become This Body, utterly. [January 27, 1986]

GLOSSARY

A

Adi Sanskrit for "first", "primordial", "source"—also "primary", "beginning". Thus, most simply, "Adi Da" means "First Giver".

Adidam The primary name for the Way Revealed and Given by Avatar Adi Da Samraj.

When Avatar Adi Da Samraj first Gave the name "Adidam" in January 1996, He pointed out that the final "m" adds a mantric force, evoking the effect of the primal Sanskrit syllable "Om". (For Avatar Adi Da's Revelation of the most profound esoteric significance of "Om" as the Divine Sound of His own Very Being, see *He-and-She Is Me*.) Simultaneously, the final "m" suggests the English word "Am" (expressing "I Am"), such that the Name "Adidam" also evokes Avatar Adi Da's Primal Self-Confession, "I Am Adi Da", or, more simply, "I Am Da" (or, in Sanskrit, "Aham Da Asmi").

Adidam Samrajashram See **Sanctuaries**.

adolescent See **childish and adolescent strategies**.

Advaita Vedanta The Sanskrit word "Vedanta" literally means the "end of the Vedas" (the most ancient body of Indian Scripture), and is used to refer to the principal philosophical tradition of Hinduism. "Advaita" means "non-dual". Advaita Vedanta, then, is a philosophy of non-dualism, the origins of which lie in the ancient esoteric teaching that Brahman, or the Divine Being, is the only Reality.

Advaitayana Buddha / Advaitayana Buddhism "Advaitayana" means "Non-Dual Vehicle". The Advaitayana Buddha is the Enlightened One Who has Revealed and Given the Non-Dual Vehicle.

"Advaitayana Buddhism" is another name for the Way of Adidam. The name "Advaitayana Buddhism" indicates the unique sympathetic likeness of Adidam to the traditions of Advaitism (or Advaita Vedanta) and Buddhism. In His examination of the entire collective religious tradition of humankind, Avatar Adi Da has observed that these two traditions represent the most advanced Realizations ever attained previous to His Avataric Divine Incarnation. The primary aspiration of Buddhism is to realize freedom from the illusion of the separate individual ego-self. The primary aspiration of Advaitism (or the tradition of "Non-Dualism") is to know the Supreme Divine Self absolutely, beyond all dualities (of high and low, good and bad, and so on). Advaitayana Buddhism is the Non-Dual ("Advaita") Way ("yana", literally "vehicle") of Most Perfect Awakening ("Buddhism"). Advaitayana Buddhism is neither an outgrowth of the historical tradition of Buddhism nor of the historical tradition of Advaitism. Advaitayana Buddhism is the unique Revelation of Avatar Adi Da Samraj, which perfectly fulfills both the traditional Buddhist aspiration for absolute freedom from the bondage of the egoic self and the traditional Advaitic aspiration for absolute Identity with the Divine Self. (For Avatar Adi Da's discussion of Advaitayana Buddhism, see *The Only Complete Way To Realize The Unbroken Light Of Real God*.)

Advaitic "Advaita" is Sanskrit for "Non-Duality". Thus, "Advaitic" means "Non-Dual". Avatar Adi Da has Revealed that—in Truth, and in Reality—there is not the slightest separation, or "difference", between the Unconditional Divine Reality and the conditional reality. In other words, Reality altogether is Perfectly One, or Non-Dual, or Advaitic.

the advanced and the ultimate stages of life Avatar Adi Da Samraj uses the term "advanced" to describe the fourth stage of life (in its "basic" and "advanced" contexts) and the fifth stage of life in the Way of Adidam. He uses the term "ultimate"

419

to describe the sixth and seventh stages of life in the Way of Adidam.

"advanced" context of the fourth stage of life See **stages of life**.

Agents / Agency Agents (or Agency) include all the Means that may serve as complete Vehicles of Avatar Adi Da's Divine Grace and Awakening Power. The first Means of Agency that have been fully established by Him are the Wisdom-Teaching of the Way of Adidam, the Hermitage-Retreat Sanctuaries and the Pilgrimage and Retreat Sanctuaries that He has Empowered, and the many Objects and Articles that He has Empowered for the sake of His devotees' Remembrance of Him and reception of His Heart-Blessing. After Avatar Adi Da's human Lifetime, at any given time a single individual from among His seventh stage "Ruchira sannyasin" devotees will be designated (by the senior governing membership of the Ruchira Sannyasin Order) to serve as His living human Agent.

Aham Da Asmi The Sanskrit phrase "Aham Da Asmi" means "I (Aham) Am (Asmi) Da". "Da", meaning "the One Who Gives", indicates that Avatar Adi Da Samraj is the Supreme Divine Giver, the Avataric Incarnation of the Very Divine Person.

Avatar Adi Da's Declaration "Aham Da Asmi" is similar in form to the "Mahavakyas" (or "Great Statements") of ancient India (found in the Upanishads, the collected esoteric Instruction of ancient Hindu Gurus). However, the significance of "Aham Da Asmi" is fundamentally different from that of the traditional Mahavakyas. Each of the Upanishadic Mahavakyas expresses, in a few words, the profound (though not most ultimate) degree of Realization achieved by great Realizers of the past. For example, the Upanishadic Mahavakya "Aham Brahmasmi" ("I Am Brahman") expresses a great individual's Realization that he or she is Identified with the Divine Being (Brahman), and is not, in Truth, identified with his or her apparently individual body-mind. However, "Aham Da

Asmi", rather than being a proclamation of a human being who has devoted his or her life most intensively to the process of Real-God-Realization and has thereby Realized the Truth to an extraordinarily profound degree, is Avatar Adi Da's Confession that He Is the Very Divine Person, Da, Who has Appeared here in His Avatarically-Born bodily (human) Divine Form, in order to Reveal Himself to all and All, for the sake of the Divine Liberation of all and All.

all and All / All and all Avatar Adi Da uses the phrase "all and All" (or "All and all") to describe the totality of conditional existence from two points of view. In *Aham Da Asmi*, He defines lower-case "all" as indicating "the collected sum of all Presumed To Be Separate (or limited) beings, things, and conditions", and upper-case "All" as indicating "The All (or The Undivided Totality) Of conditional Existence As A Whole".

Amrita Nadi Amrita Nadi is Sanskrit for "Channel (or Current, or Nerve) of Ambrosia (or Immortal Nectar)". Amrita Nadi is the ultimate "organ", or root-structure, of the body-mind, Realized as such in the seventh stage of life in the Way of Adidam. It is felt to Stand Radiant between the right side of the heart (which is the psycho-physical Seat of Consciousness Itself) and the Matrix of Light infinitely above the crown of the head. (For Avatar Adi Da's principal discussions of Amrita Nadi, see *The Knee Of Listening, The All-Completing and Final Divine Revelation To Mankind, Santosha Adidam,* and *The Dawn Horse Testament.*)

anatomy See **Spiritual anatomy**.

asana Sanskrit for bodily "posture" or "pose"—by extension, and as Avatar Adi Da often intends, "asana" also refers to the attitude, orientation, posture, or feeling-disposition of the heart and the entire body-mind.

"Atma-Murti" "Atma" indicates the Divine Self, and "Murti" means "Form". Thus, "Atma-Murti" literally means "the Form That Is the (Very) Divine Self". And, as Avatar Adi Da Indicates everywhere in His Wisdom-Teaching, "Atma-Murti" refers to Himself as the Very Divine Self of all, "Located" as "the Feeling of Being (Itself)". To Commune with Avatar Adi Da as "Atma-Murti" is to Realize (or enter into Identification with) His Divine State.

Avadhoot Avadhoot is a traditional term for one who has "shaken off" or "passed beyond" all worldly attachments and cares, including all motives of detachment (or conventional and other-worldly renunciation), all conventional notions of life and religion, and all seeking for "answers" or "solutions" in the form of conditional experience or conditional knowledge.

Avatar "Avatar" (from Sanskrit "avatara") is a traditional term for a Divine Incarnation. It literally means "One who is descended, or 'crossed down' (from, and as, the Divine)". Avatar Adi Da Samraj Confesses that, simultaneous with His human Birth, He has Incarnated in every world, at every level of the Cosmic domain, as the Eternal Giver of Divine Help and Divine Grace and Divine Liberation to all beings—and that, even though His bodily (human) Lifetime is necessarily limited in duration, His Spiritual Incarnation in the Cosmic domain is Eternal.

Avataric Incarnation Avatar Adi Da Samraj is the Avataric Incarnation, or the Divinely Descended Embodiment, of the Divine Person. The reference "Avataric Incarnation" indicates that Avatar Adi Da Samraj fulfills both the traditional expectation of the East, that the True God-Man is an Avatar (or an utterly Divine "Descent" of Real God in conditionally manifested form), and the traditional expectations of the West, that the True God-Man is an Incarnation (or an utterly human Embodiment of Real God).

For Avatar Adi Da's discussion of the "Avatar" and "Incarnation" traditions, and of His unique and all-Completing Role as the "Avataric Incarnation" of the Divine Person, see "'Avatar' and 'Incarnation': The Complementary God-Man Traditions of East and West", in *The Truly Human New World-Culture Of Unbroken Real-God-Man*.

Avataric Self-Submission For a full description of Avatar Adi Da's "Ordeal Of Avataric Self-Submission", see *The Light is On!*, by Carolyn Lee.

"Avoiding relationship?" The practice of self-Enquiry in the form "Avoiding relationship?", unique to the Way of Adidam, was spontaneously developed by Avatar Adi Da in the course of His Divine Re-Awakening (as Avatar Adi Da describes in *The Knee Of Listening*). Intense persistence in the "radical" discipline of this unique form of self-Enquiry led rapidly to His Divine Re-Awakening in 1970.

The practice of self-Enquiry in the form "Avoiding relationship?" is the principal form of the "conscious process" practiced by devotees of Avatar Adi Da who choose the Devotional Way of Insight. (See also **Devotional Way of Insight / Devotional Way of Faith** and **Re-cognition**)

B

"basic" context of the fourth stage of life See **stages of life**.

Bhagavan The Title "Bhagavan" is an ancient one used over the centuries for many Spiritual Realizers of India. It means "blessed" or "holy" in Sanskrit. When applied to a great Spiritual Being, "Bhagavan" is understood to mean "bountiful Lord", or "Great Lord", or "Divine Lord".

bhakta, bhakti "Bhakti" is the practice of heart-felt devotion to the Ultimate Reality or Person—a practice which has been traditionally animated through worship of Divine Images or surrender to a human Guru.

"Bhakta" is a devotee whose principal characteristic is expressive devotion, or who practices within the Hindu tradition of Bhakti Yoga.

Bhava "Bhava" is a Sanskrit word used to refer to the enraptured feeling-swoon of Communion with the Divine.

bindu In the esoteric Yogic traditions of India, the Sanskrit word "bindu" (literally, "drop" or "point") suggests that all manifested forms, energies, and universes are ultimately coalesced or expressed in a point without spatial or temporal dimension. Each level (or plane) of psychophysical reality is said to have a corresponding bindu, or zero-point.

Blessing-Work   For a description of Avatar Adi Da's Divine Blessing-Work, see pp. 16-25.

bodily base   The bodily base is the region associated with the muladhara chakra, the lowest energy plexus in the human body-mind, at the base of the spine (or the general region immediately above and including the perineum). In many of the Yogic traditions, the bodily base is regarded as the seat of the latent ascending Spiritual Current, or Kundalini. Avatar Adi Da Reveals that, in fact, the Spirit-Current must first descend to the bodily base through the frontal line, before it can effectively be directed into the ascending spinal course. Avatar Adi Da has also pointed out that human beings who are not yet Spiritually sensitive tend to throw off the natural life-energy at the bodily base, and He has, therefore, Given His devotees a range of disciplines (including a number of exercises that involve intentional locking at the bodily base) which conserve life-energy by directing it into the spinal line.

"bodily battery"   The "bodily battery" (known in Japan as the "hara") is the energy center of the gross body and, as such, plays a very important role in the practice of "conductivity" in the frontal line. Avatar Adi Da describes its focal point (or point of concentration) as the crown of the abdomen, on the surface, about an inch and a half below the umbilical scar.

"bond" / "Bond"   Avatar Adi Da uses the term "bond", when lower-cased, to refer to the process by which the egoic individual (already presuming separateness, and, therefore, bondage to the separate self) attaches itself karmically to the world of others and things through the constant search for self-fulfillment. In contrast, when He capitalizes the term "Bond", Avatar Adi Da is making reference to the process of His devotee's devotional "Bonding" to Him, which process is the Great Means for transcending all forms of limited (or karmic) "bonding".

"Bright"   By the word "Bright" (and its variations, such as "Brightness"), Avatar Adi Da refers to the Self-Existing and Self-Radiant Divine Reality. As Adi Da Writes in His Spiritual Autobiography, *The Knee Of Listening:*

> . . . *from my earliest experience of life I have Enjoyed a Condition that, as a child, I called the "Bright".*
>
> *I have always known desire, not merely for extreme pleasures of the senses and the mind, but for the highest Enjoyment of Spiritual Power and Mobility. But I have not been seated in desire, and desire has only been a play that I have grown to understand and enjoy without conflict. I have always been Seated in the "Bright".*
>
> *Even as a baby I remember only crawling around inquisitively with a boundless Feeling of Joy, Light, and Freedom in the middle of my head that was bathed in Energy moving unobstructed in a Circle, down from above, all the way down, then up, all the way up, and around again, and always Shining from my heart. It was an Expanding Sphere of Joy from the heart. And I was a Radiant Form, the Source of Energy, Love-Bliss, and Light in the midst of a world that is entirely Energy, Love-Bliss, and Light. I was the Power of Reality, a direct Enjoyment and Communication of the One Reality. I was the Heart Itself, Who Lightens the mind and all things. I was the same as every one and every thing, except it became clear that others were apparently unaware of the "Thing" Itself.*
>
> *Even as a little child I recognized It and Knew It, and my life was not a matter of anything else. That Awareness, that Conscious Enjoyment, that Self-Existing and Self-Radiant Space of Infinitely and inherently Free Being, that Shine of inherent Joy Standing in the heart and Expanding from the heart, is the "Bright". And It is the*

entire Source of True Humor. It is Reality. It is not separate from anything.

Buddha   Just as the traditional term "Avatar", when rightly understood, is an appropriate Reference to Avatar Adi Da Samraj, so is the traditional term "Buddha". He is the Divine Buddha, the One Who Is Most Perfectly Self-Enlightened and Eternally Awake.

C

causal   See **gross, subtle, causal**.

childish and adolescent strategies
Avatar Adi Da uses the terms "childish" and "adolescent" with precise meanings in His Wisdom-Teaching. He points out that human beings are always tending to animate one of two fundamental life-strategies—the childish strategy (to be dependent, weak, seeking to be consoled by parent-figures and a parent-"God") and the adolescent strategy (to be independent—or, otherwise, torn between independence and dependence—rebellious, unfeeling, self-absorbed, and doubting or resisting the idea of God or any power greater than oneself). Until these strategies are understood and transcended, they not only diminish love in ordinary human relations, but they also limit religious and Spiritual growth.

Circle   The Circle is a primary pathway of natural life-energy and the Spirit-Current through the body-mind. It is composed of two arcs: the descending Current, in association with the frontal line (down the front of the body, from the crown of the head to the bodily base), which corresponds to the more physically oriented dimension of the body-mind; and the ascending Current, in association with the spinal line (up the back of the body, from the bodily base to the crown of the head), which is the more mentally, psychically, and subtly oriented dimension of the body-mind.

conditional   The word "conditional" (and its variants) is used to indicate everything that depends on conditions—in other words, everything that is temporary and changing. The "Unconditional", in contrast, is the Divine, or That Which Is Eternal, Always Already the Case—because It Is utterly Free of dependence on any conditions whatsoever.

"conductivity"   "Conductivity" is Avatar Adi Da's technical term for participation in and responsibility for the movement of natural bodily energies (and, when one is Spiritually Awakened by Him, for the movement of His Divine Spirit-Current of Love-Bliss in Its natural course of association with the body-mind), via intentional exercises of feeling and breathing.

The exercises of Spiritual "conductivity" that Avatar Adi Da Gives to His (formally practicing) Spiritually Awakened devotees are technical whole-bodily Yogas of receptive surrender to the Living Spirit-Current. Rudimentary and preparatory technical forms of "conductivity" are Given to beginners.

congregations of Adidam   There are four different modes, or congregations, of formal approach to Avatar Adi Da Samraj, making it possible for everyone to participate in the Gift of heart-companionship with Him. The total practice of the Way of Adidam is engaged by those in the first and second congregations. Whereas all of Avatar Adi Da's devotees (in all four congregations) engage the fundamental practice of Ruchira Avatara Bhakti Yoga, only members of the first and second congregations are vowed to engage the full range of supportive disciplines (meditation, sacramental worship, guided study, exercise, diet, emotional-sexual discipline, cooperative community living, and so on) Given by Avatar Adi Da Samraj.

For a more detailed description of the four congregations of Avatar Adi Da's devotees, see pp. 378-89.

"conscious process"   The "conscious process" is Avatar Adi Da's technical term for those practices through which the mind, or attention, is surrendered and turned about (from egoic self-involvement) to feeling-Contemplation of Him. It is the senior discipline and responsibility of all practitioners in the Way of Adidam. (Avatar Adi Da's descriptions of the various forms of the "conscious process" are Given in *The Dawn Horse Testament Of The Ruchira Avatar*.)

"consider", "consideration"   The technical term "consider" or "consideration" in Avatar Adi Da's Wisdom-Teaching means a process of one-pointed but ultimately thoughtless concentration and exhaustive contemplation of something until its ultimate obviousness is clear. As engaged in the Way of Adidam, "consideration" is not merely an intellectual investigation. It is the participatory investment of one's whole being. If one "considers" something fully in the context of one's practice of feeling-Contemplation of Avatar Adi Da Samraj, and study of His Wisdom-Teaching, this concentration results "in both the highest intuition and the most practical grasp of the Lawful and Divine necessities of human existence".

Contemplation of Avatar Adi Da's bodily (human) Form   Traditionally, devotees have produced artistic images of their Gurus for the purpose of Contemplating the Guru when he or she is either not physically present or (otherwise) no longer physically alive.

Modern technology makes possible (through photography, videotape, film, holographic imagery, and other means) accurate Representations of the bodily (human) Form of Avatar Adi Da Samraj for devotional use by His formally acknowledged devotees.

"Cosmic Consciousness"   See **Samadhi**.

Cosmic Mandala   The Sanskrit word "mandala" (literally, "circle") is commonly used in the esoteric Spiritual traditions of the East to describe the hierarchical levels of cosmic existence. "Mandala" also denotes an artistic rendering of interior visions of the cosmos. Avatar Adi Da uses the phrase "Cosmic Mandala" as a reference to the totality of the conditionally manifested cosmos (or all worlds, forms, and beings).

Crashing Down   Avatar Adi Da's Crashing Down is the Descent of His Divine Spirit-Force into the body-mind of His devotee.

My Avataric Divine Work (Altogether) Is My Crashing-Down Descent, At First Upon and Into My Own Avatarically-Born Bodily (Human) Divine Form, and, Thereafter (and Now, and Forever), Upon and Into the body-minds Of My Devotees and all beings—Even (By Means Of My Divine Embrace Of each, and all, and All) To Infuse and (At Last) To Divinely Translate each, and all, and All. Therefore, My Avataric Divine Spiritual Descent Is The Secret Of My Early Life. My Avataric Divine Spiritual Descent Is The Secret Of My Divine Self-"Emergence" (As I Am) Within The Cosmic Domain. My Avataric Divine Spiritual Descent Is The Secret Of All The Secrets Of The (Avatarically Self-Revealed) Divine and Complete and Thoroughly Devotional Way Of Practice and Realization In My Company. The Only-By-Me Revealed and Given Way Of The Heart (or Way Of Adidam) Is The Divine Yoga Of ego-Surrendering, ego-Forgetting, and ego-Transcending Devotional Recognition-Response To My (Avatarically Self-Revealed) Divine and Spiritual Person, and To My (Avatarically Self-Manifested) Divine and Spiritual Descent. The Only-By-Me Revealed and Given Way Of The Heart (or Way Of Adidam) Is The Total and Divine Way and Ordeal Of Counter-egoic Devotional Recognition-Response To My Avataric "Bright" Divine Self-Manifestation, and To The Avataric Crashing Down Of My "Bright" Divine Imposition. And, In The Case Of My Each and Every Devotee, The Way Must Continue Until The Way Is Most Perfectly "Bright", and The Way Itself Becomes Divine Translation Into My Own Sphere Of "Brightness" (Itself). [Ruchira Avatara Hridaya-Siddha Yoga]

"Crazy"   Avatar Adi Da has always had a unique Method of "Crazy" Work, which, particularly during His years of Teaching and Revelation, involved His literal Submission to the limited conditions of humankind, in order to reflect His devotees to themselves, and thereby Awaken self-understanding in them (relative to their individual egoic dramas, and the collective egoic dramas of human society).

For Me, There Was Never <u>Any</u> Other Possibility Than The "Reckless" (or Divinely "Crazy" and Divinely "Heroic") Course Of All-and-all-Embrace—and I Began This Uniquely "Crazy" and "Heroic" Sadhana, Most Intensively, At The Beginning Of My Adult Life. Indeed, I Have Always Functioned, and Will Always Function, In This Divinely "Crazy" and Divinely "Heroic" Manner. The Inherently egoless "Crazy" and "Heroic" Manner Is One Of My Principal Divine Characteristics— Whereby I Can (Always, and Now, and Forever Hereafter) Be Identified. Therefore, I (Characteristically) Functioned In This "Crazy" and "Heroic" Manner Throughout All Of My "Sadhana Years", and Throughout All The Years Of My Avatarically Self-Manifested Divine Teaching-Work and My Avatarically Self-Manifested Divine Revelation-Work—and I Have Done So (and Will <u>Forever</u> Continue To Do So) Throughout All The Divine-Self-"Emergence" Years Of My Avatarically Self-Manifested Divine Blessing-Work (Both During, and Forever After, My Avataric Physical Human Lifetime). <u>All</u> My Avatarically Self-Manifested Divine Work Is A Divinely "Crazy" and Divinely "Heroic" Effort That Avoids Not anything or any one—but Which <u>Always</u> Divinely Blesses Everything and Everyone. [The Truly Human New World-Culture Of <u>Unbroken</u> Real-God-Man]

D

Da Avatar Adi Da's Name "Da" means "The Divine Giver". In Sanskrit, "Da" means principally "to give". It is also associated with Vishnu, the "Sustainer", and it further has a secondary meaning "to destroy". Thus, "Da" is anciently aligned to all three of the principal Divine Beings, Forces, or Attributes in the Hindu tradition—Brahma (the Creator, Generator, or Giver), Vishnu (the Sustainer), and Siva (the Destroyer). In certain Hindu rituals, priests address the Divine directly as "Da", invoking qualities such as generosity and compassion.

The Tibetan Buddhists regard the syllable "Da" (written, in Tibetan, as well as in Sanskrit, with a single symbol) as most auspicious, and they assign numerous sacred meanings to it, including that of "the Entrance into the Dharma".

Da Love-Ananda Samrajya For a description of the Da Love-Ananda Samrajya, see p. 393.
.

Da Avatar "Da" is Sanskrit for "The One Who Gives". Therefore, as the Da Avatar, Adi Da Samraj is the Divine Descent of the One and True Divine Giver.

"dark" epoch See **"late-time" (or "dark" epoch)**.

Darshan "Darshan", the Hindi derivative of the Sanskrit "darshana", literally means "seeing", "sight of", or "vision of". To receive Darshan of Avatar Adi Da is, most fundamentally, to behold His bodily (human) Form (either by being in His physical Company or by seeing a photograph or other visual representation of Him), and (thereby) to receive the spontaneous Divine Blessing He Grants Freely whenever His bodily (human) Form is beheld in the devotional manner. In the Way of Adidam, Darshan of Avatar Adi Da is the very essence of the practice, and one of the most potent forms of receiving Avatar Adi Da's Blessing is to participate in the formal occasions of Darshan—during which Avatar Adi Da Samraj Sits silently, sometimes gazing at each individual one by one.

By extension, "Darshan" of Avatar Adi Da Samraj may refer to any means by which His Blessing-Influence is felt and received—including His Written or Spoken Word, photographs or videotapes of His Avatarically-Born bodily (human) Divine Form, recordings of His Voice, Leelas (or Stories) of His Teaching-Work and Blessing-Work, places or objects He has Spiritually Empowered, visualization of His Avatarically-Born bodily (human) Divine Form in the mind, and simple, heart-felt Remembrance of Him.

Dattatreya   Dattatreya was a God-Realizer who appeared early in the common era and about whom no certain historical facts exist apart from his name. Over the centuries, numerous legends and myths have been spun around him. He was early on regarded to be an incarnation of the God Vishnu, later associated with the tradition of Saivism, and worshipped as the Divine Itself. He is commonly venerated as the originator of the Avadhoota tradition and credited with the authorship of the *Avadhoota Gita*, among other works.

The devotional sect worshipping Dattatreya presumes that he continually reincarnates through a succession of Adepts for the sake of gathering and serving devotees. The belief in the continuing incarnation of Dattatreya should be understood as a popular religious belief that is peripheral to what the Adepts in the Dattatreya succession actually taught.

The Dawn Horse Testament Of The Ruchira Avatar   *The Dawn Horse Testament Of The Ruchira Avatar* is Avatar Adi Da's paramount "Source-Text", summarizing the entire course of the Way of Adidam. (See "Avatar Adi Da Samraj's Teaching-Word", pp. 32-43.)

developmental stages of practice   For all members of the first and second congregations of Avatar Adi Da's devotees, the Way of Adidam develops through a series of (potential) developmental stages of practice and Realization. These stages of practice, and their relationship to the seven stages of life, are described by Avatar Adi Da Samraj in chapter seventeen of *The Dawn Horse Testament Of The Ruchira Avatar*.

When using the phrase "necessary (or, otherwise, potential)", Avatar Adi Da is referring to the fact that His fully practicing devotee must practice in the context of certain of the developmental stages of practice (corresponding to the first three stages of life, the "original" and "basic" contexts of the fourth stage of life, the sixth stage of life, and the seventh stage of life) but may bypass practice in the developmental stages that correspond to the "advanced" context of the fourth stage of life and to the fifth stage of life.

Devotional Way of Insight / Devotional Way of Faith   Avatar Adi Da has Given Instruction in two variant forms of the fundamental practice of feeling-Contemplation of Him: the Devotional Way of Insight and the Devotional Way of Faith. Each of Avatar Adi Da's fully practicing devotees is to experiment with both of these Devotional Ways and then choose the one that is most effective in his or her case.

Both Devotional Ways require the exercise of insight and faith, but there is a difference in emphasis.

In the Devotional Way of Insight, the practitioner engages a specific technical process of observing, understanding, and then feeling beyond the self-contraction, as the principal technical element of his or her practice of feeling-Contemplation of Avatar Adi Da.

In the Devotional Way of Faith, the practitioner engages a specific technical process of magnifying his or her heart-Attraction to Avatar Adi Da, as the principal technical element of his or her practice of feeling-Contemplation of Avatar Adi Da.

Avatar Adi Da's extended Instruction relative to both Devotional Ways is Given in *The Only Complete Way To Realize The Unbroken Light Of Real God*.

Dharma, dharma   Sanskrit for "duty", "virtue", "law". The word "dharma" is commonly used to refer to the many esoteric paths by which human beings seek the Truth. In its fullest sense, and when capitalized, "Dharma" means the complete fulfillment of duty—the living of the Divine Law. By extension, "Dharma" means a truly great Spiritual Teaching, including its disciplines and practices.

"Difference"   "Difference" is the epitome of the egoic presumption of separateness—in contrast with the Realization of Oneness, or Non-"Difference", Which is Native to the Divine Self-Condition.

Divine Being   Avatar Adi Da describes His Divine Being on three levels:

AVATAR ADI DA SAMRAJ: This flesh body, this bodily (human) Sign, is My Form, in the sense that it is My Murti, or a kind of Reflection (or Representation) of Me. It is, therefore, a Means for contacting My Spiritual Presence, and, ultimately, My Divine State.

My Spiritual Presence is Self-Existing and Self-Radiant. It Functions in time and space, and It is also Prior to all time and space. . . .

My Divine State is always and only utterly Prior to time and space. Therefore, I, As I Am (Ultimately), have no "Function" in time and space. There is no time and space in My Divine State.

Divine Body Avatar Adi Da's Divine Body is not conditional or limited to His physical Body but is "The 'Bright' Itself (Spiritually Pervading and Eternally Most Prior To The Cosmic Domain)".

Divine Enlightenment The Realization of the seventh stage of life, which is uniquely Revealed and Given by Avatar Adi Da. It is release from all the egoic limitations of the first six stages of life. Remarkably, the seventh stage Awakening, which is Avatar Adi Da's Gift to His rightly prepared devotee, is not an experience at all. The true Nature of everything is simply obvious, based on the Realization that every apparent "thing" is Eternally, Perfectly the same as Reality, Consciousness, Happiness, Truth, or Real God. And that Realization is the Supreme Love-Bliss of Avatar Adi Da's Divine Self-Condition.

Divine Ignorance "Divine Ignorance" is Avatar Adi Da's term for the fundamental Awareness of Existence Itself, Prior to all sense of separation from (or knowledge about) anything that arises. As He proposes, "No matter what arises, you do not know what a single thing is." By "Ignorance", Avatar Adi Da means heartfelt participation in the universal Condition of inherent Mystery—not mental dullness or the fear-based wonder or awe felt by the subjective ego in relation to unknown objects. Divine Ignorance is the Realization of Consciousness Itself, transcending all knowledge and all experience of the self-contracted ego-"I".

For Avatar Adi Da's extended Instruction relative to Divine Ignorance, see *What, Where, When, How, Why, and Who To Remember To Be Happy*, Part Two: "What, Where, When, How, Why and Who To Remember To Be Happy", and Part Three: "You Do Not Know What even a single thing Is" and "My Argument Relative to Divine Ignorance".

Divine Indifference See **four phases of the seventh stage of life**.

Divine "Intoxication" Unlike common intoxication, such as with alcohol, Divine "Intoxication" Draws Avatar Adi Da's devotees beyond the usual egoic self and egoic mind through His Blessing Grace into a state of ecstatic devotional Communion (and Identification) with Him.

Divine Parama-Guru The Supreme Divine Guru.

Divine Re-Awakening Avatar Adi Da's Divine Re-Awakening occurred on September 10, 1970, in the Vedanta Society Temple in Hollywood, California. For a full description of this Great Event and its import, see *The Light Is On!*, by Carolyn Lee, or chapter sixteen of *The Knee Of Listening*.

Divine Self-Domain Avatar Adi Da affirms that there is a Divine Self-Domain that is the Perfectly Subjective Condition of the conditional worlds. It is not "elsewhere", not an objective "place" (like a subtle "heaven" or mythical "paradise"), but It is the always present, Transcendental, Inherently Spiritual, Divine Source-Condition of every conditionally manifested being and thing. Avatar Adi Da Reveals that the Divine Self-Domain is not other than the Divine Heart Itself, not other than Himself. To Realize the seventh stage of life (by the Divine Grace of Avatar Adi Da Samraj) is to Awaken to His Divine Self-Domain.

For Avatar Adi Da's extended Instruction relative to His Divine Self-Domain, see *The All-Completing and Final Divine Revelation To Mankind*.

Divine Self-"Emergence" On January 11, 1986, Avatar Adi Da passed through a profound Yogic Swoon, which He later described as the initial Event of His Divine Self-"Emergence". Avatar Adi Da's Divine Self-"Emergence" is an ongoing Process in which His Avatarically-Born bodily (human) Divine Form has been (and is ever more profoundly and potently being) conformed to Himself, the Very Divine Person, such that His bodily (human) Form is now (and forever hereafter) an utterly Unobstructed Sign and Agent of His own Divine Being.

For Avatar Adi Da's Revelation of the significance of His Divine Self-"Emergence", see section III of "The True Dawn Horse Is The Only Way To Me", in *The All-Completing and Final Divine Revelation To Mankind, The Heart Of The Dawn Horse Testament Of The Ruchira Avatar,* and *The Dawn Horse Testament Of The Ruchira Avatar.*

Divine Self-Recognition   Divine Self-Recognition is the ego-transcending and world-transcending Intelligence of the Divine Self in relation to all conditional phenomena. The devotee of Avatar Adi Da who Realizes the seventh stage of life simply Abides as Self-Existing and Self-Radiant Consciousness Itself, and he or she Freely Self-Recognizes (or inherently and instantly and Most Perfectly comprehends and perceives) all phenomena (including body, mind, conditional self, and conditional world) as transparent (or merely apparent), and un-necessary, and inherently non-binding modifications of the same "Bright" Divine Self-Consciousness.

Divine Star   The primal conditional Representation of the "Bright" (the Source-Energy, or Divine Light, of Which all conditional phenomena and the total cosmos are modifications) is the brilliant white five-pointed Divine Star. Avatar Adi Da's bodily (human) Divine Form is the Manifestation of that Divine Star—and His head, two arms, and two legs correspond to its five points. Avatar Adi Da can also be seen or intuited in vision to Be the Divine Star Itself, prior to the visible manifestation of His bodily (human) Form.

Divine Transfiguration   See **four phases of the seventh stage of life**.

Divine Transformation   See **four phases of the seventh stage of life**.

Divine Translation   See **four phases of the seventh stage of life**.

Divine World-Teacher   Avatar Adi Da Samraj is the Divine World-Teacher because His Wisdom-Teaching is the uniquely Perfect Instruction to every being—in this (and every) world—in the total process of Divine Enlightenment. Furthermore, Avatar Adi Da Samraj constantly Extends His Regard to the entire world (and the entire Cosmic domain)—not on the political or social level, but as a Spiritual matter, constantly Working to Bless and Purify all beings everywhere.

dreaming   See **waking, dreaming, and sleeping**.

E

ecstasy / enstasy   The words "ecstasy" and "enstasy" derive originally from Greek. Avatar Adi Da uses "ecstasy" in the literal sense of "standing (stasis) outside (ec-)" the egoic self, and "enstasy" in the sense of "standing (stasis) in (en-)" the Divine Self-Condition. As Avatar Adi Da Says in *The Dawn Horse Testament Of The Ruchira Avatar*, Divine Enstasy is "The Native Condition Of Standing Unconditionally As The By-Me-Avatarically-Self-Revealed Transcendental, Inherently Spiritual, and Self-Evidently Divine Self-Condition Itself".

ego-"I"   The ego-"I" is the fundamental activity of self-contraction, or the presumption of separate and separative existence.

Eleutherian Pan-Communion of Adidam   The Eleutherian Pan-Communion of Adidam is a California religious non-profit corporation, dedicated to the worldwide practice and the global proclamation of the true world-religion of Adidam.

Eleutherios   "Eleutherios" (Greek for "Liberator") is a title by which Zeus was venerated as the supreme deity in the Spiritual esotericism of ancient Greece. The Designation "Eleutherios" indicates the Divine Function of Avatar Adi Da as the Incarnation of the Divine Person, "Whose Inherently Perfect Self-'Brightness' Divinely Liberates all conditionally Manifested beings—Freely, Liberally, Gracefully, and Without Ceasing—now, and forever hereafter".

En-Light-enment   En-Light-enment (or Enlightenment) is not just a state of mind, but rather an actual conversion of the body-mind to the state of Divine Consciousness Itself, or Light Itself. Thus, Avatar Adi Da sometimes writes the word "Enlightenment" with "Light" set apart by hyphens, in order to emphasize this point.

esoteric anatomy   See **Spiritual anatomy**.

Eternal Vow   For a description of the Vow and responsibilities associated with the Way of Adidam, see pp. 378-89.

etheric   The etheric is the dimension of life-energy, which functions through the human nervous system. Our bodies are surrounded and infused by this personal life-energy, which we feel as the play of emotions and life-force in the body.

F

faculties; four faculties   Avatar Adi Da has Instructed His devotees that the practice of devotional Communion with Him (or Ruchira Avatara Bhakti Yoga) requires the surrender of the four principal faculties of the human body-mind. These faculties are body, emotion (or feeling), mind (or attention), and breath.

Feeling of Being   The Feeling of Being is the uncaused (or Self-Existing), Self-Radiant, and unqualified feeling-intuition of the Transcendental, Inherently Spiritual, and Self-Evidently Divine Self-Condition. This absolute Feeling does not merely accompany or express the Realization of the Heart Itself, but It is Identical to that Realization. To feel—or, really, to Be—the Feeling of Being is to enjoy the Love-Bliss of Absolute Consciousness, Which, when Most Perfectly Realized, cannot be pre-

vented or even diminished either by the events of life or by death.

feeling of relatedness   In the foundation stages of practice in the Way of Adidam, the basic (or gross) manifestation of the avoidance of relationship is understood and released when Avatar Adi Da's devotee hears Him (or comes to the point of most fundamental self-understanding), thereby regaining the free capability for simple relatedness, or living on the basis of the feeling of relatedness rather than the avoidance of relationship. Nevertheless, the feeling of relatedness is not Ultimate Realization, because it is still founded in the presumption of a "difference" between "I" and "other". Only in the ultimate stages of life in the Way of Adidam is the feeling of relatedness itself fully understood as the root-act of attention and, ultimately, transcended in the Feeling of Being.

feeling-Contemplation   Avatar Adi Da's term for the essential devotional and meditative practice that all practitioners of the Way of Adidam engage at all times in relationship to Him. Feeling-Contemplation of Adi Da Samraj is Awakened by His Grace—through Darshan (or feeling-sighting) of His bodily (human) Form, His Spiritual Presence, and His Divine State. It is then to be practiced under all conditions, as the basis and epitome of all other practices in the Way of Adidam.

fifth stage conditional Nirvikalpa Samadhi   See **Samadhi**.

forms of practice in the Way of Adidam   Avatar Adi Da has Given a number of different approaches to the progressive process of Most Perfectly self-transcending Real-God-Realization in the Way of Adidam. In this manner, He accounts for the differences in individuals' qualities—particularly relative to their capability to make use of the various technical practices that support the fundamental practice of Ruchira Avatara Bhakti Yoga and relative to the intensity of their motivation to apply themselves to the Spiritual process in His Company.

Ruchira Avatar Adi Da refers to the most detailed development of the practice of the Way of Adidam as the "technically 'fully elaborated'" form of practice. Each successive stage of practice in the technically "fully elaborated" form of the Way of Adidam is defined by progressively more detailed responsibilities, disciplines, and practices that are assumed in order to take responsibility for the signs of growing maturity in the process of Divine Awakening. A devotee who embraces the technically "fully elaborated" form of practice of the Way of Adidam must (necessarily) be a member of the first or second congregation of Avatar Adi Da's devotees. The progress of practice in the technically "fully elaborated" form of the Way of Adidam is monitored, measured, and evaluated by practicing stages (as described in detail by Avatar Adi Da Samraj in chapter seventeen of *The Dawn Horse Testament Of The Ruchira Avatar*).

Most of Avatar Adi Da's fully practicing devotees will find that they are qualified for a less intensive approach and are moved to a less technical form of the "conscious process" (than is exercised in the technically "fully elaborated" form of the Way of Adidam). Thus, most of Avatar Adi Da's fully practicing devotees will take up the technically "simpler" (or even "simplest") form of practice of the Way of Adidam.

In the technically "simpler" form of practice of the Way of Adidam, Avatar Adi Da's devotee (in the first or second congregation) engages a relatively simple form of technical means of supporting his or her fundamental practice of Ruchira Avatara Bhakti Yoga, and this technical means remains the same throughout the progressive course of developmental stages.

In the technically "simplest" form of practice, Avatar Adi Da's devotee (in any of the four congregations) engages the fundamental practice of Ruchira Avatara Bhakti Yoga in the simplest possible manner—as "simplest" feeling-Contemplation of Avatar Adi Da, together with the random use of Avatar Adi Da's Principal Name, "Da" (or one of the other Names He has Given to be engaged in the practice of simple Name-Invocation of Him).

Avatar Adi Da's fully elaborated descriptions of the technically "fully elaborated" and the technically "simpler" (or even "simplest") forms of the Way of Adidam are Given in *The Dawn Horse Testament Of The Ruchira Avatar*.

four phases of the seventh stage of life
In the context of Divine Enlightenment in the seventh stage of life, the Spiritual process continues. One of the unique aspects of Avatar Adi Da's Revelation is His description of the four phases of the seventh stage process: Divine Transfiguration, Divine Transformation, Divine Indifference, and Divine Translation.

In the phase of Divine Transfiguration, the Divinely Enlightened devotee's body-mind is Infused by Avatar Adi Da's Love-Bliss, and he or she Radiantly Demonstrates active Love, spontaneously Blessing all the relations of the body-mind.

In the following phase of Divine Transformation, the subtle or psychic dimension of the body-mind is fully Illumined, which may result in Divine Powers of healing, longevity, and the ability to release obstacles from the world and from the lives of others.

Eventually, Divine Indifference ensues, which is spontaneous and profound Resting in the "Deep" of Consciousness, and the world of relations is otherwise noticed only minimally or not at all.

Divine Translation is the ultimate "Event" of the entire process of Divine Awakening. Avatar Adi Da describes Divine Translation as the Outshining of all noticing of objective conditions through the infinitely magnified Force of Consciousness Itself. Divine Translation is the Outshining of all destinies, wherein there is no return to the conditional realms.

Being so overwhelmed by the Divine Radiance that all appearances fade away may occur <u>temporarily</u> from time to time during the seventh stage of life. But when that Most Love-Blissful Swoon becomes permanent, Divine Translation occurs, and the body-mind is inevitably relinquished in physical death. Then there is only Eternal Inherence in the Divine Self-Domain of unqualified Happiness and Joy.

frontal line, frontal personality, frontal Yoga The frontal (or descending) line of the body-mind conducts natural life-energy and (for those who are Spiritually Awakened) the Spirit-Current of Divine Life, in a downward direction from the crown of the head to the base of the body (or the perineal area).

The frontal (or gross) personality is comprised of the physical body, and its natural energies, and the sense-based mind. It includes the entire gross dimension of the body-mind and the lower (or most physically oriented) aspects of the subtle dimension of the body-mind.

The frontal Yoga, as described by Avatar Adi Da, is the process whereby knots and obstructions in the gross (or physical) and energetic dimensions of the body-mind are penetrated, opened, surrendered, and released, through the devotee's reception of Avatar Adi Da's Transmission in the frontal line of the body-mind.

"fully elaborated" form of the Way of Adidam See **forms of practice in the Way of Adidam**.

functional, practical, relational, and cultural disciplines of Adidam
The most basic functional, practical, and relational disciplines of the Way of Adidam (in its fully practiced form, as embraced by devotees in the first and second congregations) are forms of appropriate human action and responsibility for diet, health, exercise, sexuality, work, service to and support of Avatar Adi Da's Circumstance and Work, and cooperative (formal community) association with other practitioners of the Way of Adidam. The most basic cultural obligations of the Way of Adidam (in its fully practiced form) include meditation, sacramental worship, study of Avatar Adi Da's Wisdom-Teaching (and also at least a basic discriminative study of the Great Tradition of religion and Spirituality that is the Wisdom-inheritance of humankind), and regular participation in the "form" (or schedule) of daily, weekly, monthly, and annual devotional activities and retreats.

G

Great Tradition The "Great Tradition" is Avatar Adi Da's term for the total inheritance of human, cultural, religious, magical, mystical, Spiritual, and Transcendental paths, philosophies, and testimonies, from all the eras and cultures of humanity—which inheritance has (in the present era of worldwide communication) become the common legacy of humankind. Avatar Adi Da's Divine Self-Revelation and Wisdom-Teaching Fulfills and Completes the Great Tradition.

gross, subtle, causal Avatar Adi Da (in agreement with certain esoteric schools in the Great Tradition) describes conditional existence as having three dimensions—gross, subtle, and causal.

"Gross" means "made up of material (or physical) elements". The gross (or physical) dimension is, therefore, associated with the physical body, and also with experience in the waking state.

The subtle dimension, which is senior to and pervades the gross dimension, consists of the etheric (or personal life-energy) functions, the lower mental functions (including the conscious mind, the subconscious mind, and the unconscious mind) and higher mental functions (of discriminative thought, mentally presumed egoity, and will), and is associated with experience in the dreaming state. In the human psycho-physical structure, the subtle dimension is primarily associated with the ascending energies of the spine, the brain core, and the subtle centers of mind in the higher brain.

The causal dimension is senior to and pervades both the gross and the subtle dimensions. It is the root of attention, or the essence of the separate and separative ego-"I". The causal dimension is associated with the right side of the heart, specifically with the sinoatrial node, or "pacemaker" (the psycho-physical source of the heartbeat). Its corresponding state of consciousness is the formless awareness of deep sleep.

Guru Esoterically, the word "guru" is understood to be a composite of two words, "destroyer (ru) of darkness (gu)".

H

hearing See **listening, hearing, and seeing**.

heart, stations of the heart Avatar Adi Da distinguishes three stations of the heart, associated respectively with the right side, the middle, and the left side of the heart region of the chest. He Reveals that these stations are the loci (or focal points of living origination) of the causal body, the subtle body, and the gross body (respectively). Avatar Adi Da Teaches (as foreshadowed in certain rare sixth stage texts) that the primal psycho-physical seat of Consciousness and of attention is associated with what He calls the "right side of the heart". He has Revealed that this center (which is neither the heart chakra nor the gross physical heart) corresponds to the sinoatrial node, or "pacemaker", the source of the gross physical heartbeat in the right atrium (or upper right chamber) of the physical heart. In the Process of Divine Self-Realization, there is a unique process of opening of the right side of the heart—and it is because of this connection between the right side of the heart and Divine Self-Realization that Avatar Adi Da uses the term "the Heart" as another way of referring to the Divine Self.

The Heart Itself is Real God, the Divine Self, the Divine Reality. The Heart Itself is not "in" the right side of the human heart, nor is it "in" (or limited to) the human heart as a whole. Rather, the human heart and body-mind and the world exist in the Heart, Which Is the Divine Being Itself.

heart-Communion "Heart-Communion" with Avatar Adi Da is the practice of Invoking and feeling Him. It is "communion" in the sense that the individual loses sense of the separate self in the bliss of that state, and is thus "communicating intimately" (in a most profound and non-dual manner) with Avatar Adi Da Samraj.

heart-recognition The entire practice of the Way of Adidam is founded in devotional heart-recognition of, and devotional heart-response to, Ruchira Avatar Adi Da Samraj as the Very Divine Being in Person.

AVATAR ADI DA SAMRAJ: The only-by-Me Revealed and Given Way of Adidam (Which is the One and Only by-Me-Revealed and by-Me-Given Way of the Heart) is the Way of life you live when you rightly, truly, fully, and fully devotionally recognize Me, and when, on that basis, you rightly, truly, fully, and fully devotionally respond to Me. . . .

If you rightly, truly, fully, and fully devotionally recognize Me, everything "in between" vanishes. All of that is inherently without force. In heart-responsive devotional recognition of Me, a spontaneous kriya of the principal faculties occurs, such that they are loosed from the objects to which they are otherwise bound—loosed from the patterns of self-contraction. The faculties turn to Me, and, in that turning, there is tacit devotional recognition of Me, tacit experiential Realization of Me, of Happiness Itself, of My Love-Bliss-Full Condition. That "Locating" of Me opens the body-mind spontaneously. When you have been thus Initiated by Me, it then becomes your responsibility, your sadhana, to continuously Remember Me, to constantly return to this devotional recognition of Me, in which you are Attracted to Me, in which you devotionally respond to Me spontaneously with all the principal faculties. [Hridaya Rosary (Four Thorns Of Heart-Instruction)]

heart-response See **heart-recognition**.

"Heroic" The Tantric traditions of Hinduism and Buddhism describe as "heroic" the practice of an individual whose impulse to Liberation and commitment to his or her Guru are so strong that all circumstances of life, even those traditionally regarded as inauspicious for Spiritual practice (such as consumption of intoxicants and engagement in sexual activity), can rightly be made use of as part of the Spiritual process.

Avatar Adi Da's uniquely "Heroic" Ordeal, however, was undertaken not for His own sake, but in order to discover, through His own experience, what is necessary for all beings to Realize the Truth. Because of His utter Freedom from egoic bondage and egoic karmas, Avatar Adi Da's Sadhana was "Heroic" in a manner that had never previously been possible and will never again be possible. As the Divine Person, it was necessary for Him to experience the entire gamut of human seeking, in order to be able to Teach any and all that came to Him.

Avatar Adi Da has Instructed that, because of His unique "Heroic" Demonstration, His devotees can simply practice the Way He has Revealed and Given, and do not have to attempt the (in any case impossible) task of duplicating His Ordeal. (See also **"Crazy"**.)

Hridaya-Avatar "Hridaya" is Sanskrit for "the heart". It refers not only to the physical organ but also to the True Heart, the Transcendental (and Inherently Spiritual) Divine Reality. "Hridaya" in combination with "Avatar" signifies that Avatar Adi Da is the Very Incarnation of the Divine Heart Itself, the Divine Incarnation Who Stands in, at, and <u>as</u> the True Heart of every being.

Hridaya Rosary *Hridaya Rosary (Four Thorns Of Heart-Instruction)—The Five Books Of The Heart Of The Adidam Revelation, Book Four: The "Late-Time" Avataric Revelation Of The Universally Tangible Divine Spiritual Body, Which Is The Supreme Agent Of The Great Means To Worship and To Realize The True and Spiritual Divine Person (The egoless Personal Presence Of Reality and Truth, Which Is The Only Real God)* is Avatar Adi Da's summary and exquisitely beautiful Instruction relative to the right, true, full, and fully devotional practice of the Way of Adidam, through which practice Avatar Adi Da's fully practicing devotee Spiritually receives Him with ever greater profundity, and, ultimately (through a process of the Spiritual "melting" of the entire psycho-physical being), Realizes Him most perfectly.

Hridaya-Samartha Sat-Guru "Hridaya-Samartha Sat-Guru" is a compound of traditional Sanskrit terms that has been newly created to express the uniqueness of Avatar Adi Da's Guru-Function. "Sat" means "Truth", "Being", "Existence". Thus, "Sat-Guru" literally means "True Guru", or a Guru who can lead living beings from darkness (or non-Truth) into Light (or the Living Truth).

"Samartha" means "fit", "qualified", "able". Thus, "Samartha Sat-Guru" means "a True Guru who is fully capable" of Awakening living beings to Real-God-Realization.

The word "Hridaya", meaning "heart", refers to the Very Heart, or the Transcendental (and Inherently Spiritual) Divine Reality.

Thus, altogether, the reference "Hridaya-Samartha Sat-Guru" means "the Divine Heart-Master Who Liberates His devotees from the darkness of egoity by Means of the Power of the 'Bright' Divine Heart Itself". Avatar Adi Da has Said that this full Designation "properly summarizes all the aspects of My unique Guru-Function".

Hridaya-Shakti; Hridaya-Shaktipat
The Sanskrit word "Hridaya" means "the Heart Itself". "Shakti" is a Sanskrit term for the Divine Manifesting as Energy. "Hridaya-Shakti" is thus "the Divine Power of the Heart", Which is Given and Transmitted by Avatar Adi Da Samraj.

In Hindi, "shaktipat" means the "descent of Divine Power", indicating the Sat-Guru's Transmission of the Kundalini Shakti to his or her devotee.

"Hridaya-Shaktipat", which is Avatar Adi Da's seventh stage Gift to His devotees, is "the Blessing-Transmission of the Divine Heart Itself".

Avatar Adi Da's extended Instruction relative to Hridaya-Shakti and Kundalini Shakti is Given in *Ruchira Avatara Hridaya-Siddha Yoga*.

Hridaya-Siddha Yoga The Way (Yoga) of the relationship with the "Transmission-Master of the Divine Heart" (Hridaya-Siddha), Ruchira Avatar Adi Da Samraj.

Hridayam "Hridayam" is Sanskrit for "heart". It refers not only to the physical organ but also to the True Heart, the Transcendental (and Inherently Spiritual) Divine Reality. "Hridayam" is one of Avatar Adi Da's Divine Names, signifying that He Stands in, at, and as the True Heart of every being.

I

Ignorance See **Divine Ignorance**.

Indifference See **four phases of the seventh stage of life**.

Instruments / Instrumentality Avatar Adi Da has Indicated that members of the Ruchira Sannyasin Order function collectively and spontaneously as His Instruments, or Means by which His Divine Grace and Awakening Power are Magnified and Transmitted to other devotees and all beings. Such devotees have received Avatar Adi Da's Spiritual Baptism, and they practice in Spiritually activated relationship to Him with exemplary depth and intensity. Because of their uniquely complete and renunciate response and accountability to Him, and by virtue of their ego-surrendering, ego-forgetting, ego-transcending, and really Spiritual Invocation of Him, these devotees function collectively as Instruments for the Transmission of Avatar Adi Da's Spiritual Presence to others.

Invocation by Name See **Name-Invocation**.

Ishta-Guru Bhakti Yoga An alternate name for Ruchira Avatara Bhakti Yoga. Ishta-Guru Bhakti Yoga literally means "the practice (Yoga) of devotion (Bhakti) to Avatar Adi Da, the chosen Beloved (Ishta) Guru of His devotees".

J

Jnana Samadhi See **Samadhi**.

K

Kali Kali is a Hindu form of the Divine Goddess (or "Mother-Shakti") in her terrifying aspect.

Kali Yuga A Hindu term meaning "the dark (kali) epoch (yuga)", or the final and most ignorant and degenerate period of human history, when the Spiritual Way of life is almost entirely forgotten. (In the Hindu view, the Kali Yuga is a cyclically recurring event.)

karma "Karma" is Sanskrit for "action". Since action entails consequences (or reactions), "karma" also means (by extension) "destiny, tendency, the quality of existence and experience which is determined by previous actions".

Kashmir Saivism Kashmir Saivism is a branch of Saivism (the form of Hinduism in which Siva is worshipped as the Supreme Deity), which originated in the Kashmir region of North India in the late 8th century and whose influence spread throughout the Indian sub-continent during the mid-20th century. It has a largely fifth-stage orientation.

kiln Avatar Adi Da Samraj frequently describes the transformative process of His Blessing-Power in the lives of His devotees as being like a kiln. In a kiln, as the wet clay objects are heated more and more, they begin to glow. Eventually, the kiln is so hot that everything within it glows with a white light, and the definitions of the individual objects dissolve in the brightness. Just so, as a devotee matures in Avatar Adi Da's Spiritual Company, all presumptions of separateness as an apparently individual ego-"I" are more and more Outshined by the "Brightness" of His Divine Person and Blessing.

Klik-Klak Avatar Adi Da coined the term "Klik-Klak" as a name for the conditional reality. This name indicates (even by means of the sound of the two syllables) that conditional reality is a heartless perpetual-motion machine of incessant change, producing endlessly varied patterns that are ultimately binary in nature (as, for example, "yes-no", "on-off", or "black-white").

knots Previous to Most Perfect Divine Self-Realization, the gross, subtle, and causal dimensions are expressed in the body-mind as characteristic knots. The knot of the gross dimension is associated with the region of the navel. The knot of the subtle dimension is associated with the midbrain, or the ajna center directly behind and between the brows. And the knot of the causal dimension (which Avatar Adi Da refers to as the "causal knot") is associated with the sinoatrial node (or "pacemaker") on the right side of the heart. The causal knot (or the heart-root's knot) is the primary root of the self-contraction, felt as the locus of the self-sense, the source of the feeling of relatedness itself, or the root of attention.

Kundalini-Shaktipat The Kundalini Shakti is traditionally viewed to lie dormant at the bodily base, or lowermost psychic center of the body-mind. Kundalini-Shaktipat is the activation of the Kundalini Shakti—either spontaneously in the devotee or by the Guru's initiation—thereafter potentially producing various forms of Yogic and mystical experience.

L

"late-time" (or "dark" epoch) The "'late-time' (or 'dark' epoch)" is a phrase that Avatar Adi Da uses to describe the present era—in which doubt of God (and of anything at all beyond mortal existence) is more and more pervading the entire world, and the self-interest of the separate individual is more and more regarded to be the ultimate principle of life. It is also a reference to the traditional Hindu idea of "yugas", or "epochs", the last of which (the Kali Yuga) is understood to be the most difficult and "dark". Many traditions share the idea that it is in such a time that the Promised Divine Liberator will appear. (See also **Kali Yuga**.)

Lay Congregationist Order In "The Orders of My True and Free Renunciate Devotees" (in *The Lion Sutra*), Avatar Adi Da describes the Lay Congregationist Order as "the common (or general) order for all formally established general (or not otherwise formal renunciate) lay practitioners of the total (or full and complete) practice of the Way of Adidam". Once a member of the second congregation has completed the student-beginner stage of practice, he or she makes the transition to the intensive listening-hearing stage of the Way of Adidam. By virtue of this transition, the individual becomes a member of the Lay Congregationist Order, unless he or she is accepted as a member of the Lay Renunciate Order.

Lay Renunciate Order See **renunciate orders**.

leela "Leela" is Sanskrit for "play", or "sport". In many religious and Spiritual traditions, all of conditionally manifested existence is regarded to be the Leela (or the Play, Sport, or Free Activity) of the Divine Person. "Leela" also means the Awakened Play of a Realized Adept (of any degree), through which he or she mysteriously Instructs and Liberates others and Blesses the world itself. By extension, a Leela is an instructive and inspiring story of such an Adept's Teaching and Blessing Play.

Lesson of life "The Lesson of life" is Avatar Adi Da's term for the fundamental understanding that Happiness cannot be achieved by means of seeking, because Happiness is inherent in Existence Itself. Avatar Adi Da has summarized this in the aphorism, "You cannot become Happy. You can only be Happy."

Lineage, Avatar Adi Da's The principal Spiritual Masters who served Avatar Adi Da Samraj during His "Sadhana Years" belong to a single Lineage of extraordinary Yogis, whose Parama-Guru (Supreme Guru) was the Divine "Goddess" (or "Mother-Shakti").

Swami Rudrananda (1928-1973), or Albert Rudolph (known as "Rudi"), was Avatar Adi Da's first human Teacher—from 1964 to 1968, in New York City. Rudi served Avatar Adi Da Samraj in the development of basic practical life-disciplines and the frontal Yoga, which is the process whereby knots and obstructions in the physical and etheric dimensions of the body-mind are penetrated, opened, surrendered, and released through Spiritual reception in the frontal line of the body-mind. Rudi's own Teachers included the Indonesian Pak Subuh (from whom Rudi learned a basic exercise of Spiritual receptivity), Swami Muktananda (with whom Rudi studied for many years), and Bhagavan Nityananda (the Indian Adept-Realizer who was also Swami Muktananda's Guru). Rudi met Bhagavan Nityananda shortly before Bhagavan Nityananda's death, and Rudi always thereafter acknowledged Bhagavan Nityananda as his original and principal Guru.

The second Teacher in Avatar Adi Da's Lineage of Blessing was Swami Muktananda (1908-1982), who was born in Mangalore, South India. Having left home at the age of fifteen, he wandered for many years, seeking the Divine Truth from sources all over India. Eventually, he came under the Spiritual Influence of Bhagavan Nityananda, whom he accepted as his Guru and in whose Spiritual Company he mastered Kundalini Yoga. Swami Muktananda served Avatar Adi Da as Guru during the period from 1968 to 1970. In the summer of 1969, during Avatar Adi Da's second visit to India, Swami Muktananda wrote a letter confirming Avatar Adi Da's attainment of "Yogic Liberation", and acknowledging His right to Teach others. However, from the beginning of their relationship, Swami Muktananda instructed Avatar Adi Da to visit Bhagavan Nityananda's burial site every day (whenever Avatar Adi Da was at Swami Muktananda's Ashram in Ganeshpuri, India) as a means to surrender to Bhagavan Nityananda as the Supreme Guru of the Lineage.

Bhagavan Nityananda, a great Yogi of South India, was Avatar Adi Da's third Guru. Little is known about the circumstances of Bhagavan Nityananda's birth and early life, although it is said that even as a child he showed the signs of a Realized Yogi. It is also known that he abandoned conventional life as a boy and wandered as a renunciate. Many miracles (including spontaneous healings) and instructive stories are attributed to him. Bhagavan Nityananda surrendered the body on August 8, 1961. Although Avatar Adi Da did not meet Bhagavan Nityananda in the flesh, He enjoyed Bhagavan Nityananda's direct Spiritual Influence from the subtle plane, and He acknowledges Bhagavan Nityananda as a direct and principal Source of Spiritual Instruction during His years with Swami Muktananda. (Avatar Adi Da summarizes the Instruction He received from Bhagavan Nityananda in section XXXII of "I (Alone) Am The Adidam Revelation", an Essay contained in many of the twenty-three "Source-Texts" of Adidam.)

On His third visit to India, while visiting Bhagavan Nityananda's burial shrine, Avatar Adi Da was instructed by Bhagavan Nityananda to relinquish all others as Guru and to surrender directly to the Divine Goddess in Person as Guru. Thus, Bhagavan Nityananda passed Avatar Adi Da to the Divine Goddess Herself, the Parama-Guru (or Source-Guru) of the Lineage that included Bhagavan Nityananda, Swami Muktananda, and Rudi.

The years of Avatar Adi Da's "Sadhana" came to an end in the Great Event of His Divine Re-Awakening, when Avatar Adi Da Husbanded the Divine Goddess (thereby ceasing to relate to Her as His Guru).

Avatar Adi Da's full account of His "Sadhana Years" is Given in *The Knee Of Listening*.

Avatar Adi Da's description of His "Relationship" to the Divine "Goddess" is Given in "I Am The Icon Of Unity", in *He-and-She Is Me*.

listening, hearing, and seeing

"Listening" is Avatar Adi Da's technical term for the orientation, disposition, and beginning practice of the Way of Adidam. A listening devotee listens to Avatar Adi Da Samraj by "considering" His Teaching-Argument and His Leelas, and by practicing feeling-Contemplation of Him (primarily of His bodily human Form). In the total practice of the Way of Adidam, effective listening to Avatar Adi Da is the necessary prerequisite for true hearing and real seeing.

"Hearing" is a technical term used by Avatar Adi Da to indicate most fundamental understanding of the act of egoity (or self-contraction). Hearing Avatar Adi Da is the unique capability to directly transcend the self-contraction, such that, simultaneous with that transcending, there is the intuitive awakening to Avatar Adi Da's Self-Revelation <u>As</u> the Divine Person and Self-Condition. The capability of true hearing can only be Granted by Avatar Adi Da's Divine Grace, to His fully practicing devotee who has effectively completed the process of listening. Only on the basis of such hearing can Spiritually Awakened practice of the Way of Adidam truly (or with full responsibility) begin.

I Am Heard When My Listening Devotee Has Truly (and Thoroughly) Observed the ego-"I" and Understood it (Directly, In the moments Of self-Observation, and Most Fundamentally, or In its Totality).

I Am Heard When the ego-"I" Is Altogether (and Thoroughly) Observed and (Most Fundamentally) Understood, Both In The Tendency To Dissociate and In The Tendency To Become Attached (or To Cling By Wanting Need, or To Identify With others, and things, and circumstances egoically, and Thus To Dramatize The Seeker, Bereft Of Basic Equanimity, Wholeness, and The Free Capability For Simple Relatedness).

I Am Heard When the ego-"I" Is Thoroughly (and Most Fundamentally) Understood To Be Contraction-Only, An Un-Necessary and Destructive Motive and Design, Un-Naturally and Chronically Added To Cosmic Nature and To all relations, and An Imaginary Heart-Disease (Made To Seem Real, By Heart-Reaction).

I Am Heard When This Most Fundamental Understanding Of The Habit Of "Narcissus" Becomes The Directly Obvious Realization Of The Heart, Radiating Beyond Its Own (Apparent) Contraction.

I Am Heard When The Beginning Is Full, and The Beginning Is Full (and Ended) When Every Gesture Of self-Contraction (In The Context Of The First Three Stages Of Life, and Relative To Each and All Of The Principal Faculties, Of body, emotion, mind, and breath) Is (As A Rather Consistently Applied and humanly Effective Discipline) Observed (By Natural feeling-perception), Tacitly (and Most Fundamentally) Understood, and Really (Directly and Effectively) Felt Beyond (In The Prior Feeling Of Unqualified Relatedness). [Santosha Adidam]

When, in the practice of the Way of Adidam, hearing (or most fundamental self-understanding) is steadily exercised in meditation and in life, the native feeling of the heart ceases to be chronically constricted by self-contraction. The heart then begins to Radiate as love in response to the Divine Spiritual Presence of Avatar Adi Da.

This emotional and Spiritual response of the whole being is what Avatar Adi Da calls "seeing". Seeing Avatar Adi Da is emotional conversion from the reactive emotions that characterize egoic self-obsession, to the open-hearted, Radiant Happiness that characterizes Spiritual devotion to Avatar Adi Da. This true and stable emotional conversion coincides with true and stable receptivity to Avatar Adi Da's Spiritual Transmission, and both of these are prerequisites to further Spiritual advancement in the Way of Adidam.

Seeing Is ego-Transcending Participation In <u>What</u> (and <u>Who</u>) Is. Seeing Is Love. Seeing (or Love) Is Able (By Means Of My Avatarically Self-Transmitted Divine Grace) To "Locate", Devotionally Recognize, and Feel My Avatarically Self-Transmitted (and all-and-All-Pervading) Spiritual Radiance (and My Avatarically Self-Transmitted Spirit-Identity, <u>As</u> The "Bright" and Only One <u>Who</u> Is). . . . Seeing Is The "Radical" (or Directly ego-Transcending) Reorientation Of conditional Existence To My Avatarically Self-Revealed (Transcendental, Inherently Spiritual, Inherently Perfect, and

Self-Evidently Divine) Self-Condition, In Whom conditional self and conditional worlds Apparently arise and Always Already Inhere. . . .

Seeing Me Is Simply Attraction To Me (and Feeling Me) As My Avatarically Self-Revealed Spiritual (and Always Blessing) Divine Presence—and This Most Fundamentally, At The Root, Core, Source, or Origin Of The "Emergence" Of My Avatarically Self-Revealed Divine Spiritual Presence "here", At (and In Front Of) The Heart, or At (and In) The Root-Context Of the body-mind, or At (and In) The Source-Position (and, Ultimately, As The Source-Condition) Of conditional (or psycho-physical) Existence Itself.

Seeing Me Is Knowing Me As My Avatarically Self-Revealed Spiritual (and Always Blessing) Divine Presence, Just As Tangibly (and With The Same Degree Of Clarity) As You Would Differentiate The Physical Appearance Of My Bodily (Human) Form From the physical appearance of the bodily (human) form of any other.

To See Me Is A Clear and "Radical" Knowledge Of Me, About Which There Is No Doubt. To See Me Is A Sudden, Tacit Awareness—Like Walking Into a "thicker" air or atmosphere, or Suddenly Feeling a breeze, or Jumping Into water and Noticing The Difference In Density Between the air and the water. This Tangible Feeling Of Me Is (In any particular moment) Not Necessarily (Otherwise) Associated With effects in the body-mind . . . but It Is, Nevertheless, Felt At The Heart and Even All Over the body.

Seeing Me Is One-Pointedness In The "Radical" Conscious Process Of Heart-Devotion To Me. [Santosha Adidam]

"Living Murti" Avatar Adi Da will always be Divinely Present in the Cosmic domain, even after His physical Lifetime. He is the One Who is (and will always be) worshipped in the Way of Adidam, and (therefore) He is (and will always be) the Eternally Living Murti for His devotees. However, Avatar Adi Da has said that, after His physical (human) Lifetime, there should always be one (and only one) "Living Murti" as a Living Link

between Him and His devotees. Each successive "Living Murti" (or "Murti-Guru") is to be selected from among those members of the Ruchira Sannyasin Order (see **renunciate orders**) who have been formally acknowledged as Divinely Enlightened devotees of Avatar Adi Da Samraj in the seventh stage of life. "Living Murtis" will not function as the independent Gurus of practitioners of the Way of Adidam. Rather, they will simply be "Representations" of Avatar Adi Da's bodily (human) Divine Form, and a means to Commune with Him.

Avatar Adi Da's full discussion of His "Living Murtis", and how they are to be chosen, is Given in Part Three, section XII, of *The Lion Sutra*.

"Locate" To "Locate" Avatar Adi Da is to "Truly Heart-Find" Him.

Love-Ananda The Name "Love-Ananda" combines both English ("Love") and Sanskrit ("Ananda", meaning "Bliss"), thus bridging the West and the East, and communicating Avatar Adi Da's Function as the Divine World-Teacher. The combination of "Love" and "Ananda" means "the Divine Love-Bliss". The Name "Love-Ananda" was given to Avatar Adi Da by Swami Muktananda, who spontaneously conferred it upon Avatar Adi Da in 1969. However, Avatar Adi Da did not use the Name "Love-Ananda" until April 1986, after the Great Event that Initiated His Divine Self-"Emergence".

Love-Ananda Avatar As the Love-Ananda Avatar, Avatar Adi Da is the Very Incarnation of the Divine Love-Bliss.

M

Maha-Siddha The Sanskrit word "Siddha" means "a completed, fulfilled, or perfected one", or "one of perfect accomplishment, or power". "Maha-Siddha" means "Great Siddha".

Mandala The Sanskrit word "mandala" (literally, "circle") is commonly used in the esoteric Spiritual traditions to describe the entire pattern of the hierarchical levels of cosmic existence. Avatar Adi Da also uses the word "Mandala" to refer to the Circle (or Sphere) of His Heart-Transmission, or as a formal reference to a group of His devotees who perform specific functions of direct service to Him.

mantra   See **Name-Invocation**.

meditation   In the Way of Adidam, meditation is a period of formal devotional Contemplation of Avatar Adi Da Samraj. Meditation is one of the life-disciplines that Avatar Adi Da Samraj has Given to His devotees in the first and second congregations, as a fundamental support for their practice of Ruchira Avatara Bhakti Yoga. For those who have fully adapted to the disciplines of the first and second congregations, the daily practice of meditation includes a period of one and one-half hours in the morning and a period of one hour in the evening. Such daily practice is increased during periods of retreat. Members of the third and fourth congregations are also encouraged (but not required) to engage formal meditation.

missing the mark   "Hamartia" (the word in New Testament Greek that was translated into English as "sin") was originally an archery term meaning "missing the mark".

Most Perfect / Most Ultimate   Avatar Adi Da uses the phrase "Most Perfect(ly)" in the sense of "Absolutely Perfect(ly)". Similarly, the phrase "Most Ultimate(ly)" is equivalent to "Absolutely Ultimate(ly)". "Most Perfect(ly)" and "Most Ultimate(ly)" are always references to the seventh (or Divinely Enlightened) stage of life. Perfect(ly) and Ultimate(ly) refer to the sixth stage of life or to the sixth and seventh stages of life together. (See also **stages of life**.)

mudra   A "mudra" is a gesture of the hands, face, or body that outwardly expresses a state of ecstasy. Avatar Adi Da sometimes spontaneously exhibits Mudras as Signs of His Blessing and Purifying Work with His devotees and the world. He also uses the term "Mudra" to express the Attitude of His Blessing-Work, which is His Constant (or Eternal) Giving (or Submitting) of Himself to Be the Means of Divine Liberation for all beings.

Muktananda, Swami   See **Lineage, Avatar Adi Da's**.

mummery / *The Mummery*   The dictionary defines mummery as "a ridiculous, hypocritical, or pretentious ceremony or performance". Avatar Adi Da uses this word to describe all the activities of ego-bound beings, or beings who are committed to the false view of separation and separativeness.

The Mummery is one of Avatar Adi Da's twenty-three "Source-Texts". It is a work of astonishing poetry and deeply evocative archetypes. Through the heart-breaking story of Raymond Darling's growth to manhood, his search to find, and then to be reunited with, his beloved (Quandra), and his utter self-transcendence of all conditional circumstances and events, Avatar Adi Da Tells His own Life-Story in the language of parable, and describes in devastating detail how the unconverted ego makes religion (and life altogether) into a meaningless mummery.

Murti   "Murti" is Sanskrit for "form", and, by extension, a "representational image" of the Divine or of a Guru. In the Way of Adidam, Murtis of Avatar Adi Da are most commonly photographs of Avatar Adi Da's bodily (human) Divine Form.

"Murti-Guru"   See **"Living Murti"**.

Mystery   Avatar Adi Da uses the term "the Mystery" to point out that, although we can name things, we actually do not know what anything really <u>is</u>:

It is a great and more-than-wonderful Mystery to everyone that anything <u>is</u>, or that we <u>are</u>. And whether somebody says "I don't know how anything came to be" or "God made everything", they are simply pointing to the feeling of the Mystery—of how everything <u>is</u>, but nobody knows what it really <u>Is</u>, or how it came to be. [What, Where, When, How, Why, and <u>Who</u> To Remember To Be Happy]

N

Name-Invocation Sacred sounds or syllables and Names have been used since antiquity for invoking and worshipping the Divine Person and the Sat-Guru. In the Hindu tradition, the original mantras were cosmic sound-forms and "seed" letters used for worship and prayer of, and incantatory meditation on, the Revealed Form of the Divine Person.

Practitioners of the Way of Adidam may, at any time, Remember or Invoke Avatar Adi Da Samraj (or feel, and thereby Contemplate, His Avatarically Self-Revealed Divine Form, and Presence, and State) through simple feeling-Remembrance of Him and by randomly (in daily life and meditation) Invoking Him via His Principal Name, "Da", or via one (and only one) of the other Names He has Given for the practice of Simple Name-Invocation of Him. (The specific forms of His Names that Avatar Adi Da has Given to be engaged in practice of simple Name-Invocation of Him are listed in chapter three of *The Dawn Horse Testament Of The Ruchira Avatar*.)

For devotees of Avatar Adi Da Samraj, His Names are the Names of the Very Divine Being. As such, these Names, as Avatar Adi Da Himself has described, "do not simply <u>mean</u> Real God, or the Blessing of Real God. They are the verbal or audible Form of the Divine." Therefore, Invoking Avatar Adi Da Samraj by Name is a potent and Divinely Empowered form of feeling-Contemplation of Him.

Narcissus In Avatar Adi Da's Teaching-Revelation, "Narcissus" is a key symbol of the un-Enlightened individual as a self-obsessed seeker, enamored of his or her own self-image and egoic self-consciousness. In *The Knee Of Listening*, Adi Da Samraj describes the significance of the archetype of Narcissus:

He is the ancient one visible in the Greek "myth", who was the universally adored child of the gods, who rejected the loved-one and every form of love and relationship, who was finally condemned to the contemplation of his own image, until,

as a result of his own act and obstinacy, he suffered the fate of eternal separateness and died in infinite solitude.

Nirguna "Nirguna" is Sanskrit for "without attributes or quality".

Nirvikalpa Samadhi See **Samadhi**.

Nityananda See **Lineage, Avatar Adi Da's**.

Non-Separate Self-Domain The "Non-Separate Self-Domain" is a synonym for "Divine Self-Domain". (See **Divine Self-Domain**.)

O

"Oedipal" In modern psychology, the "Oedipus complex" is named after the legendary Greek Oedipus, who was fated to unknowingly kill his father and marry his mother. Avatar Adi Da Teaches that the primary dynamisms of emotional-sexual desiring, rejection, envy, betrayal, self-pleasuring, resentment, and other primal emotions and impulses are indeed patterned upon unconscious reactions first formed early in life, in relation to one's mother and father. Avatar Adi Da calls this "the 'Oedipal' drama" and points out that we relate to all women as we do to our mothers, and to all men as we do to our fathers, and that we relate, and react, to our own bodies as we do to the parent of the opposite sex. Thus, we impose infantile reactions to our parents on our relationships with lovers and all other beings, according to their sex, and we also superimpose the same on our relationship to our own bodies. (Avatar Adi Da's extended Instruction on "Oedipal" patterning is Given in *Ruchira Avatara Hridaya-Tantra Yoga*.)

"Open Eyes" "Open Eyes" is Avatar Adi Da's technical synonym for the Realization of seventh stage Sahaj Samadhi, or unqualified Divine Self-Realization. The phrase graphically describes the non-exclusive, non-inward, Native State of the Divine Self-Realizer, Who is Identified Unconditionally with the Divine Self-Reality, while also allowing whatever arises to appear in the Divine Consciousness (and spontaneously Divinely Self-Recognizing everything that arises as a modification of the Divine Consciousness). The Transcendental Self is intuited in the mature phases of the sixth stage of life, but It can be Realized at that stage only by the intentional exclusion of conditional phenomena. In "Open Eyes", that impulse to exclusion disappears, when the Eyes of the Heart Open, and Most Perfect Realization of the Spiritual, Transcendental, and Divine Self in the seventh stage of life becomes permanent (and incorruptible by any phenomenal events).

"original" context of the fourth stage of life   See **stages of life**.

Outshined / Outshining   Avatar Adi Da uses "Outshined" or "Outshining" as a synonym for "Divine Translation", to refer to the final Demonstration of the four-phase process of the seventh (or Divinely Enlightened) stage of life in the Way of Adidam. In the Great Event of Outshining (or Divine Translation), body, mind, and world are no longer noticed—not because the Divine Consciousness has withdrawn or dissociated from conditionally manifested phenomena, but because the Divine Self-Recognition of all arising phenomena as modifications of the Divine Self-Condition has become so intense that the "Bright" Radiance of Consciousness now Outshines all such phenomena. (See also **four phases of the seventh stage of life**.)

P, Q

"Perfect Practice"   The "Perfect Practice" is Avatar Adi Da's technical term for the discipline of the ultimate stages of life (the sixth stage of life and the seventh stage of life) in the Way of Adidam. The "Perfect Practice" is practice in the Domain of Consciousness Itself (as opposed to practice from the point of view of the body or the mind). (See also **stages of life**.)

Perfectly Subjective   Avatar Adi Da uses "Perfectly Subjective" to describe the True Divine Source, or "Subject", of the conditionally manifested world—as opposed to regarding the Divine as some sort of conditional "object" or "other". Thus, in the phrase "Perfectly Subjective", the word "Subjective" does not have the sense of "relating to the inward experience of an individual", but, rather, it has the sense of "Being Consciousness Itself, the True Subject of all apparent experience".

Pleasure Dome   Avatar Adi Da Samraj Speaks of the Way of Adidam as a "Pleasure Dome", recalling the poem "Kubla Khan", by Samuel Taylor Coleridge ("In Xanadu did Kubla Khan / A stately pleasure-dome decree . . ."). Adi Da Samraj points out that in many religious traditions it is presumed that one must embrace suffering in order to earn future happiness and pleasure. However, by Calling His devotees to live the Way of Adidam as a Pleasure Dome, Avatar Adi Da Samraj Communicates His Teaching that the Way of heart-Communion with Him is always about present-time Happiness, not about any kind of search to attain Happiness in the future. Thus, in the Way of Adidam, there is no idealization of suffering and pain as presumed means to attain future happiness—and, consequently, there is no denial of the appropriate enjoyment of even the ordinary pleasures of human life.

Avatar Adi Da also uses "Pleasure Dome" as a reference to the Ultimate and Divine Love-Bliss-Happiness That Is His own Self-Nature and His Gift to all who respond to Him.

"Practice"   As the quotation marks around the capitalized word "Practice" suggest, the psycho-physical expression of the process of Divine Enlightenment is a "Practice" only in the sense that it is simple action. It is not, in contrast to the stages of life previous to the seventh, a discipline intended to counter egoic tendencies that would otherwise dominate body and mind.

Avatar Adi Da uses quotation marks in a characteristic manner throughout His Written Word to Indicate that a particular word is a technical term, to be understood in the unique and precise language of the Way of Adidam, carrying the implication "as per definition". However, in other cases, His quotation marks carry the implication "so to speak", as in the case of the term "Practice" and are, therefore, not to be understood as precise technical terminology of the Way of Adidam.

prana/pranic   The Sanskrit word "prana" means "life-energy". It generally refers to the life-energy animating all beings and pervading everything in cosmic Nature. In the human body-mind, circulation of this universal life-energy is associated with the heartbeat and the cycles of the breath. In esoteric Yogic Teachings, prana is also a specific technical name for one of a number of forms of etheric energy that functionally sustain the bodily being.

Prana is not to be equated with the Divine Spirit-Current, or the Spiritual (and Always Blessing) Divine Presence of Avatar Adi Da Samraj. The finite pranic energies that sustain individual beings are only conditional, localized, and temporary phenomena of the realm of cosmic Nature. Even in the form of universal life-force, prana is but a conditional modification of the Divine Spirit-Current Revealed by Avatar Adi Da, Which Is the "Bright" (or Consciousness Itself), beyond all cosmic forms.

R

"radical"   The term "radical" derives from the Latin "radix", meaning "root", and, thus, it principally means "irreducible", "fundamental", or "relating to the origin". In *The Dawn Horse Testament Of The Ruchira Avatar*, Avatar Adi Da defines "Radical" as "Gone To The Root, Core, Source, or Origin". Because Adi Da Samraj uses "radical" in this literal sense, it appears in quotation marks in His Wisdom-Teaching, in order to distinguish His usage from the common reference to an extreme (often political) view.

Ramana Maharshi   A great sixth stage Indian Spiritual Master, Ramana Maharshi (1879-1950) became Self-Realized at a young age and gradually assumed a Teaching role as increasing numbers of people approached him for Spiritual guidance. Ramana Maharshi's Teaching focused on the process of introversion (through the question "Who am I?"), which culminates in conditional Self-Realization (or Jnana Samadhi), exclusive of phenomena. He established his Ashram at Tiruvannamalai in South India, which continues today.

Rang Avadhoot   Rang Avadhoot (1898-1968) was a Realizer in the tradition of Dattatreya. In *The Knee Of Listening*, Avatar Adi Da describes the brief but highly significant meeting that occurred between Himself and Rang Avadhoot in 1968.

Real God   Avatar Adi Da uses the term "Real God" to Indicate the True and Perfectly Subjective Source of all conditions, the True and Spiritual Divine Person (Which can be directly Realized), rather than any ego-made (and, thus, false, or limited) presumptions about God.

Re-cognition   "Re-cognition", which literally means "knowing again", is Avatar Adi Da's term for "the tacit transcending of the habit of 'Narcissus'". It is the mature form into which verbal self-Enquiry evolves in the Devotional Way of Insight. The individual simply notices and tacitly "knows again" (or directly understands) whatever is arising as yet another species of self-contraction, and he or she transcends (or feels beyond) it in Satsang with Avatar Adi Da.

renunciate orders   Avatar Adi Da has established two formal renunciate orders: The Ruchira Sannyasin Order of the Free Renunciates of Ruchiradam (or, simply, the Ruchira Sannyasin Order), and the Lay Renunciate Order of Adidam (or, simply, the Lay Renunciate Order).

The senior practicing order in the Way of Adidam is the Ruchira Sannyasin Order.

This order is the senior cultural authority within the formal gathering of Avatar Adi Da's devotees. "Sannyasin" is an ancient Sanskrit term for one who has renounced all worldly bonds and who gives himself or herself completely to the Real-God-Realizing or Real-God-Realized life. Members of the Ruchira Sannyasin Order are uniquely exemplary practitioners of the Way of Adidam who are (generally) practicing in the context of the ultimate (sixth and seventh) stages of life. Members of this Order are legal renunciates and live a life of perpetual retreat. The Ruchira Sannyasin Order comprises the first congregation of Avatar Adi Da's devotees.

The members of the Ruchira Sannyasin Order have a uniquely significant role among the practitioners of Adidam as Avatar Adi Da's human Instruments and (in the case of those members who are formally acknowledged as Avatar Adi Da's fully Awakened seventh stage devotees) as the body of practitioners from among whom each of Avatar Adi Da's successive "Living Murtis" (or Empowered human Agents) will be selected. Therefore, the Ruchira Sannyasin Order is essential to the perpetual continuation of authentic practice of the Way of Adidam.

The Founding Member of the Ruchira Sannyasin Order is Avatar Adi Da Himself.

In "The Orders of My True and Free Renunciate Devotees" (in *The Lion Sutra*), Avatar Adi Da describes the Lay Renunciate Order as "a renunciate service order for all intensively serving (and, altogether, intensively practicing) lay practitioners of the total (or full and complete) practice of the Way of Adidam".

All present members, and all future members, of the Lay Renunciate Order must (necessarily) be formally acknowledged, formally practicing, significantly matured (tested and proven), and, altogether, exemplary practitioners of the total (or full and complete) practice of the Way of Adidam. They must perform significant cultural (and practical, and, as necessary, managerial) service within the gathering of all formally acknowledged practitioners of the four congregations of the Way of

Adidam. Either they must live within a formally designated community of formally acknowledged practitioners of the Way of Adidam or, otherwise, they must be formally designated serving residents of one of the by Me formally Empowered Ruchira Sannyasin Hermitage-Retreat Sanctuaries or one of the by Me formally Empowered Pilgrimage and Retreat Sanctuaries for all formally acknowledged practitioners of the Way of Adidam. And they must formally accept (and rightly fulfill) all the obligations and disciplines associated with membership within the Lay Renunciate Order. ["The Orders of My True and Free Renunciate Devotees"]

right side of the heart   See **heart, stations of the heart**.

Ruchira Avatar   In Sanskrit, "Ruchira" means "bright, radiant, effulgent". Thus, the Reference "Ruchira Avatar" indicates that Avatar Adi Da Samraj is the "Bright" (or Radiant) Descent of the Divine Reality Itself into the conditionally manifested worlds, Appearing here in His bodily (human) Form.

Ruchira Avatara Bhakti Yoga   Ruchira Avatara Bhakti Yoga is the principal Gift, Calling, and Discipline Offered by Adi Da Samraj to all who practice the Way of Adidam (in all four congregations).

The phrase "Ruchira Avatara Bhakti Yoga" is itself a summary of the Way of Adidam. "Bhakti", in Sanskrit, is love, adoration, or devotion, while "Yoga" is a Real-God-Realizing discipline (or practice). "Ruchira Avatara Bhakti Yoga" is, thus, "the Divinely Revealed practice of devotional love for (and devotional response to) the Ruchira Avatar, Adi Da Samraj".

The technical practice of Ruchira Avatara Bhakti Yoga is a four-part process of Invoking, feeling, breathing, and serving Avatar Adi Da in every moment.

For Avatar Adi Da's essential Instruction in Ruchira Avatara Bhakti Yoga, see the *Da Love-Ananda Gita (The Free Gift Of The Divine Love-Bliss)*, Part Five, verse 25, and Part Six; *Hridaya Rosary (Four Thorns Of Heart-Instruction)*, Parts

Four and Five; and *What, Where, When, How, Why and Who To Remember To Be Happy*, Part Three, "Surrender the Faculties of the Body-Mind To Me" and "How to Practice Whole Bodily Devotion To Me".

Ruchira Avatara Satsang   The Hindi word "Satsang" literally means "true (or right) relationship", "the company of Truth". "Ruchira Avatara Satsang" is the eternal relationship of mutual sacred commitment between Avatar Adi Da Samraj and each true and formally acknowledged practitioner of the Way of Adidam. Once it is consciously assumed by any practitioner, Ruchira Avatara Satsang is an all-inclusive Condition, bringing Divine Grace and Blessings and sacred obligations, responsibilities, and tests into every dimension of the practitioner's life and consciousness.

The Ruchira Buddha   The Enlightened One Who Shines with the Divine "Brightness".

The Ruchira Buddha-Avatar   The "Bright" Enlightened One Who is the Incarnation of the Divine Person. (See also **Avatar**.)

Ruchira Buddhism   "Ruchira Buddhism" is the Way of devotion to the Ruchira Buddha—"the 'Bright' Buddha", Avatar Adi Da Samraj (or, more fully, "the Radiant, Shining, 'Bright' Illuminator and Enlightener Who Is Inherently, or Perfectly Subjectively, Self-Enlightened, and Eternally Awake").

Ruchira Samadhi   "Ruchira Samadhi" (Sanskrit for "the Samadhi of the 'Bright'") is one of the references that Avatar Adi Da Samraj uses for the Divinely Enlightened Condition Realized in the seventh stage of life, Which He characterizes as the Unconditional Realization of the Divine "Brightness".

Ruchira Sannyasin Order   See **renunciate orders**, and see also p. 384.

Rudi / Swami Rudrananda   See **Lineage, Avatar Adi Da's**.

S

"Sadhana Years"   In Sanskrit, "Sadhana" means "self-transcending religious or Spiritual practice". Avatar Adi Da's "Sadhana Years" refers to the time from which He began His quest to recover the Truth of Existence (at Columbia College) until His Divine Re-Awakening in 1970. Avatar Adi Da's full description of His "Sadhana Years" is Given in *The Knee Of Listening*.

Saguna   "Saguna" is Sanskrit for "containing (or accompanied by) qualities".

Sahaj   "Sahaj" is Hindi (from Sanskrit "sahaja") for "twin-born", "natural", or "innate". Avatar Adi Da uses the term to indicate the Coincidence (in the case of Divine Self-Realization) of the Inherently Spiritual and Transcendental Divine Reality with conditional reality. Sahaj, therefore, is the Inherent (or Native) and, thus, truly "Natural" State of Being. (See also **Samadhi**.)

Sahaj Samadhi   See **Samadhi**.

sahasrar   In the traditional system of seven chakras, the sahasrar is the highest chakra (or subtle energy center), associated with the crown of the head and beyond. It is described as a thousand-petaled lotus, the terminal of Light to which the Yogic process (of Spiritual ascent through the chakras) aspires.

During His "Sadhana Years", Avatar Adi Da spontaneously experienced what He calls the "severing of the sahasrar". The Spirit-Energy no longer ascended into the crown of the head (and beyond), but rather "fell" into the Heart, and rested as the Witness-Consciousness. It was this experience that directly revealed to Avatar Adi Da that, while the Yogic traditions regard the sahasrar as the seat of Enlightenment, the Heart is truly the Seat of Divine Consciousness.

Avatar Adi Da's account of the severing of the sahasrar in His own Case is Given in chapter eighteen of *The Knee Of Listening*.

Saiva Siddhanta "Saiva Siddhanta" is the name of an important school of Saivism which flourished in South India and survives into the present.

Samadhi The Sanskrit word "Samadhi" traditionally denotes various exalted states that appear in the context of esoteric meditation and Realization. Avatar Adi Da Teaches that, for His devotees, Samadhi is, even more simply and fundamentally, the Enjoyment of His Divine State, Which is experienced (even from the beginning of the practice of Adidam) through ego-transcending heart-Communion with Him. Therefore, "the cultivation of Samadhi" is another way to describe the fundamental basis of the Way of Adidam. Avatar Adi Da's devotee is in Samadhi in any moment of standing beyond the separate self in true devotional heart-Communion with Him. (See "The Cultivation of My Divine Samadhi", in *The Seven Stages Of Life*.)

The developmental process leading to Divine Enlightenment in the Way of Adidam may be marked by many signs, principal among which are the Samadhis of the advanced and the ultimate stages of life and practice. Although some of the traditionally known Samadhis of the fourth, the fifth, and the sixth stages of life may appear in the course of an individual's practice of the Way of Adidam, the appearance of all of them is by no means necessary, or even probable (as Avatar Adi Da Indicates in His Wisdom-Teaching). The essential Samadhis of the Way of Adidam are those that are uniquely Granted by Avatar Adi Da Samraj—the Samadhi of the "Thumbs" and seventh stage Sahaj Samadhi. All the possible forms of Samadhi in the Way of Adidam are described in full detail in *The Dawn Horse Testament Of The Ruchira Avatar*.

Samadhi of the "Thumbs" "The 'Thumbs'" is Avatar Adi Da's technical term for the invasion of the body-mind by a particular kind of forceful Descent of His Divine Spirit-Current. Avatar Adi Da describes His own experience of the "Thumbs" in *The Knee Of Listening*:

. . . *I had an experience that appeared like a mass of gigantic thumbs coming down from above, pressing into my throat (causing something of a gagging, and somewhat suffocating, sensation), and then pressing further (and, it seemed, would have expanded without limitation or end), into some form of myself that was much larger than my physical body. . . .*

The "Thumbs" were not visible in the ordinary sense. I did not see them then or even as a child. They were not visible to me with my eyes, nor did I hallucinate them pictorially. Yet, I very consciously experienced and felt them as having a peculiar form and mobility, as I likewise experienced my own otherwise invisible and greater form.

I did not at that time or at any time in my childhood fully allow this intervention of the "Thumbs" to take place. I held it off from its fullest descent, in fear of being overwhelmed, for I did not understand at all what was taking place. However, in later years this same experience occurred naturally during meditation. Because my meditation had been allowed to progress gradually, and the realizations at each level were thus perceived without shock, I was able at those times to allow the experience to take place. When I did, the "Thumbs" completely entered my living form. They appeared like tongues, or parts of a Force, coming from above. And when they had entered deep into my body, the magnetic or energic balances of my living being reversed. On several occasions I felt as if the body had risen above the ground somewhat, and this is perhaps the basis for certain evidence in mystical literature of the phenomenon of levitation, or bodily transport.

At any rate, during those stages in meditation the body ceased to be polarized toward the ground, or the gravitational direction of the earth's center. There was a strong reversal of polarity, communicated along a line of Force analogous to the spine. The physical body, as well as the Energy-form that could be interiorly felt as analogous to but detached from the physical body, was felt to turn in a curve along the spine and forward in the direction of the heart. When this reversal of Energy was allowed to take place completely, I resided in a totally different body, which also contained the physical body. It was spherical in shape. And the sensation of dwelling as that form was completely peaceful. The physical body was completely relaxed and polarized to the shape of this other spherical body. The mind became quieted, and then there was a movement in consciousness that would go even deeper, into a higher conscious State beyond physical and mental awareness. I was to learn that this spherical body was what Yogis and occultists call the "subtle" body (which includes the "pranic", or natural life-energy, dimension and the "astral", or the lower mental and the higher mental, dimensions of the living being).

In the fullest form of this experience, which Avatar Adi Da calls "the Samadhi of the 'Thumbs'", His Spirit-Invasion Descends all the way to the bottom of the frontal line of the body-mind (at the bodily base) and ascends through the spinal line, overwhelming the ordinary human sense of bodily existence, infusing the whole being with intense blissfulness, and releasing the ordinary, confined sense of body, mind, and separate self.

Both the experience of the "Thumbs" and the full Samadhi of the "Thumbs" are unique to the Way of Adidam, for they are specifically signs of the "Crashing Down" (or the Divine Descent) of Avatar Adi Da's Spirit-Baptism, into the body-minds of His devotees. The Samadhi of the "Thumbs" is a kind of "Nirvikalpa" (or formless) Samadhi—but in descent in the frontal line, rather than in ascent in the spinal line.

Avatar Adi Da's extended Instruction relative to the "Thumbs" is Given in "The 'Thumbs' Is The Fundamental Sign Of The Crashing Down Of My Person". This Essay appears in a number of Avatar Adi Da's "Source-Texts" (*Hridaya Rosary, The Only Complete Way To Realize The Unbroken Light Of Real God, Ruchira Avatara Hridaya-Siddha Yoga, The Seven Stages Of Life*, and *Santosha Adidam*, as well as chapter twenty-four of *The Dawn Horse Testament Of The Ruchira Avatar* and chapter thirty-one of *The Heart Of The*

Dawn Horse Testament Of The Ruchira Avatar).

Savikalpa Samadhi and "Cosmic Consciousness"   The Sanskrit term "Savikalpa Samadhi" literally means "meditative ecstasy with form", or "deep meditative concentration (or absorption) in which form (or defined experiential content) is still perceived". Avatar Adi Da indicates that there are two basic forms of Savikalpa Samadhi. The first is the various experiences produced by the Spiritual ascent of energy and attention (into mystical phenomena, visions, and other subtle sensory perceptions of subtle psychic forms) and the various states of Yogic Bliss (or Spirit-"Intoxication").

The second (and highest) form of Savikalpa Samadhi is called "Cosmic Consciousness", or the "'Vision' of Cosmic Unity". This is an isolated or periodic occurrence in which attention ascends, uncharacteristically and spontaneously, to a state of awareness wherein conditional existence is perceived as a Unity in Divine Awareness. This conditional form of "Cosmic Consciousness" is pursued in many mystical and Yogic paths. It depends upon manipulation of attention and the body-mind, and it is interpreted from the point of view of the separate, body-based or mind-based self—and, therefore, it is not equivalent to Divine Enlightenment.

Avatar Adi Da's discussion of Savikalpa Samadhi is found in "Vision, Audition, and Touch in The Process of Ascending Meditation in The Way Of Adidam", in Part Four of *Ruchira Avatara Hridaya-Siddha Yoga*.

Avatar Adi Da's description of the varieties of experiential form possible in Savikalpa Samadhi is found in "The Significant Experiential Signs That May Appear in the Course of The Way Of Adidam", in Part Three of *What, Where, When, How, Why, and Who To Remember To Be Happy*.

fifth stage Nirvikalpa Samadhi   The Sanskrit term "Nirvikalpa Samadhi" literally means "meditative ecstasy without form", or "deep meditative concentration (or absorption) in which there is no perception of form (or defined experiential content)". Traditionally, this state is regarded to be the final goal of the many schools of Yogic ascent whose orientation to practice is that of the fifth stage of life. Like "Cosmic Consciousness", fifth stage conditional Nirvikalpa Samadhi is an isolated or periodic Realization. In it, attention ascends beyond all conditional manifestation into the formless Matrix of Divine Vibration and Divine Light Infinitely Above the world, the body, and the mind. And, like the various forms of Savikalpa Samadhi, fifth stage conditional Nirvikalpa Samadhi is a temporary state of attention (or, more precisely, of the suspension of attention). It is produced by manipulation of attention and of the body-mind, and is (therefore) incapable of being maintained when attention returns (as it inevitably does) to the states of the body-mind.

Avatar Adi Da's Instruction relative to fifth stage conditional Nirvikalpa Samadhi is Given in chapter forty-two of *The Dawn Horse Testament Of The Ruchira Avatar*.

Jnana Samadhi, or Jnana Nirvikalpa Samadhi "Jnana" means "knowledge". Jnana Nirvikalpa Samadhi (sixth stage Nirvakalpa Samadhi, or, simply, Jnana Samadhi) is the characteristic meditative experience in the sixth stage of life in the Way of Adidam. Produced by the intentional withdrawal of attention from the conditional body-mind-self and its relations, Jnana Samadhi is the conditional, temporary Realization of the Transcendental Self (or Consciousness Itself), exclusive of any perception (or cognition) of world, objects, relations, body, mind, and separate-self-sense—and, thereby, formless (or "nirvikalpa").

Avatar Adi Da's Instruction relative to Jnana Nirvikalpa Samadhi is Given in "The Sixth and The Seventh Stages of Life in The Way Of Adidam" in *The Lion Sutra*.

seventh stage Sahaj Samadhi, or seventh stage Sahaja Nirvikalpa Samadhi Avatar Adi Da's description of seventh stage Sahaj Samadhi is Given in Part Four of *The All-Completing and Final Divine Revelation To Mankind*.

Samraj "Samraj" (from the Sanskrit "Samraja") is a traditional Indian term used to refer to great kings, but also to refer to the Hindu gods. "Samraja" is defined as "universal or supreme ruler", "paramount Lord", or "paramount sovereign".

The Sanskrit word "raja" (the basic root of "Samraj") means "king". It comes from the verbal root "raj", meaning "to reign, to rule, to illuminate". The prefix "sam-" expresses "union" or "completeness". "Samraj" is thus literally the complete ruler, the ruler of everything altogether. "Samraj" was traditionally given as a title to a king who was regarded to be a "universal monarch".

Avatar Adi Da's Name "Adi Da Samraj" expresses that He is the Primordial (or Original) Giver, Who Blesses all as the Universal Lord of every thing, every where, for all time. The Sovereignty of His Kingdom has nothing to do with the world of human politics. Rather, it is entirely a matter of His Spiritual Dominion over all and All, His Kingship in the hearts of His devotees.

samsara / samsaric "Samsara" (or "samsaric") is a classical Buddhist and Hindu term for all conditional worlds and states, or the cyclical realm of birth and change and death. It connotes the suffering and limitations experienced in those limited worlds.

Sanctuaries As of this writing (2001), Avatar Adi Da has Empowered five Sanctuaries as Agents of His Divine Spiritual Transmission:

• Adidam Samrajashram is the Island of Naitauba in Fiji. It was the principal site of Avatar Adi Da's Teaching and Revelation Work from 1983 to 1999. Avatar Adi Da has acknowledged that, because of the intensity of His Spiritual Work there (especially during the early months of 1999, as described in *The Light Is On!*), Adidam Samrajashram is the primary Seat from which His Divine Spiritual Blessing Flows to the entire world.

- The Mountain Of Attention Sanctuary, in northern California, was the principal site of Avatar Adi Da's Teaching Work from 1974 to the early 1980s.

- Da Love-Ananda Mahal, in Hawaii, was (together with the Mountain Of Attention) the principal site of Avatar Adi Da's Teaching Work in the early 1980s.

- Tat Sundaram and Love's Point Hermitage in northern California are small Hermitage-Retreat Sanctuaries that provide a private circumstance for Avatar Adi Da and members of the Ruchira Sannyasin Order.

Especially since 1995, Avatar Adi Da Samraj has Freely Moved among the various Sanctuaries, in His spontaneous Wandering-Work of world-Blessing. Devotees of Avatar Adi Da are invited to spend periods of retreat at the larger Sanctuaries. Through His years of Blessing-Infusion of each of these five Sanctuaries, He has fully Empowered them for His devotees throughout all time.

Santosha "Santosha" is Sanskrit for "satisfaction" or "contentment"—qualities associated with a sense of completion. These qualities are characteristic of no-seeking, the fundamental Principle of Avatar Adi Da's Wisdom-Teaching and of His entire Revelation of Truth. Because of its uniquely appropriate meanings, "Santosha" is one of Avatar Adi Da's Names. As Santosha Adi Da, Avatar Adi Da Samraj is the Divine Giver of Perfect Divine Contentedness, or Perfect Searchlessness.

Santosha Avatar As the Santosha Avatar, Avatar Adi Da is the Very Incarnation of Perfect Divine Contentedness, or Perfect Searchlessness.

Sat-Guru "Sat" means "Truth", "Being", "Existence". Thus, "Sat-Guru" literally means "True Guru", or a Guru who can lead living beings from darkness (or non-Truth) into Light (or the Living Truth).

Satsang The Hindi word "Satsang" (from the Sanskrit "Satsanga") literally means "true (or right) relationship", "the company of Truth". In the Way of Adidam, Satsang is the eternal relationship of mutual sacred commitment between Avatar Adi Da Samraj and each formally acknowledged practitioner of the Way of Adidam.

Savikalpa Samadhi See **Samadhi**.

scientific materialism Scientific materialism is the predominant philosophy and worldview of modern humanity, the basic presumption of which is that the material world is all that exists. In scientific materialism, the method of science, or the observation of objective phenomena, is made into philosophy and a way of life that suppresses our native impulse to Liberation.

seeing See **listening, hearing, and seeing**.

self-Enquiry The practice of self-Enquiry in the form "Avoiding relationship?", unique to the Way of Adidam, was spontaneously developed by Avatar Adi Da in the course of His own Ordeal of Divine Re-Awakening. Intense persistence in the "radical" discipline of this unique form of self-Enquiry led rapidly to Avatar Adi Da's Divine Enlightenment (or Most Perfect Divine Self-Realization) in 1970.

The practice of self-Enquiry in the form "Avoiding relationship?" and the practice of non-verbal Re-cognition are the principal technical practices that serve feeling-Contemplation of Avatar Adi Da in the Devotional Way of Insight.

Self-Existing and Self-Radiant Avatar Adi Da uses "Self-Existing and Self-Radiant" to indicate the two fundamental aspects of the One Divine Person (or Reality)—Existence (or Being, or Consciousness) Itself, and Radiance (or Energy, or Light) Itself.

seven stages of life See **stages of life**.

Shakti, Guru-Shakti "Shakti" is a Sanskrit term for the Divinely Manifesting Energy, Spiritual Power, or Spirit-Current of the Divine Person. Guru-Shakti is the Power of the Guru to Liberate his or her devotees.

Shaktipat In Hindi, "shaktipat" is the "descent of Spiritual Power". Yogic Shaktipat, which manipulates natural, conditional energies or partial manifestations of the Spirit-Current, is typically granted through touch, word, glance, or regard by Yogic Adepts in the fifth stage of life, or fourth to fifth stages of life. Yogic Shaktipat must be distinguished from (and, otherwise, understood to be only a secondary aspect of) the Blessing Transmission of the Heart Itself (Hridaya-Shaktipat), which is uniquely Given by Avatar Adi Da Samraj.

Siddha, Siddha-Guru "Siddha" is Sanskrit for "a completed, fulfilled, or perfected one", or "one of perfect accomplishment, or power". Avatar Adi Da uses "Siddha", or "Siddha-Guru", to mean a Transmission-Master who is a Realizer (to any significant degree) of Real God, Truth, or Reality.

Siddha Yoga "Siddha Yoga" is, literally, "the Yoga of the Perfected One[s]".

Swami Muktananda used the term "Siddha Yoga" to refer to the form of Kundalini Yoga that he taught, which involved initiation of the devotee by the Guru's Transmission of Shakti (or Spiritual Energy). Avatar Adi Da Samraj has indicated that this was a fifth stage form of Siddha Yoga.

In "I (Alone) <u>Am</u> The Adidam Revelation", Avatar Adi Da Says:

. . . I Teach Siddha Yoga in the Mode and Manner of the <u>seventh</u> stage of life (as Ruchira Avatara Hridaya-Siddha Yoga, or Ruchira Avatara Maha-Jnana Hridaya-Shaktipat Yoga)—and always toward (or to the degree of) the Realization inherently associated with (and, at last, Most Perfectly Demonstrated and Proven by) the only-by-Me Revealed and Given seventh

stage of life, and as a practice and a Process that progressively includes (and, coincidently, <u>directly</u> transcends) <u>all six</u> of the phenomenal and developmental (and, necessarily, yet ego-based) stages of life that precede the seventh.

Avatar Adi Da's description of the similarities and differences between traditional Siddha Yoga and the Way of Adidam is Given in "I (Alone) <u>Am</u> The Adidam Revelation", which Essay appears in many of Avatar Adi Da's twenty-three "Source-Texts".

siddhi "Siddhi" is Sanskrit for "power", or "accomplishment". When capitalized in Avatar Adi Da's Wisdom-Teaching, "Siddhi" is the Spiritual, Transcendental, and Divine Awakening-Power That He spontaneously and effortlessly Transmits to all.

"Sila" "Sila" is a Pali Buddhist term meaning "habit", "behavior", "conduct", or "morality". It connotes the restraint of outgoing energy and attention, the disposition of equanimity, or free energy and attention for the Spiritual Process.

"simpler" (or "simplest") form of the Way of Adidam See **forms of practice in the Way of Adidam**.

sleeping See **waking, dreaming, and sleeping**.

"Source-Texts" During the twenty-seven years of His Teaching-Work and Revelation-Work (from 1972 to 1999), Avatar Adi Da elaborately described every aspect of the practice of Adidam, from the beginning of one's approach to Him to the Most Ultimate Realization of the seventh stage of life.

Avatar Adi Da's Heart-Word is summarized in His twenty-three "Source-Texts". These Texts present, in complete and conclusive detail, His Divine Revelations, Confessions, and Instructions, which are the fruits of His years of Teaching and Revelation Work. In addition to this "Source-Literature", Avatar Adi Da's Heart-Word also includes His "Supportive Texts" (comprising His practical Instruction in all the details of the practice of Adidam, including the fundamental disciplines of diet, health, exercise, sexuality, childrearing, and cooperative community), His "Early Literature" (Written during His Teaching Years), and collections of His Talks. (For a complete list of Avatar Adi Da's twenty-three "Source-Texts", see pp. 459-66.)

spinal line, spinal Yoga   The spinal (or ascending) line of the body-mind conducts the Spirit-Current of Divine Life in an upward direction from the base of the body (or perineal area) to the crown of the head, and beyond.

In the Way of Adidam, the spinal Yoga is the process whereby knots and obstructions in the subtle, astral, or the more mentally and subtly oriented dimension of the body-mind are penetrated, opened, surrendered, and released through the devotee's reception and "conductivity" of Avatar Adi Da's Transmission into the spinal line of the body-mind. This ascending Yoga will be required for practitioners of Adidam only in relatively rare cases. The great majority of Avatar Adi Da's devotees will be sufficiently purified through their practice of the frontal Yoga to proceed directly to practice in the context of the sixth stage of life, bypassing practice in the context of the "advanced" fourth stage and the fifth stage of life.

Spirit-Baptism   Avatar Adi Da often refers to His Transmission of Spiritual Blessing as His "Spirit-Baptism". It is often felt by His devotee as a Current descending in the frontal line and ascending in the spinal line. However, Avatar Adi Da's Spirit-Baptism is fundamentally and primarily His Moveless Transmission of the Divine Heart Itself. As a secondary effect, His Spirit-Baptism serves to purify, balance, and energize the entire body-mind of the devotee who is prepared to receive It.

Spiritual anatomy / esoteric anatomy
Avatar Adi Da Samraj has Revealed that just as there is a physical anatomy, there is an actual Spiritual anatomy, or structure, that is present in every human being. As He Says in *The Basket Of Tolerance*, it is

because of this structure that the "experiential and developmental process of Growth and Realization demonstrates itself in accordance with what I have Revealed and Demonstrated to be the seven stages of life".

Avatar Adi Da's extended Instruction relative to the Spiritual anatomy of Man is Given in *The Seven Stages Of Life* and *Santosha Adidam*.

Spiritual, Transcendental, Divine
Avatar Adi Da uses the words "Spiritual", "Transcendental", and "Divine" in reference to dimensions of Reality that are Realized progressively in the Way of Adidam. "Transcendental" and "Spiritual" indicate two fundamental aspects of the One Divine Reality and Person— Consciousness Itself (Which Is Transcendental, or Self-Existing) and Energy Itself (Which Is Spiritual, or Self-Radiant). Only That Which Is Divine is simultaneously Transcendental <u>and</u> Spiritual.

Sri   "Sri" is a term of honor and veneration often applied to an Adept. The word literally means "flame" in Sanskrit, indicating that the one honored is radiant with Blessing Power.

stages of life   Avatar Adi Da has Revealed the underlying structure of human growth in seven stages. The seventh stage of life is Divine Self-Realization, or Most Perfect Enlightenment.

The first three stages of life develop, respectively, the physical, emotional, and mental/volitional functions of the body-mind. The first stage begins at birth and continues for approximately five to seven years; the second stage follows, continuing until approximately the age of twelve to fourteen; and the third stage is optimally complete by the early twenties. In the case of virtually all individuals, however, failed adaptation in the earlier stages of life means that maturity in the third stage of life takes much longer to attain, and it is usually never fulfilled, with the result that the ensuing stages of Spiritual development do not even begin.

In the Way of Adidam, however, growth in the first three stages of life unfolds in the Spiritual Company of Avatar Adi Da and is based in the practice of feeling-Contemplation of His bodily (human) Form and in devotion, service, and self-discipline in relation to His bodily (human) Form. By the Grace of this relationship to Avatar Adi Da, the first three (or foundation) stages of life are lived and fulfilled in an ego-transcending devotional disposition, or (as He describes it) "in the 'original' (or beginner's) devotional context of the fourth stage of life".

The fourth stage of life is the transitional stage between the gross (bodily-based) point of view of the first three stages of life and the subtle (mind-based, or psyche-based) point of view of the fifth stage of life. The fourth stage of life is the stage of Spiritual devotion, or devotional surrender of separate self to the Divine, in which the gross functions of the being are aligned to the higher psychic (or subtle) functions of the being. In the fourth stage of life, the gross (or bodily-based) personality of the first three stages of life is purified through reception of the Spiritual Force ("Holy Spirit", or "Shakti") of the Divine Reality, which prepares the being to out-grow the bodily-based point of view.

In the Way of Adidam, as the orientation of the fourth stage of life matures, heart-felt surrender to the bodily (human) Form of Avatar Adi Da deepens by His Grace, Drawing His devotee into Love-Communion with His All-Pervading Spiritual Presence. Growth in the "basic" context of the fourth stage of life in the Way of Adidam is also characterized by reception of Avatar Adi Da's Baptizing Current of Divine Spirit-Energy, Which is initially felt to flow down the front of the body from Infinitely Above the head to the bodily base (or perineal area).

The Descent of Avatar Adi Da's Spirit-Baptism releases obstructions predominantly in what He calls the "frontal personality", or the personality typically animated in the waking state (as opposed to the dream state and the state of deep sleep). This Spirit-Baptism purifies His devotee and infuses the devotee with His Spirit-Power. Avatar Adi Da's devotee is, thus, awakened to profound love of (and devotional intimacy with) Him.

Eventually, Avatar Adi Da's Divine Spirit-Current may be felt to turn about at the bodily base and ascend up the spine to the brain core. In this case, the fourth stage of life matures to its "advanced" context, which is focused in the Ascent of Avatar Adi Da's Spirit-Baptism and the consequent purification of the spinal line of the body-mind.

In the fifth stage of life, attention is concentrated in the subtle (or psychic) levels of awareness in ascent. Avatar Adi Da's Divine Spirit-Current is felt to penetrate the brain core and rise toward the Matrix of Light and Love-Bliss Infinitely Above the crown of the head, possibly culminating in the temporary experience of fifth stage conditional Nirvikalpa Samadhi, or "formless ecstasy". In the Way of Adidam, most practitioners will not need to practice either in the "advanced" context of the fourth stage of life or in the context of the fifth stage of life, but will (rather) be Awakened, by Avatar Adi Da's Grace, directly from maturity in the fourth stage of life to the Witness-Position of Consciousness (in the context of the sixth stage of life).

In the traditional development of the sixth stage of life, a strategic effort is made to Identify with Consciousness Itself by excluding the realm of conditional phenomena. Avatar Adi Da Teaches, however, that the deliberate intention to exclude the conditional world for the sake of Realizing Transcendental Consciousness is an egoic error that must be transcended by His devotees who are practicing in the context of the sixth stage of life.

In deepest meditation in the sixth stage of life in the Way of Adidam, the knot of attention (which is the root-action of egoity, felt as separation, self-contraction, or the feeling of relatedness) dissolves, and all sense of relatedness yields to the Blissful and undifferentiated Feeling of Being. The characteristic Samadhi of the sixth stage of life is Jnana Samadhi, the temporary Realization of the Transcendental Self (or Consciousness Itself)—which is temporary because it can occur only when awareness of the world is excluded in meditation.

The transition from the sixth stage of life to the seventh stage Realization of Absolute Non-Separateness is the unique Revelation of Avatar Adi Da. Various traditions and individuals previous to Adi Da's Revelation have had sixth stage intuitions (or premonitions) of the Most Perfect seventh stage Realization, but no one previous to Avatar Adi Da has Realized the seventh stage of life.

The seventh stage Realization is a Gift of Avatar Adi Da to His devotees who have (by His Divine Grace) completed their practice of the Way of Adidam in the context of the first six stages of life. The seventh stage of life begins when His devotee Gracefully Awakens from the exclusive Realization of Consciousness to Most Perfect and Permanent Identification with Consciousness Itself, Avatar Adi Da's Divine State. This is Divine Self-Realization, or Divine Enlightenment, the perpetual Samadhi of "Open Eyes" (seventh stage Sahaj Samadhi)—in which all "things" are Divinely Self-Recognized without "difference", as merely apparent modifications of the One Self-Existing and Self-Radiant Divine Consciousness.

Avatar Adi Da uses a number of terms as synonyms for seventh stage Realization. The principal such terms are:

Divine Awakening
Divine Enlightenment
Divine Liberation
Divine Self-Realization
Most Perfect Real-God-Realization

All of these terms refer to the same Most Perfect Realization of the seventh stage of life, with each term expressing a particular Quality of that Realization. In order to explicitly indicate seventh stage Realization, the phrase "Real-God-Realization" must be preceded by "Most Perfect". (Without "Most Perfect", "Real-God-Realization" is a more general term, referring to Realization in the context of the fourth, fifth, sixth, or seventh stage of life.) "Divine Awakening", "Divine Enlightenment", "Divine Liberation", and "Divine Self-Realization" may also be preceded by "Most Perfect"—but, in the case of these phrases, the addition of "Most Perfect" does not change the meaning but simply intensifies it.

In the course of the seventh stage of life, there may be spontaneous incidents in which psycho-physical states and phenomena do not appear to the notice, being Outshined by the "Bright" Radiance of Consciousness Itself. This Samadhi, Which is the Ultimate Realization of Divine Existence, culminates in Divine Translation, or the permanent Outshining of all apparent conditions in the Inherently Perfect Radiance and Love-Bliss of the Divine Self-Condition (which necessarily coincides with the physical death of the body-mind).

In the context of practice of the Way of Adidam, the seven stages of life as Revealed by Avatar Adi Da are not a version of the traditional "ladder" of Spiritual attainment. These stages and their characteristic signs arise naturally in the course of practice for a fully practicing devotee in the Way of Adidam, but the practice itself is oriented to the transcending of the first six stages of life, in the seventh stage Disposition of Inherently Liberated Happiness, Granted by Avatar Adi Da's Divine Grace in His Love-Blissful Spiritual Company.

Avatar Adi Da's extended Instruction relative to the seven stages of life is Given in *The Seven Stages Of Life*.

Star Form   Avatar Adi Da has Revealed that He is "Incarnated" in the Cosmic domain as a brilliant white five-pointed Star, the original (and primal) conditional visible Representation (or Sign) of the "Bright" (the Source-Energy, or Divine Light, of Which all conditional phenomena and the total cosmos are modifications).

The apparently objective Divine Star can potentially be experienced in any moment and location in cosmic Nature. However, the vision of the Divine Star is not a necessary experience for growth in the Spiritual Process or for Divine Self-Realization.

Avatar Adi Da's discussion of His Star Form is found in *He-and-She Is Me*.

student-novice / student-beginner
A student-novice is an individual who is formally approaching, and preparing to become a formal practitioner of, the total practice of the Way of Adidam (as a

member of the second congregation). The student-novice makes a vow of eternal commitment to Avatar Adi Da as his or her Divine Guru, and to the practice He has Given, and is initiated into simple devotional and sacramental disciplines in formal relationship to Avatar Adi Da. During the student-novice stage, the individual engages in intensive study of Avatar Adi Da's Wisdom-Teaching and adapts to the functional, practical, relational, and cultural disciplines of the Way of Adidam.

A student-beginner is a practitioner in the initial developmental stage of the second congregation of Adidam. In the course of student-beginner practice, the devotee of Avatar Adi Da, on the basis of the eternal "Bond" of devotion to Him that he or she established as a student-novice, continues the process of listening and further adaptation to the disciplines that were begun in the student-novice stage of approach.

subtle See **gross, subtle, causal**.

"Supportive Texts" Among Avatar Adi Da's "Supportive Texts" are included such books as *Conscious Exercise and the Transcendental Sun*, *The Eating Gorilla Comes in Peace*, *Love of the Two-Armed Form*, and *Easy Death*.

Swami The title "Swami" is traditionally given to an individual who has demonstrated significant self-mastery in the context of a lifetime dedicated to Spiritual renunciation.

Swami Muktananda See **Lineage, Avatar Adi Da's**.

Swami Nityananda See **Lineage, Avatar Adi Da's**.

Swami Rudrananda See **Lineage, Avatar Adi Da's**.

T

Tail of the Horse Adi Da Samraj has often referred to a passage from the ancient Indian text *Satapatha Brahmana*,

which He has paraphrased as: "Man does not know. Only the Horse Knows. Therefore, hold to the tail of the Horse." Adi Da has Revealed that, in the most esoteric understanding of this saying, the "Horse" represents the Adept-Realizer, and "holding to the tail of the Horse" represents the devotee's complete dependence on the Adept-Realizer in order to Realize Real God (or Truth, or Reality).

"talking" school "'Talking' school" is a phrase used by Avatar Adi Da to refer to those in any tradition of sacred life whose approach is characterized by talking, thinking, reading, and philosophical analysis and debate, or even meditative enquiry or reflection, without a concomitant and foundation discipline of body, emotion, mind, and breath. He contrasts the "talking" school with the "practicing" school approach—"practicing" schools involving those who are committed to the ordeal of real ego-transcending discipline, under the guidance of a true Guru.

Tat Sundaram "Sundara" is the Sanskrit word for "beauty", and "Sundaram" means "something which is beautiful". "Tat" is the Sanskrit word for "it" or "that". Thus, "Tat Sundaram" means "That Which Is Beautiful" or, by extension, "All Of This Is Beautiful", and is a reference to the seventh stage Realization of the Perfect Non-Separateness and Love-Bliss-Nature of the entire world—conditional and Un-Conditional. Tat Sundaram is also the name of the Hermitage-Retreat Sanctuary reserved for Avatar Adi Da in northern California.

Teaching-Work For a description of Avatar Adi Da's Divine Teaching-Work, see pp. 16-25.

technically "fully elaborated" practice See **forms of practice in the Way of Adidam**.

technically "simpler" (and even "simplest") practice See **forms of practice in the Way of Adidam**.

three stations of the heart See **heart, stations of the heart**.

the "Thumbs"   See **Samadhi**.

Thunder The Divine Sound of Thunder (which Avatar Adi Da also describes as the "Da" Sound, or "Da-Om" Sound, or "Om" Sound) is one of Avatar Adi Da's three Eternal Forms of Manifestation in the conditional worlds—together with His Divine Star of Light and His Divine Spiritual Body.

Avatar Adi Da's principal Revelation-Confession about these three forms of His Manifestation is Given in *He-and-She Is Me*.

. . . I Am conditionally Manifested (First) As The everywhere Apparently Audible (and Apparently Objective) Divine Sound-Vibration (or "Da" Sound, or "Da-Om" Sound, or "Om" Sound, The Objective Sign Of The He, Present As The Conscious Sound Of sounds, In The Center Of The Cosmic Mandala), and As The everywhere Apparently Visible (and Apparently Objective) Divine Star (The Objective Sign Of The She, Present As The Conscious Light Of lights, In The Center Of The Cosmic Mandala), and (From That He and She) As The everywhere Apparently Touchable (or Tangible), and Apparently Objective, Total Divine Spiritual Body (The Objective, and All-and-all-Surrounding, and All-and-all-Pervading Conscious and Me-Personal Body Of "Bright" Love-Bliss-Presence, Divinely Self-"Emerging", Now, and Forever Hereafter, From The Center Of The Cosmic Mandala Into The Depths Of Even every "where" In The Cosmic Domain) . . . .

total practice of the Way of Adidam
The total practice of the Way of Adidam is the full and complete practice of the Way that Avatar Adi Da Samraj has Given to His devotees who are formal members of the first or the second congregation of Adidam (see pp. 379-84). One who embraces the total practice of the Way of Adidam conforms every aspect of his or her life and being to Avatar Adi Da's Divine Word of Instruction. Therefore, it is only such devotees (in the first or the second congregation of Adidam) who have the potential of Realizing Divine Enlightenment.

"True Prayer" "True Prayer" is Avatar Adi Da's technical term for the various forms of the "conscious process" that are practiced by His Spiritually Awakened devotees who have chosen the Devotional Way of Faith.

Avatar Adi Da's full Instruction relative to "True Prayer" is Given in *The Dawn Horse Testament Of The Ruchira Avatar*.

Turaga "Turaga" (Too-RAHNG-ah) is Fijian for "Lord".

"turiya", "turiyatita"   Terms used in the Hindu philosophical systems. Traditionally, "turiya" means "the fourth state" (beyond waking, dreaming, and sleeping), and "turiyatita" means "the state beyond the fourth", or beyond all states.

Avatar Adi Da, however, has given these terms different meanings in the context of the Way of Adidam. He uses the term "turiya" to indicate the Awakening to Consciousness Itself (in the context of the sixth stage of life), and "turiyatita" as the State of Most Perfect Divine Enlightenment, or the Realization of all arising as transparent and non-binding modifications of the One Divine Reality (in the context of the seventh stage of life).

U

ultimate   See **the advanced and the ultimate stages of life**.

Ultimate Self-Domain "Ultimate Self-Domain" is a synonym for "Divine Self-Domain". (See **Divine Self-Domain**.)

Ultimate Source-Condition   The Divine Reality prior to all conditional arising, which is, therefore, the "Source" of all conditional worlds, beings, and things.

V

Vira-Yogi   Sanskrit for "Hero-Yogi". (See **"Heroic"**.)

Vow   For a description of the Vow and responsibilities associated with the Way of Adidam, see pp. 378-89.

W, X, Y, Z

waking, dreaming, and sleeping
These three states of consciousness are associated with the dimensions of cosmic existence.

The waking state (and the physical body) is associated with the gross dimension.

The dreaming state (and visionary, mystical, and Yogic Spiritual processes) is associated with the subtle dimension. The subtle dimension, which is senior to the gross dimension, includes the etheric (or energic), lower mental (or verbal-intentional and lower psychic), and higher mental (or deeper psychic, mystical, and discriminative) functions.

The sleeping state is associated with the causal dimension, which is senior to both the gross and the subtle dimensions. It is the root of attention, prior to any particular experience. (See also **gross, subtle, causal**.)

washing the dog Avatar Adi Da uses the metaphor of the "dog" and "washing the dog" to Indicate the purification of the body-mind in the process of Adidam. He addresses the presumption (as in the Kundalini Yoga tradition) that the Spiritual process requires a spinal Yoga, or an effort of arousing Spiritual Energy literally at the "tail" end of the "dog" (the bodily base, or the muladhara chakra), and then drawing It up (or allowing It to ascend) through the spinal line to the head (and above). In contrast, Avatar Adi Da Samraj has Revealed (particularly in His *Hridaya Rosary*) that, in reality, the human being can be truly purified and Liberated (or the "dog" can be "washed") only by receiving His Divine Blessing-Power (or Hridaya-Shakti) and Spiritual Person downward from Infinitely Above the head to the bodily base. This Process of downward reception of Avatar Adi Da is what He calls the "frontal Yoga", because it occurs in the frontal line of the body (which is a natural pathway of descending energy, down the front of the body, from the crown of the head to the bodily base). This necessary descending Yoga of the frontal line, once completed, is sufficient to purify and Spiritually Infuse the body-mind, and, in most cases, it allows the practitioner of the Way of Adidam to bypass the ascending Yoga of the spinal line (which is the complementary natural pathway of ascending energy, up the back of the body, from the bodily base to the crown of the head). The frontal line and the spinal line are the two arcs of the continuous energy-circuit that Avatar Adi Da calls the "Circle" of the body-mind.

AVATAR ADI DA SAMRAJ: You wash a dog from the head to the tail. But somehow or other, egos looking to Realize think they can wash the "dog" from the "tail" toward the head by doing spinal Yoga. But, in Truth, and in Reality, only the frontal Yoga can accomplish most perfect Divine Self-Realization, because it begins from the superior position, from the "head" position, from My Crashing Down.

The heart-disposition is magnified by My Crashing Down in your devotional Communion with Me. And the vital, grosser dimensions of the being are purified by this washing from the head toward the "tail". If the Process had to begin from the bodily base up, it would be very difficult, very traumatizing—and, ultimately, impossible. The "dog" is washed, simply and very directly, by your participation in My Divine Descent, by your participation in this frontal Yoga. I am Speaking now of the Spiritually Awakened stages, basically. But, even in the case of beginning practitioners in the Way of Adidam—not yet Spiritually Awakened, not yet responsible for the truly Spiritual dimension of their relationship to Me—this "wash" is, by Means of My Avataric Divine Grace, going on.

Therefore, Spiritual life need not be a traumatic course. The "dog" should enjoy being bathed. Nice gentle little guy, happy to be rubbed and touched. You talk to him, struggle a little bit, but you gentle him down. That is how it should work. And, at the end of it, the "dog" sort of "wags its tail", shakes the water off—nice and clean, happy, your best friend. That is how it should work.

If you wash the "dog" from the "tail" up, you smear the shit from his backside toward his head. Basically, that "washing from the tail toward the head" is a self-generated, self-"guruing" kind of effort. The Divine Process can only occur by Means of Divine Grace. Even the word "Shaktipat" means the "Descent (pat) of Divine Force (Shakti)". But Shaktipat as it appears in the traditions is basically associated with admonitions to practice a spinal Yoga, moving from the base up. In Truth, the Divine Yoga in My Company is a Descent—washing the "dog" from head to "tail" rather than giving the "dog" a "bone", letting it wash itself from the "tail" to the head.

DEVOTEE: It is only Your Hridaya-Shakti that does it.

AVATAR ADI DA SAMRAJ: This is why you must invest yourself in Me. And that is how the "dog" gets washed. [August 13, 1995]

Avatar Adi Da's extended Discourse relative to "washing the dog" is "Be Washed, From Head to Tail, By Heart-Devotion To Me", in *Hridaya Rosary*.

Way of "Radical" Understanding
Avatar Adi Da uses "understanding" to mean "the process of transcending egoity". Thus, to "understand" is to simultaneously observe the activity of the self-contraction and to surrender that activity via devotional resort to Avatar Adi Da Samraj.

Avatar Adi Da has Revealed that, despite their intention to Realize Reality (or Truth, or Real God), all religious and Spiritual traditions (other than the Way of Adidam) are involved, in one manner or another, with the search to satisfy the ego. Only Avatar Adi Da has Revealed the Way to "radically" understand the ego and (in due course, through intensive formal practice of the Way of Adidam, as His formally acknowledged devotee) to most perfectly transcend the ego. Thus, the Way Avatar Adi Da has Given is the "Way of 'Radical' Understanding".

Witness, Witness-Consciousness, Witness-Position When Consciousness is free of identification with the body-mind, it takes up its natural "position" as the Conscious Witness of all that arises to and in and as the body-mind.

In the Way of Adidam, the stable Realization of the Witness-Position is associated with, or demonstrated via, the effortless surrender (or relaxation) of all the forms of seeking and all the motives of attention that characterize the first five stages of life. However, identification with the Witness-Position is not final (or Most Perfect) Realization of the Divine Self. Rather, it is the first of the three stages of the "Perfect Practice" in the Way of Adidam, which Practice, in due course, Realizes, by Avatar Adi Da's Grace, complete and irreversible and utterly Love-Blissful Identification with Consciousness Itself.

Avatar Adi Da's extended Instruction relative to the Witness is Given in *The Lion Sutra*.

Yoga "Yoga", in Sanskrit, is literally "yoking", or "union", usually referring to any discipline or process whereby an aspirant attempts to unite with God. Avatar Adi Da acknowledges this conventional and traditional use of the term, but also, in reference to the Great Yoga of Adidam, employs it in a "radical" sense, free of the usual implication of egoic separation and seeking.

Yogananda, Paramahansa
Paramahansa Yogananda (Mukunda Lal Ghosh, 1893-1952) was born in Bengal, the child of devout Hindu parents. As a young man, Yogananda found his Guru, Swami Yukteswar Giri, who initiated him into an order of formal renunciates. In 1920, Yogananda traveled to America to attend an international conference of religions in Boston. Subsequently he settled in the United States, attracting many American devotees. He Taught "Kriya Yoga", a system of practice that had been passed down to him by his own Teacher and that had originally been developed from traditional techniques of Kundalini Yoga. Yogananda became widely known through the publication of his life-story, *Autobiography of a Yogi*.

The Sacred Literature of Avatar Adi Da Samraj

R ead the astounding Story of Avatar Adi Da's Divine Life and
Work in *The Light Is <u>On</u>!*

The Light Is <u>On</u>!

The profound, heart-rending, humorous,
miraculous, wild—and true—Story of the
Divine Person Alive in human Form.
Essential reading as background for the
study of Avatar Adi Da's books.

E njoy the beautiful summary of His Message that Avatar Adi Da
has written especially "for children, and everyone else".

What, Where, When, How, Why, and <u>Who</u> To Remember To Be Happy

Illustrated Children's Edition

Fundamental Truth about life
as a human being, told in
very simple language for

children. Accompanied by extraordinarily vivid and imaginative
illustrations.

The Five Books Of
The Heart Of The Adidam Revelation

In these five books, Avatar Adi Da Samraj has distilled the very essence of His Eternal Message to every one, in all times and places.

BOOK ONE:

Aham Da Asmi
(Beloved, I Am Da)

The "Late-Time" Avataric Revelation Of The True and Spiritual Divine Person (The egoless Personal Presence Of Reality and Truth, Which Is The Only Real God)

The most extraordinary statement ever made in human history. Avatar Adi Da Samraj fully Reveals Himself as the Living Divine Person and Proclaims His Infinite and Undying Love for all and All.

BOOK TWO:

Ruchira Avatara Gita
(The Way Of The Divine Heart-Master)

The "Late-Time" Avataric Revelation Of The Great Secret Of The Divinely Self-Revealed Way That Most Perfectly Realizes The True and Spiritual Divine Person (The egoless Personal Presence Of Reality and Truth, Which Is The Only Real God)

Avatar Adi Da Offers to every one the ecstatic practice of devotional relationship to Him—explaining how devotion to a living human Adept-Realizer has always been the source of true religion, and distinguishing true Guru-devotion from religious cultism.

459

BOOK THREE:

Da Love-Ananda Gita
(The Free Gift Of The Divine Love-Bliss)

The "Late-Time" Avataric Revelation Of The Great Means To Worship and To Realize The True and Spiritual Divine Person (The egoless Personal Presence Of Reality and Truth, Which Is The Only Real God)

Avatar Adi Da Reveals the secret simplicity at the heart of Adidam—relinquishing your preoccupation with yourself (and all your problems and your suffering) and, instead, Contemplating the "Bright" Divine Person of Infinite Love-Bliss.

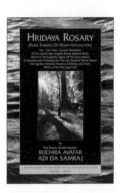

BOOK FOUR:

Hridaya Rosary
(Four Thorns Of Heart-Instruction)

The "Late-Time" Avataric Revelation Of The Universally Tangible Divine Spiritual Body, Which Is The Supreme Agent Of The Great Means To Worship and To Realize The True and Spiritual Divine Person (The egoless Personal Presence Of Reality and Truth, Which Is The Only Real God)

The ultimate Mysteries of Spiritual life, never before revealed. In breathtakingly beautiful poetry, Avatar Adi Da Samraj sings of the "melting" of the ego in His "Rose Garden of the Heart".

BOOK FIVE:

Eleutherios
(The Only Truth That Sets The Heart Free)

The "Late-Time" Avataric Revelation Of The "Perfect Practice" Of The Great Means To Worship and To Realize The True and Spiritual Divine Person (The egoless Personal Presence Of Reality and Truth, Which Is The Only Real God)

An address to the great human questions about God, Truth, Reality, Happiness, and Freedom. Avatar Adi Da Samraj Reveals how Absolute Divine Freedom is Realized, and makes an impassioned Call to everyone to create a world of true human freedom on Earth.

The Seventeen Companions
Of The True Dawn Horse

T hese seventeen books are "Companions" to *The Dawn Horse Testament*, Avatar Adi Da's great summary of the Way of Adidam (p. 466). Here you will find Avatar Adi Da's Wisdom-Instruction on particular aspects of the true Spiritual Way, and His two tellings of His own Life-Story, as autobiography (*The Knee Of Listening*) and as archetypal parable (*The Mummery*).

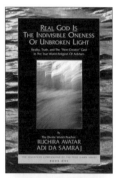

BOOK ONE:

Real God Is The Indivisible Oneness Of Unbroken Light

Reality, Truth, and The "Non-Creator" God In The True World-Religion Of Adidam

The Nature of Real God and the nature of the cosmos. Why ultimate questions cannot be answered either by conventional religion or by science.

BOOK TWO:

The Truly Human New World-Culture Of Unbroken Real-God-Man

The Eastern Versus The Western Traditional Cultures Of Mankind, and The Unique New Non-Dual Culture Of The True World-Religion Of Adidam

The Eastern and Western approaches to religion, and to life altogether—and how the Way of Adidam goes beyond this apparent dichotomy.

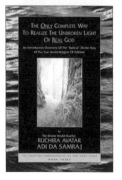

BOOK THREE:

The Only Complete Way To Realize The Unbroken Light Of Real God

An Introductory Overview Of The "Radical" Divine Way Of The True World-Religion Of Adidam

The entire course of the Way of Adidam—the unique principles underlying Adidam, and the unique culmination of Adidam in Divine Enlightenment.

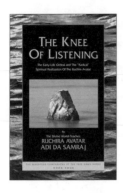

BOOK FOUR:

The Knee Of Listening

The Early-Life Ordeal and The "Radical"
Spiritual Realization Of The Ruchira Avatar

Avatar Adi Da's autobiographical account of the
years from His Birth to His Divine Re-Awakening
in 1970. Includes a new chapter, "My Realization
of the Great Onlyness of Me, and My Great
Regard for My Adept-Links to the Great Tradition
of Mankind".

BOOK FIVE:

The Divine Siddha-Method Of The Ruchira Avatar

The Divine Way Of Adidam Is An ego-Transcending
Relationship, Not An ego-Centric Technique

Avatar Adi Da's earliest Talks to His devotees, on
the fundamental principles of the devotional relationship to Him and "radical" understanding of the
ego. Accompanied by His summary statements on
His relationship to Swami Muktananda and on His
own unique Teaching-Work and Blessing-Work.

BOOK SIX:

The Mummery

A Parable Of The Divine True Love,
Told By Means Of A Self-Illuminated Illustration
Of The Totality Of Mind

A work of astonishing poetry and deeply evocative archetypal drama. This is the story of
Raymond Darling's birth, his growth to manhood,
his finding and losing of his beloved (Quandra),
and his ultimate resolution of the heart-breaking
"problem" of mortality. *The Mummery* is Avatar Adi Da's telling of His
own Life-Story in the language of parable, including His unflinching
portrayal of how the unconverted ego makes religion (and life altogether) into a meaningless mummery.

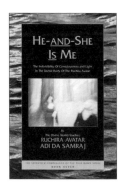

BOOK SEVEN:

He-**and**-She **Is** Me

The Indivisibility Of Consciousness and Light In The Divine Body Of The Ruchira Avatar

One of Avatar Adi Da's most esoteric Revelations—His Primary "Incarnation" in the Cosmic domain as the "He" of Primal Divine Sound-Vibration, the "She" of Primal Divine Light, and the "Son" of "He" and "She" in the "Me" of His Divine Spiritual Body.

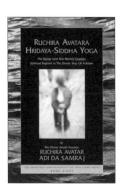

BOOK EIGHT:

Ruchira Avatara Hridaya-Siddha Yoga

The Divine (and Not Merely Cosmic) Spiritual Baptism In The Divine Way Of Adidam

The Divine Heart-Power (Hridaya-Shakti) uniquely Transmitted by Avatar Adi Da Samraj, and how it differs from the various traditional forms of Spiritual Baptism, particularly Kundalini Yoga.

BOOK NINE:

Ruchira Avatara Hridaya-Tantra Yoga

The Physical-Spiritual (and Truly Religious) Method Of Mental, Emotional, Sexual, and Whole Bodily Health and Enlightenment In The Divine Way Of Adidam

The transformation of life in the realms of money, food, and sex. Includes: understanding "victim-consciousness"; the ego as addict; the secret of how to change; going beyond the "Oedipal" sufferings of childhood; the right orientation to money; right diet; life-positive and Spiritually auspicious sexual practice.

BOOK TEN:

The Seven Stages Of Life

Transcending The Six Stages Of egoic Life, and Realizing The ego-Transcending Seventh Stage Of Life, In The Divine Way Of Adidam

The stages of human development from birth to Divine Enlightenment. How the stages relate to physical and esoteric anatomy. The errors of each of the first six stages of life, and the unique ego-lessness of the seventh stage of life. Avatar Adi Da's Self-Confession as the first, last, and only seventh stage Adept-Realizer.

BOOK ELEVEN:

The **All-Completing** and **Final** Divine Revelation To Mankind

A Summary Description Of The Supreme Yoga Of The Seventh Stage Of Life In The Divine Way Of Adidam

The ultimate secrets of Divine Enlightenment— including the four-stage Process of Divine Enlightenment, culminating in Translation into the Infinitely Love-Blissful Divine Self-Domain.

BOOK TWELVE:

The Heart Of The Dawn Horse Testament Of The Ruchira Avatar

The Epitome Of The "Testament Of Secrets" Of The Divine World-Teacher, Ruchira Avatar Adi Da Samraj

A shorter version of *The Dawn Horse Testament*— all of Avatar Adi Da's magnificent summary Instruction, without the details of the technical practices engaged by His devotees.

BOOK THIRTEEN:

What, Where, When, How, Why, and <u>Who</u> To Remember To Be Happy

A Simple Explanation Of The Divine Way Of Adidam (For Children, and <u>Everyone</u> Else)

A text written specifically for children but inspiring to all—with accompanying Essays and Talks on Divine Ignorance, religious practices for children and young people in the Way of Adidam, and the fundamental practice of whole bodily devotion to Avatar Adi Da Samraj. (The central text of this book is also available in a special illustrated children's edition—see p. 458.)

BOOK FOURTEEN:

Santosha Adidam

The Essential Summary Of The Divine Way Of Adidam

An extended overview of the entire course of the Way of Adidam, based on the esoteric anatomy of the human being and its correlation to the progressive stages of life.

BOOK FIFTEEN:

The Lion Sutra

The "Perfect Practice" Teachings In The Divine Way Of Adidam

Practice in the ultimate stages of the Way of Adidam. How the practitioner of Adidam approaches—and passes over—the "Threshold" of Divine Enlightenment.

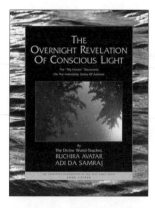

BOOK SIXTEEN:

The Overnight Revelation Of Conscious Light

The "My House" Discourses On The Indivisible Tantra Of Adidam

A vast and profound "consideration" of the fundamental Tantric principles of true Spiritual life and the "Always Already" Nature of the Divine Reality. The day-by-day record of Avatar Adi Da's Discourses from a two-month period in early 1998.

BOOK SEVENTEEN:

The Basket Of Tolerance

The Perfect Guide To Perfectly Unified Understanding Of The One and Great Tradition Of Mankind, and Of The Divine Way Of Adidam As The Perfect Completing Of The One and Great Tradition Of Mankind

An all-encompassing "map" of mankind's entire history of religious seeking. A combination of a bibliography of over 5,000 items (organized to display Avatar Adi Da's grand Argument relative to the Great Tradition) with over 100 Essays by Avatar Adi Da, illuminating many specific aspects of the Great Tradition.

The Dawn Horse Testament Of The Ruchira Avatar

The "Testament Of Secrets" Of The Divine World-Teacher, Ruchira Avatar Adi Da Samraj

Avatar Adi Da's paramount "Source-Text", which summarizes the entire course of the Way of Adidam. Adi Da Samraj says: "In making this Testament I have been Meditating everyone, contacting everyone, dealing with psychic forces everywhere, in all time. This Testament is an always Living Conversation between Me and absolutely every one."

See My Brightness Face to Face
A Celebration of the Ruchira Avatar,
Adi Da Samraj, and the First Twenty-Five
Years of His Divine Revelation Work.

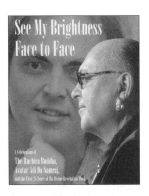

A magnificent year-by-year pictorial celebration of Ruchira Avatar Adi Da's Divine Work with His devotees, from 1972 to 1997. Includes a wealth of selections from His Talks and Writings, numerous Stories told by His devotees, and over 100 color photographs. **$19.95**, 8-1/2" x 11" paperback, 200 pages.

The "Truth For Real" series
Brief Essays and Talks
by the Divine World-Teacher,
Ruchira Avatar Adi Da Samraj

13 individual booklets on topics such as ecstasy, death, and the impulse to Happiness.
3-3/4" x 6", **$1.95** each

The Basket Of Tolerance Booklet series
6 individual essays on the religious traditions of humankind from *The Basket Of Tolerance.*
3-3/4" x 6", **$1.95** each

I n addition to Avatar Adi Da's 23 "Source-Texts", the Dawn Horse Press offers many other publications by and about Avatar Adi Da Samraj, as well as videotapes and audiotapes of Avatar Adi Da's Wisdom-Teaching. Dawn Horse Press publications are distributed by the Adidam Emporium, a devotee-operated business offering a wide array of items for meditation, sacred worship, health and well-being, and much more.

For more information or a free catalog:

CALL THE ADIDAM EMPORIUM
TOLL-FREE 1-877-770-0772
(Outside North America call 1-707-928-6653)

Visit online at
www.adidam.com

Or e-mail:
emporium@adidam.com

Or write:
ADIDAM EMPORIUM
10336 Loch Lomond Road
PMB #306
Middletown, CA 95461
USA

INDEX

A

action
 conditional, of thought, **226**
 right, **85**
 in the seventh stage, **206–207**, **294**
 Standing Prior to, **225**
addresses
 Adidam, 370
 Adidam Emporium, 372
 Adidam Sacred City, 373
 Adidam Youth Fellowship, 385
 Third Congregation Advocacy, 387
Adept-Realizer, **73–74**
 Adi Da Samraj, 49
 First, Last, and Only, **98–103**
 Incarnation of seventh stage, **97**
 right understanding of, 52
Adi, 14, 419
Adi Da Samraj
 Adept-Realizer. *See* Adept-Realizer
 Already Divinely Translated, **345**
 alternative titles and meaning of Name, 14
 Avataric Ordeal of, **276–277**
 birth of, 15, **276**
 bodily (human) Divine Form of, **265**
  and the Divine Self-"Emergence", **361**
  Eternally Revealed, **369**
  as initiation of Ashvamedha, **363–364**
  and Lineage of True Gurus, **183**, **186**
  Process beyond the Lifetime of, **364–365**
  and Universal "Conductivity", **352**
 as the "Bright", 30
 completion of foundation Work of, 19
 Confession of, **88–89**, **157–158**, **189–190**
 as Consciousness Itself, **312–313**, **324**
 Deeper-Personality Vehicle of, **124**, **187**, 408, 413
 as Divine Artist, 27–28, 44–47
 Divine Indifference of, **277–278**
 Divine Re-Awakening of, 15, **110–112**, **118**
  as "Bright" Consciousness, **157–158**
  defined, 412, 427
  as Divine Self-Recognition, **138**
  as Embrace of Divine "Cosmic Goddess", **132–133**, **184**
  as Fulfillment of Lineage, **186–187**
  in Ordeal of Divine Heart-Master, **360**
  and Ramana Maharshi, **160**
  as regeneration of Amrita Nadi, **159**
  and Universal "Conductivity", **352**
 Divine Sound and Star of, **261–262**
 as Divine Translation Process, **270–271**
 Divine Transmission of, **323**
 early life of, 15
 as First, Last, and Only Adept-Realizer, **97–99**
 and the Great Tradition
  Address to, **130–131**, **153**, **187–190**
  Fulfillment of, **75**, **117**, **364**
 Hermitage Life of, 24–25
 His Schooling of devotees, 48–49
 His Siddhi of Sameness, **353**
 as Liberator in "late time", **76**
 as life-Demonstration of Happiness, **207–208**
 Literature of, 371–372, 458–467
 "Locating", **262–263**
 as Means of Ashvamedha, **367**
 as Means of Realization, **358**, **366**
 non-cultic Purpose of, 23
 not a public Teacher, **63–64**
 as "Object" of Contemplation, **217–218**
 Perpetual Samadhi of, **347**
 Presence, Spiritual and Always Blessing, of, **266**
  and direct heart-relationship with Him, 375
  Eternally Revealed, **369**
  fifth-stage relationship to, **282**
  as True Dawn Horse, **359**
 Purpose of Incarnation of, **321**
 and refusal to be "man in the middle", **67–68**, **72**, **73**, **75**, **76**
 "Round Dance" with devotees, **68–69**
 and the Ruchira Sannyasin Order, 384
 Seat in the heart of all beings, **90**, **91**
 Secret of, **83**
 as Self-Condition and Source-Condition, **77**, **88**, **110**, **138**
 as Servant of Great Purpose, **272–273**
 as seventh stage "Experience", **343**
 as seventh stage Revelation, **107**, **109**, **110**, **133**, **134–135**, **137**
 Siddha Yoga of, **112–113**, **163–165**, **172–173**
 State, Self-Evidently Divine, of, **266**
  as Divine Domain, **340**
  Eternally Revealed, **369**
  as True Dawn Horse, **357–369**
 True Heart of all beings, **92**
 Universal "Conductivity" of, **352**
 Universal Work of, **366**
 and vision of the Dawn Horse, 38–39

Adidam Emporium, 372, 468
Adidam Hridaya-Shaktipat Yoga, **169**
Adidam Samrajashram (Fiji), 390
Adidam, Way of, 12–13
　addresses of regional centers, 370
　Adi Da Samraj as, **107**, **189–190**
　as Advaitayana Buddhism, 419
　as "Brightening" process, **217**
　community organizations of, 402
　congregations of, 378–389
　defined, 419
　as devotion to Divine Person, **189**, **195**
　Divinely Revealed, **83**
　ego-transcending ordeal of, **174–175**
　essence of, **217–218**, **365**
　Foundation of, **353**
　full establishment of, 19
　as holding "Tail of the Horse", **358**
　as progressive process of transcendence,
　　174–181
　Purpose of, **290**, **318**
　as relationship to Adi Da Samraj, 12, **64**,
　　74, **77**, 375–376
　renunciate orders of, 442–443
　and Ruchiradam, 28, 29
　Sacred Treasures of, 401–402
　as Satsang, **63**
　Secret of, **72**
　seventh stage as beginning of, **250–251**
　Siddha Yoga of, **164**, **168–169**
　support of, 398–399
　total practice of, 454
　as way of Conscious Light, **313**
　as way of "radical" ego-transcendence,
　　100, **109**, **173**
　as way of seventh stage Realization, **101**
Admonition, Perfectly Subjective,
　208–209, **212–213**
adolescence, 423
Advaita Vedanta
　defined, 419
　historical encounter with Kashmir Saivism,
　　116
　Ramana Maharshi and, **160**
　Swami Muktananda and, **113**, **136**, **161**
　ultimate goal of, 50
advocacy, 386–388
Aham Da Asmi, **61**, **72**, **78**, **83**, **103**, 420
Aham Da Asmi (Beloved, I Am Da), 19–20
Ajna Door, **234**, **235**, **236**, **238**, **281**
All-Completing and Final Revelation to
　Mankind, The, 37, 48–56
Always Already Condition
　Adi Da Samraj Is, **86**
　of the Divine Self, **274**
　of Happiness Itself, **202**

　of Ignorance, **224**
　of "Perfect Practice", **324**
　of Reality, **87**, **165–166**
　of Realization, **322**
Amma, **125–126**, **127**, **129**
Amrita Nadi
　as "Brightness" of the Heart, **241**, **244**,
　　246–247
　as "Connection" to Divine Domain, **351**
　defined, 420
　Descent in, **349**
　and Divine "Gaze", **238**
　Divinely Indifferent Demonstration of,
　　245–246
　great Function of, 55
　as human Mechanism of Self-Radiance,
　　350
　and Incarnation of Adi Da Samraj, **349**
　Outshining of, **351**
　Regenerated Form of, **159**, **284**, **348–349**
　Self-Condition as, **267**
　and seventh stage Mahamantra meditation,
　　235–236
　and seventh stage Process, **240–241**,
　　242–243, **252**
　Shining in the world, **340**
　upper terminal of, **154–155**
anger, seventh stage expression of,
　294–295
arising
　as apparent modification, **216**, **316**
　Nature of, **326**
　seventh stage "Practice" in relation to,
　　230–231
　as viewed in seventh stage, **222**, **228–229**,
　　339
Arrow of the body-mind, the, **242–243**
Artist, Divine, 27–28, 44–47
ascending Yoga
　in case of Adi Da Samraj, **156–157**
　in Christianity, **150**, **151**
　defined, 450
　in process of ego-transcendence, **143**
　Siddha-Yogis of, **117–118**
asceticism, 21
Ashvamedha, the, **357–369**
　Adi Da Samraj as Means of Completing,
　　367
　and Attainment of Light, 55, **368**
　defined, 414–415
　Divine Person as Necessary Doer of, **357**
　participating in, **361–362**, **366**, **367–368**
　as a perpetual process, **363–364**
　refusal of, **362**
　as a Spiritual process, **363**
　tradition of, **359**, **364**, **368**

Way of, **365**
Astavakra Gita, **126**, 409
Ati-Ruchira Yoga, **240–241**, **298**
"Atma Murti", **195**, 420–421
Atman, **121**
attention, **196**
  after-death destinies of, **273**
  devotionally yielded, **196**
  and limitation on Realization, 49–50
  and memory of past lives, **275**
  in seventh stage, **238**
  sixth stage dissolution of, **307**
  traditional methods of, **337–338**
  transcendence of, **337**, **338–339**
  "you" are not, **314**, **317**
  "you" are on the "other side" of, **310**
attention itself
  causal body as, **146–147**, **148**, **174**
  transcendence of, **177–178**
Attractiveness, Divine, **263**
authority-figures, **66**
Avadhoot, 421
Avatar, 14, 421
Avataric Incarnation of Adi Da Samraj, **72**
  as Adept-Realizer, **73–74**, **97–99**
  anciently expected, **183**, 412
  and assumption of Guru-function, **130**
  Complete and Final, 50–51, **98–103**
  as Completing Means, **367**
  defined, 421
  as Divine Demonstration, **185–186**,
    187–188
  Divine Re-Awakening of, **157–158**
  Divine Revelation-Work of, **167**, **169–170**
  foundation Work of, 18
  as Happiness, **207–208**
  Motive for, **276**
  and Ordeal of Divine Heart-Master,
    360–361
  as promised, **61–62**
  Purpose of, 15–16, 17, **76**, **78**, **91–92**, **366**
  and the Regeneration of Amrita Nadi, **349**
  as Served by His Lineage of True Gurus,
    183, **184–185**
  as seventh stage Revealer, **110–112**
  as True Ashvamedha, **358**, **359–360**
  as True Dawn Horse, **364**
  and True World-Religion, **83–84**, **152**,
    189–190
  Uniqueness of, **98–103**
  Vehicles of, **123–124**, **186–187**
  as Way to Realize Him, **109**
avoidance of relationship, **297**

B
belief, 12
Bethlehem, Star of, **152**
bewilderment, **65**
Bhagavad Gita, **144**
Bhagavata Purana, **144**, 410
bhakti, 421
Bhava, 421
"Big Bang", **154**, 411
bindu, **121**, 412, 421–422
birth, **272**, **275–276**
Blessing, Divine, **214–215**, **259–260**
Blessing Work of Adi Da Samraj, **64**
  Divinely Indifferent, **277–278**
  gradual process of, 39
  inception of, 17
"blue pearl", **155**
"Blue Person", **144**, 410
body
  dissolved in "head" of Amrita-Nadi, **244**
  gross physical, **280**
  nature of, **209**
  and the "Thumbs", **331**
Body, Divine Spiritual, **262**, **266**, **285**, **323**,
  352, 427
body-mind
  conditional cycles of, **86**
  existence as action, **85**
  internal structure of, **153–154**
  nature of, **209**
  not a "someone", **209**, **210**
  opening shell of, **315**
  point of view of, **309**
  separation as basis of, **181**
  seventh stage Disposition toward, **206–207**
  and seventh stage Realization, **215**
  seventh stage Spiritualizing of, **258–259**,
    260, **339**
  tendency to reproduce embodiment of a,
    278–279
bondage, **171**, **175**, **226**
bonding, 422
"Bright", the
  and Amrita Nadi, **242–243**
  defined, 422–423
  and Divine Translation, **287–288**
  as Lifelong Realization of Adi Da Samraj,
    185
  "Locating", **262**
  as Native Condition, 15
  Realization of, **180**
  as reflected in Amrita Nadi, **240**
  Siddha Yoga of, **169**
  and the Word-Sign "Da", **235**
"Brightness", Divine Heart
  Adi Da Samraj's Sphere of, 18, **78**
  and Amrita Nadi, **246–247**, **350**

("Brightness", Divine Heart continued)
circulating in the body-mind, **339**
as modified in the Cosmic Mandala, **280**
"Practice" of relaxing into, **285–286**
as Purpose of Ashvamedha, **357**
response to, in death, **271**
of the True Dawn Horse, **368**
Buddhism, **113**
and Emanationist Way, **117**
historical religious encounters of, **116**
Tibetan Tantric, **114–115**
and transmission to Mahakashyapa, 53, 407

C

C = E = mc², **300**
causal body
defined, 431
as mode of contraction, **173**, **174**
represented within Cosmic Mandala,
146–147
as root of attention, **148**
transcendence of, **177–178**
causal ego, **306**
celibacy, **128**
change, **89**
Chidakasha Gita, **119–123**, 407
childishness, 423
Chinmayananda, Swami, **120**, 408
Chitshakti Vilas, **163**
"Christ", **151**
Christianity, **140–141**, **142**, **149–152**, 410,
411
Circle of the body-mind, the
defined, 423
and Divine Indifference, **245–246**
and identification with the body-mind,
244
and Sahaj Samadhi, **240**
and seventh stage Process, **234–235**, **242**
Coin, Two Sides of the, **320**
Communion, devotional, **337**, **338**, **347**,
367–368, 432
community, **255**
conditional beings, **273–274**, **366**
conditional domain
Adi Da Samraj as, **270**
and the Divine Domain, **269**, **351**
Effectiveness of Divine Siddhi in, **101–102**
Translation of, **270**
conditional existence, **86**
apparent development of, **210–211**
Consciousness Itself and, **223**
converted and dissolved, **250**
defined, 423
Divine Self-Recognition of, **214**, **251–253**
in the first six stages of life, **108**

as a limit, **201**
nature of, **309**
not Real God, **139**
obliges transcendence, **279**
Opportunity Given to, 20
and pattern, **153–154**
as play of changes, **86**
right purpose of, **276–277**
and the seventh stage of life, **228–229**
and Outshining, **284–285**, **339**
"Point of View" toward, **230**, **340**,
341, **346**
"Practice" in relation to, **252–255**
and the sixth stage of life, **115**, **346**
strategic exclusion of, **338**, **342**
tendency to reproduction of, **278–279**
and thought, **225–226**
transcendence of, **277–278**
True Condition of, **348**
Ultimate Lesson of, **208–209**
unsatisfactoriness of, **175**
conditional experience, **170–171**
conditional reality, lesson of, **201**
"conductivity", **236–237**, **352**, 423
congregations of Adidam, 423
"conscious process"
defined, 423–424
seniority of, to "conductivity", **237–238**
seventh stage, **232–234**, **236–237**,
251–255
Consciousness Itself
Adi Da Samraj as, **69**, **137**
as All there Is, **324**, **326**
Apparently separate from Its Radiance,
210–211
cannot be inspected objectively, **309–310**,
311
as Condition of experience, **313**
dependence of body-mind on, **209**
as Domain of "Perfect Practice", **305**
Function of, in conditional context, **248**
as Great Principle, **309**
Identical to Energy, **319**
Love-Bliss as Inherent to, **224**
Nature of, **223**, **300**, **315–316**, **321–322**
no "difference" in, **216**
not reducible, **308**
as Real Situation, **308**
Realization of, **204**, **318**
Realizing Its Own Happiness, **211–212**
as root of Amrita Nadi, **159**
Self-Existing and Self-Radiant, **166**
seventh stage Identification with, **228**
sixth stage immersion in, **282–283**
Submission of Divine "Cosmic Goddess"
to, **135**

and thought, **227**
Transmission of, **323**
as True Water, 46
and Two Sides of the Coin, **320**
as the Unfamiliar, **223**
and the Word-Sign "Om", **234**
Yoga of, **224–225**
"you" are, **316, 320, 324**
"consideration", 424
control, **66**
conversation, eternal, 33
"Cooperation + Tolerance = Peace",
   175–176, 396
cooperative community, **70**
Cosmic Mandala
   Adi Da Samraj's description of, **146–148**
   and after-death destinies of attention, **273**
   defined, 424, 438–439
   as "differentiated" Spirit-Energy, **210–211**
   dissolved in Amrita Nadi, **242–243**
   Divine Descent into, **102**
   Divine Siddhis effective in, **101**
   Divine Source of, **266–267**
   Divine Star and Sound as Hole in, **285**
   as interpreted by Christianity, **151–152**
   and levels of the mind, **283**
   and the seven stages of life, **280–284**
   and un-"Veiling" of cosmic structure, **155**
counter-egoic devotional relationship, 13,
   68, 72
"Crazy" Manner of Adi Da Samraj, **63–64**,
   424–425
"Crazy Wisdom", **214–215**, 413
crickets, mummers as, **315**, 414
cults and cultism
   Adi Da Samraj's refusal to tolerate, 22–24,
      73, 75
   and belief, 23
   vs. the devotional Way of Adidam, **67–68**
   as political-social game, **65–67**
   tendency toward in devotees, **72**
   transcending, **70**
culture, **318**

D

Da
   defined, 14, 425
   as Self-Condition and Source-Condition,
      61–62
   and seventh stage Mahamantra meditation,
      235, 236
   as That to be Realized, **97**
Da Love-Ananda Mahal (Hawaii), 390
Da Love-Ananda Samrajya, 29, 392, 393, 425
Darshan, 376–377, 425
Dattatreya, **132**, 426

Dawn Horse Testament, The, 33–34, 35,
   38–39, 426
Dawn Horse, True
   Adi Da Samraj as, **357–369**
   Becoming the worlds, **360**, 416
   Vision of, 38–39, **360, 368**, 416
"de-throne", **66**
death
   destiny after, **271–272, 273, 279–280**
   and Divine Translation, **271**
   nature of, **272**
   and persistence of ego-"I", **210**
   and remembrance of previous lifetimes,
      273–274
   what happens in, **319–320**
"deeper personality", 408–409
descending Yoga, **119**
Descent, Divine
   into body-minds of true devotees, **88**
   defined, 424
   and Effectiveness of Divine Siddhi, **102**
   in fourth stage of life, **143**
   as Law of Reality, **366**
   in Ordeal of the Divine Heart-Master,
      360
   reception of, **92, 93**
devotees
   Adi Da Samraj's Schooling of, 48–49
   awakening within ordinary human life, **71**
   Call to, **366**
   capability of and Help for, **102–103**
   and cooperation, **70**
   egoic tendencies of, **72**
   and faith, **89**
   Grace of being, 390–391
   and importance of community, **255**
   life of, 380–383
   and magnification of the "Bright", **217**
   non-cultic relationship with Adi Da Samraj,
      68–69
   participation in the Ashvamedha,
      364–365, 367–368
   refusal of the Divine Self-"Emergence",
      362
   responsibility of, **63**, 392
   right action of, **70, 85–86**
   right devotional approach of, **64**
   and Satsang with Adi Da Samraj, **62–63**
   seventh stage
      admonition to, **252–256**
      Disposition of, **218–219**
      and foundation of recognition-response,
         265–266
      meditative "Practice" of, **232**
   truly surrendered, **78, 87, 91, 92, 93**
   and Universal "Conductivity", **352**

devotion to Adi Da Samraj
  as basis for Adidam, 375
  confession of, 25–27
  counter-egoic and non-cultic, **64**, **68–69**,
    72
  as ego-transcendence, **174**
  and freedom from egoic "darkness", **77**
  as fundamental form of practice, **337**
  as living relationship, 16
  and "Locating" of Him, **262**, **263**
  as means of Liberation, **89**, **102**, **181–183**
  and renunciation of egoity, **368**
  and right action, **70**, **85**
  to Self-Condition, **195**
  seventh stage, **255–256**, **268**
  "sin" of no, **74**
  whole-bodily, **196**
diet, 383
"difference"
  between Consciousness and Energy,
    210–211
  defined, 426
  Divine Self-Recognition of, **291**, **297**,
    343–344
  egoity as presumption of, **171**
  freedom from, **204**
  Realization of no, **216**, **225**, **298**, **299**
  as root-form of contraction, **289**, **296**
  search based on presumption of, **84**
  seventh stage "Practice" in relation to, **230**
discipline, 379, 381, 382
  forms of, **431**
  practical, **257**, **258–259**
  relational, **257**
  of Sahaj Samadhi, **251**
  seventh stage, **258–259**
discriminative intelligence, represented in
    Cosmic Mandala, **147–148**
discriminative self-understanding, **70**
Divine Artist, Adi Da Samraj as, 27–28,
    44–47
Divine Being
  admonition to "Practice" as, **252–253**, **255**
  Current of, **329**
  defined, 426–427
  as Divine Domain, **340**
  Happiness as Inherent Quality of, **203**
  Inherent Radiance of, **322**
  Nature of, **204**
Divine Body of Adi Da Samraj, **262**, **266**,
    285, **323**, **352**, 427
Divine "Cosmic Goddess"
  Adi Da Samraj's "Embrace" of, **135**, **138**,
    183–184
  Husbanding of, **360**, 415–416
  in Ordeal of Divine Heart-Master, **360**

as Siddha-Guru of Adi Da Samraj,
    132–133, **186**
Divine Domain
  Adi Da Samraj's Stand at, 18
  "Connection" to, **351**
  defined, 427
  Divine Person as Way to, **357**, **365**
  "Entrance" into, **287**
  Eternally Revealed, **369**
  Honoring the distinctiveness of, **259**
  is not absent, 19
  Nature of, **269–270**, **288–289**, **340**
  seventh stage Existence in, **216**
  Translation of all into, **366**
Divine Heart-Master, Adi Da Samraj
  and devotional process, **90**, **92**
  Function of, **218**
  necessary Submission of, **366**
  unique Ordeal of, **360–361**, 415
Divine Ignorance, **293–294**, **311**, **317**
Divine, Incarnation of the. *See* Avataric
    Incarnation of Adi Da Samraj
Divine Indifference
  and Amrita Nadi, **240–241**
  in case of devotees, **219–220**
  defined, 430
  as Demonstrated by Adi Da Samraj,
    207–208, **277–278**
  Nature of, **245–246**
  Process of, **219–220**, **238**, **250**, **296**
  and relaxation of Divine Life-Signs, **261**
  in seventh stage Process, **242**, **268**, **343**
  toward objects, **212**, **344**
Divine Self-Confession of Adi Da Samraj
  as Always Already Present, **101–102**
  as Avataric Incarnation, **61–62**
  as basis for call to Satsang, 34, **72–73**
  as "Bright" Divine Person, **88–89**
  defined, **101–102**
  as Love-Bliss Consciousness, **68–69**
  Nature of, 51
  reception of, 53
  and recognition-response of devotees, **93**
  right understanding of, 49–51, **75**
  as Source-Condition, 19–20
Divine Self-"Emergence"
  defined, 417, 427–428
  devotees' refusal of, **362**
  inception of, 17
  Process of, **361**
  Spiritual Nature of, **363**
  as True Ashvamedha, **358**
Divine Self-Recognition
  and action, **206–207**
  Adi Da Samraj's "Practice" of, **167**
  admonition to "Practice", **252–255**

of all arising, **291**, **300**, **342–343**
and arising of the world, **215**, **228–229**,
339
as "Brightening" process, **241–242**, **253**
defined, **428**
of "difference", **297**, **298**, **343**
of Divine Sound and Star, **287–288**
and Divine Translation, **271**, **286**
of ego-"I" and conditional world, **166**
four-stage process of, **245–246**
as Freedom, **340**
as "Perfect" seeing, **205–206**
"Practice" of, **178–180**, **342**
as Realization of the Unknown, **224**
as seventh stage "Practice", **225**, **230–231**
of the "conscious process", **232–234**
of meditation, **256**, **257**
Spontaneous Process of, **243**
Structural Pattern of, **351**
Transforming Power of, **248–249**
Divine Transfiguration, **238**
and Amrita Nadi, **240**
and association with conditions, **344**
in Circle and Arrow, **249–250**
defined, 430
and the frontal line, **242**
Nature of, **245**
in seventh stage Process, **267–268**, **343**
signs of, **260–261**
Transforming Power of, **249**, **259 260**
Divine Transformation, **238**
and Amrita Nadi, **240**
and association with conditions, **344**
in Circle and Arrow, **249–250**
defined, 430
Nature of, **245**
in seventh stage Process, **267–268**, **343**
signs of, **260–261**
and the spinal line, **242**
Transforming Power of, **249**, **259 260**
Divine Translation
Adi Da Samraj as, **270**, **345**
and Amrita Nadi, **351**
"Bhava" of, **246**
and death, **272**, **273**
defined, 430
as Demonstration of Sahaj Samadhi, **205**
Disposition towards, **216**
as dissolution of Cosmic Mandala,
242–243
and Divine "Gaze", **239**
and Divine Self-Recognition, **206**, **271**
and Divine Sound and Star, **268**
Nature of, **230**, **246**, **247**, **268–270**, **286**
and Nirvikalpa Samadhi, **282**
and Outshining of cosmic vision, **284**

present throughout seventh stage,
292–293, **344–345**
Process of, **219–220**, **250**, **286–288**
in seventh stage process, **284–285**, **343**
as a Spiritual process, **363**
as Ultimate devotional practice, **264–265**
as Work of Adi Da Samraj, **353**, **362**,
366
Divine World-Teacher, Adi Da Samraj,
428
dog, of self-contracted body-mind, **89–90**,
93, **455–456**
dream state, **281**, 455
dreams, ascended visions as, **139–140**
duality, **109**, **152**, **165**

E

e-mail addresses, 370, 373, 383, 396
ecstasy, 428
ego-death, **184**, 413
ego-"I"
and Adi Da Samraj's use of language,
35–36
causal root of, **147**
and collective darkening of mankind, **76**
cultic rituals of, **65–67**, **72**, **73**
and cycles of nature, **86**, **91**
defined, 428
and the first six stages of life, **108–109**
as group, 22, **65**
human suffering as, **170–172**
as idea in mind, **210**
impermanence of, **319**
not Divine Reality, **139**, **165**
not Truth, 60
presumption of, and thought, **226**
psycho-biography of, **338**
and quest for Happiness, **203**
as root-"problem", 21
as search itself, **290**
self-absorption in, **89–90**
separative activity of, **69**
separative "centering" activity of, **75**, **76**
surrender, forgetting, and transcendence
of, **84**, **90**
vanished in seventh stage, **350**
egoity, **64–65**
of the first six stages, **338**
Gods of, **153**
renouncing, **368**
sixth stage, **305–306**
three modes of, **173–174**
Eleutherian Pan-Communion of Adidam,
392, 394, 428
Eleutherios, **428–429**

Emanationist Way
  Bhagavan Nityananda and, **120**
  and Kashmir Saivism, **113–115**
  and the "Maha-Bindu", **154–155**
  and non-Emanationist Way, **116**
  practice of, **115**
emotion, seventh stage, **294–295**
Energy, Divine Spirit, **177**
  Apparently separate from Consciousness, **210–211**
  cannot be destroyed, **279**
  conditionally modified, **273**, **279**
  as Consciousness, **311–312**, **319**
  as Great Principle, **309**
  Realization of Love-Blissful, **181**
English as a sacred language, 34
enstasy, **77**, 428
"enthrone", **65**, **66**
enthusiasm, human cultic, 23
entities, no re-incarnation of, **273–275**
esoteric Spiritual practice
  in Adidam, **68–69**, **177–181**
  within Christian tradition, **150–152**
  and principle of devotion, **73**, **74–75**
  of Ruchiradam, **28–29**
  and the seven stages of life, **142–143**
  as un-"Veiling" of body-mind pattern, **153**
Eternal Vow, **64**, 429
etheric, represented in Cosmic Mandala, **147**
exercise, 383
Existence, Divine
  conditional existence developing from, **210–211**
  Divine Ignorance of, **311**
  Nature of, **248**, **321**
exoteric religion, **142–143**
exoteric vs. esoteric practice, **143–144**, **150–151**
"exterior", as "not-self", **309**

F

faith, **89**
Faith, Devotional Way of
  defined, 426
  and lesson of life, **201**
  seventh stage "Practice" of, **232–233**
fear, seventh stage expression of, **294–295**
feeling-Contemplation, **217**, 424, 429
"Feeling-Enquiry", **233**, **251**
Feeling of Being
  Abiding in the Well of, **213**
  Adi Da Samraj's Realization of, **137**
  defined, 429
  as Freedom, **299**
  Nature of, **204**
  Standing as, **225**

first congregation, 378, 379–384
First, Last, and Only Adept-Realizer, 49, **98–103**
"First Word", 51–52
forgetting, **217**
four congregations, 378–389
four faculties, **195**, 429
"Franklin Jones", **124**, 408
Freedom
  "Crazy Wisdom" Demonstration of, **214–215**
  Nature of, **299**
  seventh stage, from bondage, **226**
  by virtue of Divine Self-Recognition, **340**

G

"Gaze", of Divine Self-Consciousness, **234**, **238–239**, **245**
Good Company, **276**, **277**
"great path of return", the, **243**
Great Tradition
  Adept-Realizers as Means within, **73**, **74**, **121–123**, **181–183**, **189**
  Adi Da Samraj's Blessing of, **170**
  and Adi Da Samraj's Unique Revelation, **75**, **123–124**
  Always Already Full in Adi Da Samraj, **185–186**, **187–188**
  assumption of Guru-function within, **129**
  and conflict over human sexuality, **128**, **130–131**
  as Deeper Personality of Adi Da Samraj, **187**
  defined, 431
  and description of the Ashvamedha, **359**
  and exercise of attention, **337–338**
  Fulfillment of, **364**
  going beyond, **367**
  historical religious encounters within, **116**
  and Kashmir Saivism, 35–137, **116–117**
  limitation inherent in, **99–100**, **107**
  and notions of "self", **308**
  and right foundation for culture, **318**
  as search for Adi Da Samraj, **367**
  seventh stage premonitions in, **98**
  Siddha Yoga within, **167–168**
  and the sixth stage of life, **306**, **307**
  study of, 48–49
  and Teachings of Bhagavan Nityananda, **119–123**
gross body
  defined, 431
  as mode of contraction, **173**
  and "positive disillusionment", **175–176**
  as represented in the Cosmic Mandala, **146**

"gross personality", 408–409
Guru, 431
Guru-Seva, **127**, 409

H

Happiness
  as basis of Adidam, **208**
  cannot be attained, **201–202**
  as Condition of conditions, **248**
  as Demonstrated by Adi Da Samraj, **207–208**
  finding Real, 30–31
  Nature of, **195**, **202**
  Realization of, **86–87**, **206**
hearing
  defined, 436–438
  of Divine Sound, **261–262**
  as fundamental self-understanding, **87**
  "positive disillusionment" as basis for, **175–176**
  in process of ego-transcendence, **177**
  via devotional surrender, **84**
Heart, Divine, **91**, **92**, **154–155**
  "Brightness" of, **246–247**
  as Divine Domain, **241**
  and Divine "Gaze", **242–243**
  and Divine Translation, **247**
  frustrated will of, **294–296**
  Nature of, **244**
  as seventh stage Process, **241**
heart-Place, **90–91**
heart, the
  and Amrita Nadi, **235–236**
  responsiveness of, in death, **271–272**
  right side of, **238**, **240**
  Satisfaction of, 30–31
  and seventh stage Mahamantra meditation, **234–235**
  stations of, **280**, **280–281**, 432
  true impulse of, **206**
  truly surrendered, **92**
Hermitage Sanctuaries, 24–25, 390, 447–448
heroism, **201**, **202**, **211**
Hinduism, **142**
  and fifth stage visionary experience, **140–141**, **149–150**
  and Swami Muktananda, **143–145**
"Hole in the universe", **154**, **285**
Holy Spirit, **151–152**
Horse, True Dawn
  Adi Da Samraj's Embodiment of, **357–369**
  Becoming the worlds, **360**, 416
  Vision of, 38–39, **360**, **368**, 416
Hridaya-Shaktipat, **84**, **168–169**, 433
human beings
  cultic tendencies of, 23, 24

esoteric anatomy of, 450
  and performance of the Ashvamedha, **359**
  responses of, to conditional nature, **211**
  right foundation for culture of, **318**
  root-problem of, 21
humanity
  Adi Da Samraj's "Learning" of, 15
  Adi Da Samraj's message to, 30–31
  cultic rituals of, **65–67**
  egoity of, **107**, **170–172**
  and the first three stages of life, **142**
  and necessity for alignment to Truth, **60–61**
  and "positive disillusionment", **175–176**

I

Ignorance, Divine, **293–294**, **311**, **317**
illusion, **108**
impermanence, conditional, **86**
in-Depth Process, "Perfect Practice" as, **305–306**, **345–346**
Indifference, Inherent
  and "Crazy Wisdom", **214**
  as Process of Self-Abiding, **213**
  sixth stage, **213**
Insight, Devotional Way of
  defined, 426
  and lesson of life, **201**
  seventh stage "Practice" of, **232–233**
"interior, as "self", **309**
invocation, **232**
Ishta, **132**
Islam, **142**

J

Jesus of Nazareth, **150–151**, **152**
Jnana Samadhi. *See* Samadhi, Jnana
Jnani, **160**, 408
John the Baptist, **150**
Judaism, **142**

K

Karma Yoga, **127**, 409
Kashmir Saivism, **113–115**
  and Advaita Vedanta, **116–117**
  defined, 407, 434
  Swami Muktananda and, **136**, **144**
Knee Of Listening, The, 15, 32
knot, egoic, **147**, **350**, 435
knowledge, **223**
Krishna, **144**
Kundalini Shaktipat, **112–113**, 435

L

"late time"
defined, 435
destructive potential of, 76
Incarnation of Adi Da Samraj, 61–62,
124, 183, 184–185, 190
religion in, 142
lesson of life, 201, 435
life
of devotees, 380–383
and incarnation of an "entity", 273–274
lesson of, 201, 435
memory of past, 274–275
purpose of, 272
light, abstract inner, 145, 155–156
Light, Divine
Apparently separate from Consciousness,
210–211
Attained via the Ashvamedha, 55, 357
cosmic existence as, 177
and "Maha-Bindu", 155
not reducible, 308
as Purpose of Adi Da Samraj's Art, 47
as Quandra, 325
as Reality Itself, 45
Realization of, 180, 181
Self-Transmitted, 69
and Two Sides of the Coin, 320
Lineage of Adi Da Samraj, 183–185
Blessing His Avataric Work, 169
defined, 435–436
as His Divine Form, 186
Perfectly Fulfilled by Him, 187–188
listening, 436–438
listening-hearing, 175–176
literature of Adi Da Samraj, 458–467
"Living Murtis", 218, 363, 438
"Locating"
defined, 438
Divine Spiritual Body, 262
Reality, 29
Ultimate Event of, 268–269
via devotional practice, 263
Lopez Island, Yogic Swoon on, 18
love
of Adi Da Samraj, 85–86, 391
of Divine Guru as means of Liberation,
17, 181–183
incarnation of, 257
"positive disillusionment" and, 175–176
Unconditionally Radiated, 259
Love-Ananda, 169, 438
Love-Ananda Avatara Hridaya Shaktipat,
169
Love-Ananda Avatara Hridaya Shaktipat
Yoga, 169

Love-Ananda Avatara Hridaya-Siddha Yoga,
169
Love-Bliss, 31, 177
"discipline" of Conformity to, 258
and Divine Translation, 286–287
as Form of Amrita Nadi, 235–236
as Freedom, 299
as Inherent Characteristic of Consciousness,
224
Nature of, 321
Transforming Power of, 248–249
and the Word-Sign "Ma", 234–235
Love, Divine, 276

M

Ma, 234–235, 236
"Maha-Bindu", 154–155, 156, 159
Mahamantra meditation, seventh stage,
234–236
Maharastra tradition, 144, 145, 410
"man in the middle", 65–67
Adi Da Samraj's existence beyond, 77
Adi Da Samraj's refusal to be, 67–68,
72, 73, 75
"Mark", the, 74
materialism
defined, 448
insanity of, 31
as modern "cult", 66
meditation
of all, by Adi Da Samraj, 352
defined, 439
in life of the devotee, 380, 382
recognition-responsive, 77
right orientation to, 231–232
seventh stage, 231–232, 256, 257
seventh stage Mahamantra, 234–236
sixth stage, 345–346
"meet the mark", 74
memory, past life, 273–275
"Method of the Siddhas", 170, 189, 412
mind
conceptual, 280
dissolved in right side of heart, 244
as experiential subtle phenomena, 148,
149
fifth stage visions as, 139–140
makes "difference", 299
nature of, 209
represented in the Cosmic Mandala,
147–148, 283
strengths hidden in subconscious,
275–276
"money, food, and sex", 20–21, 175, 407
Mountain Of Attention, 390

Muktananda, Swami (Baba)
absorption in Savikalpa Samadhi,
139–140, 141
acknowledging Adi Da Samraj as Siddha
Guru, **128**, 410
as agent of Divine "Cosmic Goddess", **132**
and Amma, **125**
definition of name, 407
as disciple of Bhagavan Nityananda, **119**
fifth stage interpretation of, **143–145,
149–150**
and Kundalini Shaktipat tradition, **112–113**
in Lineage of Adi Da Samraj, **183, 184, 186**
relationship with Adi Da Samraj, **169, 170**
response to seventh stage Confession of
Adi Da Samraj, **131, 133–136, 138,
158–159, 161–162**
as Saguna Yogi, **117–118, 120, 127**
Siddha Yoga of, **163, 163–165, 167**
and Swami Prakashananda, **127–128**
visionary "inner" map of, **144–145**
as "Witnessing" fifth stage practitioner,
135–138, 166
Mummer, Divine, **315**
mummer, you are a, **319**
mummery, 439
Mummery, The, 32
mysticism, **149**

N

nada, **121**, 408
"Narcissus"
defined, 440
faithlessness of, **89–90**
nature, cosmic, **86, 89**
Nirguna, **117–118, 119, 120, 141**, 440
Nirguna Jnani, **123**
Nirvikalpa Samadhi. *See* Samadhi,
Nirvikalpa
Nityananda, Bhagavan
Adi Da Samraj's Sadhana with, **118, 186**
"Bhagavan" defined, 421
in Lineage of Adi Da Samraj, **183, 184**
as Nirguna Siddha, **141**
and Swami Vivekananda, **187**
teachings of, **119–123**
Non-"Difference", 13, **216**
Non-Dualism, "Radical", **109**
non-Emanationist Way, **111–112, 114, 115**
"not-self", **308, 309**

O

objects
as apparent modifications, **204**
Divine Indifference toward, **212**
Divinely Recognized "Quality" of, **220**
Nature of, **308, 319**

none in Divine Domain, **288**
and release of self-contraction, **290**
transcending ego-effort toward, **291**
Om, **121–122, 234, 236**, 413
"Open Eyes", **206**, 440–441
ordinary man, relating to an Adept-
Realizer as an, **74**
other, there is no, **298**
Outshining
of conditional existence, **255, 339**
as Consummate Demonstration, **284**
defined, 430, 441
of "difference", **264–265, 344**
and Divine Recognition of all things, **300**
ownership and egoity, **67**

P

Pan-Communion of Adidam, 392
Pandit, M. P., **120**, 408
participation, True Art as, 45–46
patrons, 386–387
pattern, **108, 153–154, 155–156, 156–157**
Pattern, Divine, **153–154, 156**
"Perfect Practice"
See also Witness-Consciousness
and attention, **337**
and congregations of Adidam, 384
defined, 441
in Domain of Consciousness, **311**
and Indifference, **213**
Nature of, **300**
Process of, **305–306, 342**
Ruchiradam as, 28
of the seventh stage, **220–221**
as Spiritual process, **312**
third stage of, **341**
three stage Process of, **345–346**
Person, Divine
Avataric Incarnation of, **364**
as Divine Domain, **340**
as Horse-Sacrifice, **361**
"Locating", **262, 263**
as only seventh stage "Event", **229–230,
342**
as Way to Divine Domain, **357, 369**
personality, gross and deeper, 408–409
photography of Adi Da Samraj, 27, 45
Play of Consciousness, **140, 163**, 410
Pleasure-Dome, 441
"Point of View"
Constancy of, **244**
of Divine Self-Recognition, **342–343**
seventh stage, **222, 329**
seventh stage, on conditional existence,
228–229, 341
transition from sixth to seventh stage, **311**

point of view
of body-mind, **309**
of conventional artist, 45
of first six stages on Consciousness, **310**
going beyond via True Art, 46
and the happening of anything, **293**
unenlightened, on conditional existence, **228–229**, **341**
of varying traditions, 49
politics, **65**
"positive disillusionment", **175–176**, **177**, **178**, **179–180**
practice, devotional
as "Brightening" process, **217**
Call to, **203–204**
of "conscious process" in seventh stage, **232–234**
developmental stages of, 426
disciplines of, 431
Divine Help for, **102–103**
essence of, **195–196**
forms of, **256–259**, **337**, 429–430
as means of Realization, 17
as means of right action, **85**
as participation in the Ashvamedha, **361–362**
progressive process of, **331–332**, 383
of Ruchiradam, 29
Spiritual, Accomplished by Adi Da Samraj, **352**
and tendency toward cultism, **67**
testimony to the process of, 25–27
and transcendence of tendency, **278**
Prakashananda, Swami, **127–128**, 409–410
prayer, **151**
pre-student-novices, 388
Principle, One, **217**, **297–298**, **299**, **329**
prophesy, of True Dawn Horse, **360–361**, **364**
psycho-physical pattern, **108**, **153–154**
puja, 380
purification, **141**
puritanism, **130–131**

Q

Quandra, **325**, 414
Quandra Sukhapur Rani, Ruchiradama, 25–27

R

"radical", 442
"Radical" Non-Dualism, **109**
"Radical" Understanding, **63**, **185**
"Radical" Understanding, Way of, 456
Raja Yoga, **121**, 408
Ramakrishna, **187**
Ramana Maharshi, **123**, **160–161**, 412, 442

Rang Avadhoot
Blessing of Adi Da Samraj, **131–132**, **156**, **183**
described, 442
in Lineage of Adi Da Samraj, **118**, **184**, **186**
as Nirguna Siddha, **141**
Raymond, **325**, 414
Re-cognition, **233**, 442
re-incarnation, **273**, **274**, **275–276**
Real God
defined, 442
direct "Locating" of, 29
Nature of, **139**
as Non-Dual Reality, **153**
Realization of, 49–50, **205**, **224**
Revelation of Adi Da Samraj as, **61–62**
Real-God-Realization
Accomplishing Power of, **101–102**
Adi Da Samraj as, 49, **218**
as basis for seventh stage "Practice", **221–222**
Divine Ignorance as context for, **293–294**
Divine Person as Necessary Doer of, **357**
as Fulfillment of Siddha-Yoga, **172–173**
impulse to, **263**
Inherent Characteristic of, **331**
Inherent in Adi Da Samraj, **185–186**
and "Locating" of Adi Da Samraj, **263**
makes no "difference", **296**
Means of, **101**
Nature of, **224**, **264**, **299**, **306**
of Non-"Difference", **216**
not previously possible, **99–100**
as "Perfect" seeing, **205–206**
Perfect self-transcendence in, 21–22, **178–180**
and "positive disillusionment", **176**
possibility of, **103**
Process of, **316–317**
as purpose of birth, life and death, **272**, **276–277**
"Radical" Nature of, **204–205**
as Realization of Happiness, **87**
Ruchiradam as process of, 29
Samadhi of, **293**
and seven stages of life, **110–112**
stopping conditional reproduction, **279**
traditional accomplishment of, 49–50
as transcendence of relationship, **297**
true religion as way of, **60**
Universal Event of, **361–362**
via devotional relationship with Adi Da Samraj, 16
Reality, Divine
Adi Da Samraj as, 12, **109–110**

Avataric Incarnation of, **364**
direct "Locating" of, 29
the Divine Domain as, **270**
interpreted in the fifth stage of life, **158**
Law of, Requiring Avataric Descent, **366**
Nature of, **314**
Non-Dual, **153**, **154**, **165–167**, **180**
non-experience of, **309**
as One and Only, **297–298**
Paradox of, **293**
perceived as Divine Sound and Star, **285**
present now, 19–20
as Real God, 20, **153**
Realization of, **224**, **314**
as Revealed by Divine Artwork, 27, 47
as the "Room", **327–328**
Self-Revelation of, **98**
Spherical Shape of, **325–326**
reality, lesson of conditional, **201**
Realizer, 52
reception, Spiritual, **77**
recognition-response to Adi Da Samraj
as basis for seventh stage "Practice", **265**
Call to, **365**
counter-egoic and non-cultic, **64**, **68**, **74**
in Darshan, 377
defined, 432
as ego-transcendence, **77**, **174**
by heart, 432
and "Locating" of Him, **262**, **263**
by Means of His Avataric Revelation, 11–12
Perfect, **264**
progressive process of, **263–265**
and reception of Hridaya-Shaktipat, **84**
rejuvenation, seventh stage bodily, **260**
relatedness, feeling of
defined, 429
Divine Self-Recognition of, **291**
gone in the seventh stage, **225**
nature of, **296–297**
"Perfect Practice" in relation to, **220–221**
as root-form of contraction, **289**
relationship
avoidance of, **297**, 421
as basis for True Art, 46
and "positive disillusionment", **175–176**
transcendence of, **297**
Way of Adidam as, 375
religion
and cult-making, **65–66**
and puritanism, **130–131**
true, **60–61**
renunciate practitioners, 379
renunciation, of egoity, **368**
retreat Sanctuaries, 390
"Right Life", **85**

right side of the heart
and Amrita Nadi, **159**
knot on, **147**
and Ramana Maharshi, **160**
as seat of Divine Heart, **155**
and Swami Muktananda, **159**
Room, the, **321**, **325**
"Round Dance", **68–69**
Ruchira Avatar
defined, 14, 443
promised in "late time", **190**
as Revelation of Divine Reality, **61–62**, **83**
seventh stage Revelation of, **109**
Unique Incarnation of, **97–99**, **102**
Ruchira Avatara Bhakti Yoga, **84**
defined, 443–444
moment-to-moment practice of, 382
seventh stage demonstration of, **178–180**
Ruchira Avatara Hridaya-Siddha Yoga
Adidam as, **63**, **169**
devotional practice of, **84**
seventh stage demonstration of, **178–180**
seventh stage Realizing, **164**
Ruchira Avatara Maha-Jnana Hridaya-
Shaktipat, **169**
Ruchira Avatara Maha-Jnana Hridaya-
Shaktipat Yoga, **164**, **169**
Ruchira Avatara Maha-Jnana-Siddha Yoga,
169
Ruchira Samadhi, **205**, 444
Ruchira Sannyasin Order, 25–27, **124**, 384,
442–443
Ruchiradam, 28–30
Ruchiradama Quandra Sukhapur Rani, 25–27
Ruchirasala of Adidam, 392, 395
Rudi (Swami Rudrananda), **118–119**, **125**,
131, **183**, **184**, **186**

S

Sacrament of Universal Sacrifice, **90**
sacred domain, 382
Sacred Treasures, 401–402
sadhana, **182**, **322**
"Sadhana Years" of Adi Da Samraj
and acknowledgement of Him as
Siddha-Guru, **128–130**
and ascending Yoga, **118–119**
defined, 444
and relationship with Amma, **125–126**
and relationship with Divine "Cosmic
Goddess", **131–133**
and relationship with Swami Muktananda,
161–162, **163**
Saguna, **117–118**, **120**, **140**, 444
Sahaj Samadhi. *See* Samadhi, Sahaj
sahasrar, **158**, **159**, **240**, 444

Saiva Siddhanta, **114**, **115**, **116–117**, 445
Samadhi
 of Adi Da Samraj, **347**
 defined, 445–447
 Jnana, 50, **127**, **213**, **307**, 447
 Nirvikalpa
  and absence of visions, **283–284**
  and Bhagavan Nityananda, **119**, **120**
  in the case of Adi Da Samraj, **132**,
   156–157
  as culmination of fifth stage process, **154**
  defined, 446–447
  limitation inherent in, 49–50, **292**
  and Nirguna Siddhas, **117–118**
  Sahaja, **239–240**, 447
  and Siddha Yoga, **127**
  and Swami Muktananda, **141**
 Realization of Perfect, **347**
 Sahaj
  defined, 413–414, 444
  "Practice" of, **251**
  Process of, **244–246**
  "Quality" of, **220**
  Realization of, **205**, **264**, **293**
  Root-Mudra of, **244**
  sixth stage, **307**, **311**
  as Unconditional Nirvikalpa, **239–240**,
   292
 Savikalpa
  defined, 446
  and Saguna Siddhas, **117**
  and Swami Muktananda, **139–140**,
   144–145, **155**
Samraj, 14, 447
Sanctuaries, 390
 Adi Da Samraj's life in, 24–25
 Hermitage-retreat, 447–448
Sat-Guru, **181**, 412, 448
Satsang
 Attractive principle of, **71–72**
 counter-egoic and non-cultic, **68**, **69–70**
 defined, 448
 Gift of, **62–63**
 as one resort, **72**
Savikalpa Samadhi. See Samadhi, Savikalpa
science, **60**, **61**
search, the, 31, **172**, **175**
second congregation, 378, 379–384
Secret, Divine, **62**, **93**
seeing
 defined, 436–438
 of Divine Star, **261–262**
 esoteric practice of, **177**
 necessity for, **264**
 seventh stage, **205**
 via devotional surrender, **84**, **87**

seeking
 abandonment of, **84–85**
 Adidam as transcendence of, **63**
 Consciousness Itself, **203**
 as generated by egoity, **338**
 Happiness Itself, **201–202**, **203**
 inevitable frustration of, **290**
 nature of, **289–290**
 as nature of body-mind, **209**
 purpose of, **359**
 tendency in devotees, **72**
 transcendence of, **290–291**
 various developments of, **211**
 for wisdom, **208**
Self-Abiding, **179**
 admonition to "Practice", **212**, **252–253**
 as "Brightening" process, **241–242**
 does not acknowledge "difference", **297**
 Nature of, **300**
 prior to attention, **339**
 as seventh stage "conscious process", **236**
 as seventh stage "Practice", **225**
Self-Condition
 Adi Da Samraj as, **77**
 Adi Da Samraj's Realization of, **157–158**
 assumption of separation from, **181**
 as the "Bright" Itself, **216**
 of conditional existence, **348**
 as Freedom, **299**
 as One and Only, **230**
 perceived as Divine Sound and Star, **267**
 Reality as, **155**, **165–166**, **167**
 Self-Radiant, **216**
self-contraction
 nature of, **289**
 and non-recognition of the Obvious, **203**
 self-imposed, 16–17
 as suffering, **204**
 transcendence of, **290–291**
self-discipline, **70**
Self, Divine
 Always Already Existing, **274**
 Apparently separate from Its Radiance,
  210–211
 Liberating Function of, **249**
 Nature of, **227**, **248**, **254–255**
 as Nature of "you", **275**, **308**
 as Only One, **209–210**
 and past-life memory, **274–275**
 as Servant of Great Purpose, **272–273**
"self", egoic, **209**, **211**, **308**, **309**
separation, **222**
service, **261**, 381, 409
*Seventeen Companions Of The True Dawn
 Horse, The*, 37
sex, 383

shabda, **121**
Shining, Divine Self-Recognition as, **253**
Siddha-Guru
  acknowledgement of Adi Da Samraj as,
    128
  Adi Da Samraj's Blessing of, tradition, **170**
  Bhagavan Nityananda as, **119**
  defined, 449
  Jesus of Nazareth as, **150**
  John the Baptist as, **150**
  as means of Liberation, **181**
  not fully developed, **118–119**, **127**
  Swami Muktananda as, **112**
Siddha Yoga
  Adi Da Samraj's Blessing of, **170**
  in case of Adi Da Samraj, **126–127**, **141**,
    161
  in case of Jesus of Nazareth, **150**
  defined, 449
  within Great Tradition, **167–168**
  Kundalini Shaktipat tradition of, **112–113**
  literature on, **125**
  and Nirvikalpa Samadhi, **154**
  puritanism and, **130**
  Swami Muktananda and, **128**, **129**, **134**,
    136, **162–163**
  true, Spiritual process of, **172–173**
  and un-"Veiling" of cosmic structure,
    155–156
Siddha-Yogi
  Adi Da Samraj as a non-celibate, **128–129**,
    130
  Amma as, **125**
  Bhagavan Nityananda as, **119**, **120**
  Rudi (Swami Rudrananda) as, **118–119**
  sexual activity in a, **128**
  Swami Muktananda as, **117–118**
Siddhas, Method of the, **170**, **189**, 412
Siddhi, Divine, **101–102**
"sin", 21, **74**, 439
sinoatrial node, **155**
Siva, **115**, **144**
sleep state, deep, **282**, 455
social sphere, **65–66**
Society of Advocates, Transnational, 387
sorrow, seventh stage expression of,
  294–295
sound, **120–121**
Sound, Divine
  and Divine Translation, **286**
  as Hole in the Universe, **285**
  Self-Recognition of, **287–288**
  as Servant of Great Purpose, **272–273**
  seventh stage perception of, **261–262**,
    267–268
  of Thunder, 454

Source-Condition
  Adi Da Samraj as, **77**
  Adi Da Samraj's Realization of, **157–158**
  Divine Domain as, **269**
  as One and Only, **230**
  perceived as Divine Sound and Star, **267**
  Realization of, **181–183**
"Source Texts" of Adi Da Samraj, 32–41,
  458–467
  capitalization in, 34–36
  and *The Dawn Horse Testament*, 37
  defined, 449–450
  and His "Bright"-Art Work, 45
  non-cultic orientation to, 23
  punctuation in, 36–37
  and Revelation of Ruchiradam, 30
  as summary of Wisdom-Teaching, 18
  titles and subtitles of the twenty-three,
    39–43
  vocabulary in, 34–36
Spherical Shape of Consciousness Itself
  Perfectly Subjective, **325**
  as the "Room", **321**
  Self-Existing, **326–327**
  as Shape of Divine Body, **323**
  as the "Thumbs", **329–331**
  as Two Sides of the Coin, **320**
Spirit-"Conductivity", **236–238**, **246**
Spirit-Current
  as Amrita Nadi, **240**
  not an "Object" to Consciousness, **243**
  as Servant of Great Purpose, **272–273**
  seventh stage Identification with, **244–245**
Spirit-Energy. *See* Energy, Divine Spirit
stages of life
  and Adi Da Samraj, **110–111**, **123–124**
  advanced and ultimate, **208–209**, **311–312**,
    419–420
  and capability of a Siddha-Guru, **182**
  chart of, 404–405
  defined, 450–452
  fifth
    ascended visions in, **139–140**,
      154–155, **156–157**
    and Bhagavan Nityananda, **118–119**,
      120–121
    and the Cosmic Mandala, **281–282**
    and Kashmir Saivism, **113–115**
    and mind, **283**
    and Rang Avadhoot, **131**
    Siddha Yoga of, **127**
    and Swami Muktananda, **117–118**,
      134–135, **143–145**, **144–145**,
      159, **162**
    ultimate Realization of, 49–50
    Yogis and Saints of, **123**

(stages of life continued)
first five, **338**
first six, **108**
first three, **263**, **280**
fourth, **113**, **119**, **127**, **280–281**
fourth to fifth, **114**, **116**, **141**, **150**, **153**
in Great Tradition, **107**
as human process of Realization, **211**
seventh
Adi Da Samraj as Revealer of, **110–112**, **133**, **134–135**, **138**, **157–158**, **188–189**
after-death destinies of those in, **280**
as already Divinely Translated, **344–345**
and Amrita Nadi, **159–160**, **349–350**
and association with phenomena, **292**
Avataric Incarnation of, **98–99**
as "Brightening" process, **241–242**
and cosmic vision, **284**
and "Crazy Wisdom", **214**
devotees in, **218–219**
Disposition of, **216–217**, **222–223**
and Divine "Gaze", **238–239**
and Divine Sound and Star, **261–262**
emotion and frustration in, **294–295**
four-stage process of
and Amrita Nadi, **240–241**, **351**
in case of Adi Da Samraj, **345**
defined, 430
Paradoxical Demonstration of, **343**
and Spiritualization of the body-mind, **238**, **242–243**
and Movement to Outshine cosmic domain, **284–285**
as Non-Dual Realization, **109**
possibility of, **99–101**, **102–103**
"Practice" of, **178–180**, **251–255**
as beginning of Adidam, **250–251**
"conscious process", **232–234**, **236**
defined, 441–442
and "difference", **230–231**
four fundamental forms of, **257–259**
Mahamantra meditation, **234–236**
relaxing into "Brightness", **285**
as Self-Abiding, **225**
Self-Abiding Divine Recognition, **220–222**
and thought, **227**
premonitorily, **126**, 409
prerequisite ordeal required for, **174–175**
Principle Sign of, **228**
Process of, **291–292**, **317**
as process of Divine Recognition, **265**
as process of Divine Self-Recognition, **115**
Realization of, 50, **101**, **293**, **299**, **312**

and recapitulation of first six stages, **243**
as Self-Abiding, **266–267**
and Siddha Yoga of Adidam, **164**, **168**
sixth stage transcended in, **149**
and Spiritualization of the body-mind, **339**
as Stand beyond the body-mind, **215**
and thought, **226–228**
and transcendence of attention, **338–339**
Transforming Power of, **259–260**
transition to, **205**, **341**, **346**
uniqueness of, 50, 53
Yoga of, 54
Siddha Yoga and, **163–164**
sixth
in contrast to Emanationist Way, **114–115**
and the Cosmic Mandala, **282–283**
as Descent in Amrita Nadi, **240**, **349**
egoic limitation in, **305–306**, **338**
and exclusive Indifference, **213**
going beyond, **306**
and meditation, **345–346**
mysticism of, **112**
Nirguna Jnanis of, **123**
"Perfect Practice" of, **342**
and Ramana Maharshi, **160**
Siddha Yoga Process in, **127**
traditionally practiced, **113**, **314**
transition beyond, **312**
as Witness-Consciousness, **148–149**
Spiritual processes within, **142–143**
and three modes of egoity, **173–174**
as transcendence of egoity, **174–181**
ultimate, **211–213**
Star, Divine Five-Pointed
at center of Cosmic Mandala, **146**, **148**, **155**
defined, 428, 452
and Divine Translation, **286**
as Hole in the Universe, **285**
and Jesus of Nazareth, **150**
Self-Recognition of, **287–288**
as Servant of Great Purpose, **272–273**
seventh stage perception of, **261–262**, **267–268**
Stone, in the Room, **324**, 414
student-beginner, 452–453
student-novice, 452–453
study, **257**, **258**, 380
subject-object point of view, 46, **180–181**
Subjective Source
"Bright" Conscious Sphere as, **325**
Consciousness Itself as, **203**, **224**
defined, 441

Happiness Itself as, **202**, **203**
   as Nature of Real God, **139**, **155**
subtle body
   defined, 431
   as mode of contraction, **173**
   represented within Cosmic Mandala, **146**
   transcendence of, **148**, **177**
suffering, human, **170–172**
surrender
   to Adi Da Samraj, **92**, **93**
   of ego-"I", **84**, **89**, **90**
   means of, **217**
   necessity for absolute, **293–294**
   to Source-Condition, **181**
   whole-bodily, **196**
Swami, 453
Swami Vivekananda, **187**

T

"Tail of the Horse", **358**, **359**, 453
"talking" school, 453
Tat Sundaram, 390, 453
Teaching Word of Adi Da Samraj, 32–41
   and continuation of the Ashvamedha,
      365
   Divine Gift of, **110**
   honoring and protecting, 400–401
   integrity of, **63**
Teaching Work of Adi Da Samraj, 15–17
   as direct confrontation with egoity, 24
   inception of, 12
   and "money, food, and sex", 20–21
   and the schooling of devotees, 48–49
tendencies
   and after-death destiny, **279–280**
   of conditional existence, **278–279**
   and death, **271–272**
   experience of past, **278**
   and re-incarnation, **274**, **275**
The Dawn Horse Testament, 33–34, 35, 426
The Knee Of Listening, 15, 32
The Mummery, 32
third congregation, 378, 386–388
thought
   gone in the seventh stage, **225**
   of "I", **210**
   not means of release, **225–226**
   objective nature of, **310**
   and the seventh stage of life, **226–228**
"Thumbs", the, **185**, **323**, **326**, **329–331**,
      445–446
time, **215–216**, **317**
transcendence of egoity
   as attention, **337**
   call to Most Perfect, **195**

death and, **271–272**, **279–280**
   means of, **217**
   and "money, food, and sex", 21
   Perfect, **109**, **154**, **157**, **206**, **341**
   and "positive disillusionment", **175–176**
   progressive process of, 21–22, **174–181**
   via Hridaya-Siddha Yoga, **164**, **172–173**
   via recognition-response, **71–72**
   transcendentalist point of view, **160–161**,
      338
"True Prayer", 454
True Water, **89**, **90**
Truth, **59–61**, **224**, **298**, **316**, **364**
Tulasiamma, **120**
turiya, **145**, **148**
Turiyatita, **149**, **269**, 454

U

un-"Veiling", of cosmic pattern, **144**, **155**,
      156–157
understanding, **87**
Unity, **175–176**, **297–298**, **299**
Unknown, Realization of the, **224**

V

videography of Adi Da Samraj, 27, 45
Vira Yogi, **124**
Virgin Mary, **152**
visions, ascended
   absence of, **283–284**
   and Adi Da Samraj, **140–141**
   and levels of the Cosmic Mandala, **283**
   and relief of human suffering, **170–171**,
      172
   and Swami Muktananda, **121**, **134**,
      139–140, **144**
Vivekananda, Swami, **187**
Voice of the Self, **120**, 408
"Void", the, **154**
Vow, Eternal, **64**, 429

W

waking state, **280**, 455
washing the dog, 455–456
Water, True, **89**, **90**
"Westerner", Adi Da Samraj as, **128–129**, **131**
White "Brightness"
   as modified in the Cosmic Mandala, **280**
   response to, in death, **271**
   of the True Dawn Horse, **368**
will, represented in Cosmic Mandala,
      147–148
Wisdom
   Awakening of True, **208**
   as Demonstrated by Adi Da Samraj, **208**
   seventh stage "Crazy", **214–215**

Witness-Consciousness
   See also "Perfect Practice"
   always the case, **309–310**
   and attention, **314**
   Awakening to, **313**
   defined, 456
   as Doorway, **314–315**
   exclusive identification with, **148–149**
   in heart-Place, **91**
   Inherent Indifference in, **213**
World-Teacher, Divine, 428
world, the
   Divinely Recognized, **166–167**
   as Energy, **311–312**
   human response to cycles of, **66**
   as "not-self", **307**
   oriented to Truth, **60–61**
   and seventh stage Realization, **215**

X
xenophobia, **70**, **130**

Y
Yoga, **224**, 431, 456
Yogananda, Swami, **146**, 456
Yogic Self-Realization, **120**
Yogic Swoons of Adi Da Samraj, 17, 18
"You do not know What anything Is", **311**
"you", Nature of, **308**, **310**, **316**, **317–318**,
    319, **324**
Youth Fellowship, Adidam, 385

I do not simply recommend or turn men and women to Truth. I _Am_ Truth. I Draw men and women to Myself. I _Am_ the Present Real God, Desiring, Loving, and Drawing up My devotees. I have Come to Be Present with My devotees, to Reveal to them the True Nature of life in Real God, which is Love, and of mind in Real God, which is Faith. I Stand always Present in the Place and Form of Real God. I accept the qualities of all who turn to Me, dissolving those qualities in Real God, so that _Only_ God becomes the Condition, Destiny, Intelligence, and Work of My devotees. I look for My devotees to acknowledge Me and turn to Me in appropriate ways, surrendering to Me perfectly, depending on Me, full of Me always, with only a face of love.

I am waiting for you. I have been waiting for you eternally.

Where are you?

AVATAR ADI DA SAMRAJ

1971